PENTAGON'S

SOUTH ASIA DEFENCE AND STRATEGIC YEAR BOOK

2014

Acknowledgements

- The data for the Country Reports has been obtained from Wikipedia, the US Library of Congress website, CIA Handbook website, UNO website, besides other sources.
- The data for the Military Balance has been obtained from the International Institute of Strategic Studies, The Military Balance 2011, US Department of Defense Annual Reports, Center for Strategic and International Studies, besides other sources.
- The data on Terrorism in South Asia has been obtained from the South Asia Terrorism Portal website, besides other sources.

PENTAGON'S

SOUTH ASIA DEFENCE AND STRATEGIC YEAR BOOK

2014

Editor
Col Harjeet Singh (Retd)

Published by
PENTAGON PRESS
206 Peacock Lane, Shahpur Jat
New Delhi – 110 049 (India)
Phones: + 91-11-64706243, 26491568
Fax: +91-11 26490600
Email: rajan@pentagonpress.in
www.pentagonpress.in

Branch Office
Prime Arcade Office #11
1154 Saifee Street
Opp. M.G. Road, Camp
Pune - 411001
Email: pentagonpresspune@gmail.com

ISBN 978-81-8574-758-6

Printed at Aegean Offset Printers Greater Noida

CONTENTS

COUNTRY STUDIES

MILITARY BALANCE

INDIA-CHINA
ROCK OF PEAC

PERSPECTIVE ON SOUTH ASIA

From the Editor's Desk

The Indian sub-continent, as a geo-political entity, does not admit of a balance of power: all of the other nations together, including Pakistan, cannot overcome India. It is like a planetary structure with the central mass provided by India, with co-existence as the goal. However, each of the constituent nations comprising South Asia has their own dynamics.

South Asian cooperation seems to be drifting between a present that cannot endure and a future that is hard to envision. Despite recent gains in regional cooperation, the region is threatening to slide back into the past. The India-Pakistan border remains turbulent, though democracy is more institutionalised in the region. The trajectory of ethnic conflict varies, but it casts a shadow over all politics. Economic cooperation is still, at best, grudging. There are the same dramas of one step forward two steps back.

There is also the familiar narrative of an obdurate military establishment in Pakistan which has no commitment to the pacification of violence; the fragmentation of the Indian political system that makes implementing any strategy difficult; and little imaginative commitment to the region. "South Asia" itself is an anodyne term. The paradox of South Asia is that the very thing it shares, a complex interconnected cultural matrix, is the thing that divides it. It works only if it is not a political agenda. The history of modern South Asia is the quest to create identity, differentiation and individuation against a common cultural mould. The region has consistently imposed huge costs on itself by frittering away the advantages of proximity. Competition between groups is a zero-sum game, territoriality trumps the well-being of people, security requires raising barriers rather than lowering them, the gains from opportunistically using external powers are greater than the gains from settling disputes and not much institutional experimentation is possible.

The main threats to the region today are: climate change; nuclear proliferation; fallouts of the global economic crises and the danger of an armed conflict; terrorism, the increased scarcity of water, criminalised governments, and structural unemployment.

Global Warming

Climate change is the greatest single threat to peace, prosperity and sustainable development. Increasingly over the last five years, national and international security organisations are recognising global warming as a potential threat to environmental security—and thus a challenge to national and regional security. The recent report by the UN Intergovernmental Panel on Climate Change has predicted dire outcomes of global warming in the years to come, if humanity fails to work together to avert this disaster. The report was in the making for six years, involving more than 800 scientists around the world. Their main finding is that it is "extremely likely" that humans are the dominant cause of global warming, with carbon dioxide emissions the main factor.

The atmosphere and ocean have warmed, the amount of snow and ice have diminished, the global mean sea level has risen and the concentrations of green house gases have increased. Unless the rise in global temperatures is kept down to two degrees by the end of this century, which seems a herculean task as the rise might reach 4.8 degrees, the world might be crossing the threshold of managing the impending disaster. As it is, each of the past three decades has been warmer than any preceding decade since 1850, and the past 30 years have been warmest since 600 AD.

The first 10 years of this century were the hottest in 160 years, and filled with more broken temperature records than any other decade, as global warming continued to accelerate. This is reflected in rising sea levels, melting of Arctic ice and the world's glaciers, thawing of permafrost releasing methane—which is even more toxic for the atmosphere than CO^2—acidification of oceans damaging coral reefs and sea life and so on. All these changes, as we are already seeing, will increase the frequency of disastrous occurrences like tropical cyclones, bush fires, floods and the likes.

There is a need, therefore, to work in harmony with nature than to confront and seek to overpower it, wherein lies the path to destruction. We need to downsize our vandalism of the planet to conserve its resources and partake of them with a sense of humility, equity and shared enterprise. And that will require a new international economic order to avert natural disasters from global warming.

Some island nations, including the Maldives, have concluded that climate change poses an existential threat, as rising sea levels could submerge their low-lying islands. Some larger nations are incorporating issues of climate change in their strategic defence planning in anticipation of a higher rate of humanitarian assistance and disaster relief missions. Their concerns centre on forecasts of a growing incidence and severity of climate-related natural disasters such as flooding, tropical cyclones and drought, and the consequent impacts on food, fresh water and infrastructure. Such events, together with their potential impacts on human disease and migration, could pose significant stresses on vulnerable nations with limited abilities and resources to respond to environmental strains.

As the security sector develops plans for adaptation and considers planning for response to the impacts of climate change, there is an emerging need for more robust institutions to support a broader and deeper dialogue between the scientific and security communities. We also need to remember that among the greatest threats to our collective rights and in particular to the rights of the poor, the weak and the vulnerable, is climate change. And why we must remember it is important that the international community acts to recognise, support and protect the world's growing number of climate refugees.

On 21 November 2013 the G77+ China group of 133 countries walked out of the United Nations climate change conference in Warsaw on the Loss and Damage mechanism after developed nations refused to agree to terms in a closed-door meeting when delegations from the industrial block refused to agree that the mechanism for such compensation is needed now and not after 2015 when a new climate change agreement is expected to be signed in Paris.

As part of the demands, the developing countries want developed nations to honour a 2009 Copenhagen pledge to provide up to $100 billion by 2020 for environmental damage. Another stumbling block in the negotiations is sharing the future emissions curbs, as developing nations want to create a UN body charged with compensating for environmental damage. Washington has opposed the position saying that a deal under which "the developed countries would be treated in one way, in one section of the agreement, and developing countries in a different part of the agreement" was a "non-starter."

Rising Military Expenditure in South Asia

Defence expenditure has been a major issue and an ongoing concern in the developing world and, in particular, in South Asia. The debate about defence versus development is perhaps one of the oldest in the discourse around planning priorities. In assessing defence spending in South Asia, we need to understand the geopolitical scenario around the region. The security of countries in South Asia is directly and indirectly affected by the military postures and policies of many countries, both within South Asia as well as beyond it. As a consequence, the defence spending of the countries of South Asia is influenced not only by countries within the traditional South Asian region, but also by others, especially those bordering the region.

Defence spending in South Asian countries, like in most other countries, is governed substantively by threat perceptions. The major spenders have been India, Pakistan, Sri Lanka, Bangladesh and Afghanistan. The proportion in terms of GDP might appear to be quite small, especially when viewed from the perspective of conventional wisdom, according to which South Asia constitutes a 'hot spot' of rivalries and conflict, and is even poised for a nuclear war. But this does not invalidate the need to further reduce levels of defence expenditure, since the region also contains great poverty and underdevelopment. What is needed is to reduce to its barest minimum the amount of national resources devoted to sustain military power.

In terms of military expenditure as percentage of GDP, Pakistan spends the most. The figures are: 3.2% in the case of Pakistan; 2.9% in the case of Sri Lanka; 2.7% in the case of India; 1.7% in the case of Nepal; 1.5% in the case of Afghanistan; 1% in the case of Bangladesh (SIPRI data on military expenditures, 2007).

Table: Military Spending by Country (All prices in $m, 2010 prices)

Country	1988	2010	2011	2011 current prices	% of GDP, 1988	% of GDP, 2010
Afghanistan	. .	576	781	**878**	. .	3.8
Bangladesh	456	1,298	1,367	**1,436**	1.0	1.1
China	. .	121,064	129,272	**142,859**	. .	2.1
India	16,705	46,086	44,282	**48,889**	3.6	2.7
Indonesia	1,405	4,663	5,220	**5,709**	0.9	0.7
Iran	1,776	. .	. .	**. .**	2.0	. .
Malaysia	1,293	3,859	4,223	**4,587**	2.4	1.6
Myanmar	. .	. .	. .	**. .**	2.1	. .
Nepal	60	255	241	**259**	0.9	1.4
Pakistan	3,657	5,661	5,685	**6,282**	6.2	2.8
Singapore	2,622	8,323	8,302	**9,475**	4.8	3.7
Sri Lanka	434	1,500	1,403	**1,557**	2.4	3.0
Thailand	3,170	4,846	5,114	**5,521**	2.9	1.5
World total	**1,511,141**	**1,622,888**	**1,624,506**	**1,727,513**		

Figures are in US $m., at constant 2010 prices and exchange rates, except for the last figure, which is in US$m at 2011 prices and exchange rates.
". ." = data unavailable.
Source: SIPRI (Stockholm International Peace Research Institute).

Despite the fact that India and Pakistan have not been recognised by the international community as nuclear weapon states, they are in truth heavily nuclearised. Also, both are non-signatories of the Comprehensive Test Ban Treaty (CTBT) and Non Proliferation Treaty (NPT). The financial burden of this nuclear race is being borne by the economies of the two countries. Pressure on budgets over a period of time has increased and will continue to do so till the process is reversed. This is over and above the expenditure on conventional weapons. The conflict and 'enmity' between India and Pakistan and the resultant insecurity in the people of both nations supports this kind of expenditure on conventional as well as nuclear or nonconventional weapons, giving it legitimacy in the people's minds.

Demographic Dividends in South Asia

In 2010, a dominant share of the world's nearly seven billion people—4.2 billion or 60.4 per cent lived in Asia. Of those, 1.7 billion lived in South Asia, a number that is projected to increase to 2.4 billion by 2050. This increase will partially reflect demographic transition within the South Asian region. It has been the result of at least two key trends—declining fertility rates and improved life expectancy.

Fertility transition in South Asia began over 40 years ago, falling from a rate of around six children per woman in the late 1960s to reach three at the beginning of the millennium. The striking aspect is the speed of the decline: fertility is below the replacement level of 2.1 in Iran and the Maldives, and close to the level in Bhutan, Bangladesh, India, Nepal and Sri Lanka.

Declining fertility rates have been accompanied by improvement in life expectancy at birth. A child born today in South Asia can expect to live on average 65 years, up from 42 years five decades ago. Countries achieving an average life expectancy of more than 70 years include Iran, Sri Lanka and the Maldives. At the other extreme is Afghanistan, with less than 50 years.

This combination of declining fertility and increased longevity has resulted in the challenging issue of population ageing. In the past six decades, South Asia's 60-plus population has increased four-fold, from 28 million in 1950 to 125 million in 2010. It is projected to increase from 7.3 per cent of the total population to 10.5 per cent in 2025, and 19.1 per cent in 2050.

Population ageing and growth in the size of elderly populations have a number of policy implications. In South Asia, the healthcare infrastructure is weak. Medical, public health, social services and other facilities required to meet the needs of the elderly are likely to put severe strain on the healthcare system and the economy. Also, old age has a major risk factor of non-communicable diseases such as cardiovascular conditions, cancer and diabetes, which will sharply increase the need for long-term health care. Another challenge is that a majority of countries do not have social security systems. Day-to-day care of the elderly requires a great many resources, including assistance from family members.

The share of the working-age population will continue to grow in almost all South Asian countries for two or three decades. This suggests that there is potential for continued economic growth. But South Asia has yet to put in place the appropriate social and economic policies that are needed to fully capitalise on the demographic dividend. Effective policies in key areas such as population and family planning, public health, education, governance and economic management will allow maximum returns, particularly from the working-age population. Policy makers and planners must be aware of the demographic dividend's relevance to investment planning and human resources development. The region must prepare itself for the irreversible demographic transition that will follow.

China-India Agreement: Interim Solution?

Following a series of alleged border incursions in 2013, China and India have signed a series of agreements, including a border pact during Indian Prime Minister Manmohan Singh's state visit to Beijing in November. While it is being labelled a 'landmark' agreement by the Indian media, there are still unresolved issues concerning the disputed Himalayan border, the so-called Line of Actual Control.

There is little doubt that the Border Defence Cooperation Agreement (BDCA) is a positive step towards smoothing tensions and rebuilding cooperation and trust between the two countries. Its main purpose, which includes provisions to improve communication between the two sides and increase military cooperation, is to reduce confrontation amid months of exacerbated tensions along the border.

The agreement emphasizes the two countries as civilisational partners who have more to benefit from mutual cooperation than conflict, specifically on trade. The agreement states that both sides will exercise maximum self-restraint and refrain from provocative actions, and not use force in situations where border forces come into contact with each other in areas that are still disputed. However, both sides have reservations on the pact's practical significance. There is still little consensus on what constitutes the border, making the likelihood of future skirmishes a near certainty despite the moves to improve communication, including a hotline between high ranking officers.

Besides the border issue, both China and India have much to gain from wider cooperation on several trans-boundary issues, including defence cooperation, intelligence sharing and people-to-people contacts. On trade and investment China and India need to maintain momentum and increase opportunities for substantive strategic dialogue if they want to deepen economic relations and achieve the pledge to increase two-way trade to $100bn a year by 2015, given that last year trade between the two countries fell 10% to $66.6bn.

Given existing sensitivities, the agreement on trans-boundary water sharing issues is an encouraging indicator of a better climate of relations between the two Asian nuclear powers. China and India have also agreed to study the possibility of an economic corridor that would run through Bangladesh and Burma (Myanmar). Although this would assist in improving trade, transport and communication links, thus far efforts towards regional economic integration have proved difficult.

China is now at a turning point. The country's economic growth has firmly cemented Chinese businesses and national interests around the globe. It has raised the living standards, but also the expectations, of China's citizens. There is a growing sense of Chinese patriotism that exists beyond the confines of the Communist Party. The emerging educated middle class has traveled the world, has seen multiple systems in action and is taking a greater interest in local and national political decisions. Modern forms of communication such as social media give Chinese citizens the ability to rapidly share successes and grievances across the country, to identify and single out cases of political corruption and to more actively keep the Party and leadership under scrutiny. At the same time, the expanded Chinese imports of raw materials and exports of commodities have substantially expanded China's active foreign interests, requiring a more nuanced and potentially a more activist foreign policy.

Iran-Pakistan Gas Pipeline

The construction of the Pakistan portion of the Iran-Pakistan gas pipeline has started. The present phase of the project involves the laying of a 780-kilometre section of the pipeline on the Pakistani side at an expected cost of $ 1.5 billion. Around 1,100 km of the pipeline in Iran between Bandar Abbas and Iranshehar has already been completed by Iran. The pipeline will terminate at Multan in Pakistan after traversing through volatile Balochistan province. The pipeline will export 8.7 billion cubic metre of natural gas to Pakistan, which will be sufficient to generate 5000 MW of power.

India withdrew from the project over pricing and security issues in 2009. Iran and Pakistan signed an agreement on the pipeline on 16 March 2010, in Ankara. According to the agreement, each country must complete its section of the pipeline by 2014. The reluctance of India to join this project in spite of perpetual shortfall in the availability of natural gas in the country was influenced by a number of factors. Most important was the security of gas supply due the volatile situation in the Balochistan area and the threat from *jihadi* terrorists to harm India's economic interest. Take and pay clause would have made India pay for the gas whether it received it or not due to these disruptions. The stoppage of the supply would have made a profound adverse economic impact on the downstream users. The high price of gas demanded by Iran was another major impediment for India in joining this project.

Another factor which came into play against India joining the pipeline project is the tremendous reduction in the cost of production, shipping and re-gassification of liquified natural gas (LNG). As a result, the transportation cost of gas through the pipeline and as LNG has become comparable within a distance range of 2000-3000 kilometres, which corresponds to the Iran-Pakistan-India pipeline length. Thus, the Indian establishment opined that LNG is a better option than a pipeline for gas transportation. A large number of LNG terminals have been already established and more are in the pipeline.

The South Par gas field from where the pipeline is originating is one of the largest gas fields in the world and is spread over 9,700 square kilometres. Out of this, 3,700 square kilometres falls in Iran and 6,000 square kilometres falls under the jurisdiction of Qatar. While Qatar is producing more than 230 billion cubic metres of gas per year, Iran is producing only 110 billion cubic metres annually.

If India joins the pipeline project at a later date when geopolitical and economic conditions get resolved, Pakistan will earn $ 500 million per year as transit fee. However, there is a flip side for Pakistan also. If the pipeline is not completed on the Pakistan side by the end of 2014, it will have to pay a daily penalty of $ 1 million to Iran until its completion. Also, from the end of 2014, Pakistan would be obliged to pay Iran for gas under a "take or pay" contract linked to the pipeline project, regardless of whether it actually receives any gas or not.

Power Politics in the Indian Ocean

The Indian Ocean Region (IOR) is becoming increasingly significant in the world arena. Recent discourse has focused on China's naval ambitions in the IOR and potential US–India cooperation in response to China's presence. To some extent, the 'China Factor' is one explanation behind the recent improvement of US–India relations, as both the US and India are anxious about Chinese entry into IOR. Particularly in India, many strategists are concerned about the imaginary Chinese 'string of pearls strategy'. However, an in-depth analysis of the three countries' strategic outlook could lead to a different conclusion.

The perception of the 'China threat' mainly derives from a fear of China's different political system and its astonishing rise, both in scale and speed. But when analysed in relation to intention, capability, or aspiration, it is clear that the potential threat of China has always been over-exaggerated. China's strategic focus is the Pacific rather than the Indian Ocean. It lags far behind the US in terms of maritime power and does not enjoy India's geographic advantages.

Today, China's naval strategy is to ensure a 'harmonious sea' through capacity building and international cooperation. China views the region surrounding the Indian Ocean as a vital energy and trade route, not a battlefield for power struggle. China's seaward policy is strongly influenced by trade and energy motives, and its open economy is becoming more interdependent with the outside world, particularly the Indian Ocean. Chinese involvement in building infrastructure in IOR littorals is part of China's economy-oriented 'going global' strategy. Although it is frequently argued that China should and must develop into becoming a strong maritime power, many Chinese scholars warn against having a military presence in the IOR. Also, the differing interests of the US and India in the IOR will be difficult to reconcile. The US and India have had contradictory strategic policies regarding the Indian Ocean since the Cold War era.

Indian politicians and strategists pay great attention to the linkages between Indian Ocean and India's national security. India's Maritime Military Strategy (2007) highlighted that 'whatever happens in the IOR can affect our national security and is of interest to us'. India's unique geographic location forms the cornerstone of India's aspiration to dominate the Indian Ocean. Many Indian strategists view the Indian Ocean as India's 'rightful domain' and contend that 'India will have to play a very large role (in the Indian Ocean) if the prospects for peace and cooperation are to grow'.

In accordance with the shift of the world power balance, the US will seek to sustain its strong presence in the Indian Ocean. The US has taken many measures to achieve this goal, including strengthening its presence in Diego Garcia and Bahrain, updating its military cooperation with established allies, and setting up forward military networks to control key choke points.

Thus, although confrontations and conflicts between China, US and India have been predicted in this region, particularly with the rise of China's maritime power, their different strategic goals may lead to different results. Given Chinese policy aims, intent and capability, they cannot afford to challenge either the United States or India. With its rapid growth of economic and military power, India is likely to adopt a more assertive maritime presence in the Indian Ocean. Thus, an India–US potential power struggle in the Indian Ocean is more likely to characterise the IOR seascape than the 'China threat'.

Militancy in Pakistan

After the invasion of Afghanistan by the US and its allies in 2001, as the Afghan Taliban and al Qaeda militants moved into tribal areas, they succeeded in networking with home-grown militant outfits due to the well-entrenched *jihadi* infrastructure. Conditions were already ripe in Pakistan for the spike in militancy at the time of the invasion of Afghanistan by the US.

The availability of supportive infrastructure spawned militancy in the country, and the religiously conservative society, fed on the steady diet of an exclusionist ideology and deprived of critical reasoning, effortlessly accepted the Taliban narrative on war. Giving in to the Taliban worldview has muddled the efforts of the Pakistan government to find military as well as political solutions to the incessant militancy.

The Taliban narrative, which has historical continuum and parallels in other Muslim countries, resonates both amongst the religious conservatives, and the educated, middle classes, who deem the rise in militancy as a natural corollary of the imperial wars of the US and other western countries, waged for control of Muslim economic resources and military bases.

Pakistani society needs to be exposed to secular, pluralistic perspectives that nullify the narrow-minded, ideological agenda of the Taliban. To undertake curricular reforms, it is important to revamp history books for teaching students a broad-based version of world history, enabling them to place historical events in context. Then, to apply lessons from history to the present world, students must be imparted knowledge through pedagogical methodologies that impart critical reasoning skills. Apart from revising history books, students must also be taught about the rituals and belief systems of different religious groups living in Pakistan to sensitise them about different religious perspectives.

Aligning of state identity with religion in Pakistan has produced fault lines in the country and increased the propensity of society to sympathise with the worldview of the militants. Institutions such as the Council of Islamic Ideology, which advises parliament and the provincial assemblies to formulate laws in conformity with the injunctions of the Quran and Sunnah, must be reconstituted to include a more modern vision of Islam.

Next, the infrastructure that is used to foster Taliban militancy and their narrative, which includes militarised *madrassas*, publishing houses printing hate literature, and certain Islamic charity organisations that collect donations to use them for funding suicide attacks against different Muslim denominations and other religious minorities must be dismantled.

Finally, the Pakistani security establishment must realise that giving support to non-state actors and the Afghan Taliban is a flawed policy. The Kashmircentric sectarian organisations that have joined hands with sectarian militant outfits to carry out their pernicious ideological agenda, while providing succour to the Afghan Taliban, has not signalled the success of the doctrine of strategic depth, but has invariably provided depth to the Taliban to carry out their attacks. Therefore the doctrine of strategic depth and the policy of using non-state actors as proxy agents, with all their unintended consequences, must be reviewed.

Understanding the numeric superiority of the state, terrorists employ the 'death by a thousand cuts' strategy, attacking the state, its institutions and its people whenever and wherever possible, then disappearing into ungoverned areas or densely populated urban and semi urban centres. The terrorists, as explained by the nature of their actions, are playing for time; time to strengthen themselves into a force that becomes an existential threat to Pakistan.

What's more, Pakistan's inability to control terror activities damages its international reputation. The world's leading financial standards body, Financial Action Task Force, declared in June 2013 that Pakistan and 11 other countries have failed to make sufficient progress in preventing money laundering and terrorist financing. This complex web of illegal financial transactions needs to be taken seriously. Pakistan must restrict and disown regional terror activities, as the country itself is internally crippled and has been one of the worst victims of terrorist violence. It may be that, finally, Pakistan has reached a point of no return in terms of terror regulation.

Water Wars

Water is the world's single most important resource. Life is not possible without it. It will likely determine our future and is becoming scarce. In the 20th century, the world's population grew by a factor of 3.8 and water use by nine. Today, more than half of humanity lives in water-stressed areas and could increase to two-thirds during the next decade. There are, incredibly, more people with a mobile phone than access to water-sanitation services. Already, bottled water costs more than crude oil on the spot market.

The Yemeni city of Sanaa, now home to two million, will be the first national capital to run dry in this century, if its groundwater reserves are depleted, which could happen as soon as 2025. Abu Dhabi and Quetta, experts believe, might also turn to dust. The international community should expect "water refugees" in just over a decade. The real geopolitical challenge of water scarcity will be national competition for rivers and glaciers—"water wars." Hydro-politics promises to become increasingly contentious and nasty.

Conflict over water arises in large part because it flows from one nation to the next or sits on geographical boundaries. Across five continents, there are 276 transnational river and lake basins separating 148 countries and accounting for three-fifths of the world's river flows. Excluding Antarctica, almost half the planet's land mass is covered by river basins spanning more than one country. Also, there are at least 274 underground freshwater basins beneath national borders. Some of these aquifers even encompass more than two countries.

The United Nations claims that more than two hundred international water agreements have been signed since World War II, but most of these deals are structurally anaemic. They lack dispute resolution mechanisms and even monitoring rules. Moreover, most have no provisions formally dividing water among users and many do not include key basin states. At this moment, there are only 18 agreements with specific allocation provisions. Significantly, none of these arrangements was signed this century, and most of them were concluded when serious water shortages were uncommon. The 1997 UN Convention on the Law of the Non-Navigational Uses of International Watercourses, intended to become the world's water law, has yet to come into effect, lacking ratification by the minimum number of countries.

The issue is highlighted most clearly by the 1960 Indus River agreement, the world's most successful water treaty. In it, India generously agreed to allocate four-fifths of the six-river Indus system to downriver Pakistan, indefinitely. It was founded on the logic that a guaranteed share of the Indus-system waters for Pakistan would ease the territorial dispute and pave the way for sub-continental peace—an assumption that helped sway India to grant the lion's share of the waters to the lower-riparian party. The agreement, however, only convinced the Pakistani political establishment that it had to control the entire river system. Ayub Khan, Pakistan's ruler at the time, wanted to grab the headwaters of the river from India after the signing, thinking the existence of the cooperative arrangement actually justified his country's aggression. Two of these six rivers are now targeted by China's dam builders.

In an analogous situation, China, the world's "hydro-hegemon," is the source of river water for more countries than any other nation. The Chinese control headwaters that are needed by almost half of the world's population, in Central, South, and Southeast Asia, as well as Russia. Yet Beijing, which annexed by force virtually all its water resources in the middle of the 20th century, is building dams at a frenetic pace—it has completed an average of one large dam per day since 1949—and obviously seeks to present downriver neighbours with a fait accompli by diverting river flows. Significantly, China is a party to no water-sharing treaties and refuses to begin negotiations on water-sharing with other countries. No other country has ever managed to assume such unchallenged riparian pre-eminence by controlling the headwaters of multiple international rivers and manipulating their cross-border flows.

The memorandum of understanding signed during Prime Minister Manmohan Singh's visit to Beijing in November 2013 merely records that both parties "recognised that trans-border rivers and related natural resources and the environment are assets of immense value," and that they "agreed that cooperation on trans-border rivers will further enhance mutual strategic trust and communication." India even expressed appreciation to China for providing flood-season hydrological data.

India is particularly vulnerable because it directly receives more than 48% of the 718 billion cubic metres of surface water that flows out of Chinese territory every year. In addition, Nepal's Tibet-originating rivers empty into India's Ganges basin. India has more arable land than China, but the source of most major Indian rivers is Chinese-controlled Tibet.

If Beijing continues on its present unilateralist path, its upstream projects could complicate India's water-sharing arrangements with Bangladesh and Pakistan. In the 1996 Ganges Treaty, India guaranteed Bangladesh an equal share of the downriver flows during the dry season. But China is now planning to build a cascade of dams on the Ganges tributaries that contribute significantly to such downstream flows.

New Delhi has been pressing Beijing for transparency on its dam projects and a commitment not to redirect the natural flow of any river or to diminish cross-border flows. But even a joint expert-level mechanism between China and India—set up in 2007 for interaction and cooperation on hydrological data—has proven of little value. China has limited its cooperation to the sale of flood-season hydrological data. India provides such data free to Pakistan year-round.

China's dam-building spree is a reminder that Tibet remains at the heart of the India-China divide. This sprawling region ceased to be a political buffer when China annexed it more than six decades ago. For Tibet to turn into a political bridge between China and India, water has to become a source of cooperation, not conflict.

The United States and Pakistan: Divided They Stand

A decade ago, George W. Bush embraced Pervez Musharraf as America's top ally in the war against terror. In the years that followed, the US has provided Pakistan with over $25 billion in military and economic aid, including 18 F-16 jet fighters and a Perry Class frigate. The goal was to fight al-Qaeda. Only Israel got more aid from America in the last decade.

In practice, however, America and its NATO allies are fighting a proxy war with Pakistan in Afghanistan. Washington, backed by the United Nations, supports the Karzai government while Islamabad backs Mullah Omar and the Afghan Taliban. A secret NATO report, titled "The State of the Taliban", held that Pakistan and the ISI are the critical patrons of the Taliban insurgency. According to over 27,000 interrogations of captured Taliban and al-Qaeda fighters in Afghanistan, the ISI not only provides safe haven, sanctuary and funds for the Taliban, its officers meet regularly to plan strategy against the NATO with Omar's Quetta Shura. Without ISI help, the Taliban would not be the force they are today.

America, of course, is also fighting a clandestine drone war in Pakistan from bases in Afghanistan. The pace of lethal drone attacks has decreased significantly in the last year, but they remain a major irritant for Pakistan. Without the drones, the US would have no means to disrupt, dismantle and defeat al-Qaeda in Pakistan, which is the goal of its Afghanistan-Pakistan policy. The US tried relying on the ISI before to fight al-Qaeda. Then it found Osama bin Laden hiding in plain sight in Abbottabad, just outside the army's top military academy. Obama rightly decided he could not trust Pakistan with intelligence about bin Laden's hideout and ordered a secret commando raid to kill him. If there is no American pressure on al-Qaeda in Pakistan after 2014, al-Qaeda and its associates will regenerate there fast and furiously.

Often forgotten is another issue that troubles the relationship behind the scenes and off camera—Pakistan's nuclear ambitions. Pakistan has the fastest growing nuclear weapons arsenal in the world today. It is under no international regime. America pointedly refuses to consider giving Pakistan an Indian-style civil nuclear deal because of Pakistan's track record as a nuclear proliferation machine.

Two key issues lie ahead. If the bilateral security agreement between Afghanistan and the US is agreed on, it will also help to stabilise the region. Once it is clear that there will be a residual NATO presence in Afghanistan after 2014, perhaps 8,000-10,000 strong, all parties will have less uncertainty to deal with in future. If the security agreement is not finalised, then uncertainty will intensify and the region will face a very unstable future.

Pakistan and Afghanistan

No country aside from Afghanistan has more to lose than Pakistan from the coming departure of international forces. All post-2014 scenarios seem dark for Pakistan should the challenged Afghan state begin to unravel. In a protracted civil war, a reluctant Pakistan stands a good chance of being drawn into the conflict along with other regional powers. Taliban gains leading to a radical Islamic regime in all or most of Afghanistan, while once welcomed by Pakistan, may now result in empowering Pakistan's own militant extremists. Intensified fighting across the border is certain to push millions of new refugees into a Pakistan unprepared and unwilling to absorb them. Prospects that a successfully negotiated political agreement might avert these outcomes seem dim.

And yet, Pakistan does have one policy option that can result in a brighter scenario for itself and its Afghan neighbour. This opportunity has, in fact, been available throughout the course of the last 12 years, but it requires a strategic reassessment by Pakistan of its long-term national security interests, recognising that they are best served when there is a stable, peaceful, prospering and independent Afghanistan. While Pakistan officially endorses this vision, its policies regularly undermine its achievement, by giving sanctuary and sustenance to Afghan insurgents. Instead, Pakistan should fully embrace efforts that improve prospects for the emergence of a moderate, economically improving, and accountably-governed Afghanistan.

Convincing Afghans of Pakistan's good intentions will not be easy. Almost regardless of their political disposition, Afghans view their neighbour as overbearing and covetous, blaming it for much of the country's problems. Building trust is bound to be a slow process. Yet Pakistan is not without the means with which to allay Afghan suspicions. It has advantages that come with geographical proximity, overlapping cultural and ethnic affinities, and established economic ties. It also has a relative abundance of human capital available with which to help strengthen the Afghan state.

To begin, Pakistan could agree to open the long denied trans-country routes that block India's trade with Afghanistan. Afghanistan's critical dependence on road links to the port of Karachi could be better secured and border impediments removed. Existing training programmes in Pakistan for Afghan civil servants could be greatly expanded. Pakistan can do more to allay Afghans' beliefs that it has no plans to divide Afghan territory ethnically. It can also help secure Afghan presidential and parliamentary elections scheduled in 2014 and 2015, respectively, by using its not inconsiderable influence to limit Taliban interference. It could also place additional troops at the border to reduce infiltration, much as it did during elections in 2004 and 2005.

Pakistan cannot continue trying to differentiate between good and bad militants and expect the country's endemic violence to end. If there is to be a reckoning, Pakistan may find that dismantling the Afghan Taliban offers a less difficult first step toward eliminating all of the militant groups that are currently or will inevitably be challenging the Pakistani state.

Pakistan has much to gain from a strategic reappraisal. Aside from possibly avoiding an Afghan civil war and its consequences, Pakistan could expect to enlist Afghan efforts to deny Pakistan's Taliban insurgents the safe haven they have found across the border. Pakistan could feel confident that the Baloch rebellion is not being fuelled from the Afghan side of the border and that India does not overplay its hand once NATO forces leave. More broadly, Pakistan should have less reason to fear India's role in Afghanistan. A stabilised, secure Afghanistan would find it unnecessary to look to India to provide a counterweight to Pakistan or worry Pakistan by maintaining an oversized army.

Building confidence between the two countries could also perhaps permanently defuse their long-standing dispute over the Durand Line that separates them. With improved security in Afghanistan, new life could be breathed into plans to construct a gas pipeline from the fields in Turkmenistan. A growing Afghan economy would open up new markets for Pakistani goods and services and improve opportunities for investment. And Pakistan's dreams of using Afghanistan as a road bridge to Central Asia to extend its commerce and political influence might finally become a reality.

Without reciprocating Afghan policies, friendly overtures by Pakistan cannot be sustained. But it is Pakistan's initiatives that will drive any embrace. More than any external power, its actions will determine whether the present Afghan state can succeed against the current odds. And through assisting its struggling neighbour, Pakistan may help secure its own future.

Afghan End-Game

For past few years, India's current as well as future role in Afghanistan has been a subject that Pakistan does not want to even consider for discussion. Delhi has its own theory of getting involved in Afghanistan. From claiming its older civilisation links with the region to helping Afghanistan to become a country worth living, India has also been trying to display the greater power its presumably assumes in the region. What helped it, to be seen in Afghanistan, was the relationship of the Karzai regime with Pakistan and its deterioration helped to open up more doors for India's involvement.

Karzai government has been at logger heads with Islamabad right from Musharraf's time as it strongly believed that certain important sections in Pakistan's security establishments had been helping Taliban to destabilize Afghanistan. Nevertheless Pakistan's geographical proximity to Afghanistan could not keep it at bay as far as its role in the post September 11 attacks is concerned.

Delhi's increasing effort to fit in the "great game" that is likely to ensue after the 2014 withdrawal, however, has not been reciprocated positively by Pakistan for varied reasons. The divergent views are part of any discourse that is shaping on these lines. The Pakistani establishment is clear that they have a lead role in Afghanistan and have concerns about what they call India's "sinister" support to certain separatist groups along the borders in Pakistan. The charge, India vehemently refutes.

This silent war has been going on for a long time. With Delhi spending more than $ 2 billion in the past several years on the reconstruction process in Afghanistan, its stakes are increasing and that is why Islamabad sees red in Delhi being too enthusiastic. India's keenness to have a greater role in Afghanistan may not be out of place. However, unless both Islamabad and Delhi are on at least a normal mode in their relations, the latter's involvement in Afghanistan is fraught with dangers.

The biggest danger that looms large in this whole game is that with continuation in bitterness on both sides, the extremists in Pakistan will not allow Islamabad to have any deal with India on Afghanistan. For them Kashmir is the best weapon to use. So the noise about militants making their way into Kashmir after the withdrawal may come true in case India's influence in Afghanistan increases without bringing a semblance in the relations with Pakistan and break ice on Kashmir. The extremists in Pakistan will hold sway and Afghanistan could well be a new battlefield for both the countries if not a direct one at least proxy.

Trouble in Kashmir

The fighting in Kashmir ebbs and flows. And after a decade of relative quiet, the Line of Control (LoC) is once more an active frontline. In 2003 India and Pakistan agreed on a ceasefire on the LoC but General Musharraf's subsequent attempt to find a settlement ran into problems. How could India be expected to make concessions after it had fought for many years to defend the status quo?

There has been a significant increase in the number of clashes on the LoC. There have been over 200 ceasefire violations since the start of 2013. There were some fatal skirmishes in January, a significantly increased number of artillery exchanges throughout the year and a single night in October when Pakistani troops fired guns and mortars at over 50 Indian border posts. Militant activity has also intensified with an increased number of attacks targeting Indian security personnel. In one incident in October as many as 40 militants crossed the line of control.

Pakistani military officials have suggested that both sides are aware that, with Sharif in power, there may be high-level talks on Kashmir. Consequently, they are trying to secure gains on the ground to strengthen their position at the negotiating table.

The 2014 reduction in the level of US forces in Afghanistan is obliging everyone to rethink. The Afghan Taliban insurgency will in all likelihood continue. A residual US force will stay in Afghanistan. The remaining US military personnel will relocate in secure bases and the Taliban, demanding the removal of all foreign forces, will keep on attacking them.

With fewer foreign forces on Afghan soil the intensity of the conflict can be expected to diminish and that means thousands of militants—especially Punjabi militants thinking of moving on from their temporary homes in the north-west—will be looking for a new frontline. There is evidence that some are already contemplating a move to Kashmir. That is what happened after the Soviet withdrawal from Afghanistan and it could happen again. In fact some Kashmiri leaders are already expressing concern that their movement could be taken over by Taliban-style fighters – a development which would surely drain it of international support. The TTP's Wali-ur-Rehman has vowed to send fighters to Kashmir and the Hizb-ul-Mujahedeen has averred that: "many Kashmiris have been martyred in Afghanistan. So it is a debt that the Afghan Mujahedeen owe us."

Increased militant activity in Kashmir could suit the Pakistan Army well as it would like to keep the Kashmir dispute alive to justify Pakistan's very high levels of defence spending. People better disposed towards the army have a more sympathetic analysis: the military wants to keep Pakistan on the front foot during any negotiations with India.

But there is another, perhaps more important, consideration. Increased militant activity in Kashmir would ensure that, at a stroke, the focus of the militants' attacks would shift from the Pakistani army towards its Indian counterpart. And continued state sponsorship of militant activity in Kashmir would give the Pakistan Army another important benefit: the biggest groups, such as the LeT, would be given a good reason to remain loyal to Pakistan's institutions.

The summer of 2014 could indeed be a hot one for Kashmir. There are many powerful organisations and institutions with an interest in Kashmir. By the time the army, the militants and the Indians have all worked out their strategies and tactics there is not much room left for the people who actually live there. And many of them will be anxious about the prospect of their long struggle being hijacked by the Taliban.

The Rising Challenge of Food and Energy Security

The world is being haunted again by the spectre of a global food shortage. Demand for food over the next decade is expected to increase by one per cent annually but global food productivity gains have declined from two per cent between 1970 and 2000 to one percent today and continuing to decline.

A 2011 study reported that the world had consumed more than it had produced for seven out of the past eight years. These concerns will lead to growing attention to the nexus between food, water and energy resources, especially as climate change is expected to have an increasing impact globally.

As China and India have opened to global trade and more wealthy societies are eating more protein, consuming more calories and enjoying more varied diets in recent years, there is growing concern with the fragility of the global food system. These concerns were highlighted by the spike in food prices and disruptions in food supply.

Robustness in food security systems is critical and that governments need to work with the private sector and other key stakeholders. Instead of piecemeal strategies, an integrated and holistic approach to policy formulation and implementation is critical to deal with the four dimensions in food security: availability, physical access, economic access and utilisation. Sharp increases in the price of key food imports, export bans by major food suppliers and difficulties in obtaining adequate supplies could have significant domestic ramifications.

Although it was earlier anticipated that energy security and food security would be competing objectives, the rise of the shale oil and gas revolution has changed the global outlook. The US will soon be self-sufficient in oil and natural gas, Australia could rival Qatar as an exporter of gas and Europe is re-thinking its opposition to exploiting its shale resources.

The issue of water management will assume growing importance as water scarcity will be a constraint in expanding food production. Pricing is a critical issue. Most governments charge farmers 10 to 20 per cent of the price paid by industrial users or households for water consumption. This leads to sub-optimal use of scarce water resources such as the growing of water-intensive crops in semi-desert conditions.

MFN Status to India by Pakistan

Most favoured nation (MFN) status to India is not being considered by Pakistan. It is an additional blow to India-Pakistan relations. While improved trade relations could significantly enhance political ties between the two countries, it more likely that bilateral relations will continue to languish at current low levels. India's 2012 trade with Pakistan accounted for a mere US$2.15 billion of its total trade of US$778 billion (less than 0.3 per cent). Exports to Pakistan accounted for only 0.56 per cent of India's exports, while imports constituted 0.11 per cent. Given the size of both countries' economies and the complementarity of their trading baskets, the present level of trade should be higher. The denial of MFN status compounds these difficulties, and arguably neutralises the positive steps taken by both countries over the last few years.

Though the positive list approach, which allowed for the import of 2,000 items from India, was abolished in 2012 and replaced with the 'negative list' approach, which prohibits listed items from import, improvement has been marginal. The negative list contains 1,500 items, with 500 being untradeable items belonging to the iron, steel and automobile sectors in which India has comparative advantage. In addition there are non-tariff barriers on both sides, including: licensing and customs requirements; visa policies and restrictions on travel; high trade and transaction costs due to long waiting periods at the borders; a lack of information on tradable items; and India-Pakistan trade compliance regulations.

India's exports to Pakistan at the industry level have witnessed negligible and fluctuating growth due to the limitations of the positive list, even in very competitive industries such as base metals and articles, and textiles. India fares better in industries where there are more items on the positive list. In recent years, India has also exported more mineral products and textiles subsequent to these products being added to the positive list. The quantity of goods moving from India to Pakistan is determined by local demand at any given point in time, and MFN status would have given stability to this demand.

On the other hand, Pakistan's exports to India are suffering from India's lack of tariff liberalisation. India has agreed to bring down all tariffs under the South Asia Free Trade Area, other than those on the negative/sensitive list. But India's negative list includes some of the top 10 import items from Pakistan, such as edible fruits and nuts, some cotton textiles materials, carpets and sacks.

MFN status would not only help provide stability in trade relations between the two countries but would also assist Pakistan in technology upgrades, greater productivity gains, and increased revenues from legal trade. It is reported that India-Pakistan informal trade (trade occurring through a third country) accounts for more than formal trade (which is around US$4 billion). Further, consumers would experience lower product prices and greater variety.

Drones and Deception

Pakistani has recently been giving a call for the US to end its drone strikes on the Af-Pak border regions. However, it is becoming clear that between 2007 and 2011, the CIA had not only been briefing Pakistan on the drone strikes but Pakistani officials also selected some of the targets.

It thus raises a tricky question: when formulating national policy on drones which Pakistani authorities count under international law? The politicians or the military? Because even as Pakistani politicians in recent years have rallied domestic and international opinion against the drones, the Pakistani military granted the Americans permission to fly them from the Shamsi air base in Balochistan. (Shamsi was only denied to the Americans in 2011).

Most obviously the provision of the air base was only for intelligence gathering by drones but it contradicted stated Pakistani government policy. It was obvious that Pakistan was also cooperating with it. In April 2013 General Musharraf admitted that he had given clearance for some strikes. The deception about the use of drones is, therefore, convoluted in the extreme. There were even suggestions that the Pakistani military attacked a target in the tribal areas and then described the strike as a drone attack which it went on to condemn. The US can hardly be accused of breaching Pakistani sovereignty. The Pakistani army's position, however, remains opaque. It is also reported that the US is still giving Pakistan briefings about against who – or where—the strikes are taking place—implying a degree of cooperation.

In terms of international law, only the state's highest authorities have the power to give consent to use force. It is not sufficient to obtain consent from particular agencies or departments of the government. The democratically elected government is the body responsible for Pakistani international relations and the sole entity able to express the will of the state in its international affairs. Suggestions of continued operation at the military or intelligence level not affect the position in international law. In other words Pakistan is like everywhere else: parliament makes laws, the government implements them and the army has to do what it's told.

Cyber Threat

A few countries along with terrorist organisations of all hues are wreaking havoc across the world, displaying their cyber prowess at crippling infrastructure—political and financial—of countries without deploying conventional violent means. The West, especially the US, is vigorously putting in place systems to combat the menace.

How prepared is India? The country's core assets such as power grids and financial and transport networks are fast getting connected to the internet and more official data are getting stored online. Hostile neighbours and wily groups of global and local extremists are equipping themselves in no-holds-barred cyber warfare—the Assam riots a few months ago that triggered a widespread exodus of north eastern students from cities such as Bangalore confirmed the subversive games they play through social networks.

The most frequently attacked networks include the Prime Minister's Office and the ministry of external affairs. Today, there can be no differentiating cyberspace from land, air and sea. Cyber defence should be an integrated effort. It is the fourth arm after the army, navy and air force. Though cyberspace is a domain of strategic importance, cyber weapons have not yet been associated with publicly well-enunciated doctrines of use comparable to that of the nuclear age.

Cyberspace is a domain of strategic importance. The threat of cyber attacks has been placed at the top of the list of national security risks in the "Intelligence Community Worldwide Threat Assessment of 2013," and computer network warfare is one of the only military areas in both the US and in NATO countries that is expected to grow.

Need to Protect the Internet

The internet as we know it is open, secure and resilient. It was designed and evolved this way. Due to its open nature, it has gained traction at a fantastic pace and transformed the world by fostering communication and innovation while generating tremendous economic growth. Roughly 2.5 billion people, more than one third of the world's population, currently use the internet, and another 2.5 billion individuals are expected to go online by the end of this decade. But the open internet that governments, corporations and individuals the world over rely on is under threat.

The internet, as it transforms, has become a victim of its own success. The various groups that rely on internet services—governments, corporations, and individuals of all types and purposes—have different needs. Sometimes these needs overlap, and sometimes they are at odds. However, sovereign governments are increasingly seeking control of their own domestic spheres as well as the flow of data and information between countries and, in doing so, are attacking the openness that represents one of the foundations of the internet.

Nation-states are increasingly attempting to regulate social, political and economic activity and content in cyberspace and, in many cases, suppress expression they view as threatening. Justifying their actions by claiming to protect national security, more than 40 governments have erected restrictions of information, data and knowledge flow on the internet. Censoring the internet takes many forms including censorship of opinions; specific websites or ISPs; specific information; demanding information be taken down; demanding users' IP addresses; and erecting regulatory barriers to cross-border, information flow. More drastically, others have considered building national computer networks that would tightly control or even sever connections to the global internet. These are broader global challenges confronting the world's internet infrastructure.

The internet facilitates communication, commerce and trade and is an integral part of modern life. The global repercussions of censorship are severe. Regulations that constrict the flow of information not only create disparities among people's access to knowledge, but also have a negative effect on the shape, architecture, safety and resilience of the internet. Future trade agreements should include the goal of fostering free flow of information across national borders. A global internet increasingly fragmented into national systems is not in the interest of the world.

How Will The New World Order Be Shaped?

We have now reached the middle years of the century's second decade, but the answers to questions about the nature of the world and how the new international political and economic order will take shape remain as obscure as ever. The last century was one of great disasters but also one of almost unbelievable progress in which the present international system was created. Now, however, the inadequacy of the system is becoming more evident.

The world we live in today is very different from that of the recent past. Inter-governmental organisations like the UN, the IMF, and the World Bank are losing their ability to function and proving themselves inadequate in providing international security and preventing economic and financial crises. The consequence is increased competition and disputes between states. The nation state is being updated. As the UN system loses functionality, a return to the balance of power and to alliances resembling those of the 19th century is gaining credence.

Globalisation, the opening of economies to international markets, leads both to great prosperity and great imbalances. At the same time it also leads to universal values, such as human rights and freedoms, spreading and being appreciated throughout different countries and continents. But in many places racial or social blockages, ethnic and religious impositions, and authoritarian administrations which mercilessly use violence even against their own people all still linger.

Absolute power has come to an end. People, goods, money, ideas, values, and technological innovations are entering into circulation in the world at unbelievable speed. The conceptions of political and military power that have prevailed for centuries are now losing their meaning. No single country, no matter how strong it may be, and no single leader, no matter how authoritarian, can single-handedly determine the agenda for the world. Non-state actors can flummox even superpowers. No one can take control of the global economy. New energy technologies are overturning traditional geopolitical strategies. Multilateral systems are being compelled to give way to bilateral agreements, balance of power politics, and the influence of regional dynamics.

What is even more important is that each country should contemplate the ways in which the new political, economic, security, and financial order of the 21st century will be shaped, the principles on which governments will rise, and where the world's centres of gravity will come into being.

ISSUES

LOOKING BEYOND SOUTH ASIA: INDIA'S 'LOOK EAST' POLICY GATHERS MOMENTUM

Harsh V. Pant, Reader in International Relations, Department of Defence Studies, King's College, London

Introduction

In a quiet stretch of water off Vietnam's coast, India and China are jockeying for position in a maritime game that serves as a microcosm of wider regional anxieties about China's claims to sovereignty over large parts of the South China Sea. By calling for international bids on an offshore oil and gas exploration lease in a block where India and Vietnam are already undertaking exploration, China has thrown down the gauntlet.[1] By deciding to stay put in the assigned block, India has indicated it is ready to take up the Chinese challenge. At stake is Chinese opposition to India's claim to be a regional power.

The conflict between India and China over the South China Sea has been building for almost two years. India signed an agreement with Vietnam in October 2011 to expand and promote oil exploration in South China Sea and then reconfirmed its decision to carry on despite the Chinese challenge to the legality of the Indian presence.[2]

By accepting the Vietnamese invitation to explore for oil and gas in Blocks 127 and 128, India's state-owned oil company ONGC Videsh Ltd, or OVL, not only expressed New Delhi's desire to deepen its friendship with Vietnam, but ignored China's warning to stay away. After asking countries "outside the region" to stay away from the South China Sea, China issued a demarche to India in November 2011, underlining that Beijing's permission should be sought for exploration in Blocks 127 and 128 and, without it, OVL's activities would be considered illegal. Vietnam, meanwhile, had relied upon the 1982 UN Convention on the Law of the Sea to claim its sovereign rights over the two blocks being explored.

India accepted Vietnam's claims and ignored China's objections.[3] India maintains that its exploration projects in the region are purely commercial. China claims Indian exploration projects in the region violate its sovereignty and views India's growing engagement within East and South-East Asia with suspicion.

[1] Pranab Dhal Samanta, "China puts Indian oil block up for auction," *Indian Express*, 12 July 2012.
[2] "India, Vietnam sign pact for oil exploration in South China Sea," *The Hindu*, 13 October 2011.
[3] Rakesh Sharma, "ONGC to Continue Exploration in South China Sea," *Wall Street Journal*, 19 July 2012.

India's decision to explore for hydrocarbons with Vietnam followed an incident in July 2011 when an unidentified Chinese warship demanded that amphibious assault vessel, INS Airavat, identify itself and explain its presence in the South China Sea after leaving Vietnamese waters.[4] Completing a scheduled port call in Vietnam, the Indian warship was in international waters at the time.

After an initial show of defiance, India appeared to have showed second thoughts about its exploration efforts in the region. In May 2012, India's junior oil minister R.P.N. Singh told the Parliament that OVL had decided to return Block 128 to Vietnam as exploration there wasn't commercially viable. Hanoi publicly suggested that New Delhi's decision was a response to pressure from China. In July 2012, after Vietnam gave OVL more time incentives in terms of a longer period to prove commercial viability, India decided to continue the joint exploration. Vietnam decided to extend the OVL contract for hydrocarbon exploration in Block 128, reiterating that it valued India's presence in the South China Sea for regional strategic balance.

In June 2012, the state-owned China National Offshore Oil Company, or CNOOC, opened nine blocks for exploration in waters also claimed by Vietnam.[5] Oil block 128, which Vietnam argues is inside its 200-nautical mile Exclusive Economic Zone granted under the UN Law of the Sea, is part of the nine blocks offered for global bidding by CNOOC.

By putting up for global bidding a Vietnamese petroleum block under exploration by an Indian oil company, China has forced India into a corner, but India was quick to show that it would not be cowed. At the July 2012 ASEAN Regional Forum in Phnom Penh, India made a strong case for supporting not only freedom of navigation but also access to resources in accordance with principles of international law.[6] New Delhi, which so often likes to sit on the sidelines and margins and avoids taking sides, seems to have recognised that it can no longer afford the luxury of inaction if it wants to preserve credibility as a significant actor in both East Asia and Southeast Asia.

In July 2013, a non-sourced report carried by the India News and Feature Alliance claimed that:

> '...of late, OVL (India's ONGC Videsh Limited) has relinquished Block no.127 and suspended work in Block no.128, which had been the epicentre of diplomatic uproar. It relinquished Block 127 after it encountered dry wells. It had already invested US $50 million in exploration in Block 128 until last year. After repeated exploration, it was found that due to the hard seabed in the area, the prospect of finding oil in the block was low. Hence, it was not a very cost effective project to continue. Besides, India had to pay US $15 million as exit fee to Petro Vietnam to get out of the block. By giving up exploration in these two blocks India has extracted itself from the SCS (South China Sea) dispute.'[7]

But, despite reports to the contrary, India has certainly not exited from Block 128. The issue of Block 127 is more complicated but there has been no official withdrawal. So officially India remains present. This continued presence, despite the apparent lack of commercial viability, further emphasises the seriousness with which New Delhi is pursuing its 'Look East' policy, notwithstanding China's displeasure. In the same month that India's withdrawal from the South China Sea oil hunt was erroneously reported, The Hindu reported that India had offered Vietnam a US$100-million credit line for the purchase of four military patrol boats.[8] This rare offer, usually reserved for India's immediate neighbours, emphasises that New Delhi's gaze remains firmly eastwards.

India's 'Look East' Policy Emerges

Despite its historical and cultural links with East and Southeast Asia, India in its post-independence foreign policy largely tended to ignore the region. The structural constraints of the Cold War proved too formidable, despite India's geographic proximity to the East Asian region. The end of the Cold War brought East Asia back to the forefront of India's foreign policy horizons. The disintegration of the Soviet Union radically transformed the structure of the then prevailing international system, and brought to the fore new challenges and opportunities for

---

[4] Ben Bland and Girija Shivakumar, "China confronts Indian navy vessel," *Financial Times*, 31 August 2011.

[5] Samanta, "China puts Indian oil block up for auction."

[6] Prak Chun Thal and Stuart Grudgings, "SE Asia meeting in disarray over sea dispute with China," *Reuters*, 13 July 2012.

[7] Amrita Banerjee, "Indo-Vietnamese Meet: Choppy Signal to China?",*India News and Feature Alliance*, 18 July 2013. http://www.sarkaritel.com/indo-vietnamese-meet-choppy-signal-to-china/ [accessed 23 July 2013]

[8] Sandeep Dikshit, "India offers $100-m. credit line to Vietnam." The Hindu, July 28, 2013.

countries like India. New Delhi was forced to reorient its approach toward international affairs in general, and towards East Asia in particular. The government of P.V. Narasimha Rao launched its 'Look East' policy in the early 1990s explicitly to initiate India's re-engagement with East Asia.

This Indian engagement of East Asia in the post-Cold War era has assumed significant proportions and remains a top foreign policy priority for the Indian leadership. India is now a full dialogue partner of the Association of South East Asian Nations (ASEAN) since 1995, a member of the ASEAN Regional Forum, the regional security forum, since 1996, and a founder member of the East Asian Summit launched in December 2005. India is also a summit partner of ASEAN on a par with China, Japan, and South Korea since 2002. Over the years, India has also come to have extensive economic and trade linkages with various countries in the region, even as there has also been a gradual strengthening of security ties. The present Indian Prime Minister, Dr. Manmohan Singh, has made it clear that his government's top foreign-policy priorities will continue to be East and Southeast Asia.

India's efforts to make itself relevant to the region come at a time of great turmoil in the Asian strategic landscape. Events in recent years have underlined China's aggressive stance towards rivals and U.S. allies in Asia, and there may be more tension to come. With its political and economic rise, Beijing has attempted to dictate the boundaries of acceptable behaviour to its neighbours. As a result, regional states have already started reassessing their strategies, and a loose anti-China balancing coalition is emerging. India's role becomes critical in such an evolving balance of power. As Singapore's elder-statesman Lee Kuan Yew has argued, he would like India to be "part of the Southeast Asia balance of forces" and "a counterweight [to China] in the Indian Ocean."[9]

India's policy trajectory is evolving as it pursues a more forceful policy of internal and external balancing to protect its core interests in response to the rise of China at a time of great regional and global power shifts. Though it is not entirely clear if there is a larger strategic framework shaping India's China policy, its approach toward China is indeed undergoing a transformation. The full consequences of these changes will not be apparent for some years.[10]

Though there has always been, and continues to be a range of opinions in India, on how best to deal with China, a consensus seems to be evolving among the highest echelons of Indian military planning and policymaking.[11] Indian defence officials have for years been warning their government in blunt terms about the growing disparity between the two Asian powers. The Indian naval chief has warned that India has neither has "the capability nor the intention to match China force for force" in military terms, while the former Indian air chief has suggested that China poses more of a threat to India than does Pakistan. But the political leadership in India has continued to act on the assumption that Beijing is not a short-term threat to India, but rather, needs to be watched over the long term. This assessment now seems to be undergoing a change. After trying to ignore significant differences with China, Indian decision-makers are finally acknowledging that the relationship between the two countries has become increasingly contentious. The Indian Prime Minister, Manmohan Singh, has suggested that "China would like to have a foothold in South Asia and we have to reflect on this reality...It's important to be prepared."[12] The Indian defence minister has argued that China's increasing assertiveness is a "serious threat."[13] And India's former National Security Advisor and Special Envoy to China, M.K. Narayanan, has openly accused Chinese hackers of attacking his website, as well as those of other Indian government departments.[14]

An elite consensus is evolving in India that China's rise is posing problems for the country. "We are friends, not rivals," said the Chinese premier in India, but a growing number of Indians now see China as a competitor, if not a rival.[15] A 2010 Pew poll in 2010 suggested that only 34% of Indians held a favourable

---

[9] P.S. Suryanarayana, "China and India cannot go to war: Lee Kuan Yew," *The Hindu*, 24 January 2011.

[10] On the various dimensions of China's rise from India's perspective, see Harsh V. Pant, *The Rise of China: Implications for India* (New Delhi: Cambridge University Press, 2012).

[11] For a good typology of India's China debate, see Mohan Malik, "Eyeing the Dragon: India's China Debate," *Asia-Pacific Center for Security Studies, Special Assessment*, December 2003, http://www.apcss.org/Publications/SAS/ChinaDebate/ChinaDebate_Malik.pdf.

[12] "PM Warns on China's South Asia Foothold," *Indian Express*, 7 September 2010.

[13] Rajat Pandit, "Assertive China a Worry, says Antony," *Times of India*, 14 September 2010.

[14] "Chinese Hacked PMO Computers, says Narayanan," *Indian Express*, 19 January 2010.

[15] Jim Yardley, "In India, Chinese Leader Pushes Trade," *New York Times*, 16 December 2010.

view of China, with four in ten viewing their neighbour as a "very serious threat."[16] More damaging is the perception gaining ground in India that China is the only major power that does not accept India as a rising global player that must be accommodated. The discord between the two countries thus remains deep-seated, and their increasing economic strength and rising geopolitical standing has only underlined their rapidly growing ambitions.[17] Though it is not entirely clear if China has well-defined external policy objectives vis-à-vis India, Beijing's economic and military capacity to pursue its goals are greater than at any time in the recent past. In response, a process of military consolidation and build-up of key external partnerships with an eye on China is underway in India, and the 'Look East' policy is part of this larger dynamic. As New Delhi has reached out to its partners in South and Southeast Asia, the regional states have also shown an unprecedented reciprocal interest in Indian foreign policy priorities.

India and Japan: A Growing Partnership

Both New Delhi and Tokyo have made an effort in recent years to put Indo-Japanese ties into high gear. India's booming economy makes it an attractive trading and business partner for Japan, as the latter tries to overcome its long years of economic stagnation. Japan is also reassessing its role as a security-provider in the region and beyond, and of all its neighbours, India seems most willing to acknowledge Japan's centrality in shaping the evolving Asia-Pacific security architecture. Moreover, a new generation of political leaders in India and Japan view each other with fresh eyes, allowing for a break from past policies that is changing the trajectory of bilateral relations.

India's ties with Japan have come a long way since May 1998, when Japan imposed sanctions and suspended its overseas development assistance over India's nuclear tests. Since then, the changing strategic environment in the Asia-Pacific region has brought the two countries closer together, culminating in Prime Minister Singh's last visit to Japan in 2010, a visit which resulted in a new roadmap to transform a low-key relationship into a major strategic partnership.[18] While China's rise figures into the evolution of Indo-Japanese ties, so, too, does the U.S. attempt to build India into a major balancer in the region.

The talks between Singh and his Japanese counterpart, Prime Minister Naoto Kan, were dominated by the enhancement of trade ties, UN reforms and civil-nuclear cooperation. After some initial obstacles and a personal intervention by Singh, talks were finally concluded on the long-awaited Comprehensive Economic Partnership Agreement, which will give a much-needed boost to Indo-Japanese trade ties. In addition, India has committed itself to providing a stable supply of rare-earth minerals to Japan, a clear response to China's reported informal blockade of the strategic minerals after the Senkaku standoff. The coming to office of Shinzo Abe as the Japanese Prime Minister in December 2012 has imparted a new momentum to the relationship as, of all recent Japanese leaders, Abe has been the most enthusiastic about the future of India-Japan relations.

Both Japan and India rely on secure sea-lanes of communication for their energy supplies and economic growth. They have a shared interest in guaranteeing the free transit of energy and trade between the Suez Canal and the Western Pacific. With this in mind they are developing maritime capabilities to cooperate with each other and other regional powers. The navies of the two are now exercising regularly, as are their coast guards, with a view to combating piracy and terrorism, and cooperating during disaster relief operations. Japan feels that only the Indian Navy is the only regional force that can be trusted to secure the sea lanes in the Indian Ocean, sea lanes that are vital for Japan's energy security. It is also important for India to join hands with the much larger Japanese Navy, Asia's most powerful, to make sure that no adversarial power controls regional waterways.

Resisting the trend towards closer ties are stalled talks on a civilian nuclear pact, with the two sides merely agreeing to speed up discussions.[19] Japan continues to insist that India sign the Nuclear Non-Proliferation Treaty and the Comprehensive Test Ban Treaty before finalising such a bilateral agreement, but India has no intention of doing so given its long-

[16] The details of this poll are available at "Key Indicators Database: Opinion of China, Percent Responding Favorable, All Years Measured," *Pew Global Attitudes Project*, http://pewglobal.org/database/?indicator=24&survey=12&response=Favorable&mode=table.

[17] For a detailed explication of the contemporary state of Sino-Indian relations, see Harsh V. Pant, *The China Syndrome: Grappling With an Uneasy Relationship* (New Delhi: HarperCollins, 2010).

[18] P. VaidyanathanIyer, "India, Japan cepa talks," *Indian Express*, 26 October 2010.

[19] Harsh V. Pant, "The Japan Roadblock to Nuclear Cooperation," *Wall Street Journal*, 28 October 2010.

standing concerns over what it sees as the discriminatory nature of these treaties. Meanwhile, the new nuclear-liability law in India—which established higher financial liability limits for accidents than the industry standard, and allows nuclear operators to sue suppliers— could also make greater civilian nuclear cooperation between the two countries more difficult to accomplish. Nevertheless, the push for an agreement will remain strong, as an India-Japan civil-nuclear pact would reinforce India's return to the global nuclear market, and both countries' want to build a partnership that reinforces regional stability.

Both India and Japan are well aware of China's not so subtle attempts at preventing their rise. It is most clearly reflected in China's opposition to the expansion of the United Nations Security Council to include India and Japan as permanent members. China's status as a permanent member of the Security Council and as a nuclear weapon state is something that it would be loath to share with any other state in Asia. India's "Look East" policy of active engagement with the ASEAN and East Asia remains largely predicated upon Japanese support. India's participation in the East Asia Summit was facilitated by Japan. The East Asia Community, proposed by Japan to counter China's proposal of an East Asia Free Trade Area, also includes India. While China has resisted the inclusion of India, Australia, and New Zealand in the ASEAN, Japan has strongly backed the entry of all three nations.

The massive structural changes taking place in the geopolitical balance of power in the Asia-Pacific are driving India and Japan into a relationship that is much closer than many could have anticipated even a few years back.

India and South Korea: Newfound Convergence

After having long ignored each other, India and South Korea are now beginning to recognise the importance of tighter ties. The resulting courtship was highlighted by South Korean President Lee Myung-Bak's state visit to New Delhi in January 2010, when he was the chief guest at the Republic Day celebrations. During his stay, New Delhi and Seoul decided to elevate their bilateral relationship to a "strategic partnership."[20]

Despite pursuing a "Look East" policy since the early 1990s, New Delhi failed to generate momentum in its ties with South Korea. South Korean businesses did not begin to view India as an important destination for investments until after the 1997 financial crisis. South Korea still remained focused on China as an economic partner, and has only recently made India a major economic and political priority. With a renewed push from both sides, things have improved dramatically on the economic front over the past few years.

The visit of former Indian President A.P.J. Abdul Kalam to South Korea in 2006 led to the signing of a Comprehensive Economic Partnership Agreement that came into force in January 2010. Even as India-Japan trade stands steady at around $11 billion annually, India-South Korea trade grew to more than $15 billion last year, with the two sides aiming to double it by 2014. South Korean firms are increasing their brand presence in India, and the Indian Chamber of Commerce has also been established in Korea.

Linkages with the Indian economy can help Korea grow at far higher rates than it is currently experiencing. Among other opportunities, Korean firms are looking to participate in India's plans to develop its infrastructure sector. In the IT sector, too, South Korea's competitive advantage in hardware complements India's software profile. India's dynamic fast-growing economy makes for a natural economic partner for South Korea, often referred to as the most innovative country in the world, with the focus of cooperation likely to be in high-priority areas like IT, civilian space, knowledge-based industries, high technology, energy, automobiles and defence.

While economic ties between India and South Korea have been diversifying across various sectors, defence cooperation between the two states has also gathered momentum, reflecting the rapid changes in the Asia-Pacific region's balance of power caused by China's rise. In 2005, India and South Korea inked a Memorandum of Understanding (MoU) on Cooperation in Defence, Industry and Logistics, which was followed in 2006 by another MoU on cooperation between the two countries' coast guards. South Korea is a leader in naval ship-building technology, and India would like to tap into South Korean naval capabilities to augment its own. As a result, naval cooperation is rapidly emerging as a central feature of bilateral defence cooperation, with the two navies cooperating in anti-piracy operations in the Indian Ocean region and the Gulf of Aden. Both states also share a strong interest in protecting

[20] Amitabh Sinha, "Choosing R-Day chief guest, Behind the warm welcome, a cold strategy," *Indian Express*, 25 January 2010.

the sea lines of communication in the Indian Ocean region.

Other sectors of convergence include nuclear energy and space. As a member of the Nuclear Suppliers Group, South Korea supported the waiver granted to India at the 45-nation grouping's September 2008 meeting.[21] Now India is looking forward to concluding a civilian nuclear energy cooperation pact between the two countries. Space cooperation is also growing. India launched South Korea's KITSAT-3 satellite in 1999 and has now invited Seoul to join the Indian expedition to the moon, — *Chandrayaan*-2.

The China factor in India-South Korea ties cannot be underestimated. India's tensions with China have increased in the past few years, with Beijing aggressively asserting its territorial claims on their shared frontier. At the same time, South Korea, too, is re-evaluating its ties with China. In recent years, China could count on South Korea as a friend in the region—a cultural admirer, with residual memories of the close political and cultural ties that existed in Ming times. For its part, Seoul counted on Beijing to help stabilise the situation on the Korean Peninsula. South Korea has become China's largest trading partner in the region and has been eagerly hospitable to Chinese visits.

Today, however, Seoul has grown disillusioned with Beijing's shielding of North Korea from the global outrage over the Cheonan incident.[22] An international investigation convened by South Korea concluded that the sinking of the warship, which killed 46 South Korean sailors in March, was likely the result of a torpedo fired by a North Korean submarine. Instead of berating Pyongyang, China watered down a U.N. Security Council presidential statement that, while condemning the incident, failed to hold North Korea responsible. As a result, no punishment has been meted out to North Korea for its brinkmanship.

As they carefully assess the evolving strategic environment in the Asia-Pacific region, New Delhi and Seoul need to advance their political ties so that a mutually beneficial and long-term partnership can evolve between the two sides. The resulting relationship could be as important for greater regional stability as it is for Indian and South Korean national interests.

India's Ties with Indonesia, Vietnam, Malaysia, and Burma: Deepening Engagement

The basis of the India-Indonesia partnership dates back to the founding fathers of these two nations – Jawaharlal Nehru and Sukarno—who offered a distinct foreign policy world view that drew on their shared colonial experiences. They visualised an Asian region that could challenge the Cold War threat perceptions of the two superpowers. Nehru and Sukarno were among the founder members of the Non-Aligned Movement.

In the contemporary context, the rise of China has drawn the two states closer. The last few years have witnessed a new phase in this relationship where the two states have pushed their ties to a historic high with strong emphasis on economic and security issues. India with its 'Look East' policy decided to substantially enhance its presence in the region, while Indonesia took the lead in bringing India closer to the ASEAN. The changing strategic landscape of Asia during the post-Cold War era has broadened the canvas of India's engagement with Indonesia. Both want to seize the opportunities being offered by the landmark economic growth being witnessed by the Asian region.

Economic engagement between the two is growing rapidly and will gain further momentum with the signing of the India-ASEAN free trade agreement last year. Indonesia is an important source of energy and raw materials for India. Bilateral trade is expected to breach the $20 billion bench-mark by 2015.[23] Major Indian companies, including the Birla group, the Tatas, Essar, Jindal Steel, Bajaj Motors, are now operating in Indonesia. Indian investment is spread across a range of areas including banking, mining, oil and gas, iron and steel, aluminium, IT, textiles and telecommunications. It was in 2005 that the two signed the strategic partnership agreement and in 2006 a defence cooperation agreement was announced. Negotiations on a Comprehensive Economic Cooperation agreement have begun.

Being the most formidable military power in Southeast Asia, Indonesia can effectively work with India in ensuring safety of the Sea Lanes of Communication (SLOCs) and tackle non-traditional security challenges in the Indian Ocean. Both have a vested interest in ensuring that China's hegemony

---

[21] On India's finalisation of civilian nuclear energy cooperation pact with the US, see Harsh V. Pant, *The US-India Nuclear Pact: Policy, Process and Great Power Politics* (Oxford: Oxford University Press, 2011).

[22] Choe Sang-Hun, "China Balks at Criticism of South Korea," *New York Times*, 30 May 2010.

[23] Veeramalla Anjaiah, "RI, India in 'new frontier' of bilateral ties," *The Jakarta Post*, 25 October 2012.

in the region does not go uncontested. Their location makes them crucial in the emerging maritime calculus in the region as they together control the entry point from the Indian Ocean to the Bay of Bengal in the north, and Malacca Straits to the east. Viewing the Indian maritime presence as largely benign, Indonesia has openly invited India to help the littoral states in the region in maintaining security in the Malacca Straits. Jakarta now also views India as a major source of military hardware. Joint naval exercises and patrols, as well as regular port calls by their respective navies, have been a regular feature of India-Indonesian naval cooperation for some time now.

Cultural links between the two nations have always been significant and they are flourishing. After all, Indonesia's name is derived from the Latin word 'Indus,' meaning India. As the most populous Islamic nation committed to pluralism and democracy, India has huge stakes in the political and economic success of Indonesia. Indonesia's role has been and will remain critical in supporting India's engagement with its Southeast Asian neighbours. And as the US tries to project Indonesia as a bastion of moderate Islam and political stability, India will only reinvigorate its ties with Jakarta.

Bilateral ties between India and Vietnam have strengthened in recent years with a focus on regional security issues and trade. Traditionally, India has had a favourable presence in Vietnam with its support for Vietnamese independence from France and eventual unification of the country, as well as its opposition to the US involvement in the Vietnam War. With the rise of China in recent years, Indo-Viet ties have become strategic in orientation. Bilateral trade has also grown since the liberalisation of the Indian and Vietnamese economies, with the trade volume now exceeding US $2 billion. The signing of the India-ASEAN free trade agreement, and India's recognition of Vietnam's market economy status, will further boost economic ties. Vietnam has backed a more prominent role for India in the ASEAN, and India's bid for the permanent membership of the UN Security Council. The two states promulgated a Joint Declaration on Comprehensive Cooperation in 2003 in which they envisaged creating an "Arc of Advantage and Prosperity" in Southeast Asia and have initiated a strategic dialogue since 2009.

Given that Vietnam and India use the same Russian and erstwhile Soviet platforms, there is a significant convergence between the two in the defence sector. Vietnam has sought Indian help in the modernisation of its military hardware, a move that assumes significance in light of the threat posed by China's diplomatic offensive to India's oil and gas exploration interests near the Vietnamese coast. Delhi and Hanoi have significant stakes in ensuring sea lanes security and preventing sea piracy, and also share concerns about Chinese access to the Indian Ocean and South China Sea. Indian strategic interests demand that Vietnam emerge as a major regional player, and India is well placed to help Hanoi achieve that objective. It has been argued in Indian strategic circles that just as China has used states in India's periphery to contain India, Delhi should build states like Vietnam as strategic pressure points against China to counter it. A common approach to the evolving balance of power is emerging, with India and Vietnam both keen on reorienting their ties with the US as their concerns about China rise.

Naval cooperation between Vietnam and India remains a the focus, with Vietnam granting India access to the port NhaTrang, situated close to the strategically significant naval base at Cam Ranh Bay. During Vietnamese President Trong Tan Sang's visit to India in October 2011, the two sides reiterated the need to enhance cooperation in ensuring safety and security of the region's sea lanes and launched a security dialogue. It was also decided to increase the trade target to $7 billion by 2015 from the present $2.7 billion.

Relations between Malaysia and India have traditionally been strong, in part due to their historical ambivalence towards the US. Malaysia under Mahathir Mohamad took a strong line against Washington and was able to steer Malaysia's economy successfully through the financial crisis of 1997. Malaysia has supported an Indian presence in the ASEAN, and in 2001 also accepted India's position that the Kashmir issue should be resolved only through bilateral negotiations. An MoU on defence cooperation was signed by the two in 1992, and a close defence relationship has emerged over the years with joint military exercises, training of defence personnel and trade in military equipment. The two have decided to work together to secure the Malacca Straits, and Malaysia has requested Indian help in protecting the Straits from emerging non-traditional security threats in the region. China's claims over the Spratly Islands remains a source of anxiety for Malaysia.

Ethnic Indians—whose forebears were forcibly relocated to work on Malaysian plantations under the British colonial habit of using indentured labour —comprise 8 percent of Malaysia's population.

Recently, some have asked the Indian government to terminate all business projects with Malaysia because of human rights violations allegedly committed against the Hindu community. Delhi, has taken up this issue up informally, through back channels, to avoid harming Indo-Malaysian ties.

Trade was the focus of the Indian Prime Minister's visit to Malaysia in 2010, when he made a strong pitch for greater Malaysian investment in India. Singh and Malaysian Prime Minister Najib Tun Razak signed an array of agreements aimed at galvanising bilateral economic cooperation and liberalising their respective investment regimes to facilitate greater mutual foreign direct investment.[24] The leaders also decided to strengthen the security partnership by exploring collaborative defence projects and enhancing cooperation in counterterrorism through information-sharing and the establishment of a joint working group.

Burma too has made its own overtures to India. President Thein Sein has pursued a range of reforms in the domestic realm that include opening substantive talks with opposition leader Aung San Suu Kyi, declaration of an amnesty for political prisoners, and cancellation of the Chinese-funded Myitsone Dam project. These efforts could be viewed as an attempt to seek a rapprochement with the democratic world, and that may be why for his first visit abroad as president of a nominal civilian government, Thein Sein chose India.[25]

During his visit, Burma's President Then Sein sought greater Indian investment in Burma's energy sector, expanded cooperation in oil and gas exploration, open border trade, and accelerated construction of natural gas pipelines. India, which is investing in the Kaladan multimodal transport system to connect India's eastern seaboard to its north-eastern states through Myanmar, further offered $500 million in credits for infrastructure projects.

Despite pressure from the West to demand more democratic reforms, pragmatic self-interest continues to guide India's relations with Burma. Putting its strategic interests first, New Delhi has only gently nudged the Burmese on the issue of democracy, gradually gaining a sense of trust at the highest echelons of the junta. India would be loath to lose this relationship. As such, India remains opposed to Western sanctions on the country. Burma's recent moves towards democratic transition will give India a larger strategic space to manoeuvre. Compared to Beijing, New Delhi will be a more attractive partner for Burma as it tries to find a modus vivendi with the West.

At the broader regional level, India and the Association of South East Asian Nations marked their twenty years of partnership with a commemorative summit in New Delhi in December 2012. The significance that ASEAN members are increasingly according India was illustrated by the presence in New Delhi of the prime ministers of Singapore, Cambodia, Malaysia, and Vietnam, along with the presidents of Myanmar and Indonesia and the vice-president of the Philippines, in attending the India-ASEAN-India summit. The highlight of the summit was the conclusion of talks on a Free Trade Agreement (FTA) on services and investment, which is expected to increase bilateral trade to $200 billion by 2022. Further talks on the Regional Comprehensive Economic Partnership, which also includes Australia, China, Japan, South Korea and New Zealand, are expected. As Indian Prime Minister, Manmohan Singh, has said, India and the AESAN states "constitute a community of 1.8 billion people, representing one-fourth of humanity, with a combined GDP of $3.8 trillion" and therefore "it is only natural that India should attach the highest priority to its relationship with ASEAN."[26]

India was admitted as sectoral dialogue partner of the ASEAN in 1992 and went on to become a full-fledged dialogue partner in 1996. There has been a significant increase in India-ASEAN trade from $42 billion in 2008 to $80 billion in 2012. This trade relationship will get a further boost with the signing of the services and investment agreement. The FTA on goods was signed in 2010 despite some significant opposition in India, and since its implementation last year India has been keen on expanding trade in services in order to leverage its own strengths. The relationship is now officially 'strategic' with the two sides deciding to elevate their ties from a mere dialogue partnership.

India and Australia: Mending Fences

In 2009, New Delhi and Canberra decided to elevated their ties to the status of a "strategic partnership."But little of substance was achieved until Prime Minister Julia Gillard's state visit to India in October 2012,

---

[24] "Malaysia rolls out red carpet for Manmohan Singh," *The Hindu*, 27 October 2010.

[25] Sandeep Dikshit, "India, Myanmar agree to resolve border issues," *The Hindu*, 14 October 2011.

[26] See the Opening Statement of the Indian Prime Minister at Plenary Session of India-ASEAN Commemorative Summit, December 20, 2012, available at http://www.mea.gov.in/Speeches-Statements.htm?dtl/20981/

when she declared that "Australia's future in Asia is finally grounded in relationships of respect with Washington, Tokyo, Beijing, Jakarta, Seoul and Delhi." Australia, said Gillard, recognised "India's importance in the Asian century", and India was "one of the handful of countries which matter most to Australia." At the same time, she candidly admitted that "the strong relationship between our peoples has not been matched by the strength of the connection between our governments."[27]

The highlight of the visit was the decision by the two nations to pave the way for a uranium safeguards agreement that will finally allow Australia to export uranium to India. Australia has the world's largest deposits of uranium, and its big mining companies are looking to expand production as global demand for nuclear power grows over the next decade. India's civilian nuclear industry is expanding, with the number of operating plants expected to increase from 20 to more than 60 over the next decade. Gillard's predecessor, Kevin Rudd had banned uranium sales on the grounds that India was not a signatory to the NPT, placing the bilateral relationship in cold storage. But at the ruling Labour Party's national conference in 2011, Gillard succeeded in overturning party policy. Though the safeguards pact will take time finalise, the change of policy by Canberra is a remarkable development and needs to be recognised as such. That an Australian Labour government, traditionally considered a non-proliferation hawk, should take such a decision is reflective of the Canberra's changing priorities, and perhaps, pressure from Washington not to upset its regional calculations.

Washington had to pull out all the stops in convincing the Julia Gillard government that, given the strategic importance of India, Canberra needed to change its policy on uranium sales. And Gillard could point to the U.S.-India civil nuclear pact that has brought India into the global nuclear mainstream.

Australia has the world's largest deposits of uranium, so it always made economic sense for it to sell more to an energy-hungry India. Moreover, it is difficult for Canberra to justify a ban on uranium exports to India, a fellow democracy and a country with impeccable non-proliferation credentials while continuing to send uranium to China, which has been the most important factor in the weakening of the non-proliferation regime in view of its relationship with Pakistan. Australia has 22 bilateral nuclear cooperation pacts with countries including the US, China, Taiwan and South Korea.

Even as other nuclear-supplier nations have been lining up to sign civil nuclear pacts with India, Australia found itself marginalized. After the Nuclear Suppliers Group meeting in 2008 granting it a special waiver, there was no logical reason for Australia to continue with its policy of a ban on uranium sales to India.

The changes in Australia's policy towards India signal new thinking with regard to the tectonic shifts occurring in the regional geostrategic environment. Washington has been working to transform the U.S.-Australian partnership from "an Asia-Pacific alliance to an Indo-Pacific alliance." India and Australia have a shared interest in managing the Indo-Pacific commons, including the very important sea-lanes of communication. Closer maritime cooperation between New Delhi and Canberra is crucial in managing the growing turbulence in the Indian Ocean region. Indian Defence Minister, A.K. Antony, was in Australia in June 2013, the first trip to the country by any Indian defence minister. During Antony's visit, the two nations decided to step up military exchanges and pursue a regular dialogue on maritime security. A joint naval exercise has been scheduled for 2015 with the two states underlining that maritime security and freedom of navigation, in accordance with principles of international law, is critical for the growth and prosperity of the Asia-Pacific and the Indian Ocean region.

Bilateral trade between Australia and India has increased from $3.3 billion in 2000 to $20 billion in 2011, and is projected to reach $40 billion by 2016 as negotiations on the Comprehensive Economic Cooperation Agreement continue. India is now the fourth largest market for Australian exports. As the Indian economy grows, Australia will continue to be a major supplier of minerals and fuel. Despite recent tensions over attacks on students of Indian origin, Australia remains an important destination for Indian students. The Indian community is Australia's fastest growing immigrant community.

Finally, it seems that New Delhi and Canberra have realised that their bilateral relationship goes beyond "cricket, Commonwealth and a common language". The two sides no longer seem shy of taking advantage of this growing convergence.

[27] Philip Hudson, "Julia Gillard will elevate India to the highest priority for Australia," *The Australian*, 17 October 2012.

Conclusion

India is emerging as a serious player in the Asian strategic landscape as smaller states in East Asia reach out to it for trade, diplomacy and, potentially, as a key regional balancer. The "Look East" policy initiated by one of India's most visionary prime ministers, P.V. Narasimha Rao, is now the cornerstone of India's engagement with the world's most economically dynamic region. States in South and Southeast Asia remain keen on a more pro-active Indian role in the region.

China is too big and too powerful to be ignored by the regional states. States in China's vicinity are now seeking to expand their strategic space by reaching out to other regional and global powers. Smaller states in the region are now looking to India to act as a balancer in view of China's growing influence, and America's anticipated retrenchment from the region in the near future, while larger states see India as an attractive engine for regional growth. To live up to its full potential and meet the region's expectations, India must do more if it is to emerge as a credible strategic partner. Neither India nor the regional states in East Asia have a desire to frame their relations with China in negative terms. But they are certainly interested in leveraging their ties with other states to gain benefits from China, and bring a semblance of equality to their relationships with Beijing.

Great power politics in the region have only just begun. The rapid rise of China in Asia and beyond is the main pivot, even as Delhi seeks to expand economic integration and interdependence with the region. India is also developing strong security linkages with regional partners, and trying actively to promote and participate in regional and multilateral initiatives. New Delhi's ambitious policy in East and Southeast Asia is aimed at significantly increasing its regional profile. It remains to be seen if India can indeed live up to its full potential, as well as to the region's expectations.

CHINA'S TIBET POLICY UNDER A NEW LEADERSHIP

Claude Arpi, Independent Journalist, Pondicherry, India

In March 2013, a new leader walked onto the stage in the Great Hall of the People in Beijing; Xi Jinping had been selected to lead the Middle Kingdom for the next 10 years. A few months earlier, he had been nominated Secretary General of the Chinese Communist Party (CCP) and Chairman of the powerful Central Military Commission.

At the end of the National People's Congress, the composition of the State Council (or Cabinet) was announced, with Li Keqiang stepping into Wen Jiabao's boots as China's Premier. Li has four vice-premiers and five state councillors to help him carry out his difficult task.

As the new leadership takes over the command of the second largest world economy, an issue which remains alive and could create serious problems for China in the near future, is the unstable situation on the Tibetan plateau.

It needs to be carefully watched by India which shares a 4,000 kilometre border with China. For centuries, the Sino-Indian border was the Indo-Tibetan border; India had a peaceful neighbour and a peaceful border. Today, it is not the case: whatever happens on the Roof of the World has implications for India and the sub-continent; this is particularly true for the rivers flowing from the Tibetan plateau to the Indian plains and the social instability on the Roof of the World.

The Central Working Coordination Small Group on Tibet

It is necessary to say a few words about China's decision mechanism for policies on Tibet, particularly about the Central Working Coordination Small Group on Tibet.[1]

Since the beginning of the Deng Xiaoping's era, the Tibet Policy of the People's Republic of China has been formulated during the five Tibet Work Forums.[2] A Tibet Work Forum is usually held every five or ten years to discuss the CCP's Tibet policies. These large meetings are attended by some 200 to 300 senior cadres, amongst others by the members of the all-powerful Politburo's Standing Committee, senior PLA generals, representatives of the People's Armed Police, United Front Work Department officials, regional leaders, etc. The last Tibet Work Forum (the Fifth) was held in January 2010 in Beijing.

[1] Also known as Small Group on Tibet, one of the Leading Small Groups (LSG) on the Central Committee of the Communist Party of China.

The Small Group on Tibet is responsible for the implementation of the policies decided during the Tibet Work Forum. The chair of the Small Group on Tibet is usually held by the Chinese People's Political Consultative Conference (CPPCC) chairman. During the CCP's 17th Congress, the Chairman of the Small Group on Tibet was Jia Qinglin, the then CPPCC chairperson. Other probable members were Ma Kai,[3] Meng Jianzhu,[4] Ling Jihua, and Du Qinglin and other unnamed officials.

After the 18th Party Congress leadership change, these leaders have secured good jobs,[5] they will probably continue to participate in the deliberations of the Small Group on Tibet.

The reconstituted Group, under the Chairmanship of Yu Zhengsheng and with more or less the same membership than the previous one, has been immediately involved in the implementation of China's Tibet policy. This implies that no or little improvement can be expected in Tibet in the near future.

Yu Zhengsheng

During an inspection tour in Sichuan Province from 6 to 8 January 2013, Yu Zhengsheng called on monks and nuns to be patriotic and observe Chinese laws as well as monastic rules. Yu was participating in a seminar along with Tibetan Buddhist representatives in Ganzi Tibetan Autonomous Prefecture of Sichuan.

Yu pleaded with the monks, that they should support the government's efforts to manage monasteries in accordance with the law. His argument was that the government should offer public services to monasteries and manage them as a socialist society. He wanted a unified and strong motherland, while developing 'stabilised Tibetan areas' which would, in turn help "ethnic groups improve the lives of the people and brighten the prospects for Tibetan Buddhism".

Yu also said that the fight against the Dalai Lama clique should continue, adding that it was necessary "'to create a favourable social and political environment for economic development and the improvement of people's well-being".

Ganzi became the first ethnic minority autonomous prefecture after the People's Republic of China was founded in 1949. The prefecture is still one of the poorest in China. Yu assured the monks that the key to development in the Tibetan areas was the development of infrastructure and the public services. Once done, it would help to increase the incomes of farmers and herdsmen. Yu asked the cadres and officials to improve their work style and serve the masses wholeheartedly.

This gives some indication of the direction in which the Small Group on Tibet is likely to proceed. After visiting Ganzi Tibetan Autonomous Prefecture (Kham) in January, Yu Zhengsheng visited Gansu (in the former Amdo province) in early July 2013.

In Gansu, Yu called for "for lasting prosperity and stability in China's Tibetan regions by improving local livelihoods and fighting the 14th Dalai Lama clique." More importantly, from 1 to 6 August 2013, Yu Zhengsheng conducted an 'inspection tour' in the Tibetan Autonomous Region, particularly Lhasa and Ngachu; the most extraordinary part was that nothing appeared in the Chinese (or local) press before Yu was back in Beijing on 6 August evening. It shows the level of nervousness of the leadership.

Outside China, it is difficult to believe that an official responsible for a region at the highest level of the government can stay for nearly one week in this region with the world being informed of it only after he had left. Xinhua quoted Yu Zhengsheng saying that development remains 'fundamental and the key' to addressing all issues related to Tibet. The Chairman of the National Committee of the Chinese People's Political Consultative Conference was keen "to promote efforts to rule Tibet by law and seek a regional development path with Chinese and local characteristics."

Like Xi Jinping, when he addressed the Tibetan delegation in March in Beijing, Yu spoke of "achieving leapfrog economic and social development in Tibet and long-term stability". Yu referred to (and rejected) the Dalai Lama's proposal for 'high-degree autonomy in Greater Tibet'; he said that it "runs counter to China's Constitution, the law, and the fundamental interests of Tibetan Buddhism."

---

[2] The five Tibet Work Forums were held in 1980, 1984, 1991, 2001 and 2010.

[3] Ma Kai was President of the National School of Administration. In 2012, he became member of the Politburo of the 18th CPC Central Committee. In 2013 he became Vice-Premier of the State Council. Ma will be responsible for the economy and internal party matters. He was part of former Premier Wen Jiabao's staff and advisor to former Secretary General Zhao Ziyang.

[4] Member of the Politburo of the 18th Central Committee. Secretary of the CPC Central Committee Politics and Law Commission, in other words, the new security boss of China. Meng takes on the mantle of Zhang Yongkang as the boss of the security apparatus.

[5] Ma Kai and Meng Jianzhu are part of the Politburo, while Ling Jihua is now heading the United Front Work Department. Du Qinglin is part of the CCP's General Office, a crucial posting.

Yu asked the monks to "have a clear understanding of the secessionist nature of the Dalai Lama clique and resolutely safeguard national unification, ethnic unity and Tibet's harmony and stability ...and comprehensively implement the ethnic and religious policies of the Communist Party of China and actively guide religions so they adapt to a socialist society." Nothing new, except that his words did not help in calming down the situation.

The 'secret' visit was unusually long (six days) and seems to have focused on the way "to scientifically develop ideas for the development of Tibet, strengthen infrastructure construction and cultivate industries." In this context, it is interesting a look at the officials who accompanied Yu to understand the true objectives of this long visit. They were:

- Zhang Yijiong, the Executive Vice Minister of the United Front Department. He stepped into the shoes of Zhu Weiqun and is 'responsible for any future dialogue with Dharamsala.
- Du Ying, a Deputy Director of the State Development and Reform Commission, in other words, the Planning Commission.
- Sithar, a German-speaking Tibetan earlier posted in Europe, now working for the United Front Department.
- Weng Mengyong, a Vice Minister in the Transportation Ministry. His boss and minister, Yang Chuantang, used to be vice-chairman of the Tibet Autonomous Regional Government.
- Shuai Junqing, Vice-President of the State Grid Corporation of China who obviously accompanied Yu to study the feasibility of harnessing Tibet's hydropower potential.

Interestingly, despite this high-level visit and the 'instructions' given by the Central leadership, Driru, one of the main towns of Nagchu remained in turmoil.

The Case of Ngachu

The case of Ngachu is interesting: despite regular 'inspection tours' by several high-level dignitaries of the Communist Party (including Yu Zhengsheng), the Prefecture is still boiling.

Nagqu Prefecture is one of the seven prefectures of the Tibet Autonomous Region; it is the largest with an area of 450,537 square kilometres for a population of 400,000. The prefecture is divided into 11 counties with Nagchu Town as capital. As Nagqu is located on the Qinghai-Tibet railway line, Beijing plans to make the prefecture one of the main economic hubs on the Tibetan plateau.

In May 2013, Yu Zhengsheng chaired his first Small Group on Tibet in Beijing. Apart from the Central officials, the meeting of the Small Group on Tibet is said to have been attended by cadres from Gansu, Qinghai, Yunnan, Sichuan provinces as well as the Tibetan Autonomous Region (TAR).

Soon after the meeting, the Party Secretaries from these areas went back to their respective provinces and gave speeches on the importance of Yu's instructions and comments. A few days later, Yu visited Xinjiang; from his declarations, one can guess what Yu told the Party cadres in Beijing. He called for greater efforts for improving people's living conditions, 'promoting ethnic solidarity' and 'social harmony'; he also emphasised 'social stability'.

On his return to Tibet, Chen Quanguo, the TAR's Party Secretary went for an inspection tour of the Nagchu Prefecture; he carried Yu's message to "bring stability and harmony to Nachu." Unfortunately for Secretary Chen, the day he was returning to Lhasa, thousands of Tibetans gathered in Driru county (Chinese: Biru in Nagchu Prefecture). They met at a sacred Tibetan mountain to demonstrate against the Chinese government's planned mining projects in Driru County. *The Tibet Post* reported: "On 24 May 2013, over 1,000 trucks [probably cars] loaded more than 5,400 Tibetans from the four major areas, including Pekar, Nagshoe Phudha and Tsala gathered in Dathang town, near the sacred mountain in protest of the growing Chinese mining tensions in the county".

The mountain, called Lhachen Naglha Dzambha, is rich in mineral resources. It was said that the local Tibetans ultimately managed to stop the mining at the holy Mountain, though for days, the situation was reported tense in the Driru county, on the protest site where the local authorities deployed a large number of paramilitary personnel, especially after two protesters Gonp and Abu are said to have died in a car accident on their way to the site.

According to Radio Free Asia (RFA): "Mining operations in Tibetan regions have led to frequent standoffs with Tibetans who accuse Chinese firms of disrupting sites of spiritual significance and polluting the environment as they extract local wealth. ...Waste from the mines, in operation since 2005, has been dumped in the local river, and mining activities have polluted the air." This was bad luck for Mr. Chen who had just preached 'stability'. It was however not the first time that such an incident has happened.

In October 2012, two Tibetan cousins Tsepo, 20 and Tenzin, 25, self-immolated in front of a school in Driru. Tibetans in exile told RFA that the cousins shouted slogans calling for freedom in Tibet and the return of Tibet's spiritual leader the Dalai Lama before setting themselves alight. They also pleaded for all Tibetans to be 'united like brothers'. RFA commented: "Tibetans in Driru have been in the forefront of opposition to Chinese rule in the Tibet Autonomous Region since deadly riots in the region in 2008, with monks and nuns protesting and abandoning monasteries in order to defy 'intrusive' new Chinese regulations."

At that time, Lobsang Gyaltsen, who has since become the head of the government in the TAR, had stayed two weeks in the area to pacify the Tibetans. The Party's senior cadres' exhortations do not seem to work on the local population.

This goes in parallel with the recurring looting of the underground wealth of Tibet. A website, *Meltdown in Tibet*, highlighted the crucial role of the railway line: "Mining and mineral exploration have increased dramatically on the Tibetan Plateau since the 2006 arrival of the Golmud-Lhasa railway link, and due to government programmes and promotion. Along with the large government and business controlled mines, small unregulated mining operations are popping up all over the plateau. Due to low salaries, minimal health and safety standards, and weak environmental laws, normally uneconomic mineral deposits can be mined profitably by Chinese companies. Corrupt officials are willing to cut costs even more."

In 2007, Xinhua had announced: "Chinese geologists have discovered 16 large copper, iron, lead and zinc ore deposits along the Qinghai-Tibet Railway route since 1999, said the country's top geological surveyor." Meng Xianlai, director of the China Geological Survey (CGS) under the Ministry of Land and Resources told the Chinese agency: "Geologists initially found five non-ferrous metal deposits along the 1,956-kilometre railway with total possible reserves of more than 20 million tons of copper and 10 million tons of lead and zinc."

In early October 2013, The Tibetan Centre for Human Rights and Democracy (TCHRD) reported that the People's Armed Police had beaten and detained 40 Tibetans. The local government apparently used threats and intimidation tactics to enforce the 'mass-line'[6] policy, a brain child of President Xi Jinping. The TCHRD says: "Touted by the Chinese government as a means to bring the party leadership closer to the needs and concerns of the masses, the reality is the policy is aimed at bringing every Tibetan under the direct surveillance of the party's human and technological surveillance machinery."

The human rights organisation mentions: "A host of highly-intrusive mass surveillance campaigns such as the '*Benefit the Masses, Solidify the Foundation*', '*The Grid Management*' system, '*New Socialist Villages*' and the recently-announced '*Advanced Joint Household*' system are now being implemented in TAR. The official justification behind all these campaigns is that these campaigns would benefit the Tibetans in two ways: by providing long term stability and prosperity." Those who do not comply with these regulations are severally punished. According to the TCHRD, on 28 September 2013, a serious confrontation occurred between the Chinese security forces and the local Tibetans in Mowa Village in Diru County. The Tibetans rebelled against the compulsory order (under the 'Nine Must Haves' campaign[7]) to fly the five-starred red flags during the National Day celebrations.

TCHRD explains: "Local Tibetans in Mowa had refused to fly Chinese flags on their rooftops, a space

---

[6] The Mass Line is the political, organizational and leadership method developed by Mao Zedong. In 2013, the CCP launched a year-long 'mass line' education campaign to strengthen Party-people relations. On June 18, Xi Jinping declared that the 'mass line' is the lifeline of the Party and the campaign will act as a 'thorough cleanup' of harmful and undesirable work styles such as formalism, bureaucratism, hedonism and extravagance. He urged the Party's members to boost ties with the people and fight corruption.

[7] According to *The Tibet Daily*, the United Front Department decided to promote the 'Nine Haves Monasteries'

1. Have a poster of the four national leaders
2. Have a national PRC flag
3. Have a motorable road to the monastery
4. Have a good source of water
5. Have electricity
6. Have a TV set
7. Have the capacity to show films
8. Have a reading room for books
9. Have *The People's Daily* and the *Tibet Daily* newspapers.

traditionally reserved for sacred prayer flags; instead they threw the flags into a nearby river to express their disapproval. Armed police and the military arrived later to rein in the Tibetans." This led to an inevitable confrontation. The local authorities in Diru County announced that the Tibetans who refuse to comply with official rules would be punished; Tibetan protesters would have their children expelled from schools; their sick relatives would not receive medical care in hospitals; and they would not get licenses to harvest the famous *Ophiocordyceps sinensis*, a pricey caterpillar fungus used as an aphrodisiac in China.

Since 10 September 2013, the Tibetan Autonomous Region authorities have sent some 18,000 Chinese cadres to Diru to intensify the party's 'mass line' policy. These cadres have been conducting 'patriotic education' campaigns among local Tibetans, demanding them to pledge their 'love and gratitude' to the Party and the nation.

The same day, Wu Yingjie, a TAR Deputy Party Secretary, who has been camping for weeks in Nagchu and Dortho, a Chinese born in Tibet who is Nagchu Prefecture Party Secretary (and TAR's Standing Committee member) ordered the release of the 40 arrested Tibetans. On 29 September 2013, another protest took place with 4,000 students of County Primary and Middle schools after they were informed about the threat to expel their classmates whose parents had participated in the earlier protests. The County Middle School has later been closed indefinitely.

A day after the National Day (on 2 October), local Tibetans in Diru County once again defied the security forces by putting up human blockades along the major highways which had been occupied by the security forces. They demonstrated against the annihilation of the Tibetan identity. Four Tibetans are said to have been killed by bullets in the demonstrations.

To give an idea of the scale of the 'monitoring' of Tibetan activities, Xinhua recently admitted that 60,000 cadres had been stationed in 5,459 villages and 1,877 monastic institutions in TAR. According to TCHRD: "These cadres will either work as village level party secretary or as 'work team' cadres running political education campaigns and espionage activities under another controversial campaign known as 'The Six Ones'. It reminds many of the black day of the Cultural Revolution. What is strange is that despite the visits of so many dignitaries (including Yu Zhengsheng) the situation remains extremely volatile.

The Party Prepares for the post-Dalai Lama Period

The Communist Party of China seems to be preparing for the period post-Dalai Lama. This translates into the 'spiritualisation' of the Communist leadership on the Tibetan plateau. It seems paradoxical, but the atheist Communist Party of China (CCP) is getting increasingly interested in spiritual matters. The CCP has started promoting some reincarnated Lamas, known in China as 'Living Buddhas', in a much larger way than in the past.

Ironically, the atheist regime in Beijing seemed more and more interested in the system of governance through 'reincarnation'. In 2007, the Chinese State Administration for Religious Affairs in Beijing issued State Order No.5 stating the "Management Measures For the Reincarnation of Living Buddhas in Tibetan Buddhism". Beijing then started to promote 'Living Buddhas' in the name of the Communist Party. Beijing has recently been trying its utmost to increase its control over reincarnations of Tibetan lamas (and ultimately the Dalai Lama), thus legitimising the Communist rule over the Himalayan region. The Party has obviously decided to play the 'religion' card to resolve the Tibet issue.

On 11 March, *China Tibet Online* published a photograph of the 'Chinese' Panchen Lama,[8] Gyaltsen Norbu[9] taken as he was casting his vote. The caption reads: "The 11th Panchen Lama fulfils his role as a Chinese People's Political Consultative Conference (CPPCC) member."[10]

The Communist Government seems determined to fully play the 'Panchen' card against what it calls 'the Dalai and his clique'. At that time, the Chinese government announced that the 11th Panchen Lama had been elected member of the Standing Committee of the CPPCC National Committee, China's top political advisory body: "Three years after making his political debut, [he] has been entrusted with a more important role of advising China on state affairs."[11]

---

[8] Gedun Choeki Nyima, the boy recognised by the Dalai Lama as the real Panchen Lama is still under house arrest somewhere in China.

[9] Bainqen Qoigyijabu in pinyin

[10] http://www.china.org.cn/opinion/2011-03/14/content_22131847.htm

[11] http://www.chinadaily.com.cn/china/2013npc/2013-03/12/content_16303296.htm

Beijing anticipated that the 23-year old Panchen Lama could contribute politically because of his 'religious influence'. The Chinese-selected Panchen Lama visited Tibet between 27 August and 13 October. Xinhua reported: "The 23-year-old Panchen Lama, one of the two most revered living Buddhas in Tibetan Buddhism, has performed religious rituals, including sutra interpretations and giving blessings, for thousands of Tibetan Buddhists at several monasteries in the region since 27 August."

Who is the other most revered 'Living Buddha' in Tibetan Buddhism? The Dalai Lama! Beijing does not like to write his name or even hear his name, though his status seems to be acknowledged. Even more interesting, Xinhua reveals: "The Panchen Lama lived in seclusion at the Zhaxi Lhunbo Lamasery [Tashilhunpo monastery] in Xigaze [Shigatse] Prefecture, the traditional residence of reincarnated Panchen Lamas, from 12 September to 7 October."

Why in 'seclusion' when he is on his 'annual inspection tour'? This gives some indication about the difficulties Beijing has to control the Tibetans. According to earlier reports, Gyaltsen Norbu was staying at the Dechen Phodang, the 'summer' residence of the Panchen Lamas, outside the main Tashilhunpo monastery. Some of the photos published by the Chinese news agency showed Gyaltsen Norbu performing a puja, but with very few monks around.

Xinhua reminds us: "As a member of the Standing Committee of the Chinese People's Political Consultative Conference National Committee, China's top political advisory body, the Panchen Lama also held discussions with members of Tibetan religious circles and visited local farmers and schools to gather their opinions on social and religious issues." No photos were published of these meetings and encounters. Did they really take place?

On 10 October, Gyaltsen Norbu visited the Sakya monastery. Here again, the crowds seemed sparse, if not to say nonexistent. The Lama is said to have looked at some palm-leaf manuscripts of Buddhist texts, met a few devotees and 'worshiped' inside one of the temples. Where were the Tibetans? Gyaltsen Norbu's other public appearance was at the end of August in the Jokhang Cathedral in Lhasa. At that time, he had discreetly met with the TAR Party officials. This was not reported in the Chinese English media.

The question is 'why such a low profile visit/ inspection tour' after all the noise in March? After all, Gyaltsen Norbu is supposedly the main tool for the Chinese propaganda in Tibet. Has something gone awry?

This perhaps explains an interview given by Prof. Jin Wei of the Central Communist Party School to a Hong Kong weekly, earlier this year. She said: "Under the current circumstances, there will be 'Twin Dalai Lamas', with one reincarnation recognised abroad and one domestically, leading to more complicated issues, having great impact on the stability and security of the Tibetan region. If the 'Dalai Lama impasse' can be broken, we should fight to have the Dalai Lama reincarnation arise within the country. Although we can use 'Drawing Lots from the Golden Urn' to prevent the reincarnation from arising overseas, there is a historical precedent for Living Buddhas designating their own successors. We must use every effort to avoid the embarrassment of the 'Twin Panchen Lama' event."

She admits that the 'Golden Urn' process was manipulated; this has been described in detail by Arjia Rinpoche, a former Abbot of Kumbim monastery who participated in the 'ceremony'. Arjia Rinpoche, who now lives in exile in the US, recounts: "I boarded a chartered jet for the return trip to Beijing. On the airplane, Li Tieying, the Chinese delegate,[12] called Jamyang Shepa Rinpoche and me into a private sitting room. Ye Xiaowen[13] was also there. Both of them looked especially pleased with themselves. Li Tieying placed the event in the context of great moments in China's history, while Ye Xiaowen dutifully took notes. After a while Li Tieying, looking a bit tired, donned an oxygen mask in the unpressurized cabin and went to sleep."

Then, the true story came out: "Ye Xiaowen, a large, dark-complexioned man, continued to chat informally with us. Exuberant with the success of the past several days, he unwittingly revealed a shocking secret: 'When the Dalai Lama announced the name of his chosen candidate, the government immediately sent out charter jets, usually reserved for members of the Politburo, to the birthplaces of the three final candidates in the Naqu district of Tibet. They put the boys and their families on the three jets and whisked them away into hiding'. He proudly continued, 'When we made our selection we left nothing to chance. In the silk pouches of the ivory pieces we put a bit of cotton at the bottom of one of

---

[12] Head of the Chinese delegation during the selection process.

[13] Minister in the State Administration for Religious Affairs. He was responsible for the selection of a new Panchen Lama.

them, so it would be a little higher than the others and the right candidate would be chosen.' We were dumbfounded! Certainly we had had our suspicions, but we never expected proof that the process was completely rigged. Goose bumps rose on my skin, but Jamyang Shepa Rinpoche and I kept silent, our heads lowered, pretending we had heard nothing unusual. After we were dismissed and heading back to our seats, Jamyang Shepa Rinpoche looked at me incredulously and shook his head."

But now, even the well-scripted selection of a Chinese Panchen Lama seems to fail; if the trustworthy candidate is not that dependable, the situation becomes delicate for the Chinese authorities. Further, if everything had worked as planned by the Party, Gyaltsen Norbu being a 'Nagchu boy', he should have been the one to go and extinguish the fires in the restive Prefecture. In other words, the 'selection' process through the Golden Urn may reveal itself a complete flop for Beijing. It is probably why 'thinkers' such as Prof. Jin Wei have started offering of other solutions.

In the meantime, the Panchen Lama selected by the Dalai Lama remains under house arrest. On 26 and 27 September, in Geneva, the UN Committee on the Rights of the Child reviewed China's record, including in Tibet, as part of its compliance review under the UN Child Rights Convention.

International Campaign for Tibet reported: "The Committee questioned the Chinese delegation on the whereabouts of Gedhun Choekyi Nyima, who was disappeared by Chinese authorities in 1995 after he was recognised by the Dalai Lama as the 11th Panchen Lama. The Committee asked if China's contention that the Panchen Lama had been given higher education and living a happy life had been confirmed by an independent authority, as had already been asked by the Committee in 2005. The Chinese government refused to answer this question".

One more embarrassment for Beijing! All this creates an atmosphere of instability not favourable to stability. One can understand Beijing, the legitimacy of their 'liberation' of Tibet may be postponed for several decades if the Dalai Lama takes birth in India.

Post-trauma Stress Disorders

One strange phenomenon has to be mentioned here. It demonstrates the difficulty faced by Beijing to 'stabilize' Tibet. While Beijing's propaganda likes to state that the Tibetans enjoy 'unprecedented freedoms', its People's Armed Police (PAP) suffers in an unprecedented manner on the Roof of the World.

This emerges from a secret Chinese document which has been smuggled out of Tibet and later translated by the Tibetan Centre for Human Rights and Democracy, in Dharamsala. The document, dated October 2008 is called *"A Handbook on Psychological Counselling and Protection During Stability Maintenance Work in Tibetan Areas"*. It was drafted by the medical staff department of the Sichuan's PAP Corps. Its objective is to counsel the paramilitary forces doing 'maintenance stability work in Tibetan areas', a euphemism for repression of peaceful gatherings on the Tibetan plateau. The 'handbook' was prepared to take care of the psychological health of the armed police. Various hospitals and heath institutes participated in drafting the document which explained: "The purpose of this handbook is to create awareness on common psychological problems faced by PAP soldiers in stability maintenance in Tibetan areas and to identify common psychological problems to strengthen the ways and means to handle such problems while carrying out stability maintenance tasks" Because the PAP's 'psychiatric well-being is needed to maintain stability'.

The handbook answers the questions of the stressed soldiers in a question and answer format. First question: How to ease mental stress faced by stability maintenance troops in Tibetan areas? The answer gives the background of 'the work': "Ever since the soldiers began their responsibility of maintaining stability in Tibetan areas, despite all the risks and dangers, on the whole they have kept a determined mind, without succumbing to fear, and made lots of efforts bearing all hardships."

But it is not so easy to control unarmed non-violent Tibetan crowds. The handbook says: "However, the environment of Tibetan areas is very unique and special, and carrying out activities there entails lots of complexities."

Indeed, 60 years after the so-called Liberation of Tibet, the Chinese stress out as soon they reach the plateau. The handbook goes in detail into different cases of severe headaches, nightmares, flashbacks of brutal episodes such as beating (self-immolations had not begun when the manual was written): "if you face unbearable experiences such as insomnia, it would have an extremely negative impact on your responsibility to carry out work successfully." The unnecessary psychological traumas should be resolved in an appropriate time, says the manual. It explains further: "If you are suffering flashbacks, you should close your eyes and imagine that you are zooming in on the scene like a camera. It may feel uncomfortable. Then zoom all the way out until you cannot see anything. Then tell yourself the flashback has gone."

It appears now that special teams have been visiting the region, spending months at a time counselling Chinese troops.

Some Conclusions

First, let us see the 'stability' of the Tibetan plateau.

In May 2013, Meng Jianzhu, a member of the all-powerful Communist Party's Politburo, in-charge of the security in China visited Zhejiang Province. He spoke to the CCP's cadres about developing the 'Fengqiao Experience' to be emulated elsewhere in China.

What is this Fengquiao Experience?

Fengqiao is a town in Zhuji City in Zhejiang Province. According to *The People's Daily*, in Fengquiao "the Party and government bear their respective responsibilities for definite work, relying on the masses, diffusing contradictions, safeguarding stability and promoting development to ensure that minor problems can be settled without going out of the village, major problems can be resolved without going out of the town and contradictions are not passed on to the leadership". Thc Party's conclusion is "the experience of Fengqiao is worth being popularised". It is clear that China faces such a serious problem in Nagchu and other areas on the Tibetan plateau that it is unable to implement the Fengqiao experience. Beijing has to constantly intervene in Tibetan issues, which often gives a bad image to the Party.

This is a big thorn in the Middle Kingdom's foot. India should be aware of it and keep watching how the situation develops.

Second issue: the infrastructure development on the plateau.

The Indian Defence Minister A.K. Antony recently assured the Parliament: "After 'years of neglect', India is fast developing capabilities near the China border, including building of roads, raising of two mountain Divisions, many new airfields and landing grounds." Mr. Antony conceded that China was 'superior' in terms of border infrastructure as India, "because of the 1962 war, India was late in deciding on building roads and other capabilities near the Line of Actual Control." On the ground the situation remains grim and the ministerial promises may take time to materialize.

On the other side of the border, two more airports have recently been put into service on the Tibetan plateau. One is the Daocheng Yading airport, located in Daocheng County, Kardze Tibetan Autonomous Prefecture of Sichuan Province which started operating on 16 September. On 19 August, Xinhua had reported the arrival of an A319 passenger plane from Sichuan Airlines which "marked the opening of the Xiahe Airport of Gannan Tibetan Autonomous Prefecture. It is the first 'civil' aviation airport built in ethnic [Tibetan] areas of Gansu Province as well as the only plateau airport at an elevation of 3,198 metres in Gansu," said the official news agency.

Then, the construction of a new airport to serve Dawu Township, capital of Golog (Golok) Tibetan Autonomous Prefecture (TAP) in Qinghai Province will begin later this year. For Beijing, it will also help control the 'restiveness' of the Tibetans in the area.

One could cite many more examples of Chinese advance in terms of infrastructure, nonetheless the fact remains that after more than 60 years, Beijing has not been able to 'liberate' Tibet; the situation is extremely worrisome for the leadership.

In the remote likelihood of a conflict, the 'instability' on the plateau would in some way, balance India's unpreparedness on the Himalayan slopes.

NUCLEAR DETERRENCE IN SOUTH ASIA—POSSIBILITIES AND LIMITS

Klaus Lange, Institute for Transnational Studies, Germany/Italy

Some General Introductory Remarks

Since the book by Herman Kahn "On Escalation" was published in 1965 the world has been accustomed to look at questions of nuclear deterrence from a widely different perspective. The nuclear arms race as it had developed throughout the so called "Cold War" was finally stopped as the main rivals, the USA and the Soviet Union realised that the reciprocal quest for nuclear dominance was about to endanger the strategic stability and to increase the probability of nuclear exchange cum escalation. Notwithstanding quite a number of crises, misperceptions and technical faults, the history of which still remains to be written, in the first place there was one main reason which prompted the adversaries to look at the nuclear arms race with different eyes: Based on experiences in situations of crises but also on game theoretical analysis the insight spread that strategic stability or the improbability of nuclear exchange was in inverse proportion to the level of nuclear armament achieved on both sides:

The more nuclear weapons both sides could field, the more likely it was that one side would push the button in order to avoid neutralisation of its nuclear potential by the other one. Comprehension began to dawn on the adversaries that more nuclear weapons do not equal more stability—at least not from a certain level of armament. This is to say that answering the question whether possession of nuclear weapons implies more or less stability with a simple 'Yes' or 'No' is not doing sufficient justice to the underlying complexity. A closer look at—let us say two adversaries'—nuclear arms race shows that the process can be seen as going through three stages:

1. The stage at which the competitors start showing intention to acquire nuclear weapons. At this stage stability is very low because the stronger competitor will do nearly everything in order to stop the weaker one in his efforts to get hold of nuclear weapons.
2. The second stage, at which the different sides dispose of relative modest nuclear capacities whereby distribution of those capacities will be more or less symmetrical. Since nuclear weapons are something like a "great equalizer" the weaker competitor will be relatively safe because the stronger one will always try to avoid the risk of a nuclear

second strike. Stability at this stage is relatively high.

3. The stage of high-level and further increasing nuclear capacities and also of increasing efficiency of delivery systems at which tension is growing in direct proportion to the efficiency of weapons systems on both sides. On the one hand, either side is tempted to risk a first strike in order to disarm the adversary. On the other hand, such a first strike is pondered because the adversary is perceived as calculating in exactly the same way and must thereby be pre-empted. That stage is characterised by, again - growing instability.

Therefore, if we look at nuclear armament or a nuclear arms race in a more differentiating way we find that the second stage implies least probability of military confrontation. I should add: If we have to deal with more or less rational players.

After these introductory and general remarks we look at the situation of nuclear armament and nuclear strategy in South Asia.

Nuclear armament in South Asia: Some aspects to be taken into consideration

If we refer to nuclear armament, nuclear strategy and nuclear policy in South Asia we have to narrow down our focus to the Indian–Pakistani relationship. The reason why "South Asia" has been integrated in the title has to do with the fact that South Asia as a whole is negatively affected by the Indian–Pakistani antagonism which in itself is to a great degree characterised by the – hitherto in vain - attempt at finding a stability-prone approach to the problem that we have two nuclear armed states which still struggle with the fact that their nuclear strategy –if we euphemistically want to call the ongoing quest for a rational approach a "strategy", is not helpful yet to rule out a nuclear exchange within a sufficient scope of probability. At first glance one tends to believe that the process of procuring nuclear arms has reached the above mentioned second stage, where, in spite of a still comparatively "modest" (when I am saying "modest", I do not overlook the fact that the nuclear arsenal of India and Pakistan is about to overtake that of other traditional nuclear powers) level of nuclear armament on both sides, either side is able to inflict damage on the adversary to a degree which would seriously question the survival of the nation in each conceivable sense. Neither India nor Pakistan has the ability to launch a disarming strike which would annihilate the ability of a second strike.

Moreover, in the foreseeable future none of the two will possess the BMD–capacities to render a second strike useless. In other words: Both are vulnerable to a degree which forbids any thought of using nuclear weapons. This again will also limit military clashes with conventional means to a level of very low intensity because large-scale conventional clashes would sooner or later move dangerously close to the red line beyond which use of nuclear weapons and the start of nuclear escalation becomes a realistic possibility. Presupposing rational actors one could thereby arrive at the conclusion that the stage of nuclear armament reached by both sides not only rules out the use of nuclear weapons but even forces both sides to keep conventional clashes at the lowest possible level.

From this point of view, possession of nuclear weapons by both adversaries has implied a lower probability of military conflict altogether. Never in the history of India and Pakistan has the probability of major military conflict been lower than since 1998 when both sides demonstrated their nuclear capacities. Pointing to the variety of nuclear weapons both countries have at their disposal and which allow for thorough use from the tactical up to the strategic level one could argue that the present factual situation of mutually assured destruction could be followed by doctrines of flexible response whereby conventional challenges will be answered by conventional means, use of tactical nuclear weapons will be answered by use of respective tactical ones and so forth.

This, as the theory of "flexible response" holds, would provide opportunities to stop the turning of the escalation spiral and to do a cost –benefit analysis at each level of escalation and thereby provide an option of ceasefire even after nuclear weapons have been used already.

I do not believe that, in the case of a major military conflict between India and Pakistan, flexible response is a realistic option. Escalation management will spiral out of control as soon as Indian conventional superiority would seriously question the territorial integrity of Pakistan. There is no doubt that, in such a case, Pakistan would resort to the use of tactical nuclear weapons instead of getting used to the idea of another war lost. The only possibility for India to dissuade Pakistan from the use of tactical nuclear weapons would be the threat of massive retaliation, an approach which was advocated earlier this year by Shyam Saran, convener of the NSAB. It has not yet become really clear to which degree this approach is an official one or not. In any case, there is reason to doubt that in case Pakistan uses tactical nuclear weapons in order to stop Indian troops advancing onto Pakistani territory, India would resort to massive retaliation as this again would no doubt trigger a similar reaction on the part of Pakistan.

In other words: In case a conflict would take such a course, there would be no winner but only losers in the most dramatic sense. Therefore one must be inclined to believe that the Pakistani decision to balance Indian conventional superiority by employment of tactical nuclear weapons has in fact annihilated any option of "cold start" or the like. (For a thorough analysis of this see: Zafar Nawaz Jaspal: "Tactical Nuclear Weapons: Deterrence Stability between India and Pakistan", CCC, Monterey 2012)

Against this background it makes sense to expect that Indian reaction to, for instance, Pakistani sponsored terrorist attacks would be very carefully calibrated in such a way that they would remain below the threshold beyond which Pakistan would feel compelled to react with the use of tactical nuclear weapons. Accordingly, Indian reaction would be limited to conventional surgical strikes or/and economic sanctions.

In a nutshell: The present stage of nuclear armament on both sides implies a maximum of stability or in other words a maximum of credible minimum deterrence. This, of course, is no reason to firmly trust without any reservation that there is a watertight guarantee of 100% absence of a possible nuclear conflict.

The history of the Cold War gives very disturbing examples of growing possibility of nuclear war due to the specific psychological conditions in situation of crises, wrong perceptions regarding intentions of the other side or simply technical deficiencies.

Another disquieting aspect lies in the fact that one cannot rule out with absolute certainty that unauthorised entities, the mindset of which is not influenced by rational cost – benefit calculation, can gain control of nuclear weapons. But this refers to the problem of safeguarding nuclear weapons which is a topic in itself. Given safety measures and procedures in place and the degree of professional expertise in place the likelihood that doomsday—minded groups can get hold of nuclear weapons and unleash nuclear Armageddon, can be considered extremely small, at least for the foreseeable future.

There are nevertheless two developments which have the potential to undermine the present situation of stability:

1. Miniaturisation of nuclear weapons; and
2. Increase of nuclear stockpiles, together with increasing sophistication of delivery systems.

On point 1: Conventional wisdom holds that there is, in principle, a floating transition between the category of small nuclear weapons and powerful conventional weapons. This is not a really realistic assessment if one considers that the yield of the most powerful conventional weapons, so-called thermobaric weapons around 40 tons of TNT, while a standard nuclear artillery shell such as the W48 equals ca. 80 tons of TNT.

Irrespectively, it may well be though, that through use of new and more potent conventional explosives or further miniaturisation of nuclear weapons the difference in terms of yield between conventional weapons and small nuclear devices may be further blurred. But there will still always be one qualitative difference regarding the use of conventional and nuclear battlefield weapons - the nuclear pollution caused by employment of the latter. And this fact has not only, as one might be inclined to assume, a bearing upon the post-war situation in the regions where nuclear battlefield weapons have been used, but also on the military strategy and tactics as such. This becomes understandable if one looks at possible scenarios:

The first one is based on the case that conventionally superior Indian forces break through the Pakistan defence which sees no other means than to stop the Indian advance through the use of tactical nuclear weapons. In this scenario, Pakistani tactical nuclear weapons would be used on Pakistani soil and irrespective of whether thereby Indian troops can be stopped or not, it would in first place be Pakistani territory to be affected by radioactive pollution. If one additionally assumes that the Indian side, in such a case, would respond on its part with nuclear weapons, be it nuclear artillery or nuclear-tipped short range missiles, the collateral damage in this scenario would be greater than any Pakistani leadership could accept.

Accordingly, a second scenario becomes more realistic, namely pre-emption of a conventional Indian attack on Pakistani territory through attempts at annihilating Indian troop concentrations as long as those are still on Indian territory. This scenario carries nightmarish implications insofar as the decision on the use of Pakistani nuclear weapons would depend on the quality of intelligence regarding Indian intentions.

History, in at least one known example, shows that

questionable intelligence can lead to the brink of nuclear war: the KGB—project RYaN (attack by nuclear rockets), launched by former KGB director Yuri Andropov in 1981 had created such a strong belief-cum-hysteria in a forthcoming nuclear strike by NATO that during the NATO manoeuvre "Able Archer" in 1983 false intelligence on the Soviet side would nearly have triggered a nuclear war.

There is no reason to believe that the Pakistani side will never mistakenly consider Indian troop concentration as being based on intention to launch an attack which would have to be pre-empted by nuclear means. And there is equally no guarantee that the Indian side would under no circumstances anticipate Pakistani nuclear strikes on Indian troop concentrations and on its part not try to pre-empt such Pakistani pre-emption with whatever suitable means, not least with nuclear ones.

At this point of the discussion a lot of criticism is imaginable. Such criticism can be based on the argument that the rationality of both players is greatly underestimated, that confidence building measures can be developed to such a degree as to rule out a development whereby the rationality of deterrence by means of small nuclear weapons would metamorphose into the irrationality of pre-emption-cum-escalation and that the positive sum game of increasing economic interaction would contribute to the nearly 100% unlikelihood of nuclear warfare.

All these are valid arguments but they are questioned by a second scenario: If we presuppose that miniaturisation of nuclear weapons, which allows for their use as battlefield weapons, is progressing on both sides, then we also have to take into account that this process will additionally imply decentralisation of the decision-making process regarding use of nuclear weapons respectively devolution of the command authority from a National Command Authority to regional or local commanders. The smaller nuclear weapons are, the shorter the lines of command, which determine their use, have to be.

It makes no sense to have nuclear artillery or/and other battlefield nuclear weapons if, in the fluid battlefield situation, decision on their use must come from the very top each time. Thus it will be the limited perspective of regional or local commanders which governs a decision on the use of nuclear weapons. Their overriding rationale will always be survival on the battlefield, and no other aspect whatsoever, and the decision in favour of use of nuclear weapons will not take into account the likely course of ensuing escalation but will exclusively aim at carrying the day at one concrete and short point in time.

What do these few remarks boil down to? It has been stated that due to reciprocal vulnerability, since 1998, a stage of relative deterrence stability between India and Pakistan has been reached. But this stage is only transitory in nature to the degree to which development of nuclear battlefield weapons is moving forward together with the overall increase of the nuclear arsenal of both sides.

If the development of more, new and also smaller nuclear weapons is not stopped, the presently reached deterrence stability will erode and the probability of nuclear war will start increasing again.

This not only has to do with implications of the fielding of battlefield nuclear weapons I have alluded to, but also with the logic of a nuclear arms race as such. As indicated in the introductory remarks the relationship between the level of nuclear armament of two adversaries follows a development which could be illustrated by a curve very similar to the "Laffer–curve" which describes the relationship between taxation and revenues of the state derived from taxation. In our case we have to depict the relationship between deterrence stability and the level of nuclear armament: The respective curve runs from a low level of stability in correlation to low levels of armament over high stability related to a minimum credible second strike capacity of both adversaries to decreasing stability in spite of growing armaments levels. The reason for decreasing stability is the growing constraint to pre-empt. Translated into our concrete case one can say that deterrence stability has more or less reached a maximum over the years. The duration of this stage of relative stability depends on the speed with which armaments' levels are increased.

After this period, the duration of which is very difficult to estimate, there will be a decrease of stability and the probability of nuclear exchange will grow due to a growing affinity to a pre-emptive mindset.

In order to illustrate what is being said one could imagine two hostile persons who are both not armed. The probability that the two will start fighting each other physically is high because none of the two is in danger to get killed. If both dispose of weapons which, in principle, could lead to the death of both (for instance hand grenades) they would be much more careful, watch the adversary carefully but try to avoid throwing the hand grenade. Stability in such a case would be relatively high. But, if both adversaries point with a loaded gun at each other, at short notice the inclination to press the trigger in order to pre-empt shooting by the other person is very high. This stage has, in my view, not been reached yet in the concrete case of the two nuclear armed adversaries. But it will become a gruesome reality if nothing is done about the factors which sooner or later will imply the third stage of increasingly likely pre-emption.

Some Concluding Trains of Thought

There is a precarious situation because the phase of relative stability will be followed by growing instability, if determining factors cannot be changed. Those factors are: Pakistani awareness of Indian conventional superiority which is the main reason of the Pakistani nuclear arms program; Indian quest for deterrence stability not only vis-à-vis China but increasingly also vis-à-vis Pakistan; lack of a nuclear doctrine on both sides which in combination with suitable confidence-building measures would allow for a freeze of the nuclear armaments process.

All this is in place and it makes little sense to believe that those determining factors can easily be changed: India will hardly cut down on its conventional strength, which, although it is in fact mainly China–specific, is considered a threat by Pakistan.

There is also little hope that both countries would enter into an agreement on strategic–cum-nuclear arms reduction.

And finally, it would be overoptimistic to assume that incidents between the two states which, again and again, will lift tensions to dangerous levels can be avoided in future. There is not much hope that those factors can be changed before the phase of decreasing stability is being reached. Such a pessimistic expectation doesn't necessarily have to come true, because, as Karl Popper claims, today we cannot know what we will know tomorrow.

Yet, it would be questionable to draw comfort from this and stop thinking about possibilities to avoid the dangers of nuclear war.

Taking into account the apocalyptic implications of nuclear war, it is more rational to start from a worst case–scenario. This might point into the direction where a solution to the problem of increasing risk could be found: The problem we have to deal with has a lot to do with the modular character of thinking about socio-economic problems and security-related reasoning.

In both countries there is very little interaction, communication and feedback between economic rationality and the rationality which governs deliberations on security.

War, particularly nuclear war, would appear the greatest possible irrationality in the eyes of the economic players. On the other hand, while for decision makers in the field of security, every decision, which does not justice to the worst-case regarding security, is considered as irresponsible if not as forfeiting national interest or even national existence.

If one communicates in India and Pakistan, on the one hand with representatives of the business community, and on the other hand with representatives of the security establishment it is like moving between completely different worlds. What is at the heart of the danger I have tried to allude to, is the lack in both countries of a more holistic approach when looking at each other.

The hope must therefore be to overcome the modular character of thinking in terms of socio –economic rationality and of exclusively thinking in terms of security. There are indications in my view that such modular thinking is being increasingly questioned. One would wish that this process becomes a determining one before time runs out.

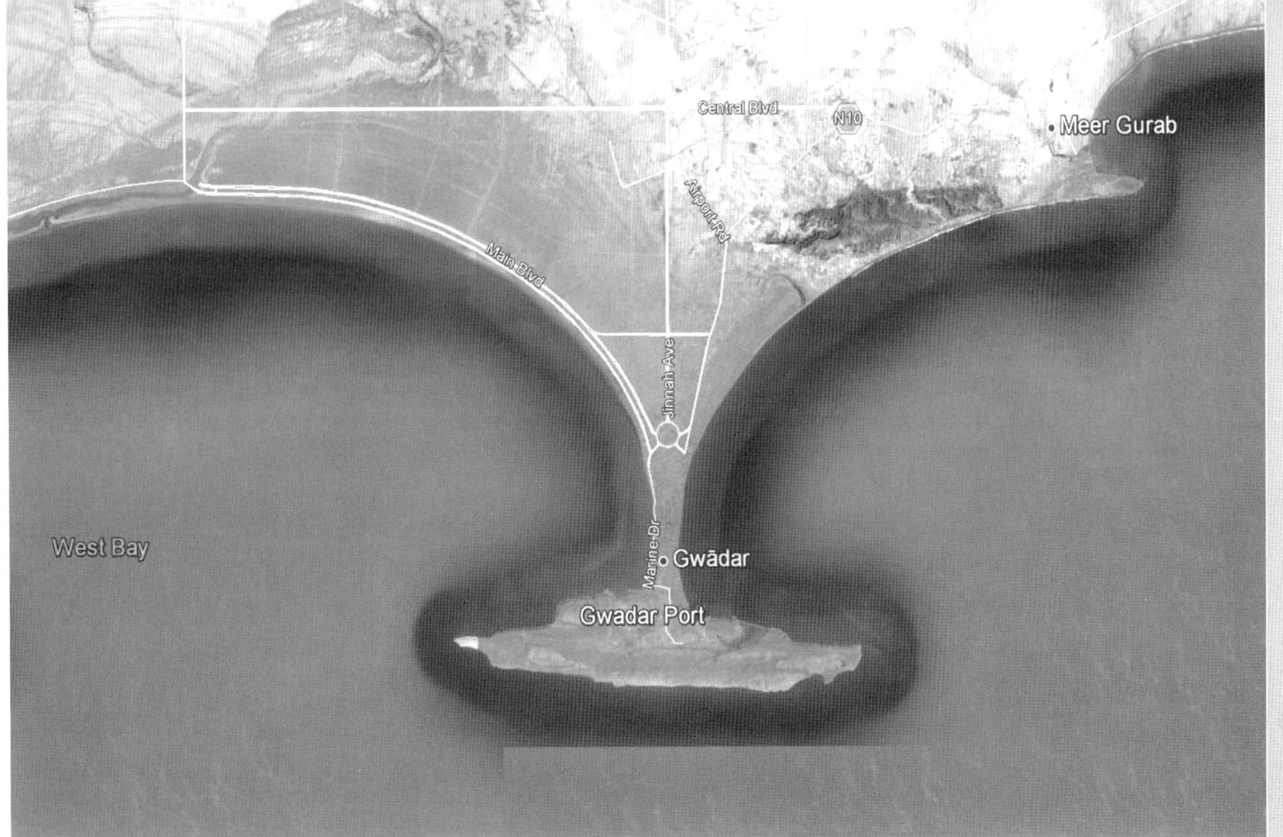

PAKISTAN'S BALOCHISTAN

Brig VP Malhotra, Author and Defence Analyst, New Delhi

Baloch population is concentrated on the Iranian Plateau[1] between Pakistan, Iran and Afghanistan. The Pakistan province of Balochistan, towards its southwest, is composed of barren, rugged mountainous and fertile land. Most of the land in the west is barren and is sparsely populated. The southern part, known as Makran, is generally desert. It is the largest province of Pakistan with an area of 347,190 square kilometres and population of around 13 million. The population density is only 38 per square kilometre due to the rugged terrain and water shortage. 75 per cent of the population lives in rural areas which is poor. Balochistan comprises 44 per cent of the country's area and only around 14 per cent of its population, and is the least developed of all provinces. Its neighbouring regions are Iranian Balochistan to the west, Afghanistan and FATA to the north, and Punjab and Sindh to the east. Balochistan shares a 1173 kilometres-long border with Iran and 837 kilometres with Afghanistan. The principal languages in the province are Baluchi, Brahui, Sindhi, Pashto and Urdu. Most Balochis are Sunni Muslims. About 60 per cent live in Balochistan, 25 per cent inhabit Sistan and Baluchestan province (one province) of the Islamic Republic of Iran, and many also live in southern Afghanistan, besides Sindh and south Punjab in Pakistan. Most of the rest live in Turkmenistan, Oman, Bahrain, Kuwait and some parts of Africa. Small numbers also live in Europe (particularly Sweden and Norway) and in Perth, Western Australia. Quetta is the capital and the largest city with Pashtun majority.

Balochistan has a 770 kilometres-long coast line, which is 70 per cent of the total coast line of Pakistan with tremendous potential for fisheries, tourism and sea ports. At Gawadar, the Government is currently completing a project with Chinese help to build a large port to provide the Pakistan Navy with another base to reduce its reliance on Karachi and Port Qasim. Gawadar is strategically important, situated close to the Indian Ocean and the Strait of Hormuz.

It is assessed that Pakistan has its nuclear, possibly also chemical weapons developing sites, and missile testing range at Wazir Khan Khoso, Ras Koh and Sonmiani in Balochistan.

There is scanty rain in Balochistan. Water is being fed to it through Sukkur and Kashmore barrages (on River Sindh). Agriculture is the mainstay of the

[1] From the Caspian in the northwest to Balochistan in the south-east, the Iranian Plateau extends for close to 2,000 km. It encompasses the greater part of Iran, Afghanistan and Pakistan west of the River Indus.

60 per cent of the work force linked directly or indirectly with it. Fruit production contributes to 16 per cent of the Pakistan's total fruit production. But for the infrastructure, more fruit products could be sold in other states of Pakistan or exported to neighbouring countries. The prominent fruits grown are dates, grapes, pomegranates, apples, almonds, apricots, plums and peaches.

GAWADAR

Gawadar, a fishing village at the apex of Arabian Sea and Gulf of Oman, was bought by Pakistan in 1958 from Oman for $3 million. It was integrated in to Balochistan in 1977 and a deep sea port has been completed in 2009 with Chinese help. 500 Chinese worked for the project over a period of time. A green field airport has also been completed concurrently. Simultaneously, a road network has been developed linking the port with Karachi and the road network of Pakistan.

The port is presently being operated by China Overseas Port Holding Company Limited (COPHCL). China's investment in the development and operation of the port is heavy and aims at developing an energy corridor to Xinjiang. The project will cut down oil and gas transportation distance from Africa and Middle East by thousands of kilometres.

China also participates in development projects like development of ports, deep sea mining, ocean-research and antipiracy operations in the IOR. China's presence will attract international presence in the region.

Balochistan is endowed with rich natural, mineral and energy resources. It has significant reserves of coal, copper, gold, zinc, lead, iron, chromite, lime stone and marble. Pakistan receives 40 per cent of its natural gas from Balochistan. Most of the proposed gas pipelines, like Iran-Pakistan-India, Turkmenistan-Afghanistan-Pakistan, and Qatar-Pakistan-India, have to pass through Balochistan.

The region became part of Afghan Empire in the mid-18th century. Western Balochistan was invaded and taken by Iran in the 19th century. Balochistan commanded a strategic position being a communication centre between South West Asia, Central Asia and South Asia. The 'Great Game' of the 19th century led to division of the Baloch between British India, Iran and Afghanistan in order to appease Iran and Afghanistan to keep the Russians away from the Indian subcontinent.

Originally a loose tribal confederation, Balochistan was later divided into principalities that were under Persian or Afghan suzerainty. In the 19th century, British troops tried to subdue the inhabitants until a Treaty in 1876 gave them autonomy in exchange for British Army outposts along the Afghan border and strategic roads. The treaty was concluded by Sir Robert Sandeman with the Khan of Kalat[2] which brought his territories including Kharan, Makran and Las Bela under British suzerainty. This was a turning point in the history of Balochistan. After the Second Afghan War of 1878-80, in the Treaty of Gandamak, concluded in 1879, the Afghan Amir ceded the districts of Quetta, Pishin, Sibi and Harnai to the British. In 1883 the British leased the Bolan Pass, south of Quetta, from the Khan of Kalat on permanent basis.

In 1893, Sir Mortimer Durand negotiated an agreement with Amir Abdur Rahman, Khan of Afghanistan to fix the border between Afghanistan and British India (Durand Line). The Khans of Kalat, the rulers, somehow were never completely independent. There was always a power they were reporting to. They reported to Delhi, Kandahar and Kabul from time to time. Afghan kings conferred titles on Kalat chiefs like Beglar Begi (Chief of Chiefs) and Wali-i-Kalat (Governor of Kalat). The situation in 1947 was that the Baloch had been split into Pakistani Balochistan, Iranian Balochistan and the Baloch in Afghanistan.

THE DURAND LINE

The Durand Line was created as the border between British India and Afghanistan in 1893 through an agreement between Sir Mortimer Durand and Amir Abdur Rahman, the Khan of Afghanistan. This Agreement has been accepted internationally, but Afghanistan does not accept it due to the following reasons:

- *It divided three sovereign countries, namely Afghanistan, Balochistan and British India. It did not include Balochistan which was an affected party and was only in treaty relationship with the British.*
- *It was fixed as a result of an unequal treaty and was only meant to be a line of control.*
- *The drawing of the border was arbitrary and divided the ethnic Baloch and Pashtun.*
- *The boundary did not follow defined geographical features.*
- *Access to sea was denied to Afghanistan.*

Although recognised internationally as the western border of Pakistan, it remains unrecognized in Afghanistan. It has been described as one of the most dangerous borders in the world.

On 11 August 1947, the British returned control of Kalat to His Highness Mir Ahmad Yar Khan, the Khan of Kalat. The Khan immediately declared independence of Kalat, and Mohammad Ali Jinnah signed the proclamation of Kalat's sovereignty under the Khan. The New York Times reported on 12 August 1947, "Under the agreement, Pakistan recognizes Kalat as an independent sovereign state with a status different from that of the Indian States". An announcement from New Delhi said "Kalat, Moslem State in Balochistan, has reached an agreement with Pakistan for free flow of communications and commerce, and would negotiate for decisions on defence and external affairs".[3] The next day, the NY Times even printed a map of the world showing Balochistan as a fully

[2] Kalat was a princely state located generally in centre of modern day Balochistan. It was the most significant state in the region and the British dealt with it to enhance their interests like drawing of boundaries, direct British control of territories, ceding of territories and extending suzerainty etc. Balochistan was an independent state before 15 August 1947. Its boundaries are supposed to extend to areas where Baloch inhabit and that includes areas in Iran and Afghanistan.

[3] The region of Balochistan was an independent country before the advent of the British. It is for this reason that independence was declared, but it was advised that an independent Balochistan would not be a viable option. India concurred with this view.

independent country. On 15 August 1947, the Khan formally declared full independence of Balochistan and proclaimed 15 August a day of celebration. The Khan formed the lower and upper houses of Kalat Assembly, and during the first meeting of the Lower House in September 1947, it confirmed the independence of Balochistan. From 15 August 1947 to 27 March 1948, the region was *de facto* independent before acceding to Pakistan on 27 March 1948. The Government of Pakistan took complete control of Balochistan and several political leaders were taken into custody. Khanate was reverted to its previous status as it had existed under the British rule. The Khan of Kalat, however, was persuaded or coerced to accede to Pakistan.

The education system in Balochistan is dismal. There are not enough primary schools and many children do not have access to education at all. Even the ones who enrol, the dropout rate is rather high.[4] Net primary school enrolment stands at 52 per cent in 2010-11 (age group 6-10) against 61 per cent at the national level. 14 per cent enrol for matriculation and lesser in higher grades. There are seven main universities, in addition to a few private institutes. Two more universities have been approved. Balochistan has a literacy rate of 39 per cent against the national average of 52 per cent. Thus, 61 per cent of the population is illiterate. With least educational institutions and lowest literacy rate, Balochistan is home to the largest number of school buildings that are falling apart.

Balochistan has the highest infant and maternal mortality rate in South Asia. According to a Ministry of Health policy paper, 'Gender Awareness Policy Appraisal 2006', one of the major reasons for this high mortality rate is hunger and malnutrition. Successive findings indicate that maternal mortality rate is 785 per 100,000 against the national average of 272 per 100,000; child mortality is 89 deaths per 1,000 against the national average of 61.

Balochistan has the lowest water and sanitation indicators. The poor are particularly vulnerable. The urban poor spend a disproportionately large part of their income buying water, while in the rural areas fetching water from long distances is the burden of women-folk and children. Nearly half the population relies on wells, ponds, rivers, canals or streams for their drinking water needs. In the urban areas, 80 per cent of the population has access to piped water and another 10 per cent to other improved sources.[5] In rural areas, these figures are 18 per cent and 26 per cent respectively; with only 38 per cent of the rural population having access to improved sources of water within two kilometres. Electricity is supplied to barely 25 per cent of the population in Balochistan.

Only 40 per cent of the population has access to excreta disposal, 10 per cent to waste water disposal and 5 per cent to solid waste disposal. Adequate excreta disposal facilities are not available to 71 per cent of the rural population; waste water disposal is available to barely 1 per cent, and there is no solid waste collection and disposal system. Most schools lack proper toilets, posing problems, especially to girls. Garbage litters are common, particularly in urban areas.

The presence of Afghan refugees (unofficially 4 million) has disrupted the delicate ethnic balance in the province by raising the Pashtun numerically nearly equal to the Baloch. There are also a growing number of Sindhis, Kurdish, Punjabis, Mohajir and Iranians who have made Balochistan their home. The indigenous Baloch is not only not happy with this demographic invasion, but also sees this as a conspiracy against them by the Federal Government.

According to the UNDP 2005 Human Development Index Report, Balochistan figures lowest with .5557 against the national average of .6196 and .6699 in the Punjab province. Amongst the top 31 districts with the highest HDI, Punjab was at 59 per cent, while Balochistan was at the tail end at 9 per cent. 92 per cent of Balochistan's districts are classified as 'high deprivation' compared to 50 per cent in Sindh.[6] Balochistan has 60 per cent poor as compared to 45.7 per cent in the country. According to a study conducted by Dr Talat Anwar, a senior development expert, rural poverty in Balochistan increased by 15 per cent between 1999 and 2005.

In a bid to counter the majority of Bengalis in East Pakistan, in 1955 entire West Pakistan was converted into one single province, with Lahore as its capital. The "One Unit", with linguistic and ethnic diversity, led to emergence of a large "anti-One Unit" movement in West Pakistan. The Pakistan Army invaded Balochistan in 1958 to crush the movement. A 1,000-strong militia fought the army in pitched battles for over a year. In May 1959, Nauroz Khan,

---

[4] Federal Bureau of Statistics on Pakistan Social and Living Standards Measurement (PSLM) Survey 2010-11

[5] An improved drinking-water source is defined as one that, by nature of its construction or through active intervention, is likely to be protected from outside contamination, in particular contamination with fecal matter.

[6] The Express Tribune (Pakistan), Editorial, Overwhelmed by Poverty, 26 February 2013

the leader of the militia, was arrested and died in captivity in 1964, becoming a symbol of Baloch resistance. Five of his relatives, including his son, were hanged. "One Unit" continued until General Yahya Khan dissolved it and Balochistan received provincial status on 1 July 1970 by merger of Quetta and Kalat. The unicameral Assembly of Balochistan comprises 65 seats, of which 51 are directly elected members representing constituencies from each district, 11 reserved seats for women and three reserved seats for minorities. In addition, five territories are designated as Provincially Administered Tribal Areas (PATA).[7]

Balochistan is predominantly a tribal structure, each tribe headed by a *sardar,* who rules by their tradition and need. There are around 400 tribes. The tribal heads are hereditary and powerful, even to the extent that they matter in the state affairs. Marris and Bugtis are among the major tribes. There are three major ethnic groups viz. the Baloch, the Pathan and Brauhi among many others. Each tribe has its own tradition and systems with intra-tribe and inter-tribe rivalries. Balochistan, as such, has not been able to unify internally resulting in lack of coordination in every field, be it business, trade or projection of the state interests. The polarization affects the developmental plans adversely and keeps the state away from meaningful integration with Pakistan. Along with the tribal governance, the tribes and ethnic groups maintain their armed forces which are equipped with modern weapons. The situation suits the powerful *sardars* who would rather have *status quo* maintained. The *sardars,* rather than leading their tribes, tend to become mediators between the state and the tribe. The *sardari* system is so deeply entrenched that no government has been able to make a meaningful change. The divisive system is also exploited by the Federal Government, when required.

Balochistan was divided into 'A' and 'B' areas by the British to manage law and order, and governance through proxy. 'A' areas are urban areas where the provincial police is effective and 'B' areas are governed by the *sardars* through tribal levies. The major towns fall under 'A' areas and the remaining 95 per cent under 'B' areas. The system further strengthens the writ of the *sardars*. 'B' areas, as such, have become a safe haven for anti-social elements, insurgents and terrorists. Following the anti-terror drive in the wake of 9/11, a major initiative was undertaken to convert the 'B' areas into 'A' areas. Towards this effort, the Government raised a 6,000-strong Baloch Constabulary to enforce the new policies. The Federal Government has also committed over Rs 5 billion to raise more forces, procure arms and ammunition and create infrastructure. The drive, however, has encountered major resistance from the tribes and the *sardars*. They contend that the levy system, which is over 100 years old, is more suited to the tribal areas and is manned by the locals; as such is cost effective. The decision to convert "B" areas in to "A" areas, it appears, lacked analysis and was rather hasty. While most of the decision has been reversed, 70 per cent of the resources allotted have already been committed. The levies which were to be replaced by regular police and Frontier Corps (FC) are back. The writ of the *sardars* continues.

The Pakistan Army had to subdue insurgents based in Kalat, who rejected Kalat's decision to accede to Pakistan in 1947. The Baloch separatist movement gained momentum, which led to serious conflicts during 1948, 1958-59, 1963-69, 1973-77 and 2004 onwards. The Dera Bugti district has been the site of intense operations by the Pakistan military in 2005-07. The Pakistan military laid siege to Dera Bugti, employing artillery and air power. More than 900 Baloch were killed, 450 political activists (mainly from the Baloch National Party) disappeared and 4,000 arrested. The Meingal (the second largest tribe) and the Marri are in open revolt against the Government in the province. With the killing of Nawab Akbar Khan Bugti in 2006 and Nawabzada Balach Marri, the Chief of the Balochistan Liberation Army (BLA) in 2007, the momentum of the insurgency declined, as some leaders either fled Pakistan or were neutralized. However, insurgencies do not cease with temporary setbacks, particularly when none of the underlying causes have been addressed in the right earnest. Insurgency has picked up again as the militants have re-grouped. Quetta, Sibbi, Dera Bugti, Turbat and Khuzdar have volatile situation. Reportedly CIA, RAW, Mossad, MI 5/6 are active in Balochistan.

Pakistan has resorted to military expeditions against the people of Balochistan again and again. Thousands of insurgents and Pakistani soldiers were killed and wounded during these operations. According to UN estimates, as of December 2006, there were 84,000 internally displaced persons (IDPs) in Balochistan, of whom 26,000 were women and 33,000 children. The largest and richest state of Pakistan has become the poorest, discontented and

[7] The Provincially Administered Tribal Areas (PATA) are Pakistani administrative sub-divisions where no Act of Provincial Assembly can be applied unless specifically extended by the Governor with consent of the President of Pakistan.

alienated. Approximately 4 lakh refugees from Afghanistan, the IDPs and other outsiders from Pakistan give the Baloch and the *sardars* a feeling of marginalization in their home land. The situation added to the illiteracy and poverty, which were already high. Economy became a serious casualty.

On 11 August 2013, Chief Justice of Pakistan, Iftikhar Chaudhry took *suo motu* notice of the deteriorating law and order situation in Balochistan following Eid and pre-Eid attacks that caused over 40 deaths and inadequate preventive action by the Government. On 13 August 2013, the Interior Minister Chaudhry Nisar Ali Khan announced that the Federal Government would provide a 15,000-strong security force to the Balochistan Government to rid the province of terrorists and insurgents.

Despite Balochistan's rich natural resources; due to sparse population, low level of human development, the *sardari* system, tribal nature of society, ethnic contiguity with Iran and Afghanistan, Federal policy and the security environment, industry has not developed in keeping with its potential. These are also the cause of unrest. The Baloch are also not happy with the development of the Gawadar port and Saindak Copper-Gold projects in collaboration with China without their involvement in decision making, even though these will act as major commercial and military hubs with collateral developments like Makran Coastal Highway, Mirani Dam Water Project, Kachhi Canal, Quetta water and sewerage scheme, export and industrial zones, international airport etc.[8]

The discontent has resulted in demands which range from greater cultural, economic and political autonomy, to outright secession and creation of an independent state of Balochistan. It claims to receive considerable support from the Baloch diaspora in Oman, the UAE, Sweden, Norway, Europe and North America. The agitation has led to emergence of a number of militant organisations. The more prominent ones are:

- **The Baloch Liberation Front (BLF).** A political as well as militant group founded in 1964 in Damascus, and played an important role during 1968-1980 Insurgency in Pakistani Balochistan and Iranian Balochistan. The BLF had support from Arab nationalist's leaders. In 1974, the Pakistani army started widespread operations, resulting in fleeing of the cadres to Afghanistan, where Iraq and the Soviet Union helped them reorganise.
- **The Baloch Students Organization (BSO).** Founded in 1967, it organized the guerrilla groups for the 1973-1977 Insurgency. It now comprises three groups viz. BSO (Pajjar), BSO (Meingal) and BSO (Azad). While all three are militant groups, only BSO (Azad) advocates independence of Balochistan.
- **The Baluch People's Liberation Front (BPLF).** Formed in 1976 after developing irreconcilable differences with the Baloch Students Organisation on the question of strategies to be adopted. The group seems to be dormant since 2006, but retains links with Afghanistan.
- **The Balochistan Liberation Army (BLA).** Formed in 1999, it calls for the creation of a Greater Balochistan, to include the Baloch territories in Iran and Afghanistan. BLA is a well organised and motivated clandestine force, with a high degree of invisibility. It was declared a terrorist organisation by Pakistan and UK in April 2006 after a series of attacks on security personnel, civilians, gas and oil establishments, Sui Airport and journalists. The group has an estimated strength of 500 fighters. BLA's allies include Baloch Liberation Front, Baloch Republican Army, Lashkar-e-Balochistan, Balochistan Liberation United Front and BSO (Azad).
- **The Baloch Republican Army**. It seeks an independent homeland for the Baloch people. Formed in 2006, its targets are primarily security forces and infrastructure including railway lines, communication systems, gas pipelines, wells and plants, electricity pylons and any other system.
- **Lashkar-e-Balochistan (LeB).** A terrorist separatist group, which surfaced in 2012 after it claimed responsibility for several bombings in Lahore, Karachi and Quetta. The organization is an off-shoot of the Baloch Liberation Army and operates in far flung areas of Balochistan. It is believed to have several training camps in Balochistan as well as in Afghanistan. It is divided into battalions, each consisting of 20 guerillas. Every battalion commander works under LeB Chief.
- **The Baloch National Party (BNP).** An amalgam of moderate forces, it calls for extensive provincial autonomy, limiting the Federal

[8] Makran Highway has been completed and has cut down travelling time from Gawadar to Karachi from 48 hours to about 7 hours.
Mirani Dam has also been completed and its water is being used for irrigation in Balochistan.
Kachhi Canal is half completed and suffers from cost and time overrun.

Government to control of defence, foreign affairs, currency, and communications. Party also believes in de-nuclearisation and de-militarisation of Balochistan.

There are other outfits which have not been included here to keep the paper precise.

On April 18, 2006, Government of Balochistan-in-Exile, was established somewhere in the Middle East, and His Highness Mir Suleman Dawood Khan (heir apparent of the Khan of Kalat, Mir Ahmad Yar Khan Baloch) was nominated as King. The objective is to liberate Balochistan from the occupying forces. On 12 August 2009, he formally announced a Council for Independent Balochistan. The Council's claimed domain includes the Baloch of Iran and Afghanistan, apart from Pakistani Balochistan.[9] Red, green and blue with sun was chosen as flag with Kalat as the capital. Location of the Government-in-Exile may well be:

Desk of the Government of Balochistan-in-Exile
The World Baloch Jewish Alliance Building
PO Box 5631, Jerusalem, 91000 Israel
(In actual fact this organization may be a floater, or a cyber space HQ)

The above-described scenario makes Balochistan one of the most strategic and volatile regions of the world. Virtually all major powers like USA, China, Russia, Iran, India and Pakistan itself have stakes and capability to intervene overtly and covertly:

- Gawadar has a key strategic position for shipping oil and gas from Turkmenistan to the Arabian Sea via Afghanistan towards western shores. The US and allies may intervene directly or indirectly to control Gawadar at the mouth of Strait of Hormuz/Gulf of Oman, through which over 40 per cent of world's oil passes, thus controlling the energy resources of Middle East. A peaceful Balochistan will permit oil and gas to flow east and west. A disturbed Balochistan will interfere in the flow.
- To Iran, Gawadar is a rival to Chabahar from which oil and gas is shipped. A peaceful Balochistan facilitates Iran for trading its oil and gas.
- China seeks a gas pipeline from Iran through Balochistan into Xinjiang. China has strategic and economic interests in tranquil Balochistan.
- The disturbance in Pakistani Balochistan tends to spill over to Iranian Balochistan. Iran is aware of *Jundallah's* (Soldiers of God) role in support of Sunni Muslims in its territory from Balochistan.
- Shifting of trade from Central Asia southwards is not what Russia desires, thus it would prefer a turbulent Afghanistan and Balochistan.
- Pakistan and Afghanistan have been running militant training camps against each other since the 1970s. In the wake of the Russian invasion of Afghanistan in 1978-79, USA and Pakistan have been employing the Taliban for operations in Afghanistan. In retaliation, the Afghans provide bases to Baloch insurgents in southern Afghanistan to create unrest in Balochistan and Pakistan. Currently the BLA is reported to be operating from Kandahar.
- USA may exploit the situation in Balochistan to address Pakistan and Iran, taking advantage of ethnicity, secessionist activity and the Sunni-Shia divide. *Jundallah* is already active in Iran and may be supported. US Congressman Dana Rohrabacher even introduced a bill in Congress, calling for US support for the outright independence of Balochistan.
- Pakistan and China like to keep Afghanistan disturbed and weak in order to control Balochistan to exploit its strategic potential. This leads to interference both in Balochistan and Afghanistan.
- To counter Pakistan's active support to Kashmiri terrorists, India could well use the insurgency in Balochistan as leverage. Pakistan has repeatedly accused India of funding the Baloch nationalists, which has been denied by India.
- Balochistan also provides another route into Southern Afghanistan from south.

The situation in Balochistan is complex and intertwined. Either way it provides opportunities to competing nations of the world. Pakistan is facing unprecedented challenges — economic turbulence and poverty, law and order issues in Sind, insurgency in Balochistan and the Northern regions, internal terrorism, recoil of its sponsored insurgency in Afghanistan, perpetual conflict with India and unequal collaboration with the US and her allies in the war on terror. Pakistan cannot survive even a day without Balochistan. In the overall interest of Pakistan and the people of Balochistan, the legitimate grievances of the Baloch must be addressed in order to integrate heart and soul of Balochistan in the fabric of Pakistan, and allow much needed industry and foreign investment to come into the region.

[9] Government of Balochistan-in-Exile website.

Balochistan's revenue resources are predominantly Federal with only 6-7 per cent generated in the province. Balochistan has to help itself, improve its youth development and rise above the *sardari* system to allow economic development to enable much more contribution to its budget and reduce dependence on Federal transfers. It must consciously restructure its societal system to fall in tune with the modern times and integrate with the rest of the country. Emotional links with the Baloch in Iran and Afghanistan must give way to logic as exemplified by the Indian and Pakistani Punjab(s) and West Bengal and Bangladesh. Punjabi domination is because of their numbers, competence and hard work. The perceived or real exploitation by the Federal Government will cease only when Balochistan becomes strong internally in tune with its potential. Economic development will calm the agitating minds despite complex historical, internal and external factors.

Perpetual unrest in Balochistan provides leverage to countries inimical to Pakistan which are not few. The situation is absorbing Pakistan's scarce resources to restore normalcy and disturbs the flow of strategic material to the rest of Pakistan and operation of the Gawadar port. The military option, which is often adopted, needs to be abandoned in favour of a political and economic solution. Overbearing responses have not accrued dividends. Given the state of governance, acts of violent responses are not restricted to a few areas, but occur in practically each of the districts, including the capital, Quetta. Radicalised Balochistan can further lead to turmoil and severely affect the economy. The situation may force Federal military intervention, as in the past.

A disturbed Balochistan suits western powers who eye the oil and gas of the Middle East. A disturbed Balochistan also takes away attention and scarce resources of Pakistan from the Indian borders, which is against the state policy of Pakistan. A disturbed Balochistan also does not make economic sense for Pakistan, India and China. Balochistan has tremendous strategic potential, whichever angle you view it from. Pakistan has the pivotal stake; other countries have their national interests and priorities.

STRATEGIC STABILITY IN SOUTH ASIA: PAKISTAN'S "NEW CONCEPT OF WAR FIGHTING"—INTERFACE WITH NUCLEAR DOCTRINAL THINKING

Brigadier Arun Sahgal (Retd), Distinguished Fellow,
School of Geopolitics, Manipal Academy of Higher Education

Introduction

Pakistan is attempting to undermine India's favourable conventional asymmetry through its nuclear doctrine and posturing of thresholds. India developed a pro-active doctrine of "cold start" to dissuade Pakistan from prosecuting sub-conventional war with impunity. Doctrinal thinking aimed at exploiting conventional superiority through massive and punitive retaliation while pushing back the Pakistani nuclear thresholds, creating space for "Limited War under Nuclear Overhang". This doctrinal thinking is posited in the backdrop of the doctrine of massive punitive retaliation to underplay Pakistani attempts to play the brinkmanship card through threshold ambiguity and nuclear coercion.

The Pakistanis, on the other hand, believe that India's pro-active conventional thinking has adversely impacted the prevailing state of regional deterrence. Resultantly, it is attempting to deal with Indian conventional superiority and pre-emptive doctrine at two levels, through the recently articulated New Concept of War Fighting (NCWF); second, and more importantly, by linking NCWF with sub-strategic nuclear response as a means of enhancing conventional deterrence, should Indian pre-emptive offensives manage significant penetrations making their operational posture untenable in politically and strategically sensitive sectors.

The Pakistani military establishment believes that three factors have impacted the prevailing nuclear restraint regime:

- Growing Indian conventional capabilities and threat perceptions. Pakistan believes these are increasingly unmanageable, leaving it open to coercion.
- Indo–US nuclear and follow on nuclear fuel deals with other countries is creating strategic imbalance in India's favour forcing Pakistan to upgrade its arsenal. Fast breeder technology is seen as adding to this imbalance?
- Third, BMD and sea-based nuclear deterrence, currently under development, are potential game changers. With technological access from US and Israel these will result in dangerous asymmetry degrading its first-use doctrine.

Pakistan is aiming to address this imbalance by creating an "**interface between conventional and nuclear strategy**". The overall aim is to deter war through a combination of credible conventional and unconventional means as part of an overall strategy aimed to deny India space for ***'limited war under nuclear overhang'***. Lowering of nuclear threshold is a deliberate attempt at providing requisite relief to the conventional strategy and to reduce the space for war. It also helps in maintaining widespread speculation regarding lowering of thresholds that enable prosecution of war in more offensive manner. Lastly, it is an attempt to exploit the perceived notion of *"Nuclear Irrationality"* propounded by Pakistan.

Preview

Within the above backdrop the paper will focus on the following aspects:

(a) Outline of Indian Pro-active doctrine.
(b) Pakistan's NCWF as a response.
(c) Pakistan's nuclear doctrinal thinking and Interface of TNW with conventional strategy.
(d) Indian Response.

Indian Pro Active Doctrinal Thinking

The genesis of the cold start doctrine lies in the lessons learnt during "Operation Parakram", the year long standoff with Pakistan, where limitations of the prevailing war fighting doctrine failing to force a strategic decision on its adversary stood starkly exposed. There is a widespread view that "Operation Parakram," as an exercise in coercive diplomacy to dissuade Pakistan from waging proxy war and to punish it for terrorist strikes against India, failed to achieve both strategic or operational objectives. The asymmetric option of waging proxy war and destabilising India was further exhibited by Pakistan through its orchestrated terror strikes in Mumbai.

There are two broad rationales for the cold start doctrine. One; the long and arduous mobilisation period of the army's offensive strike reserves from their peace locations to their operational areas, running into weeks on account of exterior lines, led to loss of strategic surprise allowing Pakistan to counter mobilise. Second; it allowed credible international intervention to diffuse the crisis thus effectively restraining India from exercising any planned offensive options. These perceptions are further reinforced by the declining edge in conventional force ratios, owing to declining budgetary allotments, and tedious and time consuming acquisition procedures together with underdeveloped defence industrial base.

The edifice of the cold start doctrine highlights a shift in Indian Armed forces in general and Army in particular from a defensive reactive strategic thinking to a more proactive approach to leverage conventional Indian force superiority by seizing early initiatives in any confrontation. In some ways it is quite akin to ***"active defence and anti-access doctrines"*** of the Chinese PLA. The fundamental perspective being swift and effective synergised joint response before the adversary is able to carry out credible operational deployment. The idea was to leverage conventional superiority for punitive employment to inflict unacceptable costs.

The Indian Pre Emptive Doctrine

The doctrine envisages converting holding troops (deployed on defensive tasks on the border) into strong pivot formations capable of undertaking limited offensive operations with minimum reorganisation. The major change is in conceptual thinking in terms of organisation for combat of large strike formations, seen as huge and unwieldy. The thought process revolves around creating a number of divisional-sized all-arms integrated battle groups capable of being launched at shortest possible notice (48 to 72 hours) without awaiting full-scale mobilisation.

The operational shift is reflected in close synergy between the three services, and all arms within the army, as part of joint integrated operations. Operational objectives largely relate to breaching operational depths to pose a threat to hinterland. Some analysts look upon this doctrinal thinking in terms of punitive retaliation by quickly massing firepower together with air and naval strikes to deliver punishing blows, and degrading war waging potential without serious collateral damage.

Pakistan's NCWF

NCWF is the Pakistani attempt to develop an effective response to the Indian pro-active doctrine. It forms a critical part of Pakistan's overall national deterrence strategy. It is a hybrid concept that entails employing a combination of conventional, unconventional and sub-strategic means as part of a *'whole of nation'* approach. It is aimed to reinforce deterrence through communication, capability and credibility. Pakistani military planners believe that credible conventional capability gives credence to the notion of nuclear deterrence/threshold. It provides an interface between its conventional and nuclear strategies thereby developing disincentives for India in undertaking proactive operations.

Pakistan's new war fighting doctrine is a distillation that emerged from a series of war games and operational discussions, backed by field manoeuvres, in an exercise code named *"Azm-e-Nau"* (New Beginning) from February to May 2010. Another series of these exercises were conducted in October 2013, which included live firing of *Nasr* salvos.

Doctrinal Percept

NCWF is the first tier conventional response to Pakistan's multi-tier response strategy to growing conventional asymmetry with India. It entails 'forward deployment and quick reaction to degrade Indian offensives in early stages of operations through the judicious use of brigade and divisional-sized Integrated Combat Groups (ICGs) that would aim to drive a wedge between Indian pivot (holding) forces and strike offensives (Integrated Battle Groups and Theatre Force Reserves (TFR).

Pakistan believes that Indian proactive strategy, although a reality, is still 'transient' and will further mature based on the response by Pakistani Army. A major shortcoming of the Indian Pro Active doctrine, according to Pakistani planners, is inability to achieve strategic or even tactical surprise. Early loss of surprise provides both time and opportunity to adopt a strong defensive posture. Second, the Indian concept relies heavily on integration of the three services, which it believes is India's Achilles heel; they cite the Indian Air Force's reservations on the efficacy of the doctrine. Insofar as the navy is concerned, given the differential in mobilisation, it may not be able to generate the desired combat effects in terms of time and space in these operations.

Pakistani perception is that the Indian Pro Active doctrine revolves around seamless fusion and synergy, in sequential application of forces having tenuous time linkages. The mobilisation of Indian battle groups is deemed to be susceptible to 'selective interdictions' along choke points resulting in delay in application of their offensive potential. Predictably the application of the IBGs and their sustenance beyond 72-96 hours is also seen as questionable. Last, is the belief that post culling out of IBG's from the defensive formations creates operational voids /gaps that could be exploited.

NCWF Doctrine

Nonetheless, it is taken seriously enough and has forced Pakistan to make important operational changes. First, taking cognizance of Indian quick proactive response, Pakistani planners are coming around to the view that it's current 14 days warning period for mobilisation is outdated. Second, and more importantly, its overall defensive posture is based on large-scale commitment of auxiliary forces, given their commitments on counter terrorism and militancy operations precludes availability at short notice. Lastly, the current logistic system is seen to be unsuitable for a short-duration war of high intensity.

Pakistani military planners are also convinced that, despite overt nuclearisation, there is no respite from the conventional threat. It is in this context that they are planning to interface/integrate nuclear and conventional strategies in an endeavour to reduce space for conventional war by lowering the nuclear thresholds, while maintaining a requisite level of readiness to meet projected levels of deterrence

Based on the foregoing, the overall concept envisages mitigation of strategic surprise, through vigilant intelligence-gathering by a combination of ISR/air power, HUMINT and third country sources. Second, it is reworking its defensive posture through a combination of exaggerated forward defensive posture in Punjab and exploiting forward zones between its defences and the international border through a strong mechanised forces-based presence to attrite, delay and deflect Indian IBG's. The concept also envisages strengthening the defensive posture astride delay lines, based on obstacle systems and astute employment of reserves at various levels, to limit Indian spatial gains and preventing projection into depth areas that could threaten its heartland and open it to exploitation. It is in this construct that its defensive thinking is incrementally shifting from holding defensive lines strongly to one based on creating strong reserves for counter strike or riposte while holding forward defences lightly.

Pakistan believes that by enhanced Command Control Communications and Computers, Information and Intelligence, Surveillance and Reconnaissance (C^4I^2SR) it is possible to interdict Indian IBGs and theatre reserves before they become effective. The concept's major focus is on employing operational reserves created through revised deployment at each successive stage of the offensive i.e. tactical and operational, to enhance the defensive balance and provide multiple options for employment of strategic and command reserves, leading to blunting the Indian offensive and its piecemeal destruction.

One of the consequences of restructuring is re-designation of command responsibilities, reconstituting of armoured and infantry divisions into multi-role divisions, and most importantly rearticulating of reserves. Pakistan has recently raised Headquarters (HQ) Southern Command responsible for command of all forces in the desert and semi-desert sectors of Punjab and Sind. Similarly, there are plans to raise HQ Northern Command with HQ 1 Corps as the Army Strike Reserve (North), for defence of the strategically-sensitive Punjab theatre.

To facilitate rapid grouping and regrouping in fluid operational situations it is planning to reorganize the traditional infantry and armoured divisions into multi-role divisions with balanced grouping of armour and infantry. In so far as reserves are concerned it is learnt that with the raising of command headquarters, Pakistan is reconstituting its strike corps based on 1 Corps and 2 Corps into Army and Command reserves. Structurally, the Army HQ reserve will be constituted from some elements of the strike corps.

Structurally, each corps will be expected to form up to three to four command reserves to retain flexibility, and enable the strike corps to take on both defensive and offensive tasks. Defensive tasks include maintenance of operational balance and restoration of adverse situations. Offensive tasks comprise exploiting the success of corps and other operational reserves or launch a counter offensive to capture sensitive objectives in India for post-conflict bargaining. Similarly, reserves at corps and divisional levels are also envisaged based on armoured and infantry brigades. These are being termed as Integrated Combat Groups (ICG's). Pakistan plans to pre-locate these astride the intended thrust line, based on the assumption that there is little or no strategic or tactical surprise allowing time for pre location. To enhance its information dominance Pakistan is upgrading its ISR capability and creating "Information Cells" from GHQ down to divisional level, for continuous flow of a composite battle picture.

To mitigate effects of operational/tactical surprise Pakistan is planning to position ICG's at sensitive locations together with developing capacities to reach intended operational areas in the shortest possible time. It can resort to pre-emptive deployment without formally declaring mobilisation. To achieve this, a number of existing cantonments are being expanded and new ones constructed such as Pasrur, Zafarwal, Narowal, Surihan and Chistian Mandi.

Pakistani Discourse on TNW and Options for Employment

The TNW's are increasingly being seen by the Pakistani strategic planners as part of its design to achieve conventional parity through strategic coercion. To understand their likely employment there is a need to examine Pakistani nuclear thinking beyond the normal hyperbole, highlighted by their military and civilian leadership. First and foremost, it is important to recognise the pride of place nuclear weapons occupy in Pakistani psyche. In its sixty-six year history there have been few achievements to celebrate; the success of the nuclear programme therefore is central to Pakistani national identity, seen as an equaliser in dealing with an enemy six times larger in size. Pakistani Prime Minister Muhammad Ali Bogra stated in 1954 that "when there is more equality of military strength, then I am sure that there will be a greater chance of settlement." His words expressed a national obsession of seeking military parity with India.

This among others is the major reason for Pakistan today possessing the world's fastest growing nuclear arsenal. According to estimates. Pakistan's inventories of enriched uranium and plutonium places the potential number of weapons that can be produced at 160–240 (although international estimates put these as 110–130). As a result of its persistent efforts, today it possesses the fourth largest inventory of warheads of the nine nuclear classified countries. Pakistan professes the concept of 'credible minimum' weapon capability but always fights shy of indicating any defined numbers or rationale that will give them a sense of security. During discussions in the ongoing Track II discussions on nuclear CBM's, Pakistani interlocutors do indicate that they have a blue print that defines both the quality and quantity of the nuclear warheads and vectors that they perceive as adequate.

To understand what is driving this feverish pace of nuclear capability development it is important to first consider Pakistani nuclear doctrinal precepts. The Pakistani concept of mutual nuclear deterrence rests on the logic that, in the backdrop of growing conventional asymmetry, the only way the unfavourable conventional deterrence can be compensated is by unmistakable linkage to nuclear deterrence. This is qualified by the doctrine of 'First Use', based on the belief that in a conventionally asymmetric environment 'if there is no first use than there is no nuclear deterrence; giving strategic advantage to the side with a strong conventional capability. Certainty about the use of nuclear weapons is critical to the balance of forces in a crisis situation. When the balance of forces favours the defender (Pakistan), immediate deterrence is likely to hold. However, in case response is weak on account of conventional asymmetry, it will open exploitation by the strong (India). It is this thinking, based on strategic balance, that provides doctrinal rationale for developing strong and credible nuclear capability.

Interplay of Nuclear and Conventional Forces

The Pakistani military establishment has sought to link nuclear and conventional forces as part of an all-encompassing 'deterrence doctrine'. In its thinking, the degree of nuclear deterrence depends upon the nature of the equilibrium produced by nuclear forces. Therefore, the influence of nuclear weapons upon conventional forces is deemed to be *total, partial or non-existent*. It is in the above context that the capability and capacity of conventional forces are deemed as both important and necessary; their role being either to round off nuclear deterrence if it is not complete, or even to replace it if influence at the conventional level is negligible.

Thus, in the India–Pakistani context, two things stand out. One, the imperative need to balance India's growing conventional superiority both in terms of capability enhancement and nuclear weapons. Its belief is that weak conventional forces tend to lower the nuclear threshold to a dangerously low level leading to pronounced instability. Therefore, in the Pakistani mindset, conventional forces with the ability to thwart enemy incursions are absolutely essential. In its absence, the enemy can mount a swift offensive, capture major objectives, declare a ceasefire and present a fait accompli, leaving Pakistan to be confronted with an excruciating choice of either accepting the loss or opting to commit mutual suicide. Conventional capability that has the ability to successfully thwart any conventional aggression by the adversary, therefore, is deemed to complement nuclear deterrence and help in keeping thresholds low. Flowing from above the fundamental doctrinal objective is to convince India that there is a ***clear linkage between conventional and nuclear strategies, and that the nuclear threshold exists which is low and ambiguous, specifically aimed at contracting the space for conventional war***. It also helps Pakistan conduct proxy war with impunity using cross border infiltration and terrorism as instruments.

Tactical Nuclear Weapons and Overall Deterrence

At the grand strategic level, Pakistan sees India as a revisionist military power (and itself as a 'status quoist') that is involved in tilting the regional military balance in its favour through build up of conventional and nuclear capabilities including an effective 'Nuclear Triad' and 'Ballistic Missile Defence' as a shield against Pakistani nuclear escalation and response. Consequently, Pakistan believes that the unfolding scenario of pronounced and growing conventional and nuclear asymmetry is perilous to deterrence stability in South Asia.

In Pakistani thinking, India's pre–emptive conventional doctrine provides the following strategic challenges to Pakistan:

(a) India can launch a pre-emptive offensive at short notice with a credible element of surprise. Growing Indian ISR and non-contact capabilities are seen as extending its operational advantage.

(b) The IAF, with its significant and growing superiority both in numbers and quality, can create a favourable air situation through effective counter air and interdiction (strategic and operational) campaign, providing a significant strategic advantage to India.

(c) Development of credible BMD over a period of time would greatly negate Pakistan's first strike option.

(d) A massive Indian offensive, launched over a wide front, significantly increases the challenge for Pakistani intelligence's limited reconnaissance assets, improving the chance of major breakthrough in critically sensitive areas.

These assumptions have forced Pakistan to relook at the functional efficacy of its doctrine of 'First Use'. What appears to be unnerving the Pakistani military establishment is the growing Indian ISR capability resulting in greater battlefield transparency, backed by precision strike capabilities, together with long range artillery fire support through multi-barrel weapons systems such as Smerch and Pinaka. These developments have exposed Pakistan's conventional and nuclear limitations. In the absence of the option of a flexible, measured, and proportionate response, Pakistan faces the grim option of either resorting to massive and suicidal nuclear attacks against India, as a single rung response, or face strategic losses of grave political consequences. These limitations appear to have necessitated the development of tactical nuclear weapons and miniaturisation of nuclear warheads for its cruise and other missile systems.

Pakistani planners appear to be increasingly concerned about the credibility of the 'doctrine of use (first use) as a last resort' particularly in the face of military pressure from India. Should Pakistan launch a credible first strike or should it doctrinally develop a graded and proportional punitive retaliation option? There is also a perception that while the nuclear deterrence can prevent major escalation, it does leave adequate space for a limited conflict. In its perception, space for limited conflict exists precisely because of the confidence that these can be contained and if an escalation is feared, ceasefire can be declared before the matter goes out of hand. Thus, one of the methods for stabilising an increasingly asymmetric conventional deterrence is introduction of low-yield nuclear weapons at the conventional level. Pakistan's decision to develop TNW is predicated on the following factors:

(a) Low-yield-battle field nuclear weapons help solidify its defensive fence and assist in tackling the eventualities sprouting due to increasing conventional asymmetries between India and Pakistan.
(b) Second; the threat of employment of a new weapon previously untried in battle, Complete uncertainty is created as to the tactical result of the battle and therefore to the entire course of a campaign;
(c) Third; the employment of low yield nuclear weapons creates the fear of near certainty of escalation on to the nuclear level. The stability achieved at the nuclear level thus gets extended to the conventional level as well.

Although Pakistan accepts the fact that development of these weapons require specific technical knowhow as indeed their integration into existing nuclear command and control requires sophisticated and fool proof arrangements, nonetheless Pakistan is willing to pay the price and take the attendant risk to make nuclear deterrence more effective at the conventional level by taking what they understand as a tactical risk.

Pakistani Operational Thresholds for Use of TNWs

Given the fact that Pakistan has purposely not articulated a nuclear doctrine, any analysis of likely employment of TNW's is based on the examination of existing literature, discussions with Pakistani interlocutors during Track II meetings, on Nuclear CBM's etc. Fundamentally, taking cognizance of the fact that Pakistan is following a strategy of "Defensive Denial" and concerned about implications of "Surprise or pre–emptive disarming conventional strike" would like to keep nuclear response option but keep escalation at the lowest levels, in a strategy of graded response. It is in above context that its use of TNW's can be contemplated at any of the following thresholds:

(a) Pre-emptive Response Threshold.
(b) Early Response Threshold.
(c) Delayed Response Threshold.
(d) Accumulated Response Threshold.

Pre–emptive Response Threshold

This relates to pre-mediated, use of nuclear weapons to prevent, as Pakistan puts it, an 'incautious' pre-emptive Indian attack in response to major terrorist incident or any other provocation. Such a scenario could come about if India is able to achieve both tactical and strategic surprise and the Pakistani military establishment, prone to perceiving Indian political leadership weak and vacillating, is caught unprepared. Such a option is predicated upon India's growing ability to execute a successful "Non-Contact Campaign" in terms of surgical and calibrated air strikes that inflict credible damage on Pakistan's operational and strategic assets backed by asymmetric means, such as cyber attacks and information operations, increasingly feasible by enhanced battle space awareness and credible C^4ISR systems.

Another scenario is that of a jittery Pakistani military leadership resorting to low yield nuclear weapons. This could also be an action of a rogue corps commander to whom tactical control has been delegated by the Pakistani Nuclear Command Authority (NCA). In any of these scenarios use of tactical weapons will be against Indian military formations at their launch pads, logistic installations, choke points etc. to dissipate the offensive before or immediately on launch.

Early Response Threshold

The scenario for such a use will be based largely on unexpected success of Indian offensives, particularly into politically sensitive sectors in Punjab or even Sindh, considered sacrosanct in its political and territorial domains. Fundamentals of exercising such an option would be dictated by the relationship between the territorial threat posed by Indian offensives, and/or degree of force degradation, in particular air power and strategic reserves. The decision to use will rest on the perceptions of the Pakistani military leadership in terms of nature of an adverse situation and the threat it poses to politically sensitive areas.

The potential for use could also be if key strategic and operational targets, with serious economic and political ramifications, are attacked or degraded as part of an Indian non-contact campaign. This option appears to be most realistic to employment of TNW's, something which Pakistan can sell as an act of self defence and credible war termination strategy.

Delayed Response Threshold

This threshold essentially relates to saturation of conventional options resulting in a situation of great strategic vulnerability to politically sensitive and strategically important areas or important economic targets are attacked. An imbalance in Pakistani defences in critical sectors e.g. Sialkot, Lahore, Multan or Rahimyar Khan, threatening the severance of North–South Super Highway could result in such a situation. The scenario replicates the 'Early Threshold'; the difference being delay in decision making creating a situation of grave political or military ramifications.

The targets here include, forward echelons, logistic installations, forward airfields, choke points, C^4ISR infrastructure etc. Weapon use will be aimed at causing severe damage to advancing Indian offensives, as also war waging potential. Given the prevailing scenario, the number of TNW being employed will be much higher than the previous option. A high degree of political signalling and brinkmanship is likely to ensue before use.

Accumulative Response Threshold

This relates to major strategic gains by India, leading to unacceptable loss of territory or unacceptable force degradation indicating strategic and operational ineptness of Pakistani military yet again. Such a scenario would create a major decision dilemma with regard to deterrence breakdown. Essentially this option relates to Pakistan suffering major operational defeat e.g. Indian military inroads in the Lahore or Sialkot sectors, or serious degradation to Pakistani strategic reserves, backed by major losses of its air and sea power.

Such a scenario could call for a 'massive nuclear first strike' as part of 'use it or lose it' strategy. However, given the certainty of Indian response and cold rationality, Pakistan may like to keep thresholds low and use TNW's to indicate its desperation while indicating certainty of larger response. Pakistan could, in such a scenario use, limited *Nasr* salvos and nuclear-tipped cruise missiles against Indian forces and military assets in the first instance. Fundamentally, such a scenario has the potential for dangerous nuclear escalation and deterrence failure.

Analysis of Thresholds and Indian Response

Pakistan is likely to use TNW as a perceived low-cost strategic option under conditions when it is faced with either major operational defeat, or loss of important territory, or critical infrastructure important to its war waging effort. Going by delayed/accumulated response it is apparent that Pakistan is unlikely to use TNW's in the first instance, acknowledging thereby space below the nuclear threshold, although both doctrinally and through posturing it wants to deny it to India.

It is in the above context that Pakistan's "New Concept of War Fighting" as a quick reaction strategy against India's pre-emptive doctrine finds resonance with Pakistani military planners. Its interface with TNW is deemed as a low cost option that helps preventing tangible military losses while lowering nuclear thresholds.

Importantly, it underscores an early deployment of TNW which would in itself be an act of escalation that could lead to concurrent or near simultaneous deployment of strategic weapons almost concurrently with conventional force mobilisation. This correlation between conventional and strategic mobilisation constitutes major escalation, bringing nuclear weapons into the equation, at the first instance, even before there is any concern for deterrence failure?

Such a scenario will further contribute to instability with both sides shifting from recessed deterrence to alerted deployment, which then could become targets for conventional missile strikes. Pakistani military planners appear to be miscalculating that in such a scenario India will hedge its bets on early deployment for fear of premature nuclear confrontation, and international opprobrium, thereby further constraining space for conventional conflict. This will at best be a prevarication based on Pakistani military leadership's misunderstanding of Indian will and resolve.

Another important aspect is posturing and signalling. This could take the form of assertive and pro-active verbalisation, including demonstrative strikes to indicate firmness of resolve and criticality of the situation. It needs to be noted that use of nuclear weapons is likely to be preceded by fair amount of posturing and signalling, heightening the chances of miscalculation. At another level, the nature of escalation will be reflected by the competing risk-taking behaviour in a way that

Pakistan may attempt to increase the risk by aggressive posturing and signalling. Inadequacy of response could lead to miscalculations.

A number of scenarios/simulation exercises have indicated misreading of signals leading to either complete surprise; resulting in jittery and premature response or inability to take timely political decision leading to delayed response. While decision making and timing are functions of the Nuclear Command Authority, a credible C⁴ISR would help in decision making, including correct reading of signals. Development of these capabilities is becoming an imperative for India to ensure it is not surprised.

The logic of Pakistani use of TNWs is largely being driven (assumption) by the 'strategy of denial', which essentially means that even if India was to launch massive retaliatory counter value-cum-counter force strikes in response to sub-strategic use, its growing credibility of assured second strike capable of inflicting critical damage would act against such massive use as part of the Indian deterrence of punishment. Thus, Pakistani planners believe in the construct of graduated escalation and flexible response, something they believe can be managed both by its own arsenal and leveraging international opinion.

Upgradation in situational awareness through military cooperation with China – in terms of improvement in optical and ELINT capabilities is another factor that could induce Pakistani military leadership to respond pre-emptively. Fielding of Chinese Beidou navigation satellites, and its availability to Pakistan, would lead to enhanced strike accuracy of Pakistani weapon systems. These technological developments, together with perception of Indian political vacillation and lack of resolve, could induce a sense of overconfidence, resulting in premature use. There is a tendency among the Pakistani SPD to factor India's response thresholds and preparedness, both loosely and negatively, based in the belief that Indian NCA being too diffused, bulky and incapable of taking timely decision.

On the issue of command and control of TNW's, open source literature is vague. However discussion with Pakistani interlocutors and others indicate these weapons will be tightly controlled by Pakistani NCA in the same manner as strategic weapons. This however does not appear logical given the nature of weapons and their tactical deployment. At some stage their control will have to be delegated, as was the experience of NATO, creating potential for 'rogue' use.

Yet another issue is the security of these weapon systems in the tactical battle area. The range of '*Nasr*' is 60 – 80 kilometres; given its limited range perforce these weapon systems would have to be deployed at least 15 to 20 kilometres from the forward defended localities, so as to cover targets up to the operational depth to cover the full length of Indian offensives while also being in a position to target forward airfields and logistic installations, bridgeheads etc. It is important to note that these locations will be within the range of Indian multi-barrel rocket launch (MBRL) systems, apart from many other systems. This would require their initial deployments to be in hides with forward deployment on orders according to standard SOP's. During such moves these systems would be vulnerable, with tenuous command and control, and an obvious target for Indian ground and air weapon systems, creating a scenario of great instability.

Use of nuclear tipped cruise missiles, both ground and air-launched, also need to be factored in the operational planning. These could be employed for counter force targeting along with TNW's or used to take out Indian deployed vectors as part of the larger nuclear attack plan. The fact that these can be employed both at tactical and strategic levels is an important consideration.

Indian Response and Options

The edifice of Indian cold start doctrine is based on speedy political clearance, quick mobilisation and tempo of operations. It first demands both political acceptability in terms of military capability to prosecute such a strategy and even more importantly the resolve to persist in the face of likely international pressure. Second is speed of mobilisation and achievement of at least operational if not strategic surprise. This requires development of asymmetric non-contact capabilities, pre-planned mobilisation schedules and back up logistics. A third aspect relates to maintenance of tempo to ensure attempts by Pakistan to coincide its lines of denial with Indian operational lines are prevented. Simply put prevent sidestepping of Corps/Command or the GHQ reserves.

This essentially requires Indian armed forces to showcase structural, doctrinal and operational capabilities to undertake proactive operations that can achieve operational surprise. Fundamental to this is unilateral ability to project power through contesting and degrading the opponent's centres of gravity. This requires preparedness to seize initiative at the early stages of standoff. It also requires focus on devising strategies that maximize relative strengths and create opportunities to exploit the adversary's weaknesses. It entails both physical capabilities and operational thinking to deter, threaten, strike and neutralize Pakistani formations attempting to sidestep or deploy opposite own projected thrust lines.

The major take away from the Pakistani doctrine is its belief that through enhanced ISR it will be able to pick up Indian forces well in time to undertake pre emptive deployment. This is the key, and suggests two things, early identification of Pakistani defensive forces and reserves i.e. ICG and those at Command and GHQ level, while simultaneously denying Pakistan the ability to pick up own movements through credible degradation of its sensors and other surveillance assets. This entails credible surveillance cover not only over the projected TBA but over entire Pakistan, through C^4ISR capacities that transcend, optical, ELINT, COMINT and all associated means. Similarly capabilities will need to be developed to keep important airfields down during the critical stage as also to deny or degrade trans-regional build up of forces.

An equally important perspective is both speed and the agility of mobilisation. This essentially entails restructuring of pivot corps with adequate mobile reserves to launch speedy offensives supported by credible logistics. Achieving agility entails a higher state of operational readiness in terms of equipment serviceability, and training, backed by non-contact capability, both in the cyber and kinetic domains.

The next important issue is forward basing of selected mechanised formations by prepositioning and maintenance of defensive balance at all times. This will create multiple options and help in reducing launch time. In the process of trying to create dedicated reserves in the form of ICGs and other task forces certain voids would be created. Credible ISR cover should be able to discern these and exploit them through innovative planning.

The Indian army has recently completed a major transformation study that is aimed at actualising Indian army's proactive strategy. Important aspects include, restructuring of both offensive and defensive formations as well as theatre-based combat and logistic support.

The greatest credibility of proactive operations will rest on creating and maintenance of favourable air situation over projected area of operations through substantial combat edge of the IAF. Growing Indian air power backed by improved ISR capability allowing precision strikes will be the game changer. However, the greatest single factor that will contribute to the success of the strategy will be 'tri-service integration' and not merely 'jointmanship'.

Indian Doctrinal Response to TNW's

Pakistan is consciously shifting the strategic focus of its nuclear option to low-level graduated escalation using TNW's as a conflict prevention or termination strategy. It appears to be shifting from what is termed in nuclear lexicon from "Offensive Disarmament" through pre emptive first use to one of Defensive Denial—a category located in the middle of the nuclear spectrum—where the principal intention consists of denying the assailant either its operational objectives on the battlefield or its strategic interests through employment of nuclear weapons. Nuclear weapons, in this conception, are treated as war fighting instruments as well but they are intended less for exploitation and *more to reinforce deterrence and avert military defeat*, with all the disastrous political consequences that flow from such an outcome. Sub-strategic use or 'Tactical Nuclear Weapons' fall in this category, and could be conceived as a shift from 'Pre–emptive' or 'First Strike' doctrinal thinking.

The dilemma of TNW's for India is how should it respond? Should it continue with 'no first use' doctrine clearly dispelling the notion of graduated response or by clearly articulating and more importantly signalling massive punitive retaliation through both deployments and political articulation? This issue is need to be examined at the doctrinal and operational levels, in terms of effects on Indian operations.

In terms of response strategy, despite a clearly enunciated doctrine of massive retaliation, political considerations - particularly the likely impact—will be factors that will that would weigh heavily in the response options of India. The response matrix will be dictated by use and the effects. Early threshold where the use is at tactical level could be an option of graduated response. However in 'Delayed' or 'Accumulated Threshold' scenarios, options could range from strong conventional response in the form of precision missile strikes on Pakistani nuclear assets, limited nuclear response against Pakistani conventional forces, to massive nuclear strikes both on counter force and counter value targets, including decapitation. Another option for India is to launch 'on warning' strikes once it sees Pakistan getting its strategic weapons ready. India would need to issue credible declaratory warning to leave Pakistani leadership in no doubt that attempts to escalate will result in more devastating response.

Another message India could send is that any deployment of TNW in the TBA would not preclude Indian proactive options and that it reserves the right to take out these weapons as part of its battlefield interdiction campaign. Any attempt to coerce India through use of tactical battlefield weapons will invite full-fledged nuclear response.

Coupled with the above is the detailed analysis of the impact of these weapons on the battlefield. Since the 1980s, the Indian Army has been making preparations for NBC warfare. It is producing indigenous NBC suits, decontamination suits, facelets, overboots and NBC tents. As regards training, from 1987 onwards, the Indian army, through its College of Military Engineering, began running familiarisation courses in NBC warfare, while scientists conduct courses at brigade level. A series of studies have been undertaken to provide for both active and passive defence against nuclear attack for army combat formations.

Conclusion

Pakistan's logic and rationale of first use driven by its perception of nuclear weapons deterrence effect lies only in use or intended use; hence nuclear war fighting remains an inherent construct of its doctrinal thinking. It has clearly attempted to link conventional and strategic deterrence to deal with what it perceives as a growing conventional asymmetry. Indian pre-emptive offensives are part of the punitive response strategy, through orchestrated military action. If not contained, the Pakistani new concept of war fighting will result in use of TNW as an effective means to provide credibility to its conventional deterrence.

Even more importantly, Pakistani doctrinal thinking certainly indicates pre-emptive deployment of TNW into the battle area. Given the range of the *'Nasr'* missile system these perforce will have to be deployed within the immediate depth areas of the corps zone. In the same vein, Pakistan will certainly deploy cruise missiles both on board ships and aircrafts, leading larger strategic mobilisation in near simultaneity with conventional, constituting a dangerous escalation.

Although Pakistan attempts to convey threshold ambiguity; ***nuclear tripwire*** is not uniform. It appears to be much shorter and tighter in the Punjabi heartland and relatively more stretched in Sindh and loose in POK. Thus Pakistani response would be different depending upon the sector addressed.

It is important to recognize that TNW, given the technological and economic investments, are part of Pakistani doctrinal reality. It is, therefore, incumbent on India to develop its own counter TNW doctrine, to convey unambiguously both the certainty and credibility of response.

CHINA'S ECONOMIC MIRACLE: ROLE OF THE MARITIME SECTOR

Dr. Vijay Sakhuja, Director (Research), Indian Council of World Affairs (ICWA), New Delhi

China has experienced impressive economic growth and its economy has grown at nearly 10 per cent annually during the last three decades. The manufacturing sector has been the most dynamic and China has risen from the seventh position in the 1980s, to emerge as the world's largest producer of manufactured goods. The economic miracle has prompted a number of global corporate houses to establish commercial links and set up production units in China.

China's coastal areas contribute significantly to the national economy. It is estimated that nearly 40 per cent of the population, 50 per cent of cities, 70 per cent of GDP and 84 per cent of direct foreign investment and export products are generated within 200 kilometres of the coast; that corresponds to a little less than 30 per cent of China's landmass.

The maritime dimension of Chinese economic power is highly dependent on merchant shipping assets, port infrastructure to transact large volume of trade, ability to build ships to conduct maritime trade, and the availability of quality human resources that shape and conduct maritime business. Likewise, China's ability to exploit living and non-living marine resources has contributed to its food and energy security. It is also developing technology to exploit deep seabed minerals which would help China's economic growth in the future. Further, technology development and inflow of investments in the maritime sector has been instrumental in the growth of the marine economy. In the above context, this paper attempts to highlight the role of the maritime sector in China's economic miracle.

China's Maritime Geography

China is a maritime country and is endowed with a long coastline of 6,000 nautical miles on the mainland. Its deeply indented coast is fringed with some 3,500 islands including Taiwan. There are also a large number of island territories in distant waters and these geographical constants generate an additional coastline of 5,000 nautical miles. China is signatory to the 1982 United Nations Convention on the Law of the Sea (UNCLOS) and claims an Exclusive economic Zone (EEZ) of 3,877,019 square kilometres, of which 3,000,000 square kilometres is disputed.

China does not border an ocean and its shores are washed by the Yellow Sea (400,000 square kilometres), East China Sea (700,000 square kilometres) and South China Sea (3,400,000 square kilometres). The latter is home to four principle island groups: the Palawan, Spratly Islands, Paracel Islands and the Natuna group.

China's Marine Economy

In China, the marine economy has witnessed impressive investments that have contributed significantly to its national growth. In 1998, the Chinese government published a White Paper on its maritime economy titled 'Development of China's Marine Programs' which lists 20 different sectors of China's marine economy including shipbuilding, shipping, ports and harbours, inland waterways, fish industry, offshore minerals and salt industry, offshore oil and gas resources, seabed minerals and marine leisure industry, etc. Several high-tech marine industries have been setup in the coastal areas that are engaged in exploitation of seawater, sea energy and seabed resources resulting in a comprehensive development of the national economy.

The White Paper notes that the Chinese maritime economy grew at 17 per cent annually in the 1980s, and 20 per cent in the 1990s. In January 2013, China's State Council released the 12th Five-Year Development Plan for National Marine Economy, which highlights the major achievements of the marine economy during the 11th Five-Year Plan (2006-2010). During this period:

(a) The average growth of the marine economy was 13.5 per cent annually, reaching RMB4 trillion in 2010;

(b) 33.5 million jobs were created by the end of 2010; and

(c) The marine economy's share in the national GDP was 9.9 per cent.

Further, under the 12th Five Year Plan, China's marine economy is expected to grow at 8 per cent annually up to 2015, generate 2.6 million new jobs, and could be about 10 per cent of the national GDP. The total marine output volume in 2020 is set to be double that of 2010, which was pegged at 3.84 trillion Yuan.

The Chinese leadership is conscious of the importance of the marine economy and its contribution to the national GDP. In August 2013, President Xi Jinping, while chairing a group study session of the Political Bureau of the Communist Party of China Central Committee, tasked to discuss a roadmap to become a maritime power, noted that 'A developed marine economy is an important part of building maritime power.'

Shipbuilding

There are several reasons for an upsurge in Chinese shipbuilding capacity and its popularity among international buyers. These range from its long coastline which allows development of shipyards, plentiful of cheap labour and domestic ancillary industry and engineering skills. Besides, Chinese shipbuilding labour is relatively cheaper.

In the international market, China is ranked third in shipbuilding behind Japan and Korea who are the leaders in the global shipbuilding industry. However, in 2012, China's shipbuilding totalled 60.21 million dwt down 21.4 per cent year on year, and new shipbuilding order quantity was 20.41 million dwt, down 43.6 per cent year on year. There has been a sharp shrinking (about 20 per cent) of order completion and more than 40 per cent decrease of new orders. This can be attributed to the European debt crisis which had an adverse impact on the Chinese shipbuilding companies.

Chinese shipyards are also proficient in building warships and in the past constructed submarines, destroyers, frigates, auxiliary and logistic vessels, space monitoring ships and more recently hospital ships. Perhaps the refitting of the Ukrainian carrier Varyag and making it operational as the PLA Navy's first aircraft carrier, the Liaoning (CV-16), is a very good example of the capability of Chinese shipyards. China now plans to build aircraft carriers indigenously and China Shipbuilding Industry Co. Ltd (CSIC) could be 'one of those that is going to either build, or fit out the new domestically manufactured aircraft carrier.' Likewise, China is also building an icebreaker research vessel for undertaking voyages in the Arctic sea/ice. It will be jointly designed by the Finland-based Aker Arctic Technology Inc. and the Chinese Arctic and Antarctic Administration (CAA), under the State Oceanic Administration (SOA) and the Polar Research Institute of China. The vessel is expected to be of 8,000 tons dwt, an endurance of 20,000 nautical miles and is capable of navigation through 1.5 metres of ice. It will be ready for operations in 2014. Chinese shipyards have built merchant ships for international customers and warships for a number of navies in Asia and Africa.

Shipping

The manufacturing industry pivots on assured and timely supply of resources and carriage of finished goods to international markets, bulk of which is carried in the hulls of merchant vessels. Being the world's biggest importer of a variety of metallic ores, second-largest oil importer and the third-largest exporter of finished goods Chinese shipping industry has come to play an important role in China's economic growth.

In China, the shipping industry is an integral part of economic growth and 90 per cent of the Chinese trade is carried out by ships. The Chinese fleet is built around a variety of vessels that include bulk carriers, oil tankers, LNG and gas carriers, container vessels, Ro/Ro ships and passenger liners. In 2012, China emerged as the world's third-largest shipping fleet in terms of capacity, after Japan and Greece. It now has about 10 per cent of global capacity, up from 6.3 per cent in 2006. However, due to the global economic crisis and a near recession in some of the economies, there is slump in the Chinese shipping industry.

China has decided to 'shift towards a domestic consumer demand-oriented economy [which] could provide a significant boost to the global shipping industry, as the world's second largest economy targets for more sustainable growth'. Under the circumstances, the Chinese shipping will play an important role in domestic trade and transport of materials and goods to different parts of China. The domestic market is expected to grow keeping in mind that 'about half of the country's population will join the middle classes by 2020. Annual income is projected between US$ 7,000 and US$ 23,000'.

The Chinese oil and gas tanker fleet has been in great demand. As China's economy grows, the need for energy has increased correspondingly; China became a net importer of oil in 1993 and since then has been importing large proportions of its needs from the Persian Gulf, Latin America, Africa and Southeast Asia. This aspect is also discussed later in the paper.

Ports

In China, bulk of the sources of raw materials are located in the hinterland and the industrial infrastructure is located in the coastal provinces thus necessitating a robust and well developed land, sea and inland waterway transportation network. As one of the world's largest growing economies, China is engaged in expanding transportation infrastructure both on land and along the coast to meet the ever growing demand by the industrial centres for raw materials and transportation of finished goods.

In China there are two types of ports: seaports along the long coastline and inland ports that lie astride the rivers and waterways. There are over 460 seaports and about 26 of these are major ports that handle more than 80 per cent of the cargo coming in and moving out of China. There are about 2,000 river ports controlled mainly by local municipalities. The 2004 government statistics note that China has 1,430 ports with a combined throughput of 4.17 billion tons that service a fleet of 210,000 ships used for ocean shipping.

One of the greatest success stories of China's economic success has been the development of container ports and international container shipping. Seven of the top ten global container ports are in China.

Table: World's Busiest Container Ports: 2012

Rank	Country	Port	Million TEUs
1	China	Shanghai	32.6
2	Singapore	Singapore	31.7
3	China	Hong Kong	23.1
4	China	Shenzen	22.9
5	South Korea	Busan	17.0
6	China	Nngbo-Zaoshan	16.8
7	China	Giangzho harbour	14.7
8	China	Qingdao	14.5
9	Jabel Ali	Dubai, UAE	13.3
10	China	Tainjin	12.3

Source: World Shipping Council.

Large infrastructure projects such as ports require immense financial capital. China receives enormous support from international financial institutions such as the World Bank, Asian Development Bank and Japanese Overseas Corporation Fund, etc. including developed countries for aid to build new ports and augmenting the existing port facilities to meet the growing shipping traffic. Some ports in China are of international standard and can compete with ports in the US and Europe, and occupy top positions in the Asian port sector.

Fishing Industry

Lester R. Brown's book titled *Who Will Feed China: A Wake Up Call for Small Planet*, had alarmed the international community that the rising Chinese population would create a food crisis due to the grain demand and result in high food prices. The Chinese government published a White paper, *The Grain Issue in China*, which dismissed Brown's hypothesis and argued that China has favourable land conditions and rich water resources to meet its requirements of food and will be no threat to the world food market. According to '*The Agricultural Outlook, 2013-2022* ' published by the Organisation for Economic Co-operation and Development (OECD) and the Food and Agriculture Organisation (FAO) under the United Nations, China's 'rapid growth in both national income and agricultural output has contributed to substantially higher national food availability and a much improved access to food.'

The report also notes that China's capture and aquaculture fisheries production is projected to reach about 69 Mt by 2022, a growth of 26 per cent above the average level for 2010-12. Aquaculture is expected to rise by 37 per cent while there would a marginal decline of capture fisheries by 3 per cent. As far as fish imports for human consumption is concerned, it will touch 4.4 Mt, growing by 2.1 per cent per annum in the next decade and its share of domestic consumption in China will gradually rise from 7 per cent to 8 per cent. Perhaps what is significant is that China will continue to be top world exporter with 10 Mt by 2022, an increase of 28 per cent.

In essence, Chinese fisheries production has witnessed impressive growth in the last few decades. The industry has evolved into a powerful industrial system consisting of aquaculture, sea based fishing, processing, marketing, fishing vessels, shipbuilding, ports, science and technology and fisheries management. It forms an important part of China's maritime economy and contributes towards economic development.

Offshore Oil and Gas

As noted earlier, China's economy is highly dependent on the manufacturing sector which requires enormous amounts of energy resources. China became a net importer of energy in 1993 and imports nearly 60 per cent of its needs. It consumes nearly 4.5 - 5.0 million barrels of foreign crude a day (in 2010 and 2011) and would overtake the United States as the world's largest importer by the end of the decade as a result of the shale revolution.

According to the Energy Information Administration (EIA), China's onshore and offshore oil production was pegged at 4.3 million barrels per day in 2011, and it was the fourth largest oil producer in the world, after Saudi Arabia, Russia and the United States. In the 12th five year plan, i.e. 2011–2015, China is expected to "strengthen the exploration and development of petroleum and natural gas resources, stabilize domestic petroleum output, and the development and utilisation of unconventional oil and gas resources, such as coal-bed gas and shale gas."

The shore based production is limited, and China has been exploring the offshore regions for oil and gas. The disputed South China Sea is expected to contain nearly 17 billion barrels of oil and 498 trillion cubic feet of natural gas, which according to the Chinese state owned oil and gas company CNOOC is 'a tiny fraction of the potential unproven resources'. Likewise, in East China Sea, China has proven gas reserves of nearly 18 million barrels of oil and 300 billion cubic feet. This is also a disputed area where Japan and China have overlapping maritime claims.

Further, the Energy Information Administration (EIA) has noted that 'billions more barrels of both conventional and unconventional oil and gas are likely to be found off the southern and eastern coasts of China'. Also, the possibility of oil and gas deposits off the southern and eastern coasts is prompting China to take an assertive stance on sovereignty issues in the South China Sea and East China Sea islands. China's quest for oil has taken it to the Arctic region where it is in advanced talks with a number of oil and gas companies from Russia, Norway, Canada and Greenland.

China is also developing offshore wind, sea water and tidal energy. For instance, the China's State Oceanic Administration has commenced 100 marine economy projects in the Shadong province that will use marine resources such as wind power, seawater and tides in a sustainable way and 30 pilot zones by the end of 2015. These projects aim to generate 12.6 GW of offshore wind capacity by 2030 in six areas.

Seabed Resources

In the last few decades, China's industrial output has witnessed enormous growth and it has emerged as the largest importer of a number of basic metals (chemicals, metals and minerals) and energy. During the 1990s, the international investor sentiment was high and witnessed foreign direct investment in new manufacturing plants. By the mid-2000s, China emerged as a major manufacturing hub for textiles, auto parts, electronics and other domestic durable products. This was a welcome development that resulted in substantial increase in labour costs and labour availability. Further, the population control measures had an impact on the supply of labour pool.

China has over 170 different mineral resources; and among them 158 are proven. There are nearly 18,000 production areas of mineral resources and more than 7,000 of these are either big or medium-sized. China's demand for a number of basic metals such as iron ore, nickel, copper, aluminium, zinc and lead etc. has witnessed a steady increase. China began to explore international markets to fulfil its needs and began to look towards the seabed to meet the demand. It dispatched two ships Xiangyanghong 16 and Xiangyanghong 9 to undertake seabed surveys and on 5 March 1991, China registered with the UN as a Pioneer Investor of deep-sea bed exploitation. It was granted 300,000 square kilometres in the Clarion–Clipperton area in the Pacific Ocean.

In 2011, China was awarded 10,000 square kilometres seabed area in southwest Indian Ocean for exploiting poly-metallic sulphide deposits. The China Ocean Mineral Resources Research and Development Association (COMRA), the nodal agency for mineral research has a number of survey vessels, submersible manned and unmanned robots to mine Cobalt, Titanium, Nickel, Platinum, Molybdenum, Tellurium, Cerium and other metals and rare earth elements.

Marine Tourism

China's long coastline and island territories are dotted with pristine beaches and marine tourist sites. These are known to offer a number of recreational activities such as water sports, scuba diving and marine resorts. The burgeoning marine tourism industry in China is built along the 14,000 km long coastline that is home to over 160 bays and more than 1,500 tourism related scenic and recreational sites. The coastal states have developed more than 300 marine parks and recreational zones, with a variety of marine leisure infrastructure such as marinas, water sport parks and beach sports centres. There are also 90,000 lakes that are home to yachting & sailing clubs and other spectacular marine tourism sites. China has also invested in Marine Nature Reserves (MNR).

A number of marinas are being developed in China to attract international and national tourists. Sanya, Qingdao and Xiamen are home to the growing yacht and luxury boating industry and a number of international manufacturers of marina equipment from around the world are setting up operations to take advantage of the new market. For instance, the Wuyuan Bay Marina in Xiamen is experiencing inflow of capital for development of yachting and tourism. The marina will include berths for 600 boats, a yacht club and business centre, and host exhibitions and regattas.

According to the United Nations World Tourism Organisation (UNWTO), China ranked third largest tourist destination in 2012, a position it has held since last two years, and received 58 million international tourists. Tourist arrivals in China have witnessed a phenomenal growth and the revenue has increased from US $40.8 billion dollars in 2009 to US $50 billion in 2012. The tourism industry is expected to grow at 10.4 per cent in the coming decade, and this could result in the development of hotel industry as well. China has declared 2013 as 'Year of Marine Tourism' with the theme 'Beautiful China'. The associated slogans are 'Experience the Sea, Tour China', 'Marine Tourism Shapes the Future' and 'Marine Tourism, Unlimited Excitement'.

Human Resource

China's seafaring labour has witnessed extraordinary expansion and emerged as a dominating workforce. Chinese seafarers are employed on Chinese-flagged (coastal and ocean going) vessels and international shipping. Significantly, Chinese seafarers have not been immune to globalisation and are common sight onboard foreign flag vessels and have earned for themselves a reputation of being a human capital to reckon with.

Current estimates point to the fact that the global seafaring labour market is led by the Philippines followed by China, which has more than 650,000 sailors working onboard Chinese flagged ships and foreign ships. However, in recent times, shipping companies are turning away from the Chinese market to other markets such as South Asia. According to the Director of I.D. Maritime Singapore, "As we all know now Chinese are the biggest vessel owners and they depend on Chinese seafarers and in turn Chinese seafarers prefer to work on Chinese-owned ships. With the Chinese seafarers' pool being shared by Chinese owners we had to look for an alternate seafarers' pool. That is how we also started banking on the South Asian seafarers' pool and started taking Indians and we find it is a very successful innings with them on board."

China has set up a world class infrastructure for marine education and training, and Chinese seafarers have been accepted by international employers. There are nearly 4,000 maritime education specialists and 60 per cent of these have both teaching and maritime qualifications. Besides, China has established seven higher education institutions that have a maritime department and prominent among these are the Dalian and Shanghai Maritime Universities. There are also 18 intermediate schools and 43 training institutions that support maritime training infrastructure and nearly 5,000 students graduate with maritime expertise annually.

China has also set up a Maritime Safety Administration (MSA), which is responsible for quality control of education and training, curriculum and examination system. There is a greater stress on the teaching of English to ensure that the Chinese seafarers are internationally competitive and nearly 20 per cent of courses are conducted in English. This is so because, in the past, lack of English language communication skills had been a barrier for integrating Chinese seafarers into international market.

China's maritime industry is harnessing the advantages of globalisation and in that context, in August 2013, China University of Nottingham, Ningbo Municipal Government and Wanli Education Group (WEG) established the International Academy for the Marine Economy and Technology (IAMET) at the University of Nottingham Ningbo China (UNNC). This £25 million cooperative initiative involves an international centre of excellence in marine economy, delivering transformative technologies, and managing sustainable industry and enterprises.

Inland Waterways

China is endowed with 5,800 rivers of which 15 are over 1,000 km long and 12 lakes with an area greater than 1,000 square kilometres. Among the rivers, the Yangtze, Pearl, Heilongjiang, Huaihe, Qiantang, Minjiang and the Huangpu are navigable. The Hangzhou-Beijing waterway is called the Grand Canal.

The Yangtze River runs 6,418 kilometres from the Tibetan Plateau and drains into the East China Sea. The river has witnessed impressive traffic growth and some of the provinces along the Yangtze such as Anhui, Chongqing and Hunan have recorded 364 million tons, 117 million tons and 179 million tons freight, respectively. Further, in 2011, nine provincial capitals that are astride the Yangtze and its major tributaries had a combined GDP of US $1 trillion, up from $155 billion in 2001.

There are a number of ports along the Pearl River waterway; the major ports such as Foshan, Zhaoqing and Guigang have an annual freight between 30 million and 60 million tonnes which comprises mostly of dry-bulk. The Pearl River waterway is subjected to regular dredging and vessels up to 3,000 dwt can dock in some of the ports.

The Beijing-Hangzhou Grand Canal is 1,800 kilometres long and is the longest artificial waterway in the world. It is 22 times longer than the Panama Canal and 10 times longer than the Suez Canal. It connects Beijing in the north with Hangzhou in the south and only 883 kilometres is navigable.

Concluding Remarks

The maritime sector plays a major role in China's economic growth and it has developed a sophisticated strategy that not only aims to enhance capacity to exploit marine resources but also to safeguard maritime rights and interests. The strategy also envisages sustainable exploitation of resources and instituting stringent measures to prevent pollution and ecological remediation measures.

China is developing advanced oceanic technologies to exploit offshore and seabed resources. The stress is on research and development of core technologies for marine economic development. There are a number of emerging sectors of the marine economy which include marine bio-pharmaceuticals, seawater utilisation and renewable energies, and offshore equipment manufacturing.

While these are critical components of China's marine economy, China must contend with a number of offshore boundary disputes. China will have to adopt the process of dialogue 'on an equal footing and friendly consultation' to peacefully exploit marine resources. In that context, it has now proposed a new 'maritime silk road' to strengthen maritime cooperation with ASEAN countries and set up a China-ASEAN Maritime Cooperation Fund.

SALIENCE OF NON-STATE ACTORS AND THEIR IMPACT ON THE SECURITY AND DEVELOPMENT OF SOUTH ASIA

Major General (Retd) JS Kataria, Defence Analyst, New Delhi

"A fanatic is one who can't change his mind and won't change the subject."

—Winston Churchill

Preface

The last two decades of the twentieth century witnessed two watershed events in the history of warfare and international affairs. The first was the rise of the *mujahedeen* in Afghanistan. They were Non-State Actors (NSAs) (funded by the US and raised by Pakistan) who played a key role in defeating the Soviet forces in Afghanistan, and eventually leading to the disintegration of the USSR in 1991. Later the *mujahedeen* were turned into an Islamic political entity called the 'Taliban' and given legitimacy to capture power in Afghanistan.[1] It was followed by the rise of Al Qaeda, in 1998. The second was the end of the cold war and the emergence of the lone super power—the USA. For discerning strategists and analysts of security and international affairs, these developments were harbingers of the arrival of NSAs, with religious fundamentalism.

South Asia is home to one-fourth of the world's population which is currently pegged at 7 billion. Most of the nations that form part of South Asia were under British rule till the end of World War II. The British left a legacy of acrimonious boundary disputes amongst the newly formed states. Since the inception of India and Pakistan, the boundary dispute between the two has led to three major wars. In the 1971 War, Pakistan was comprehensively defeated by the Indian Armed Forces leading to the creation of Bangladesh. In the aftermath of the 1971 war, military thinkers in Pakistan started looking for an alternative strategy against India. The raising of the *mujahedeen* with US support provided an opportunity for Pakistan to ferment terrorism in India by siphoning weapons and funds from the Afghan front. This was the turning point in the rise of NSAs (Islamic Fundamentalists) in the region.

South Asia has emerged as the hub of NSAs with Pakistan being the mother of the Islamic fundamentalist organisations. This is impeding the development, growth and security of the region.

[1] http://en.wikipedia.org/wiki/Taliban

What should be the strategy of India and other states in South Asia to counter this fast growing menace?

Westphalian State and its Impact

The Westphalian state—the contemporary system of nation states with integral territory, without any influence from external forces, in which the national aims and goals reign supreme over any individual citizen or ruler has its roots in the Treaty of Westphalia in 1648.[2] The treaty had led to a strong surge in nationalism and recognition of national suzerainty within national boundaries. It became the bedrock of other treaties in Europe thereby reducing the role of NSAs viz. pirates and privateers. However, other NSAs like the East India Company continued to operate under the garb of commerce and trade and acquire colonies in Asia and Africa for their mother states.

The subject of NSAs has a host of ambiguities and questions. Varied thinkers have different perceptions of NSAs. What is their origin? Should their ambit include terrorists, religious zealots, freedom fighters and business houses with political/state lineage? What has been the impact of the Westphalian state on their evolution?

Today, the rise of Muslim fundamentalist terrorist organisations has challenged the concept of the Westphalian state. This phenomenon emerged after the raising of Taliban/Al Qaeda by Pakistan with the US support in Afghanistan. It was a clear use of NSAs by the established nations for their hegemonic national aim.[3] Lewis Atiyyatullah, who claimed to be a representative of Al Qaeda, stated in the aftermath of the 2004 Madrid attacks that the international system built by the West since the treaty of Westphalia will collapse and a new system under the leadership of a mighty Islamic state will rise. Paradoxically, these NSAs created by various nations for their vested interests are directly impacting the security of the international community and challenging the very existence of the Westphalian system of governance.

The available indicators clearly point that the threat from NSAs is on the increase and is breaking new bounds of intensity, employing all available tools of technology with regular proclivity. These new breeds of warriors are faceless and operate seamlessly in an unrestricted manner to pose a major challenge to the safety, security and cohesion of the nation state. Are special organisations needed to counter the NSAs or will a synergetic and harmonious operations by all organs of the state be a potent deterrence? What should be the role of the international community in terms of enacting policies, plans and cooperative mechanisms to counter this menace of security to mankind?

South Asia and the Non-State Actors

Geo-Strategy. South Asia comprises of Afghanistan, Bangladesh, Bhutan, India, Maldives, Nepal, Pakistan, and Sri Lanka. Myanmar and Iran are also considered a part of the outer core of South Asia. Majority of these countries were under the British Empire till the middle of the twentieth century. India is the largest nation in the region and shares its land and maritime boundaries with all except Iran. South Asia is a reservoir of abundant natural resources, varied culture, diverse ethnicity and vast markets for trade and industry. Ecologically, it is a coherent region sharing common river systems, mountain ranges, oceans and ecological system; but with the rising pressure of population and conflicting national interests these can become a serious bone of contention in the times to come. The region occupies a strategically pivotal geographical position by virtue of its domination over the Indian Ocean, proximity to the oil-rich region of West Asia and the Straits of Malacca, a major shipping lane connecting the Indian and Pacific Ocean. These facets elevate the importance of the region in the international power play.

Geo-Politics. Geo-politically, South Asia is in a constant state of turmoil since the departure of the British from the region. The key factors that have impacted the region are acute poverty, varied political set-ups ranging from democracy to military rule, religious fundamentalism and acrimonious division with ill-defined boundaries.

Economics. The region shares an unenviable record of being the poorest in the world after Sub-Saharan Africa.[4] More than 31% of its people live below the poverty line (earning below $1.25 a day). It is under intense pressure of population explosion. It has more than 20% of the world population, only 3% of the land area and the biggest youth bulge in the world but lacks the requisite resources to exploit this demographic advantage to its benefit. More than 125 million children have no basic education which makes them vulnerable to the NSAs, the religious fundamentalist organisations in particular.

---

[2] http://en.wikipedia.org/wiki/Westphalian_sovereignty

[3] Exclusive Al Qa'ida Islamic State will control the world by Yaniv Burman, Media Line, 01 Apr 2004.

[4] http://data.worldbank.org/topic/poverty

Fault Lines of South Asia

Legacy of the Boundary Dispute. Today, South Asia is one of the most conflict-prone and dangerous regions in the world. India and Pakistan, the two biggest nations of the subcontinent are nuclear powers with large standing armies. They have fought three major wars since their independence, primarily on account of boundary disputes, a major fault line-legacy of the British partitioning of the Indian subcontinent. In the 1971 Indo-Pak War, India comprehensively defeated Pakistan and paved the way for the creation of Bangladesh. To avenge its defeat, Pakistan has been supporting NSAs to ferment insurrection in the Indian states, especially J&K and Punjab.

World Power Play. Historical complexities of the region are linked to South Asia's pivotal geo-strategic position, its proximity to China, Russia, oil-rich West Asia and Central Asia. It is further compounded by the interests of the world powers who have always endeavoured to retain their influence in the region through the application of soft/ hard power. The power play by the world powers was at its peak in 1980s, when the *mujahedeen* were raised by the ISI of Pakistan at the behest of the US. This gave a much wanted opportunity to Pakistan to rack up resources to ferment terrorism in India through the modicum of Islamic Jihadist organisations. The funds and warlike material provided by the US for operations in Afghanistan during the 1980s were siphoned to ferment terrorism in India.

Impact of Pakistan's Radicalisation

Founding Fault Line. The founding fathers of Pakistan conceived it as a Muslim state. Thus Pakistan came up as an 'ideological state' with Islam as its political orientation. In contrast, India remained a secular state. The two states with diametrically conflicting ideologies and the boundary dispute had a fault line embedded in their very inception.

Seeds of Radicalism. The seeds of current radicalism in Pakistan were sown in the very first year of independence, when *jihad* was invoked by mobilising tribesmen from the Northwest Frontier region to raid and seize Kashmir, after the Maharaja of Kashmir had signed the instrument of accession to join the Union of India. Later, General Ayub Khan, the first military ruler advocated that Pakistan should turn to its ideology i.e. *jihad*. The actual radicalisation of Pakistan and its armed forces took place under the rule of Zia-ul-Haq in the 1970s/1980s. His rule witnessed a tectonic shift in Pakistan's *madrasas* which embraced the idea of *jihad* whole-heartedly. It also spread to the Urdu and public schools, but with lesser intensity. The young men of that era now form part of the rank and file of the Pakistan army and their society in general. The killing of the moderate leader, Salman Taseer, the Governor of Punjab by his security guard; the 2007 Lal Masjid standoff; the attack on a key naval base at Karachi;[5] the torture/killing of the brave Pakistani journalist, Syed Saleem Shahzad by the ISI and Osama Bin Laden remaining ensconced for years in Abbottabad under the nose of the Pakistan Army are clear pointers towards radicalisation of Pakistan's army and the society at large.

Rise of Jihadist Groups (NSAs). The period between the 1980s to the first decade of the twentieth century witnessed the emergence of various *jihadist* groups in Pakistan. These groups could be classified into four broad categories. The first being the Taliban which is Pakistan's creation and has close links with their Army/ISI. The second is Al Qaeda, the ideological twin of Taliban, an indirect product of Pakistan's *jihadi* factory. The ties between the two are deep-rooted. Both the groups have their bases in Afghanistan as well as FATA, Khyber Pakhtunkhwa and other provinces of Pakistan. The third category comprises Lashkar-e-Jhangvi and Shia Tehrik-e-Jafria which is largely responsible for violent bouts within Pakistan. The fourth category includes Lashkar-e-Taiba, Hizbul Mujahedeen and Jaish-e-Muhammad responsible for operations within India. These groups are armed, trained and funded by the ISI.

Pakistan's Connexion. Consequent to 9/11, the US and the international community took notice of the rise of Islamic NSAs in Pakistan. The launch of 'Operation Enduring Freedom' by the US put Pakistan authorities under pressure to act against the *jihadist* elements. Pakistan deftly managed to avoid confrontation with the Taliban and Al Qaeda by acting against their low-level cadres only. Leaders like Osama Bin Laden and others were made to cool their heels in Abbottabad and elsewhere. The fourth category of *jihadists* was protected under the charade of freedom fighters. It was the third category that became the main target to project Pakistan's sincerity to the US and the international community of their commitment to support the 'war against terror'.

---

[5] The Radicalisation of Pakistan's Military by Fareed Zakaria, Top Opinion, 22 June 2013

Other Nations of South Asia

Afghanistan. This land-locked country with one of the most rugged terrains in the region is a link between Central Asia, South Asia and to some extent West Asia. It has a highly volatile history and has never been subjugated by any power for long. Pakistan has been treating Afghanistan as its strategic backyard. Today the nation is host to Taliban and Al Qaeda, the two most notorious fundamentalist Islamic organisations (NSAs). They are now threatening world peace and the very existence of the nation state. It also hosts the Golden Drug Crescent with the drug trade running into millions of dollars which helps the NSAs to finance their activities.[6] According to the UN Office on Drugs and Crime, in 2012 Afghanistan produced 74% of the world drug output which is estimated to be a little less than 5,000 tons. It is smuggled across the world using routes that pass through Pakistan/Iran, the Middle East and Iraq. Afghanistan's continuous dominance in drug production and the emergence of Pakistan as a focal point in the world drug trade route has a direct bearing on the safety, security and development of South Asia.

Bangladesh. The state came into existence following a guerrilla struggle, headed by select army officers under the banner of Mukti Bahini in response to the tyrannical rule of Pakistan. The period witnessed a million people fleeing to India and leading to the 1971 Indo-Pak war, surrender of Pakistan's army in the east and creation of the state of Bangladesh. Ironically, the public memory of rape, vandalism and massacre at the hands of the Pakistan army appears to have faded and the armies of the two countries have established harmonious relations. The Bangladesh army has been interfering in state affairs like the Pakistan army. The strong Islamic beliefs of the people, coupled with abject poverty, have been exploited by the Pakistan based *jihadists*. Today the country has twelve Islamic fundamentalist organisations with their links in Pakistan and they act as a conduit for operations against India.[7] They have a strong influence in the polity of Bangladesh with direct impact on the security and development of the region.

Bhutan and Nepal. These two Himalayan states have a history of peaceful existence except for the recent rise of violence in Nepal, owing to the emergence of Maoists and their struggle against the monarchical system that had been ruling the country for centuries. They are on the threshold of becoming full-fledged democracies. Nepal has been the centre of ISI activities against India which include planning and execution of terrorist activities by exploiting its open border with India. *Madrasas* have mushroomed along the Indo-Nepal border and these act as safe havens for infiltrating/ex-filtrating terrorists and induction of fake currency into India.

Maldives. The country got its independence in 1965 and became a republic in November 1968. It has been largely peaceful except for a series of coup attempts in the 1980s by some NSAs with business interests. The 2012 public uprising was against the mismanagement of the government. Initially the protests remained peaceful but later turned violent with the supporters of the ruling and opposition parties clashing to snatch power. Maldives is one nation in South Asia that has been the play field of NSAs with commercial interests owing to its economic and trade treaties with India.

Sri Lanka. Located in the Indian Ocean, it occupies an important geo-strategic position. It became a democratic republic after independence in 1948. The country got involved with Tamil insurgency commencing from 1982 and remained embroiled till 2009 when the LTTE finally conceded defeat. Should LTTE be seen as NSA or an internal freedom struggle actor?

Myanmar. Myanmar is deemed as an extension of South Asia. It shares its boundary with India, China, Bangladesh and Thailand. It acts as a link between South Asia and South-East Asia. The country has been ruled by the military from 1962 till early 2011, when the military rule was dissolved and restoration of democracy commenced. In October 2012, Myanmar witnessed large scale civil riots between Rakhine Buddhists and Rohingya Muslims in the northern Rakhine state. In 2007, the German professor Bassam Tibi[8] had suggested that the Rohingya conflict may be driven by an Islamic political agenda to impose religious laws. In 2013, these riots re-emerged with violence spreading to towns close to Yangon with the Buddhist hardliners taking the centre-stage. It is a route often adopted by the NSAs to put a weak/vulnerable government on the back foot.

Significance for India

Internal Dynamics. India, the biggest democracy in the world, which is founded on the principles of

[6] http://www.unodc.org/unodc/secured/wdr/wdr2013/World_Drug_Report_2013.pdf

[7] http://www.observerindia.com/cms/export/orfonline/modules/analysis/attachments/Bangladesh-Militant-Groups_1246945884723.pdf

[8] http://en.wikipedia.org/wiki/Burma

sovereignty, social equality and secularism has been the subject of terrorist activities (NSAs) in J&K, abetted by Pakistan. The eastern states of the country have been facing insurgency since independence of which most are heading towards normalcy, except for Manipur where the violence is still above the threshold of tolerance. Indian Mujahedeen and Maoists are the indigenous by-product of ill-fated politics and poor administration – fuelled by Pakistan. Most of the NSAs have little local support. Their self-proclaimed support is largely driven through the fear of the gun. They mostly survive due to the external support of either Pakistan or China. Despite the yeoman services rendered by the Indian Defence Forces; corruption and political misdemeanours—the two banes of society have been supplying the requisite oxygen needed for the survival of NSAs in India.

External Influences. India is vulnerable to external infiltration by the NSAs due to its open/porous borders. Besides, India hosts the third-largest Muslim population in the world after Indonesia and Pakistan. Exploiting the Muslim card, the ISI has deployed its covert *jihadist* cells in India, Bangladesh and Nepal for multi-directional infiltration into India. Their attempt to complete the *jihadist* encirclement of India appears to have been stalled by the rise of Buddhist fundamentalism in Myanmar. The ISI has been employing all dirty tricks available i.e. gun running, drug trafficking, fake currency, detonation of improvised explosive devices and *fidayeen* attacks on Indian civilian/military targets. The 2001 attack on the Indian Parliament by Lashkar-e-Taiba and Jaish-e-Mohammad, the two Pakistan-based NSAs had brought the two nations on the brink of a full-fledged war which was prevented with the intervention of the international community. Paradoxically, Pakistan is back to its old ways. The 26/11 Mumbai attack, blasts in Bodh Gaya and the recent attacks in Kathua and Samba Districts[9] of Jammu and Kashmir are cases in point.

Evaluation of Twenty-First Century's Non-State Actors

Categorisation. The NSAs of the current era could be broadly clubbed into three categories. The armed rebel groups like the Maoists, insurgents of Manipur, Indian *Mujahideens* and LTTE of Sri Lanka constitute the first category. Their prime motive is to challenge/ overthrow the legitimate state government through armed struggle. The second category is the religious/ social ideologues like Deobandis (Darool Uloom Deoband), Bajrang Dal and even Khap Panchayats whose writ often goes beyond the law of the land. The third category is the Islamic fundamentalist organisations supported by Pakistan/others. The last category has been the by-product of international political rivalry and hegemonic designs of the nations involved that is jeopardising the international safety and security.

Causative Factors. An analysis of the rise and growth of the NSAs points towards the weak and corrupt state machinery where they have grown and sustained. Misdemeanours of political leaders are a critical cause of the growth of this deadly virus. It is compounded by the lack of education and abysmal poverty. Lastly, the international/ inter-state rivalries and their funding/ protection by the state agency have been the source of oxygen essential for their survival. The technological explosion, real-time communication and ability to travel across the globe have made the NSAs virtually omnipresent and nondescript.

Deterrence—The Way Out

Strategy. Deterrence in the current context cannot be applied in a linear fashion, as was the case during the cold war when it was used purely in the nuclear context. The current dynamics of threat from the NSAs is nebulous, multi-faceted and represents fear of their presence anywhere and everywhere. They are highly motivated and are even ready to die for their cause. Therefore, the strategy of deterrence should encompass their physical elimination and also address their minds to weaken the belief in their cause. Good governance, effective administration, speedy delivery of justice and a strong security system backed by real time intelligence should be the cornerstone of any strategy. India should think beyond the boundary resolution and appeasement of Pakistan to resolve the ongoing imbroglio. It should redefine its foreign and economic policies with a long-term perspective and in-built deterrence for Pakistan, should it persist with the ongoing misdemeanour of nurturing and supporting J-*jihadi* operations against India. Towards this end, India has to move forward on the path of economic and social development taking along other states of South Asia, sans Pakistan till it mends its ways.

Integrated Approach. The NSAs often have a lead over the government agencies since they remain incognito till forced out of their shell. The existing state organs are competitive to counter NSAs threat but they must keep abreast with the latest technology.

[9] 12 Killed in Fidayeen Strike in Jammu, The Hindu, 26 Sep 2013.

A proactive vis-à-vis a reactive approach would deny the advantage to NSAs and provide an early lead to the state agencies to target them physically and mentally. This demands that all state agencies should work in concert with each other. One-upmanship, if any, would be detrimental, as was seen between the Delhi and Mumbai police in the aftermath of the arrest of Syed Zabihuddin Ansari aka Abu Jindal.[10]

Centralised Decision and Decentralised Execution. To remain proactive, it is vital that centralised decision making should be restricted to key policy areas and critical facets of operations. There should be optimum decentralisation to execute operations within the bounds of pre-defined policies. The conduct of operations by the US forces in Afghanistan and the border provinces of Pakistan, especially the drone strikes and the killing of Osama Bin Laden are excellent examples to be studied and applied appropriately.

Understanding the Fibre. The fibre of NSAs comprises ideologues, military leaders, foot soldiers, financers, couriers, explosive experts, technology/ communication specialist, gun runners, and drug peddlers and so on. All those involved in the decision making and countering them should have the requisite knowledge and understanding of their modus operandi to be able to effectively contribute. The current trend of bureaucrats/officials with little or no knowledge of the subject sitting in key decision making positions is catastrophic.

Choking Financial Support. Financial support is the key to all operations of NSAs. Drying of finances can kill an idea and embed a death nail in the coffin of such organisations. It requires a coordinated effort both at the national and international levels to check the flow of black money, drug money and other funds by specially trained financial crime prevention cells.

International Cooperation. The global intelligence services and the comity of nations, especially those with high level of technology need to come forward to put a coordinated deterrence plan in place. It must be supported by the requisite technological tools to counter the growing menace of NSAs. The international community under the UN should have clearly defined policies to deter rogue states like Pakistan by way of punitive actions to stall any support to NSAs for any kind of violence, gun running, drug peddling or any other nefarious activity.

Conclusion

NSAs have been challenging the rulers/ legitimate state authorities and have left indelible footprints in the history of mankind. They have been soaked in various hues of classifications varying from freedom fighters, nationalists, robbers and terrorists. With the growth of the Westphalian state and the ushering of democracy, nationhood has gained more sanctity than ever before. It has also led to the rise of nationalism and the overriding importance of national interest over the individual. The emergence of nuclear weapons led to the rise of the two super powers and intense international rivalry in the form of cold war. With this emerged the concept of nuclear deterrence and mutually assured destruction. It made military strategists look for alternate ways to defeat the adversary which led to the emergence of NSAs, supported and funded by the opponents. The world witnessed the defeat of the mighty US at the hands of the Vietcong in the 1960s. Later, the US avenged their defeat when the Soviets decided to intervene in Afghanistan. It paved way for the rise of *Mujahideen*/Taliban/Al Qaeda and other Islamic fundamentalist organisations in South Asia, mostly supported by Pakistan/the US. Though the US achieved its aim of decimating the Soviet Union, the Islamic *Jihadists* raised for the purpose have now acquired a mammoth magnitude. These NSAs are impacting the safety, security and development of India/South Asia and the international community. They will continue to be a challenge for the international security strategist in the twenty first century.

> *"The international community is worried about the rise of NSAs.*
> *Well, there is a way out – stop sponsoring and supporting them."*

[10] Delhi, Mumbai Police fight over Abu Jindal, The Times of India, 28 Jun 2012.

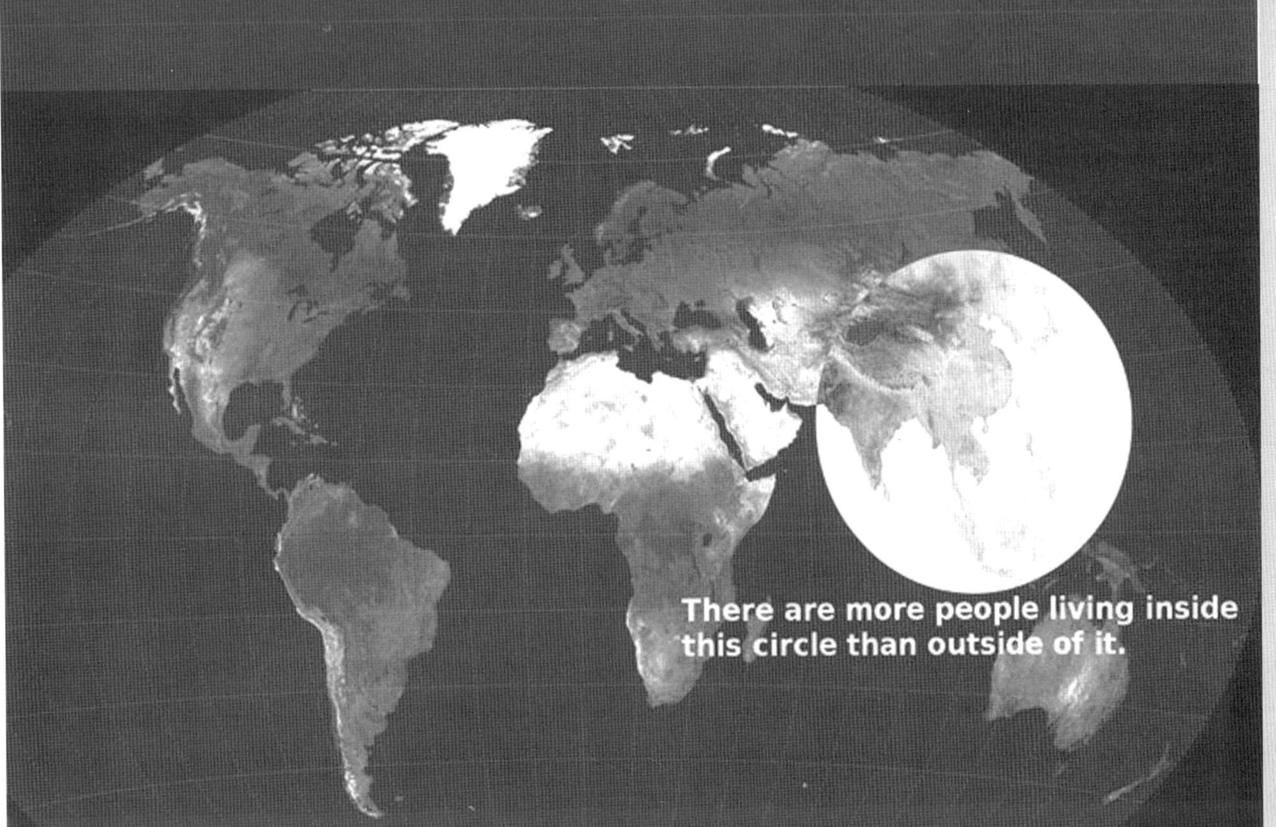

CONSTRUCTING A REGIONAL SECURITY PARADIGM AND AN "IMAGINED REGION" OF SOUTH ASIA: A SUB-CONTINENTAL SECURITY PERSPECTIVE

Dr. Iqbal Shailo, Carleton University, Ottawa, Canada

Introduction

Since the 9/11, security narratives in South Asia have taken a new dimension and the geopolitical codes of sovereignty and territory have also changed in state policies of the South Asian region. Thus, the term 'security' in its conventional geopolitical connotation has undergone a dramatic change, and the events of September 11 have forced so many countries, especially India to adopt and enforce measures to root out terror networks inside and outside of the country. India has been accusing Pakistan of imparting training to non-state actors to carry out terror acts on Indian soil.[1] Following the attacks on the Twin Towers, President Bush's rhetoric 'the enemy other' became vividly clear to the world. His sentiments were echoed by some of the world's most controversial leaders such as Ariel Sharon of Israel, Tony Blair of the UK, and Atal Bihari Vajpayee of India.[2]

This article demonstrates how the security of the South Asian region, specifically within the context of Bangladesh, India and Pakistan, is an epistemological question especially with regard to how cultural and political identities are structured and how hegemonic power, especially the role of India, is a threat to its neighbours and remains an obstacle to establish a concerted security paradigm in the region. This study is organised as follows: First, it briefly discusses India's role in forming a regional security community. Second, it sets out a prelude to imagine and reframe the geopolitical map of the South Asian region along with the causes and objects of territorial demarcation of the Sub-continent. Third, it focuses to include economic, environment, military, and societal factors to construct South Asian security paradigms in the region. Fourth, it highlights the role of the SAARC, and some perspectives to construct trans-border security paradigm for the sub-continent in particular and the South Asian region in general.

---

[1] Chandran, Suba and Rajmohan, P.G. 2007. "Soft, Porous or Rigid? Towards Stable Borders in South Asia," *South Asian Survey*, Vol. 4(1), pp. 117-128.

[2] Jones, Reece. 2009. "Geopolitical boundary narratives, the global war on terror and border fencing in India," *Transactions*, The Institute of British Geographers, pp. 290-304.

South Asian Security, India's Role and the Sub-continental Perspectives

In a regional context, India's strength in forming any regional security community should not be underestimated. Recently India has emerged as an economic tiger not only in the South Asian region but also in the whole of Asia after China. India has focused on the rapid modernisation of its economic, technological and military capabilities and "globalisation has been embraced as an integral part of India's economic growth, and industrial and technological transformation."[3] India has been playing the role of hegemonic power in the region since its independence and it has intervened at certain times in some neighbouring states. In order to face challenges from its neighbours, such as Pakistan and China, India acquired nuclear bombs and long-range missiles. India's "Look East" and "South Asia" policy now comprises a region of regions that extends widely from Southeast Asia to the Pacific and Southwest Asia to Central Asia (i.e. its horizon includes the Persian Gulf in the west to the Malacca Straits in the east and from Central Asia in the north to near the equator in the south).[4] "Because of India's geostrategic location, its maritime horizon covers the entire northern arch connecting Australia, Southeast Asia, South Asia, the Persian Gulf region, and the African littoral up to the Cape of Good Hope, as also the island states in Indian Ocean."[5]

Alternatively, Pakistan defines security very narrowly. One might suggest that Pakistan is always suspicious of the possible threats to its security and attacks from neighbouring India. This attitude is prevalent in its public discourse and has become an orthodox pattern of elite thinking in Pakistan. Pakistan does not have any positive inclination to build a good relationship with India. Pakistan's geopolitical gestures and words tend to challenge the political superiority of India. Still, there are many unsolved emerging issues as Malone notes, "Kashmir remains at the crux of tortured relationship between India and Pakistan."[6] He further highlights that "the growing asymmetry in economic performance, as well as in geostrategic significance builds in a powerful structural dimension to Pakistan's resentments."[7] Political analysts observe that Pakistan's present political position and its geostrategic structures are genuinely anti-Indian although its foreign policies remarkably advocate for a congenial atmosphere in the region. Here Cohen's words are noteworthy, "India and Pakistan are two countries in the region that suffer from an allergy to each other."[8] Incidents like the Kargil operation of 1999, the hijacking of the Indian Airlines flight by Pakistani-backed terrorists in December 1999, terrorist attack on the Indian Parliament in December 2001, a suicide car bomb attack on the Indian Embassy in Kabul in July 2008, and the Mumbai attack in November 2008 are testimonies of Pakistani motives and India's attempts to place responsibility on the shoulder of Pakistan.[9]

New Delhi's strategic plan has long been a problem for Bangladesh; the people of Bangladesh have mixed reactions about India's role in the region, especially with regard to Bangladesh. Some groups believe that during the colonial era, the rule of Hindu feudal lords was representative of domination and exploitation, therefore any relationship with India ideologically will turn hegemonic by any means.[10] Both countries experience deep mistrust and suspicion of each other. The degree of cooperation and collaboration between them varies from regime to regime and it depends on the political parties of both sides and the level of trust existing between each other. "Bangladeshi perceptions *vis-à-vis* India are based on historical baggage, deep-seated suspicions, reality of power gap, the communal dimension of partition, construction of an 'enemy image' through politically-motivated media campaigns and highly nationalistic and sovereignty-sensitive elites that seek their political sustenance through non-cooperation."[11] Jones believes that any attempt to formulate a security framework in South Asia relies on the active

---

[3] Dutta, Sujit. 2009. "The Asian Transition and India's Emergency Strategy," In N.S. Sisodia and V. Krishnapada (eds.) *Global Power Shifts and the Strategic Transition in Asia*, Academic Foundation, New Delhi, pp.19-32.

[4] Shailo, Iqbal. 2010. "The Maritime Boundary Claims of Bangladesh, India and Myanmar: The Challenge of Security Integration in South Asia," *Pentagon's South Asia Defence and Strategic Year Book*: Pentagon Press, pp. 131-141.

[5] Ibid., p. 137.

[6] Malone, David M. 2011. *Does the Elephant Dance? Contemporary Indian Foreign Policy*, Oxford University Press, pp. 109-110.

[7] Ibid., p.110.

[8] Cohen, Stephen, P. 2001. *India: Emerging Power*, Washington DC: Brookings Institution Press.

[9] Malone, David M. 2011. *Does the Elephant Dance? Contemporary Indian Foreign Policy*, Oxford University Press, p.110.

[10] Pattanaik, Smruti S.2010. "India's Neighbourhood Policy: Perceptions from Bangladesh," *Strategic Analysis*, Vol. 35 (1), pp.71-87.

[11] Ibid. p.74.

participation of India. Quoting from Adler and Barnett, Jones suggests "the existence of powerful states that are able to project a sense of purpose, offer an idea of progress, and/or provide leadership around core issues can facilitate and stabilise this phase."[12]

Framing an "Imagined Region" of South Asia

The framing of any region depends on the interest of the framers, geopolitical players and stakeholders, and is a normative political exercise to serve specific goals and objectives. The construction of the South Asian region is a product of a 'power-knowledge nexus' in which different regional and global political actors are engaged in order to manage and control the region for their benefit and interest. Hence, we cannot ignore the importance of cartography to divide the region where geography plays an important role.

The contemporary geographical literature has considered South Asia as a "geographically discrete region"[13] surrounded by natural barriers, oceans, mountains and forests. But various embodied and embedded narratives have shaped the regional perception, trans-border relations and collective memory of the South Asian region. Lewis and Wigen (1997) note the derogatory Euro-centric regional nomenclature that considers South Asia a "sub-continent'.[14] The legacy of the British regime, post-colonial anxiety and insecurities, and mostly the 'Two-Nations' theory have shaped and reshaped the people's memory and imagination. The identity of the region has been constructed ideally by the political elites, but identity is a construction of political and social processes, something given and fragmented.[15]

The 'imagined region' of South Asia is constituted by particular processes and practices such as cartography, geography, language, culture, religion, historical specificity, trans-border economy and geopolitics, not only by universal timeless fixed entities.[16] Geopolitics is also a strategic mechanism that can formulate a region. Buzan and Wæver's (2003) concept of a South Asian Sub-Complex is the best example how geopolitics and world order divide the region and frame a regional geopolitical order.[17] Explaining the distinctiveness of the region, Cohen (2009) notes that "South Asia is a distinct geopolitical region, separated from surrounding realms and regions by nature, culture, social differences, politics, and, to a considerable extent, religion."[18] Before Buzan and Wæver, Saul Bernard Cohen (1963), a political geographer, defined the South Asian region. He claimed that "the concept of South Asia as an independent geopolitical region separated from surrounding strategic realms and their regional subdivisions was first advanced by this writer [Cohen himself] in 1963", and accordingly he argued that "while South Asia is not, and never was, a completely unified geopolitical region, it is a distinct geographical region, possessing many cultural and human similarities and separated from the rest of Asia."[19]

The region has some extraordinary qualities since long and "it can be neither dominated by Great Powers nor absorbed into adjoining geopolitical frameworks, although Pakistan and Myanmar, on the region's western and eastern margins, respectively, have strong links with the bordering geopolitical region."[20] But still great powers are included in decision making processes and policies, making plans to hold strategic resources, facilitating trade business and investment for their own benefit. Accordingly, great powers are doing the same thing in the South Asian region.

China and Myanmar are excluded from the territorial boundaries of the South Asian region and the Himalayan Mountains work as a demarcation line between South Asia and China. But one may raise a question: If China is not a part of the South Asian

---

[12] Jones, Peter. 2008. "South Asia: Is A Regional Security Community Possible?," *South Asian Survey*, Vol. 15(2), pp.183-93

[13] Ayoob, Mohammed. 1999. "From Regional System to Regional Society: Exploring Key Variables in the Construction of Regional Order," *Australian Journal of International Affairs*, Vol. 53(3): Australian Institute of International Affairs, pp. 247-260

[14] Lewis, Martin W. and Wigen, Karen E.1997. *The Myth of Continents—A Critique of Metageography*, University of California Press

[15] Hall, Stuart. 1996. "Introduction: Who Needs "Identity?," In Stuart Hall and Paul Du Gay (eds.), Questions of Cultural Identity, London: Sage, pp.1-17.

[16] Singh, Sinderpal. 2001. "Framing "South Asia": Whose Imagined Region," IDSS working paper series (9), IDSS, Singapore & Lewis, Martin W. and Wigen, Karen E.1997. *The Myth of Continents—A Critique of Metageography*, University of California Press.

[17] Buzan, Barry and Wæver, Ole. 2003: *Regions and powers: The Structure of International Security*, Cambridge University Press.

[18] Cohen, Saul Bernard. 2009. *Geopolitics: The Geography of International Relations* (Second Edition), Rowman & Littlefield Publishers, Inc., p. 348.

[19] Ibid., p. 330.

[20] Ibid., p. 330.

region then why the Indo-China border war took place in 1962 which was fought on the ownership of the borderlands by both countries. Also, the Maldives are included in the South Asian region, which are thousands of miles far away from India. According to some scholars, the South Asian region is culturally framed and the basis of the demarcation of the region is culture. In *Defending India*, Jaswant Singh (1999), the former external and defence minister of India, stated the British India as 'self-contained civilisational areas of the world'.[21] The then education minister of India in the 1950s Maulana Abul Kalam Azad (1959) in *India wins Freedom* has established that communal harmony and collective culture and shared values are the essence of the population of this Sub-continent. Even the first prime minister of India, Jawaharlal Nehru, describes the tradition of *The Discovery of India* (2004), the Indian Sub-continent boasts of its a 5,000 year of cultural history and tradition.[22] Still West Bengal and Bangladesh belong to a similar culture in various ways such as dress, language, rituals, food habits and folk-traditions. The Punjabis of both India and Pakistan are identical in attire, traditions, food and rituals (except some religious events). The Muslims of Pakistan and the Muslims of India are quite similar in culture, traditions and rituals. There is huge cultural affinity between and among the Nepalese, Bhutanese and Hindus in India. The people of Waziristan, in the northwest mountainous region of Pakistan, are closely related with the bordering populations of Afghanistan and the people of both regions speak Pashto, Persian and rarely Urdu. Thus there is some cultural affinity between and among the populations of the South Asian region.

Religion is also one of the factors in the formation of a region. Afghanistan, Bangladesh, Pakistan, the Maldives are mostly Muslim countries. More than 160 million Muslims also live in India. Hindus also live in Bangladesh and a few Hindus and Sikhs also live in Pakistan. This religious faith can play a greater role in the formation of a region. A religious affinity also remains between Sri Lanka and Bhutan. Almost 70% people of Sri Lanka are Buddhists while the two-thirds of Bhutanese populations are also Buddhists. About 23% of the Bhutanese are Hindus who belong to same religion as Indian Hindus. The cultural and religious affinity of Tamil Nadu of India is equal to those of Sri Lanka.

Historical specificity sometimes becomes imperative to form a region. Lewis and Wigen (1997) argue that there is no confusion about Pakistan to be a part of South Asia because of "solid historical and cultural reasons; and many Pakistanis would agree with this designation."[23] They further elaborate that after the rise of fundamentalism and radical groups in Pakistan and frequent tensions between Hindus and Muslims in India, "many Pakistanis now are arguing that their country should be included in the primarily Islamic region centred on Southwest Asia and North Africa. For now, it is perhaps best to regard Pakistan as Janus-faced country, looking both east to South Asia and west to the "Middle East."[24] Even a few organisations and websites, though they are not famous and popular in both sides of the borders of Bangladesh and West Bengal of India, have been campaigning since long for the reunification of Bangladesh and West Bengal of India. They advocate for a greater Bengal stretching out from the Himalayas to the Bay of Bengal including Bihar, Jharkhand, Orissa, Meghalaya, Manipur, Nagaland, Tripura, Mizoram, Arunachal Pradesh and Assam of India. Historically these places were together and the British rulers conquered these places in the 18th and 19th centuries and put them under the Bengal Presidency, the largest British province in India.

Trans-border economic interaction also works as a mechanism to establish a region, such as NAFTA for Canada, Mexico and the USA. South Asia has established its economic network called South Asian Association for Regional Cooperation (SAARC) in 1985 and opened its borders for its member-states to do trade and business. SAARC consists of Bangladesh, Bhutan, India, the Maldives, Nepal, Pakistan, Sri Lanka (Afghanistan joined in 2006). The role of the SAARC is to ease trade cooperation among the countries, but still the members face obstacles and complexity to run business. This trade and business are under the South Asian Free Trade Area (SAFTA) which was signed in January 2004, but it came into force in January 2006. Thus, economic and trans-border business relations can play a great role to form a region. The trade volume of the countries is less than expected, as noted on the SAARC website. "The total cumulative value of exports under SAFTA has crossed US$2 billion but is far below the potential."[25]

[21] Singh, Sinderpal. 2001. "Framing "South Asia": Whose Imagined Region," IDSS working paper series (9), IDSS, Singapore.

[22] Ibid.

[23] Lewis, Martin W. and Wigen, Karen E.1997. *The Myth of Continents—A Critique of Metageography,* University of California Press.

[24] Ibid., p.199.

[25] SAARC website. 2013. http://www.saarc-sec.org/areaofcooperation/detail.php?activity_id=5 Retrieved on 30th May, 2013.

Various western universities have established South Asian research centres and they undertake research on various countries of the South Asia region. For example, the Centre of the South Asian Studies at Cambridge University identifies the South Asian region in the following way: "It is primarily responsible for promoting within the University the study of India, Pakistan, Sri Lanka, Bangladesh, the h[H]imalayan Kingdoms and Burma, but has also, over the last twenty years, extended its activities to include Thailand, Malaysia, Singapore, Vietnam, Cambodia, Laos, Indonesia, the Philippines and Hong Kong."[26] The South Asian Studies at both the University of Toronto and York University, Canada have emphasised the present SAARC countries but the South Asian centres at the University of Michigan, and the University of Virginia include Tibet as one of its member countries while the Rutgers University and the University of California does not consider the Maldives in the South Asian region.

It is interesting that Burma was excluded from the South Asian region, while it was a part of the British India and included in Southeast Asia.[27] Here also we find a link of power-knowledge nexus works.[28] The British ruled the country since 1886 and Rangoon became the capital of the British Burma to link Kolkata (Calcutta) and Singapore. During World War II, Japan occupied Burma in 1942 and British rule collapsed. In 1944, the Allied forces occupied Burma and Japanese rule ended in July 1945. The exclusion of Burma from South Asia is the result of the interest of the great powers and to include it in Southeast Asia by the desire of the western allied forces to regain their colonial empire for strategic planning in the post-colonial period. "The neighbouring countries of Thailand and Burma can be expected to fall under Communist domination if a communist-dominated government controlled Indo-China. The balance of Southeast Asia would then be in grave threat."[29] As the USA is already in the political intervention of the Southeast region thus it will facilitate to dominate Burma which is ruled by the communist military rulers. And the influence of the domino theory, failure in Vietnam and encountering communism, the USA strategically does not want to see the map of Burma with South Asia. That's why Burma was erased from the South Asian region.

If we critically examine the various concepts behind the formation of the South Asian region, it can be said that the demarcation of geographical space and giving a particular name to it such as British India or the Indian sub-continent as categories in political processes and knowledge systems. The colonial mapping of the Indian sub-continent and the British rule in the region were the desire of the Britons who ruled the region. As Edney indicates, "the creation of British India required the prior acceptance by the British of 'India' as signifying a specific region of the earth's surface."[30] Thus the formation of the Indian sub-continent created by the British from the essence of knowledge of whom to rule, which space to rule and what resources to extract. So it was their imagination to demarcate, delineate, include and exclude the region. The British did demarcate the region through the disciplines of geography, cartography, human culture, political division and natural unity of the region.

Given the above discussion, it can be said that Bangladesh, Bhutan, India, Nepal, Pakistan, Sri Lanka (only six countries) can be an imagined South Asian community. Because they belong to similar geographical location, and most of the borders of these countries are somehow related to each other. Although Sri Lanka does not have any land boundary with India but it has maritime borders with India to the northwest. These countries have almost same historical backgrounds, and culturally they are similar to each other. In the SAARC, the Maldives is included but there is no significance to include the Maldives in the South Asia region, as the distance of the Maldives from India is about 2,154 kilometres. The reason behind the inclusion of the Maldives in SAARC is to include Muslim population into a regional bloc and the architects to incorporate the country are Bangladesh and Pakistan.

Afghanistan has been included in SAARC in 2006 although Afghanistan is very close to Iran and Central Asia or the Gulf countries. It does not fit within the framework of the South Asian region. Earlier the country was excluded on the basis of culture, social taboos, warlords and societal practices and most importantly, its location belongs to Southwest Asia including Iran and Iraq. If we

[26] Centre for South Asian Study (CSAS) website, Cambridge. http://www.s-asian.cam.ac.uk/ Retrieved on June 5, 2013.

[27] Singh, Sinderpal. 2001. "Framing "South Asia": Whose Imagined Region," IDSS working paper series (9), IDSS, Singapore.

[28] Ibid.

[29] Pentagon Papers (Gravel edition). 1950. "Summary of Existing Policy on Indochina for the Joint Chiefs of Staff," Vol. 1, Document 9: 25 July, pp.373-4.

[30] Edney, Mathew H. 1997. *Mapping an Empire: The Geographical Construction of British India, 1765-1843:* University of Chicago Press, p.3.

critically analyse both the Maldives and Afghanistan then they cannot be a part of South Asia; neither geographically nor culturally but they can only be merged as Muslim populated countries in the South Asian region. Buzan (2000) in his analysis has regarded Afghanistan as an insulator between the Gulf and South Asia, a zone that demarcates South Asia from geopolitical dynamics.[31] Burma might be included in the South Asian region as some parts of the country border with Bangladesh. In addition, it has historical linkages with the sub-continent in trade and business and above all, during the British period farmers and labourers of India and Bangladesh used to go to Burma as seasonal workers. In addition, the southern-east part of Bangladesh is related with Rakhine state (formerly Arakan) of Burma and there is cultural and religious affinity with the populations of Cox's Bazar and that of Rakhine Muslim ethnic community.

The Role of the SAARC, Trans-border Security and the Sub-continent

SAARC has not proven effective since its inception and has even allegedly failed in achieving its well-defined goals and "falls far short of being an instrument for furthering regional unity."[32] The organisation has not taken any bold initiatives to resolve internal security and conflicts between member states, including issues of border disputes and border security between Bangladesh and India, infiltration, internal terror attacks and trans-border terrorism in Bangladesh, India, Pakistan and Sri Lanka. The SAARC summit in 2009 did highlight the issue of regional and global terrorism but failed to reach consensus as to how to tackle it. If internal and external security issues are resolved by SAARC initiatives, economic ties and partnership might gain momentum. India and Pakistan are devastated by the on-going terror attacks that frequently break or delay progress with regard to negotiations, dialogues and overtures between both countries.

SAARC as a mechanism is a very limited in taking forward economic and security issues.[33] But each country within SAARC wants to cooperate with each other. SAARC is largely seen as a redundant mechanism. Political mistrust and lack of honesty are the two most important things that damage relations; India and Pakistan are no exception. India is exploring possibilities to increase friendship with its neighbouring countries. Bilaterally India had good relations during the Parvez Musharraf regime and the UPA (United Progressive Alliance) led by Prime Minister Dr. Singh's government during the period of 2004 to 2007. Political will on both sides is required to run SAARC actively. In respect of SAARC, economic and national security issues are prominent in its charters for the member-countries but it does not advocate and take initiatives to form a security alliance sub-regionally or regionally.

Any regional security integration or a formation of security community in South Asia needs to be organised not only by maintaining economic treaties and settlements but ecological, cultural and societal issues must be considered as they are an integral component in pushing countries and communities towards cooperation within regional security framework. These days, actors behind any regional cooperation are no longer states, as there are so many stakeholders such as political elites, civil societies, think tanks, NGOs, different types of institutions, organisations, people's movements and mass populations. The South Asian security perspectives might involve economic, environmental, militarily and societal sectors to reformulate the security paradigm bilaterally, trilaterally or regionally.

The following can be considered to define a security paradigm of the South Asian region.

First, security can be redefined and reconstructed in terms of economic criteria. An economic globalising dynamic is the main factor that brings countries, mostly neighbours, closer to each other which Barnet (1981) terms as a global interdependence. Since the inception of SAARC, South Asian countries have not shown any desire of signing a trade agreement. India has several bilateral trade agreements with Bhutan, Maldives, Nepal and Sri Lanka. But it has restricted some trade relations with Bangladesh and Pakistan by putting some barriers on the cross-border movement of goods. The member-countries envisaged to initiate a free trade zone (South Asian Free Trade Area [SAFTA]) within the regional boundaries.

---

[31] Buzan, Barry. 2000. "The Logic of Regional Security in the Post-Cold War World," In Bjone Hettne, Andras Inotali and Osvaldo Sunkel (eds.) *The New Regionalism and the Future of Security Development*, Macmillan Press Ltd, pp.1-25.

[32] Chapman, Graham P. 2003. *The Geopolitics of South Asia: from early empires to the nuclear age*, Ashgate.

[33] Shailo, Iqbal. 2010. "The Maritime Boundary Claims of Bangladesh, India and Myanmar: The Challenge of Security Integration in South Asia," *Pentagon's South Asia Defence and Strategic Year Book*: Pentagon Press, pp. 131-141.

Second, the concept of security can be reformulated in respect of human security. While the concept of human security has earlier roots, its recent prominence comes from the 1994 *Human Development Report* of the United Nations Development Program (UNDP). The report has helped solidify the concept of human security, although recognition of people's security independent of state security is nothing new (Axworthy, 2001).[34] In respect of the sub-continent, millions of people suffer from insecurity. Ethnic conflicts in both India (Muslims, *Dalits*, tribal) and Pakistan (the *Shiites* and the *Ahmadiyas*), poverty stricken-people of the sub-continent and lack of human rights, injustice and fair trial is alarming for any developing and advanced nation. Thus security should be considered in human aspects too.

Third, the environment is an important aspect of human security and any threats to human security includes environmental degradation. However, environment as a security issue is not widely accepted and has not received enough attention either by the governments or the public in the South Asian region. Global warming, erosion, water scarcity, drought, floods, climatic hazards and other disasters might be issues requiring consideration in a broad regional discussion of security. Bangladesh, India and Pakistan have also been facing environmental disasters whose roots are regional, not local. Indian rivers often cause floods in Bangladesh and Pakistan, and Bangladesh is dependent on upstream states, including India, to meet its water needs.[35] The Farakka Barrage built in India on the Ganges has made the northern part of Bangladesh a desert and people are gradually becoming climate refugees. Thus any security pact taking environmental issues as a priority would reduce the negative effects in national life.

Fourth, the concept of security in the sub-continent may include the issue of arms control and the theme of non-proliferation. The problem of nuclear non-proliferation has become an issue of anxiety in the region and antagonism and hostility between India and Pakistan might escalate to nuclear war, as some pundits suggest at any time for any causes accidentally. Both parties are holding various initiatives, meetings and dialogues to reduce the risk of accidental use of nuclear weapons in the region.

Fifth, the sub-continent can expand security in terms of societal aspects such as friendship and alliances with ethnic units/groups within the country. The sub-continent can drive for more engagement in cultural aspects such as sports (cricket, soccer, and SAARC inter-state game), cultural programmes (musical programmes, dances, competition in literary programmes), and education and training (exchange of students, SAARC scholarships and cross-country tours).

A host of security scholars of the sub-continent believe that political elites have a greater role and they should be more positive towards establishing a well-developed relationship and mutual affinity between and among the countries of the South Asian region. The first condition they suggest is to resolve mutual disputes and long-awaited border demarcation to reach a consensus in the region for promoting peace, development and democratic growth. And the second condition is to make strong regional institutions to better serve the people and to promulgate laws that would ease the bureaucratic bottlenecks and red-tape in trans-border economic transaction and movement of the people and goods. They claim that visas should not be required for the people of the South Asian region to move from one country to another country. A few of them seem to be biased and prefer to uphold the images of their respective countries and they passionately narrate the supremacy of their country. They do not like to criticize their own country or to explore the issues that need to be mutually resolved by the respective stakeholders of the region.

It may be said that India and Pakistan operate in a system of geopolitical representations, and the bleak colonial ideologies have transformed into visions of development and economic growth in the context of a new array of regional and global power. For more than sixty years, there is rivalry and hostility relation between India and Pakistan and for decades together governments of both countries attempted to explore negotiation and the third party participation like the World Bank initiated to resolve the Indus water problems in 1960 resulted less success to ensure peaceful solutions to outstanding problems.[36] Although some initiatives adopted by both countries have been under process to increase economic relations, but India is more sensitive about its security and domestic development.

---

[34] Axworthy, Lioyd. 2001. "Human Security and Global Governance: Putting People First," *Global Governance*, Vol. 7(1), p. 19-23.

[35] Chapman, Graham P. 2003. *The Geopolitics of South Asia: from early empires to the nuclear age*, Ashgate.

[36] Malone, David M. 2011. *Does the Elephant Dance? Contemporary Indian Foreign Policy*, Oxford University Press, pp. 109-110.

India has been facing violence and conflicts between different groups and tensions between religious communities since its birth. Its prime concern is to combat terrorist groups that are active inside and outside of India and are adversely affecting its economic growth, progress and development. Even some political elites of India believe that insurgency in various states of India and India's internal leftist attacks on civilians and paramilitaries including Maoists and Naxalites, are financed and supported by some neighbouring countries including Pakistan and China.

In geopolitical actions, Bangladesh lags behind "at the margins of power" in comparison to both India and Pakistan. It has been struggling between democracy and military rule since its birth. Although Bangladesh connects itself to the regional and global geopolitics it is hampered by internal political tensions, slow economic growth, environmental degradation and overpopulation. The concept of security in Bangladesh and India differs. Bangladeshis believe that India is unfriendly, uncooperative and unwelcoming and has been suppressing Bangladeshis by negotiating mutual conflicts and disputes which are continuing for decades.

Since the birth of Bangladesh, the relationship of India with the country has been fluctuating. India has alleged several times that Bangladesh, with the help of ISI (Pakistani Intelligence), gives shelter to some of the leaders of its separatist groups who are hiding in Bangladesh. Bangladesh has repeatedly been denying such allegations. As such the friendship of both countries has been in mistrust and confusion and the decade-long attitude towards each other as 'We' and 'They' remains unchanged. The discourse of the Global War on Terror and global security concerns have changed the geopolitical narratives of the sub-continent and the events of 9/11 have forced India to take three rapid actions: a) to adopt resolutions that require security forces to take extra caution including extensive surveillance of individuals suspected of terrorism and intercepting phone calls; b) to increase the security relationship and intelligence sharing with the USA; and c) to fence off the borders with Pakistan.[37] Also, "by the end of 2007, 2,535 kilometres of barbed wire fencing were completed along the Bangladesh border and 3,250 kilometres of roads have been constructed to facilitate the movement of Indian Security Forces (BSF)."[38]

The narratives of foreign policies, speeches of political elites and foreign policy strategy of the sub-continent are somehow consistent for years together in some aspects. On the one hand, there is an emergence of a new range of challenges. Changes that take place in the geopolitical landscape are the reflection of new forms of conflict and chaos between the two regional nuclear powers, India and Pakistan, and a geopolitical tension remains across the countries of the South Asian region. India is a regional hegemonic power facing obstacles from its neighbours due to its geopolitical codes, political rhetoric and lack of dynamism. The foreign policy discourses of the sub-continent can play a greater role to emphasise upon allies and adversaries to make a framework to construct security and formulate a regional collective voice on security, trans-border peace, growth and development.

[37] Jones, Reece. 2009. "Geopolitical boundary narratives, the global war on terror and border fencing in India," *Transactions*, The Institute of British Geographers, pp. 290-304.

[38] Ibid., p. 293.

THE WAR IN SHADOWS

Vice Admiral (Retd) Vijay Shankar, former Commander-in-Chief of the Andaman & Nicobar Command, Commander-in-Chief of the Strategic Forces Command and Flag Officer Commanding Western Fleet

A century ago it was Japan's uncompromising and resolute political culture, superior operational savvy, doctrinal cohesion and tactical preparation that permitted comprehensive strategic success in a Fleet on Fleet clash over the Russian challenge, in the process upsetting the status quo. Today the emergence of China falls into a similar mould. It has the political will, the economic power and the selective military capability to challenge and revise the status quo. But the nature of War has changed. In this era calibrated escalation of power antagonisms, pressure diplomacy, economic influence and coercion as opposed to a destructive conflict find more favour as political tools. The current situation in Syria, Iran, West Asia, North Korea, weaponising of space, disruptive control of cyber space, resource capturing and indeed the South China Sea imbroglio are marked by a 'War in Shadows' where the principal tools are persuasive in their threat to dent the adversaries comprehensive power. In all cases there is not just a compelling military posture that notifies antagonists but also one that reassures Allies.

Consequences of Strategic Enlargement: Battle of Tsushima 1905

On 08 February 1904 Admiral Heihachiro Togo fired the first salvo in the Russo-Japanese War with a surprise attack on the Russian Far Eastern Fleet harboured at Port Arthur. In one strategic stroke the Russian Fleet was annihilated and the balance of maritime power in the North West Pacific careened in favour of Japan. The attack preceded a formal declaration of War. Termination of the conflict occurred under equally stunning circumstances when Russia's Baltic Fleet, now seconded to retrieve the balance of power, was routed a year and a half later in the Battle of Tsushima.[1]

The war grew directly out of competing imperialism in Korea and Manchuria between, what was rated as, a first rate European Power pitted against a developing 'second' rate Oriental Power. What astounded the West was that the latter emerged victorious with consummate ease despite strong European alliances on both sides. Unnoticed was Japan's national tenacity driven by a deep sense of

[1] Chant, Holmes and Koenig, *Two Centuries of Warfare-Tsushima*, Octopus Books Ltd, London, 1978, pp 187-209.

veneration of the State, the Samurai spirit and ethos of militarism which nurtured a fiercely nationalistic political culture. It also propelled its extension into "Greater East Asia" for strategic security and resource access. Few in Japanese government circles of that day dissented with Baron Hayashi's severe resolve (so reminiscent of China's contemporary status): "If new warships are considered necessary we must, at any cost, build them; if the organisation of the army is inadequate we must start rectifying it from now, if need be our entire military system must be changed. At present Japan must keep calm and sit tight so as to lull suspicions against her; during this time the foundations of national power must be consolidated; and we must watch and wait for the opportunity in the Orient that will surely come one day. When this day arrives Japan will decide her own fate."[2] Victory in the Russo-Japanese War announced Japan's day for Great Power status had arrived.

But there was a more significant impact of Japanese enlargement of its sphere of influence which coincided with the draw down of European naval power from their many overseas commitments in the run up to the looming conflict in Europe. Of more than six major powers exploiting the geo political situation in the Far East during the period of the Russo-Japanese War, all but the United States and Japan remained in the ring to contend for mastery of the Pacific. This fact was not only recognised by the two protagonists, but also set in motion a phase of intense strategic engagement that sought to remedy the imbalance caused by the termination of Russia's ambitions in the region. The Root-Takahari Agreement of 1908 between the United States and Japan went so far as to delineate spheres of accepted influence.[3]

The world at large and navies in particular drew important lessons from the Russo-Japanese War and the Tsushima action. Consequences of the encounter were felt at three different levels which were to usher a new era in strategic thought and concepts in maritime war fighting. Firstly, at the politico-strategic level the emergence of a new power centre had to be accompanied not just by recognition but also with strategic engagement, realistic accommodation backed by balance if friction and hostility was to be avoided. Secondly, at the Operational level the pivot of maritime power had shifted to the all-big-gun fast and accurate Dreadnought type platform. Lastly, at the tactical level doctrines and training provided the key to success in engagement.

The Sum of Anxieties

We note with some disquiet that the emergence of China in the second decade of the of the twenty first century falls into the same mould as Japan a century ago. It was strategic security and resource access that provided the context for Japan's extension into the "Greater East Asia" region; today it is strategic security, resource access and access denial that provide the logic for China's extension across the South China Sea into the Indian Ocean. A century ago it was the decline and destruction of Russian naval power and the consequent disruption of the balanced antagonism between Russia and Japan that left the USA and Japan to contend for mastery over the Pacific; today it is the dissolution of the erstwhile Soviet power, an inward looking Europe and stifling of Japan that has left a rising China to contend for domination of the West Pacific and influence in the Indian Ocean with a flagging USA. A hundred years ago it was Japan's uncompromising and resolute political culture, superior operational savvy, doctrinal cohesion and tactical preparation that permitted comprehensive success over the Russian Challenge and upsetting the status quo; today China has the political will, the economic power and the selective military capability to challenge and revise the status quo. The question really is what form revision will take and whether a balance of power will succeed in reigning in China's aspirations. The paper will focus on the maritime dimension of this looming entanglement.

A Theory of Maritime Warfare

A fourfold classification of maritime forces has dominated naval thought since the Second World War. The grouping is largely functional and task oriented. The differentiation comprises of aircraft carriers, strike units and denial forces, escorts and scouts, and auxiliaries (the last include logistic and other support ships such as landing ships, mine layers, sweepers, tenders etc). In addition contemporary thought has given strategic nuclear forces a restraining role to define and demarcate the limits within which conventional forces operate. Through the years there have been other concepts governing the constitution of the Fleet and its development, often driven by well reasoned logic

[2] Kennedy Paul, *The Rise and Fall of the Great Powers*, Vintage Books, New York, 1989, pp. 208-209. Baron Hayashi Gonsuke a career diplomat from the samurai tradition was a career diplomat and the resident minister of Japan in the court of the Qing.

[3] Gould, Lewis L. *The Presidency of Theodore Roosevelt*, University Press of Kansas, 1992, p. 268.

and at other times motivated by nothing beyond the instantaneous intimidation. That being as it may, clearly the make up of fleets must logically be a material articulation of the strategic concepts and ideas that prevail. The principal demand of the theory of naval war is to attain a strategic posture that would permit control of oceanic spaces in order to progress and influence the course of conflict.

Against this frame of reference the fundamental obligation is therefore to provide the means to seize and exercise that control (it therefore comes as no surprise that China develops forces necessary to realize 'access denial'). Pursuing this line of argument, the rational formulation that remains consistent with our theory of naval warfare is that upon the escorts and scouts depends our ability to exercise control over the objective maritime space or of Sea Lines of Communication (SLOC); while on the Aircraft Carrier group and its intrinsic air power assisted by strike and denial forces depends the security of control. Control and Security of Control is the relationship that operationally links all maritime forces. It may be argued that the best means of achieving control is to incapacitate the adversary's ability to interfere. It would then appear that even in the maritime environment the doctrine of destroying the enemy's armed forces reasserts itself as the paramount objective. This is what must concern the planner to the extreme; that is, should we not concentrate our maritime exertions with the singular aim of dealing that knock out punch. But the maritime environment and the vastness of the hydrosphere that we choose to influence is of a nature that compromises will have to be made in force deployments. At the same time the antagonist may hardly be expected to be so accommodating as to expose his main forces in unfavourable circumstances. As Corbett so eloquently put it "the more closely he induces us to concentrate in the face of his fleet, the more he frees the sea for the circulation of his own trade, and the more he exposes ours to cruiser raids."[4] Indeed, there is no correct solution to this dilemma of how best in time, space and most economically, can Sea Control be established as this would often be dictated by the relative strength, structure and constitution of the fleet, intentions and the geographic character of the theatre of operations which favours one or the other protagonist. However, we may draw a general conclusion that the object of maritime power is to establish control over a pre designated area for a desired period of time. The process may be preceded by strikes against the foe and actions to deny that sea space. The consequence of control may either be operations to secure the object on land or an assurance of passage on that sea area in order to further the war effort. To achieve this state efficiently it is necessary that maritime power be equipped with the appropriate mix of vessels specially adapted for the purpose.

We have thus far noted that our theory of maritime warfare is governed by the ability to control maritime space and put it to use that furthers the national effort. However it is the conditions of use of sea power and the nature of twenty first century conflicts that is now of significance. The adoption of a cogent theory which integrates the promotion, nurturing and maintenance of force with a convincing contract for use is one of the first imperatives that the State must seek to reconcile.

From this resolution emerges the concept of 'Strategic Poise'. India's armed forces have traditionally evolved to cope with operational scenarios. But the operational canvas (inexplicable not to have been apparent), is a transient that abhors futuristic force planning. So it was year-after-every-five-year the planner was condemned to an exercise that perceived possible threats and acquiring/building force structures that attempted to cope with those threats. It was, therefore, the immediate intimidation of the changing global scenario that drove plans and consequently resulted in the accretion of forces. Unfortunately, this inspiration of the instantaneous intimidation is the pretender that serves to fill the strategic space. The significant pitfall that plagues the operational perspective is the continuous struggle to catch up and keep pace with a future that the planner neither sought to shape nor forecast and contend with.

The War in Shadows

Strategic maritime thought and its manifestations in the twenty first century have long supplanted the Mahanian concept of Command of the sea which envisaged a life and death fleet-on-fleet mortal struggle for domination.[5] Corbett's formulation, adapted for the present, of 'Control-for-Causes' is far more sophisticated and appropriate to contemporary geo political circumstances.[6] Its application will have far reaching relevance in an era when calibrated escalation of power antagonism, pressure diplomacy, economic influence and coercion

[4] Corbett Julian S. *Some Principles of Maritime Strategy*, Longmans Green and Co., New York, 1911, p. 115.

[5] Mahan A.T., *The Influence of Sea Power on History* the theme of Command of the Sea is a recurrent theme through the text.

[6] Corbett Julian. S, *Some Principles of Maritime Strategy*. Longmans Green and Co. New York, 1911, pp. 110-121.

as opposed to a destructive and economically debilitating conflict finds favour as a political tool.

The current situation in Syria, Iran, West Asia, North Korea, weaponising of space, access denial strategies, disruptive control of cyber space and indeed the South China Sea imbroglio are marked by just such a 'War in Shadows' where the principal tools are persuasive in their threat to dent the adversaries comprehensive power. In all cases there is not just a compelling military posture that notifies antagonists but also one that reassures Allies. Decisive action seen as the clash of battle fleets, which naval strategists of the late nineteenth and most of the twentieth century considered the key to all strategical problems at sea is today displaced by the interplay and competition of the comprehensive national power of states.

In concept, the comprehensive capability of a country to pursue its strategic objectives through freedom of action internally and externally defines its national power. In achieving this freedom of action, three core factors play a disproportionate part. The first and primary of these is strategic capability in all dimensions. Second, is the resolve of the nation to power as underscored by the will of its people and leadership. And lastly, is the state's ability to face up to and manipulate strategic outcomes. Klaus Knorr, an American academic influenced greatly by the First and Second World Wars and the Cold War, while putting forth an analysis of the war making potential of states, went beyond the characteristics of economic and military potential to include such components as "the will to fight" and "administrative capacity." He defined national power as the aggregate of a state's economic capability, its administrative competitiveness in terms of the influence it was willing to bring to bear globally and its readiness to use its military in order to bring about favourable conclusions.[7] The Ray Cline expression, though one that emerged during the height of the cold war, moves away from the Second World War mould and introduces soft power attributes. It placed before the statesman the natural subjectivity which arises, when dealing with strategic factors and the will and vigour of people; at the same time it did not lose sight of the hard objective factors that contribute to power. This blend of the abstract with the realist's point of view is its most abiding virtue. The other significant feature of the latter paradigm is that it sees power through the eyes of the international system or a potential adversary.[8] Dealing in abstract matters related to the correlation of power was a fresh and sophisticated approach.

This then is the nature of the 'War in Shadows'. If, now, we search for a practical expression we need go no further than the current situation in Iran. The nature of war that we are currently witness to does not readily fall into any mould other than one in 'Shadows'. Covert action, cyber attacks and political alienation sufficiently reinforced by economic sanctions and intrusive nuclear inspections on the one hand, has unleashed globally disruptive nationalism on the other. The South China Sea imbroglio is another manifestation of a 'War in Shadows'; the rise of a new hegemon in China and the slow decline of the current Principal, the USA stimulates the former to develop forces and alliances necessary to realize its grand strategy which China has unambiguously articulated as: stability of dispensation, unimpeded resource access to spur growth and regional pre eminence.[9]

China's Strategic Proposition for Sea Control

Julian Corbett made a convincing argument when he stated that control of sea spaces is neither identical nor analogous in its strategic conditions with the conquest of territory.[10] The reasons are amply clear for the seas are not susceptible to ownership (outside territorial waters) because neither can neutrals be excluded from it nor can forces and populations subsist on it for any cognisable duration of time. Therefore the only deliberate consideration is how best to secure the right of free and unfettered passage for both commercial and, should the need arise, military purposes.

Consistent with this strategy is China's shipbuilding programme of escorts and scouts to exercise Control over sea spaces and Aircraft Carriers assisted by strike and denial forces for security of Control. Control and Security of Control is the classic model that China's naval revival has been inspired by. The problem with the guiding Grand Strategy and its implementation, specifically the coming 'Third

---

[7] Knorr, Klaus. *The Power of Nations: The Political Economics of International Relations*, Basic Books, 1975, Definition and expansion of the National Power of a State is the central theme of the book.

[8] Cline, S. Ray, *'World Power Assessment: A Calculus for Strategic Drift'* Washington: Center for Strategic and International studies, Georgetown University, 1975, p. 11.

[9] Ma Cheng-Kun, PLA News Analysis, *Significance of 2008 China's National Defence White Paper No. 15,* pp. 49-60.

[10] Corbett, Julian S. *Some Principles of Maritime Strategy*, Longmans Green and Co., London, 1911, pp. 88-90.

Island Security Chain'[11] superimposed on 'Access Denial'[12] is its blindness to recognize that we are dealing with a hydro space that is the busiest of all the "vast commons". The reluctance for collaboration makes the potential for friction high, the impulse to alter the status quo stimulates counter alliances, a revisionist strategy will generate turbulence while aggressive resource garnering sets into motion precarious trade practices.

China's commercial and military engagement of Africa and West Asia, quest for an alternative secure and controlled strategic energy and raw material corridor and its vigorous involvement in sea bed mining in the Indian as well as the Pacific Oceans is no aberration but the start of a strategic multi pronged resource access trend. Like the Imperial Powers of the colonial era before and Super Powers in more recent times, China's charge to acquire other discrete supply lines will demand that the primary prong to the 'trend' embrace continued enhancement of it's naval capabilities in-region and exploit the willingness of Pakistan to replace the influence played by America in her affairs. The second prong is on the diplomatic front; its growing assertiveness is evident in the stance it has taken on Syria in the UN, its influence over North Korea, continued technological and material support it provides to Pakistan; it's blocking of sanctions and refusal to cut back on oil sourced from Iran and its very keen attention to the course of the confrontation there; and its rapid mending fences with Russia and Central Asia. In these dealings, what is most remarkable is the absence of political or ideological baggage. The third prong is its deployment of soft power in the region in terms of infrastructural, educational, technological, financial and other aid programmes.

Against this backdrop is the centrality, to China, of continued rapid growth and regime perpetuation and therefore the imperative to temper and balance her strategic aspirations with a non-confrontational posture when dealing with other key regional players even at the cost of relations with secondary players. This, despite the fact that recent American actions in the region to replace unpalatable dispensations are seen as destabilising events. Two conditions will govern Chinese moves; China has little incentive in catalysing unrestricted rivalry with regional players, as such a situation will only serve to close markets and draw down resources which could better be used in the cause of growth and development. Yet at the same time, it is rational to assume that China would extend themselves to ensure that their interests are not degraded either by inimical forces or as consequence of unrelated political or military action even if it means waging a 'War in Shadows'. The significance of the Gwadar-Xinjiang energy and raw material passage, its sea lines of communications across the Indian Ocean and 'the string of pearls' in both conditions remains strategically pivotal.

For China, it is securing the 'control and right of passage' in the Indian Ocean and South China Sea that is of critical consequence. The 'string of pearls' provides to its nascent 'blue water' Navy a reach and control capability that would assure security of its energy lines and sanctuary to its raw materials emanating from Africa. It is towards this end that Chinese strategic policy is directed. The development of 'Access Denial' capabilities has shown impressive growth over the last decade and a half, not just in terms of material progress but also in terms of doctrinal foundations and operational precepts. China's force modernisation along with their investments in cyber warfare, anti air, anti ship weaponry and anti carrier hardware in addition to the thrust on nuclear submarines, both strategic and nuclear powered attack submarines, a carrier group centred on the Liaoning (ex *Varyag*) aircraft carrier with its suite of SU30s all make for a force that is increasingly lethal in effectiveness and enhanced in reach. Operating from infrastructure that they have cultivated from Sittwe and Aan in Myanmar to Hambantotta in Sri Lanka, Maroa in the Maldives and Gwadar in Pakistan (collectively the so called string of pearls) would gives teeth to the long range access denial within the coming Third Island Security Chain.

Specific operational deployments may include one carrier group operating in the Indian Ocean; a Jin class Ballistic Missile Nuclear Submarine (SSBN) on deterrent patrol; two Nuclear powered Submarines (SSN) on SLOC patrol with cooperating surface group and maritime patrol aircrafts; long range

---

[11] Authors monograph titled *Strategic Posture in the Eastern Ocean*, USI New Delhi, 2011, pp. 20-21.

[12] Security analysts have examined China's efforts to develop weapons systems that can retard or even stop a potential adversary from entering an area of interest. Dubbed "access-denial," the aim of such a strategy is to use weapons that deter and should the need arise challenge or indeed prevent inimical forces from operating in conflict zones or oceanic areas of interest. The cutting edge of this strategy is the long range anti-ship ballistic missile. Such a missile, fired from land, sea, underwater or air can cause tremendous damage to an enemy surface vessel particularly an aircraft carrier. While such technology isn't new, the effective ranges of such weapons have increased tremendously, along with their accuracy, speed of delivery and precision. Defending against such systems is therefore a major problem for planners.

maritime strike air crafts operating from Aan or Gwadar; one amphibious brigade standby with transports on hand at one of the 'string of pearls.' Also one regiment of ASAT missiles along with cyber warfare teams to manipulate, black out, control and wage information warfare that will seek to paralyze operations in the Indian Ocean or the Western Pacific Ocean. Whether development as an international maritime power is going to cause friction with regional players such as India and other stake holders remains the moot question.

A Conclusion: Challenges and Policy Urge the Strategic Entente

India's interests in the region is strategic, enduring and diversifying just as China's is while that of the sole superpower's and her allies cannot be set aside. What form this strategic rivalry will take and the substance of it will perhaps only be clear when the dust of USA's involvement in Iran, Afghanistan and Iraq settles down. However there is considerable congruence of interests between USA (and its Allies), Japan and India which provides a substructure for strategic entente.

The challenge before Indian Planners begins with an understanding of the significance of China's rise. Just as Japan, a century ago in the post Tsushima era, propelled herself into "Greater East Asia" in the quest for strategic security, great power status and resource access; China's move into the Indian Ocean may be seen as analogous. Divergences from the analogy lie in the fact that there are other competing stake holders (which includes India, Japan, Russia the USA and allies) in the region and significantly the change in the nature of warfare. The probability of a Fleet on Fleet conflict when there is balance in the correlation of power is low but friction and tensions are more than likely to take the 'War in Shadows' form. So the first task before the Planner is to ensure the building of an entente with like minded nations and the second is to structure and deploy forces such that the balance of power is not upset and the resolve to confront the 'War in Shadows' is not weak. From this strategic posture leadership may attempt to identify areas of common and overlapping interests with China and to enhance cooperation in these areas. The new found strategic Indo-US relationship provides leverage to promote the areas that lie in the domain of vitally common interest of the entente, such as guaranteed energy security, safety of production facilities, protection of transportation infrastructure and the right to unimpeded passage. The stake holders also share a common sensitivity to terrorism emanating from the Afghanistan-Pakistan area. Measures to arrest it may translate to joint naval patrols working in tandem with littoral states and the use of commercial and diplomatic clout to rein-in maverick states. The relationship that oil producers have with their consumers is a symbiotic one; this interdependence also provides the basis of a new framework which could be driven by action to promote security to both consumer and producer in such a manner that stability becomes of interest to all parties.

Participation of the stake holders in forums such as India Africa Forum Summits (IAFS) and the Indian Ocean Naval Symposium (IONS) would give relevance and substance to these institutions. After all not to include the main actors with governing stakes in the area, not withstanding the fact that China, Japan, Russia and the USA are extra regional powers, is to denude these associations of context. This may cue the next logical step to give regulatory teeth to these institutions. Given the stakes that China has in her own development and her security concerns, there are adequate signals to suggest that India needs to pull out of the state of paranoia that she transits through every time that China collaborates with Pakistan and replace it with an understanding of and preparedness for the 'War in Shadows' on the one hand, while on the other a willingness to leverage its burgeoning trade with China which is expected to reach $100 billion by 2015. In this deepening of commercial relations lies the germ of friction resolution.

A PERSPECTIVE ON SOUTH ASIA IN CHINA'S STRATEGIC OUTLOOK AND SECURITY CALCULUS

Major General BK Sharma, (Retd), Distinguished Fellow, United Service Institution of India, Delhi

Historical Perspective

China's strategic outlook is shaped by her ancient culture and contemporary geopolitical imperatives. China's profound self-concept of grandiose is anchored in the 'Middle Kingdom' mind-set. The noted Chinese expert Lee Kuan Yew (founder of modern Singapore) observes that, "in Chinese, China means Middle Kingdom—recalling a world in which they were dominant in the region and other states related to them as supplicants".[1] *The Classics of History*; a document of the 6th Century BC, visualised the world in five major concentric geographical zones emanating outwards from the capital—the royal domains, the princely domains, a pacification zone, the zone of allied barbarians and the zone of savagery.[2]

This ancient belief impelled the Chinese rulers to expand outwards and intervene in the peripheral regions to 'civilise the barbarians' and restore order (a euphemism for expanding politico-economic-military control over outer regions). Paradoxically, this outlook was punctuated by unsavoury developments of the 19th Century, what they call as the 'Century of Humiliation'. The Chinese believe that they are victims of '100 years of shame and humiliation' at the hands of Western and other foreign powers, especially her oriental neighbour Japan. Beginning with the Opium War, China was invaded, divided and weakened by external powers until Mao Zedong re-unified China and founded the People's Republic of China (PRC). This legacy has left a deep impression on the perceptions and national identity of the Chinese. Having been forced to subjugation by Western powers, and partially due to its own inertia to think beyond her periphery, this siege mentality weighs heavily on its psyche. Apropos; any perceived expansion by her neighbours is seen as a potential threat to its sovereignty.

Throughout the period of the Long March and thereafter, the Communist Party, as part of shoring up its identity and securing its legitimacy, fostered the narrative of the Chinese peoples having been

---

[1] Graham Allison and Blackwill D. Lee Kuan Yew, *The Grand Master's Insights on China, United States, and the World* (MIT Press: London, Kindle edition, 2012).

[2] Martin Jacques, *When China Rules the World: The End of the Western World, and Birth of New Global World* Order (London: Penguin Books Ltd, 2009) p. 242.

victims of persecution by barbaric non-Chinese races and that the Party alone would restore their lost glory. This victimisation narrative has created an acute Chinese sensitivity to potential infringements on China's sovereignty and territorial integrity. Indeed, China's victim-mentality and its effort to reclaim lost status are two sides of the same coin that collectively shape China's effort to regain its 'rightful role' in modern international relations. In Chinese thinking subjugation by colonial powers in the 19th century has been an aberration in the shinning historical narrative of their great civilisation.

During the 20th Century, Mao perceived the world through a prism of 'Three World Theory' namely 'Imperialists', the 'Revisionist' and 'International Proletariats', and in terms of three adversaries as arch-rivals, secondary enemies and potential enemies, arrayed against revolutionary forces.[3] Therefore, the contemporary self–concept of China is shaped by a bruised psyche, perception that rest of world is inimical to China's rise, as well as a sense of past grandeur. The slogans of "unfinished historical agenda" and "China Dream" allude to revival of her past glory and integration of Taiwan and other contested territories. This historical narrative is influenced by the contemporary geopolitical imperatives that further shape China's strategic security outlook.

Geo-political Imperatives

Geospatially, China resembles a rooster whose potbelly protrudes into the Pacific Ocean. A good insight on the geopolitical imperatives of China is offered by Stratfor in its exclusive analysis reports titled, *'Geopolitics of China: a Great Power Enclosed'* [4] and the series published on geopolitics of the Yangtze River.[5] Three geopolitical imperatives shape China's strategic security calculus. First, the prosperity of the Chinese 'Heartland'; which is bounded by the Pearl River in the South, the Yellow River in the North and Yangtze River running through the middle. About one billion Han agriculturists who inhabit this region suffer from a relative sense of deprivation.[6]

Development of the 'Heartland' is a major socio-economic challenge for the Communist Party of China (CPC). Major social unrest in the 'Heartland' can undermine the legitimacy of the CPC and undermine the very survival of the regime. From ancient times the ruling regime of the day has often been brought down by a combination of internal dissonance and external abetment. The collapse of Ming Dynasty in 1644 was caused after rebelling peasants took Beijing and the Manchu, with the collusion of Ming genereals invading from the north. Manchu's own Qing dynasty fell three hundred years later after a series of internal conflicts coincided with Western and Japanese invasions.[7]

The CPC continues to face an inner-power struggle between the Youth Communist League, Shanghai Gang and *Prince-lings*. At the same time, the party is debating ideological, political and organisational issues with its cadres and factions expressing divergent views on the relevance of communist ideology, type of democracy, re-structuring of the Politburo, and whether the PLA should continue to be an organ of the Party or be nationalised. Xi Jinping has embarked upon a reformation programme, called the "Campaign on Mass-line, Education and Practice" that seeks a thorough cleanup of the party to get rid of formalism, bureaucratise, hedonism and extravagance. His 'Eight Point' reform agenda programme is being monitored by specially-constituted teams that strive to enlighten provincial leaders, educational heads, managers of state-owned enterprises and the military hierarchy about the morals and ethics of good governance. However, the success of this new purge strategy is yet to be seen.

The new leadership faces challenges from an assertive media and burgeoning middle class that harbours capitalistic ambitions and democratic aspirations. Therefore, the new regime faces a major challenge of transformation of its neo–capitalist society. The Xi Jinping regime seems to be fully seized of this challenge and have announced during the recently concluded "Third Plenum" some economic reforms , introduced right to property and set up a new committee to oversee internal security problems, due to simmering social unrest.[8]

---

[3] Mao Zedong, "On the Question of the Differentiation of the three Worlds", www.revolutionarydemocracy.org, quoting Mao Zedong on Diplomacy, Foreign Languages Press, Beijing, 1998, p. 454.

[4] Stratfor, The Geopolitics of China, A Great Power enclosed, Jun 2008.

[5] Stratfor, The Geopolitics of Yangtze River, April 2013.

[6] "Geopolitics of Yangtze river", Stratfor, 1 April, 2013.

[7] Wang Jixi, "China's Search for a Grand Strategy, Foreign Affairs", March /April, 2011, p. 68.

[8] BBC news-China Third Plenum: Leaders Unveil Key Reforms, 12 November 2013.

The second geopolitical imperative is that of Sinocisation of the restive non–Han 'Buffer' region. This region—comprising Xinjiang, Tibet, Inner Mongolia and Manchuria, accounts for about sixty percent of Chinese territory but is inhabited by only seven percent of its population. Historically, these 'Buffer' regions have been under Chinese rule whenever China was strong and had broken away when China was weak; hence, Beijing's emphasis on the 'Unity of Motherland.' China's security concerns relating to her strategic periphery pertain to the threat from the 'Three Evils', namely Separatism, Extremism and Terrorism. Sub-national movements in Xinjiang and Tibet fall under the rubric of the 'Three Evils'. The Uighurs in China number about eight million which is less than one percent of China's population but they account for 45 percent of Xinjiang's. The impetus to economic growth and social re-engineering have not been able to assuage sub-national sentiments in Tibet and Xinjiang, and growing anti-Han sentiments in Inner Mongolia. It is in this socio-political milieu that the CPC stokes ultra-nationalist sentiments from time to time on the emotive issues that China has with its neighbours and the US.

The third and the most important geopolitical imperative for China is the security of its coastal areas, the country's economic centres of gravity. Geographical restrain in the Western Pacific region imposes a kind of a siege mentality on China. Taiwan is a strategic pivot in the Western Pacific that abuts the East China Sea and South China Sea. Macarthur aptly described Taiwan as an, "unsinkable aircraft carrier".[9] China's claims in the East China Sea are founded on historical basis and on the 'Principal of Extended Continental Shelf', which extends beyond the 200 Nautical Miles (NM) limit. China claims 80 percent of the South China Sea, based on a 'Nine-Dotted Claim Line'. This claim is based on an earlier territorial claim known as Eleven-Dash Line, drawn up in 1947 by then ruling Kuomintang government. This map, despite its lack of specific coordinates, was adopted by the PRC, with minor modifications, in 1953. The CPC leadership transcribed its island claims by enacting a 'Domestic Law on the Territorial Sea and Domestic Zone', in 1992. The new Chinese maps met with little resistance from the other littorals, many of which were focused on their own national independence movements. However, in due course these countries have come to challenge China's stand and stake their respective claims over the island territories.

The issue of contested sovereignty in the two seas with Japan, Philippines, Vietnam and some other States and the vulnerability of the Western and the Eastern SLOCS markedly shape China's threat perception. This strategic reality explains China's Taiwan sensitivity, the oft—repeated 'Malacca Dilemma' and growing security concerns over the US Pivot to Asia Policy or the Trans Pacific Partnership (TPP), which excludes China. China's 'Two Ocean and Counter Intervention Strategy' are driven by the aforesaid security calculus.

Grand Strategic Orientation

China's strategic outlook is influenced by a hegemonic notion of strategic space. The Chinese view strategic space as a living space of its people that spans beyond strategic frontiers and expands and constricts with the ebb and flow of Comprehensive National Power (CNP). China's grand strategy entails development of CNP (*Zhonghe Guoli*) and its strategic configuration (*Shi*) to achieve strategic objectives in a time frame of the coming decade – what they call the "Strategic Window of Opportunity". China's leaders from Deng Xiaoping through Jiang Zemin to Hu Jintao have adopted a consensus grand strategy that emphasizes securing the external conditions conducive to internal economic growth and social change. At the same time, there is seriousness of purpose in modernising China's military and using it, if need be, in the Taiwan Strait and in possibly not too distant future to protect the nation's stated core interests.[10]

In a forecast carried in the Economist publication titled, "20 MEGACHANGE 50: The World in 2050", by 2040 China's economy would have surpassed that of the US. The forecast is based on the assessments of the Asian Development Bank (ADB), Carnegie Endowment for International Peace, Goldman Sachs and Pricewaterhousecooper. In Goldman Sachs projections, if the US economy grows at 2 percent and China's at 6 percent, China will overtake the US by 2027. China is already the second largest defence spender in the world. According to SIPRI, by the year 2035, if China's economic growth continues, her defence spending will surpass that of the US.[11]

---

[9] Michael Mazza, "Why Taiwan Maters," http://thedeplomate.com/china-power/why-taiwan-matters/

[10] Aaron L. Friedberg, "Going Out": China's Pursuit of Natural Resources and Implications for the PRC's Grand Strategy, "Thinking about Power," Vietnamese official, Hanoi, March 2006.

[11] Simon Cox, "The of Emerging Markets", 20 Megachange 50 - the World in 2050, the Economist, Profile Books Ltd, 2012, pp. 153-169.

China strives to become a pre-dominant military power in the Asia-Pacific by 2020-2025, and a world-class military power by 2050. In the short–term, she seeks to reduce the military capability gap with major powers; in the mid-term, the focus would be on modernising high-technology weapons to enable Naval and Aerospace power. In the long-term, China intends developing potent capabilities in outer space, cyber space, nuclear weapons and disruptive technologies. China's approach to military transformation is based on 'Revolution in Military Affairs (RMA) with Chinese Characteristics i.e. imbibe modern technology, keep Sun Tzu's intent in mind and contextualise Mao's principles of war fighting.

South Asian in China's Strategic Calculus

South Asia assumes added importance in China's strategic calculus from the perspective of securing her regional periphery, combating the three evils to her security, gaining access to the Indian Ocean Region (IOR) and restraining India—the only potential competitor in the region. China perceives India as part of the 'Grand Encirclement Design' being weaved by the US to contain her rise. India is deemed to be a competitor in the IOR and South Asia, vying for domination of strategic resources, locations and influence. China is pursuing a well-crafted twin strategy of balancing India in the IOR and South Asia. This strategy is manifest in her endeavours to alter the geopolitical and security landscape of the region along India's continental borders and maritime boundary and at the same time engage India, thus preventing New Delhi from band-wagoning with the US. The new leadership in China has taken strides to ease tensions with India, albeit without compromising its fundamental stand on the issue of contested territory.

Tibet is essential to China's territorial self-conception and it affects China's external relations, particularly with India, Bhutan, Nepal and Pakistan. Mao termed Tibet as China's palm with five fingers extending as Arunachal Pradesh, Sikkim, Bhutan, Nepal and Ladakh.[12] Tibet constitutes about 26 percent of China's landmass. Robert Kaplan writes in *Foreign Affairs* (2011), "without Tibet China would be but a rump and India would add another zone to its sub continental powerbase."[13] Tibet is known as the water tower of Asia.[14] China is a water-stressed country, with 26 percent of world population and only about eight percent of water resources. China's water resources are skewed with 81 percent of water resources located in relatively less-populated northern areas and only 19 percent of water resources available in the high population density areas of the South. China has outstanding border disputes with Bhutan and India and leverages this factor in her creeping assertive strategy against both the countries. Tensions at the border are compounded by China's concerns over the Tibetan movement that seeks more autonomy and a role for the Dalai Lama in Tibetan affairs. The issue of succession of the Dalai Lama is yet another flash point with potential to impact Sino-Indian relations.

China is developing massive infrastructure in Tibet. As part of a 'National Trunk Highway System' (NTHS), China has improved the Central, Eastern and Western Highways and a large number of roads to border areas opposite India. The Qinghai-Tibet-Railway (QTR) is being extended to Shigatse and the Chumbi Valley. New railway freight corridors from Kunming to Ngiti, Xining to Naqu and Chamdo to Ngiti are being developed. It is also improving military airfields and signal communication infrastructure in Tibet. A large number of logistics hubs, with underground facilities, have been constructed to achieve a 'Single-Season Military Campaign' capability. China regularly conducts 'Trans-Regional Support Operations' (TRSO) rehearsing mobilisation of formations from one Military Area Command (MAC) to another. In 2011, PLA conducted military exercises during which the PLAAF rehearsed bombing operations and PLA mechanised forces trained in capture of passes in the high attitude terrain of Tibet. The PRC has developed close relations with Maoist-led Government in Nepal. China plans to extend the railway link from Shigatse to Kathmandu and construct road links along the ancient trade routes into Nepal. It is also modernising police stations in Nepal and has set up a number of 'Maoist Cultural Centres' in Eastern Nepal, bordering the Indian states of Sikkim and West Bengal.

China seeks to alter the strategic transportation landscape of the region to boost commerce and trade and address her needs of energy security. In Greater Central Asia, China is developing the 'East-West Eurasian Corridor and 'Pan Asian Energy Grid'

---

[12] Ajoy Chatterjee, "Liberation of Tibet's Five Fingers", www.globalpolitician.com, 28 September 2011.

[13] Robert D. Kaplan, op cit.

[14] https://en.wikipedia.org/wiki/Tibet.

[15] Ananth Krishnan, "China-Pakistan Deal on Economic Corridor passing Through POK", *Hindu*, 23 May 2013.

through the Central Asian landmass to Eastern Europe and Middle East. From Xinjiang, China is developing an economic corridor to Pakistan.[15] The project entails development of Gwadar in the IOR as a petro-chemical hub and construction of a Karakoram overland bridge, across the Khunjerab pass to Kashgar in the Xinjiang province of China. This corridor passes through the 'Northern Areas' of Pakistan-Occupied Kashmir (POK)—a region that lies close to the Line of Control (LOC) between India and Pakistan. Contiguous to the Northern Areas is the strategically important Shaksgam Valley, which was illegally ceded by Pakistan to China in 1963. China is the major supplier of military hardware and nuclear technology to Pakistan. There is a strong strategic nexus between the two countries which impinges on India's security.

These developments impact regional strategic dynamics and play vividly on India's national security concerns. China is incementally increasing its influence in Nepal, particularly in the Eastern districts which border West Sikkim and the Siliguri Corridor, and pursuing Bhutan to settle the boundary issue with China independent of the India-China boundary dispute. China will not be averse to make lucrative package deals on the border, except in the strategically-important Doklam Plateau which lies at the tri-junction of the India-China-Bhutan border and in proximity to the strategically sensitive Siliguri Corridor.The underlying design of these moves is to undermine the status of these two land-locked countries as strategic buffers and alter the dynamics of India's security calculus.

Another strategic transportation corridor being developed by China is from Myanmar to Kunming. Kyaukpu (Bay of Bengal) in Myanmar has been developed into a petro-chemical hub with facilities for super-tankers to discharge crude. The strategic transportation corridor from Kyaukpu comprising, rail-road-energy-pipelines runs to Kunming.[16] This strategic transportation corridor is being extended to Chittagong port in Bangladesh. China–Bangladesh bilateral relations are on the upswing. China has invested in a large number of infrastructure projects in Bangladesh and is the main supplier of military hardware to its armed forces. China is constructing a 1,736 kilometre-long road from Kunming via Myktina in Myanmar to Pangsau pass on the border with the Indian state of Assam. These developments have serious implications on India's influnce in the strategic neighbourhood and 'Look East Policy'.

As regards the IOR, looking from a broad strategic perspective, this region and the Western Pacific, connected through the South China Sea, form a common strategic space from the trade and security point of view. The Indian Ocean contains several important minerals: 80.7 % of world extraction of gold, 56.6 % of tin, 28.5 % of manganese, 25.2% nickel and 77.3% natural rubber. The highest tonnage of the world goods; at least 40 per cent of the world's sea-borne trade, 50 per cent of its container traffic and 70 percent of the traffic in hydro-carbon products transits through the region. About 80 percent of oil imports to China pass through the IOR. From the Chinese perspective, domination of the IOR is vital for uninterrupted flow of oil and natural resources and transportation of manufactured goods to export markets.

The IOR, therefore, is emerging as China's major security concern. In China's calculus, IOR is the arena where India-US-Japan strategic interests coalesce against China and present a formidable threat to Chinese SLOCs, the very lifeline of China's economy. China's "Far Seas Ocean Strategy", is aimed at *inter alia* safeguarding her interests in the IOR. In PLAN's definition, the "Far Seas" area stretches from the Northwest Pacific to the East coast of the Indian Ocean, and beyond to the East coast of Africa. For domination of such a vast area, development of 'Blue Water' maritime capability becomes a strategic imperative. Such a capability *inter alia* would mean creation of 'Maritime Domain Awareness' and sustainable logistics support facilities.

It is axiomatic that, after China consolidates her economic gains and develops political influence in the IOR, the next logical step should be to build infrastructure for military usage such as command, control, communication, surveillance and intelligence posts, berthing and logistic servicing facilities and facilities for ocean geological, hydrological and meteorological observation posts. Having successfully developed Hambantota, Chinese interests lie in construction of Colombo port in Sri Lanka, Lamu in Kenya, ports in Djibouti and Sonadia in Bangladesh.[17]

China has reportedly evinced keen interest in developing facilities in Maldives, Seychelles, Mauritius and Oman. These emerging port facilities are described by Booz Allen Hamilton—a known US

[16] Ho Qiang, "China-Myanmar Pipelines to be completed in May", www.english.news.cn.

[17] Robert D Kaplan, "China's Port Expansion in Indian Ocean", Stratfor, 29 June 2012.

defence contractor as "String of Pearls". China is likely to augment her naval deployment in the Gulf of Aden and increase frequency of port calls. PLAN hospital ships are known to visit along the East African coast, providing medical aid to the local population. Strategic experts are of the view that it is not long before China's commercial endeavours will assume a military dimension. The emerging developments in the IOR will have long-term strategic implications for the region and impact India's security scenario.

Appraisal of Sino-India Relations

China and India are the world's most populated countries and the second and third largest economies. The two countries are natural competitors in the Asian strategic space for access to resources, domination of locations and influence. India-China relations are characterised by the three Cs; Cooperation, Competition and Conflict. The two countries show conditional cooperation in the arena of global commons and reformation of international institutions, except that China opposes Indian candidature for a permanent seat at the UNSC and Shanghai Cooperation Organisation.They compete for resources, export markets and influence in the transitional world order. If they are unable to manage ensuing competition, they could drift towards a conflictive course.

The boundary dispute, Tibet, accidental standoff in the IOR, Pakistan and the water issue are drivers of conflict with a potential to exacerbate mistrust and spark off tensions. A dispassionate analysis of the comprehensive national power would suggest that, in terms of hard power, China has a competitive advantage over India, be it strategic orientation, size of economy, defence spending, infrastructure, defence industry, the pace of military modernisation and politico-military decision making. The trend lines analysis indicates that if India fails to act with a sense urgency her power asymmetry vis-a-vis China will further grow.

From a short to long-term perspective such an outcome is not desirable for India's national security. With the increase in comprehensive national power, China may be emboldened to subject India to strategic coercion or even be tempted to exercise a military option to subdue the country. It is, therefore, incumbent for India to strengthen her comprehensive national security and skillfully configure it achieve a favourable strategic balance in South Asia.

Concluding Remarks

India should seize a window of opportunity offered by the upswing in the political relations. Signing of nine agreements with India during the visit of Prime Minister Manmohan Singh on 23 October 2013 is a significant step in the direction of improving Sino-India relations.[18] Of particular significance are the Border Defence Cooperation Agreement and Memorandum of Understanding on strengthening cooperation on trans-border rivers. It is imperative for both sides to implement these agreements in letter and spirit by creating instrumentalities and mechanisms to ensure peace and tranquillity at the border. Of utmost importance in this regard would be to create an enabling environment that facilitates maintaining a status quo at the LAC. This is extremely important to create that much-needed window of opportunity for the political leadership and diplomatic community to work on the other areas of divergence, build strategic trust and develop political will to resolve the boundary issue. India should utilise this window of relative peace to address the issues of comprehensive national development, mitigate internal security challenges and create a credible deterrence capability to nudge China and Pakistan to understand the futility of a military option against India.

China, due to her economic power and defence diplomacy, is well poised to induce a gravitational pull on the small and relatively weak South Asian states. It is incumbent for India to pursue a proactive and astute foreign policy, backed by economic and military diplomacy, to bring about a regional economic and security integration of South Asia, if need be sans Pakistan. India has the potential to emerge as an important regional economic vector, a net security provider and a role model of secularism, pluralism and democracy. Such a desired end-state will result in harmonisation of India's strategic interests with aspirations of regional countries and establish India's primacy in the balance of power in South Asia. Retaining her pre-eminent position and creating a favourable strategic balance in South Asia is a strategic imperative for India to play a larger role in the Indo–Pacific and the world at large.

[18] Ministry of External Affairs, Government of India, Media Centre, 23 October 2013.

SINO-INDIAN BORDER DISPUTE: BACKGROUND, INDIA's CASE, BORDER TALKS AND BORDER MANAGEMENT

Maj Gen (Retd) Sheru Thapliyal, Defence Analyst, India

Introduction

Boundaries are the lines of political zones. Generally, the boundaries of the nations are demarcated on the ground on the basis of geographical, cultural, historical and political factors. The boundaries unite an area and the people under one sovereign Government. The boundaries are the limits within which the municipal law takes effect and proves effective barriers to social, political, economical and cultural exchange. The boundary is a meeting place of two socio-political bodies each having it's particular "interest", "structure", and "ideology". The American scholar Stephen B. Jones (Geographer Yale University) proposed two kinds of boundaries—Natural and Artificial.

After 1945, most of the Afro-Asian countries achieved independence with a partition of their natural homelands; e.g. Egypt and Sudan, North Korea and South Korea. It is a matter of historical record that the Afro-Asian countries were partitioned under pressure, as a part of super power politics, and not on social, cultural or economic considerations. "War" as a means of settlement of the border disputes has become the prominent feature of the developing countries in the post-World War-II era; e.g. Iraq-Iran War, Sino-Indian War of 1962, Libya-Chad boundary dispute etc.

HISTORICAL EVIDENCE OF INDIA'S NORTHERN FRONTIERS

Mythological Background

The Himalayas are regarded as the northern frontier of India since ancient times and its mythology and literature support this boundary alignment; e.g. *Vishnupurana, Mahabharata, Upanishads, Bhagvad Gita and Rig Veda*. The unity of the Himalayan region during the period is evinced by the statement in the *Shubha Parwa* of the Mahabharata that:

> "Arjun on one of his campaigns returned from Pragjyotisha (Assam) to Uluka (in northern Punjab) through the inner, outer and adjacent belt of Himalaya."

It is mentioned in the *Upanishads, Rig Veda* and *Bhagvad Gita* that the Himalayas were the frontier of India and brought under the control and dominated from time to time by the political powers. The *Vibhnu*

Purana makes it clear that the Himalayas formed the frontier and not the dominance of contiguous power in those days. It states that the land south of the Himalayas and north of the ocean is called *Bharat* and all born in it are called *Bharatiyas* (Indians). The empire of Chandragupta Maurya, towards the end of the 4th Century B.C., comprised the whole of India, except Assam, as well as Afghanistan, Baluchistan, Nepal up to Mysore and Madras. It shows that the Himalayas were a part of India and the people were familiar with it.

Early History

The Tibetan and Chinese influence, in fact, never gained a permanent footing on the Indian side of the Himalayas throughout the centuries of Hindu rule in India. The Himalayan region often changed hands, but it was always between Indian rulers. Indian literature, from the earliest days down to modern times, shows that India's present northern frontier is along the whole stretch of the historic frontier. Indian political history, throughout, clearly brings out that the Himalayas formed the Northern borders of India. Kautilya's *Arthashastra* also focused on this aspect. In addition, there is considerable evidence to show that Indian control extended through the ages right up to the Himalayan watershed and even beyond in some cases. The Mauryan Empire, the Ashokan Empire, the Kushan Empire and the Gupta empire all extended to the Himalayan watershed and even beyond. There is evidence in the way of inscriptions on monuments, numismatic, and philological evidence which confirms the existence of Indian rule in these areas.

Hieun Tsiang, the well-known Chinese monk, brings out that Kashmir, Ladakh, Nepal and the bulk of Assam (including North East Frontier areas i.e. the present Arunachal Pradesh) were ruled by Indians. During the Muslim rule, the rulers consolidated their empire right up to the Himalayas and some cases even carried out expeditions into Tibet; e,g. Khilji A.D. 1205 and Tughlak A.D. 1327. Baluchisthan, Skardu and Ladakh were traditionally under Hindu rule and the original population in Ladakh was Dardi (Indo-Iranic). Periodically, campaigns were launched by Kashmiri kings right across Ladakh. After the extension of the Mughal rule to Kashmir, Ladakh also came under its sway. Subsequently, during the British period, exploration and survey parties operated in Ladakh and depicted their findings in successive Indian maps. The British brought under their control the present States of Punjab, Himachal Pradesh and Uttar Pradesh by the mid-19th Century and after extensive survey work, issued authoritative maps.

In the case of Assam the original Hindu kings of the Varna Salasthambha and Pala dynasties were displaced by the Ahoms, who themselves got assimilated into the Hindu main stream. Subsequently the British brought their control over the entire province of Assam including the "North East Frontier Agency".

Historic-Political Status of Ladakh

In 400 B.C. Sargyal established his kingdom at Ladakh and Tibet. Niathichen was the next ruler who established the rule of the Thi Dynasty. The Gyalpo established his rule in 333 A.D. After that Gyalpo Showang-Chen-Izghimpo came to power in 650 A.D. The history of Ladakh has been recorded in Laduagas – Rigyal – Rabis and its translation into English was prepared by A.H. Franke in 1926. Skyed-Ilde-Negma Gon is considered the founder of the Lah-Chen Dynasty. This dynasty ruled over Ladakh up to the end of 15th Century. The son of Skyed-Ilde Negma Gon, Gyalpo Rinchin became the ruler of Kashmir and accepted Islam and assumed the name of Sultan Sadar-Ud-din. He ruled from 1324 to 1327 and was the first ruler of Kashmir. After that Ladakh was invaded by Mirza Haider Dughlat in 1531. He has given an account of the campaigns in his Tarikh-i-Rashidi as under:

> At Lahore some Kashmiris requested me to come to their rescue and attack Kashmir. I led an attack and defeated the enemy. The battle was very desperate. I conquered Kashmir on the second August of 1541.

This shows that Mirza Haider Duglat conquered Kashmir. After that Namgyal came to power in the 16th Century. Sovang Namgyal subdued the whole of Ladakh and established his capital at Leh in 1533 A.D. He succeeded in extending his kingdom to the outskirts of Lhasa. Sovang Namgyal passed away in 1555 A.D. and was succeeded by his brother Jamyang Namgyal. After that, in 1610, Namgyal became the king of Ladakh. He subdued Purang Zanskar, Spiti and even Tibet but failed to achieve complete success. After that he planned to annex Skardu but the latter obtained the help of Mughals and, after minor skirmishes, Singe Namgyal agreed to pay homage to Ladakh,

Singe Namgyal was succeeded by his son Deldan Namgyal in 1645 A.D. During his regime the ruler of Skardu invaded Ladakh. During the same period the Mughals also invaded Ladakh. At last Deldan Namgyal entered in an alliance with Mughals.

Deldan Namgyal was succeeded by his son Delek Namgyal in 1666 A.D. During his regime Tibet invaded Ladakh and defeated the Ladakhis. Delek implored help from the Mughal Governor of Kashmir and at last succeeded in driving out the Tibetans from Ladakhi soil. In return, he continued to pay homage to the Mughals. Nyima Namgyal came into power in 1695 A.D. and died in 1750 A.D. Ladakh continued to be ruled over by weak kings of the Namgyal dynasty. Tundop Namgyal came to power in 1820 A.D. He was succeeded by his son Sovang who spent his time in merry making and affairs of the state fell to disorder. This state of affairs led to others entering Ladakh. The Dogra General, Wazir Zorawar Singh, invaded and conquered Ladakh in 1883 A.D. and Ladakh became a part of Jammu and Kashmir state which had come into existence by the Treaty of Amritsar with the then British Government of India.

This historical account shows that the Ladakh has always been dominated by Indian rulers. This part of Jammu and Kashmir was neither dominated by the Chinese nor by Tibetans but ruled by Indians only. During the First Century A.D. Indian control over Ladakh in this period was reaffirmed as late as 733 A.D. by Lalitaditya Muktyapida. Even after the Tibetan influence reached Ladakh, the latter never constituted an integral part of Tibet. Ladakh came under the influence of Tibet due to socio-religious factors and not as a part of Tibetan sovereign power.

After the 10th Century A.D. Tibet's influence declined. Kashmir's influence was again to be found in the 12th Century A.D. Tributes were sent by Tibet to Kashmir in the 15th Century and periodic campaigns were waged by Kashmiri kings right across Ladakh. From 1586 onwards, with the commencement of Mughal rule in Skardu, Ladakh too came under the Mughal Empire in 1664. After that Ladakh was conquered by Gulab Singh of Jammu. The year 1841 saw battles between one of the Generals of Gulab Singh and Tibetan armies and, at this juncture, the Tibetans were joined by the Chinese. The venture was hardly successful enough to initiate any possession rights as the Chinese Tibetan armies were defeated before they reached Leh. However, a peace treaty was concluded in 1842 A.D. Four years later, in 1846, Kashmir came under the suzerainty of the British. The British recognised Gulab Singh as a Maharaja of the entire Ladakh Kashmir sector.

Indo-Tibet Border in the Middle Sector

In the Central Sector of the Indo-Tibet Border, from river Sutlej to the border of Nepal, the territorial extent of each country has been established by centuries of usage. Both sides of the border were inhabited by civilised people. Movement of traders and pilgrims across the border, based on the Himalayan crest line, was frequent. Barring a few small localities where minor disputes existed, the crest line of the great Himalayan range has been a tacitly agreed border and so far the Chinese have made no attempt to alter the status quo except in some isolated pockets in Bara Hoti, Jedong and Shipkila.

Evolution of India-Tibet Border in the Eastern Sector

In the Eastern sector, the sweep of the Himalayan crest between Bhutan in the west, and the Myanmar (then Burma) in the East was not recognised as the border by the Chinese. Although the Brahmaputra valley was always part of the Hindu cultural system during the last two millennia, it had not politically formed part of the Indian State. Moghul attempts to subjugate Assam had always ended in failure. The Ahoms of Burma invaded Assam in the early 17th Century and established their kingdom. The early settlers, however, retained their tribal independence.

DELIMITATION AND DEMARCATION OF INDIA'S NORTHERN BOUNDARY BY TREATIES

It is a reality that India's northern frontier has not been formally demarcated along its entire length. In fact the terrain of the northern frontier is very difficult and makes the demarcation on ground impossible at various places. However, India's northern frontier has been a recognised frontier on account of tradition, customs and geography. In the past, India's northern boundaries have been delimited and demarcated in a few sectors through the following treaties and agreements:

1. Peace Treaty of 1684 A.D.
2. Sanganli Treaty of 1815 A.D.
3. Peace Treaty of 1842 A.D.
4. An Agreement of 1852 A.D.
5. Sinchu La Pass treaty 1865 A.D.
6. Anglo-Chinese Convention of 1890 A.D.
7. Simla Convention of 1914 A.D.

Peace Treaty of 1684

Ladakh was an independent state which, in 1664 A.D., came under the suzerainty of the Mughal empire. The Treaty of 1684 A.D. was signed at the end of Ladakh-Tibet war in which the frontier between Ladakh and Tibet was determined. The final "delimitation" of the boundary line was approved by the treaty which was signed by the King of Ladakh Skyed-Ida-Ngeema-Gon and Mee-Pham-Wang-Po, the Tibetan plenipotentiary.

Sanganli Treaty of 1815

In the middle and the eastern sector of the India-China Border, Nepal, Sikkim and Bhutan are of concern to India. Bhutan is bound by a treaty with India, wherein her defence is India's responsibility. The Indo-Nepal boundary is peaceful and not disputed. It has evolved in two phases. The first phase was drawn up on the basis of the Sanganli Treaty in 1815 and the second phase was on the basis of the Anglo-Nepalese Treaty of 1921. The boundary has been successfully demarcated on the ground.

The total length of the "Sino-Nepal" border is 800 kilometres. The important passes on the border are Mustang, Kuti, Kindari, Wahug, Chung, Gola and Hethia. The world famous Mount Everest stands along this border. It follows the watershed principle and the Sino-Nepal border dispute was settled in 1960 with minor adjustments.

The Chinese have claimed near about 300 square miles of Bhutanese territory. The border dispute is yet to be settled and political negotiations for the settlement of the border continue.

Peace Treaty of 1842

After the treaty of 1684 A.D. the boundaries in the western sector were again confirmed and demarcated by the Treaty of 1842. It was signed on 16 and 17 September 1842. The parties of the treaty were on the one hand, Shri Khalsaji and Shri Maharaj Sahib Bahadur Raja Gulab Singh and on the other hand the Emperor of China and the Lama Guru of Lhasa; By this treaty the traditional boundary of Ladakh and Tibet was reaffirmed.

Treaty of 1852

This agreement was signed between the two Garpons or provincial Governors appointed by the Dalai Lama and the representative of Maharaja of Kashmir. The ancient demarcation of boundary between Ladakh and Tibet was once again reaffirmed by the treaty. The Treaty lays down that both the parties shall adhere strictly to the agreement thus arrived at between Tibet and Singpas (Kashmir) and the two frontier officers shall act in perfect accord and cooperation.

Anglo-Chinese Convention of 1890

The boundary of Sikkim with Tibet extends over about 225 kilometres. In 1890 Great Britain and China concluded a treaty whose conventions laid down that boundary between Sikkim and Tibet is the crest of mountain ranges separating the water flowing into Teesta in Sikkim from the water flowing into the Ma Chu of Tibet. This treaty was signed in Calcutta on 17 March 1890 and the border was demarcated in 1895. There is no dispute concerning Sikkim's boundary with Tibet as it was jointly demarcated. It is only now that the Chinese are trying to create a dispute in the Plateau area of North Sikkim.

Simla Conference of 1914

At this conference, the British Government proposed that an imaginary line be drawn along the Himalayan crest line from the Tri-junction of India-Bhutan and Tibet towards the eastern extremity of the Lohit division and this proposal approved the boundary between India and Tibet. The word imaginary was used for the reason that in those days it was not physically possible to reach the snow covered mountains peaks and set boundary identification marks. This proposal was drafted by Sir Henry McMahon, who was Secretary in the Political Department of British India. It was attended by the plenipotentiaries of the Government of India, Tibet and China having equal status. An exchange of notes between the Tibetan and India representative took place in March 1914, confirmed the boundary between India and Tibet. The Tibetan representative Lohchen Shatra accepted the proposal. It was actually delineated on two large scale maps, after full discussion, and these maps were signed and sealed by the Indian and Tibetan Plenipotentiaries. The boundary as delimited on the maps was later confirmed by the formal exchange of notes and the map itself was attached to the draft convention. The Chinese representative Ivan Chan, explained that unless he went back to Peking and explained the proposal to his Government he would not be able to sign it, although he had put his initials on the maps.

ARRIVAL OF THE BRITISH AND AN ATTEMPT AT DEMARCATION

Between 1684 and 1914 an attempt was made to delimit and demarcate India's northern border with Tibet and China. To check the Russian threat, the British sincerely made efforts to demarcate Ladakh's border with Tibet and Sinkiang but due to poor response from the Chinese and their internal problems, Ladakh's frontier with Tibet and Sinkiang remained un-demarcated.

Vance Agnew and Alexander Cunningham Survey

Boundary Commissioner Vance Agnew and his assistant Capt. Alexander Cunningham were among the pioneers in fixing the boundary between Tibet and Ladakh. Agnew's proposal for the boundary was the most westerly of the many variants. It linked Chushul Donchok and Lanak La. Northwards the border ran along the general line of the Karakoram range and included the valleys of Shyok, Galwan and Chipchap rivers to the Karakoram Pass. This was the first attempt to define the boundary in Ladakh by an officer of the Government of India. The area left out however, was Aksai Chin, the unexplored desolation that stretches eastward from Ladakh.

The Johnson Line 1865

Since the whole substance of India's title to Aksai Chin derives from Johnson's claim and his survey, it is necessary to examine his attempt in detail. He was a junior civilian sub-assistant in the Survey of India. Since he was Indian-born the British treated him as inferior which forced him to go into the service of the Maharaja of Kashmir and carry out the survey on his behalf in 1864-65. This survey was eventually accepted by the British and maps handed over by them to India at the time of Independence showed the Johnson Line as the border between India and Tibet. The Chinese transgressed this line, on their occupation of Tibet in 1950-51, to construct their Western Highway through it from 1952 onwards. Later, in order to give depth to this highway, the Chinese extended their occupation of Aksai Chin further westwards. India has weakened its case in Aksai Chin because, in 1951, the Indian Government published a White Paper on Aksai Chin and attached a Survey of India map which showed Aksai Chin in colour wash and the Johnson Boundary not marked on the map. Although the map was withdrawn later, but the damage has been done.

Map 1: Ladakh and Aksai Chin

McCartney McDonald Line 1899

Later, the British felt that perhaps the Johnson Line had moved too far forward to the North East and also it did not follow any watershed in the Aksai Chin area. Sir C. McDonald, a Secretary in the Government of India and his assistant McCartney then proposed another boundary in 1899. The proposal was like this:

> "Commencing on the little Pamir from the point at which the Anglo-Russian Boundary Commission of 1895 A.D. completed their work. It runs south-east crossing the Karachikar stream and Mintaka, Aghazi, then proceeding in the same direction, it joins at Karchenai Pass the crest of the main ridge of the Muztagh range. It follows this to the south passing by Khunjerab Pass and continues southwards to the peak just north of the Shimshal Pass. At this point, the boundary leaves the crest and follows a spur running approximately parallel to the road from the Shimsal to the Hunza Post at Darwaza. The line turning South through the post crosses the road at this point and then ascends the nearest high spur and rejoins the main crest line and follows it through Muzlagh, Gasherbrun, Saltoro and passes through the Karakoram Pass. From the Karakoram Pass, the crest of the range runs East for about half a degree and then turns to little below the 35th Parallel of North Latitude. Rounding it, what in our maps is shown as the source of the Karakash, the line of hills to be followed runs Northeast to the point East of Kizil Jilga and from there in a South easterly direction follows the Lak Tsung range until that meets the spur running South from the Juen Lun range which hitherto had been shown on our maps as the Eastern boundary of Ladakh. This is little East of 80° East Longitude.

This is the only proposal conveyed by the British to the Chinese. When no response was received from them, the British started regarding the Johnson Line as the boundary between British India and Tiber and this was shown on the maps handed over to India at the time of Independence.

The McMahon Line

In the West, a trade route from Lhasa passed through Towang, over the Sala Pass through Dirang to the market town of Udalgudi. This area was inhabited by the Monpa tribe which paid obeisance to the Dalai Lamas. Later, a monastery was built at Towang, the birth place of the 5th Dalai Lama and the Towang salient down to Dirang was administered by Tibetan Lamas. It was only in 1951 that Indian control was extended to Towang and further to the McMahon Line.

It needs to be clearly understood that, historically, the Manchus never administered Tibet. Their claim to suzerainty dates back to a temporary occupation of Lhasa in 1720. The Manchus perceived a direct threat to their suzerainty only when Col. Younghusband led an expeditionary force to Lhasa in 1904. Determined to assert its rights, the Manchu Government sent a force under Gen. Chavo Erhfeng to Tibet 1910 and for the first time Chinese rule was extended to Tibet. However, the sudden collapse of the Manchu empire in China, in 1911, weakened the Chinese hold on Tibet and it became an independent country till 1950 when it was invaded by the communist forces and forcibly made a part of China.

Even after the fall of Manchu empire, the Chinese did not cede control of Tibet. The President of the

Map 2: The McMahon Line

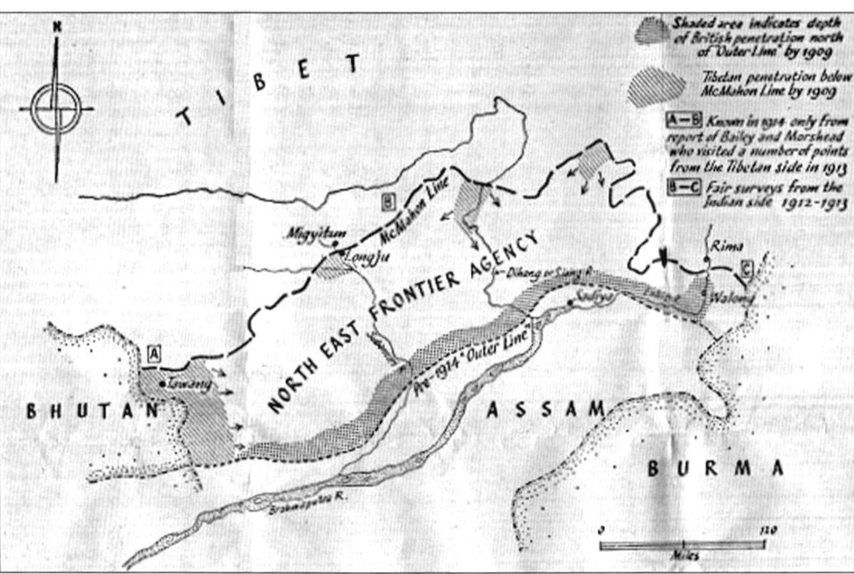

newly formed republic, Dr. Sun Yat Sen, publicly issued a decree that Tibet was treated as an integral part of China. It was then that the British Government began to formulate plans for a tripartite conference of British, Chinese and Tibetan representatives to determine trans-Himalayan realities such as the fact of Tibetan autonomy and the nature of Chinese rights in Tibet and the alignment of the Indo-Tibet border in the North Eastern sector. This resulted in the famous Simla conference of October 1913 chaired by Sir Henry McMahon, the Foreign Secretary of Government of India. According to the agreed boundary it ran along the highest crest of Assam Himalayas, from the Bhutan border in the west all the way to border of Burma with Chinese Yunan province. Interestingly the Tibetan Government agreed to concede the Towang salient to India. The British however, did not insist on its vacation by the Tibetan representative and they continued to rule it till 1951 when India extended their control over the Towang salient. At that time the Chinese made no protest. It was only later, in order to force its illegal occupation of Aksai Chin, that the Chinese started denouncing the McMahon Line as an imperialist legacy forced on them when they were weak. This is where the dispute started.

TERRITORIAL CLAIMS BY CHINA AND INDIA'S STAND

According to Beijing, the boundary as drawn in Indian maps cut about 38,000 square kilometres deep into Chinese territory. The Chinese claim that neither British nor Indian administration has ever extended to these places in the past or the present. The Chinese claim some 50,000 square miles of Indian territory. The border dispute generally relates to these areas.

(a) **Western Sector**: The boundary of Jammu and Kashmir with Sinkiang and with Tibet is a disputed territory measuring some 13,000 to 15,000 kilometres. In this area, China claims the Aksai Chin district, the Changchenmo valley, Pangong Lake and the Spangur Tso area of Northern Ladakh as well as a strip of land about 5,000 square kilometres down the entire length of Eastern Ladakh.

(b) **The Middle Sector**: Conforms to the boundary with Himachal Pradesh and Uttar Pradesh with Tibet. The Chinese claim nearly 1,300 square kilometres in this area. Barahoti, Nilang Jadhang Sangcha Milla, Lapthal Chue-Chuje, Shipki Pass and Pussing, Sundo Barahoti with an area of about a four square kilometres. Nilang Jadhang belongs to Tibet. Tibet has been exercising jurisdiction over this area. Sangcha Mall and Lapthal, claimed by China, are other areas situated in the Almora district of Uttar Pradesh. They are 3 to 10 kilometres South of the border. Another claim of China pertains to Nilang Jadhang, an area of about 140 square kilometres on the main watershed and to the North of the main Himalayan range.

(c) **The Eastern Sector**: Conforms to the boundary of Arunachal Pradesh with Tibet. In this sector, the Chinese claim about 94,700 square kilometres of Indian territory, including the Kameng Frontier division and three fourths of the Lohit division of the erstwhile North East Frontier Agency, Tawang and Longju area are the most critical in this area. (Sikkim's border with Tibet is already demarcated on ground. There is no dispute regarding Sikkim's boundary with China (Tibet).

India's Claim

India's northern border is defined and recognised by various treaties, customs and traditions by both the countries. India claims that Chinese have occupied 2,500 square miles in the Western Sector (Ladakh) in addition to 12,000 square miles occupied in 1962 through aggression. In the Eastern Sector, 2,000 square miles of Indian territory is under illegal occupation of China after declaring a unilateral cease fire on 21 November 1962. China has also occupied Longju which is on the McMahon Line.

BORDER TALKS

Border Talks Prior to the 1962 War

In Ladakh and Assam, the Nehru Government without initiating negotiations with the Chinese decided to claim the Johnson line in the West and Mc Mahon Line in the east as the boundary with Tibet. In the early 1950s, Zhou En Lai suggested to the Indian ambassador in Beijing that since there was no territorial dispute or controversy between India and China, the question of their border should be settled as early as possible. Since there was no follow up to that proposal, the Government of India presumed that China accepted the Johnson Line in the West and McMahon Line in the East as the border and decided not to raise this issue officially with the Chinese Government. In the mid-1950s, a Chinese map showed Assam as Chinese territory. Nehru raised this issue with Zhou En Lai. Zhou's glib reply was that these were old maps and the communist government had not got time to revise them.

From Zhou En Lai's statements about border

problems between 1954 and 1956, it appears that the Chinese attitude at that time was moderate enough only the Eastern sector because in the West the Chinese had started construction of the strategically important western highway between Xingjian and Tibet which passes through Aksai Chin. India remained unaware of this activity till 1958 when the Indian Embassy in Beijing sent a report about it. A patrol was sent by India to Haji Langar, in Aksai Chin, was taken prisoner by Chinese and not released for two months. The Government of India protest was summarily rejected by the Chinese who claimed Aksai Chin to be Chinese territory against all historical evidence and treaties. The period of goodwill was over. The Chinese repressive measures in Tibet resulted in the Dalai Lama's flight to India in March 1959. The enthusiastic welcome given to him started a confrontation along the eastern borders. It was at that time that the Chinese started talking of an east – west swap wherein India were to acknowledge Chinese de facto occupation of Aksai Chin in return for China agreeing to the McMahon Line as the boundary in the eastern sector. India however, hardened its stance. China, thereafter, decided to teach India a lesson which resulted in the border war in 1962. Negotiations were thereafter frozen till the 1988 visit of Rajiv Gandhi to China.

Border Talks post-1988

The Chinese very seriously and sincerely expressed their desire to resolve the border question at the earliest. During the discussion, both the parties suggested a set of guiding principles as a basis for Sino-Indian dialogue. China put forward five principles:

1. Equality.
2. Friendly consultation.
3. A fair and reasonable settlement.
4. Mutual understanding and accommodation.
5. A comprehensive solution.

India suggested a set of six principles as against the Chinese set of five principles:

1. An early solution of the border problem.
2. A just solution taking into account the legitimate interests of both the sides.
3. A common approach and a basis for discussion.
4. Steps to create an appropriate climate.
5. Efforts to settle the border issue in each Sector.

Joint Working Group

During Rajiv Gandhi's visit to China, both countries agreed to set up a "Joint Working Group" to evolve a consensus border between India and China. The Joint Working Group was also bound to a time frame of two to three years. This attempt was perhaps the most serious one to resolve the border dispute on the principle of mutual understanding and accommodation which would be acceptable to the people of both the countries in terms of mutual interests and benefits.

The Joint Working Group is led by the foreign secretary on the Indian side and the Deputy Foreign Minister from the Chinese side. During Rajiv Gandhi's visit to China, it was also determined that JWG will meet at stipulated intervals and make recommendations to their respective government.

There were three main objectives of establishing Joint Working Group:

(a) Make concrete recommendations for an overall solution to the boundary question within a definite time frame. That solution must be acceptable to both the parties which would be in their mutual interests and mutual benefits.

(b) Ensure the peace and tranquillity in the border area, until the final settlement is arrived at.

(c) The working group conceived as a joint undertaking involves institutions like foreign minister, military experts, surveyors, communications experts and legal bodies on both the sides.

India China Expert Group

An "Expert Group" has been set up to assist the Joint Working Group in implementation of the Agreement on Maintenance of Peace and Tranquillity along the Line of Actual Control in the India-China border areas, which was signed in Beijing on 7 September 1993 during Prime Minister Mr. P.V. Narasimha Rao's visit to China.

The first meeting of the India-China Expert Group was held at New Delhi from 2 to 4 February 1994. The Indian delegation was led by Shri Shivshankar Menon, Joint Secretary (North-East), Ministry of External Affairs. It consisted of representatives from the Ministries of External Affairs, Defence and Home Affairs, the Army Headquarter and the Survey of India. The Chinese delegation, which also included experts from their concerned departments, was led by Mr. Fu Xuezhang, Deputy Director Asian Department, Ministry of Foreign affairs of the People's Republic of China.

During the first meeting of the Expert Group, after discussion, both the sides reached basic agreement on many issues relating to its mandate, future tasks and methodology and noted with satisfaction that the situation along the India-China border area is peaceful. The issues agreed upon were:

(a) The importance of effective confidence-building measures and discussed on furthering such measures.
(b) The two sides exchanged views on the drafts on prior notification of military exercises and prevention of air intrusions across the India-China LAC. (These drafts were prepared by Indian side).
(c) The two sides also agreed that additional designated points for meetings between the border personnel of the two countries will be established at Nathu La Pass in the Sikkim sector and a point to be agreed in the middle sector of the India-China border areas. It important that the Border Security personnel of India and China hold scheduled and flag meetings at Bum La Pass and Spanggur Gap Pass in the eastern and western sectors respectively.

Status Report—Special Representatives' Talks

A joint status report of the 15 rounds of special representatives' talks to resolve the vexed India-China boundary dispute has concluded that both sides are far from their goal despite some stated accomplishments. A bigger concern that has emerged is that there are serious differences in interpreting the 2005 agreement on the political parameters and guiding principles for the settlement of the boundary question, which is so far the most importance achievement of the three-stage process to arrive at a political solution. Significantly, sources said, these differences seem to wax and wane depending on the strategic climate at that point in time.

The exercise has shown that differences dominate despite positive proclamations. To begin with, the Chinese side has claimed close to 60,000 square kilometres in Arunachal Pradesh, which may be lesser than its earlier claims but remains significant and includes Tawang. The Chinese believe this is in tune with Article III of the Guiding Principles, which states that both sides will "make meaningful and mutually acceptable adjustments to their respective positions on the boundary question, so as to arrive at a package settlement to the boundary question".

The Indian understanding of meaningful adjustments is, however, different and does not involve large chunks of land. New Delhi believes that adjustments would mean minor territorial give-and-take in the border areas during the process of demarcating a common line. These extreme interpretations on both sides have meant that Chin's emphasis on concessions from India in the eastern sector has only increased through the dialogue process, particularly in the rounds after 2005. This is when the Special Representatives' started working on a framework agreement – the second stage of what is a three-stage settlement process.

The political impossibility of any Indian government giving up large territory in the eastern sector to achieve this settlement has not been recognised by the Chinese side in all these rounds. Instead, China has thrown back the argument that an Indian concession in this sector is a political pre-requisite for any leadership in Beijing, pointing to Article V of the guiding principles that mentions taking into account "national sentiments".

BORDER MANAGEMENT

The First Attempt—Colombo Conference Proposals, 10-12 December 1962

1. The Conference considers that the existing de facto ceasefire period is a good starting point for a peaceful settlement of the Indian Chinese conflict.
2. (a) With regard to the Western Sector, the Conference would like to make an appeal to the Chinese Government to carry out their 20 kilometres withdrawal of their military posts as has been proposed in the letter of Prime Minister Chou En-lai to Prime Minister Nehru of November 21 and November 28, 1962.
   (b) The Conference would make an appeal to the Indian Government to keep their existing military position.
   (c) Pending a final solution of the border dispute, the area vacated by the Chinese military withdrawals will be demilitarised zone to the administered by civilian posts of both sides to be agreed upon, without prejudice to the rights of the previous presence of both India and China in that area.
3. With regard to the Eastern Sector, the Conference considers that the line of actual control in the areas recognised by both the Governments could serve as a ceasefire line to their respective positions. Remaining areas in this sector can be settled in their future discussions.
4. With regard to the problems of the Middle Sector, the Conference suggests that they will be solved by peaceful means, without resorting to force.
5. The Conference believes that these proposals, which could help in consolidating the ceasefire,

once implemented should pave the way for discussions between representatives of both parties for the purpose of solving problems entailed in the ceasefire position.

6. The Conference would like to make it clear that a positive response for the proposed appeal will not prejudice the position of either of the two Governments as regards its conception of the final alignment of the boundaries.

Clarifications Given By the Representatives of the Colombo Powers to the Government of India, 13th January, 1963

Upon request from the Government of India, the following clarifications of paragraphs 2, 3 and 4 of the Colombo Conference proposals were given by the delegations of Ceylon, U.A.R. and Ghana:

Western Sector

(a) The withdrawal of Chinese forces proposed by the Colombo Conference will be 20 kilometres as proposed by Prime Minister Chou En-lai to Prime Minister Nehru in the statement of the Chinese Government dated 21 November, and in Prime Minister Chou En-lai's letter dated 28 November 1962, i.e. from the line of actual control between the two sides as of 7 November 1959, as defined in Maps III and V circulated by the Government of China.

(b) The existing military posts which the forces of the Government of India will keep will be on and up to the line indicated in (i) above.

(c) The demilitarised zone of 20 kilometres created by Chinese military withdrawals will be administered by civilian posts of both sides. This is a substantive part of the Colombo Conference proposals. It is as to the location, the number of posts and their composition that there has to be an agreement between the two Governments of India and China.

(d) Chinese forces will continue to remain in the areas captured in 1962 War.

Eastern Sector

The Indian forces can, in accordance with the Colombo Conference proposals, move right up to the south of the line of actual control, i.e. the McMahon Line except for the two areas on which there is difference of opinion between the Governments of India and China. Chinese forces, similarly, can move up to the north of McMahon Line except for these two areas. The two areas referred to as the remaining areas in the Colombo Conference proposals, arrangements in regard to which are to be settled between the Governments of India and China, according to the Colombo Conference proposals, are Chedong or the Thagla ridge area and the Longju area, in which cases there is a difference of opinion as to the line of actual control between the two Governments.

Middle Sector

The Colombo Conference desired that the status quo in this sector should be maintained and neither side should do anything to disturb the status quo.

Western Sector

Chinese forces continue to remain in the areas captured in the 1962 war.

Conclusion

Sino-Indian border dispute has defied solution for over six decades now. While India is keen to resolve it, the Chinese uses this dispute as a means to keep India unbalanced and anxious. Their strategic aim is to keep India tied down in South Asia so that it does not emerge as a competitor to China on the bigger state in Asia. A prudent course of action will, therefore, be to enhance economic engagement with China while keeping the border issue on the back burner. Implicit in this is that capacity building must continue. It needs to be borne in mind that the Chinese only understand the language of power and have no time or respect for those who try to appease them—a lesson that ought to have been learnt after the 1962 war. Hopefully it is not too late.

EXAMINING PAKISTAN ARMY'S RADICAL TILT

Wilson John, Senior Fellow, Observer Research Foundation, New Delhi

Introduction

There is a renewed global focus on Pakistan Army today because of its covert and overt alliance with extremist and terrorist groups, creating an ever-increasing threat to the world. This duplicitous policy of a nuclear-armed force has allowed al Qaida, the Taliban, and its various criminal, sectarian and extremist surrogates to transform a part of Pakistan into a sanctuary of radical ideology and terrorism. These developments threaten the world in many unpredictable ways; one of the most perilous being the possibility of nuclear weapons, materials or even a nuclear establishment falling into the maverick hands of terrorist groups or extremist elements operating within or outside Pakistan.

This paper explores, within the above context, a disturbing but a palpable possibility: Is the Pakistan Army transforming itself from a still somewhat professional armed force of a Muslim nation into an Army of Islam?

Today's Pakistan faces three major threats that have converged since the 11 September 2001 attack on the US, posing an 'existential threat' to the country and, as a consequence, to global stability. These are:

(a) the alignment of State-supported home-grown *jihadi* groups with al Qaida,

(b) persistent fears of degeneration into a failed State, and

(c) increasing unease over the security of the nation's nuclear establishment.

Although there are many who argue, with vehement conviction, that Pakistan is neither a Somalia-in-the-making nor is there any possibility of its nuclear weapons and materials falling into the hands of extremist elements, there nevertheless are adequate indicators in recent events to disallow one to take any comfort from such assurances.

Two factors suffice to keep one on tenterhooks over such a possibility. First is the very real presence of al Qaida-linked terrorist groups in Pakistan and their increasing strength in some regions of the nation. These groups today control over 11 per cent of Pakistan's territory—about 89,568 sq kms.[1] A 2009 BBC survey[2] estimated that 24 per cent of North West

[1] Dr Farrukh Saleem, Where is the Pakistan Army?, *The News*, April 26, 2009. Dr Saleem is the executive director of the Centre for Research and Security Studies.

[2] Pakistan conflict map, *BBC*, 13 May 2009.

Frontier Province (NWFP) and Federally Administered Tribal Areas (FATA) were under 'permanent' Taliban presence while an additional 38 per cent showed fluctuating Taliban presence.

Second is the increasing number of terrorist attacks carried out by these groups in several parts of Punjab[3] in the past few years (particularly after the Lal Masjid military operations of July 2007). These attacks have taken place in Islamabad, Rawalpindi, Wah, Sargodha and Lahore—all of them the nucleus of Pakistan's nuclear establishment. Most of these attacks have been suicide bombings, but many of them were armed assaults,[4] clearly indicating the capability of the terrorist groups to build up and exploit a 'local support base' in these cities.

Table 1: Casualties of Violence - 2013[5]

Month	Killed	Injured	Total Casualties
January	591	373	964
February	454	324	778
March	570	392	962
April	429	544	973
May	622	914	1536
June	616	535	1151
July	572	642	1214
August	432	342	774

Equally distressing has been Pakistan Army's dithering attitude towards these groups. The Army's action has swung back and forth between all-out offensive actions, with combat helicopters and artillery guns, to hastily signed peace deals.[6] General Pervez Musharraf, in his years as the President (2002-2007), engaged in such policy shifts with alarming alacrity. The heavy bombardment of towns and villages in southern and northern Waziristan between 2002 and 2004 was followed by a series of peace deals with various Taliban/tribal leaders –acts of compromise which only encouraged the terrorist groups to coalesce into a stronger *jihadi* network.

His successor, General Ashfaq Parvez Kayani, was part of these policy decisions, first as the Director General Military Operations and subsequently as the DG ISI. It is not really surprising, therefore, to witness such tactical swings between muscular military responses and 'operational pauses' in Malakand division, a large chunk of NWFP which was effectively ceded to a local militant group in February 2009. It is undeniable that such frequent 'operational pauses' have helped the Taliban and its allied groups to create a support base among the people, first in the tribal areas and subsequently in North West Frontier Province (NWFP), as also to regroup and challenge, with greater ferocity and audacity, the writ of the State.[7]

For the Army, the Taliban has never really been an adversary but a 'strategic asset'.[8] Terrorist groups have been an integral part of the Army's arsenal against its eastern neighbour, India and, on its volatile western border, the dysfunctional state of Afghanistan. Taliban's presence and strength in Afghanistan offer a 'strategic depth' to Pakistan, by strengthening Islamabad's hand in the affairs of Kabul, thereby helping to keep India at bay. Islamabad has long viewed Indian presence in Afghanistan as an obstacle to Pakistan's influence over its extended neighbourhood—the Islamic republics' in Central Asia. This tacit as well as open support has been evident even after the Mumbai terrorist attacks in November 2008.[9]

---

[3] For a detailed examination of the issue, see Dr Hassan Abbas, Defining the Punjabi Taliban Network, *CTC*, Volume 2, Issue 4, April 2004; Prof. Kalim Bahadur, Islamisation of Pakistan: A case study of Punjab, *Issue Brief*, Observer Research Foundation, New Delhi, 2007.

[4] Attack on a Mianwali police post, suicide bombing near the Sargodha Air Base (where F-16s designed to carry nuclear weapons operate from) and Wah cantonment, a major military industrial complex closely linked to the nuclear weapons programme.

[5] http://crss.pk/story/4756/monthly-report-august-2013

[6] A good reference is Pervez Musharraf, *In the Line of Fire - A Memoir*, Simon & Schuster, New York, 2006; A balanced critique can be found in Ashley Tellis, Pakistan's Record on Terrorism: Conflicted Goals, Compromised Performance, *The Washington Quarterly*, Spring, 2008. A defence on Pakistan's record can be seen at Seven Questions: Pakistan's War on Terror, *Foreign Policy*, July 2006.

[7] The ferocity of military offensives after the collapse of every peace deal has been an indication of the recouping of the Taliban and other terrorist elements in FATA and elsewhere. The recent military offensive in Swat and Buner (May 2009), where the Taliban was allowed to usurp the State through a controversial peace deal, witnessed a fierce fighting and a very high displacement of residents from the area. Refer to Farhat Taj, The army finally gets it right, *The News*, May 9, 2009; Troops kill at least 180 militants in Swat *Dawn*, May 10, 2009; Sceptics question Pakistan's anti-Taliban resolve, *Dawn*, May 10, 2009.

[8] David Sanger, *The Inheritance: The World Obama Confronts and the Challenges to American Power, Harmony, 2009*. Sanger, a New York Times correspondent, referred to a transcript given to Mike McConnel, the Director of National Intelligence in May 2008, which had Pakistan Army chief General Ashfaq Pervez Kayani calling Taliban leader Jalaluddin Haqqani as a 'strategic asset".

Though many believe that the Pakistani state was incapable of dealing with these powerful terrorist groups,[10] the real reason for the civilian and military leadership to stay away from taking the battle home lies elsewhere. The Army was simply not keen on taking on its 'strategic assets' and 'patriots'[11] while launching military offensives against those who refused to follow the GHQ command. Noted US counter-insurgency expert, David Kilcullen, summed it up with a typical military bluntness –"substantial parts of the Pakistani security establishment are complicit with the enemy, whether through incompetence, intimidation or ill intent".[12] The problem was not merely that of skill but also of will.[13]

This complicity, to the Pakistani mind, is justified where India is concerned. A majority of Pakistanis have for long been made to believe that it is the looming military presence of a 'hostile' India on its eastern borders which compels Pakistan to adopt countervailing covert strategies. This is only a part of the picture. The other part, largely unstated and absent in western discourses, is the Pakistan Army's raison d'être, which is to complete the 'unfinished agenda' of Partition,[14] which is to annex Kashmir[15] and keep India engaged in a prolonged battle with terrorist groups "groomed and financed" by different Islamabad agencies.[16]

What complicates the situation many times over is the fact that the Pakistan Army, over the years, has become "culturally sympathetic to the extremists". Not only have the armed forces and its intelligence wing, the Inter Services Intelligence (ISI), been exploiting religion for years as an instrument of covert war, but there is also evidence of their office cadre and its rank and file are increasingly becoming ideologically aligned with terrorist groups[17] like LeT and TNSM.

Well known expert, Ahmed Rashid has pointed out that Frontier Corps, a paramilitary force led by officers deputed from Pakistan Army, was "imbued with *jihadist* ideas and motivations".[18] There are numerous instances of regular officers and men from the Army involved in terrorist activities either directly or indirectly as facilitators and trainers for groups like LeT and JeM.

Tanzeem-ul Ikhwan, for instance, is a radical group of retired army men and officers which has been advocating a 'one-per cent' formula to convert Pakistan into an Islamic country. Ikhwan has often trained and sent cadres to train with LeT.[19] The fact that its leaders were all retired senior Army officers drew 'hundreds of serving officers and soldiers' to the group's ideological training sessions. Lt. General Hamid Gul, a former chief of ISI who was involved in the Afghan jihad, called it a 'soft Islamic revolution'. He argued that "Pakistani Army soldiers have always been religious, but now a growing number of officers have turned Islamist".[20]

1947 and Kashmir

In August 1947, about 200,000 Muslim soldiers, drawn out of the erstwhile British Indian Army, formed part of the Pakistan Army. It was certainly not a very homogenous group, though they shared a common faith. There were apparent differences among the Muslim soldiers and officers. One, the

---

9 For a succinct analysis of this relationship, refer to author's *ORF Policy Brief*, Concerted International Action Needed to Rein in Pakistan Terror Groups, Feb. 17, 2009. Accessed at http://www.orfonline.org/cms/export/orfonline/modules/policybrief/attachments/Policy-brief_1234853722674.pdf

10 Shuja Nawaz, Pakistan's Army: fighting the wars within, *Seminar*, April 2008.

11 Army official calls Baitullah Mehsud, Fazlullah 'patriots', *The News*, December 1, 2008.

12 Ibid.

13 See the testimony of Lt. General David W Barno, a former commander of the U.S. and Coalition Forces in Combined Forces Command-Afghanistan as part of Operation Enduring Freedom before the *US House Armed Services Committee*, April 23, 2009.

14 National Security and Pakistan's Foreign Policy. *Pakistan Horizon*., April 1990, The article was based on the address by Mr Iqbal Akhund, Advisor to the Prime Minister on Foreign Affairs and National Security, on "National Security and Pakistan's Foreign Policy in a Changing World" at the Pakistan Institute for International Affairs, April 5, 1990.

15 An excellent reference to Pakistan Army's Kashmir agenda is Praveen Swami's *India, Pakistan and the Secret Jihad: The covert war in Kashmir*, 1947-2004, Routledge, 2007.

16 Hassan Abbas, *Pakistan's Drift into Extremism: Allah, the Army, and America's War on Terror*, Pentagon Press, India, 2005, pp 201-216.

17 Daveed Gartenstein-Ross, Fixing Our Pakistan Problem, *The Journal of International Security Affairs*, Spring 2009.

18 Ahmed Rashid, Pakistan's Continued Failure to Adopt a Counterinsurgency Strategy, *CTC Sentinel*.

19 Ikhwan's one per cent formula is that even if one per cent of Pakistan's population—1.7 million (170 million)—is converted to its idea, the objective of converting Pakistan into a fully Islamic nation would be achieved. Details of the group can be found in the author's yet-to-be published *Coming Blowback: How Pakistan is endangering the world*, Rupa, 2009.

20 Zahid Hussain, Young holy warriors, *Newsline*, February 2001.

new army consisted largely of Punjabis and Pathans, with the former in majority among both the officers and the troops. This was because the Punjabis formed the biggest ethnic bloc in the British Indian Army. But despite their overwhelming majority, the Punjabis remained deprived of the top slots in the Army between 1947 and 1972—Ayub Khan was a Hindko speaking Pathan, Musa a Persian speaking Mongol-Hazara and Yahya Khan a Persian speaking Qizilibash. General Tikka Khan was the first Punjabi Chief of Army Staff.[21] It was natural that the Punjabi officers nursed a grudge against the Pathan domination of the higher offices.[22]

Table 2: Ethnic Composition of the Pakistani Army

Ethnic Groups/ Provinces	Percentage of population	Percentage of Officers	Percentage of Other Ranks
Punjab	56%	65%	70%
NWFP (Pathans)	16%	22%	25%

Adapted from Anita M Weiss, and S Zulfiqar Gilani (eds), Power and Civil Society in Pakistan (Karachi: Oxford University Press, 2001), p. 200.

Second was the impact of the newly formed State's challenge of integrating the 'Bengali sub-nation'[23] within the federation. Though the Bengalis formed the largest ethno-cultural group and, in fact, were in majority (almost 54 per cent of the population), their poor representation in the forces presented unique challenges to the process of integration. Aware of these problems, the founding President, Jinnah, had ordered the raising of Bengali units, but Ayub Khan, who had a poor opinion of the Bengali's martial qualities, discontinued the practice, a retrogressive step which had its fall out in 1971.

The third visible difference among the new soldiers was caused by sectarian identities. Though the Army was predominantly Sunni, Shia men and officers had their representation in the force, although the exact number of such men and officers remain undocumented. These differences came out in the open after Zia began sending officers on deputation to Saudi Arabia. Since the Saudis insisted on Sunni officers, Shias felt aggrieved.[24] The most credible conspiracy theory, involving the role of a Shia officer from Pakistan Air Force in the assassination of President Zia-ul Haq in August 1988, could be taken as an indicator of the sectarian divides within the military.

At the time of Independence, there were men and officers from other sects as well, among whom Ahmadia officers merit a special mention. The Ahmadia officers had risen to higher positions in the British Indian Army, but found themselves isolated soon after Independence. The killing of an Ahmadia officer[25] near a military station in Quetta in 1947 became a precursor to the bloody anti-Ahmadia riots of 1953 in Punjab. The riots not only saw the Ahmadias, a sect within Islam, marked as *'kafirs'* or infidels like Hindus and Christians, but also set the tone for Pakistan to become a Sunni State. The riots and the subsequent actions taken by the Army to quell the riots accelerated the process of the Army's transformation into a political entity, and paved the way for the first Pakistani Chief of Army Staff, General Ayub Khan, to take over power from the civilian leadership.

These differences were subsumed, forcibly and otherwise, by using Islam as a political tool by the senior leadership to bind the new force together. This is how General Ayub Khan, widely perceived to be a liberal General and indeed carried on a running feud with radical parties like Jamaat-e-Islami (JI), articulated the Army's ideological compulsions succinctly in 1962. He said:

> "Pakistan came into existence on the basis of an ideology, which does not believe in differences of colour, race or language. It is immaterial whether you are a Bengali or a Sindhi, a Balochi or a Pathan or a Punjabi—we are all knit together by the bond of Islam".[26]

Such a process of 'artificial and forced homogenisation of diverse cultures and people' by the Army, ironically supported with equal fervour by Islamist parties like JI, has been one of the primary drivers of sectarian conflicts and *'jihadi'* struggles in Pakistan,[27] altering attitudes and inclinations within the armed forces.

Two strands of Islamisation were evident in the force's early years. Although the first generation of

[21] Major Agha Humayun, The Pakistan Army-From 1965 to 1971, Defence Journal, November 2007.

[22] Ibid.

[23] Raunaq Jahan, *Pakistan: Failure in national integration*, Columbia University Press, 1972, New York.

[24] Lt. General Faiz Ali Chishti, *Betrayals of Another Kind*, Asia Publishing House, London, 1989.

[25] Lawrence Zirring, *Pakistan in the Twentieth Century—A Political History*, Oxford, 1999.

[26] *Speeches and statements of Field Marshal Ayub Khan, Vol. 5*, Pakistan Publications, Karachi, 1962.

[27] Rubina Saigol, *The State and the limits of Counter-Terrorism: The Case of Pakistan and Sri Lanka*, Council of Social Sciences Pakistan (COSS), Islamabad, 2006.

officers came from the British Indian Army, trained at the Military Academy at Sandhurst, they were quick to adopt Islamic symbols. For instance, number 786 became the tactical number for the General Headquarters at Rawalpindi. In Islamic numerology, '786' represents the Arabic religious term, *Bismillah IrRahman IrRahim*. The number was etched or painted on all gateposts and army vehicles. The Army badge was designed as two crossed swords holding up an Islamic rising crescent and a five-pointed star against a green background, all equally evocative Islamic symbols. Although majority of the officers were not overtly fundamentalist in their belief, there was a general belief that "religious symbols and zeal in appropriate doses can boost the fighting abilities of rank and file, and battlefield commanders".[28]

The first example of Pakistan Army's use of religion as a weapon was the Kashmir raids of 1947-48. Incensed by the Maharaja of Kashmir's decision to go with India, Major General Akbar Khan,[29] Military Advisor to Pakistan's first Prime Minister Liaqat Ali Khan, launched an 'irregular' offensive to wrest Kashmir from India. It was not a religious but a political war aimed to correct what the Pakistan Army felt was a grossly erroneous demarcation of the political boundaries. Khan styled himself as 'General Tariq'[30] and invoked the cause of Islam to gather a *lashkar* (army) from the tribal areas to infiltrate and hold the ground thereafter. The move succeeded only partially, as Khan did not anticipate a determined counter-offensive by the Indian Army, a mistake which many successive Generals would continue to make.

Even though the Kashmir raids had failed to achieve its primary objective, it taught some key lessons to the Generals. First, they saw the immense potential of exploiting the power of religion and second, they discovered the tactic of using 'irregular forces' to act as the first line of offence—soldiers of a proxy war. The strategy was further reinforced when a study to craft military strategy, commissioned by General Ayub Khan in the early 50s, recommended the use of 'irregular' force to supplement the regular army, which was smaller than the Indian Army.[31]

This became quite apparent during the 1965 War when a wave of *jihadi* ideology, encouraged indirectly by Ayub Khan himself, swept through the officer cadre and men, especially when "Pakistan's military gains in the Rann of Kutch against India swept the country with an overwhelming Islamic sentiment and pride".[32] Sindh was renamed 'Babul Islam' to revive the great dream of an Islamic (Pakistani) re-conquest of India. The media fanned up a frenzy of *jihad*, extolling the virtues of Pakistan's soldiers of Islam.[33] Several junior officers who saw action in that war, came back to describe it as a "struggle of Islam and Un-islam".[34] Brigadier Gulzar Ahmad, a 1965-war veteran, was delirious enough to claim that "there was a hidden hand deflecting the rounds which would otherwise have taken a heavy toll of the advancing troops".[35]

The Army, later that year, launched Operations Gibraltar and Grand Slam 'to reinforce the Islamic orientation of an armed conflict with India'. When the Indian forces reached the doorstep of Lahore, Ayub Khan, in a broadcast to the nation, declared 'we are at war', invoking the *Kalima-e-Tayyaba* "to project the war as a virtual *jihad*: a conflict between Islam and *Kufr*".[36] This was the first time that the *jihadi* theme found place in the soldier's vocabulary.

There were other, clearly visible, signs of radicalisation taking place within the armed forces. Brigadier AR Siddiqui[37] was witness to such changes: "During my own extensive tours of the operational areas after the ceasefire, I found the front-line soldiers resonant with the *Kalima-i-Tayyaba* and the *Kalima-i-Shahadat*. Nothing uncommon for a Muslim soldier or civilian, only practised and recited louder than

---

[28] Hamid Hussain, The Martial Mind: Pakistan Officer Corps' thought process about defence, *Defence Journal*, September 2000.

[29] Major General Akbar Khan, *Raiders in Kashmir*, National Book Foundation, Islamabad, 1970; Rizwan Hussain, *Pakistan and the emergence of Islamic militancy in Afghanistan*, 2005, Ashgate Publishing, 2005. The tribal lashkars were drawn from the Mehsuds. Incidentally, one of the Mehsud leaders, Baitullah Mehsud, is spearheading the spread of Taliban in Pakistan.

[30] Moorish General Tariq ibn-Ziyad had invaded Spain in 711.

[31] Altaf Gauhar, Ayub Khan: *Pakistan's First Military Ruler*, p. 93.

[32] AR Siddiqui, Islam and the Military, *The Nation*, February 28, 2001.

[33] AR Siddiqui, *The Military in Pakistan-Image and Reality*, Vanguard Publications, Lahore,1996.

[34] Major General Tajammul Hussain Malik, *The Story of My Struggle* (Lahore, Jang Publishers, 1991). Malik was retired by Zia in 1976 for his fanaticism.

[35] Quoted in Hamid Hussian, The Martial Mind: Pakistan Officer Corps thought process about defence, *Defence Journal*, November 2000.

[36] Ibid.

[37] Brigadier Siddiqui was General Yahya Khan's public relations officer and remained the head of Inter Services Public Relations (ISPR) till his retirement.

usual. More bearded faces were in evidence than normal on the battle fronts....A number of officers I happened to meet would be reluctant even to have their pictures taken for the I.D. Cards. One of them carried an I.D. without the regulation photograph".[38]

Yahya and Bhutto Years

Although the Army under General Yahya Khan retained its professionally secular image with religion given importance only as a personal faith, things changed with the appointment of retired Major-General Sher Ali Khan as the Minister of Information and National Affairs. Sher Ali, a fundamentalist by belief and a strong Jamaat-e-Islami (JI) supporter, took it upon himself to work for the glory of Islam. Khan, a Pathan officer like his superior, indicated the increasing incidence of *'jihadi'* mindset among the officer cadre. Influenced by 'Islamic warriors' and 'defenders of Islam' concepts, these officers were far from averse to using religion as an instrument of State policy.

Khan and his men recruited 'volunteers' from JI and its student wing, Islami Jamiat Talaba (IJT) to fight the Bengali insurgency in East Pakistan. A large number of these 'volunteers' were drawn from the Punjab University's IJT cadres and were well educated; the Army trained them to crush secessionists—political leaders, journalists, artists, writers, activists and judicial officers—in the nation's eastern wing. JI also formed peace committees in East Pakistan to facilitate intelligence gathering for the Army. In return, the Army rewarded JI with seats in the East Pakistan Assembly.[39]

The Army began using Islamic slogans during the East Pakistan crisis. "For instance, during the fight for East Pakistan, the local commander, Lt. General Tikka Khan, quoted freely from Islamic texts in his talks to the beleaguered West Pakistani garrison reminding his forces of the great battles against infidels a proof of what Muslims could do".[40]

The anglicised Zulfiqar Ali Bhutto, who came to power after Yahya Khan was not averse to exploiting religion when it suited his political aims and encouraged the use of Islamic symbols and themes like "Islam our Faith, Democracy our Polity and Socialism our economy". Bhutto "openly championed Islamisation so that he could co-opt part of the opposition party".[41] He allowed regulations which let officers keep beards. Short pants were discarded from the uniform. He prohibited alcohol from the military messes and shifted the day off from Sunday to Friday. And, call it an irony of fate or a fatal mistake, it was Bhutto who picked up an obscure, orthodox General, Zia-ul Haq, over other more deserving officers to be his Chief of Army Staff.

Bhutto's efforts fell woefully short of winning the Army to its side. The force remained deeply sceptical of his intentions, more so after he commissioned a White Paper on Higher Defence Organisation which called for an absolute civilian supremacy over the military. Even though Bhutto deserved credit for putting the country on the path of becoming a nuclear power ("we will eat grass but make nuclear bombs!"), the Army developed an intense dislike for Bhutto's Pakistan People's Party (PPP). This propelled the military to develop closer alliance with Islamist parties like JI. Moreover, gross political manipulations and rampant corruption weakened political institutions, boosted Islamist organisations and strengthened the Army's hold over the country.

The ignominious surrender at Dhaka, the dismemberment of the country's eastern wing and the civilian premier's manipulations to subjugate the Army had a deep and lasting effect on the officers recruited during that critical period. Those who took part in the 1971 War against India and suffered the humiliation of defeat and dissection of the country developed an intense hatred towards India and realised the futility of engaging its neighbour on the east in a conventional war. The disillusioned officers crafted the strategy of an irregular warfare—a proxy war—choosing Kashmir as the first theatre for this experiment.

The most abiding influence on these officers and those who followed them in the period between 1978 and 1988 was the feverish pace of Islamisation that General Zia-ul Haq, a Mohajir General, had set in motion. Nicknamed *'maulvi'* among his peers, it was Zia, son of an overtly religious clerk, who systematically and radically changed what was, till then, essentially a professional army in the tradition of the British period. He invoked the triple motto of *Taqva* (piety), *Iman* (Islamic faith) and *Jihad-fi-Sabil-Allah* (Fight in the name of Allah).

---

[38] Ibid.

[39] Vali Nasr, *The Vanguard of Islamic Revolution*; Hussain Haqqani, *The Military and Mullah Alliance*, Stephen Cohen, *The Idea of Pakistan*, Oxford, 2005.

[40] Stephen Cohen.

[41] Vali Nasr.

Explaining the concept, Zia, in a Foreword to Brigadier General SK Malik's *Quranic Concept of War,* wrote "*Jihad fi sabilallah* is not the exclusive domain of the professional soldier, nor is it restricted to the application of military force alone...The professional soldier in a Muslim army, pursuing the goals of a Muslim state, cannot become 'professional' if in all his activities he does not take the 'colour of Allah'. The non-military citizen of a Muslim state must, likewise, be aware of the kind of soldier that his country must produce and the only pattern of war that his country's armed forces may wage".

The Pakistan Army later expanded these themes more elaborately. Iman, it said, is: to have faith and trust in Allah and consider oneself:

> A follower of none but Allah.
> And a follower of none but his messenger.
>
> The concept of "no deity except Allah" is always alive in the Muslim's heart. A Muslim recognizes that Allah alone is the Creator; that He alone is the Provider and Sustainer that He is the true Reality, the source of all things of all benefits and harms. This requires that He alone be worshiped and obeyed. "No deity except Allah" also includes the question of authority as the right to govern belongs to the One Who created him.
>
> Belief in Allah's messenger means accepting Prophet Muhammad (PBUH) as the last messenger sent by Him. Prophet Muhammad (PBUH) is the spokesman for God by His authority. The duty of Prophet Muhammad (PBUH) was not only to deliver the message which Allah revealed but also to explain it and put it into practice as an example to be followed by mankind.

Taqwa was explained as:

> The fear of Allah.
> Guarding ones tongue, hands and heart from evil.
> Righteous, piety and good conduct.

Taqwa connotes the sense of protecting oneself from moral peril, preserving one's virtue, and guarding oneself against the displeasure of Almighty. It is, thus, a kind of awareness or consciousness by means of which one protects oneself from sliding into evil.

Jihad-fi-Sabilillah was explained as:

> The real objective of Islam is to shift the lordship of man over man to the lordship of Allah on the earth and to stake one's life and everything else to achieve this sacred purpose. The Arabic word "Jihad" means to struggle "or" to strive. Inasmuch as "Jihad" is a struggle, it is a struggle against all that is perceived as evil in the cause of that which is perceived good, a cosmic and epic struggle spanning time and all dimensions of human thought and action, and transcending the physical universe. The Islamic Law regulates declaration of Jihad as also the limitations are imposed on its conduct. In Chapter II verse 190 of The Holy Quran the reference to the duty of the Muslims to "fight in the cause of God those who fight you and be not aggressors. God loveth not those who are aggressors".
>
> The Muslims when they are engaged in fighting are not to transgress the limits within which war is allowed to be waged and, in principle, they are not to be cruel or become revengeful. The general command to be just and fair is discernible from Chapter V. Verse 8:
>
> Oh, ye who believe stand out firmly for God as witness To fair dealings,
> And let not the hatred of other people to you make you swerve to wrong and depart from justice.
> Be just, that is next to piety. And fear God,
> Surely, Allah is aware of what you do

To encourage a faster Islamic transformation of the army, Zia saw to it that: new mosques were built within cantonments and training areas; Islamic texts were introduced into training courses; staff college libraries stocked with books on Islam, Islamic military ideology and practices and; middle-level officers were made to study and give examinations on Islam and Islamic military doctrine. Islamic teachings were introduced in the Pakistan Military Academy, Kakul.

Changes were made in the curriculum at staff colleges where new officers began studying and researching Islamic military practices, doctrine and strategy. A lecture series run by officer-scholar, Col. Abdul Qayyum, at the Command and Staff College formed the intellectual basis for the Islamic drive.[42] Qayyum lectured on Islamic theology and doctrine but adopted a more open and rationalist approach that made him a much sought after ideologue. The post of army '*mullahs*' was created to act as a bridge between profession and faith. The *mullahs* accompanied units into combat zones.[43] A Directorate of Religious Instruction was established at GHQ and religious handouts were published occasionally for the troops.

---

[42] FS Aijazuddin, *The Shifting Qiblah, Islamisation under General Zia ul Haq and Secularism under General Pervez Musharraf—The Pakistani Experience,* Paper presented at Conference on the Future of Secularism, Yale Center for International and Area Studies and Yale Center for the Study of Globalisation, Yale University, March 26-27, 2004.

[43] Stephen Cohen, *Pakistan Army.*

Zia was the first army chief and head of State to attend the annual meeting of the *Tablighi Jamaat* at Raiwind in Punjab.[44] Zia believed that "nobody but Allah made him the Chief of Army Staff and that he was on a divine mission to impose Islam in Pakistan".[45] He encouraged officers and troops to frequent *Tablighi* meetings more openly. *Tablighi Jamaat*, an organisation engaged in preaching and practicing Islam, has since been accused of encouraging radicalisation of Islam. A known *Tablighi* officer was Lt. Gen. Javed Nasir, the first in this rank with a full beard, who took over as the Director General of ISI in 1992. Nasir extended patronage to Deobandi *jihadi* groups to launch a proxy war in Kashmir and "authorised ISI collaboration with Dawood Ibrahim, a Muslim leader of the Bombay underworld, who organised the attack on the Bombay Stock Exchange on 12 March 1993".[46]

Zia openly encouraged his men and officers to pray, fast and distribute Islamic literature within the force.[47] Those who prayed five times a day, though it was not mandatory, found themselves in the shortlist for promotions more easily than others. Religious fervour became a passport to higher ranks and membership of JI and IJT proved to be useful.[48] In selection boards for officers, religious knowledge and habits received positive marks.[49] Hassan Askari Rizvi said "public display of Islamic orthodoxy and conservatism was an asset" and even "a method of career enhancement".

The Islamisation influenced ISI men and officers more because many of them, at least in the lower ranks, were recruited from the *madaris* immediately after the Afghan *jihad*.[50] (1990-1993) Recruits during this phase were made to take oath on the Koran and were taught Islamic subjects. They were also tested regularly for their grasp of religious knowledge to "raise the level of religious awareness among Pakistani troops and ensure indoctrination". [51] Many officers in the Army became attracted to JI's ideology and Mawdudi's teachings.[52] Zia in fact used to reward men and officers with a copy of Mawdudi's books.

Zia even wanted to redesign the national flag by inserting Arabic inscriptions and shift the Independence Day from August 14 to its equivalent in the Islamic calendar.[53] The proposals met with strong opposition from within the Army and he eventually dropped them. Stephen Cohen noted that "Zia's emphasis on Islam, in an already conservative society, encouraged fundamentalism in the Army".[54] Zia opened the door to intolerant bigots and fanatics. During his spell as the Army Commander, a number of subordinates got religious. A harmful legacy of the Zia years was the attempted coup in September 1995, led by Major General Zahir-ul Islam Abbasi, who spoke publicly about the need to Islamise both Pakistan and its Army. He wrote in the Staff College's professional journal of the importance of Islamisation and resisting the "domination of an aggressive, sinister India and other foreign, anti-Muslim states."

Musharraf and Kayani

The influences on the officer corps during the Musharraf regime (October 1999 -November 2007) and Kayani's tenure (November 2007 – November 2013) could provide clues to the Army's attitude towards religion in future. A study of the undercurrents of feelings and opinions within the senior and middle-ranking officers can help answer the principle question of this paper: is the Pakistan Army poised to become an Army of Islam?

The developments during Musharraf's tenure can be instructive in this regard. Musharraf had considerable public support when he took over power from an increasingly unpopular Nawaz Sharif, in October 1999. His popularity remained high until 11 September 2001, after which the US leaned on him to become a 'staunch non-NATO ally' of the US in the Global War on Terror. Although he

---

[44] Amir Mir, *The True Face of Jihadis*, Roli Books, 2006.

[45] Lt. Gen. Faiz Ali Chishti, *Betrayals of Another Kind*, Asia Publishing House, London, 1989.

[46] Hussain Haqqani, *Pakistan—Between Mosque and Military*, Vanguard Books, Lahore, 2005.

[47] Hussain Haqqani, Vali Nasr.

[48] Amir Mir.

[49] Hassan Abbas, *Pakistan's Drift into Extremism—Allah, the Army and America's War on Terror*, Pentagon Press, India 2005.

[50] PW Singer, 'Pakistan's Madrassas: Ensuring A System of Education, Not *Jihad*", *Analysis Papers #41*, Brookings Institution, January 2002.

[51] Mohamed Nawab Osman and Barkha Shah , Is Pakistan lost to the extremists?, *RSIS Commentaries*, July 18, 2007. Accessed at http://www3.ntu.edu.sg/rsis/publications/Perspective/RSIS0752007.pdf

[52] Hassan-Askari Rizvi, *Military, State and Society in Pakistan*, Sange-e Maal Publications, Lahore, 2002.

[53] Lt Gen. Faiz Ali Chishti, *Betrayals of Another Kind.*

[54] Stephen Cohen, *The Idea of Pakistan*, Oxford, 2005.

projected himself to be a moderate Army Chief, he made no changes in the Army's traditional policy of supporting *jihadi* groups to foment trouble in India and Afghanistan. He was, in fact, quite frank about this—at least before the 9/11. In an interview to the New York Times magazine in 2000, the General justified his support for *jihad* on these lines. "There is no question that terrorism and *jihad* are absolutely different. You in the West are allergic to the term *jihad* but *jihad* is a tolerant concept." Referring to terrorist groups, he said "these people are not terrorists. They are fighting a *jihad*."

Contrary to what most of his supporters in the West believed, Musharraf allowed extremist and terrorist organisations to expand in different parts of Pakistan and promoted *madrasas*, many of them becoming centres of radicalism. In 1971, there were 900 such *madrasas* in Pakistan; today these institutions of sectarian learning exceed 13,000 with an enrolment of 1.5 million. Unregistered *madrasas* could be 25,000 or higher. Under the General's watch, terrorist training camps mushroomed in Punjab, Khyber Pakhtunkhawa, Sindh and Balochistan.

When General Ashfaq Kayani took charge in November 2007, there was a high expectation that he would not only clean up the image of the army sullied by his predecessor's actions but also do away with the past policies of using terror as an instrument of policy. A clear-headed assessment of Kayani's actions first as the head of ISI and then as the Army chief (2007-2013) show how erroneous such expectations were.

Of particular interest should be Kayani's actions as the DG ISI under Musharraf. During his command of the ISI HQ at Aabpara, Islamabad, the agency oversaw the release of Harkat-ul Mujahideen chief Fazlur Rehman Kahlil (December 2004) and Harkat-ul Jihad al Islami chief Qari Saifullah Akhtar (May 2007), two of the Afghan *jihad* veterans who were instrumental in re-organising terrorist strategies and operations on behalf of the ISI and the Army. In September 2006, the ISI agreed to release more than 2,600 terrorist suspects; two of them were HuJI operational commander Sohail Akhtar (involved in the suicide attack in Karachi that killed 11 French engineers in May 2002) and Fazl Karim (one of the prime suspects in the 2002 Daniel Pearl murder).

Kayani was also aware that several ISI officials, forcibly retired in a purge carried out by his predecessor, Lt. Gen. Ehsan ul Haq, had returned to work for the agency as contractual employees to aid the Taliban network in Afghanistan and Pakistan. These re-employed ISI officials are part of the clandestine group or division created to pursue the Army's two-track policy. Offices were established in private homes in Peshawar, Quetta and other cities. The group has no direct link with ISI or GHQ. It works more like an NGO with a flat hierarchy and informal operational rules. One such officer, whom the CIA tracked down was 'General Yusef', who recruited and trained men to fight in Nuristan and Kunar provinces. He reported to an ISI office in Chitral and received a monthly stipend. The training camp was run by the LeT.

The ISI, under Kayani, established new terrorist training camps in North West Frontier Province (NWFP). *Herald*, a widely read English monthly published by the Dawn group of publications, reported in June 2006 about the fresh recruitment drive launched by the terrorist groups and the sprouting of training camps. Dozens of aspiring recruits from the Frontier and FATA towns were sent each month to training camps in Wana in South Waziristan. In August 2006, when Musharraf was striking deals with the Taliban and its allies in the tribal areas, *Herald* reported the presence of more than a thousand trained militants in three camps in the Hazara region of Khyber Pakhtunkhawa alone. Of these, the Hisari and Batrasi camps were located in the Manshera District while a third camp was located in Boi in district Abbottabad.

Kayani, as the DG ISI, chose to follow the tradition, a characteristic which became more evident after he took over as the Army Chief from Musharraf. Kayani, though faced with increased threat from terrorist groups like Tehrik-e-Taliban Pakistan (TTP), chose to protect equally violent groups like the Taliban, the Haqqani Network and LeT. He called them 'strategic assets'. [55] Sectarian extremist groups like Lashkar-e-Jhangvi not only remained untouched during Kayani's term but in fact have grown in strength and influence. The Sunni sectarian group has been involved in killing Shias, Hazaras and other minorities in Karachi, Quetta, Peshawar and other major cities without any military intervention. The principle accused in the Mumbai attacks, Hafiz Saeed, remains free and a key ally of the army in negotiating with anti-Pakistan militants, in countering TTP in the tribal areas and in keeping alive the '*jihad*' against India.

---

[55] Huma Imtiaz, 'Strategic assets': ISI must disengage from proxies: Mullen, *The Express Tribune*, September 21, 2011.

Nuclear jihad?

Since 2002, there has been a growing confluence of interest among three different actors in Pakistan—al Qaida, LeT and Pakistan Army—over the use of nuclear weapons or materials for '*jihad*' against their enemies.[56] There is enough evidence that al Qaida has been nursing such an idea for quite some time. Back in 1999, Osama had mentioned with pride to the western media that Pakistan, a Muslim country, possessed nuclear weapons to counter the Christian and Jewish bombs. The Pakistan's nuclear weapons capability, facilitated in substantial measure by billions that poured in from all sides for the so-called Afghan *Jihad*, was hailed in the Muslim world as the Islamic Bomb. AQ Khan, often wrongly called the 'Father of the Islamic Bomb', has justified his proliferation activities on the ground that it was his religious duty as a Muslim.

The Global War on Terror and Pakistan's decision to join the US after 9/11, however, changed this friendly equation dramatically. As Pakistan launched military offensives (even if many of them were half-hearted and gross failures) in the tribal areas, surrogates of al Qaida in the Taliban constellation turned against the army and launched a series of spectacular suicide bombings across Pakistan. Even though Pakistan allowed al Qaida and the Taliban elements to find shelter in the tribal areas and, arguably, facilitated the creation of a sanctuary in the Waziristan area, the State resisted the expansion of this 'Islamic Emirate of Waziristan' beyond a certain 'red' line.

The Lal Masjid operation of July 2007, in which over 300 men (mostly Pashtun *madrassa* products) were killed, firmly turned the al Qaida leadership against the Pakistani State with Ayman al Zawahari calling upon the people to overthrow President Musharraf time and gain. The group has kept up with the tirade against the Army, even after Musharraf left his position in August 2008. In the recent times, al Qaida has sharpened its attacks on the Pakistan establishment including the Army. Zawahari has even called up on the armed forces to mutiny and establish the Islamic law, or *Sharia*, in Pakistan which, he and others argued, was created as a nation of Muslims and should remain so.

A debate on the internet forums dealing with Pakistan and nuclear weapons could offer a glimpse into the debates within the *jihadi* circles. In March 2009, al-Fajr Media Centre, a *jihadi* media outlet, published a 29-page book—*Sharpening the Blades in the Battle against the Government and Army of Pakistan*—written by a senior al-Qaeda leader, Abu Yahya al-Libi.[57] Libi argues that since the government of Pakistan and the Army has prevented the implementation of *Sharia*, it had become a religious duty to take over the country. He quoted Hadith and Quranic verses to buttress his argument.

The book provoked considerable chatter on the *jihadi* internet forums with many arguing the imperative need to control Pakistan's nuclear weapons. Some forum members contended that the time was ripe to convert Pakistan into the base for establishing an Islamic Emirate and it was therefore important to seize its nuclear weapons before it fell into the hands of the US. There are references to getting hold of secret documents and maps pertaining to the location of these nuclear weapons—apart from nuclear installations in India—with the objective of keeping the 'enemies of Islam, the Hindus' at bay. A key argument was that it was more pragmatic to plan the takeover of nuclear weapons in Pakistan than pursue a '30-year *jihad* '.

One of the important strains of the discussion involved the co-opting of nuclear, military and civilian officials in Pakistan sympathetic to their cause. A.Q. Khan was singled out as one who should be persuaded to align with their cause, along with other nuclear scientists. One forum member said Khan and other scientists should be protected if a conflict broke out in Pakistan.

There is a still more recent reference to Pakistan's nuclear weapons made by a senior al Qaida leader from Afghanistan. In June 2009, Mustafa Abu al-Yazid told al Jazeera channel that "God willing, the nuclear weapons will not fall into the hands of the Americans and the *mujahideen* would take them and use them against the Americans."[58]

Such declarations and invitations might seem rhetorical and therefore not so serious in intent. But it would be a grave error to ignore them, for two simple reasons. First, these statements show a heightened interest in the *jihadi* circles about Pakistan

[56] A major part of the argument here are reproduced from author's chapter on Islam, WMDs and al Qaida's final goals from the ORF-ECC edited volume, *Radical Islam*, 2011.

[57] Abdul Hameed Bakier ,"Jihadis discuss plans to seize Pakistan's Nuclear Arsenal," Jamestown terrorism Monitor, Vol 7 (14), May 26, 2009.

[58] Mustafa Abu al-Yazid's Interview on al-Jazeera ,June 22, 2009, http://www.nefafoundation.org/miscellaneous/FeaturedDocs/nefa_yazidqa0609.pdf

and its nuclear weapons. Ideologues like al-Libi have quoted verse and chapter to prove that it was the religious duty of a Muslim to acquire such weapons. The argument is that these weapons must not fall into the hands of the enemy, the US, thereby making the forcible or illicit acquisition of these weapons an obligation on the part of Muslims to defend or protect themselves, all of which have explicit sanctions in the Quran. Second, there are enough people within Pakistan, both in and outside the establishment, who might not be immune to such exhortations, particularly when their idea of 'enemy' coincides with the 'enemy' of al Qaida, the Zionist-Christians represented by the US and Israel, and the Hindus by India.

A closer scrutiny of the 'sympathisers' in Pakistan is therefore imperative. These are the people who could become the 'vanguards of Islam' as Qutb and Laden have argued, and facilitate al Qaida's quest for WMD parity with the US. They are the game changers at the civilisational level, as former CIA Director George Tenet had argued in his autobiography.

For the sake of brevity and comprehension, it would be useful to divide these people into three groups: *jihadi* groups aligned to al Qaida; radicalised elements in the nuclear establishment and; sympathisers within the Pakistan Army or other wings of the armed forces, including the ISI. Without such a coterie of sympathisers, al Qaida's plans to breach Pakistan's nuclear weapons infrastructure would be impossible. Any such attempt would be fiercely opposed and repelled.

First, the *jihadi* groups sympathetic to al Qaida. There are a quite few that have a shared history with al Qaida, but it is Lashkar-e-Tayyeba (LeT) which is ideologically as well as operationally linked to the radical Salafi movement. Both al Qaida and LeT were inspired by the Arab Palestinian ideologue, Dr Abdullah Azzam, a close ally and teacher of Osama bin Laden, and Hafiz Saeed. The seed money for setting up the LeT headquarters at Muridke, Lahore, was given by bin Laden or one of his close associates. Such linkages are further strengthened by the commonality of objectives, attitudes and operational doctrines. The LeT was created as a Trojan Horse for al Qaida and others in the movement to infiltrate Pakistan and its society, an 'attack from within' as opposed, notably, from that of Jamaat-e-Islami (JI) which has been advocating the theory of 'attack from above' to transform Pakistan into a fully Islamic State. The LeT's presence in Pakistan indicates a far more serious threat to the State as well as its nuclear infrastructure simply because it has, largely due to the complicity of the State as well as the society, created over the years a subterranean as well as over ground network of schools, hospitals and charity organisations, besides political, economic and social alliances. These networks offer LeT a virtual invincibility from the State and a platform for a grand strategic alliance with its ideological hub, al Qaida.

Three other reasons could be cited for the LeT's insidious threat in the overall context of this paper's central thesis. First, there are references which show that the group was not averse to the use of nuclear weapons to achieve its goals. A relevant reference can be found in an English daily published from Lahore, *Daily Times,* (6 February 2004) which quoted Hafiz Saeed as saying that "atomic weapons, traditional weapons, a strong army and voluntary *mujahideen* are obligatory for *jihad* and the Jamat-ud-Dawa will continue protecting and arranging these resources for *jihad* against Hindus." More notable was how he contextualised the call more broadly—"Muslims throughout the world have a bond of *kalma*. From Lahore to Srinagar, Kabul to Baghdad, Basra to Chechnya, they are fighting under this *kalma*, but the infidel world doesn't like it and describes it as terrorism...only *jihad* could guarantee the security of Pakistan and the whole Islamic world". [59]

There have been at least two instances where LeT's role in training cadres in chemical and radiological weapons were detected in the past. A French-born terrorist named Willie Brigitte, arrested in Australia, admitted to being a member of LeT and disclosed that his targets were the electrical grid, Lucas Heights nuclear research centre outside Sydney and other military facilities and natural-gas pipelines. Investigations revealed that Brigitte and his associate, Faheem Lodhi, were funded and controlled by a LeT commander by the name Sheikh Sajid. A piece of evidence which Brigitte disclosed to the investigators was that he had seen a "Chechen" terrorist Abu Salah experimenting with chemical weapons in a LeT camp.

Second was the case of Joe Padilla (an American citizen of Puerto Rican descent) alias Abdullah Al Muhajir. He was planning to detonate a radioactive bomb in the US on the orders of Al Qaeda. Padilla had trained how to wire explosive devices and researching radiological dispersion devices at LeT safe houses in Pakistan. His handler was Abu Zubaida, a key Al Qaeda operative, arrested in 2002

[59] "We need atomic weapons and mujahideen, says Daawa", Daily Times, 6 February 2004.

from a LeT safe house in Faisalabad, Pakistan.

More important than these cases has been the involvement of the Pakistan nuclear establishment in illegal nuclear trade. Interestingly, LeT chief Saeed made it a point to praise the notorious nuclear scientist, AQ Khan in article: "He shared the technology for the supremacy of Islam and he acted on the Allah's command. He is our hero, will remain our hero, and the Government can't undermine his honour under American pressure." This was not an isolated comment. Khan has been a frequent visitor to LeT's annual congregations in the past. Interestingly, Khan attended these meetings not alone, but along with his other colleagues in the nuclear establishment, including Sultan Bashiruddin Mehmoud, former director of Pakistan Atomic Energy Commission and the man who enriched uranium at Khushab. Another key nuclear scientist who had been a regular visitor to LeT rallies was Abdul Majid, a close associate of Khan. Both Bashiruddin and Majid, and of course Khan, believed that Pakistan should generously help other Muslim nations with nuclear technology and materials.

Since Khan's proliferation activities have been documented in extensive detail by several authors since 2004 (when the network was busted by the CIA), it would suffice to limit this enquiry to the al Qaida connections these scientists have had. Most notable was the association Mahmoud and Majid had with bin Laden. After the bombing of Kabul in October-November 2001, the US troops discovered documents in a safe house that indicated Majid and Mahmoud had met Laden, raising fears in Washington that these scientists might have transferred their knowledge, and perhaps materials, to Laden. Bashiruddin, who spent 20 years of his career at Kahuta enriching uranium, was an ideal source for such knowledge transfer.

Mahmoud first denied discussing nuclear matters with Laden and al-Zawahari, but the CIA's search of his charity organisation, Umma Tameer-e-Nau (UTN), in Kabul disclosed documents relating to the construction of nuclear weapons. There were maps and diagrams. The investigators also found letters exchanged between UTN and LeT. Both the scientists subsequently admitted that they had a theoretic discussion on nuclear weapons with Laden and his deputy, al-Zawahri. Mahmoud also admitted telling Laden that "the most difficult part of the process is obtaining the necessary fissile material". At least Mahmoud had advocated in the past (1999) that it was obligatory on the part of Pakistan to share nuclear technology and materials with other Muslim nations, a belief which AQ Khan shared. Notably, there are references to such an acquisition of WMD within al Qaida's debate on the subject.

Although both the scientists were let off after detailed interrogation and investigation, the case of two other nuclear scientists in Pakistan, Suleman Asad and Muhammad Ali Mukhtar, raised further suspicion about the influence of radical groups within Pakistan's nuclear establishment. Both Asad and Mukhtar were spirited out of Pakistan and given asylum in Myanmar. It was reported that President Musharraf had personally called up his counterparts in Myanmar to ensure their safe passage and housing. Their whereabouts and involvement with extremist groups remain a mystery till date.

The third reason to suspect LeT's role in furthering the al Qaida cause is its expanding network of schools, particularly the science colleges, and its insistence on imparting science education to is students. Saeed has advocated promotion of scientific temperament along with *jihad* as part of his campaign to indoctrinate the young Pakistanis. LeT is part of al Qaida's Long War and is following JI's path of 'revolution from the top'. Although it is hard to document how many graduates from these institutions have joined the government, the army or the nuclear establishment, it can be safely assumed that at least some of the recruits to these institutions in future will have affiliations with LeT-run educational institutions. It is hard not to, since LeT runs more than 175 English-medium schools in Punjab, a province from which the maximum number of candidates are recruited to the Army, government and the nuclear establishment.

The third entity that can be influenced by al Qaida and bin Laden is the Army, which controls the nuclear establishment. The Army's al-Qaida and Taliban links have been well documented and need no repetition. What, however, must be emphasised is that the Army's strategic relationship with extremist groups like LeT and the Taliban have influenced at least some of the young and middle-ranking officers who cherish visions of leading an Army of Islam. In 2003, More than 20 officers, many of them of the rank of Lt. Col., were arrested for their linkages with the Taliban. The arrests were made on the US intelligence reports. Six of them were held after the al Qaida operational commander Khaled Mohammad Sheikh, arrested from Rawalpindi, snitched on them. Although the Army refused to identify the officers, one of the officers was identified as Lt. Col. Khalid Abbassi from the Corps of Signals, posted at Kohat. He was known to be well respected among his peers and delivered daily lessons from the Holy Quran to his troops. Several junior Pakistan Air Force officers were arrested a few years ago for taking part in the conspiracy to assassinate President Musharraf. These officers had aligned with terrorist groups close to al Qaida for this task.

Conclusion

From the above discussion, it is fair to draw the conclusion that there has been no serious attempt to 'de-radicalise' the armed forces. Instead, successive Generals have kept the force imbued with extremist fervour to achieve traditional 'strategic' objectives of deeply hurting India, deepen influence in Afghanistan and keep control over resources in Pakistan. There is a strong belief within the military establishment that the strategy of using terror as an instrument of state policy has been successful in the past and is likely to offer similar returns in the future.

Noted commentator, Vali Nasr, summed up the military mindset by pointing out that "Pakistan was able at the time to perpetuate its regional interests by adroitly using extremism with minimal investment in resources. That Pakistan's strategic outlook on the Afghanistan and Kashmir issues has not changed suggests that the military is likely to continue to use extremism to achieve it strategic objectives".[60]

With no sign of the army giving up its terrorist assets in the near future, the likely impetus on the growth of extremism within force, and the country, remains a strong possibility, and a great peril.

[60] Vali Nasr, *Testimony to the US Senate Foreign Relations Committee*, July 14, 2004.

THE FLIGHT OF THE DRONE

Ajay Singh, Strategic Analyst & Author

The CIA.s Special Activities Division at Langley in Virginia, USA is not a very imposing location. From outside it is unobtrusive and insignificant. Yet, within its grey confines, the deadly drone attacks of the CIA are planned and conducted across three continents. From its air-conditioned, neon-lit cubicles, UAVs are launched and retrieved, flight paths fed and changed, missions executed and monitored. Its computers receive video images beamed back by the UAVs at three second intervals. Should the cameras identify a suspect, his identity is confirmed and, if required, a strike is initiated Once the strike is activated the target is tracked relentlessly through the optical sights of a drone. At the opportune moment the command is given and 8,000 miles away a Hellfire missile would be released from a Predator drone, to ride a laser-designator beam and home unerringly on to the target. A second missile, a third or fourth or more could be launched, other drones could be called in to help complete the destruction. Then the drones would continue their mission, silent and unseen, tirelessly beaming back images for post-strike analysis. For the UAV controllers in the air-conditioned offices of mainland USA, the battlefield is just a computer console, the target just pixels on a computer screen and the attack just a routine activity on a eight hour shift. It is not really a bad way to fight a war, is it?

That, of course would depend on which side of the attack you were at. Badruddin Haggani, at the receiving end of the most recent attack would have viewed it differently. Like most of the Al Qaeda and Taliban leadership he knew of the dangers of the lethal drone strikes and took elaborate precautions to avoid detection. But, in spite of his precautions, his movements had been detected and he was being continuously tracked by a drone for over a week. The drone's cameras had followed him to his village, caught the movements of his bodyguards at their windows and kept tab of every action in the vicinity. When he drove away to attend a meeting of the local *shura*, just before dawn, the cameras even picked up the number from the number plate of his pick-up truck and provided the controllers with pin-point identification of Haqqani and his followers. He had no idea when the Predator drone trained its laser designator on the cab of his vehicle. Nor did he see the flash of the Hellfire missile released from four kilometers away, or have any inkling of its flight till it smashed into his vehicle. When the remaining vehicles converged in a futile attempt to aid their chief the second Hellfire missile exploded in their midst, killing all including the two women who part of the entourage.

This drone attack was just one of the 447 that have

been conducted by the USA in the Af-Pak region. Haqqani was one of the estimated 3400 militants that have been claimed by these attacks—a figure which includes an estimated 780 civilians who are passed off as the ubiquitous 'collateral damage'. The casualty list is quite long. It includes Mullah Dadullah, head of the Taliban, Ilyas Kashmiri, Haqqani and Osama's son, Saad Bin Laden; virtually the entire top tier of the Al Qaeda leadership. As per US intelligence, eleven of the top twenty terrorist leaders have been eliminated in these attacks. Even Osama Bin laden was kept under surveillance by a drone for weeks before the raid on his Abbotabad hide-out. Many of the top and middle level functionaries have been eliminated while moving from their hide-outs towards Afghanistan; others have been targeted in the mud-houses of their villages. Their efficacy has seen many of the remaining cadres move towards safer sanctuaries in Quetta and Karachi. Others have been deflected even further towards Yemen and Somalia. In the twelve year long quagmire of the "War against Terror", the drone stands out as a success story and fast becoming the weapon of choice in this form of conflict.

Yet the very success of these drone attacks has been clouded by the public resentment that they have generated. Notwithstanding the US claims of 'minimum collateral damage', an estimated thirty percent of the casualties are civilians. US agencies deny the figure and attribute the civilian casualties to the propensity of Al Qaeda and Taliban leaders to keep women and children in their entourage to divert attention. The locals claim that most innocent casualties are caused by follow-up strikes when civilians rush to help in the aftermath of an attack. Deliberate strikes have also been launched at funerals and weddings to target militants present there – a tactic which has recently been suspended after wide-spread condemnation. These drone attacks are perhaps the single most factors for the rising anti-US sentiment in Pakistan and the Muslim world. Its operational success has to be balanced with the psychological fall-out and a balance between the two has to be achieved if the success of the drone is to be fully exploited in the long-term.

The Rise of the Drone

The Unmanned Aerial Vehicle has come a long way since its inception in 1916, as a remote controlled aerial target for anti-aircraft gunners. It seems strange that a weapon of such potential remained dormant for almost 60 years thereafter. Hitler attempted to use them in World War II but had limited success. It was first used actively in Vietnam, when the USAF, concerned over the rising pilot casualties began using UAVs for reconnaissance duties. Over 3500 missions were flown and though over 550 UAVs were lost to all causes (usually bad weather) they saved valuable pilot lives. Till then their task was largely surveillance. Their active operational role came about in 1982, when the Israelis used them as decoys to activate Syrian Air Defence batteries during their attack on Lebanon. The drone really came into its own as a weapon system in the First Gulf war of 1993. Over 1200 missions were flown over Iraq in a range of roles. The war also saw the first drone versus aircraft dogfight when an Iraqi MIG 25 and a US UAV fired missiles at each other—the drone emerged second best and was shot down. In one notable case, a company of Iraqi soldiers actually surrendered to a drone. Yet it really emerged with the development of the Predator armed with AGM-114 Hellfire missiles. This hunter-killer 'avatar' was a handy weapon. At around $5 million per piece it was not really cheap but still came at the fraction of the cost for an aircraft. Plus there was none of the inconvenience of dead or captured pilots- especially if it had to be used in covert roles.

Controlling the operations of these drones – or Remotely Piloted Vehicles as they came to be called is quite easy. A RPV station usually consists of four drones, a ground control station and specialised data links to receive information and transmit orders to the drone. The drones are launched from an unnamed base, and remotely flown using K band satellite data links. A camera mounted in the nose of the UAV helps in piloting the aircraft and in receiving real-time information. Most modern UAVs also have a laser designator for firing their own missiles or guiding munitions from other UAVs onto the target. The flight path, camera actions and even the firing of weaponry are all remotely controlled via fast and secure satellite links which gives it an ease of operation and safety of use that few other weapon systems can provide.

Drone Operations in Af-Pak

Shadow and Predator drones were inducted into the Afghan theater in 2002, basically to assist in the search for Osama Bin Laden. In the rugged mountains of Tora Bora, they were used for the first time to assassinate high profile Al Qaeda leaders. In that difficult, inaccessible terrain, they were used in a variety of roles, surveillance, close support, strikes on militant hide-outs, elimination of leaders and their cadres. It was only a matter of time that the strikes crossed the Durand Line and began targeting terrorists in their sanctuaries in Waziristan.

During the initial years of the "War against Terror", drone strikes inside Pakistan were few and selective, just 45 in the first five years. Each strike was judiciously selected. A team of CIA lawyers prepared a brief justifying each attack which was then approved from the very top. The trend changed with the arrival of President Obama in 2006 and his willingness to carry the 'War against Terror' to its sanctuaries inside Pakistan. Drone attacks inside Pakistan intensified, with 265 being conducted in the first three years itself. Drone attacks became the fulcrum of US counter-insurgency strategy, especially after the surge of 30,000 additional US troops to Afghanistan in 2008. Drone strikes were launched not on concrete target identification, but often on mere 'signatures'. Any suspected behavior observed —usually the movement of cadres towards the Afghan border—was tracked and if confirmed, attacked. This helped eliminate a number of lower and middle level functionaries, but correspondingly, also increased the quantum of 'collateral damage'.

Pakistan's military and political establishment seems to have played a very "Yes-No" kind of role in this. For all their public protestations, in private many military leaders actually wanted intensification in the drone campaign – especially after the Taliban turned against them. Musharraf, in a recent interview, admitted to secretly clearing drone strikes during his presidency. In fact, Shamsi Air Base in Baluchistan was handed over to the USAF for launching drone operation in 2002- an arrangement which continued till 2011 when US –Pak relations broke down.

Yet, there has been complicity between the CIA and ISI on the drone attacks inside Pakistan. The CIA Counter Terrorism cell usually sent a fax to the ISI counterpart notifying the date and general area of attack. The Pak authorities would acknowledge receipt of the fax but neither write a note of approval or dissent. The fax system was designed to provide legal cover, but US agencies soon realised that the designated targets would often get tipped off and simply move or go underground. The fax system soon stopped and the US merely proceeded with their attacks without any form of notification. These arbitrary attacks heightened the sense of mutual distrust and highlighted Pakistan's perceived loss of sovereignty. The blatant use of military force on the soil of another nation showed the US as an aggressor and not an ally. The rising civilian casualties too amplified the growing wave of anti-US sentiment. In spite of the operational success of these drone attacks, they remain a major bone of contention. It is only now when the US has become more dependent on Pakistan to facilitate its exit strategy from Afghanistan that the intensity of drone strikes have reduced, perhaps to assuage public sentiment.

As the hydra of Al Qaeda rises in other regions of the world, nations such as Yemen, Sudan and Somalia are increasingly coming under focus. High profile leaders, such as the American- Arabic cleric Anwar-al-Awlaki and the firebrand radical Salim Harethi have been eliminated in recent drone strikes. Drones were also responsible for locating and tracking Muammar Gaddafi he attempted to flee Libya in his convoy. The relaying of this information led to his detection and death by a vengeful Libyan mob. The drone strategy of surveillance and selective assassination is likely to be replicated in this emerging arena as well.

The success of drone warfare has led to the development of a new generation of smaller, more lethal drones with greater range and endurance. The recently developed Global Hawk can loiter at altitudes of over 60,000 feet for over two days, and circumvent half the globe without refueling with the help of solar panels. At the other end of the spectrum, drones which can fit in a soldier's knapsack are also being developed. These can be launched by hand to provide a "Over-the-Horizon" capability to a Combat team or an infantry squad. They can also identify a hidden enemy and eliminate snipers with a tiny explosive warhead. Drones have recently been developed which can carry a small load of ammunition and supplies to forward troops under fire. The very versatility of the system makes its applications virtually limitless. Perhaps the day is not far when small, pint-sized drones will become the standard supporting weapon system for each squad/platoon.

Today, almost unbelievably, over 450 projects are being pursued across 20 nations to develop different types of UAVs—whether for civilian or military use. In India too, drones have increasingly entered the arsenal. The Heron and Searchers UAVs have been used for surveillance along the border fence on the Line of Control and to peer across. They have proved successful in anti-Naxalite operations allowing its operators to keep track of their suspected movements. DRDO too is working on the Nishant UAV, a truck launched UAV with a low logistic footprint which can undertake missions up to five hours. When fitted with a Foliage Penetration Radar it can peer into thick forest and vegetation. This is to be followed up by their own Medium Altitude Long

Endurance UAV, the RUSTOM– I. With an increase in technology, especially GPS technology, and the development of miniaturised cameras and nano-sized circuits, the potential for developing smaller and even more potent drones is increasing. Its applications too would increase to encompass a wider range of tasks, including police duties, riot control, and even for disaster relief and rehabilitation.

The drone has fast emerged as one of the most potent weapon systems of the time. In many ways it is changing the manner in which wars—both conventional and unconventional—will be fought. Yet it's very simplicity and ease of operations has a flip side. It can soon be adopted by terrorist organisations for early warning of the move of security forces, attacks on government installations and even political assassinations—perhaps it will soon replace the suicide bomber with time. The long flight of the drone is just beginning. Yet, its use must be tempered with caution. Else, the indiscriminate nature of its use could have an adverse psychological impact that far outweighs its immediate tactical gains.

Table: US Drone Attacks in Pakistan

Year	Number of Attacks	Number Killed	
		Min.	Max.
2004	1	5	8
2005	3	12	13
2006	2	90	102
2007	4	48	77
2008	36	219	344
2009	54	350	721
2010	122	608	1,028
2011	72	366	599
2012	40	188	299
Total	334	1,886	3,191

GENERAL ATOMICS—PREDATOR

Crew: none on-board
Length: 27 ft (8.22 m)
Wingspan: 48.7 ft (14.8 m); *MQ-1B Block 10/15:* 55.25 ft (16.84 m)
Height: 6.9 ft (2.1 m)
Wing area: 123.3 sq ft (11.5 m²)
Empty weight: 1,130 lb (512 kg)
Loaded weight: 2,250 lb (1,020 kg)
Max. takeoff weight: 2,250 lb (1,020 kg)
Powerplant: 1 × Rotax 914F turbocharged four-cylinder engine, 115 hp (86 kW)
Maximum speed: 135 mph (117 knots, 217 km/h)
Cruise speed: 81–103 mph (70–90 knots, 130–165 km/h)
Stall speed: 62 mph (54 knots, 100 km/h) (dependent on aircraft weight)
Range: 675 nmi (675 mi/1,100 km)
Endurance: 24 hours
Service ceiling: 25,000 ft (7,620 m)
Armament

- 2 hardpoints
- 2 × AGM-114 Hellfire (MQ-1B)

- 4 × AIM-92 Stinger (MQ-1B)
- 6 × Griffin air-to-surface missiles

Avionics

- ASIP-1C
- AN/AAS-52 Multi-Spectral Targeting System
- AN/ZPQ-1 Synthetic Aperture Radar (early airframes only)

NISHANT—UAV

Developed by:	Aeronautical Development Establishment, DRDO
Role:	Battlefield Surveillance, Reconnaissance, Target Acquisition, Damage assessment and electronic surveillance.
Weight:	380 kgs
Payload	45 kgs
Length:	4.6 m
Wingspan:	6.57 m
Cruise Speed:	125 kmph
Max Speed:	185 kmph
Range:	160 kms
Endurance:	4.5 hours
Launch System:	Vehicle mounted. Rail launch from hydro-pneumatic launcher
Recovery:	Parachute plus landing bags system.
Engine:	1 × RE 2-21-P
Target Designation:	Integral Laser Target Designation
Cameras:	35 mm Mini Pad; FLIR; IRLS

BEYOND WARFIGHTING: ROLES OF MILITARIES IN NATION STATES

Lt Gen Vijay Oberoi, former Vice Chief of Army Staff, Indian Army

PREAMBLE

Militaries have existed in one form or another for ages. Initially, they lacked formalised structures and were mostly bands of armed personnel with no permanent allegiance to a person or a state. With the passage of time and especially with the emergence of nation-states, militaries started being formally structured, with an accepted hierarchy. The period following the Middle Ages saw the emergence of modern defence forces. It was the European powers who started to develop military establishments with a standing army; and during the 19th century the military became a specialised institution. It expanded with a professional leadership and started being stationed away, but in proximity of the civil populace. This was how cantonments and military stations were formed. Colonialism gave further impetus to military organisations and structures. Most third world countries inherited the structures of the colonial era.

During the monarchical as well as the colonial eras, militaries enjoyed pride of place, with military commanders enjoying great privileges. They were the confidants of the kings and no major decisions were taken without consulting them in the formulation of grand strategies. With the advent of democracies, wherein civil control assumed great importance, the militaries lost some of their standing but barring the odd exception like India, their status continued to be high.

In most countries, the role of the military, i.e. the army, the navy and the air force, is to defend the nation from external threats and ensure that the borders of the country are safe and secure from adversaries. The nature of the threats, their likely intensity and the aims of the adversaries are taken into account while deciding on the size and the capabilities the military must have to meet the types of threats that may arise.

Besides defence against external threats, defence forces have to meet those internal threats that cannot be tackled by other instruments of the state, like different types of police forces. The military has also played an important, if not a central role, in the process of nation-building in many diverse ways.

Some militaries in democratic countries have resorted to military takeovers for varied reasons, ranging from gross dissatisfaction on how the political leadership runs the affairs of the state to seeking of power by a person or a group. In dictatorial countries, military takeovers rarely take place as either the military already shares power with the dictators or the country is already a military dictatorship.

It can thus be seen that besides meeting external threats, militaries have to deal with many other threats and contingencies. In democracies, these tend to have added meaning, as the defence forces are, after all, the people's forces and must act as such and must be available for carrying out non-military tasks with the same efficiency as war fighting, as long as these do not result in diluting their readiness to carry out their primary role effectively. It is a truism that if militaries fail to deliver when confronted by external threats, then any amount of efficiency displayed in carrying out secondary tasks comes to nought.

SCOPE

This paper focuses on all tasks that militaries are required to carry out, but analyzes, in greater detail, those tasks that are beyond the primary task of the military, viz. war fighting. These need to be performed by the defence forces to strengthen the state, especially in those states that are wholly committed to democracy and its perpetuation. It is dealt with in the following parts:

- Part I - Characteristics of Militaries
- Part II - Importance of Primary Tasks.
- Part III - Relationship of Militaries with Political Leaderships.
- Part IV - Secondary Tasks and Nation Building.
- Part V - Military and Bureaucracy.

PART I
CHARACTERISTICS OF MILITARIES

The modern military is an important institution of nation-states, with distinct features, i.e.:

a) It is an instrument of war and thus enjoys a monopoly and total control of weaponry and coercive power of a state. Its loyalty and support is essential for the survival of the state and the government.
b) Militaries are highly disciplined and are formally organised. They have a hierarchical structure with ranks and a culture of command and obedience.
c) Militaries are characterised by a set of principles, rules and values, that prepare their personnel to fight and kill enemies and if required make the supreme sacrifice.
d) All militaries feel that they are 'special', as they are directly responsible for the security and integrity of the nation and tend to regard themselves as being 'above' politics.

All these features give them a special status, respect and an advantage over civilian organisations and institutions. However, sometimes there are aberrations, which if not corrected are likely to result in negative connotations.

The nature and character of defence forces is shaped both by internal and external factors, like the history and traditions of military units; the nature of the political system; political culture; values of the people; and so on. In fact it is difficult to generalize the nature and significance of the military. It plays different roles in different political systems and the relationship between the political leadership and the military also differs in different set ups. For example, the political orientation of the People's Liberation Army (PLA) in China is influenced by the role it played in establishing the communist regime in 1949 and by the strict control of the Communist Party of China.

Besides being instruments of war, the other features of militaries are that they are guarantors of political order and stability and are also an interest group in their own right. Militaries are not alternatives to civilian rule, but they assume power in certain circumstances, either on their own or when called upon to do so. This aspect will be discussed in some detail later.

The capability of militaries for defending their countries against external aggressors depends on their strength, preparedness and modernisation. When the armed forces are used by the state to pursue an expansionist agenda by waging war against other states, their strength and capability must necessarily be greater than that of the adversary; there must be people's support; and the tasks for the military must be well-defined and unambiguous. Such tasks require a high level of military spending and enhanced amalgamation of senior military leaders in the process of policy making. The danger here is that this may lead to militarism and a changeover to a dictatorial regime. Hitler's Nazi regime in Germany is an example of such a state.

Hierarchies of the defence forces are well versed in technical knowledge and expertise in foreign and defence policy matters. At times they may act as interest groups that seek to shape or influence government policy that is favourable to the military, though not necessarily against the nation. The political leadership usually depends on the advice of senior officers of the military during deliberations relating to defence and strategic issues. In this respect, India is probably the sole exception, as there is little direct interaction between the political leadership and the military hierarchy.

The public attaches great significance to defence issues, as well as the status of military personnel as the guarantors and defenders of national security and the integrity of the state. This, when correctly highlighted by the media, benefits the military, including in its efforts to influence the Government regarding strengthening their capacity and increasing allocations for defence. As an example, the role of the senior military officers in USA to justify high levels of military spending and demonstrating the effectiveness of new technologies led to added allocations to pursue successful operations during the two Gulf Wars.

In many countries, militaries are stationed in areas where day to day interaction with the populace is limited. This has both plus and minus points, especially in democracies, as the ethos of democracies is maximum inclusiveness.

The above features of militaries automatically curb their democratic rights, when compared to other citizens of the nation. In countries having dictatorships, the roles are reversed, wherein there are more curbs on the citizenry than on military personnel. Our world also has quasi democracies, also known as 'cosmetic' democracies! As far as the rights of militaries in such countries are concerned they are at par with those existing in overt dictatorships.

Militaries do not and should not have a role in making or implementing policies of routine governance, but they do have and must have a major role in the formulation of security strategies of nations. This is true for democracies, quasi-democracies and dictatorships alike. Countries that tend to keep militaries out of such formulations suffer in the long run as neither the political leadership nor their civilian advisers (including diplomats) have the training, abilities or experience to fully understand the nuances of strategic issues. The case of India is a pointer, as it has no security strategy worth the name and plods along from one crisis to another, with no long term security outlook. In actuality it does not have long term strategies in even non-military fields, but that is another story and beyond the purview of this essay.

India is fortunate to have a highly professional military, which is also completely apolitical, that has so far risen to the occasion and pulled the governments chestnuts out of the fire, but this arrangement is not open-ended at all and the country is bound to suffer and suffer heavily if amends are not made on an urgent basis.

PART II
IMPORTANCE OF PRIMARY TASKS

General

In the last few decades, the nature of wars and conflicts has changed. The reasons range from increasing technological breakthroughs in weapons and equipment; the availability of weapons of mass destruction (WMD's); the information revolution; and the resort by some countries to the employment of non-state actors to further their interests. Consequently, most militaries need to be capable of fighting a variety of diverse conflicts in an ever-changing security environment.

There are broadly two methods of determining the size of militaries. Some militaries are capability-based while others are threat-based. Nations that have well-defined threats and have a broad defensive outlook usually base the size of their forces on the latter. Others, who may or may not have well-defined threats, choose the capability-based approach, as it gives them more flexibility. Most countries in South Asia have developed their militaries using the threat-based approach, while countries like the United States, Russia and to an extent China, that have plans to project power outside their countries, have adopted the capability-based approach. Both approaches have strengths and weaknesses.

National defence is the core function of any national military. In most democracies, military officers are always involved in the formulation of defence policies and provide expertise and professional advice to the political decision-makers. Effective defence policy-making requires that the political leadership makes use of the military's professional expertise. There are the odd exceptions, e.g. in India, where there is little interaction between the military and the political leadership because the political leaders in India prefer to have a layer of separation by placing bureaucrats between themselves and the military. The result is lack of any coherent security strategy and an overwhelming dependence on 'fire fighting'. Consequently, the system in India is not one that should be recommended to any state.

Structuring of the military comprises decisions on the size and organisation of the armed forces, their command structures, as well as the general guidelines of recruitment, education, appointments and equipment. Such organisational autonomy is necessary for the military to fulfil its functions. However, civilian control is maintained by the political leadership, which is assisted by the bureaucracy. Doctrinal issues should be the sole prerogative of the militaries, the only caveat being that they are in consonance with the overall national policy or grand strategy of the government.

Advancements in Military Technology

Rapid advancements in technology, in the fields of information; nuclear energy; biotechnology; aviation; and underwater operations, are changing the concept of warfare. Capabilities for all-weather surveillance; night vision devices; extensive use of satellites; and multiplicity of sensors; have also affected all types of military operations. In the field of information technology (IT), digitisation; networked communications; electronic warfare; as well as information warfare (IW); have highlighted the importance of systems integration. This has lead to the concept of system of systems, which is a complete architecture of detection, selection, display, targeting and attack.

The Revolution in Military Affairs (RMA) has also affected the security environment as well as military operations. RMA is the direct outcome of the development of the microchip, triggering technological advancements in the field of communications and information processing. Warfare in this information age requires highly-complex planning and coordination and massive data-base and information-exchange capabilities. Militaries in South Asia and its periphery are now focusing on rapidly imbibing the latest technological tools, albeit at a slower pace than their western counterparts, so that they are not left behind and are able to field modern military forces.

Changing Nature of War

The proliferation of Nuclear Biological and Chemical (NBC) weapons, increased use of precision-guided and terminally-guided munitions (PGMs and TGMs), imaginative employment of IT, more lethal and precise weapons, the fielding of many types of missiles and major up-gradation of aviation assets, have made substantive changes to the concepts and methodologies of waging war. Asymmetric warfare, for example, focuses on fighting a stronger enemy and still winning. In the same context, non-nuclear deterrence, which is aimed at deterring regional conflicts with only conventional weapons, continues to be important.

Operations in the future may not be easily compartmentalised into conventional and low intensity conflicts. The shadow of nuclear weapons would also influence the planning and conduct of operations. The modern battlefield will be characterised by short, intense operations, against a nuclear backdrop. There will be a large number of short, swift, and lethal engagements, using precision weapons, with heavy attrition, but with minimum collateral damage. Increased use of various types of sensors will bring total transparency to the battlefield. This will affect the achievement of surprise, both strategic and tactical, and there would be an overload of information at the command posts.

In conventional operations, front, depth and rear areas would be engaged simultaneously with real time surveillance; integrated command, control, intelligence and information; target acquisition; and highly lethal precision weapon systems. The battlefield will become more digitised, more transparent and would experience a major increase in deployment of electronic devices, signalling the growing primacy of the electromagnetic spectrum. Escalation will have to be carefully controlled to ensure that no nuclear red lines are crossed. Despite this constraint, sufficient space for conventional operations will continue to be available. The ability of ground forces will depend upon the speed with which they can move, concentrate and regroup rapidly over any type of terrain.

Overall, armies will require flexible organisations to meet the diverse needs of future operations. The fast pace of operations, day and night battles and high attrition rates will result in greater physical and psychological strain on all combatants. This will have to be factored in by leaders at all levels.

Joint and combined operations are already the norm. IT, in all its manifestations, will increasingly affect decision-making. At the same time, IW, including the creation of a favourable public opinion, is a necessary adjunct to the higher direction of war. Military planners will need to give considerable thought to the likelihood of terrorist threats, along with fighting conventional operations. Resultantly, greater number of troops and equipment would be required to cope with such threats.

Future military strategies would need to be effective across the entire spectrum of possible conflicts, from a brief but intense conventional war under the backdrop of a nuclear threat, to low intensity conflicts. Militaries, especially land forces also need to be cognizant of the need to transit from manpower orientation to high technology, but tempering it with the knowledge that sub-conventional operations are manpower intensive.

While limited conventional conflicts are still likely to occur, they are gradually giving way to trans-border terrorism, engineered ethnic strife and sponsored insurgency. Deterring war would be the primary aim of the armed forces. This implies the maintaining of a potent force in being.

PART III
RELATIONSHIP OF MILITARIES WITH POLITICAL LEADERSHIP

Civil-Military Relations

Nations which fail to develop a balanced pattern of civil-military relations squander their resources and run uncalculated risks.

—Admiral Vishnu Bhagwat, October 1998

The contours of civil–military relations, a *sine qua non* of democracies, are usually not understood by everyone. These relations are those interactions between the military and the political leaders that cover military inputs in making political decisions relating mainly to issues that concern the security of the nation. This is predominantly in the sphere of external threats but also relate to internal threats of a serious nature that are beyond the capability of the other instruments of the state.

The term military in this equation needs to be defined unambiguously, lest there be doubts. The military is defined as those permanent state organisations that are authorised by law to apply coercive power in order to provide security for society and state, primarily against external threats. This definition includes the army, navy and air force, as well as various military sub-organisations and specialised military units under formal command lines, such as military police; military intelligence services; communications units; and all arms and corps of the army. Those excluded are paramilitary forces, all types of police forces, and non-state security forces (private security companies or party militias). It needs to be noted that civilian officials (bureaucrats) or diplomats and other categories of civil officials do not feature in the above definition.

The military has no role in what may be termed 'public policy'. This encompasses decision-making and implementation in all political affairs except security and defence policies, e.g. all fiscal and economic policies, foreign policy (except that relating to security strategies) and public welfare. Examples of the breaching of civilian control are any occurrences of autonomous military policy-making or the formation of military structures which take over functions from civilian administrative organisations in the areas of 'public policy'.

The principles of civilian control are violated if:

a) The military enjoys constitutionally-reserved representation in the cabinet and/or parliament.
b) The state has informally recognised or institutionalised veto powers by the military regarding the appointment of members of the government or public administration.
c) The armed forces control aspects of the electoral process.
d) Active service personnel hold positions of political leadership.

Military Takeovers

The reasons for militaries intervening in politics and their return to the barracks need to be analysed, so that such contingencies can be avoided. In most cases, militaries use 'nationalism' to justify their interventions in politics while ensuring that withdrawal only occurs if national identity is protected.

In actuality, the excuse of nationalism by the military strengthens the praetorian state and not the nation-state. Nations with an unstable political system appear to be more vulnerable to military takeovers. Equally vulnerable are those nation-states where political stability has been eroded on account of bad governance, rampant corruption and the state's inability to meet the legitimate aspirations and requirements of its citizens.

It should never be forgotten that most militaries have the capability of taking over the government for a short time and/or for a specific purpose. However, they will not do so if their reasonable aspirations are met to a fair degree; the military gets its legitimate status; is kept modernised; and is amalgamated in those affairs of governance that are its legitimate concerns. Military coups in many under-developed and developing countries bear ample testimony to this.

Recent history indicates that in most newly-independent countries, politicians fought for power, often with motives that contradicted those of the military. The military, being the strongest institution in new states, was not happy with the ineffectiveness of politicians to address the security of the nation. The inability of political institutions to cope with increasing social mobilisation caused disorder and chaos, thereby increasing the likelihood of military intervention. The weakness of civilian institutions and civilian politicians to deal with such problems resulted in the politicisation of the military. Breakdowns in domestic security tended to feed the population's dislike for civilian politicians and the popularity of the military increased, with the perception of the military as the nation's saviour.

This is in line with Samuel Huntington's view in his book *The Soldier and the State* that *"the political systems of a society best account for military intervention"*. But that may not present the full picture. As Shuja Nawaz, in *Crossed Swords: Pakistan, Its Army, and the Wars Within (2008)* states: *"It may well be the inadequate interaction of military and political leaders, as also their respective ambitions and inclinations that account for some of these interventions. Many countries stumble on their way to nationhood and stable polities without fully developed political systems"*.

Generally, a military's disposition to intervene in politics has been due to the following:

a) The national interest;
b) Corporate self-interest;
c) Social (especially ethnic or class) self-interest;
d) Individual self-interest.

Militaries believe that it is their duty to be the custodians of the national interest. Historically, this role has taken a number of forms. Either the military overtly rules the nation and establishes a political agenda, or the military becomes an arbiter that intervenes if a decision or policy by civilian politicians is perceived as a threat to the permanent interest of the nation. Intervening on behalf of the national interest is often used by militaries as justification to hide their real motives, that of self-interest and corporate interest.

The control of weaponry and coercive power does give the military the capacity to intervene directly in governance, which may lead to the establishment of military rule. Military rule implies that the armed forces displace the civilian political leadership, directly or indirectly. It is direct when there is no civilian government and the military leaders are the supreme decision makers. It is indirect when the military leaders have a definite and major influence upon the civilian government and thereby mould its policies according to their will. The best example of both is Pakistan, where the military has wielded both direct and indirect power at different times.

One type of direct military rule is the rule by a military junta (derived from the Spanish word *'junta'*, meaning council or board). The military junta is a form of collective military government, centred on a council of officers, whose members usually represent the three services (army, navy and air force). Militaries in countries of Latin America tend to favour such juntas. The second type of takeover by the military is a coup leading to direct military rule by a single powerful individual. This type of takeover is characterised by a sudden and forcible seizure of the government in power through illegal and unconstitutional action. All military takeovers in Pakistan have been of this category.

In some countries, effective military governments can be established without a formal act by the armed forces, as had occurred in the Philippines under President Marcos, after the declaration of Martial Law in 1972. The recent seizure of power by the military in Egypt from President Morsi and his Muslim Brotherhood party is a case where the takeover is sought to be legitimised as a result of the wishes of a large majority of citizens.

Negating Military Takeovers

Most militaries understand that they are not to dabble in politics in any manner. This does not mean that they are not to be aware of politics but that they cannot and must not take sides or promote any political leader or party. The *'mantra'* for the military is that it is their duty to serve 'the government of the day', without overtly or covertly siding with any political entity. Huntington has stated that *"managing the coercive power of the military—making sure that those who govern do not become tyrants to the governed—is the central focus of civil-military relations"*. He has suggested that if the military was allowed to be autonomous in maintaining its professionalism and professional responsibility, it would contribute to make it stay out of politics.

Considering the trend towards increased democratisation throughout the world, a coup to overthrow a civilian regime is now less likely in most countries. A major reason is that militaries have learnt that while it may be easy to launch a coup, governing the country after the coup is not at all easy for any military, especially if the country is large and there is major diversity in the people. Military leaders realize that the problems facing nations are highly complicated and the military is not really equipped to tackle them. Moreover, there would be strong resistance against a coup in a country that has been under democratic rule for decades.

There are a few other issues involving democracy and civil-military relations that merit attention. Some suggest that the military is a part of the political establishment. However, it may be true of only some countries, e.g. Pakistan, where the political leadership has subordinated itself to the military in many fields. What is more important is the role of the military in the areas of national and regional security. The problems connected with security are now complex and multi-faceted. They include military security, non-traditional security and human security. These are interrelated. It is worth studying how the military perceive their role in this respect under the framework of civil-military relations and of democracy.

The institutionalisation of civilian control over the armed forces has in many countries remained a crucial issue. This owes to the fact that weak civilian control has generally coincided with democratic frailty. The result has been a preponderance of power by the military over civilian governments, a condition that has eroded political rights and civil liberties. Some militaries have shown a great deal of maturity in this respect by remaining apolitical even when civilian governments have shown a propensity for bad governance and have ignored the aspirations of the military. The case of the Indian military is by far the best example, especially when seen in the light of the political leadership placing a layer of civilian officialdom between the military and the political leadership. Unless the civilian leadership carries out major reforms in the existing standoff arrangement of civil-military relations in India, even a highly professional military may start having second thoughts.

Unlike bureaucracies, militaries do not deal with the citizens on a day-to-day basis. They prefer to remain in their own environment, where they get a chance to train extensively and hone their war fighting skills. Governments need to ensure that the militaries are treated impartially and their status is not lowered. This, along with a professional hierarchy devoted to ensure that the legitimate requirements of the rank and file are fully met will preclude any thinking of a military takeover.

The past three decades have seen a global trend of democratic transition going hand in hand with the decline of military regimes and open military intervention. Democracy has replaced all of the military or "quasi-civilian" regimes in Latin America. In the Middle and Near East, military rule has almost universally transformed into civilian strongman rule. In Asia, Bangladesh, Indonesia, South Korea, Thailand and Pakistan have moved from military domination to democracy or mixed patterns of civilian-military authority. Even in Myanmar, military rule of long-standing is giving way to civil rule, although it is still at a nascent stage.

Notwithstanding the above trend, in the emerging democracies of Indonesia, the Philippines, Thailand, Bangladesh, and especially Pakistan, the military has shown itself more or less resilient in guarding its prerogatives in the post-authoritarian era. This seriously impedes the democratically elected authorities' effective power to govern in these countries and has facilitated democratic deterioration in virtually all these countries. Such military resilience stems from the fact that their disengagement from political and economic governance was only partial at best.

Pakistan has evolved into a classic "*praetorian* state" where the Army feels it is the only true guardian of national sovereignty; political integrity; the principal initiator of any national agenda; and the chief resolver of socio-political conflicts. The military holds enormous sway over civilian governments in terms of political decision-making in spheres like elite recruitment, public policy, internal security, national defence, and military organisations. The military will certainly maintain itself as the chief stakeholder in Pakistan's political system. Although currently the Army has withdrawn from directly ruling the country, it will definitely resume its interest in the political process whenever it feels that its professional or corporate interests are being challenged.

In Bangladesh, the armed forces have on occasion managed to play a significant role in politics since independence in 1971, though their influence appears to be receding. While security needs have contributed to unity among soldiers, there continue to be some inhibitions. These include factionalism and politicisation in the military. Civilian government strategies have in general proven successful in ensuring civilian control. Though the military will continue playing a major political role in Bangladeshi politics, it will increasingly be confronted by civilian governments that have successfully led Bangladesh for many years.

PART IV
SECONDARY TASKS AND NATION BUILDING

Secondary Roles of Militaries

In addition to the primary role of meeting external threats, most militaries also have to be ready to face other threats in their secondary role. Such employments on non-military tasks vary from state to state. They may range from fighting militants, insurgents and other similar entities who have resorted to taking up arms against the state and who have become so strong that the police, including armed police forces of the nation, are unable to subdue them. Besides this, the military is also called out for the maintenance of law and order when the police forces are unable to do so, on account of the severity of the problem.

Other tasks of militaries are to assist the civil authorities in coping with natural and man-made calamities that are beyond the capability of the instruments available with the civil authorities. While providing aid to the civil authorities is a secondary task of the armed forces, the two major caveats are that they must be employed as a last resort and such employment must be for the minimum period. However, the reality is that because the army delivers efficiently and with alacrity, both these caveats are being ignored in India. The involvement of the Indian military in counter-insurgency operations appears to be open-ended as it has been operating for decades in the north eastern states and J&K, with no end in sight. Such long deployments on secondary roles adversely affect the combat potential of the army, alienate the populace and lower the morale of the troops. The prolonged employment in fighting insurgents and terrorists has taken stress and fatigue of the military personnel to extremely high levels in the Indian Army. These operations are extremely difficult and full of tension, especially on account of scrupulously adhering to human rights norms.

In a few countries, the military has been used as a 'political' tool to meet the partisan goals of the government in power, but when used in this manner, the government runs the risk of a military takeover in the long term. On the other hand, when employed to control major civil unrest or counter popular insurrections during serious religious, ethnic or national conflicts, it is the only guarantee of the unity and integrity of the state.

The implications of all these tasks/roles of most militaries are as under:

a) Military is the ultimate instrument the state has for applying in the most serious situations.
b) Militaries should be preserved for application after all other instruments have failed and the issue is so serious that it needs to be resolved urgently.
c) Militaries need to be kept modernised in terms of both weapons and equipment and trained man-power at all times and their leadership must be of the highest order.
d) The élan and the exclusiveness of militaries need to be maintained at a high state, so that their mere employment acts as a deterrent. This can only come about when governments ensure a higher status for the militaries than other instruments of the state.

Nation Building by the Military

There are many definitions of 'nation building'. A comprehensive one is that *"it is the development of behaviours; values; language; institutions; and physical structures that elucidate history and culture; concretize and protect the present; and ensure the future identity and independence of a nation"*. A briefer definition is that *"it is the process of structuring a national identity"*. This process aims at the unification of the people within the state so that it remains politically stable and viable in the long run. Nation-building can involve the use of propaganda and/or major infrastructure development to foster social harmony and economic growth.

The defence forces have played an important, if not a central role in the process of nation building and state formation over the past many decades. In the majority of nation-states during the 19th and 20th centuries, the military played a crucial role in nation building by providing security and stability. It continues to do so even now.

When India gained Independence, it was burdened with the collective baggage of over two centuries of alien rule. In most fields of state endeavour, there were many discords, mass illiteracy, total absence of economic development, lack of socio-political cohesion and widespread poverty. The political leaders of that era had brought about many changes that contributed to building the newly-independent nation. Many well thought-out policies and programmes aimed at nation-building were launched. Some have worked, while many others did not. Many institutions of the government and in later years many non-government organisations contributed to this effort. The defence forces of India have also contributed to nation-building in a big way, although their contribution has never been formally appreciated. Lately, governance in India has deteriorated, resulting in an adverse impact on nation building. However, the Indian military continues to add to nation-building as it has been doing for the last six decades since Independence.

The pillars of nation building are usually stated as security, justice, economic development and a democratic polity. Security comes first in the pecking order because the other three pillars function effectively only if the security of the nation remains intact. This in turn facilitates smooth functioning of democracy and brings in its wake social justice and economic development.

Democracy in India, albeit tenuous, has managed to hold and indeed flourish in many respects. The Constitution continues to be sacrosanct and is respected. This has been facilitated by the armed forces of India who have scrupulously maintained the ideals enshrined in the Constitution and have contributed significantly towards nourishment of democracy. Thus, if any institution is to be singled out in nation-building, it is the Indian military that has upheld two pillars of nation-building, viz. security and a democratic polity.

The strength of the armed forces lies in their high standards of discipline and morale, supported by a secular outlook and an apolitical demeanour. The armed forces of India faced all challenges posed to the nation and have been a pillar of support to the people, who look up to the most dynamic institution of the country – the Indian Army, in times of crises. The niche carved by the army's selfless service has been an enduring institution of the country – always dependable, standing rock-like in the service of the nation, and religiously adhering to the Chedwodian motto *"The safety, honour and welfare of your country come first, always and every time ..."*.

While the Indian Army did not fight a war of independence in the classic sense, it did contribute to the British decision to leave India. The factors included the formation of the Indian National Army (INA) in Singapore and the Indian Legion in Germany during World War II; the mutinies in the Navy and the Air Force, the post-War demobilisation of nearly two million soldiers and 12,000 Emergency Commissioned Officers; the outcry at the court martial of three INA officers; and the demeanour of the Indian officers of the Army, who could not hide their nationalist feelings. This had prompted General Auchinleck, then C-in-C, to write to the Army Commanders *"Every Indian commissioned officer is a nationalist and rightfully so, provided he hopes to attain independence for India by constitutional means."*

Following independence in 1947, organisational changes strengthened civilian control over the military. The position of Commander-in-Chief was abolished in 1955, and the three services were placed under the civilian ministry of defence. These changes reflected the ambiguous feelings of the civilian leadership toward the military. Nehru and other Indian political leaders ignored how the armed forces of India had served the nation both during the blood-bath of Partition and the invasion of Kashmir by Pakistan in 1947, but instead looked at the Indian military as an institution strongly wedded to the colonial past and looked at it with suspicion and distrust, as it was perceived as an imperialist tool. Nearly six decades later, even after the Army has proved its credentials repeatedly and has endeared itself to the people, it is sad that the political leadership (goaded by their bureaucratic advisors) still see the Army as a threat! This is despite even one act of disloyalty.

It was the derided Indian Army that did so much to reduce the flow of blood in 1947 and provided safe transit to the large movement of the population to and from the newly-created dominion of Pakistan and rose to meet every adverse situation which confronted the nation. Although time for consolidation was badly needed after Independence, there was none as the army was operationally committed in Kashmir, Junagadh and Hyderabad. Despite all these major constraints, the achievements of the army are a tribute to the leadership, fighting spirit and patriotic fervour of all ranks.

1971 was a defining moment for the Indian military, when it achieved total victory. However, what the military won on the battlefield was frittered away at the conference table, as indeed it had been after every war which the Indian military had fought, since Independence. The reason was the ignoring of military advice and keeping the military out of the decision-making loop.

The Indian military has been engaged in active operations on a sustained basis, since Independence, with only short periods of peace. Its involvement in Low Intensity Conflicts (LIC) has been extensive. Starting with deployment for about a year to curb the communist insurgency in Telengana in the 1950's, the army's involvement with LIC still continues, nearly sixty years later. These challenges have helped it to earn a formidable reputation of a force that delivers, usually against heavy odds. It will continue to fight the nation's wars, giving its best, but the nation must also support it to the maximum extent, meet its aspirations and restore its *"izzat"*, besides alleviating its concerns and misgivings.

PART V
MILITARY AND BUREAUCRACY

Effective civilian leadership is central to desired civil-military rapport. Civilian leadership implies elected representatives and not the bureaucracy. Unfortunately, in India the bureaucracy has unilaterally abrogated this right to itself, on account of the indifference of the political class! Inadequacies of the political leadership result in their over-dependence on the bureaucracy for governance.

In democracies the world over, the political leadership makes national policy and the national security strategy, with the active participation of civil and military officials of the country. Not so in India, where the military has been deliberately kept out of the policy formulation loop and even after over six decades of loyal, patriotic and dedicated service to the nation, it is obvious that it is still not trusted! Nothing else explains the reasons for its exclusion from the government and the inability to evolve a viable and comprehensive structure for higher defence.

For inexplicable reasons, the political leadership in India is highly uncomfortable in dealing with military officers and prefers to let the bureaucracy handle them. There is a total disconnect between the political leadership and the military. The overall result is that the military has little faith in the ability of the political leadership to do anything substantive for them.

Although the bureaucrats wield authority, their knowledge about military matters is shallow. Their misplaced sense of importance is the biggest impediment in the relationship of civil and military officials in India. It appears that the bureaucrats try to overcome their sense of inadequacy and endeavour to 'keep the military in its place'. There is no denying that the bureaucracy has been responsible for continued damage to the esteem of the armed forces of India.

Since Independence, the Indian political leadership has displayed a congenital fear of its armed forces. Playing on this insecurity, the bureaucratic establishment has created a web of officialdom to ensure that it effectively calls the shots. Resultantly, India has the most lopsided civil-military 'command and control' structure anywhere in the world, where policy makers are not accountable at all, while the military that is kept out of policy making is accountable for everything!

CONCLUSION

Militaries the world over have served their respective nations in ensuring the security of their nations, largely against external threats but also in restoring internal conflicts that are beyond the capabilities of other forces available. The militaries can do so only if they are well-trained, well-led and are equipped with modern weapons and equipment. The political leadership of nations, especially of democratic countries, needs to appreciate that militaries can only deliver if they are professionally capable and this depends on their status, leadership, equipment and assimilation in the national mainstream. In democracies, there are many institutions that make democracies work. If any of these institutions are allowed to be down-graded in any manner, the adverse effects become starkly visible. Hence, it is important to meet the legitimate requirements of the military by the political leadership.

The relationship of the military with the political leadership and the citizens in democracies and authoritarian states is different. In the former case, militaries accept the supremacy of the political leadership, while in the latter, either the military is supreme as in states ruled by militaries or the military has a prominent role in governance, as in non-military dictatorships. Political leaders in democracies therefore need to have a correct and balanced relationship with the military, so that it can operate as a reliable and effective institution of the nation that provides security and stability for the other pillars of nation-building to flourish.

In India, it is unfortunate that the civil-military relationship, post-Independence in 1947, has been hijacked by the bureaucracy and the political leadership has abrogated its legitimate authority. Resultantly, the last six decades are full of episodes that suggest a constant state of tension between the 'generalist' bureaucracy and the 'specialists' military leaders, with the political executive watching and sometimes encouraging the bureaucracy to cut the military down to size. That this needs to change at the earliest is axiomatic, if the country has to progress steadily and find its rightful place in the comity of nations.

The reasons behind the antipathy against the military displayed by the civil bureaucracy have been adequately brought out earlier. It is apparent that non-military officials resent the armed forces because of their evidently orderly and efficient ethos, the tightly-bound camaraderie and distinct standing in the society. This is not unique to India. Renowned sociologist Morris Janowitz had famously said: *"The intimate social solidarity of the military profession is both envied and resented by civilians."*

Indian military prides itself in its professionalism and being apolitical. It is fully convinced that a politicised military is the worst thing that can happen to a country, as no country has ever prospered under military control. It entertains no political ambitions whatsoever. Civilian supremacy is never doubted or even remotely questioned. During India's long history, there has been only one instance when the military had grabbed power, and that happened way back in 185 B.C. when Pushyamitra dethroned the last Mauryan emperor. The record of the modern Indian military is thus unblemished!

COUNTRY STUDIES

AFGHANISTAN

The Islamic Republic of Afghanistan (Dowlat-e Eslami-ye-Afghanestan) recognizes its independence day as 19 August 1919 when it became fully independent of British rule. The background of the Afghan flag is three equal vertical sections of black, red, and green from left to right. In the centre of the flag in yellow is the national coat of arms, which portrays a mosque with a banner and a sheaf of wheat on either side. In the upper-middle part of the insignia are the lines "There is no God but Allah and Muhammad is his prophet" and "Allah is Great," together with a rising sun. The word "Afghanistan" and the year 1298 (the Muslim calendar equivalent of the year of independence, 1919) are located in the lower part of the insignia.

Recent History

In December 2001, Afghan leaders in exile signed the Bonn Agreement, forming an interim government, the Afghan Interim Administration, under the leadership of Hamid Karzai. In 2002 Karzai was selected president of the Transitional Islamic State of Afghanistan, whose ruling council included disparate leaders of the anti-Taliban Northern Alliance. A new constitution, written by a specially convened Loya Jirga, or constituent assembly of regional leaders, was ratified in early 2004. In October 2004, an overwhelming popular vote elected Karzai president of the Islamic Republic of Afghanistan. However, regional warlords and large areas of Afghanistan remained beyond the control of the Karzai government. Despite substantial international aid, the Afghan government was unable to address numerous social and economic problems.

The Bonn Agreement lapsed after the 2005 elections. The agreement's successor, the Afghanistan Compact, went into effect in January 2006 to set goals for international assistance in economic development, security, protection of human rights, and the fight against corruption and drug trafficking.

In the meantime, the resurgent Taliban intensified terrorist activities in areas beyond government control, particularly the south-eastern provinces. Beginning in 2007 the Taliban utilised safe havens in adjacent Pakistan to gradually restore and expand its control in Afghanistan. In early 2008, it controlled an estimated 10% of the country while the government controlled only an estimated 30%. Local tribes controlled the remaining territory. Despite U.S.-aided efforts to reduce cultivation of poppies for narcotics production, that crop accounted for an increasing percentage of Afghanistan's economy and was a major support of the Taliban. Meanwhile, widespread economic hardship increasingly weakened the Karzai government's support among the population.

The Taliban-led insurgency in Afghanistan has continued unabated and spread into new areas. Counterinsurgency efforts were forced to adapt to changes in Taliban tactics. Tensions within NATO over mission objectives have undermined the mission's effectiveness and a broader debate over how the international community should define 'success' in Afghanistan.

Capital	-	Kabul
Government	-	President Hamid Karzai
	-	Vice President Mohammad Fahim
	-	Vice President Karim Khalili
	-	Chief Justice Abdul Salam Azimi
Formation	-	Independence 19 August 1919
AREA	-	647,500 square kilometres
Population	-	31,108,077 (2013 estimate)
GDP (PPP)	-	$33.740 billion (2012 estimate) Per capita - $ 1,053
GDP (nominal)	-	$19.906 billion (2012 estimate) Per capita - $621
Defence Minister	-	Bismillah Khan Mohammadi
Chief of Staff	-	Lieutenant General Sher Mohammad Karimi
Commander ISAF	-	General Joseph Dunford

Despite lack of troop numbers, ISAF forces were tasked for interdicting drug traffickers and destruction of opium factories within Afghanistan in a bid to hinder insurgents' sources of funds, while troops remained heavily engaged in combat and stabilisation operations across the country. Insurgents have moved into previously quiet provinces, increased their use of suicide bombing and of improvised explosive devices, and launched attacks on a number of high-value targets, including President Hamid Karzai and local government and security officials. The suicide attacks on the Serena Hotel and on the Indian Embassy have showed the relative ease with which insurgents move within Kabul.

After suffering a series of defeats in open combat with international forces in the heartland areas of Helmand, Kandahar and Urzgan, insurgents established bases in areas where government and ISAF forces were fewer in number, such as the south-western provinces of Nimruz and Farah, while becoming more active in the north, especially in Badghis, Faryab, Faizabad and Badakhshan.

Over five million Afghan refugees were repatriated in the last decade, including many who were forcefully deported from NATO countries. This large return of Afghans may have helped the nation's economy but the country still remains one of the poorest in the world due to the decades of war, lack of foreign investment, ongoing government corruption and the Taliban insurgency. According to a report by the United Nations, the Taliban and other militants were responsible for 76% of civilian casualties in 2009, 75% in 2010, 80% in 2011, 80% in 2012. In 2011 a record 3,021 civilians were killed in the ongoing insurgency, the fifth successive annual rise.

After the May 2011 death of Osama bin Laden in Pakistan, many prominent Afghan figures were assassinated, including Mohammed Daud Daud, Ahmed Wali Karzai, Jan Mohammad Khan, Ghulam Haider Hamidi, Burhanuddin Rabbani and others. Also in the same year, the Pak-Afghan border skirmishes intensified and many large scale attacks by the Pakistani-based Haqqani Network took place across Afghanistan. This led to the United States warning Pakistan of a possible military action against the Haqqanis in the Federally Administered Tribal Areas. The U.S. blamed Pakistan's government, mainly Pakistan Army and its ISI spy network as the masterminds behind all of this.

Attempts to turn Taliban fighters away from insurgency have met with limited success, though in the long run this would seem essential to any solution to Afghanistan's problems. The National Peace Commission was given the task of fostering reconciliation, but its mandate is unclear and the process is slow, allowing for the reconciliation only of individuals rather than groups. In anticipation of the 2014 NATO withdrawal and a subsequent expected push to regain power by the Taliban, the anti-Taliban United Front (Northern Alliance) groups have started to regroup under the umbrella of the National Coalition of Afghanistan (political arm) and the National Front of Afghanistan (military arm).

Geography

Location: Afghanistan is located in Central Asia, north and west of Pakistan, east of Iran, and south of Turkmenistan, Uzbekistan, and Tajikistan. The narrow Wakhan Corridor extends from north-eastern-most Afghanistan to meet with China. The land boundaries are with China (76 kilometres); Iran (936 kilometres); Pakistan (2,430 kilometres); Tajikistan (1,206 kilometres); Turkmenistan (744 kilometres); and Uzbekistan (137 kilometres).

Topography: The terrain of Afghanistan is dominated by rugged mountain ranges, which generally run from the northeast to the southwest. Mountains occupy all but the north-central and south-western regions of the country, which are dominated by plains. Nearly half the country has an elevation of 2,000 metres or more, and the highest peaks in the northeastern Hindu Kush range exceed 7,000 metres. Historically, mountain passes along the northeastern border with present-day Pakistan have been of great strategic importance. Significant parts of the southwestern plains region are desert.

Principal Rivers: The main rivers are the Amu Darya, 800 kilometres; the Harirud, 850 kilometres; the Helmand, 1,000 kilometres; and the Kabul, 460 kilometres. Afghanistan's chief tributaries to the Amu Darya, which forms much of the country's northern border, are the Koshk and the Qonduz.

Climate: Afghanistan's climate generally is of the arid or semi-arid steppe type, featuring cold winters and dry, hot summers. The mountains of the northeast have subarctic winter conditions. Farther south, monsoon effects moderate the climate near the Pakistan border and increase rainfall as far inland as central Afghanistan. The highest precipitation occurs in the Kabul region of the northeast. The highest temperatures and lowest precipitation are in the south-western plains region, where summer temperatures reach 49° C. Low temperatures in the north-eastern mountains range from –15° C in winter to 0° C in summer. The climate of the north-central Turkistan Plain is increasingly arid closest to the northern borders with Turkmenistan, Uzbekistan, and Tajikistan.

Natural Resources: Agricultural resources are primarily grazing land; fertile crop-growing land is concentrated in Kondoz Province in the north and Helmand Province in the south. Afghanistan is known to have major deposits of chrome, coal, copper, iron, and salt, as well as lesser amounts of a wide variety of minerals including gold, silver, and uranium. Natural gas is the most abundant hydrocarbon resource. Substantial oil deposits are recognised but not yet quantified. Water for all purposes is in critically short supply.

Land Use: Some 12.1% of Afghanistan's land is classified as arable; however, in the early 2000s a four-year drought cut that figure in half. In 2007 only 0.2% of the total was planted to permanent crops.

Environmental Factors: The environment of Afghanistan is assumed to have been spared large-scale disturbances until the Soviet invasion of 1979. Since that time, however, numerous events have caused severe damage. Afghanistan, which has no appreciable bodies of water, suffers from a limited freshwater supply that makes potable water unavailable to more than half the population. In recent years, groundwater quality has deteriorated because of agricultural and industrial runoff, and water quantity has been diminished by large-scale land clearing and desertification. Because of insufficient water treatment, the incidence of water-borne diseases is very high. Widespread overgrazing, soil erosion, salinisation, and water logging have reduced agricultural productivity. Although Afghanistan has little industry, particulate pollutants from the Aral Sea and industrial complexes in Iran, Turkmenistan, and Uzbekistan contaminate the atmosphere in northern Afghanistan. Chemical use and physical destruction in recent military conflicts have damaged the environment, and landmines and unexploded shells are residual hazards endangering an estimated 4 million Afghanis in 32 provinces. North-eastern Afghanistan is considered an earthquake hazard zone; in 1998 an earthquake along the Tajikistan border resulted in an estimated 4,000 fatalities.

Society

Population: Population assessment is difficult because many people do not have fixed residences. In 2008 the estimated population was 32.7 million. The population growth rate was 2.6% per year. The population is approximately 75% rural; in 2008 the six most populous cities accounted for less than 10% of the population. In 2006 net out-migration was 0.4 per 1,000 population. After heavy out-migration and internal displacement in the 1980s and 1990s, an estimated 2.5 million Afghans returned to Afghanistan in 2003–4 before the numbers began to decrease. The United Nations reported that in 2007 some 365,400 Afghanis returned to their country, bringing the total of repatriations since 2002 to 4.1 million. In 2007 more than 2 million Afghans were living in Pakistan and 1.5 million in Iran. In 2007 both countries, the main recipients of Afghan refugees, began preparations for large-scale deportation. Tajikistan closed its border with Afghanistan in 2007. Meanwhile, in that year insecure conditions in Afghanistan noticeably decreased the rate of return. In the early 2000s, hundreds of thousands were internally displaced within Afghanistan, mainly from rural to urban areas, because of drought and instability. In the first quarter of 2008, an estimated 13,000 people fled their homes as conflicts occurred in previously safe regions.

Ethnic Groups: Afghanistan is a multiethnic society, and its historical status as a crossroads has contributed significantly to its diverse ethnic makeup. The population of the country is divided into a wide variety of ethno-linguistic groups. Because a systematic census has not been held in the nation in decades, exact figures about the size and composition of the various ethnic groups are unavailable. The main ethnic groups are Pashtun, 42%; Tajik, 27%; Hazara, 9%; Uzbek, 9%; Aimak (a Persian-speaking nomadic group), 4%; Turkmen, 3%; and Baloch, 2%. Other ethnic groups include Pashayi, Nuristani, Arab, Brahui, Pamiri, Gurjar, etc. are 4%.The largest remaining nomadic group is the Kuchis, a Pashtun group whose population has dwindled to about 1.5 million since 1979. The Pashtuns are the major ethnic group in the south and the east, the Tajiks in the northeast. The predominant groups in north-central Afghanistan are the Hazaras, Tajiks, and Uzbeks.

Languages: More than 30 languages are spoken in Afghanistan. The official languages are Dari (Afghan Persian) and Pashtu. Dari is spoken by 50% of the population, and Pashtu is spoken as a first language by 35%. Turkic languages (primarily Turkmen and Uzbek) are spoken by 11% of the population. Of the languages spoken by smaller segments of the population, the most important are Balochi and Pashai. Many Afghans speak more than one language; Dari is the most common second language.

Economy

The economy of Afghanistan has improved significantly since 2002 due to the infusion of billions of US dollars in international assistance and investments, as well as remittances from expats. It is also due to dramatic improvements in agricultural production and the end of a four-year drought in most of the country. However, Afghanistan still remains one of the poorest and least developed countries in the world that is highly dependent on foreign aid. As of 2009, the nation's GDP is $14 billion and the GDP per capita is $1,000.

About half the population suffer from shortages of housing, clean drinking water, electricity and employment. The Government of Afghanistan and international donors have remained committed to improving access to these basic necessities by prioritising infrastructure development, education, housing development, jobs programs, medical care, and economic reform over the recent years. Historically, there has been a dearth of information and reliable statistics about Afghanistan's economy.

Agriculture. The Afghan economy continues to be overwhelmingly agricultural, despite the fact that only 12% of its total land area is arable and less than 6% currently is cultivated. Agricultural production is constrained by an almost total dependence on erratic winter snows and spring rains for water; irrigation is primitive. Relatively little use is made of machines, chemical fertilizer, or pesticides. The country's fruit and nut exports are at $113 million per year and could grow to more than $800 million per year in 10 years given the proper investment. Badghis and Samangan Province in the north of the country are famous for pistachio cultivation but the area lacks proper marketing and processing plants.

Wheat and cereal production is Afghanistan's traditional agricultural mainstay. The overall agricultural production dramatically declined following four years of drought as well as the sustained fighting and instability in rural areas. Some studies indicate that agricultural production and livestock numbers may only be sufficient to feed about half of the country's population. Shortages are exacerbated by the country's limited transportation network, which is currently being rebuilt. A report by the Food and Agriculture Organisation (FAO) states that Afghanistan was nearing self-sufficiency in grain production.

Livestock. The availability of land suitable for grazing has traditionally made animal husbandry an important part of the economy. There are two main types of animal husbandry: sedentary, practiced by farmers who raise both animals and crops; and nomadic, practiced by animal herders known as Kuchis. Natural pastures cover some 30,400 square kilometres but are being overgrazed. The northern regions around Mazar-e Sharif and Maymanah were the home range for about six million karakul sheep in the late 1990s. Most flocks move to the highlands in the summer to pastures in the north. Oxen are the primary draft power and farmers often share animals for ploughing. Poultry are traditionally kept in most households.

Much of Afghanistan's livestock was removed from the country by early waves of refugees who fled to Pakistan and Iran. In 2001, the livestock population in Afghanistan had declined by about 40% since 1998. In 2002, this figure was estimated to have declined further to 60%. An FAO survey done in the northern regions in spring 2002 showed that in four provinces (Balkh, Juzjan, Sar-e Pol, and Faryab), there was a loss of about 84% of cattle from 1997 to 2002 and around 80% of sheep and goats. In recent years, USAID has been helping to improve animal husbandry in Afghanistan.

Fishing. The nation has plenty of water reserves and suitable climate for fish farming. Fishing takes place in the lakes and rivers, such as in Sarobi and Mahipar area. Fish constitute a smaller part of the Afghan diet today because fish farmers are unable to produce enough fish to keep up with the demands of customers. The annual catch was about 900 tons in 2003. Most fish and seafood is imported from neighbouring Pakistan, Iran, the United Arab Emirates and other countries. There are about 300 fish farms throughout the country and the largest one is at the Qargha.

Forestry. Afghanistan's timber has been greatly depleted, and since the mid-1980s, only about 3% of the land area has been forested, mainly in the east. Exploitation has been hampered by lack of power and access roads. Moreover, the distribution of the forest is uneven, and most of the remaining woodland is presently found only in mountainous regions in the southeast and south. The natural forests in Afghanistan are mainly of two types: dense forests of oak, walnut, and other species of nuts that grow in the southeast, and on the northern and northeastern slopes of the Sulaiman ranges; and sparsely distributed short trees and shrubs on all other slopes of the Hindu Kush. The dense forests of the southeast cover only 2.7% of the country. Roundwood production in 2003 was 3,148,000 cubic metres, with 44% used for fuel. The destruction of the forests to create agricultural land, logging, forest fires, plant diseases, and insect pests are all causes of the reduction in forest coverage. Illegal logging and clear-cutting by timber smugglers have exacerbated this destructive process.

Trade and industry. The current trade between Afghanistan and other countries is at US$5 billion a year. In 1996, legal exports (excluding opium) were estimated at $80 million and imports estimated at $150 million per year. Since the collapse of the Taliban government in 2001, new trade relations are emerging with the United States, Pakistan, Iran, Turkmenistan, the EU, Japan, Uzbekistan, India and other countries. The Afghan hand-woven rugs are one of the most popular products exported from the country. Other products include hand crafted antique replicas, precious and semi-precious stones as well as leather and furs.

Mining. Afghanistan is endowed with a wealth of natural resources, including extensive deposits of natural gas, petroleum, coal, marble, gold, copper, chromite, talc, barites, sulfur, lead, zinc, iron ore, salt, precious and semi-precious stones, and many other materials. If Afghanistan generates about $10 bn per year from its mineral deposits, its gross national product would double and provide long-term funding for Afghan security forces and other critical needs. The United States Geological Survey (USGS) estimated in 2006 that northern Afghanistan has an average 2.9 billion (bn) barrels (bbl) of crude oil, 15.7 trillion cubic feet (440 bn m3) of natural gas, and 562 million bbl of natural gas liquids. In December 2011, Afghanistan signed an oil exploration contract with China National Petroleum Corporation (CNPC) for the development of three oil fields along the Amu Darya river in the north.

Other reports show that the country has huge amounts of lithium, copper, gold, coal, iron ore and other minerals. The Khanashin carbonatite in Helmand Province contains 1,000,000 metric tons (1,100,000 short tons) of rare earth elements. In 2007, a 30-year lease was granted for the Aynak copper mine to the China Metallurgical Group for $3 billion,[216] making it the biggest foreign investment and private business venture in Afghanistan's history. The state-run Steel Authority of India won the mining rights to develop the huge Hajigak iron ore deposit in central Afghanistan. Government officials estimate that 30% of the country's untapped mineral deposits are worth between $900 bn and

$3 trillion. One official asserted that "this will become the backbone of the Afghan economy" and a Pentagon memo stated that Afghanistan could become the "Saudi Arabia of lithium". The United States and other Western nations that have borne the brunt of the cost of the Afghan war have been conspicuously absent from the bidding process on Afghanistan's mineral deposits, leaving it mostly to regional powers.

Economic development and recovery. Afghanistan embarked on a modest economic development program in the 1930s. The government founded banks; introduced paper money; established a university; expanded primary, secondary, and technical schools; and sent students abroad for education. In 1956, the government of Afghanistan promulgated the first in a long series of ambitious development plans. By the late 1970s, these had achieved only mixed results due to flaws in the planning process as well as inadequate funding and a shortage of the skilled managers and technicians needed for implementation.

Afghanistan is an impoverished and least developed country, one of the world's poorest because of decades of war and lack of foreign investment. As of 2012, the nation's GDP stands at about $34.29 billion with an exchange rate of $19.91 billion, and the GDP per capita is $1,100. The country's export was $2.6 billion in 2010. Its unemployment rate is about 35% and roughly the same percentage of its citizens live below the poverty line. About 42% of the population live on less than $1 a day, according to a 2009 report. The nation has less than $1.5 billion external debt and is recovering by the assistance of the world community.

The Afghan economy has been growing at about 10% per year in the last decade, which is due to the infusion of over $50 billion in international aid and remittances from Afghan expats. It is also due to improvements made to the transportation system and agricultural production, which is the backbone of the nation's economy. The country is known for producing some of the finest pomegranates, grapes, apricots, melons, and several other fresh and dry fruits, including nuts.

While the nation's current account deficit is largely financed with the donor money, only a small portion is provided directly to the government budget. The rest is provided to non-budgetary expenditure and donor-designated projects through the United Nations system and non-governmental organisations. The Afghan Ministry of Finance is focusing on improved revenue collection and public sector expenditure discipline. For example, government revenues increased 31% to $1.7 billion from March 2010 to March 2011.

Da Afghanistan Bank serves as the central bank of the nation and the "Afghani" (AFN) is the national currency, with an exchange rate of about 47 Afghanis to 1 US dollar. Since 2003, over 16 new banks have opened in the country, including Afghanistan International Bank, Kabul Bank, Azizi Bank, Pashtany Bank, Standard Chartered Bank, First Micro Finance Bank, and others.

One of the main drivers for the current economic recovery is the return of over 5 million expatriates, who brought with them fresh energy, entrepreneurship and wealth-creating skills as well as much needed funds to start up businesses. For the first time since the 1970s, Afghans have involved themselves in construction, one of the largest industries in the country. Some of the major national construction projects include the $35 bn New Kabul City next to the capital, the Ghazi Amanullah Khan City near Jalalabad, and the Aino Mena in Kandahar. Similar development projects have also begun in Herat in the west, Mazar-e-Sharif in the north and in other cities.

In addition, a number of companies and small factories began operating in different parts of the country, which not only provide revenues to the government but also create new jobs. Improvements to the business-enabling environment have resulted in more than $1.5 billion in telecom investment and created more than 100,000 jobs since 2003. The Afghan rugs are becoming popular again and this gives many carpet dealers around the country to expand their business by hiring more workers.

Afghanistan is a member of SAARC, ECO and OIC. It is hoping to join SCO soon to develop closer economic ties with neighboring and regional countries in the so-called New Silk Road trade project. Foreign Minister Zalmai Rassoul told the media in 2011 that his nation's "goal is to achieve an Afghan economy whose growth is based on trade, private enterprise and investment". Experts believe that this will revolutionize the economy of the region. Opium production in Afghanistan soared to a record in 2007 with about 3 million people reported to be involved in the business but then declined significantly in the years following. The government started programs to help reduce cultivation of poppy, and by 2010 it was reported that 24 out of the 34 provinces were free from poppy grow.

Government and Politics

Overview: Politics in Afghanistan has historically consisted of power struggles, bloody coups and unstable transfers of power. With the exception of a military junta, the country has been governed by nearly every system of government over the past century, including a monarchy, republic, theocracy and communist state. The constitution ratified by the 2003 Loya jirga restructured the government as an Islamic republic consisting of three branches, executive, legislative and judicial.

Judicial Branch: To replace the ad hoc system in place under the transitional government, the constitution of 2004 stipulated that the Supreme Court include nine justices appointed by the president, with approval of the Wolesa Jirga, for 10-year terms. Those justices have particular importance because they are responsible for managing the personnel, budgets, and policy decisions of the entire national, regional, and local court system. At the level below the Supreme Court are high and appeals courts. A National Security Court handles cases of terrorism and other threats to national security.

Administrative Divisions: The major sub-national administrative division is the province (*wilayat*), numbering 34 in 2008. The two newest provinces were added in 2004. Each province has between five and 15 districts. In 2006 some 361 districts were in existence, but the number changes frequently as districts split or combine. Each province has one designated provincial municipality; some but not all provinces also have a single rural municipality. The municipalities fall under the direct jurisdiction of the Ministry of Interior.

Mass Media

The media was tightly controlled under the Taliban and other periods in its history, and was relatively free in others. Under the Taliban, television was shut down in 1996, and print media were forbidden to publish commentary, photos or readers letters. The only radio station broadcast religious programmes and propaganda, and aired no music.

After the overthrow of the Taliban in 2001, press restrictions were gradually relaxed and private media diversified. Freedom of expression and the press is promoted in the 2004 constitution and censorship is banned, though defaming individuals or producing material contrary to the principles of Islam is prohibited. 400 publications are now registered and 60 radio stations, a major source of information, currently exist. Foreign radio stations, such as the BBC World Service, also broadcast into the country.

Transport and Communications

Afghanistan has about 53 airports, with the biggest ones being the Kabul International Airport, serving the capital and nearby regions followed Kandahar International Airport in the south, Herat International Airport in the west, and Mazar-i-Sharif Airport in the north. Ariana Afghan Airlines is the national carrier, with domestic flights between Kabul, Kandahar, Herat and Mazar-i-Sharif. International flights include to United Arab Emirate, Saudi Arabia, Germany, Turkey, India, Iran, Pakistan and a number of other Asian destinations.

There are also domestic and international flight services available from the locally owned Kam Air, Pamir Airways and Safi Airways. Airlines from a number of regional nations such as Turkish Airlines, Gulf Air, Air Arabia, Air India, PIA and others also provide services to Afghanistan. Flights between Dubai and Kabul take roughly 2 hours to reach.

The country has limited rail service with Uzbekistan and Turkmenistan in the north. The government plans to extended the rail line to the capital and then to the eastern border town of Torkham by 2014, connecting with Pakistan Railways. Long distant road journeys are made by older model company-owned Mercedes-Benz coach buses or carpool and private cars. Newer automobiles have recently become more widely available after the rebuilding of roads and highways. They are imported from the United Arab Emirates through Pakistan and Iran. As of 2012, vehicles that are older than 10 years are banned from being imported into the country. The development of the nation's road network is a major boost for the economy due to trade with neighbouring countries. Afghanistan's postal and package services such as FedEx, DHL and others make deliveries to major cities and towns.

Telecommunication services in the country are provided by Afghan Wireless, Etisalat, Roshan, MTN Group and Afghan Telecom. In 2006, the Afghan Ministry of Communications signed a $64.5 million agreement with ZTE for the establishment of a countrywide optical fibre cable network. As of 2011, Afghanistan has around 17 million GSM phone subscribers and over 1 million internet users. It only has about 75,000 fixed telephone lines and little over 190,000 CDMA subscribers. 3G services are provided by Etisalat and MTN Group.

National Security

The final tranche of the transfer of security responsibilities to Afghan security forces was announced on 18 June 2013. It signified Afghan institutions' assumption of full responsibility for security of the country over the summer. On the occasion, President Karzai appealed to the international community "to equip Afghan forces according to the region's realities and according to existing security threats". The Commander of the International Security Assistance Force (ISAF), General Joseph Dunford, publicly emphasised that a post-2014 support presence would be essential to the sustainability of efforts.

At present there are approximately 183,000 Afghan National Army personnel (against a goal of 187,000 personnel) and 6,700 Afghan Air Force personnel (with a target of 8,000). Of these, some 630 are female, including one general and about 100 working with the Special Forces to address gender sensitivities during night raid operations. The United Nations-administered Law and Order Trust Fund for Afghanistan supported 139,631 police, against a target of 157,000. Of these, 1,974 are women. Efforts to continue strengthening the capabilities of Afghan security forces continue, although there remains a notable shortage of logistical capacity, air support and medevac, as well as of assets to counter improvised explosive devices.

With Afghan security forces conducting most operations, the number of casualties they endure has risen considerably. During the second quarter of 2013, over 3,500 Afghan service personnel were reportedly wounded or killed in action. On 1 July, the Ministry of the Interior reported that 299 police officers were killed in the Afghan month of *Jawza* (mid-May to mid-June), a 22% increase over the same period in 2012. Large-scale unauthorised absences, in the army in particular, remain an issue. Attrition, from all causes, is as high as 2.4 per cent per month. "Insider attacks" also continued. There were two incidents against the international military—in Kandahar and Paktika Provinces—for which the Taliban took responsibility, and five attacks involving Afghan forces in Herat, Helmand and Kunar.

In the context of reshaping the Afghan National Police from a security force to a law enforcement and community policing service, on 25 June the Minister of the Interior convened Afghanistan's first Community Policing Conference to discuss how to strengthen the relationship between the police and the community. A new Justice and Rule of Law Trust Fund for Afghanistan is planned for early 2014. The Law and Order Trust Fund for Afghanistan will be housed under the fund to support an integrated justice and rule of law approach.

Separately, the expansion of the Afghan Local Police programme continued. As at 14 August, the total number of personnel stood at 23,550. Initially focused on the north and north-east of the country, the major expansion is now in the southeast, with Nimroz, Panjshir, Samangan and Nuristan the only provinces without the programme. The Afghan Local Police has borne an increasingly disproportionate brunt of attacks by anti-Government elements. At the same time, in spite of continued efforts, there continues to be concern at a lack of vetting and accountability mechanisms, with reports of serious abuses and intimidation levelled against the Afghan Local Police.

The United Nations continued to monitor security-related incidents relevant to the work, mobility and safety of civilian actors, particularly those events that affect the delivery of activities and programmes mandated by the United Nations. No respite was evident during the holy month of Ramadan. From 16 May to 15 August, 5,922 incidents were recorded, an 11 per cent increase compared with the same period in 2012 (5,317 incidents), while still a 21 per cent decrease from 2011 (7,482 incidents). Tactically, armed clashes and improvised explosive devices constituted the majority of events (4,534 of the total). There has also been an insurgent focus on attacking security checkpoints and bases handed over to Afghan forces by the international military. Generally effective resistance by Afghan security forces focused on protecting key urban and district administrative centres as well as strategic transport routes.

Geographically, the southern, south-eastern and eastern provinces continued to account for the bulk of the security incidents—69 per cent between 16 May and 15 August. Sangin district in Helmand Province remained one of the most contested areas in the country. The Wardoj district of Badakhshan Province remained fragile following armed clashes earlier in the year. On 28 June, foreign elements were reportedly involved and directly engaged in a clash between anti-Government elements and the Afghanistan National Border Police. Road transport in the district has been impacted, reducing access to four border districts. Across the North, the Al-Qaida-linked Islamic Movement of Uzbekistan is reported to have developed a field presence in several provinces.

Anti-Government elements conducted a number of "spectacular" attacks in urban areas. Between 16 May and 15 August, there were 33 suicide incidents, of which 7 occurred in the heavily protected capital, compared to 7 for all of 2012 and 16 in 2011. On 2 July, a truck bomb, aimed at a logistics base contracted by the international military near the largest United Nations facility in Afghanistan, killed six people and is believed to have used the largest explosive charge to date in Kabul. On 3 August, in Jalalabad, the Consulate of India was the subject of a complex suicide attack, in which all casualties were Afghan security personnel and civilians.

The United Nations, its implementing partners and other humanitarian entities came under a variety of direct and collateral attacks. On 22 June, in Farah City, a homemade improvised explosive device targeted a United Nations compound, although no casualties or damage were reported. On 1 August, a UNAMA vehicle travelling to Taloqan (Takhar Province) came under small arms fire as it evaded an illegal checkpoint. The United Nations was made aware of specific threats against agencies in Kunduz, Herat, Gardez, Khost, Jalalabad and Kabul, with staff temporarily withdrawn from premises in several cases.

Regional Cooperation

New Governments in the Islamic Republic of Iran and Pakistan presented opportunities for Afghanistan to build on and consolidate relationships with those neighbours. On 26 and 27 August, President Karzai undertook an official visit to Islamabad, emphasising that for both countries the "primary concern" was lack of security and the menace of terrorism. Prime Minister Nawaz Sharif stated Pakistan's "strong and sincere support for peace and reconciliation in Afghanistan" and emphasised a policy of cooperative relations with all neighbours as vital to stable external relations and a focus on domestic priorities. A number of economic and connectivity projects were also agreed.

On 4 August, President Karzai attended the inauguration in Tehran of Hassan Rouhani as President of the Islamic Republic of Iran. During the visit, a memorandum of understanding on strategic cooperation between the National Security Council of Afghanistan and the Supreme National Security Council of the Islamic Republic of Iran was signed. Areas of mutual interest include intelligence sharing in combating security threats such as terrorism, narcotics and organised crime. On 1 August, the Ministers for Foreign Affairs of Afghanistan and the United Arab Emirates signed a long-term strategic partnership agreement and agreements on security cooperation and the transfer of prisoners.

On 7 July, Afghanistan became the fifty-fourth member of the Energy Charter Treaty. On 9 July, progress was made on the Turkmenistan-Afghanistan-Pakistan-India (TAPI) gas pipeline project with a contract signed in Ashgabat between Afghanistan and Turkmenistan on the sale and purchase of gas. On 13 July, in Kyrgyzstan, a meeting of the Foreign Ministers' Council of the Shanghai Cooperation Organisation reaffirmed support to Afghanistan as an "independent, peaceful, neutral and prosperous State free from terrorism and drug-related crime".

Counter-narcotics

On 26 June, the World Drug Report 2013 was launched. It highlighted that Afghanistan had accounted for 74% of the world's illicit opium production in 2012. The global area under poppy cultivation rose by 15% in 2012, driven largely by increases in Afghanistan. Global production, however, fell by almost 30%, mainly as a result of poor yields in Afghanistan owing to adverse weather conditions. The report further assessed that nearly 1 million Afghans were affected by drug use—one of the world's highest levels of addiction—with only 10% receiving any form of treatment.

An early assessment for 2013 estimated an increase in opium cultivation in 12 provinces. Governor-led eradication activities in the reporting period aimed to reduce production figures. As at 13 July, up to 8,262 hectares of opium poppy were estimated to have been eradicated. In undertaking this effort, 132 lives have been lost and 89 persons injured.

BANGLADESH

History

Bangladesh, formerly the East Wing of Pakistan, emerged as an independent nation in December 1971. One of the most divisive issues confronting Pakistan in its infancy was the question of what the official language of the new state was to be. Jinnah yielded to demands that Urdu be Pakistan's official language. In East Pakistan, the dissatisfaction turned to violence. (The Bengalis of East Pakistan constituted an estimated 54% of Pakistan's entire population). Jinnah visited East Pakistan only once after independence, shortly before his death in 1948. In the Constituent Assembly frequent arguments voiced the fear that the West Pakistani province of Punjab would dominate the nation. An ineffective body, the Constituent Assembly took almost nine years to draft a constitution, which was never put into effect.

At a 1966 Lahore conference of both the eastern and the western chapters of the Awami League, Mujib announced a controversial six-point political and economic programme for East Pakistani provincial autonomy. He demanded that the government be federal and parliamentary in nature, its members to be elected by universal adult suffrage with legislative representation on the basis of population; that the federal government have principal responsibility for foreign affairs and defence only; that each wing have its own currency and separate fiscal accounts; that taxation would occur at the provincial level, with a federal government funded by constitutionally guaranteed grants; that each federal unit could control its own earning of foreign exchange; and that each unit could raise its own militia or paramilitary forces.

Mujib's six points ran directly counter to greater national integration. It would divide Pakistan by encouraging ethnic and linguistic cleavages in West Pakistan, and would leave East Pakistan, with its Bengali ethnic and linguistic unity, by far the most populous and powerful of the federating units. It was tantamount to a call for independence.

On 25 March 1969 General Yahya Khan placed under martial law and assumed the titles of chief martial law administrator and president. He announced elections to take place on 7 December 1970 and East Pakistan was awarded 162 seats out of the 300-member National Assembly. On 12 November 1970, a cyclone devastated an area of almost 8,000 square kilometres of East Pakistan's mid-coastal lowlands and its outlying islands in the Bay of Bengal. As many as 250,000 lives were lost. Two days after the cyclone hit, Yahya arrived in Dhaka after a trip to Beijing, but he left a day later. His seeming indifference to the plight of Bengali victims caused a great deal of animosity.

The elections on 7 December 1970 were the first in the history of Pakistan when voters were able to elect members of the National Assembly directly. In a convincing demonstration of Bengali dissatisfaction with the West Pakistani regime, the Awami League won all but 2 of the 162 seats allotted to East Pakistan in the National Assembly. Bhutto's Pakistan People's Party came a poor second nationally, winning 81 out of the 138 West Pakistani seats in the National Assembly. The Awami League's electoral victory

Capital	-	Dhaka
Official language	-	Bengali
Government	-	Parliamentary Democracy
	-	President Abdul Hamid
	-	Prime Minister Sheikh Hasina Wajed
	-	Speaker Shirin Sharmin Chaudhury
Formation	-	Independence from Pakistan
	-	Declared 26 March 1971
	-	Victory Day 16 December 1971
Area	-	Total 147,570 square kilometres
Coastline	-	580 kilometres
Population	-	150,039,000 (2013 estimate)
	-	Density 1,033/square kilometre
GDP (PPP)	-	$306.0 billion (2012 estimate)
	-	Per capita $2,100
GDP (nominal)	-	$153.6 billion (2012 estimate)
	-	Per capita $1,044
Defence Minister	-	Sheikh Hasina Wajed
Chief of Army Staff	-	General Iqbal Karim Bhuiyan
Chief of Navy Staff	-	Vice Admiral Vice Admiral M Farid Habib
Chief of Air Staff	-	Air Marshal Muhammad Enamul Bari

promised it control of the government, with Mujib as the country's prime minister, but the inaugural assembly never met.

Yahya and Bhutto vehemently opposed Mujib's idea of a confederated Pakistan. Mujib was adamant that the constitution be based on his six-point programme. Bhutto, meanwhile, pleaded for unity in Pakistan under his leadership. As tensions mounted, Mujib suggested he become prime minister of East Pakistan while Bhutto be prime minister of West Pakistan. This triggered mass civil disobedience in East Pakistan. Yahya decided to ignore Mujib's demands and on 1 March 1 postponed indefinitely the convening of the National Assembly.

West Pakistani troops were sent to East Pakistan as tensions rose. Talks between Yahya and Muhib collapsed, and on March 23 Bengalis following Mujib's lead defiantly celebrated "Resistance Day" in East Pakistan instead of the traditional all-Pakistan "Republic Day." Yahya decided to "solve" the problem of East Pakistan by repression. On 25 March the Pakistan Army launched a terror campaign to intimidate the Bengalis into submission. Within hours a wholesale slaughter had commenced in Dhaka, with the heaviest attacks concentrated on the University of Dhaka and the Hindu area of the old town. Bangladeshis remember the date as a day of infamy and liberation. The Pakistan Army killed several hundred Bengalis. Mujib was captured and flown to West Pakistan for incarceration.

The West Pakistani press waged a vigorous but ultimately futile campaign to counteract newspaper and radio accounts of wholesale atrocities. The civil war was played down by the government-controlled press as a minor insurrection quickly being brought under control. After the tragic events of March, India became vocal in its condemnation of Pakistan. An immense flood of East Pakistani refugees, between 8 and 10 million according to various estimates, fled across the border into the Indian state of West Bengal. In April an Indian parliamentary resolution demanded that Prime Minister Indira Gandhi supply aid to the rebels in East Pakistan. She complied but declined to recognize the provisional government of independent Bangladesh.

On 4 December 1971 the Indian Army executed a 3-pronged pincer movement on Dhaka launched from West Bengal, Assam, and Tripura, taking only 12 days to defeat the 90,000 Pakistani defenders. On 6 December, India became the first nation to recognize the new Bangladeshi government.

At independence, Bangladesh was scarred by civil war. The new nation faced many other seemingly insurmountable problems inhibiting its reconstruction. The most glaring was the breakdown of law and order. In the wake of the war of independence, numerous bands of guerrillas roamed the countryside, fully armed and outside control of the government.

Despite substantial foreign aid, mostly from India and the Soviet Union, food supplies were scarce, and there was rampant corruption and black marketeering. Mujib's economic policies also directly contributed to his country's economic chaos. His large-scale nationalisation of Bangladeshi manufacturing and trading enterprises and international trading in commodities strangled Bangladesh entrepreneurship in its infancy. However, at the time of the first national elections held in 1973 the Awami League won 282 out of 289 directly contested seats. After the election, the economic and security situations began to deteriorate rapidly, and Mujib's popularity suffered further as a result of what many Bangladeshis came to regard as his close alliance with India.

On the morning of 15 August 1975, Mujib and several members of his family were murdered in a coup engineered by a group of young army officers, most of whom were majors. The diplomatic status of Bangladesh changed overnight. One day after Mujib's assassination President Bhutto of Pakistan announced that his country would immediately recognize the new regime and offered a gift of 50,000 tons of rice in addition to a generous gift of clothing. India, however, suffered a setback in its relations with Bangladesh.

After several coups Ziaur Rahman, the Chief of Army Staff became the Chief martial Law Administrator of Bangladesh in November 1976. Zia made repatriate Major General Hussain Muhammad Ershad the deputy army chief of staff. Having consolidated his position in the army, Zia became president on 21 April 1977 and seemed to be supported by a majority of Bangladeshis.

In May 1977, with his power base increasingly secure, Zia drew on his popularity to promote a nineteen-point political and economic program. Zia focused on the need to boost Bangladeshi production, especially in food and grains, and to integrate rural development through a variety of programs, of which population planning was the most important.

He heeded the advice of international lending agencies and launched an ambitious rural development program in 1977, which included a highly visible and popular food-for-work program.

One of the most important tasks Zia faced was to change the direction of the country. Zia altered the Constitution's ideological statement on the fundamental principles, in particular changing the Mujibist emphasis on secularism to "complete trust and faith in almighty Allah." While distancing Bangladesh from India, Zia sought to improve ties with other Islamic nations. Throughout his regime, Zia pursued an active foreign policy, and the legacy of his efforts continued to bear fruit in the late 1980s. In 1980 Zia proposed a conference for the seven nations of the subcontinent (Bangladesh, Bhutan, India, Maldives, Nepal, Pakistan, and Sri Lanka) to discuss the prospects for regional cooperation in a number of fields. This initiative was successful in August 1983 when the South Asian Association for Regional Cooperation (SAARC) was established.

In April 1978, Zia announced that elections would be held to "pave the way to democracy," adding that the Constitution would be amended to provide for an independent judiciary as well as a "sovereign parliament." Zia also lifted the ban on political parties. He was supported by a "national front," whose main party was the Jatiyo Ganatantrik Dal (National Democratic Party). As the candidate of the Jatiyo Ganatantrik Dal-led Nationalist Front, Zia won overwhelmingly, taking 76.7% of the vote. After campaigning by Zia, the Bangladesh Nationalist Party won 207 of the 300 seats in Parliament with about 44% of the vote.

Zia was assassinated in Chittagong on 30 May 1981,

in a plot allegedly masterminded by Major General Manzur, the army commander in Chittagong. The army, under its chief of staff, Major General Ershad, remained loyal to the Dhaka government and quickly put down the rebellion, killing Manzur. In the trials that followed, a sizable number of officers and enlisted men received the death penalty for complicity.

After Zia's assassination, Vice President Sattar became acting president and, as the Constitution stipulates, called for new elections for president within 180 days. Although there was some speculation that Zia's widow, Begum Khalida Ziaur Rahman, and Mujib's daughter, Sheikh Hasina Wajed, would be candidates, Sattar ran against a number of political unknowns in the November election and won the presidential election with two-thirds of the vote. Immediately following the 1981 election, Ershad pushed Sattar for a constitutional role for the military in the governance of the country. On 24 March 1982, Ershad dismissed Sattar, dissolved the cabinet and the Parliament, and assumed full powers under martial law.

In January 1985, it was announced that parliamentary elections would be held in April, to be preceded by a partial relaxation of martial law: the Constitution was to be fully restored after the elections. In order to be eligible to contest the elections as a candidate in the presidential election in October 1986, Ershad Joined the Jatiya Dal, being elected as Chairman of the party and nominated as its presidential candidate. In the presidential election, which was boycotted by both the Bangladesh Nationalist Party (BNP) and the Awami League (AL), Ershad won an overwhelming victory.

In the Parliamentary elections, which were held in February 1991 the BNP alliance won an overall majority and, following discussions with the Jamaat-e-Islami, as a result of which the BNP was ensured a small working majority in the Jatiya Sangsad, Begum Khaleda Zia assumed office as Prime Minster. In September the BNP had gained an absolute majority in the Jatiya Sangsad, following the party's victory in a number of by-elections.

The main political parties are the Awami League and the Bangladesh Nationalist Party (BNP). The AL, which spearheaded the war of independence under Sheikh Mujib, is now led by his daughter, Sheikh Hasina. The differences between the AL and the BNP in terms of official economic policy have largely disappeared. While AL plays on its leading role during the war of liberation in 1971 and attacks those who opposed it, the BNP appeals more broadly to nationalist forces, drawing support from forces that had been on both sides of the liberation war.

On 11 January 2007, following widespread violence, a caretaker government was appointed to administer the next general election. The country had suffered from extensive corruption, disorder and political violence. The new caretaker government made it a priority to root out corruption from all levels of government. To this end, many notable politicians and officials, along with large numbers of lesser officials and party members, were arrested on corruption charges. The caretaker government held a fair and free election on 29 December 2008. Awami League's Sheikh Hasina won the elections with a landslide victory and took oath of Prime Minister on 6 January 2009. The ruling alliance got 230 seats among 300 seats in the parliament.

Geography

Bangladesh is a country of 144,000 square kilometres with a land area 133,910 square kilometres. Its topography is of a broad deltaic plain besides the Chittagong Hills in the southeast, low hills in the northeast and modest-elevation highlands in the north and northwest.

Bangladesh is located in the low-lying Ganges-Brahmaputra River Delta or Ganges Delta. This delta is formed by the confluence of the Ganges (Padma), Brahmaputra (Jamuna), and Meghna rivers and their respective tributaries. The Ganges unites with the Jamuna (main channel of the Brahmaputra) and later joins the Meghna to eventually empty into the Bay of Bengal. The alluvial soil deposited by these rivers has created some of the most fertile plains in the world. Bangladesh has 58 trans-boundary rivers, making water issues politically complicated to resolve - in most cases as the lower riparian state to India. Most parts of Bangladesh are less than 12 metres (39 ft) above sea level, and it is believed that about 50% of the land would be flooded if the sea level were to rise by 1 metre.

The highest point in Bangladesh is in Mowdok range at 1,052 metres in the Chittagong Hill Tracts to the southeast of the country. A major part of the coastline comprises a marshy jungle, the Sundarbans, the largest mangrove forest in the world and home to diverse flora and fauna, including the Royal Bengal Tiger. In 1997, this region was declared endangered.

Straddling the Tropic of Cancer, Bangladeshi climate is tropical with a mild winter from October to March, a hot, humid summer from March to June. A warm and humid monsoon season lasts from June to October and supplies most of the country's rainfall.

Natural calamities, such as floods, tropical cyclones, tornadoes, and tidal bores occur almost every year, combined with the effects of deforestation, soil degradation and erosion. Cox's Bazar, south of the city of Chittagong, has a beach that stretches uninterrupted over 120 kilometres.

In September 1998 Bangladesh saw the most severe flooding the modern world has seen. Although only 1,000 people were killed, 30 million were made homeless and 130,000 cattle were killed, 50 square kilometres of land were destroyed and 11,000 km of roads were damaged or destroyed. 66% of the country was underwater. There were several reasons for the severity of the flooding. Firstly, there were unusually high monsoon rains. Secondly, the Himalayas shed off an equally unusually high amount of melt water that year. Lastly, trees that usually intercept rain water were cut down for fire wood or to make space for animals.

Population

Bangladesh is the 7th most populous nation in the world. With a land area of 144,000 square kilometres, the population density is remarkable. Bangladesh's population growth was among the highest in the world in the 1960s and 1970s, when the country grew from 50 to 90 million, but with the promotion of birth control in the 1980s, the growth rate slowed.

The majority ethnic group of Bangladesh is the Bengali people, comprising 98% of the population. The remainder are mostly Bihari migrants and indigenous tribal groups. There are thirteen tribal groups located in the Chittagong Hill Tracts, the most populous of the tribes are the Chakmas. The region has been a source of ethnic tension since the inception of Bangladesh. The largest tribal groups outside the Hill Tracts are the Santhals and the Garos (Achiks). There are also Kaibartta, Meitei, Mundas, Oraons, and Zomi ethnic groups. Human trafficking has been a lingering problem in Bangladesh and illegal immigration has remained a cause of friction with Burma and India.

The official and most widely used language in Bangladesh is Bengali or Bangla. English is used as a second language among the middle and upper classes and in higher education.

Health and education levels have recently improved. Most Bangladeshis are rural, living on subsistence farming. Health problems abound, ranging from surface water contamination, to arsenic contamination of groundwater, and diseases including malaria, leptospirosis and dengue. The literacy rate in Bangladesh is approximately 41%. There is gender disparity, though, as literacy rates are 50% among men and 31% among women.

Religion

The major religion practiced in Bangladesh is Islam (89.7%) and a sizable minority adheres to Hinduism (9.2%). About 96% of the Muslims are Sunni while over 3% are Shi'a. Ethnic Biharis are predominantly Shia Muslims. Other religious groups include Buddhists (0.7%, mostly Theravada), Christians (0.3%, mostly of the Roman Catholic denomination), and Animists (0.1%). Bangladesh ranks fourth after Indonesia, Pakistan, and India by the number of Muslims, with over 130 million. Islam is the state religion of Bangladesh.

Economy

Bangladesh has seen a dramatic increase in foreign direct investment. In order to enhance economic growth, the government set up several export processing zones to attract foreign investment. These are managed by the Bangladesh Export Processing Zone Authority.

The insufficient power supply constitutes an obstacle to growth. According to the World Bank, "among Bangladesh's most significant obstacles to growth are poor governance and weak public institutions." In April 2010, Standard & Poor's awarded Bangladesh a BB- for a long term in credit rating which is below India and well over Pakistan and Sri Lanka in South Asia.

One significant contributor to the development of the economy has been the widespread propagation of microcredit by Muhammad Yunus (awarded the Nobel Peace Prize in 2006) through the Grameen Bank. By the late 1990s, Grameen Bank had 2.3 million members, along with 2.5 million members of other similar organisations.

Bangladesh government is planning for construction

of the largest deep sea port in South Asia at Sonadia Island. The 500 billion taka project will be completed in multiple phases and enable Bangladesh to service the whole region as a maritime transport and logistics hub. India, China, Bhutan, Nepal and other neighbouring countries will be able to take full advantage of the strategic location and Bangladesh's LDC status for exporting their goods, which are manufactured in Bangladesh. Furthermore, with $7.5 billion a new international airport will be constructed. The airport is being modelled on Thailand's Suvarnabhumi Airport in size and capacity.

To ease the chaotic traffic congestion in the capital Dhaka the government plans to construct more expressways, freeways, and flyovers. There is a plan to build an overhead Rapid transit called Dhaka Metro, but the progress is slow and controversial because of contracts and agreements.

Recently the government of Bangladesh signed a deal with a Chinese company to provide high-speed modern DEMU trains and is also going to construct metro rail system and high-speed electric powered inter-city rail network. More airports, bridge (such as the multi-billion Padma Bridge project) national highways are also being constructed to facilitate trade and regional development.

Infrastructure

Rivers. Bangladesh has as extensive and complex network of some 700 rivers. The major systems are the Jamuna-Brahmaputra, Padma-Ganges, Surma-Meghna, and Padma-Meghna, all of which flow south into the Bay of Bengal. It is the primary transportation system employing nearly 300,000 small and medium-sized country boats, with about 8,430 kilometres of navigable waterways.

Roads. About 16,890 kilometres of motorable roads. Despite severe flooding, it is an important means of moving people and goods, with an extensive network of bridges and ferries cross numerous inland waterways all over the country.

Railroads. About 2,818 kilometres of track, operated by Bangladesh Railways.

Ports. Chittagong and Chalna are major freight-handling ports.

Airports. Largest near Dhaka (Zia International Airport) and at Chittagong and Sylhet.

Government and Politics

Bangladesh has a parliamentary form of government with a popularly elected prime minister. The 1972 Constitution amended numerous times to reflect new political realities as the country has also had a presidential form of government. There is a unicameral Parliament (known as Jatiyo Sansad, or House of the People) with 300 members.

Authoritarian or military regimes have run Bangladesh almost since its inception. The regime in power traditionally controls government and Parliament through a single national political party: under Sheikh Mujibur Rahman (1972-75), the Awami League (People's League); under Ziaur Rahman (1977-81), the Bangladesh Nationalist Party; and under Hussain Muhammad Ershad, and the Jatiyo Party (National Party). Numerous opposition parties joined periodically in fractious alliances against the party in power e.g. Awami League, centrist Bangladesh Nationalist Party, leftist Jatiyo Samajtantrik Dal (National Socialist Party), and conservative, pro-Islamic Jamaat e Islami (Congregation of Islam). Student and workers' wings of these parties are important players in national politics.

Two radical Islamist parties, Jagrata Muslim Janata Bangladesh (JMJB) and Jama'atul Mujahideen Bangladesh (JMB), were banned in February 2005. Bomb attacks taking place since 1999 have been blamed on those groups, and hundreds of suspected members have been detained in numerous security operations, including the head of those two parties in 2006. The first recorded case of a suicide bomb attack in Bangladesh took place in November 2005.

Foreign Policy

Bangladesh pursues a moderate foreign policy that places heavy reliance on multinational diplomacy, especially at the United Nations. In 1974 Bangladesh joined both the Commonwealth of Nations and the United Nations and has since been elected to serve two terms on the Security Council in 1978–1979 and 2000–2001. In the 1980s, Bangladesh played a lead role in founding the South Asian Association for Regional Cooperation (SAARC) in order to expand relations with other South Asian states.

India. Bangladesh's most important and complex foreign relationship is with India. This relationship is formed by historical and cultural ties and is strengthened because of India's involvement in liberating the people of Bangladesh from Pakistan. This forms an important part of the domestic political discourse. Over the years, the relationship between the two countries has fluctuated for a number of reasons. A major source of tension between

Bangladesh and India is the Farakka Dam. However, both countries recognize the importance of good relations, regional security and South Asian economic integration. In 2009, Bangladeshi security forces launched a crackdown on Indian insurgents hiding in the country's border regions, captured and deported the leaders of several insurgent groups. Bangladesh and India have also agreed to develop regional connectivity and economic integration, along with Nepal and Bhutan. India's eastern states, as well as Nepal and Bhutan, are keen to gain access to Bangladesh's Chittagong and Mongla ports. With India its common history, many shared natural and geographical resources and a long border with an unresolved status presents security challenges. These include:

a) Water sharing of 54 common rivers.
b) Implementation of the 1974 Mujib–Indira Border Agreement.
c) Demarcation of maritime boundaries and the ownership of South Talpatty Island.
d) Burgeoning trade imbalances in favour of India and the reluctance to allow export of Bangladesh goods mostly on non-tariff grounds.
e) Smuggling and illegal cross-border activities.

China. Bangladesh enjoys very warm ties with the People's Republic of China, and particularly in the past decade, there has been increased economic cooperation between them. Between 2006 and 2007, trade between the two nations rose by 28.5% and there have been agreements to grant various Bangladeshi commodities tariff-free access to the Chinese market. Cooperation between the Military of Bangladesh and the People's Liberation Army is also increasing, with joint military agreements signed and Bangladesh procuring Chinese arms which range from small arms to large naval surface combat ships such as the Chinese Type 053H1 Missile Frigate.

Pakistan. Pakistan was hostile to Bangladesh in the early 1970s, but by 1974 it was apparent that the new nation would stand on its own, and Pakistan recognised Bangladesh. Diplomatic relations were established in January 1976, followed by the reestablishment of communications and transportation links. Two major areas of disagreement between Bangladesh and Pakistan stem from the dislocations resulting from the independence struggle. The first concerned the finances of united Pakistan. After the war, Bangladesh claimed that it deserved a share of the US$4 billion worth of pre-independence exchange, bank credit, and movable assets protected in West Pakistan. In a 1975 agreement, Bangladesh accepted half of Pakistan's pre-1971 external debt, but asset sharing issues remain unresolved. The second issue concerns the emigration of nearly 540,000 Biharis (non-Bengali Muslims) to Pakistan after the war.

Myanmar. It is the only nation besides India that shares a border with Bangladesh. Relations between the two countries have generally been cordial, but relations have deteriorated with Myanmar pushing out its Rohingya Muslim population into Bangladesh from time to time destabilising Bangladesh's fragile economic and social order, which is a matter of deep concern for Bangladesh. There are also issues of maritime territorial expansion.

The United States. The US is a major development partner of Bangladesh, and has given over five billion dollars in aid since 1972. The two countries also cooperate in counter-terrorism and promote regional cooperation in South Asia. Bangladesh participated in the US-led coalition during the 1991 Gulf War to liberate Kuwait, and supports the US-led reconstruction of Afghanistan. The US Military has also engaged in disaster management and relief operations in Bangladesh, in the aftermath of several devastating floods and cyclones, including the 1991 Bangladesh cyclone and Cyclone Sidr. On the economic front, the US is Bangladesh's largest export destination. American companies are also the largest foreign investors in Bangladesh, with major investments in the country's natural gas reserves by Chevron and Conoco Philips.

Armed Forces

Since its establishment in 1972, immediately after independence in 1971, the military of Bangladesh was not required to fight any war against an external force. It has, however, faced a troubled situation in maintaining law and order in the Chittagong Hill Tracts of the country for a protracted period of time since 1980s. The role of the Navy in containing smuggling through the seaways is insignificant. However, in November 2008, Bangladesh Navy effectively staved off economic aggression by Myanmar in the seas of Bangladesh. Occasionally the military forces have been called to participate in social activities like rehabilitation of people following a flood or cyclone. Since 2002, it has been involved in maintaining law and order situation within the country. This was institutionalised through formation of a military based police force called Rapid Action Battalion, RAB in short, of Bangladesh Police.

Since the 1990s, it has earned international reputation by working as part of UN Peace Keeping Missions in different countries of the world. In popular perception, the Bangladesh military is a privileged class of the society and recognised as a disciplined and well-trained national institution that can tackle critical national phases. However assassination of two presidents of the country in 1975 and 1981 and overthrow of an elected government in 1982 by the military has rendered it a potential opponent to the political and democratic system of the country. In 1996 too, the military made a mobilisation without presidential authority. Yet, all political government in effect patronize the military, reflected in higher budgetary provision and enhancement of seniority vis-a-vis civil bureaucrats. Critics often call into question the necessity of a full-fledged military in a small country like Bangladesh, engulfed by India on three sides.

The budget allocated for the military is considered inordinately high leaving lesser resources for the country's growth and development. In all, the role of the military is opaque. However, its power-base remains unquestionable. The Bangladesh military killed President Sheikh Mujibur Rahman in 1975 and President Ziaur Rahman in 1981. It toppled the democratically-elected government of the country and captured state power in 1982. Besides the illegitimate and bloody incidents of 1975, 1981 and 1982, the military determined the course of the country politics after the end of the Bangladesh Nationalist Party (BNP) regime in October 2006. The change-over of January 2007, is popularly known as a silent coup, when Professor Iajuddin Ahmed was made to declare state of emergency and resign as Chief Adviser of the Caretaker government.

On 25 February 2008 more than one thousand personnel of the Bangladesh paramilitary force, Bangladesh Rifles (BDR) staged a mutiny at its headquarters in Dhaka at Pilkhana. For the next 33 hours, the mutineers held the BDR HQ, keeping several officers and civilians as hostage. Initially confined to Pilkhana, the mutiny spread to other outposts of BDR. There were reports of disobedience or violence from at least twelve other BDR outposts. The killings, however, were confined to the HQ. By the end of the mutiny, 74 people including 56 officers had lost their lives. The mutiny shocked the entire nation leaving a question mark on the state of security in Bangladesh.

In addition to traditional defence roles, the military has been called on to provide support to civil authorities for disaster relief and internal security during periods of political unrest. Bangladesh contributed 2,300 troops during Operation Desert Storm in 1991, and is the world's largest contributor (10,736) to UN peacekeeping forces.

Environmental Challenges

Climate change poses a grave threat to Bangladesh. The country faces possible loss of large areas of land to sea level rise over the next decades. In the shorter term, Bangladesh has to deal with more frequent and intense cyclones and floods. In addition, the direct and indirect consequences of climate change on countries upstream of it would likely affect it as well.

The various vulnerabilities combine to compound the impact of climate change on the country, threatening water, food, health and livelihood security. Those pressures could lead to a dramatic rise in the number of refugees, which would put further stress on resources and create further tensions both within the country and with its neighbour, India.

Threats to the environmental security of Bangladesh are a cause of concern. They are floods, salinity, siltation, and cyclones. The dry season leads to recession of water in the Ganges, causing increased salinity in the rivers and streams, posing a serious threat to agriculture and industrial activities. Salinity also affects the flora and fauna in the Sunderbans forests. The soil character of Bangladesh is undergoing changes because of siltation and salinity. Bangladesh holds the view that construction of barrages, in India, upstream of the river has aggravated the situation. Periodic floods also cause destruction to agriculture, roads and human lives affecting the economic and social life of Bangladesh. Also, the level of arsenic in the ground water has reached a dangerous level. Bangladesh is in the midst of the biggest mass poisoning in history, having more than five times the amount considered acceptable in 46 districts.

BHUTAN

Bhutan is a landlocked nation in the Himalaya Mountains. Its flag is rectangular and divided diagonally from the lower left side corner. The upper part is yellow, symbolising the secular power of the king, while the lower part is orange, representing the Buddhist religion. Across the middle a white dragon (druk) is depicted, which symbolizes purity. The jewels held tightly in the dragon's claws symbolize wealth. The roaring mouth represents the strength of deities protecting the country.

Bhutan has a land boundary of 1,075 kilometres (China 470 kilometres, India 605 kilometres). Bhutan is one of the most isolated and least developed nations in the world. Nonetheless, it has been described as the happiest least developed country on earth. Foreign influences and tourism are heavily regulated by the government to preserve the country's traditional culture and national identity. The landscape ranges from subtropical plains in the south to the Himalayan heights in the north, with some peaks exceeding seven thousand metres. Mahayana Buddhism is the state religion and the population is predominantly Buddhist, with Hinduism being the second most dominant. Thimphu is the capital and largest city.

History

Until the early 17th century, Bhutan existed as a patchwork of minor warring fiefdoms when the area was unified by the lama and military leader Shabdrung Ngawang Namgyal. To defend the country against intermittent Tibetan forays, Namgyal built a network of impregnable dzong (fortresses), and promulgated a code of law that helped to bring local lords under centralised control.

During the 1870s, power struggles between the rival valleys of Paro and Trongsa led to civil war in Bhutan, eventually leading to the ascendancy of Ugyen Wangchuck, the ponlop (governor) of Tongsa. From his power base in central Bhutan, Ugyen Wangchuck defeated his political enemies and united the country following several civil wars and rebellions in the period 1882–1885.

In 1907, an epochal year for the country, Ugyen Wangchuck was unanimously chosen as the hereditary king of the country by an assembly of leading Buddhist monks, government officials, and heads of important families. The British government promptly recognised the new monarchy, and in 1910 Bhutan signed a treaty which "let" Great Britain "guide" Bhutan's foreign affairs. In reality this did not mean much. It also did not seem to apply to Bhutan's traditional relations with Tibet. The greatest impact of this treaty seems to be the perception that it meant Bhutan was not totally sovereign. After India gained independence from the United Kingdom on 15 August 1947, Bhutan became one of the first countries to recognize India's independence. A treaty similar to the one of 1910 was signed on 8 August 1949 with India.

In 1953, King Jigme Dorji Wangchuck established the country's legislature—a 130-member National Assembly—to promote a more democratic form of governance. In 1965, he set up a Royal Advisory Council, and in 1968 he formed a Cabinet. In 1971,

Capital	-	Thimphu
Official language	-	Dzongkha
Government	-	Constitutional democratic monarchy
	-	King Jigme Khesar Namgyel Wangchuck
	-	Prime Minister Tshering Tobgay
Area	-	38,394 square kilometres
Population	-	742,737 (2012 estimate) Density 18/ square kilometre
GDP (PPP)	-	$4.287 billion (2011 estimate) Per capita $6,112
GDP (nominal)	-	$1.488 billion (2011 estimate) Per capita $2,121
Chief Operations Officer	-	Maj Gen Batoo Tshering

Bhutan was admitted to the United Nations, having held observer status for three years. In July 1972, Jigme Singye Wangchuck ascended to the throne at the age of 16 after the death of his father, Dorji Wangchuck.

In the 1980s, in order strengthen Bhutan's identity as a nation, the "one nation, one people" campaign was started to foster greater integration of the peripheral ethnic and cultural groups into main stream Bhutanese society. The age old code of conduct, known as Driglam namzha and usage of the official national language Dzongkha was promoted. Around the same time, a nation-wide census revealed a huge influx of illegal immigrants of Nepali origin, into Southern Bhutan. When the government attempted to remove the illegal settlers, there was a violent backlash; numerous acts of terrorism were carried out against government schools, hospitals, offices and neutral Southern Bhutanese. In order to re-establish order in the south, the government was forced to draft many young men and able bodied civil servants into a militia force. Eventually order was restored; along with the illegal settlers, a number of political dissidents and Southern Bhutanese who had rebelled against the country, fled to Nepal, where they were admitted into United Nations run camps and given refugee status. Despite the best efforts of the governments of Bhutan, Nepal and India, as well as outside parties such as the United Nations, European Union and the United States, a viable solution to this problem proves to be still elusive.

In 1998, King Jigme Singye Wangchuck introduced significant political reforms, transferring some of his powers to the Prime Minister and allowing for impeachment of the King by a two-thirds majority of the National Assembly. In late 2003, the Bhutanese army successfully launched a large-scale operation to flush out anti-India insurgents who were operating training camps in southern Bhutan.

In 1999, the government lifted a ban on television and the Internet, making Bhutan one of the last countries to introduce television. In his speech, the King said that television was a critical step to the modernisation of Bhutan as well as a major contributor to the country's Gross National Happiness (Bhutan is the only country to measure happiness) but warned against the misuse of television which may erode traditional Bhutanese values. Some believe it has indeed affected Bhutan in a negative way.

Bhutan is a predominantly Buddhist country, with the religion forming an integral part of everyday life. A new constitution was presented in early 2005 which will be put up for ratification by a referendum before coming into force. King Jigme Singye Wangchuck introduced significant political reforms, transferring most of his administrative powers to the Council of Cabinet Ministers. On 14 December 2006, Jigme Singye Wangchuck announced that he was abdicating his throne. Bhutan entered a new era of democracy, starting with its first elections in 2008. On 6 November 2008, 28-year old Jigme Khesar

Namgyel Wangchuck, eldest son of King Jigme Singye Wangchuck, was crowned King of the Himalayan Kingdom, becoming the world's youngest reigning monarch and head of the newest democracy.

On 8 February 2007, the Indo-Bhutan Friendship Treaty was substantially revised. Whereas in the Treaty of 1949 Article 2 read as "The Government of India undertakes to exercise no interference in the internal administration of Bhutan. On its part the Government of Bhutan agrees to be guided by the advice of the Government of India in regard to its external relations." In the revised treaty it now reads as "In keeping with the abiding ties of close friendship and cooperation between Bhutan and India, the Government of the Kingdom of Bhutan and the Government of the Republic of India shall cooperate closely with each other on issues relating to their national interests. Neither Government shall allow the use of its territory for activities harmful to the national security and interest of the other." The revised treaty also includes in it the preamble "Reaffirming their respect for each other's independence, sovereignty and territorial integrity;" an element that was absent in the earlier version. The Indo-Bhutan Friendship Treaty of 2007 strengthens Bhutan's status as an independent and sovereign nation.

The new democratic system comprises an upper and lower house, the latter based on political party affiliations. Elections for the upper house (National Council) were held on 31 December 2007, while elections for the lower house, the 47-seat National Assembly, were held on 24 March 2008. Two political parties, the People's Democratic Party (PDP) headed by Sangay Ngedup, and the Druk Phuensum Tshogpa (DPT) headed by Jigmi Thinley, competed in the National Assembly election. The Druk Phuensum Tshogpa won the elections taking 45 out of 47 seats in the parliament. Judicial power is vested in the courts of Bhutan. The Chief Justice is the administrative head of the Judiciary.

Economy

The Ngultrum is the currency of Bhutan and its value is pegged to the Indian rupee. The rupee is also accepted as legal tender in the country. Incomes of over Nu 100,000 per annum are taxed, but very few wage and salary earners qualify. Bhutan's inflation rate was estimated at about 3% in 2003. Bhutan has a Gross Domestic Product of around USD 2.913 billion (adjusted to Purchasing Power Parity).

Though Bhutan's economy is one of the world's smallest, it has grown very rapidly with about 8% in 2005 and 14% in 2006. This was mainly due to the commissioning of the gigantic Tala Hydroelectricity project. As of March 2006, Bhutan's per capita income was US$ 1,321 making it one of the fastest growing in South Asia. Bhutan's standard of living is growing faster than that of its neighbouring countries and is one of the highest in South Asia. Bhutan's small

economy is based on agriculture, forestry, and the sale of hydroelectric power to India. Agriculture provides the main livelihood for more than 80% of the population. Agrarian practices consist largely of subsistence farming and animal husbandry. Handicrafts, particularly weaving and the manufacture of religious art for home altars are a small cottage industry and a source of income for some.

A landscape that varies from hilly to ruggedly mountainous has made the building of roads, and other infrastructure, difficult and expensive. This, and a lack of access to the sea, has meant that Bhutan has never been able to benefit from significant trading of its produce. Bhutan does not have a railway system, though Indian Railways plans to link up southern Bhutan with its vast network under an agreement signed in January 2005. The historic trade routes over the high Himalayas, which connected India to Tibet, have been closed since the 1959 military takeover of Tibet (although smuggling activity still brings Chinese goods into Bhutan).

The industrial sector is minimal, production being of the cottage-industry type. Most development projects, such as road construction, rely on Indian contract labour. Agricultural produce includes rice, chillies, dairy (yak) products, buckwheat, barley, root crops, apples, and citrus and maize at lower elevations. Industries include cement, wood products, processed fruits, alcoholic beverages and calcium carbide.

Government revenues total € 122 million ($146

million), though expenditures amount $152 million. 60% of the budget expenditure, however, is financed by India's Ministry of External Affairs. Bhutan's exports - principally electricity, cardamom, gypsum, timber, handicrafts, cement, fruit, precious stones and spices - total $154 million. Imports, however, amount to $196 million, leading to a trade deficit. Main items imported include fuel and lubricants, grain, machinery, vehicles, fabrics and rice. Bhutan's main export partner is India, accounting for 87.9% of its export goods. Bangladesh (4.6%) and the Philippines (2%) are the other two top export partners. As its border with Tibet is closed, trade between Bhutan and China is now almost non-existent. Bhutan's import partners include India (71.3%), Japan (7.8%) and Austria (3%).

Demographics

Among the Bhutanese people, several principal ethnic groups may be distinguished. The second dominant group is the Ngalops, a Buddhist group based in the western part of the country. Their culture is closely related to that of Tibet. Much the same could be said of the Sharchops ("Easterners") the dominant group, who are associated with the eastern part of Bhutan (but who traditionally follow the Nyingmapa rather than the official Drukpa Kagyu form of Tibetan Buddhism). They are called the Eastern Bhutanese and Western Bhutanese respectively. In modern times, with improving transportation infrastructure, there has been much intermarrying between Easterners and Westerners, due to the closeness of their cultures and traditions. In the early 1970s, intermarriage between the Lhotsampas and main stream Bhutanese society was encouraged by the government.

The national language is Dzongkha, one of 53 languages in the Tibetan language family. The script, here called Chhokey ("Dharma Language"), is identical with the Tibetan script. A number of Nepali dialects are spoken in parts of southern Bhutan. Khengkha is spoken in central Bhutan. In the schools English is the medium of instruction and Dzongkha is taught as the national language. 24 languages are currently spoken in Bhutan, all of them in the Tibeto-Burman family, except Nepali, an Indo-Aryan language. Till the 1980's the government sponsored the teaching of Nepali in schools in Southern Bhutan. However, after the violent insurgency in the south, Nepali was removed from the curriculum. The languages of Bhutan are still not well-characterised, and several have yet to be recorded in an in-depth academic grammar. English now has official status as well.

The literacy rate is only 42.2% (56.2% of males and 28.1% of females), 14-year olds and younger comprise 39.1%, while people between 15 and 59 comprise 56.9%, and those over 60 are only 4%. The country has a median age of 20.4 years. Bhutan has a life expectancy of 62.2 years (61 for males and 64.5 for females) according to the latest data from the World Bank. There are 1,070 males to every 1,000 females in the country.

Military and Foreign Affairs

The Royal Bhutan Army is Bhutan's military service. It includes the Royal Bodyguard and the Royal Bhutan Police. Membership is voluntary, and the minimum age for recruitment is 18. The standing army numbers about 6,000 and is trained by the Indian Army. It has an annual budget of about US$13.7 million—1.8% of the GDP.

Though the 1949 Treaty with India is still sometimes misinterpreted to mean that India controls Bhutan's foreign affairs, Bhutan today handles all of its foreign affairs itself including the sensitive (to India) border demarcation issue with China. Bhutan has diplomatic relations with 22 countries, including the European Union, with missions in India, Bangladesh, Thailand and Kuwait. It has two UN missions, one in New York and one in Geneva. Only India and Bangladesh have residential embassies in Bhutan, while Thailand has a consulate office in Bhutan.

By a long standing treaty, Indian and Bhutanese citizens may travel to each other's countries without a passport or visa using their national identity cards instead. Bhutanese citizens may also work in India without legal restriction. Bhutan does not have formal diplomatic ties with its northern neighbour, China, although exchanges of visits at various levels between the two have significantly increased in the recent past. The first bilateral agreement between China and Bhutan was signed in 1998, and Bhutan has also set up consulates in Macau and Hong Kong. Bhutan's border with China is largely not demarcated and thus disputed in some places.

On 13 November 2005, Chinese soldiers crossed into Bhutan under the pretext that environmental conditions had forced their retreat south from the Himalayas. The Bhutanese government allowed this incursion (after the fact) on humanitarian grounds. Soon after, the Chinese began building roads and bridges within Bhutanese territory. Bhutanese Foreign Minister Khandu Wangchuk took up the matter with Chinese authorities after the issue was raised in Bhutanese parliament. In response, Foreign

Ministry spokesman Qin Gang of the People's Republic of China has said that the border remains in dispute (completely ignoring the original official pretext for the incursion) and that the two sides continue to work for a peaceful and cordial resolution of the dispute.

Security Issues

Bhutan is bounded on three sides by India. From east to west, the Indian states of Sikkim, West Bengal, Assam, and Arunachal Pradesh border Bhutan. In view of the long-standing political disputes and border confrontations between India and China, Bhutan has long been part of India's strategic defence plan. In the view of some Indian strategists, Bhutan is a weak link in India's defence against China.

The key document guiding relations with India is the Treaty of Friendship between the Government of India and the Government of Bhutan of 1949. The ten-article treaty, in force in perpetuity, calls for peace between the two countries and assures Indian non-interference in Bhutan's internal affairs in return for Bhutan's agreeing "to be guided by the advice of the Government of India in regard to its external relations". It also guarantees free trade between the countries and duty-free transit across India of Bhutan's imports. Furthermore, the treaty assures the rights of citizens of each country and the extradition of criminals seeking refuge in either country.

Events in Tibet have had causal effects on Bhutan-Indian relations. The Indo-Bhutanese border was delineated in the Treaty of Peace of 1865 between Bhutan and Britain, but it was not until the period between 1973 and 1984 that a detailed delineation and demarcation was made. Border demarcation talks with India generally resolved disagreements except for several small sectors, including the middle zone between Sarbhang and Geylegphug and the eastern frontier with Arunachal Pradesh.

In the 1960s Bhutan joined international organisations. It first became a member of the Colombo Plan in 1962, which put the kingdom into contact with member states throughout South Asia and Southeast Asia for fostering cooperative economic development. UN membership was achieved in 1971. A founding member of SAARC in 1983, Bhutan has also established relations with the Coordination Bureau of the Nonaligned Countries (the headquarters of the Nonaligned Movement), the Group of 77, the Asian Development Bank, and the European Community. In 1975 Bhutan and four other landlocked Asian countries (Afghanistan, Laos, Mongolia, and Nepal) were granted a special status as "least developed landlocked countries" by the UN Economic and Social Commission for Asia and the Pacific (ESCAP) in coordination with the United Nations Conference on Trade and Development (UNCTAD) and UNDP. Despite these organisations' intentions to assist Bhutan and the other countries in dealing with international transit problems, Bhutan declined to participate in their work.

Perhaps the most significant international participation Bhutan embarked on in the 1980s was membership in SAARC. Bhutan became involved in useful working group discussions on agriculture and livestock, rural development, meteorology, telecommunications, science and technology, health and population, transportation, postal cooperation, and trade and industrial cooperation.

CHINA

The outbreak of revolution on 10 October 1911 signalled the collapse of the Qing Dynasty (1644–1911), which was formally replaced by the government of the Republic of China on 12 February 1912. The People's Republic of China was officially established on 1 October 1949, replacing the Republic of China government on mainland China.

The flag of China is red with a large yellow five-pointed star and four smaller yellow five-pointed stars (arranged in a vertical arc toward the middle of the flag) in the upper hoist-side corner. The colour red symbolizes the spirit of the revolution, and the five stars signify the unity of the people of China under the leadership of the Chinese Communist Party.

Since the introduction of economic reforms in 1978, China has become the world's fastest-growing major economy. As of 2012, it is the world's second-largest economy, after the United States, by both nominal GDP and purchasing power parity (PPP), and is also the world's largest exporter and second-largest importer of goods. On a per capita income basis, China ranked 90th by nominal GDP and 91st by GDP (PPP) in 2011, according to the IMF. China is a recognised nuclear weapons state and has the world's largest standing army, with the second-largest defence budget. In 2003, China became the third nation in the world, after the former Soviet Union and the United States, to independently launch a successful manned space mission. China has been characterised as a potential superpower by a number of academics, military analysts, and public policy and economics analysts.

History

The communist takeover of the mainland in 1949 set the scene for building a new society built on a Marxist-Leninist model replete with class struggle and proletarian politics fashioned and directed by the CCP. The People's Republic of China was barely established when it perceived a threat from the United States, which was at war in North Korea, and elected to support its neighbour, the new communist state, the Democratic People's Republic of Korea. The Chinese People's Volunteer Army invaded the Korean Peninsula in October 1950 and, along with its North Korean ally, enjoyed initial military success and then a two-year stalemate, which culminated in an armistice signed on 27 July 1953. Meanwhile, China seized control of Tibet. It also had embarked on a political rectification movement against "enemies of the state" and promoting "class struggle" under the aegis of agrarian reform as part of the "transition to socialism."

Periods of consolidation and economic development facilitated by President Liu Shaoqi (1898–1969) and Premier Zhou were severely altered by disastrous anti-intellectual (such as the Hundred Flowers Campaign, 1957), economic (the Great Leap Forward, 1958–59), and political (the Great Proletarian Cultural Revolution, 1966–76) experiments directed by Mao and his supporters. During this time, China had broken with the Soviet Union by 1959, fought a border war with India in 1962, and skirmished with Soviet troops in 1969. The 1976 death of Mao ended

Capital	-	Beijing
Largest city	-	Shanghai
National language	-	Standard Mandarin (spoken)
	-	Simplified Chinese (written)
Ethnic groups	-	91% Han; 11+ minor ethnic groups; 55 recognised minorities
Government	-	Single-party communist state
	-	President Xi Jinping
	-	Premier Li Keqiang
Legislature	-	National People's Congress
Establishment	-	People's Republic of China proclaimed 1 October 1949
Area	-	9,596,960 square kilometres
Coastline	-	14,500 kilometres
Population	-	1,358,821,000 (2012 estimate)
	-	Density 363/square kilometre
GDP (PPP)	-	$12,405 trillion (2012 estimate)
	-	Per capita $9,233
GDP (nominal)	-	$8,227 trillion (2012 estimate)
	-	Per capita $6,076
Defence Minister	-	General Chang Wanquan
Chief of General Staff	-	General Fang Fenghui
Chief of Navy	-	Admiral Wu Shengli
Chief of Air Force	-	General Ma Xiaotian
Chief of Missile Forces	-	Gen Jing Zhiyuan

the extremist influence in the party, and, under the leadership of Deng Xiaoping and his supporters, China began a period of pragmatic economic reforms and opening itself to the outside world.

Reform-era activities began in earnest in 1978 and eventually made China one of the largest world economies and trading partners as well as a regional military power. The Four Modernisations (agriculture, industry, science and technology, and national defence) became the preeminent agenda within the party, state, and society. The well-being of China's people increased substantially, especially along coastal areas and in urban areas involved in manufacturing for the world market. Yet, politics, the so-called "fifth modernisation," occurred at too slow a pace for the emerging generation. The democracy movement, however, was violently suppressed by the military in the 1989 Tiananmen incident.

In the years after Tiananmen, conservative reformers led by Deng protégé Jiang Zemin endured and eventually overcame world criticism. When Deng went into retirement, the rising generation of technocrats ruled China and oversaw its modernisation. Political progress gradually occurred. Term limits were placed on political and governmental positions at all levels, succession became orderly and contested elections began to take place at the local level. Tens of thousands of Chinese students went overseas to study; many returned to participate in the building of modern China, some to become millionaires in the new "socialist economy with Chinese characteristics."

As the 21st century began, a new generation of leaders emerged and gradually replaced the old. Hu Jintao emerged—by 2004—as the preeminent leader (president of China, chairman of both the state Central Military Commission and party Central Military Commission, and general secretary of the CCP). A concern is that the benefits of economic development has not been distributed evenly, resulting in a wide development gap between urban and rural areas. As a result, under President Hu Jintao and Premier Wen Jiabao, the Chinese government initiated policies to address these issues of equitable distribution of resources, though the outcome remains to be seen. More than 40 million farmers have been displaced from their land, usually for economic development, contributing to the 87,000 demonstrations and riots across China in 2005. Living standards have improved significantly but political controls remain tight. During China's 18th National Communist Party Congress in November 2012, Hu Jintao and Wen Jiabao were replaced as President and Premier by Xi Jinping and Li Keqiang, who formally took office in 2013. Under Xi, the Chinese government began large-scale efforts to reform its economy, which has suffered from structural instabilities and slowing growth.

By 2030, the global economy is likely to have regained its momentum, and the outlines of a new geopolitical order will be much clearer. China is likely to have assumed additional global responsibilities.

Geography

China has a total of 22,117 kilometres of land boundaries with 14 other nations. These borders include. Afghanistan (76 kilometres), Bhutan (470 kilometres), Burma (2,185 kilometres), India (3,380 kilometres), Kazakhstan (1,533 kilometres), North Korea (1,416 kilometres), Kyrgyzstan (858 kilometres), Laos (423 kilometres), Mongolia (4,677 kilometres), Nepal (1,236 kilometres), Pakistan (523 kilometres), Russia (4,300 kilometres), Tajikistan (414 kilometres), and Vietnam (1,281 kilometres). China's coastline extends 14,500 kilometres from the border with North Korea in the north to Vietnam in the south. China is involved in a complex dispute with Malaysia, Philippines, Taiwan, Vietnam, and possibly Brunei over the Spratly (Nansha) Islands in the South China Sea. China also occupies the Paracel (Xisha) Islands, which are also claimed by Vietnam and Taiwan, and asserts a claim to the Japanese-administered Senkaku Islands (Diaoyu Tai) in the Pacific Ocean.

Most of the mountainous and militarised boundary with India is in dispute. China's de facto administration of the Aksai Chin section of Kashmir is the subject of a dispute between China and India. India does not recognize Pakistan's ceding lands to China in a 1964 boundary agreement. In October 2004, China signed an agreement with Russia on the delimitation of their entire 4,300-kilometre-long border, which had long been in dispute.

Principal Rivers. Mountains cover 33% of China's landmass, plateaus 26%, basins 19%, plains 12%, and hills 10%. Thus, 69% of China's land is mountains, hills, and highlands.

China has 50,000 rivers totaling some 420,000 kilometres in length and each having a catchment area of more than 100 square kilometres. Some 1,500 of these rivers each have catchment areas exceeding 1,000 square kilometres. Most rivers flow from west to east and empty into the Pacific Ocean. The Yangzi (Changjiang or Yangzte River), which rises in Tibet, flows through Central China, and, having traveled 6,300 kilometres, enters the Yellow Sea near Shanghai. The Yangzi has a catchment area of 1.8 million square kilometres and is the third longest river in the world after the Amazon and the Nile. The second longest river in China is the Huanghe (Yellow River), which also rises in Tibet and travels circuitously for 5,464 kilometres through North China before reaching the Bo Hai Gulf on the north coast of Shangdong Province. The Heilongjiang (Heilong or Black Dragon River) flows for 3,101 kilometres in Northeast China and an additional 1,249 in Russia, where it is known as the Amur. The longest river in South China is the Zhujiang (Pearl River), which is 2,214 kilometres long.

Natural Resources. China has substantial mineral reserves and is the world's largest producer of antimony, natural graphite, tungsten, and zinc. Other major minerals are bauxite, coal, crude petroleum, diamonds, gold, iron ore, lead, magnetite, manganese, mercury, molybdenum, natural gas, phosphate rock, tin, uranium, and vanadium. With its vast mountain ranges, China's hydropower potential is the largest in the world.

Land Use. 14.86% (about 1.4 million square kilometres) of China's land is arable. About 1.3% (some 116,580 square kilometres) is planted to permanent crops. With comparatively little land planted to permanent crops, intensive agricultural techniques are used to reap harvests that are sufficient to feed the world's largest population and still have surplus for export. An estimated 544,784 square kilometres of land is irrigated.

Environmental Factors. The major current environmental issues in China are air pollution (greenhouse gases and sulfur dioxide particulates) from over reliance on coal, which produces acid rain; water shortages, particularly in the north; water pollution from untreated wastes; deforestation; an estimated loss of 20% of agricultural land since 1949 to soil erosion and economic development and desertification. Deforestation has been a major contributor to China's most significant natural disaster—flooding. China's national carbon dioxide (CO_2) emissions are among the highest in the world and increasing annually. The CO_2 emissions are estimated at 2.8 billion tons. These amounts cited by the UN are more than double those of India and Japan but still less than half those of the United States. China's ozone depleting potential also is high. The CO_2 emissions are mostly produced by coal-burning energy plants and other coal-burning operations. Better pollution control and billion-dollar cleanup programmes have helped reduced the growth rate of industrial pollution.

Time Zone. Although China crosses all or part of five international time zones, it operates on a single uniform time, China Standard Time (CST; Greenwich Mean Time plus eight hours), using Beijing as the base.

Society

Population. The most densely populated provinces are in the east. Jiangsu (712 persons per square kilometre), Shangdong (587 persons per square kilometre), and Henan (546 persons per square kilometre). Shanghai is the most densely populated municipality at 2,646 persons per square kilometre. The least densely populated areas are in the west, with Tibet having the lowest density at only 2 persons per square kilometre. Sixty-two% of the population lived in rural areas in 2004, while 38% lived in urban settings. About 94% of population lives on approximately 46% of land. In the long term, China faces increasing urbanisation; according to predictions, nearly 70% of the population will live in urban areas by 2035.

Demography. China has been the world's most populous nation for many centuries. China now has an increasingly aging population; it is projected that 11.8% of the population in 2020 will be 65 years of age and older. Based on 2006 estimates, China's age structure is 0–14 years of age—20.8%; 15–64 years—71.4%, and 65 years and older—7.7%. Estimates made in 2006 indicate a birth rate of nearly 13.3 births per 1,000 and a death rate of 6.9 per 1,000.

Ethnic Groups. Besides the majority Han Chinese, China recognizes 55 other nationality or ethnic groups, numbering about 105 million persons, mostly concentrated in the northwest, north, northeast,

south, and southwest but with some in central interior areas. Based on the 2000 census, some 91.5% of the population was classified as Han Chinese (1.1 billion). The other major minority ethnic groups were Zhuang (16.1 million), Manchu (10.6 million), Hui (9.8 million), Miao (8.9 million), Uighur (8.3 million), Tujia (8 million), Yi (7.7 million), Mongol (5.8 million), Tibetan (5.4 million), Bouyei (2.9 million), Dong (2.9 million), Yao (2.6 million), Korean (1.9 million), Bai (1.8 million), Hani (1.4 million), Kazakh (1.2 million), Li (1.2 million), and Dai (1.1 million). All nationalities in China are equal according to the law.

Languages. The official language of China is standard Chinese or Mandarin (Putonghua, which means standard speech, based on the Beijing dialect). Because of the many ethnic groups in China, numerous minority languages also are spoken. All of the Chinese dialects share a common written form that has evolved and been standardised during two millennia and serves as a unifying bond amongst the Han Chinese. The government has aggressively developed both shorthand Chinese and Pinyin (phonetic spelling) as ways to increase literacy and transliterate Chinese names. The Pinyin system was introduced in 1958 and was approved by the State Council in 1978 as the standard system for the romanisation of Chinese personal and geographic names.

Religion. The traditional religions of China are Confucianism, Daoism, and Buddhism.

Confucianism is not a religion, although some have tried to imbue it with rituals and religious qualities, but rather a philosophy and system of ethical conduct that since the 5th century B.C. has guided China's society. Kong Fuzi (Confucius in Latinised form) is honored in China as a great sage of antiquity whose writings promoted peace and harmony and good morals in family life and society in general. Ritualised reverence for one's ancestors, sometimes referred to as ancestor worship, has been a tradition in China since at least the Shang Dynasty (1750–1040 B.C.). In 2005 the Chinese government acknowledged that there were an estimated 100 million adherents to various sects of Buddhism and some 9,500 and 16,000 temples and monasteries, many maintained as cultural landmarks and tourist attractions. Approximately 8% of the population is Buddhist, approximately 1.5% is Muslim, an estimated 0.4% belongs to the government-sponsored "patriotic" Catholic Church, an estimated 0.4 to 0.6% belongs to the unofficial Vatican-affiliated Roman Catholic Church, and an estimated 1.2 to 1.5% is registered as Protestant. Most adherents of Islam are members of the Uighur and Hui nationality people.

Education and Literacy. The population has had on average only 6.2 years of schooling, but in 1986 the goal of nine years of compulsory education by 2000 was established. The education system provides free primary education for five years, starting at age seven, followed by five years of secondary education for ages 12 to 17. Since free higher education was abolished in 1985, applicants to colleges and universities compete for scholarships based on academic ability. Private schools have been allowed since the early 1980s. In 2003 China supported 1,552 institutions of higher learning (colleges and universities) and their 725,000 professors and 11 million students. While there is intense competition for admission to China's colleges and universities among college entrants, Beijing and Qinghua universities and more than 100 other key universities are the most sought after. The literacy rate in China is 90.9%, based on 2002 estimates.

Economy

As of 2013, China has the world's second-largest economy in terms of nominal GDP, totalling approximately US$8.227 trillion according to the International Monetary Fund (IMF). If PPP is taken into account (US$12.405 trillion in 2012), China's economy is again second only to the United States. In 2012, its PPP GDP per capita was US$9,161, while nominal GDP per capita was US$6,075. Both cases put China behind around ninety countries (out of 183 countries on the IMF list) in global GDP per capita rankings.

From its founding in 1949 until late 1978, the People's Republic of China was a Soviet-style centrally planned economy. Following Mao's death in 1976 and the consequent end of the Cultural Revolution, Deng Xiaoping and the new Chinese leadership began to reform the economy and move towards a more market-oriented mixed economy under one-party rule. Agricultural collectivisation was dismantled and farmlands privatised, while foreign trade became a major new focus, leading to the creation of Special Economic Zones (SEZs). Inefficient state-owned enterprises (SOEs) were restructured and unprofitable ones were closed outright, resulting in massive job losses. Modern-day China is mainly characterised as having a market economy based on private property ownership, and is one of the leading examples of state capitalism. The state still dominates in strategic "pillar" sectors such as energy production and heavy industries, but private enterprise has expanded enormously, with around 30 million private businesses recorded in 2008.

Since economic liberalisation began in 1978, China's investment- and export-led economy has grown more than a hundredfold and is the fastest-growing major economy in the world. According to the IMF, China's annual average GDP growth between 2001 and 2010 was 10.5%. Between 2007 and 2011, China's economic growth rate was equivalent to all of the G7 countries' growth combined. According to the Global Growth Generators index announced by Citigroup in February 2011, China has a very high 3G growth rating. Its high productivity, low labour costs and relatively good infrastructure have made it a global leader in manufacturing. However, the Chinese economy is highly energy-intensive and inefficient; China became the world's largest energy consumer in 2010, relies on coal to supply over 70% of its energy needs, and surpassed the US to become the world's largest oil importer in September 2013. China's economic growth and industrialisation has caused damage to its environment. In the early 2010s, China's economic growth rate began to slow amid domestic credit troubles, weakening demand for exports from China, and global economic turmoil.

China is a member of the WTO and is the world's largest trading power, with a total international trade value of US$3.87 trillion in 2012. Its foreign exchange reserves reached US$2.85 trillion by the end of 2010, an increase of 18.7% over the previous year, making its reserves by far the world's largest, China owns an estimated $1.6 trillion of US securities. China, holding over US$1.16 trillion in US Treasury bonds, is the largest foreign holder of US public debt. China is the world's third-largest recipient of inward foreign direct investment (FDI), attracting $115 billion in 2011 alone, marking a 9% increase over 2010. China also increasingly invests abroad, with a total outward FDI of $68 billion in 2010, and a number of major takeovers of foreign firms by Chinese companies. China's undervalued exchange rate has caused friction with other major economies, and it has also been widely criticised for manufacturing large quantities of counterfeit goods.

China now ranks 29th in the Global Competitiveness Index, although it is only ranked 136th among the 179 countries measured in the Index of Economic Freedom. In 2011, 61 Chinese companies were listed in the Fortune Global 500. Measured by total revenues, three of the world's top ten most valuable companies are Chinese, including fifth-ranked Sinopec Group, sixth-ranked China National Petroleum and seventh-ranked State Grid (the world's largest electric utilities company).

China's middle-class population (defined as those with annual income of at least US$17,000) had reached more than 100 million by 2011. The number of US dollar billionaires in China increased from 130 in 2009 to 251 in 2012, giving China the world's second-highest number of billionaires. China's domestic retail market was worth over 20 trillion yuan (US$3.2 trillion) in 2012 and is now growing at over 12% annually, while the country's luxury goods market has expanded immensely, with 27.5% of the global share. However, in recent years, China's rapid economic growth has contributed to severe consumer inflation, leading to increased government regulation. China has a high level of economic inequality, which has increased in the past few decades.

Communications

China currently has the largest number of active cellphones of any country in the world, with over 1 billion users as of May 2012. It also has the world's largest number of internet and broadband users, with over 591 million internet users as of 2013, equivalent to around 44% of its population. According to the China Internet Network Information Centre (CNNIC), China's average internet connection speed in 2011 was 100.9 kbit/s, less than half of the global average of 212.5 kbit/s. However, a 2013 report also confirms the national average speed as 3.14 MB/s as of July 2013, China accounts for 24% of the world's internet-connected devices.

China Telecom and China Unicom, the country's two largest broadband providers, accounted for 20% of global broadband subscribers, whereas the world's ten largest broadband service providers combined accounted for 39% of the world's broadband customers. China Telecom alone serves 55 million broadband subscribers, while China Unicom serves more than 40 million. The massive rise in internet use in China continues to fuel rapid broadband growth, whereas the world's other major broadband ISPs operate in the mature markets of the developed world, with high levels of broadband penetration and rapidly slowing subscriber growth. Several Chinese telecommunications companies, most notably Huawei and ZTE, have become highly profitable in overseas markets, but have also been accused of spying for the Chinese military.

Infrastructure

Since the late 1990s, China's national road network has been significantly expanded through the creation of a network of highways, known as the National Trunk Highway System (NTHS). In 2011 China's highways had reached a total length of 85,000 km, making it the longest highway system in the world. Private car ownership is growing rapidly in China, which surpassed the United States as the world's largest automobile market in 2009, with total car sales of over 13.6 million. Analysts predict that annual car sales in China may rise as high as 40 million by 2020. A side-effect of the rapid growth of China's road network has been a significant rise in traffic accidents, mostly caused by poorly enforced traffic laws – in 2011 alone, around 62,000 Chinese died in road accidents, and efforts to improve traffic safety have had limited success.

China also possesses over 9,676 km of high-speed rail. In December 2012, China opened the world's longest high-speed rail line, running from Beijing to Guangzhou. China intends to operate approximately 16,000 km of high-speed rail lines by 2020. Rapid transit systems are also rapidly developing in China's major cities, in the form of networks of underground or light rail systems. China is additionally developing its own satellite navigation system, dubbed Beidou, which began offering commercial navigation services

across Asia in 2012, and is planned to offer global coverage by 2020.

As of 2012, China is the world's largest constructor of new airports, and the Chinese government has begun a US$250 billion five-year project to expand and modernize domestic air travel. However, 80% of China's airspace remains restricted for military use; long-distance transportation remains dominated by railways and charter bus systems. Railways are the vital carrier in China; they are owned by the state, and divided into various railway bureaux in different regions. Due to huge demand, the system is regularly subject to overcrowding, particularly during holiday seasons, such as Chunyun during the Chinese New Year. The Chinese rail network carried an estimated 1.68 billion total passengers in 2010 alone. In urban areas, bicycles remain an extremely common mode of transport, despite the increasing prevalence of automobiles – as of 2012, there are approximately 470 million bicycles in China.

Government and Politics

Executive Branch. The government is led by the State Council, the equivalent of a cabinet. There also are four vice premiers and five state councillors. In 2006 there were 22 ministries and four commissions subordinate to the State Council. In addition, the People's Bank of China (China's central bank) and the National Audit Office are part of the State Council system. The five-year terms of office run concurrently with those of the National People's Congress (NPC) and are limited to no more than two consecutive terms.

Legislative Branch. The National People's Congress (NPC) is the highest organ of state power and exercises the legislative power of the state. Deputies to the NPC are elected from the provinces, autonomous regions, centrally administered municipalities, special administrative regions, and the armed forces. Elections are conducted by the permanent body of the NPC, the Standing Committee, and normally are held at least two months before the end of the current NPC. Deputies serve five-year terms and meet annually for two or three weeks, typically in March or April; 2,979 deputies were elected to the current 10th NPC. The NPC is empowered to amend the constitution; supervise the enforcement of the constitution; and elect the president and vice president of the People's Republic, chairman of the state Central Military Commission, president of the Supreme People's Court, and procurator general of the Supreme People's Procuratorate. The NPC Standing Committee consists of a chairman, 15 vice chairmen, a secretary general, and 153 members, including the officers. Standing Committee members are not allowed to hold administrative, judicial, or procuratorial posts and, in practice, are often senior CCP and former state leaders and officials. As with the NPC membership, the chairman and vice chairmen may serve no more than two consecutive terms.

Judicial Branch. China has a four-level court system. At the top is the Supreme People's Court in Beijing. Lower courts are the higher people's courts in provinces, autonomous regions, and special municipalities; intermediate people's courts at the prefecture level and also in parts of provinces, autonomous regions, and special municipalities; and basic people's courts in counties, towns, and municipal districts. Special courts handle matters affecting the military, railroad transportation, water transportation, and forestry. Constitutionally, the court system exercises judicial power independently and technically is free of interference from administrative organs, public organisations, and individuals. The Supreme People's Court supervises the administration of justice by local courts and special courts, while courts at higher levels oversee the administration of courts at lower levels. At each level, the courts are "responsible to the organs of state power which created them." Judges are limited to two consecutive terms running concurrently with the National People's Congress or local people's congresses.

Administrative Divisions. China has 22 provinces, five autonomous regions, and four municipalities. The provinces are, in the northeast. Heilongjiang, Jilin, and Liaoning; in the north. Shandong, Hebei, Shanxi, and Shaanxi; in central China. Jiangsu, Anhui, Henan, Hubei, and Zhejiang; in the south. Hunan, Jiangxi, Fujian, Guangdong, and Hainan (an island in the South China Sea); in the southwest. Guizhou, Yunnan, and Sichuan; and in the northwest. Gansu and Qinghai. The autonomous regions—Guangxi Zhuang, Tibet (Xizang), Xinjiang Uighur, Inner Mongolia, and Ningxia Hui—are in border areas with large non-Han ethnic minority populations. The four municipalities—Beijing, Tianjin, Shanghai, and Chongqing—are directly controlled by the central government. China also has two special administrative regions (SARs), Hong Kong and Macau. Beijing also claims Taiwan as a province.

Electoral System. Under the Organic Law of the Village Committees, all of China's approximately 1 million villages hold competitive, direct elections for sub-governmental village committees. The revised law also explicitly transferred the power to nominate candidates to villagers themselves, as opposed to village groups or Chinese Communist Party (CCP) branches. Deputies to local people's congresses of provinces, centrally administered municipalities, and cities divided into districts are elected by the people's congress at the next lower level. Deputies to people's congresses of counties, cities not divided into districts, municipal districts, townships, ethnic townships, and towns are elected directly by their constituencies to five-year terms. The local congresses each have corresponding standing committees that exercise legislative authority when the full congresses are not in session. Elected leaders, however, remain subordinate to the corresponding CCP secretary, and most are appointed by higher-level party organisations. Although China's constitution guarantees suffrage for citizens age 18 and older, the CCP maintains a close watch on electoral democracy at the grassroots levels and controls the outcome of elections at other levels.

Mass Media. China's electronic mass media are regulated by the State Administration of Radio, Film, and Television, a subordinate agency of the Ministry of Information Industry. The Chinese Communist Party's Propaganda Department traditionally has played a large role as arbiter of standards for appropriate broadcasts. The People's Broadcasting Station transmits radio broadcasts in standard Chinese (Putonghua) and the various dialects and minority languages throughout China. China National Radio, headquartered in Beijing, transmits programmes in standard Chinese, Kazakh, Korean, Mongolian, Tibetan, and Uighur. The government has been active in regulating newspapers. The Ministry of Information Industry regulates access to the Internet while the Ministry of Public Security and the Ministry of State Security monitor its use. A broad range of topics that authorities interpret as potentially subversive or as slanderous to the state, including the dissemination of anti-unification information or "state secrets" that may endanger national security, are prohibited by various laws and regulations. Internet service providers (ISPs) are restricted to domestic media news postings and are required to record information useful for tracking users and their viewing habits, install software capable of copying e-mails, and immediately abort transmission of material considered subversive. As a result, many ISPs practice self-censorship to avoid violations of the broadly worded regulations.

Foreign Relations

Sweden was the first western country to establish diplomatic relations with the People's Republic on 9 May 1950. In 1971, the PRC replaced the Republic of China as the sole representative of China in the United Nations and as one of the five permanent

members of the United Nations Security Council. The PRC was also a former member and leader of the Non-Aligned Movement, and still considers itself an advocate for developing countries.

Under its interpretation of the One-China policy, the PRC has made it a precondition to establishing diplomatic relations that the other country acknowledges its claim to Taiwan and severs official ties with the Republic of China government; it has acted furiously when any country shows signs of diplomatic overture, or sells armaments to Taiwan. It also opposes publicised foreign travels by pro-Taiwan-independence ROC officials, and other separatist figures, such as the 14th Dalai Lama.

The PRC has been playing an increasing role in calling for free trade areas and security pacts amongst its Asia-Pacific neighbours. The PRC is also a founding member of the Shanghai Cooperation Organisation (SCO), with Russia and the Central Asian republics. In 2000 the U.S. Congress approved "permanent normal trade relations" with China, allowing Chinese exports in at the same low tariffs as goods from most other countries. China has a significant trade surplus with the United States, its most important export market. U.S. politicians have recently argued that the Chinese yuan is undervalued, giving China an unfair trade advantage.

Sinophobic attitudes often target Chinese minorities and nationals living outside of China. Anti-Chinese sentiment is often rooted in socio-economics.

Much of the current foreign policy is based on the concept of Five Principles of Peaceful Coexistence of Zhou Enlai—non-interference in other states' affairs, non-aggression, peaceful coexistence, and equality and mutual benefits. China's foreign policy is also driven by the concept of "harmony without uniformity" which encourages diplomatic relations between states despite ideological differences. This has led China to support states that are regarded as dangerous by Western nations, such as Zimbabwe, North Korea, or Iran. Conflicts with foreign countries have occurred at times in its recent history, particularly with the United States; for example, the US bombing of the Chinese embassy in Belgrade during the Kosovo conflict in May 1999 and the US-China spy plane incident in April 2001. Its foreign relations with many Western nations suffered for a time following the Tiananmen Square protests of 1989, though they have since recovered.

The relationship between China and Japan has been strained at times by Japan's refusal to acknowledge its wartime past to the satisfaction of the PRC. Another point of conflict between the two countries is the frequent visits by Japanese government officials to the Yasukuni Shrine.

Equally bordering the most countries in the world alongside Russia, the PRC was in a number of international territorial disputes. China's territorial disputes have led to localised wars in the last 50 years, including the Sino-Indian War in 1962, the Sino-Soviet border conflict in 1969, and the Sino-Vietnamese War in 1979. In 2001, the PRC and Russia signed the Sino-Russian Treaty of Friendship, which paved the way in 2004 for Russia to transfer Yinlong Island as well as one-half of Heixiazi to China, ending a long-standing Sino-Russian border dispute. Other territorial disputes include islands in the East and South China Seas, and undefined or disputed land borders with India and Bhutan.

While accompanying a rapid economic rise, the PRC since the 1990s seeks to maintain a policy of quiet diplomacy with its neighbours. It does so by keeping economic growth steady and participating in regional organisations and cultivating bi-lateral relations in order to ease suspicion over China's burgeoning military capabilities. The PRC has started a policy of wooing African nations for trade and bilateral co-operation. (There are no less than 750,000 Chinese nationals working or living in Africa). There are some discussions about whether China will become a new superpower in the 21st century, with certain commentators pointing out its economic progress, military might, very large population, and increasing international influence but others claiming it is headed for economic collapse.

National Security

Overview. The armed forces of China are officially and collectively known as the People's Liberation Army (PLA). With 2.3 million active troops, the People's Liberation Army (PLA) is the largest military in the world. The PLA consists of an army, navy, air force, and strategic nuclear force. The Chinese Communist Party (CCP) Central Military Commission sets policy for the PLA. The commission, which is chaired by China's president, has three vice chairmen, each a general in the PLA ground forces, and seven members representing various components of the PLA. Operational control is administered dually by the CCP Central Military Commission and the State Central Military Commission and the Ministry of National Defence. PLA headquarters is organised into the General Staff Department, General Political Department, General Logistics Department, and General Armaments Department.

China, with possession of nuclear weapons and delivery systems, is considered a major military regional power and an emerging military superpower. China is the only member of the UN Security Council to have limited power projection capabilities. As a consequence, it has been establishing foreign military relationships that have been compared to a 'String of Pearls'.

Much progress has been made in the last decade and the PRC continues to make efforts to modernize its military. It has purchased state-of-the-art fighter jets from Russia, such as the Sukhoi Su-30s, and has also produced its own modern fighters, specifically the Chinese J-10s and the J-11s. It has also acquired and improved upon the Russian S-300 surface-to-air missile systems, which are considered to be among the best aircraft-intercepting systems in the world, albeit Russia has since produced the new generation S-400 Triumf, with China reportedly already having spent $500 million on a downgraded export version of it. The PRC's armoured and rapid-reaction forces have been updated with enhanced electronics and targeting capabilities. In recent years, much attention has been focused on building a navy with blue-water capability.

Defence Budget. The official announced budget of the PLA for 2009 was $70 billion. However, the United States claims China does not report its real military spending. The Defense Intelligence Agency estimates that the real Chinese military budget for 2008 could be anywhere from US$105 to US$150 billion.

Internal Threat and Terrorism. Although the government defines the outlawed Falun Gong movement as the major internal threat and the People's Armed Police Force actively pursues its members, Falun Gong is, nevertheless, not classified as a terrorist group, and it has not committed or sponsored acts of violence. Muslim separatists in Xinjiang Uighur Autonomous Region present China with its most significant terrorist threat, which emerged in the late 1980s. In 2003 Beijing published an "East Turkistan Terrorist List," which labelled organisations such as the World Uighur Youth Congress and the East Turkistan Information Centre as terrorist entities. These groups openly advocate independence for "East Turkestan," and, although they have not been publicly linked to violent activity, the separatists have resorted to violence, bomb attacks, assassinations, and street fighting, which Beijing responds to with police and military action. The Tibet Autonomous Region has also seen unrest.

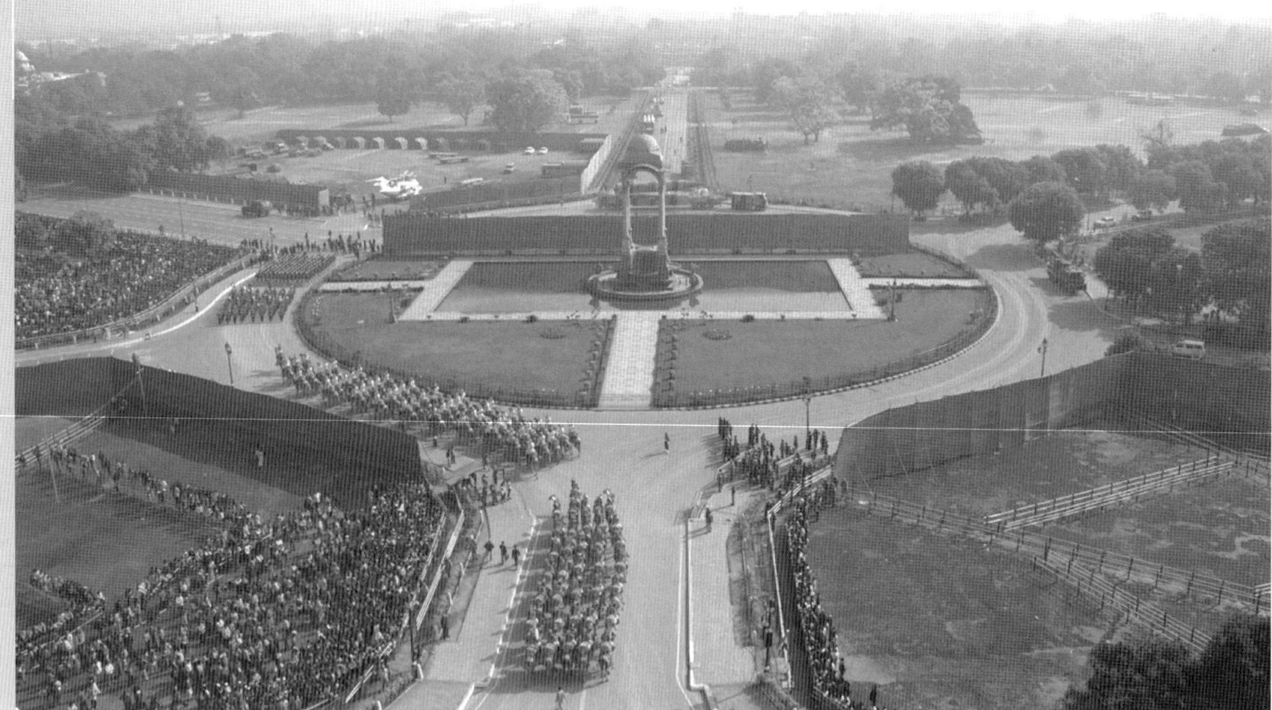

INDIA

The Republic of India (official Sanskrit name is *Bharat*) occupies much of the Indian subcontinent. On the north, India borders China, Nepal, and Bhutan, Pakistan in the west, and Bangladesh and Myanmar in the east. The Indian Ocean to the south, the Arabian Sea to the west, and the Bay of Bengal to the east form the country's coastline. Non-contiguous to the mainland are the Lakshadweep Islands in the Arabian Sea and the Andaman and Nicobar Islands located 1,300 kilometres from the mainland in the Bay of Bengal. India has 35 cities and urban agglomerations with more than 1 million persons. The most populous cities are Mumbai (16.4 million people), Kolkata (13.2 million), New Delhi (12.8 million), Chennai (6.4 million), Bangalore (5.7 million), Hyderabad (5.5 million), and Ahmadabad (4.5 million).

India's national flag has three horizontal bands. The upper band is saffron in colour, the lower is green, and the middle is white with a 24-spoke dark blue wheel in its centre. The saffron symbolizes courage, sacrifice, and renunciation; the white represents purity and truth; and the green signifies faith and fertility. The wheel is the Dharma Chakra, an ancient Buddhist symbol used by the Indian king Ashoka to represent the "wheel of law."

Historical Background

On 15 August 1947, the country was partitioned into India and Pakistan, which led to massive migration of Hindus and Muslims and substantial communal conflict. Furthermore, the British had left India with a rudimentary industrial and scientific base; tremendous poverty; a large and growing population; social cleavages along caste and economic lines; and contentious territorial boundaries that have led to armed conflicts with Pakistan (1947 to 1949, 1965, 1971, 1999), China (1962), and numerous insurgent groups.

In spite of such difficulties, India can count a number of successes. India has maintained a democratic political system. India has developed an educational infrastructure that has trained one of the world's largest scientific and technical populations. Using Green Revolution agricultural technologies, the country has become self-sufficient in food production. A combination of socialist planning and free enterprise from the 1950s to the 1970s led to substantial industrialisation with the goal of making India economically self-sufficient. In the 1980s and 1990s, socialist economic planning and import substitution industries were slowly replaced by liberalisation measures, a large middle class emerged, information technology developed into an important economic sector, and economic growth has been impressive. India has also become influential in international political and economic matters and appears set to continue those trends.

Numerous problems remain, however, such as substantial poverty, large income gaps between wealthy and poor, a large mass of people who lack the skills to participate in the new economy, and numerous insurgencies that threaten the nation's territorial integrity. Some social issues remain unresolved, and the rise of Hindu nationalism has

Capital	-	New Delhi
Official languages	-	Hindi, English (Constitutional languages – Assamese, Bengali, Bodo, Dogri, Gujarati, Hindi, Kannada, Kashmiri, Konkani, Maithili, Malayalam, Manipuri, Marathi, Nepali, Oriya, Punjabi, Sanskrit, Santhali, Sindhi, Tamil, Telugu, Urdu)
Government	-	Federal republic, parliamentary democracy
	-	President Pranab Mukherjee
	-	Prime Minister Manmohan Singh
	-	Chief Justice P Sathasivam
Formation	-	Independence 15 August 1947 Republic 26 January 1950
Area	-	3,287,263 square kilometres
Coastline	-	7,516 kilometres
Population	-	1,210,193,422 (2011 census) Density 371/square kilometre
GDP (PPP)	-	$4.711 trillion (2012 estimate) Per capita $3,851
GDP (nominal)	-	$1.825 trillion (2012 estimate) Per capita $1,592
Defence Minister	-	AK Antony
Defence Secretary	-	RK Mathur
Chief of Army Staff	-	General Bikram Singh
Chief of Navy Staff	-	Admiral Devendra Kumar Joshi
Chief of Air Staff	-	Air Chief Marshal Arup Raha

become a particularly contentious topic in both Indian society and politics. Some observers believe India is facing difficulties in the political capacity to address these problems. Intense multi-party political competition over numerous economic and social issues has resulted in often-fragile coalitions of political parties, and no single political party has held a parliamentary majority since 1989. The government changed nine times from December 1989 to the elections in May 2009 in which the Indian National Congress returned to power under Prime Minister Manmohan Singh. Increasing pluralism of political parties, growing diversity in interest-group representation, and substantial ideological divisions among parties are significant obstacles in policy implementation.

Geography

India's exact size is subject to debate because some borders are disputed. The Indian government lists the total area as 3,287,260 square kilometres and the total land area as 3,060,500 square kilometres; the United Nations lists the total area as 3,287,263 square kilometres and total land area as 2,973,190 square kilometres. In either case, India is the seventh largest country in the world.

Land Boundaries. Land boundaries total 15,200 kilometres. India shares common borders with Pakistan (3,325 kilometres; the Jammu and Kashmir border is 1,085 kilometres), China (line of actual control is 3,439 kilometres), Bhutan (605 kilometres), Nepal (1,690 kilometres), Burma (1,452 kilometres), and Bangladesh (4,339 kilometres). Although India and Sri Lanka do not share a land boundary, the narrowest distance between the two countries is only 64 kilometres across the Palk Strait. Most of Jammu and Kashmir is contested with Pakistan, and the Aksai Chin area of Jammu and Kashmir is disputed with China, as is the border of Arunachal Pradesh in northeast India. Nepal claims a 75-square-kilometre area called Kalapani. Possession of recently emerged New Moore Island (South Talpatty) in the Bay of Bengal has been disputed by Bangladesh, and much of the border with Bangladesh is not demarcated.

Coastline. India's total coastline is 7,516 kilometres in length, which comprises 5,422 kilometres for the mainland, 132 kilometres for the Lakshadweep Islands, and 1,962 kilometres for the Andaman and Nicobar Islands. The Indian peninsula juts 1,980 kilometres into the Indian Ocean. 50% of the Indian Ocean basin lies within a 1,500 kilometre radius of India, a reality that has strategic implications.

Maritime Claims. Under the 1982 United Nations Convention on the Law of the Sea, India has a 200 nautical mile exclusive economic zone, a 12 nautical mile territorial sea, a 24 nautical mile contiguous zone, and a legal continental shelf extending to a depth of 2,500 metres or to the end of the continental margin. India has 1,197 islands in the Indian Ocean. (572 in the Andaman and Nicobar – 38 of which are inhabited and 23 in the Lakshadweep – 10 of which are inhabited. In addition, there are 447 islands off the Western coast and 151 islands off the Eastern Coast).

Topography. There are three main geological regions, the Indo-Gangetic Plain and the Himalayas—collectively known as North India—and the Peninsula, or South India. India has diverse physiological regions that include highlands, plains, deserts, and river valleys. The country's highest elevation is 8,598 metres at Kanchenjunga, which is the third highest mountain in the world and located in the Himalayas.

Principal Rivers. India's longest rivers are the Brahmaputra and Indus, which are both 2,896 kilometres long, although neither is entirely within India. Other major rivers are the Ganga (2,525 kilometres), Godavari (1,465 kilometres), Kaveri (Cauvery, 800 kilometres), Krishna (1,401 kilometres), Mahanandi (851 kilometres), Narmada (1,312 kilometres), and Yamuna (1,370 kilometres).

Climate. Climate in India varies significantly from the permanently snow-capped Himalayas in the north to the tropics in the south. The country has four seasons. December to February is relatively dry and cool, March to May is dry and hot, from June to September predominating southwest maritime winds bring monsoon rains to most of the country, and in October and November there are retreating dry monsoons originating from the northeast. Average temperatures range from 12.5° C to 30° C in the northwest, 17.5° C to 30° C in the north and northeast, and 22.5° C to 30° C in the south. Average annual rainfall is around 1,000 to 1,500 millimetres for much of the country, but can be quite low in some parts of the northwest (150 to 300 millimetres annually) and very high in the northeast and along the west coast (1,500 to 2,500 millimetres annually).

Natural Resources. Commercially important natural resources include arable land, bauxite, chromite, coal (fourth-largest reserves in the world), diamonds, iron ore, limestone, manganese, mica, natural gas, petroleum, and titanium ore.

Land Use. The total arable land and land planted under permanent crops combined is about 1,697,000 square kilometres, and total irrigated land is about 548,000 square kilometres. The total of non-arable land and land not under permanent crops is about 1,276,190 square kilometres.

Environmental Factors. India is vulnerable to various natural hazards, particularly cyclones and annual monsoon floods, and various combinations of poverty, population growth, increasing individual consumption, industrialisation, infrastructural development, poor agricultural practices, and poor resource distribution have led to substantial human transformation of India's natural environment. An estimated 60% of cultivated land suffers from soil erosion, water logging, and salinity. It is also estimated that between 4.7 and 12 billion tons of topsoil are lost annually from soil erosion. From 1947 to 2002, average annual per capita water availability declined by almost 70% to 1,822 cubic meters, and overexploitation of groundwater is problematic in the states of Haryana, Punjab, and Uttar Pradesh. Forest area covers 19.4% of India's geographic area (63.7 million hectares). Nearly half of the country's forest cover is found in the state of Madhya Pradesh (20.7%) and the seven states of the northeast (25.7%); the latter is experiencing net forest loss. Forest cover is declining because of harvesting for fuel wood and the expansion of agricultural land. These trends, combined with increasing industrial and motor vehicle pollution output, have led to atmospheric temperature increases, shifting precipitation patterns, and declining intervals of drought recurrence in many areas. The Indian Agricultural Research Institute has estimated that a 3° C rise in temperature will result in a 15 to 20% loss in annual wheat yields. These are substantial problems for a nation with such a large population depending on the productivity of primary resources and whose economic growth relies heavily on industrial growth.

Society

Ethnic Groups. The exact number of ethnic groups depends on source and method of counting, and scholars estimate that only the continent of Africa exceeds the linguistic, cultural, and genetic diversity of India. 72% of the population is Indo-Aryan, 25% Dravidian, and 3% Mongoloid and other. Each of these groups can be further subdivided into various combinations of language, religion, and caste. About 16% of the total population is "untouchable" (Scheduled Castes is the more formal, legal term; *Dalit* is the term preferred by "untouchables" and roughly translates to downtrodden); around 8% of the population belongs to one of 461 indigenous groups (often called Scheduled Tribes for legal purposes, although the term adivasi is commonly used).

Languages. The total number of languages and dialects varies by source and counting method, and many Indians speak more than one language. The Indian census lists 114 languages (22 of which are spoken by one million or more persons) that are further categorised into 216 dialects or "mother tongues" spoken by 10,000 or more speakers. An estimated 850 languages are in daily use, and there are more than 1,600 dialects. Hindi is the official language and the most commonly spoken, but not all dialects are mutually comprehensible. English also has official status and is widely used in business and politics, although knowledge of English varies widely. The teaching of Hindi and English is compulsory in most states and union territories. 22 languages are legally recognised by the constitution for various political, educational, and other purposes - Assamese, Bengali, Bodo, Dogri, Gujarati, Hindi, Kannada, Kashmiri, Konkani, Maithili, Malayalam, Manipuri, Marathi, Nepali, Oriya, Punjabi, Sanskrit, Santhali, Sindhi, Tamil, Telugu, and Urdu. The most commonly spoken languages are Hindi (40.2% of the population), Bengali (8.3%), Telugu (7.9%), Marathi (7.5%), and Tamil (6.3%).

Religion. Approximately 80.5% of the population is Hindu, 13.4% Muslim, 2.3% Christian, 1.9% Sikh, 0.8% Buddhist, and 0.4% Jain; another 0.6% belongs to other faiths, such as Zoroastrianism and numerous religions associated with Scheduled Tribes. The Indian constitution confers religious freedom for individuals and prohibits religious discrimination, but in spite of this, there have been enduring tensions among religious communities, most notably between Hindus and Muslims.

Education and Literacy. In 2000 the adult literacy rate (% aged 15 or older) was 58.5% (72.3% for males, 44.4% for females). These figures have all nearly doubled since 1961 and are higher than in most other South Asian nations. In 2001 the combined primary, secondary, and tertiary enrolment ratio was 55% of

the population of official school age for the three levels. Total government expenditures on education in 2001 were 13.2% of all government expenditures and 4% of GDP. Government expenditures on education have increased steadily, as have the number of educational institutions from the primary to the university level. The majority of states and union territories have free education up to the seventh-grade level, and the majority of primary schools are government funded and managed. 34% of secondary institutions are government funded but privately managed, and 25% are privately managed without government funding.

Health. National health indicators are generally lower than in many developing countries but have shown dramatic improvement nationwide, although there are variations among states in India. An estimated 21% of the total population is malnourished. In 2001 public health expenditures were 3.1% of total general government expenditures but only 17.9% of total health expenditures. By contrast, private expenditures were 82.1% of total health expenditures. Furthermore, total health expenditures per capita represented 5.1% of GDP The population's health is also a function of the relatively low number of health personnel and low level of infrastructure, which are on a par with many countries in Sub-Saharan Africa.

Welfare. Generally, central government welfare expenditures are a substantial portion of the official budget, and state and local governments play important roles in developing and implementing welfare policies. In 2000 union government expenditures on social services (includes education, health, family welfare, women and child development, and social justice and empowerment), rural development, and basic minimum services were approximately US$7.7 billion, which was 11.1% of total government expenditures and 1.7% of GDP. Furthermore, the union and state governments maintain a plethora of reserved seats in various political and education institutions for lower castes, indigenous persons, and others based on their percentage of the population.

Economy

From the 1950s to the 1980s, India followed socialist-inspired policies. The economy was shackled by extensive regulation, protectionism, and public ownership, leading to pervasive corruption and slow growth. Since 1991, the nation has moved towards a market-based system. The policy change in 1991 came after an acute balance of payments crisis, and the emphasis since then has been to use foreign trade and foreign investment as integral parts of India's economy.

According to the World Bank, the Indian economy is the tenth-largest economy by market exchange rates, and the third-largest by purchasing power parity, or PPP. With its average annual GDP growth rate of 5.8% over the past two decades, and reaching 6.1% during 2011–12, India is one of the world's fastest-growing economies. However, the country ranks 140th in the world in nominal GDP per capita and 129th in GDP per capita at PPP.

The 486.6-million worker Indian labour force is the world's second-largest, as of 2011.The service sector makes up 55.6% of GDP, the industrial sector 26.3% and the agricultural sector 18.1%. Major agricultural products include rice, wheat, oilseed, cotton, jute, tea, sugarcane, and potatoes. Major industries include textiles, telecommunications, chemicals, pharmaceuticals, biotechnology, food processing, steel, transport equipment, cement, mining, petroleum, machinery, and software. In 2011, India was the world's tenth-largest importer and the nineteenth-largest exporter. Major exports include petroleum products, textile goods, jewellery, software, engineering goods, chemicals, and leather manufactures. Major imports include crude oil, machinery, gems, fertiliser, and chemicals. Between 2001 and 2011, the contribution of petrochemical and engineering goods to total exports grew from 14% to 42%.

Averaging an economic growth rate of 7.5% for several years prior to 2007, India has more than doubled its hourly wage rates during the first decade of the 21st century. Some 431 million Indians have left poverty since 1985; India's middle classes are projected to number around 580 million by 2030. Though ranking 51st in global competitiveness, India ranks 17th in financial market sophistication, 24th in the banking sector, 44th in business sophistication, and 39th in innovation, ahead of several advanced economies, as of 2010. With 7 of the world's top 15 information technology outsourcing companies based in India, the country is viewed as the second-most favourable outsourcing destination after the United States. India's consumer market, currently the world's eleventh-largest, is expected to become fifth-largest by 2030.

India's telecommunication industry, the world's fastest-growing, added 227 million subscribers during the period 2010–11, and after the first quarter of 2013, India surpassed Japan to become the third largest smartphone market in the world after China and the U.S.

Its automotive industry, the world's second fastest growing, increased domestic sales by 26% during 2009–10, and exports by 36% during 2008–09. Power capacity is 250 gigawatts, of which 8% is renewable. At the end of 2011, Indian IT Industry employed 2.8 million professionals, generated revenues close to US$100 billion equaling 7.5% of Indian GDP and contributed 26% of India's merchandise exports.

The Pharmaceutical industry in India is among the significant emerging markets for global pharma industry. The Indian pharmaceutical market is expected to reach $48.5 billion by 2020. India's R&D spending constitutes 60% of Biopharmaceutical industry. India is among the top 12 Biotech destinations of the world. The Indian biotech industry grew by 15.1% in 2012-13.

Despite impressive economic growth during recent decades, India continues to face socio-economic challenges. India contains the largest concentration of people living below the World Bank's international poverty line of US$1.25 per day, the proportion having decreased from 60% in 1981 to 42% in 2005. Since 1991, economic inequality between India's states has consistently grown: the per-capita net state domestic product of the richest states in 2007 was 3.2 times that of the poorest. Corruption in India is perceived to have increased significantly, with one report estimating the illegal capital flows since independence to be US$462 billion. Driven by growth, India's nominal GDP per capita has steadily increased from US$329 in 1991, when economic liberalisation began, to US$1,265 in 2010, and is estimated to increase to US$2,110 by 2016; however, it has always remained lower than those of other Asian developing countries such as Indonesia, Iran, Malaysia, Philippines, Sri Lanka, and Thailand, and is expected to remain so in the near future.

According to one report, India's GDP at purchasing power parity could overtake that of the United States by 2045. During the next four decades, Indian GDP is expected to grow at an annualised average of 8%, making it potentially the world's fastest-growing major economy until 2050. Key growth factors are a young and rapidly growing working-age population; growth in the manufacturing sector because of rising education and engineering skill levels; and sustained growth of the consumer market driven by a rapidly growing middle class. The World Bank cautions that, for India to achieve its economic potential, it must continue to focus on public sector reform, transport infrastructure, agricultural and rural development, removal of labour regulations, education, energy security, and public health and nutrition.

Infrastructure

India's transportation infrastructure has undergone tremendous change since independence. While traditional, non-mechanised transport means are still quite common, roads, railroads, ports, and aviation continue to expand. India now has the world's second largest road network, and its rail network is among the most used in the world for passengers and freight. Furthermore, increasing incomes and government liberalisation measures have contributed to tremendous growth in the numbers of automobiles, two- and three-wheeled vehicles, private and public buses, and urban rail networks. However, there are significant, accompanying problems with pollution, increasing traffic density, unauthorised transportation providers, and high numbers of traffic fatalities.

Roads. There were about 3.3 million kilometres of roads by 2002, of which 1.4 million kilometres were surfaced and more than 1 million kilometres were covered with gravel, crushed stone, or earth. More than 150 highways are rated as national highways and carry about 40% of road traffic on a total length of 65,569 kilometres. Around 85% of all passenger traffic and 70% of all freight traffic travel by road. By 2007, highways have expanded by 13,146 kilometres, with road projects aimed at linking the country's major cities and spanning the entire country north-south and east-west. Modes of road transport are a mix of traditional and modern means. Urban transit is dominated by motor vehicles, with increasing use of automobiles, minibuses, buses, trucks, and particularly two- and three-wheeled vehicles.

Railroads. All railroads are government-owned and operated by Indian Railways. In 2002 total route length was 63,028 kilometres and double and multiple tracks resulted in a total track length of 108,706 kilometres. Of the total track length, 86,526 kilometres were 1.676-millimeter gauge, 18,529 kilometres were 1.000-millimeter gauge, and 3,651 kilometres were 0.762- and 0.610-millimeter gauge. About 16,000 kilometres were electrified, mostly 1.676 millimetre gauge. The rail system includes 7,566 locomotives, 37,840 coaches, 222,147 freight wagons, 6,853 stations, and nearly 116,000 bridges. Both passenger and freight carriage continue to expand annually, and the rail system is the fourth most heavily used in the world, both for passengers and freight. For the financial year 2004, Indian Railways carried 557 million freight tons and more than 5 billion passengers. There are some high-speed routes and increasing use of them. Most rolling stock and other components are still domestically produced, but they are increasingly manufactured through commercial agreements with foreign companies. There have been major government investments in modernisation since the early 1990s, but Indian Railways has also experienced dwindling government budgetary support and has suffered from the dual role of being both a public utility and a commercial enterprise.

Ports. India has 12 major ports and 185 minor and intermediate ports along the country's coastline. There are also 7 shipyards under the control of the central government, 2 shipyards controlled by state governments, and 19 privately owned shipyards. The major ports handled 344.6 million tons of cargo for the financial year 2004, with Chennai,

Vishakhapatnam and Kandla carrying the greatest tonnage. Major ports can collectively handle 390 million tons of cargo annually, and port operations have improved since the mid-1990s. All major ports, except one (Ennore), are government administered, but private-sector participation in ports has increased. In 2000 there were 102 shipping companies operating in India, of which five were privately owned and based in India and one was owned by the government (Shipping Corporation of India). In 2000 there were 639 government-owned ships, including 91 oil tankers, 79 dry cargo bulk carriers, and 10 cellular container vessels. Indian-flagged vessels carried about 15% of overseas cargo at Indian ports.

Inland and Coastal Waterways. India has approximately 14,500 kilometres of inland waterways, but their transportation potential is vastly underused. More than 3,600 kilometres are navigable by large vessels, although only about 2,000 kilometres are used. For purposes of navigational development and conservation, three inland waterways have been declared national waterways. The Allahabad-Haldia portion of the Ganga-Bhagirathi-Hooghly rivers (1,620 kilometres), the Sadiya-Dhubri section of the Brahmaputra River (891 kilometres), and a combination of western canals (205 kilometres).

Civil Aviation and Airports. The government owns two airlines (Air India and Indian Airlines) and one helicopter service (Pawan Hans), and there are twelve privately owned airlines. Private airlines account for about 45% of domestic air traffic, and the government has divested more than 50% of the equity in both government-owned airlines. Of 288 airports, 208 have permanent-surface runways, and there are two runways of more than 3,659 meters. The Airports Authority of India administers 126 airports - 11 international, 89 domestic, and 26 for defence purposes.

Pipelines. In 2003 India had an estimated 5,798 kilometres of gas pipelines, 1,195 kilometres for liquid petroleum gas, 5,613 kilometres for oil, and 5,567 kilometres for refined products. India and Iran have discussed constructing a gas pipeline, but the Indian government and oil industry analysts have expressed concerns about the pipeline's security because of its proposed route through conflict-prone areas of Pakistan.

Telecommunications. India is witnessing its greatest period of change in communications, with shifts from government to private providers and greater public use of various technologies. From 1995 to 2003, the number of Internet users increased from 250,000 to 18.4 million. Since the late 1990s, the number of telephones, mobile phones, and personal computers has increased substantially. In 2004 there were 40.9 million telephones and 26.2 million mobile phones, and in 2003 there were an estimated 7.5 million personal computers. Some basic telephone services were opened to private-sector competition in 1994, and portions of state-owned telecommunications services have been purchased by private entities. Government-owned radio (All India Radio) and television (Doordarshan) networks have extensive national and local coverage, but domestic and international private television networks are increasingly prolific through cable and satellite.

Government and Politics

India is a democratic republic with a system of government legally based on the often-amended 1950 constitution. The central government is also known as the union government, and its structure is much like the British parliamentary system, with distinct, but interrelated executive, legislative, and judicial branches. State governments are structured much like the central government, and district governments exist in a variety of forms. The Indian parliament is a bicameral legislature composed of a lower house (the Lok Sabha or House of the People), with 543 popularly elected members and 2 members appointed by the President and an upper house (the Rajya Sabha or Council of States), with 12 appointed members and 233 members elected by state and union territory assemblies. Lok Sabha members serve five-year terms, and Rajya Sabha members serve six-year terms, with one-third of members up for election every two years. The legislature passes laws on constitutionally specified matters, such as central government finances and constitutional amendments. The two houses have the same powers, but the Rajya Sabha's power in the legislative process is subordinate to the Lok Sabha. India has both a prime minister and a president. Members of parliament and state legislative assemblies elect the president. Prime ministers are leaders of the majority party in parliament but are formally appointed by the president. In 2004 Manmohan Singh became prime minister. Over time, political power has become increasingly concentrated in the prime minister and Council of Ministers (cabinet), although they are responsible to the parliament. The president's duties are mostly ceremonial, although the president formally approves the prime minister and also approves the Council of Ministers based on the prime minister's advice. Furthermore, all bills require presidential approval before becoming law.

The vice president is ex officio chairperson of the Rajya Sabha and acts in place of the president when the president is unable to perform his or her duties.

Judicial and Legal System. The Supreme Court is the top legal entity, and it is composed of a chief justice appointed by the president and 25 associate judges also appointed by the president in consultation with the chief justice. The Supreme Court has numerous legal powers, such as appellate jurisdiction over all civil and criminal proceedings, with the potential of influencing interpretation of the constitution. The parliament and Supreme Court have maintained a contentious relationship on issues related to judicial review and parliamentary sovereignty. Below the Supreme Court are high courts, followed by a hierarchy of subordinate courts, and some states also have *panchayat* (village level) courts that decide civil and criminal matters. Some high courts serve more than one state, and all are independent of state legislatures and executives. The judiciary is regarded as slow and cumbersome but is also widely respected and often takes an activist role in protecting citizens' rights.

Administrative Divisions. There are 28 states and 7 union territories including the national capital territory of New Delhi. State boundaries are often based on language or other social characteristics, and union territories tend to be geographically smaller and less populous than states. States and union territories contain 601 districts that are further subdivided into townships containing from 200 to 600 villages. The union government exercises greater control over union territories than over states. Relationships between some state governments and the union government have been contentious, particularly when state governments are run by political parties that oppose the governing party or coalition in parliament. The tremendous variations in economic and social development among states suggest that state governments can have a greater influence on their populations than the union government. However, the union government exercises considerable influence on states through numerous financial resources and its authority to assume control of states during times of emergency (called President's Rule).

Electoral System. The Election Commission is the independent government body that supervises parliamentary and state elections, which are massive and sometimes marred by violence. Elections for state assemblies and the Lok Sabha are held every five years unless called earlier, such as through a no-confidence vote of the government by the Lok Sabha.

Indeed, elections are often held before the five-year limits because governments have often had difficulty staying in power for the full five-year term. In the 2004 general elections, there were more than 687,000 polling stations and 671.5 million voters. Since 1952, there have been 14 general elections, with voter turnout ranging from 55 to 64% of eligible voters. The legal voting age is 18. National and state legislative elections are similar to the British House of Commons and United States House of Representatives, in which members gain office by winning a plurality of votes in their local constituency. There are 543 parliamentary constituencies. The number of constituencies for state legislatures ranges from 32 to 403, with a total of 4,120 state constituencies nationwide.

Politics and Political Parties. From 1947 until 1989, the left-of-centre Indian National Congress and its factions dominated national politics. In the 1990s, the centre-right Bharatiya Janata Party (BJP) and the centrist Janata Dal emerged as influential political parties, although Congress returned to power in May 2004. There are numerous national and state parties. Among the best known and most prominent are Akali Dal, All-India Anna DMK (AIADMK), Asom Gana Parishad, Bahujan Samaj Party (BSP), Bharatiya Janata Party (BJP), Communist Party of India (CPI), Communist Party of India-Marxist (CPI-M), Dravida Munnetra Kazhagam (DMK), Indian National Congress, Rashtriya Janata Dal (RJD), Samajwadi Party, Samata Party, Shiv Sena, and Telugu Desam. Since the late 1960s, minority parties in Parliament have often been majority parties in state legislatures. Since 1989, single political parties have generally failed to win a parliamentary majority. As a result, parliament is often run by coalitions of political parties.

Mass Media. India has more newspapers than any other nation, and newspaper readership annually grows by millions. There are a few state-run newspapers, but most print media are privately owned. There are more than 5,600 daily newspapers and more than 46,000 non-daily newspapers and print periodicals. In 2002 the government allowed print media to be up to 26% foreign owned, but the most powerful publishers are joint stock companies that frequently have other commercial and industrial holdings. Government authorities control most television channels, yet the growth of private FM and television stations has marked a shift away from mostly state-run electronic media such as Doordarshan (television) and All India Radio. Foreign television channels are available through cable television or Indian broadcasters. An estimated 42.3% of Indian households have a television, and 52.2% of those have cable or satellite transmission. Similarly, the number of Internet users has rapidly to an estimated 18.4 million users in 2003. India has a high degree of press and speech freedom.

Foreign Relations. India's Ministry of External Affairs is the governmental body that is officially responsible for making and implementing foreign policy, although India's prime ministers have often exercised substantial influence in foreign policy decision making. India's parliament and armed forces historically have had very limited roles in the formulation of foreign policy. India is the second most populous country and the world's most-populous democracy and recently has one of the fastest economic growth rates in the world. With the world's tenth largest military expenditures, and eleventh largest economy by nominal rates or fourth largest by purchasing power parity, India is considered to be a regional power, and a potential global power. It is India's growing international influence that increasingly gives it a more prominent voice in global affairs.

India has a long history of collaboration with several countries and is considered a leader of the developing world. India was one of the founding members of several international organisations, most notably the United Nations, the Non-Aligned Movement, the Asian Development Bank and the G20 industrial nations. India has also played an important and influential role in other international organisations like East Asia Summit, World Trade Organisation, International Monetary Fund (IMF), G8+5 and IBSA Dialogue Forum. Regional organisations India is a part of include SAARC and BIMSTEC. India has taken part in several UN peacekeeping missions and is the second-largest troop contributor to the United Nations. India is currently seeking a permanent seat in the UN Security Council, along with the G4 nations.

Post-Cold War shifts in military power and concerns with terrorism have led India to create stronger bilateral relations with China, Israel, the United States, and other nations. The Ministry of External Affairs has generally been most concerned with relations with neighbouring Nepal, Sri Lanka, and particularly Pakistan on issues concerning unresolved borders, natural resource distribution, immigration, and insurgent activity. India's security concerns have been most pronounced with Pakistan. In spite of these difficulties, tensions between India and Pakistan have periodically thawed, and the two countries have demonstrated interest in resolving their enduring dispute over Jammu and Kashmir.

As promotion of democracy around the world is one of the most important foreign policy objectives of the USA, India – as the largest democracy of the world - can hardly be ignored by the USA. Cooperation in promotion of democracy in the world has become one of the most important facets of Indo-USA relations in recent times.

Major International Treaties. India is a signatory to numerous international treaties. India is not a party to the Treaty on the Non-Proliferation of Nuclear Weapons (NPT) or the Missile Technology Control Regime. Indian governments have argued that the NPT does not reduce nuclear weapons proliferation by states already possessing nuclear weapons and that the NPT denies non-nuclear states the right to have nuclear weapons.

National Security

The prime minister and Council of Ministers formulate national security policy. Below this level is the civilian bureaucracy, which exercises important influence, primarily through the Defence Minister's Committee of the cabinet. The third tier of defence policy making is the Chiefs of Staffs Committee. These three levels are supported by intelligence organisations, scientific and technical advisory committees, defence production, and research and development groups. There are three military services—army, navy, and air force—and a number of paramilitary and reserve forces. The army has been the dominant service in terms of both percentage of budget allotted to the armed forces and percentage of persons serving in the armed forces.

India maintains the third-largest military force in the world. The President of India is the supreme commander of the Indian Armed Forces. India maintains close defence cooperation with Russia, Israel and France, who are the chief suppliers of arms. The Defence Research and Development

Organisation (DRDO) oversees indigenous development of sophisticated arms and military equipment, including ballistic missiles, fighter aircraft and main battle tanks, to reduce India's dependence on foreign imports. India became a nuclear power in 1974 after conducting an initial nuclear test, and further underground testing in 1998. India maintains a "no first use" nuclear policy. On 10 October, 2008 Indo-US civilian nuclear agreement was signed, prior to which India received IAEA and NSG waivers, ending restrictions on nuclear technology commerce with which India became de facto sixth nuclear power in world.

Service chiefs and military officers continually suggest that the military should have greater input into defence policymaking and national security, and generally such a role is not viewed as a threat to civilian control of the military. Since 2001, the government has established the Defence Intelligence Agency (DIA), the Defence Acquisitions Council (DAC, which now controls the DRDO), and the National Security Council (NSC), which suggests that India has rethought its defence policymaking structure. The government has also proposed creating a Chief of Defence Staff. However, these changes have yet to make a major impact.

Foreign Military Relations. Indian peacekeeping forces have been sent to Sri Lanka from 1987 to 1990 and to the Maldives in 1988. Indian military and police contingents have participated in United Nations (UN) peacekeeping forces in Angola, Bosnia and Herzegovina, Cambodia, Democratic Republic of the Congo, Costa Rica, Cyprus, Dominican Republic, El Salvador, Ethiopia and Eritrea, Gaza, Guatemala, Honduras, Iraq, Korea (during the Korean War), Kuwait, Laos, Lebanon, Liberia, Mozambique, Namibia, Nicaragua, Rwanda, Sierra Leone, Somalia, Vietnam, West New Guinea (West Irian), Yemen, and Yugoslavia. India has also provided police personnel and monitors for UN peacekeeping operations in Angola, Bosnia and Herzegovina, Cambodia, Haiti, Kosovo, Mozambique, Sierra Leone, and Western Sahara.

Foreign Military Forces. The only foreign military forces in India are with the United Nations Military Observer Group in India and Pakistan (UNMOGIP), which has 45 military observers from 9 countries stationed in Jammu and Kashmir.

External Threat. External security threats come from neighbouring countries and insurgents using foreign border areas as havens for activities in India. Countries such as Bangladesh, Bhutan, and Sri Lanka present no conventional military threat to India, but their inability to police and control areas bordering India has provided Indian insurgents with havens. Indian government and military officials have publicly expressed concern about the political instability in its neighbourhood. As far as external threats posed by other countries, popular opinion tends to regard Pakistan as the principal enemy, largely because of the Kashmir conflict and Pakistan's suspected links to numerous South Asian militant groups. However, the defence establishment generally regards China as the chief external threat, because of perceived Chinese attempts to isolate India militarily and diplomatically from the rest of Asia and perceived Chinese efforts to prevent India from becoming a permanent member of the UN Security Council. While China-India border issues remain unresolved from the Indian point of view, Sino-Indian relations have improved.

Internal Threats and Terrorism. India's top security concerns are mostly internal. Much of the national security apparatus is directed to maintaining territorial integrity as dozens of groups push for varying degrees of political or social autonomy, sometimes violently. India treats separatism with extreme concern given the possibility that successful separatism may establish a precedent that other groups might seek to follow. Internal threats can be categorised as religiously oriented conflict or ethnic violence, usually with separatist objectives. Separatist violence periodically escalates in Jammu and Kashmir. Numerous separatist insurgent groups are active in the northeast. Left-wing Extremism (Naxalite) remains the largest internal security threat to India.

Human Rights. Although human rights problems exist in India, the country is generally not regarded as among the world's serious human rights violators. Human rights problems appear to be acute in areas and periods of communal violence, and security forces, insurgents, and various ethnic-based groups have all been accused of human rights violations in

Jammu and Kashmir, Gujarat, Maharashtra, Uttar Pradesh, and various north-eastern states. Both international human rights organisations and India's National Human Rights Commission have questioned the impartiality of police and judicial authorities in various locales. On the other hand, human rights groups have praised India's repeal of the Prevention of Terrorism Act, which both the newly elected government and international organisations criticized as enabling human rights abuses by security forces. Indian media routinely address controversial issues, such as political corruption and discrimination against women, sexual minorities, indigenous peoples, and "untouchables." In response to cyber-crime and cyber-terrorism perpetrated by parties in both India and Pakistan, India passed the Information Technology Act of 2000, which allows cyber cafés and Internet users homes to be searched without warrants at any time as part of criminal investigations.

INDONESIA

The Republic of Indonesia (the word Indonesia was coined from the Greek *indos*—for India—and nesos—for island) proclaimed independence on 17 August 1945, from the Netherlands. The Hague recognised Indonesian sovereignty on 27 December 1949. Estimates of the size of Indonesia's total area vary. Officially, the Indonesian government says the total land area is 1.9 million square kilometres and total sea area, 7.9 million square kilometres, including an exclusive economic zone. The Indonesian flag has two equal horizontal bands of red (top) and white.

History

The struggle between the Dutch colonial government and the Indonesian nationalist movement was well under way when the Japanese occupied the Indies in 1942. They remained until the end of World War II in August 1945.

On 17 August 1945, Sukarno and Mohammad Hatta proclaimed the independent Republic of Indonesia with Sukarno as president and Hatta as vice president. Allied forces (mostly British and British Indian troops) did not arrive until six weeks later, by which time the republic had begun to establish itself and nationalist pride had burgeoned. The period October-December 1945 was filled with violent conflict in which Indonesians made it clear they would defend their independence with their lives. The republic survived two Dutch "police actions" and an internal communist rebellion, and on 27 December 1949, The Hague formally recognised the sovereignty of a federated republic, which a year later was formed into a unitary Republic of Indonesia.

The years following the struggle for independence were characterised by political and economic difficulty, regional dissidence, attempted assassinations and coups d'état, military-civilian conflict, and economic stagnation. A period of Guided Democracy was announced in 1959 by Sukarno, who in September 1963 proclaimed himself president-for-life and presided over a political system in which the civilian nationalist leadership, much of the Islamic leadership, the large Indonesian Communist Party (PKI), and the army were all at odds. This tense and hostile atmosphere was broken on 30 September 1965, with what appears to have been an attempted PKI coup against the Sukarno government. The precise circumstances remain unclear, but the immediate result was that a "New Order" coalition of students, intellectuals, Muslims, and the army brought about a military-dominated government that removed Sukarno and permitted a broad and deadly assault on communists, especially on Java, Bali, and Sumatra. On 11 March 1966, power was transferred from a seriously ill Sukarno to Suharto, an army officer. The PKI was formally banned the following day and Suharto became the acting president, and the New Order era began.

The New Order era, which lasted for more than 30 years, has a mixed record. Like Guided Democracy, it was authoritarian, but it was more successful in bringing stability to the nation. Unlike Guided Democracy, its economic achievements were enormous and the well-being of the majority of Indonesians undeniably improved, e.g. average life expectancy increased from 46 to 65.5 years. On the other hand, the state's heavy involvement in banking

Capital	-	Jakarta
Official language	-	Bhasha Indonesian
Government	-	Presidential republic
	-	President Susilo Bambang Yudhoyono
	-	Vice President Boediono
Formation	-	Independence from the Netherlands Declared 17 August 1945 Acknowledged 27 December 1949
Area	-	1,904,569 square kilometres
Population	-	237,424,363 (2011 estimate) Density 322.76/ square kilometre
Coastline	-	54,716 kilometres
GDP (PPP)	-	$1,314 trillion (2013 estimate) Per capita $5,302
GDP (nominal)	-	$946.391 billion (2013 estimate) Per capita 3,816
Defence Minister	-	Purnomo Yusgiantoro
C-in-C Armed Forces	-	General Moeldoko
Chief of Army Staff	-	General Budiman
Chief of Navy Staff	-	Admiral Marsetio
Chief of Air Staff	-	Air Chief Marshal Ida Bagus Putu Dunia

and industry, especially the petroleum and natural gas sectors, worked against competition and encouraged corruption on a large scale. Suharto provided strong leadership, but he did not provide for a wise transition and, in his last years, clung to power and favoured family and friends. East Timor, which had been forcibly annexed by Indonesia in 1976, saw bitter conflict between the Indonesian military and local independence movements. When the Asian financial crisis hit in 1997–98, the New Order lost the economic justification that had guaranteed much of its public support, and there was a widespread call for Suharto to step down. He resigned on 21 May 1998, little more than two months after being elected for his seventh term as president.

Suharto was succeeded by Bucharuddin Jusuf Habibie, who sought first to resolve the East

Timor situation and begin a new and more open electoral process. In 1999, following Indonesia's first freely contested parliamentary elections since 1955, Abdurrahman Wahid, well-known as both a progressive intellectual and as leader of Indonesia's largest Muslim became president. His quirky leadership style and questions about both his competency and his health, brought increasing opposition and eventually serious threats of impeachment. He was dismissed from office in July 2001 in favour of Megawati Sukarnoputri, the vice president and head of the Indonesian Democratic Party of Struggle (PDI-P). Megawati, Sukarno's eldest daughter, was decisively defeated in the September 2004 presidential runoff election by the Democratic Party candidate, retired army general Susilo Bambang Yudhoyono. Yudhoyono was sworn in as president in October 2004. In the last five years the economy has performed strongly. Although relations among different religious and ethnic groups are largely harmonious, sectarian discontent and violence has occurred. A political settlement to an armed separatist conflict in Aceh was achieved in 2005.

Geography

Topography. Indonesia's land boundaries total 1,758 kilometres, including 1,107 kilometres with Malaysia, 820 kilometres with Papua New Guinea, and 288

kilometres with East Timor. Indonesia's coastline totals 54,716 kilometres on the Indian Ocean, Strait of Malacca, South China Sea, Java Sea, Sulawesi Sea, Maluku Sea, Pacific Ocean, Arafura Sea, Timor Sea, and other smaller seas. Indonesia is the largest archipelagic nation in the world. It encompasses 17,508 islands. About 6,000 of these islands are named, and about 1,000 are permanently settled. The five main islands are Java, Kalimantan, Papua (formerly called Irian Jaya), Sumatra, and Sulawesi. There are two major archipelagos, Nusa Tenggara and Maluku, and about sixty smaller archipelagos. The larger islands of Indonesia are mountainous, with some peaks reaching 3,800 metres above sea level on the western islands and as high as 5,000 metres on Papua. The highest point is Puncak Jaya (5,030 metres) on Papua. The region is tectonically unstable with some 400 volcanoes, of which 100 are active.

Principal Rivers. Indonesia's waterways total 21,579 kilometres. The principal rivers are the Musi, Batanghari, Indragiri, and Kampar rivers on Sumatra; the Kapuas, Barito, and Mahakam rivers on Kalimantan; the Memberamo and Digul rivers on Papua; and the Bengawan Solo, Citarum, and Brantas rivers on Java, which are used primarily for irrigation.

Climate. Indonesia's maritime equatorial climate typically produces high, even temperatures and heavy rainfall; temperature variations are generally due to elevation and time of day, while rainfall may vary across the archipelago as a result of many different factors, among them monsoon patterns, which themselves vary according to location. Average temperatures at or near sea level range from about 23° C to 31°C. In most of the country, rainfall is comparatively heavy throughout the year, with a pronounced rainy season roughly between December and March. East of Surabaya, however, a dry season is increasingly noticeable, especially between June and October.

Natural Resources. Petroleum and natural gas are among Indonesia's most important natural resources. Indonesia is the world's largest exporter of liquefied natural gas. Most petroleum production is on central Sumatra, but Java also has significant production, and there are substantial proven offshore reserves. There are also large coal reserves. Other significant minerals are bauxite, copper, gold, iron, manganese, nickel, sulfur, silver, and tin. An important non-mineral resource is timber.

Land Use. 11.3% (206,753 square kilometres) of Indonesia's total land area is arable, and land planted in permanent crops, including an irrigated area of 48,150 square kilometres, represents 7.2% of the total (132,051 square kilometres). There are 1,619,687 square kilometres of non-arable land and land not under permanent crops.

Environmental Factors. Indonesia's geography leaves the nation vulnerable to severe flooding, unpredictable drought and plant pest attacks, volcanic activity, and earthquakes, which are sometimes associated with tidal waves (tsunami). The most important environmental issues associated with human activities are forest degradation (unregulated cutting, fires, smoke and haze, and erosion); water pollution from industrial wastes and sewage; air pollution from motor vehicles and industry in urban areas, and generally from smoke and haze caused by forest fires; and threats to biodiversity and rare plant and animal species.

Time Zones. Indonesia has three time zones.

Society

Population. Indonesia has the world's fourth largest population after China, India, and the United States, totaling an estimated 238,452,952 in July 2004, with a 1.5% annual growth rate. 69% of the population lives in rural areas. Java is one of the most densely populated areas in the world, with more than 120 million people, or some 945 persons per square kilometre. By contrast, the most densely populated Outer Islands have 90 persons or fewer per square kilometre. Jakarta, on the western end of Java, is the largest city, with an estimated population of 12 million.

Ethnic Groups. Indonesia is a culturally diverse nation. Ethnic identities are not always clear, stable or agreed upon; ethnic groups may appear or profess to be more distinct socially or culturally than they actually are. There are about 350 recognised ethno-linguistic groups in Indonesia, 180 of them located in Papua; 13 languages have more than a million speakers. Javanese are 45% of the population, Sundanese 14%, Madurese 7.5%, coastal Malays 7.5%, and others 26%.

Languages. The official national language is Bahasa Indonesia, a modified form of Malay, with an estimated 17 million to 30 million mother-tongue speakers and more than 140 million second-language speakers or readers. Additionally, as many as 725 other languages and dialects are spoken. Since independence, and particularly since 1965, English has replaced Dutch as the main Western language spoken and is widely used in government and business circles.

Religion. Indonesia has the largest Islamic population of any nation. Most Indonesians (88%) count themselves as Muslims and observe Islamic practices to varying degrees; another 5% of Indonesians are Protestant, 3% are Roman Catholic, 2% are Hindu, 1% are Buddhist, and 1% observe other religions. In some remote areas, animism is practiced. The constitution guarantees religious freedom for the five religions (the first five mentioned) recognised by the state. In 2002 the People's Consultative Assembly rejected a proposal to introduce Islamic law as a constitutional requirement.

Health. Indonesia had a three-tiered system of community health centers in the late 1990s, with 0.66 hospital beds per 1,000 population, the lowest rate among members of the Association of Southeast Asian Nations (ASEAN). In the mid-1990s, there were 16 physicians per 100,000 population in Indonesia, 50 nurses per 100,000, and 26 midwives per 100,000. Both traditional and modern health practices are employed. Government health expenditures are about 3.7% of the GDP. There is about a 75.25% ratio of public to private health-care expenditures. Human immuno-deficiency virus/acquired immune deficiency syndrome (HIV/AIDS) has posed a major public health threat since the early 1990s. Other health hazards are dengue fever and avian influenza.

Economy

Indonesia has a mixed economy in which both the private sector and government play significant roles. The country is the largest economy in Southeast Asia and a member of the G-20 major economies. The industry sector is the economy's largest and accounts for 46.4% of GDP (2012), this is followed by services (38.6%) and agriculture (14.4%). However, since 2012, the service sector has employed more people than other sectors, accounting for 48.9% of the total labour force, this has been followed by agriculture (38.6%) and industry (22.2%). Agriculture, however, had been the country's largest employer for centuries.

According to World Trade Organisation data, Indonesia was the 27th biggest exporting country in the world in 2010. Indonesia's main export markets (2009) are Japan (17.28%), Singapore (11.29%), the United States (10.81%), and China (7.62%). The major suppliers of imports to Indonesia are Singapore (24.96%), China (12.52%), and Japan (8.92%). In 2005, Indonesia ran a trade surplus with export revenues of US$83.64 billion and import expenditure of US$62.02 billion. The country has extensive natural resources, including crude oil, natural gas, tin, copper, and gold. Indonesia's major imports include machinery and equipment, chemicals, fuels, and foodstuffs. And the country's major export commodities include oil and gas, electrical appliances, plywood, rubber, and textiles.

Indonesia was until recently Southeast Asia's only member of OPEC, and the 1970s oil price raises provided an export revenue windfall that contributed to sustained high economic growth rates, averaging over 7% from 1968 to 1981. Following further reforms in the late 1980s, foreign investment flowed into Indonesia, particularly into the rapidly developing export-oriented manufacturing sector, and from 1989 to 1997, the Indonesian economy grew by an average of over 7%.

Indonesia was the country hardest hit by the Asian financial crisis of 1997–98. During the crisis there were sudden and large capital outflows leading the rupiah to go into free fall. Against the US dollar the rupiah dropped from about Rp 2,600 in late 1997 to a low point of around Rp 17,000 some months later and the economy shrank by a remarkable 13.7%. These developments led to widespread economic distress across the economy and contributed to the political crisis of 1998 which saw Suharto resign as president. The rupiah later stabilised and a slow but steady economic recovery ensued. However political instability, slow economic reform, and corruption slowed the recovery. Since 2007, however, with the improvement in banking sector and domestic consumption, national economic growth has accelerated to over 6% annually and this helped the country weather the 2008–2009 global recession. The Indonesian economy performed strongly during the Global Financial Crisis and in 2012 its GDP grew by over 6%. The country regained its investment grade rating in late 2011 after losing it in the 1997. However, as of 2012, an estimated 11.7% of the population lived below the poverty line and the official open unemployment rate was 6.1%.

Infrastructure

Roads. Indonesia has a total of 342,700 kilometres of roads, mostly (about 60%) located on Java,

Madura, Bali, and Sumatra; 158,670 kilometres (46%) were paved, of which 27,358 kilometres were classified as main roads and 40,490 kilometres as secondary roads. Another 184,030 kilometres (54% of the total) were unpaved. About 32% of the roads were classified as highways. There are smaller networks of roads on Sulawesi and Kalimantan, while smaller islands often have limited roads within or connecting major settlements. Urban transit is dominated by motor vehicles; the use of automobiles, buses, minibuses, and motorcycles is widespread, even in seemingly remote areas.

Railroads. Track length totalled 6,458 kilometres in 2002, of which 125 kilometres were electrified. All rail facilities were government-owned and -operated until 1991, when government liberalisation created a public corporation, now called PT Kereta Api, which operates Indonesian Railways. The corporation possesses almost total commercial freedom, with the exception of some passenger fares that remain fixed by the government, but it continues to face financial problems as the rising demand for its services is coupled with shortfalls in investment and revenues. However, some of this demand has been met by private passenger and freight service operators that have entered the market since 1995. All railroads are narrow gauge, with 5,931 kilometres 1.067 meter gauge, and 497 kilometres 0.750 meter gauge in 2002. Some 211 kilometres of roadbed are double-track, and 125 kilometres of 1.067 gauge electrified, all on Java.

Ports. Indonesia has 379 ports and harbours controlled by the Ministry of Communications for international and inter-island trade. The four main ports are at Tanjung Priok (near Jakarta), Tanjung Perak (near Surabaya), Belawan (Medan), and Makassar (South Sulawesi). Other major ports are at Cilacap, Cirebon, and Semarang (all on Java), Kupang (Timor), and Palembang (Sumatra). Some 127 ports are classified as capable of handling international shipping.

Inland and Coastal Waterways. Inter-island transportation is critical to domestic commerce. Traditional sailing craft are widely used, but they increasingly are motorised. The merchant fleet is composed of 718 ships of 1,000 gross registered tons or more. These ships include, by type, the following. cargo (398), refrigerated cargo (2), container (57), bulk carrier (47), roll on/roll off (15), petroleum tanker (128), chemical tanker (13), specialised tanker (12), liquefied natural gas (6), passenger (10), passenger/cargo (13), short-sea passenger (9), vehicle carrier (7), and livestock carrier (1). There also are 35 oceangoing vessels, 259 inter-island vessels, more than 1,000 modernised local-use vessels, almost 4,000 traditional vessels, and 1,900 special bulk carriers. River transport plays a major role in eastern Sumatra, Kalimantan, and Papua. Most of Indonesia's major rivers are at least partly navigable, but those on Java are used primarily for irrigation.

Civil Aviation and Airports. The government owns one airline, Garuda Indonesia, and one smaller subsidiary, Merpati Nusantara Airlines. Civil aviation as a private-sector venture has greatly increased from one private airline in 1993 to 27 private domestic airlines by 2004. In 2003 there were an estimated 661 airports in Indonesia, of which 154 had paved runways (four with more than 3,000-metre runways) and 507 had unpaved runways. Six of the larger airports can accommodate wide-bodied aircraft. Additionally, there were 22 heliports in 2003. Indonesia had a fledgling domestic turbo-prop airliner industry under development under the government-owned Indonesia Aerospace in the late 1990s, but it reached only a prototype-level of production.

Pipelines. In 2003 Indonesia had 672 kilometres of condensate, 125 kilometres of condensate/gas, 8,183 kilometres of gas, 7,429 kilometres of oil, 66 kilometres of oil/gas/water, 1,329 kilometres of refined products, and 72 kilometres of water pipelines.

Telecommunications. Indonesia has been a pioneer in national satellite communications since 1975. A third generation of satellites, known as Palapa C1 and C2, was launched in 1996; these satellites provide

a number of inter-island and international telecommunications services. In 2002 there were some 7.8 million telephones and 11.7 million mobile cellular telephones in use, producing a ratio of some 91 units per 1,000 people. International telephone service was widely available. Radio and television were long dominated by government networks, but private stations have been on the rise since the early 1990s. As of 1998, there were 678 AM, 43 FM, and 82 shortwave radio stations and more than 31 million radios. In 2000 more than 31.7 million television receivers were in use. Estimates vary as to the number of Internet users in Indonesia— between nearly 4 million and 8 million. By 2002 there were more than 2.3 million personal computers, producing a ratio of 11.9 units per 1,000 people.

Government and Politics

Indonesia is a republic based on limited separation of powers among the executive, legislative, and judicial branches. The constitution of 1945 is in force, but, based on a constitutional amendment of August 2002, beginning with the 2004 presidential elections, the once powerful, party-centred presidency is subject to popular election and limited to two five-year terms. Prior to the 2004 elections, the People's Consultative Assembly (Majelis Permusyawaratan Rakyat—MPR) chose the president and vice president, who were not necessarily from the same political party. Under the new law, the president and vice president are elected on a single ticket and the winning ticket must win more than 50% of the popular vote and at least 20% of the vote in half of the provinces. If these percentages are not met, a second-round runoff election is held. The president is both chief of state and head of government.

The MPR, the highest authority of the state, has both elected and appointed members. Under the amendment that surrendered its presidential election powers, the MPR also replaced its 200 non-elected members (representatives of provinces and various social groups) with elected members of a new legislative body, the 200-seat House of Regional Representatives (Dewan Perwakilan Daerah—DPD), which was established by constitutional amendment in 2001. The DPD joins the existing 500-seat House of People's Representatives (Dewan Perwakilan Rakyat—DPR) in a bicameral, all-elected legislature. The members of both houses make up the MPR. The highest court of the land is the Supreme Court (Mahkamah Agung), composed of justices appointed by the president from a list of candidates approved by the legislature. In 2004 the Supreme Court was preparing to assume administrative responsibility for the lower-court system, currently run by the Ministry of Justice and Human Rights. Under the Supreme Court is a quadripartite judiciary of general, religious, military, and administrative courts. Appeals can be made, sequentially, from a district court to a high court to the Supreme Court. A separate Constitutional Court was established in 2003. The Supreme Audit Board (Badan Permeriksa Keuangan) oversees accountability of public finance and is independent of the chief executive, but its members are chosen by the president.

The judicial branch is theoretically equal to the executive and legislative branches and has the right of judicial review over laws passed by the DPR, as well as government regulations and presidential, ministerial, and gubernatorial decrees. In practice, however, the judiciary is less influential than the executive and legislative branches, and it has often been heavily influenced by the executive branch. Indonesia has not accepted compulsory International Court of Justice jurisdiction.

Administrative Divisions. Indonesia has 30 provincial-level units. 27 provinces (*propinsi*), two special regions (*daerah istimewa*; Aceh and Yogyakarta), and one special capital city region (*daerah khusus*; Jakarta). Since January 1, 2001, when central control over local affairs was lessened, the 357 districts (*kabupaten*) and municipalities (*kotamadya*)—the first-level provincial subdivisions—became the administrative units responsible for providing most government services. Following a 1999 referendum agreed to by the legislature, and a period of United Nations stewardship, the province of Timor Timur became the independent nation of the Democratic Republic of Timor-L'este (East Timor) on 20 May 2002.

Provincial and Local Government. Provinces (*propinsi*) are divided into districts or regencies (*kabupaten*), which are further divided into subdistricts (*kecamatan*). There also are some municipalities or city governments (*kotamadya*) that are on the same administrative level as the districts and others that are on the subdistrict level. The lowest level of the administrative hierarchy is the village (*desa*). The chief executives are provincial governors, district or regency heads, mayors of cities, and village heads. Legislation is handled by provincial and district parliaments. Under the revised election laws, governors, mayors, and district heads (regents) were to be directly elected for the first time in 2004.

Judicial and Legal System. The legal system is based on Roman-Dutch law, modified by indigenous concepts and by new criminal procedures and election codes. There are 2,418 district courts, each of which has a panel of judges that conducts trials by posing questions, hearing evidence, deciding on guilt or innocence, and assessing punishment. Both the defence and prosecution can appeal verdicts. Arbitrary arrest and detention are prohibited, but the government lacks adequate enforcement mechanisms, and authorities have routinely violated the Criminal Procedures Code. The code provides prisoners with the right to notify their families promptly, and specifies that warrants must be produced during an arrest. Exceptions are allowed if, for example, a suspect is caught in the act of committing a crime. The law allows investigators to issue warrants; at times, however, authorities make arrests without warrants.

Politics and Political Parties. Whereas the official government party, Golkar, once held an absolute majority, there are now numerous parties vying for power, and none enjoys national majority support. These parties include the Crescent Moon and Star Party (PBB), Democratic Party (PD), Indonesia Democratic Party-Struggle (PDI-P), National Awakening Party (PKB), National Mandate Party (PAN), Prosperous Justice Party (PKS), and United Development Party (PPP).

Mass Media. The constitution provides for freedom of speech and freedom of the press; however, the government has a history of restricting these rights in practice. Private press in current operation includes nearly 50 daily newspapers, dozens of magazines, 10 foreign press bureaus, and five private commercial television stations. There are also 10 foreign press bureaus, two government radio stations (Radio Republik Indonesia and Voice of Indonesia), one government news agency (Antara), and one independent national news agency (Kantorberita Nasional Indonesia). The government does not restrict Internet usage or content.

Foreign Relations. Indonesia is a charter member of the Nonaligned Movement, which was established in September 1961. The April 1955 Asian-African Conference—held in Bandung, Indonesia—was an important milestone in the development of the Nonaligned Movement's goal of independence from the Cold War superpowers (the United States and the Soviet Union) and the former colonialist powers and put Indonesia on the international stage for a time. As the Sukarno era progressed, however, Indonesia's government was at odds with the Dutch over West New Guinea (now called Papua) and increasingly hostile toward neighbouring Malaysia to the point that Sukarno withdrew Indonesia from the United Nations when Malaysia was appointed a non-permanent member of the Security Council in 1964. In 1967 Indonesia participated in establishing a new officially nonaligned grouping of neighbours, the Association of Southeast Asian Nations (ASEAN), which was friendly toward the Western powers. Its secretariat was placed in Jakarta, and its first secretary general was an Indonesian.

The commemoration of the 30th anniversary of the Bandung Conference in 1985 saw Indonesia's full reemergence on the world stage, allowing Jakarta to project itself as a leading voice in the Nonaligned Movement and providing it with an extra-regional platform for claiming proper international standing. Indonesia's diplomatic relations with China had been reinstituted in 1990. Indonesia continues to play an important role in ASEAN affairs. Indonesia's most contentious regional relations are those with Australia, mostly over the situation in East Timor.

Separatist movements in the provinces of Aceh and Papua have led to armed conflict, and subsequent allegations of human rights abuses and brutality from all sides. Following a sporadic thirty-year guerrilla war between the Free Aceh Movement (GAM) and the Indonesian military, a ceasefire agreement was reached in 2005. In Papua, there has been a significant, albeit imperfect, implementation of regional autonomy laws, and a reported decline in the levels of violence and human rights abuses, since the presidency of Yudhoyono.

National Security

Armed Forces. The Indonesia Armed Forces (Tentara Nasional Indonesia—TNI) component services are the Army (TNI—Angkatan Darat), 265,000; Navy (TNI—Angkatan Laut); and Air Force (TNI—Angkatan Udara). There is a reserve force of 400,000. With the transition to democratic rule beginning in 1998, the government endeavoured to undertake steps to reform the TNI in order to improve public opinion about the military and to bring the military under civilian control. Among such steps were the devolution of the national police from the armed forces to the Office of the President and official transfer of responsibility for internal security from the TNI to the police in April 1999, focusing the military's attention on national defense rather than domestic policing. Another important reform was a provision that military personnel had to retire or resign before occupying an elected or appointed civilian government position. However, the TNI successfully resisted transformation of its territorial command structure because of threats of terrorism and separatism, and because it needs this structure to support its huge business empire, from which it obtains an estimated two-thirds of its funding (the government budget provides only one-third of the funds needed to operate and equip the military and national police). After several years in disrepute because of revelations of extensive human rights abuses, the TNI has regained much of its lost prestige. Many Indonesians appear to favour military firmness as the country is facing terrorist, separatist, and ethnic conflict as well as a moribund economy.

Foreign Military Relations. Indonesia enjoys cordial military-to-military relations with a wide range of nations. Its closest ties are with fellow members of Association of Southeast Asian Nations (ASEAN). Formerly close ties to the United States, Australia, and some European countries became strained in the 1990s over human rights issues; many countries cut back their military relations with the TNI after the rampage of army and army-supported militia forces in East Timor in 1999. Because of arms sales embargoes imposed by its primary sources in the United States, Indonesia has turned to Russia and other nations of the former Soviet Union, South Korea, and Poland, among others, for major arms purchases.

Human rights and political issues have also affected sales of foreign military equipment to Indonesia, but such tensions eased after East Timor gained independence in 2002. In 1992 the U.S. Congress terminated grant military training assistance (International Military Education and Training—IMET) after learning of Indonesian military human rights abuses in East Timor. This restriction was partially relaxed in 1995, but assistance was suspended again in 1999 as a result of violence following the referendum on East Timor's separation from Indonesia.

External Threat. Indonesia has no conventional external threat to its security. The primary outside threat is that of international terrorism. Terrorists belonging to the regional terrorist group Jemaah Islamiyah (Community of Islam) have conducted a number of recent bomb attacks, including the bombing of two night clubs on Bali in October 2002 that killed 202 people and injured more than 300, while a bombing at the Marriott Hotel in Jakarta in August 2003 killed 12 people and injured 150. Other threats to Indonesian security include piracy, particularly in the Strait of Malacca, smuggling, and maritime poaching.

Internal Threats and Terrorism. There are two general threats to Indonesian domestic security: terrorism and ethnic and religious conflict. The terrorists causing the greatest problems in Indonesia are members of the regional group, Jemaah Islamiyah (Community of Islam). Although Jemaah Islamiyah operates primarily in Indonesia, it has operational units in peninsular Malaysia, Singapore, Australia, and Papua New Guinea. Jemaah Islamiyah has perpetrated significant terrorist acts and is believed to have strong links with al-Qaeda. The government announced at the time of the October 2002 Bali bombings that terrorism was "a real and potential threat to national security" and has called upon the public to confront domestically based terrorists.

Centre-region relations have been perennially problematic, with the government continuing to experience difficulties in maintaining order and the rule of law in outlying regions. The most pressing threats are separatists in Aceh and Papua (formerly Irian Jaya). The major insurgent groups are Gerakan Aceh Merdeka (GAM—Free Aceh Movement), which wants an independent Islamic state in Aceh and has an estimated strength of 2,000 armed activists; and Organisasi Papua Merdeka (OPM—Free West Papua Movement), which seeks independence for Papua and has an estimated 150 activists.

Other regions also experienced outbreaks of violence, some of them very serious, after 1996. These include religious violence in Maluku and Central Sulawesi, ethnic violence over land use and local power in Kalimantan and other locales, and violence involving both political-religious hostility as well as hysteria about the misuse of supernatural powers in East Java. There have been many incidents of anti-Chinese riots in urban areas, some of them very destructive. On several occasions, most notably in 2001, radical Muslim groups have "swept" parts of Jakarta, cities in central Java, and other tourist areas, threatening Westerners.

IRAN

Iran is home to one of the world's oldest civilisations. The Islamic Republic of Iran, *Jomhuri-ye Eslami-ye Iran,* was known as Persia until 1935. It became an Islamic republic in 1979 after the ruling monarchy was overthrown and Shah Mohammad Reza Pahlavi was forced into exile. Conservative clerical forces led by Ayatollah Ruhollah Khomeini established a theocratic system of government with ultimate political authority vested in a learned religious scholar referred to commonly as the Supreme Leader who, according to the constitution, is accountable only to the Assembly of Experts - a popularly elected 86-member body of clerics.

The Iranian flag consists of three equal horizontal bands of green (top), white, and red; the national emblem (a stylized representation of the word Allah in the shape of a tulip, a symbol of martyrdom) in red is centred in the white band; *Allah Akbar* (God is Great) in white Arabic script is repeated 11 times along the bottom edge of the green band and 11 times along the top edge of the red band; green is the colour of Islam and also represents growth, white symbolizes honesty and peace, red stands for bravery and martyrdom.

A geographically diverse but mostly mountainous country, Iran has always been of significant geopolitical importance, owing to its location at the crossroads of Central Asia, Western Asia, and South Asia. Iran is a major regional and middle power, exerting considerable influence in international energy security and the world economy through its large reserves of fossil fuels, which include the largest natural gas supply in the world and the fourth-largest proven petroleum reserves. Iran has a strategic location on the Persian Gulf and Strait of Hormuz, which are vital maritime pathways for crude oil transport.

Geography

Iran consists of the Iranian Plateau with the exception of the coasts of the Caspian Sea and Khuzestan Province. It is one of the world's most mountainous countries, its landscape dominated by rugged mountain ranges that separate various basins or plateaux from one another. The populous western part is the most mountainous, with ranges such as the Caucasus, Zagros and Alborz Mountains; the last contains Iran's highest point, Mount Damavand at 5,610 metres, which is also the highest mountain on the Eurasian landmass west of the Hindu Kush.

The terrain is rugged, mountainous rim; high, central basin with deserts, mountains; with small, discontinuous plains along both coasts. The northern part of Iran is covered by dense rain forests called *Shomal*. The eastern part consists mostly of desert basins such as the *Dasht-e Kavir*, Iran's largest desert, in the north-central portion of the country, and the *Dasht-e Lut*, in the east, as well as some salt lakes. This is because the mountain ranges are too high for rain clouds to reach these regions. The only large plains are found along the coast of the Caspian Sea and at the northern end of the Persian Gulf, where Iran borders the mouth of the Shatt al-Arab river. Smaller, discontinuous plains are found along the remaining coast of the Persian Gulf, the Strait of Hormuz and the Gulf of Oman.

Capital	-	Tehran
Official language	-	Persian
Spoken languages	-	Persian, Azerbaijani, Kurdish, Lurish, Gilaki, Balochi, Mazandarani, Arabic, Turkmen, Armenian, Georgian,
Government	-	Islamic Republic
	-	Supreme Leader Ali Khamenei
	-	President Hassan Rouhani
Constitution	-	24 October 1979
Area	-	1,648,195 square kilometres
Coastline	-	2,440 kilometres includes the Caspian Sea (740 kilometres)
Population	-	77,176,930 (2013 census) Density 48/square kilometre
GDP (PPP)	-	$999.199 billion (2013 estimate) Per capita $12,803
GDP (nominal)	-	$548.895 billion (2013 estimate) Per capita $5,039
Defence Minister	-	Brigadier General Ahmad Vahidi
Chief of Armed Forces	-	Major General Hassan Firuzabadi
Chief of Army	-	Lieutenant General Ataollah Salehi
Chief of Navy	-	Rear Admiral Habibollah Sayyari
Chief of Air Force	-	Brigadier General Hassan Shahsafi
Commander-in-Chief IRGC	-	Major General Mohammad Ali Jafari

Iran has land boundaries over a length of 5,440 kilometres, with Afghanistan (936 kilometres), Armenia (35 kilometres), Azerbaijan-proper (432 kilometres), Azerbaijan-Naxcivan exclave (179 kilometres), Iraq (1,458 kilometres), Pakistan (909 kilometres), Turkey (499 kilometres) and Turkmenistan (992 kilometres). Its climate is mostly arid or semi-arid, and subtropical along the Caspian coast. Its natural resources include petroleum, natural gas, coal, chromium, copper, iron ore, lead, manganese, zinc, and sulphur.

The arable land is 10.05% and the area of irrigated land is about 87,000 square kilometres. Iran is prone to periodic droughts, floods; dust storms, sandstorms and earthquakes.

Ethnic groups in Iran are Persian 61%, Azeri 16%, Kurd 10%, Lur 6%, Baloch 2%, Arab 2%, Turkmen and Turkic tribes 2%, other 1%. Religion-wise Iran is 98% Muslim (Shia 89%, Sunni 9%), other (includes Zoroastrian, Jewish, Christian, and Baha'i) 2%.

The major population centres are Tehran (7.19 million); Mashhad (2.592 million); Esfahan (1.704 million); Karaj (1.531 million) and Tabriz (1.459 million).

Administrative Divisions

Iran has 31 provinces—Alborz, Ardabil, Azarbayjan-e Gharbi (West Azerbaijan), Azarbayjan-e Sharqi (East Azerbaijan), Bushehr, Chahar Mahal va Bakhtiari, Esfahan, Fars, Gilan, Golestan, Hamadan, Hormozgan, Ilam, Kerman, Kermanshah, Khorasan-e Jonubi (South Khorasan), Khorasan-e Razavi (Razavi Khorasan), Khorasan-e Shomali (North Khorasan), Khuzestan, Kohgiluyeh va Bowyer Ahmad, Kordestan, Lorestan, Markazi, Mazandaran, Qazvin, Qom, Semnan, Sistan va Baluchestan, Tehran, Yazd, and Zanjan.

Government

Cabinet: The Council of Ministers is selected by the

president with legislative approval; the Supreme Leader has some control over appointments to the more sensitive ministries.

Executive: It has three oversight bodies:

1) Assembly of Experts (*Majles-e Khoebregan*), a popularly-elected body charged with determining the succession of the Supreme Leader, reviewing his performance, and deposing him if deemed necessary;
2) Expediency Council or the Council for the Discernment of Expediency (*Majma-ye-Tashkhis-e-Maslahat-e- Nezam*) exerts supervisory authority over the executive, judicial, and legislative branches and resolves legislative issues when the *Majles* and the Council of Guardians disagree and since 1989 has been used to advise national religious leaders on matters of national policy; in 2005 the Council's powers were expanded to act as a supervisory body for the government;
3) Council of Guardians of the Constitution or Council of Guardians or Guardians Council (*Shora-ye Negban-e Qanon-e Asasi*) determines whether proposed legislation is both constitutional and faithful to Islamic law, vets candidates in popular elections for suitability, and supervises national elections.

Elections: The Supreme leader is appointed for life by the Assembly of Experts; The president is elected by popular vote for a four-year term (eligible for a second term and additional non-consecutive term).

Legislative branch: Unicameral Islamic Consultative Assembly or *Majles-e Shura-ye Eslami* or *Majles* (290 seats; members elected by popular vote from single and multimember districts to serve four-year terms).

Judicial branch: The Supreme Court president is appointed by the head of the Supreme Judicial Council in consultation with judges of the Supreme Court; and appointed for a 5-year term. Subordinate courts include Penal Courts I and II; Islamic Revolutionary Courts; Courts of Peace; Special Clerical Court (functions outside the judicial system and handles cases involving clerics); military courts.

Political parties and leaders: Formal political parties are a relatively new phenomenon in Iran and most conservatives still prefer to work through political pressure groups rather than parties. Often political parties or coalitions are formed prior to elections and disbanded soon thereafter.

Economy

Iran's economy is marked by statist policies and an inefficient state sector, which create major distortions throughout the system, and reliance on oil, which provides a large share of government revenues. Price controls, subsidies, and other rigidities weigh down the economy, undermining the potential for private-sector-led growth. Private sector activity is limited to small-scale workshops, farming, some manufacturing, and services. Significant informal market activity flourishes and corruption is widespread. Tehran since the early 1990s has recognised the need to reduce these inefficiencies, and in December 2010 the Majles passed President Mahmud Ahmadi-Nejad's Targeted Subsidies Law (TSL) to reduce state subsidies on food and energy. This was the most extensive economic reform since the government implemented gasoline rationing in 2007. Over a five-year period the legislation sought to phase out subsidies that previously cost Tehran \$60-\$100 billion annually and mostly benefited Iran's upper and middle classes. Cash payouts of \$45 per person to more than 90% of Iranian households mitigated initial widespread resistance to the TSL program. However, inflation in 2012 reached its highest level in four years, eroding the value of these cash payouts and motivating the *Majles* to halt planned price increases. New fiscal and monetary constraints on Tehran, following international sanctions in January against Iran's Central Bank and oil exports, significantly reduced Iran's oil revenue, forced government spending cuts, and fuelled a 20% currency depreciation. Economic growth turned negative for the first time in two decades. Iran also continues to suffer from double-digit unemployment. Underemployment among Iran's educated youth has convinced many to seek jobs overseas, resulting in a significant "brain drain."

Agriculture constitutes 11.3% of the economy, Industry 37.6% and Services 51%.Agriculture products include wheat, rice, other grains, sugar beets, sugarcane, fruits, nuts, cotton; dairy products, wool and caviar.

Industries include petroleum, petrochemicals, fertilizers, caustic soda, textiles, cement and other construction materials, food processing (particularly sugar refining and vegetable oil production), ferrous and non-ferrous metal fabrication, armaments

Petroleum constitutes 80% of its exports. Other commodities include chemical and petrochemical products, fruits and nuts, carpets. Exports–partners are China (22.1%), India (11.9%), Turkey (10.6%), South Korea (7.6%) and Japan (7.1%).

Imports include industrial supplies, capital goods, foodstuffs and other consumer goods, technical services. Imports partners are UAE (32.2%), China (13.8%), Turkey (11.8%), South Korea (7.4%).

Energy

Iran has the largest proved gas reserves in the world, with 33.6 trillion cubic metres. It also ranks third in oil reserves. It is OPEC's 2nd largest oil exporter and is an energy superpower. In 2005, Iran spent US$4 billion on fuel imports, because of contraband and inefficient domestic use. Oil industry output averaged 4 million barrels per day (640,000 m3/d) in 2005, compared with the peak of six million barrels per day reached in 1974. In the early years of the 2000s (decade), industry infrastructure was increasingly inefficient because of technological lags. Few exploratory wells were drilled in 2005.

In 2004, a large share of natural gas reserves in Iran was untapped. The addition of new hydroelectric stations and the streamlining of conventional coal and oil-fired stations increased installed capacity to 33,000 megawatts. Of that amount, about 75% was based on natural gas, 18% on oil, and 7% on hydroelectric power. In 2004, Iran opened its first wind-powered and geothermal plants, and the first solar thermal plant is to come online in 2009. Iran is the third country in the world to have developed GTL technology.

Demographic trends and intensified industrialisation have caused electric power demand to grow by 8% per year. The government's goal of 53,000 megawatts of installed capacity by 2010 is to be reached by bringing on line new gas-fired plants and by adding hydroelectric, and nuclear power generating capacity. Iran's first nuclear power plant at Bushehr went online in 2011.

- Electricity production is 213.7 billion kWh and consumption is 173.1 billion kWh. Iran exports 6.154 billion kWh.
- Crude oil production is 4.231 million bbl/day (2011 estimate)
- Crude oil - exports: 2.295 million bbl/day (2009 estimate)
- Crude oil - proved reserves: 151.2 billion bbl (2013 estimate)
- Refined petroleum products - production: 1.801 million bbl/day (2008 estimate)
- Refined petroleum products - consumption: 1.694 million bbl/day (2011 estimate)
- Refined petroleum products - exports: 246,500 bbl/day (2008 estimate)
- Refined petroleum products - imports: 187,200 bbl/day (2008 estimate)
- Natural gas - production: 146.1 billion cu m (2010 estimate)
- Natural gas - consumption: 144.6 billion cu m (2010 estimate)
- Natural gas - exports: 8.42 billion cu m (2010 estimate)
- Natural gas - proved reserves: 33.07 trillion cu m (2012 estimate)

Communications

Iran had estimated 27.767 million telephones main lines in use in 2011. Mobile cellular connections were 56.043 million (2011). The telephone system is currently being modernised and expanded with the goal of not only improving the efficiency and increasing the volume of the urban service but also bringing telephone service to several thousand villages, not presently connected.

The addition of new fibre cables and modern switching and exchange systems installed by Iran's state-owned telecom company have improved and expanded the fixed-line network greatly; fixed-line availability has more than doubled since 2000; additionally, mobile-cellular service has increased dramatically; combined fixed and mobile-cellular subscribership now exceeds 100 per 100 persons

Broadcast media

Iran has a state-run broadcast media with no private, independent broadcasters; Islamic Republic of Iran Broadcasting (IRIB), the state-run TV broadcaster, operates 5 nationwide channels, a news channel, about 30 provincial channels, and several international channels; about 20 foreign Persian-language TV stations broadcasting on satellite TV are capable of being seen in Iran; satellite dishes are illegal and, while their use had been tolerated, authorities began confiscating satellite dishes following the unrest stemming from the 2009 presidential election; IRIB operates 8 nationwide radio networks, a number of provincial stations, and an external service; most major international broadcasters transmit to Iran (2009).

- Internet hosts: 197,804 (2012)
- Internet users: 8.214 million (2009)

Transportation

Iran has 319 airports (2013); 140 with paved runways.

Pipelines: condensate 7 kilometres; condensate/gas 973 kilometres; gas 20,794 kilometres; liquid petroleum gas 570 kilometres; oil 8,625 kilometres; refined products 7,937 kilometres (2013)

Railways have a length of 8,442 kilometres broad gauge: 94 kilometres 1.676-m gauge standard gauge: 8,348 kilometres 1.435-m gauge (148 kilometres electrified) (2008)

Length of roadways is 198,866 kilometres

Waterways extend over a length of 850 kilometres (on Karun River; some navigation on Lake Urmia) (2012)

Ports and terminals: Bandar-e Asaluyeh, Bandar Abbas, Bandar Emam Khomeyni

Military

Military branches: Islamic Republic of Iran Regular Forces (Artesh): Ground Forces, Navy, Air Force (IRIAF), Khatemolanbia Air Defense Headquarters; Islamic Revolutionary Guard Corps (Sepah-e Pasdaran-e Enqelab-e Eslami, IRGC): Ground Resistance Forces, Navy, Aerospace Force, Quds Force (special operations); Law Enforcement Forces.

Transnational Issues

Iran protests Afghanistan's limiting flow of dammed Helmand River tributaries during drought; Iraq's

lack of a maritime boundary with Iran prompts jurisdiction disputes beyond the mouth of the Shatt al Arab in the Persian Gulf; Iran and UAE dispute Tunb Islands and Abu Musa Island, which are occupied by Iran; Azerbaijan, Kazakhstan, and Russia ratified Caspian seabed delimitation treaties based on equidistance, while Iran continues to insist on a one-fifth slice of the sea; Afghan and Iranian commissioners have discussed boundary monument densification and resurvey

Refugees and Internally Displaced Persons

Iran has an estimated 2.4 million refugees (1 million registered, 1.4 million undocumented) (Afghanistan); 42,500 (Iraq) (2013).

Illicit Drugs

Despite substantial interdiction efforts and considerable control measures along the border with Afghanistan, Iran remains one of the primary transhipment routes for Southwest Asian heroin to Europe; suffers one of the highest opiate addiction rates in the world, and has an increasing problem with synthetic drugs; lacks anti-money laundering laws; has reached out to neighbouring countries to share counter-drug intelligence.

MALAYSIA

Malaysia is a federation of 13 states and three federal territories in Southeast Asia. The country consists of two geographical regions divided by the South China Sea. Peninsular Malaysia (or West Malaysia) on the Malay Peninsula shares a land border on the north with Thailand and is connected by the Johore-Singapore Causeway and the Malaysia-Singapore Second Link to the south with Singapore. It consists of nine sultanates (Johor, Kedah, Kelantan, Negeri Sembilan, Pahang, Perak, Perlis, Selangor and Terengganu), two states headed by governors (Malacca and Penang), and two federal territories (Putrajaya and Kuala Lumpur). Malaysian Borneo (or East Malaysia) occupies the northern part of the island of Borneo, bordering Indonesia and surrounding the Sultanate of Brunei. It consists of the states of Sabah and Sarawak and the federal territory of Labuan.

Its land boundaries total 2,669 kilometres with Brunei (381 kilometres), Indonesia (1,782 kilometres) and Thailand (506 kilometres). Its coastline extends 4,675 kilometres. Putrajaya is the newly created administrative capital for the federal government of Malaysia, aimed in part to ease growing congestion within Malaysia's capital city, Kuala Lumpur. Kuala Lumpur remains the seat of parliament, as well as the commercial and financial capital of the country.

The Malaysian flag has 14 equal horizontal stripes of red (top) alternating with white (bottom); there is a blue rectangle in the upper hoist-side corner bearing a yellow crescent and a yellow 14-pointed star (the crescent and the star are traditional symbols of Islam). Malaysia adopted its Constitution on 31 August 1957 (amended on 16 September 1963)

History

Britain established its first colony in the Malay peninsula in 1786, with the lease of the island of Penang to the British East India Company by the Sultan of Kedah. In 1824, the British took control of Malacca following the Anglo-Dutch Treaty of 1824 which divided the Malay archipelago between Britain and the Netherlands, with Malaya in the British zone. In 1826, Britain established the crown colony of the Straits Settlements, uniting its three possessions in Malaya: Penang, Malacca and Singapore. The Straits Settlements were administered under the East India Company in Calcutta until 1867, when they were transferred to the Colonial Office in London.

During the late 19th century, many Malay states decided to obtain British help in settling their internal conflicts. The commercial importance of tin mining in the Malay states to merchants in the Straits Settlements led to British government intervention in the tin-producing states in the Malay Peninsula. British gunboat diplomacy was employed to bring about a peaceful resolution to civil disturbances caused by Chinese gangsters, and the Pangkor Treaty of 1874 paved the way for the expansion of British influence in Malaya. By the turn of the 20th century, the states of Pahang, Selangor, Perak, and Negeri Sembilan, known together as the Federated Malay States were under the de facto control of British Residents appointed to advise the Malay rulers. The British were "advisers" in name, but in reality they

Capital	-	Kuala Lumpur Putrajaya (administrative centre)
Official languages	-	Bahasa Malaysia, English
Ethnic groups	-	54% Malay, 25% Chinese, 7.5% Indian, 11.8% other
Government	-	Federal constitutional elective monarchy and Federal parliamentary democracy
	-	Head of State Tunku Abdul Halim
	-	Prime Minister Najib Tun Razak
Formation	-	Independence from Britain - 31 August 1957 Federation (with Sabah, Sarawak and Singapore) 16 September 1963
Area	-	329,847 square kilometres
Coastline	-	4,675 kilometres
Population	-	28,334,135 (2010 census) Density 86/ square kilometre
GDP (PPP)	-	$472.942 billion (2012 estimate) Per capita $16,186
GDP (nominal)	-	$278.680 billion (2012 estimate) Per capita $10,446
Defence Minister	-	Datuk Seri Ahmad Zahid Hamidi
Chief of Defence Forces	-	General Dato' Sir Azizan Ariffin
Chief of Army	-	General Tan Sri Dato' Sri Hj
Chief of Navy	-	Admiral Tan Sri Abdul Aziz Bin Hj Zafar
Chief of Air Force	-	General Tan Sri Dato' Sri Rodzali bin Daud

exercised substantial influence over the Malay rulers.

The remaining five states in the peninsula, known as the Unfederated Malay States, while not directly under rule from London, also accepted British advisors around the turn of the 20th century. Of these, the four northern states of Perlis, Kedah, Kelantan and Terengganu had previously been under Siamese control. On the island of Borneo, Sabah was governed as the crown colony of British North Borneo, while Sarawak was acquired from Brunei as the personal kingdom of the Brooke family, who ruled as White Rajahs.

Following the Japanese occupation of Malaya during World War II, popular support for independence grew. Post-war British plans to unite the administration of Malaya under a single crown colony called the Malayan Union foundered on strong opposition from the Malays, who opposed the emasculation of the Malay rulers and the granting of citizenship to the ethnic Chinese. The Malayan Union, established in 1946 and consisting of all the British possessions in Malaya with the exception of Singapore, was dissolved in 1948 and replaced by the Federation of Malaya, which restored the autonomy of the rulers of the Malay states under British protection.

During this time, rebels under the leadership of the Communist Party of Malaya launched guerrilla operations designed to force the British out of Malaya. The Malayan Emergency, as it was known, lasted from 1948 to 1960, and involved a long anti-insurgency campaign by Commonwealth troops in Malaya. Against this backdrop, independence for the Federation within the Commonwealth was granted on 31 August 1957.

In 1963 Malaya along with the then-British crown colonies of Singapore, Sabah (British North Borneo) and Sarawak formed Malaysia. The Sultanate of Brunei, though initially expressing interest in joining the Federation, withdrew from the planned merger due to opposition from certain segments of the population as well as arguments over the payment of oil royalties and the status of the Sultan in the planned merger.

Independence was marred by conflict with Indonesia (Konfrontasi) over the formation of Malaysia, Singapore's eventual exit in 1965, and racial riots in 1969. The Philippines also made an active claim on Sabah in that period based upon the Sultanate of Brunei's cession of its north-east territories to the Sultanate of Sulu in 1704. The claim is still ongoing. After the racial riots of 1969, the controversial New Economic Policy—intended to increase the share of the economic pie owned by the bhumiputras ("indigenous people", which includes the majority Malays, but not always the indigenous population) as opposed to other ethnic groups—was launched by Prime Minister Tun Abdul Razak. Malaysia has since maintained a delicate ethno-political balance, with a system of government that has attempted to combine overall economic development with political and economic policies that favour Bhumiputras.

Geography

The two distinct parts of Malaysia, separated from each other by the South China Sea, share a largely similar landscape in that both West and East Malaysia feature coastal plains rising to often densely forested hills and mountains, the highest of which is Mount Kinabalu at 4,095.2 metres on the island of Borneo. The local climate is equatorial and characterised by the annual southwest (April to October) and northeast (October to February) monsoons.

The Strait of Malacca, lying between Sumatra and Peninsular Malaysia, is arguably the most important shipping lane in the world. Malaysia's natural resources include tin, petroleum, timber, copper, iron ore, natural gas, and bauxite. Malaysia is the world's primary exporter of natural rubber and palm oil, which together with sawn logs and sawn timber, cocoa, pepper, pineapple and tobacco dominate the growth of the sector. Palm oil is also a major generator of foreign exchange.

The country has 5.46% of arable land of which 17.54% is under permanent crops. Irrigated land covers an area of 3,650 square kilometres. Natural hazards include flooding, landslides, forest fires. Environmental issues include air pollution from industrial and vehicular emissions; water pollution from raw sewage; deforestation and smoke/haze from Indonesian forest fires.

Tin and petroleum are the two main mineral resources that are of major significance in the Malaysian economy. Malaysia was once the world's largest producer of tin until the collapse of the tin market in the early 1980s. In the 19th and 20th century, tin played a predominant role in the Malaysian economy. It was only in 1972 that petroleum and natural gas took over from tin as the mainstay of the mining sector. Meanwhile, the contribution by tin has declined. Petroleum and natural gas which were discovered in oilfields offshore Sabah, Sarawak and Terengganu have contributed much to the Malaysian economy particularly in those three states. Other minerals of some importance or significance include copper, gold, bauxite, iron-ore and coal together with industrial minerals like clay, kaolin, silica, limestone, barite, phosphates and dimension stones such as granite as well as marble blocks and slabs. Small quantities of gold are produced.

In 2004, Minister in the Prime Minister's Department, Datuk Mustapa Mohamed, revealed that Malaysia's oil reserves stood at 4.84 billion barrels while natural gas reserves increased to 89 trillion cubic feet. The government estimates that at current production rates Malaysia will be able to produce oil up to 18 years and gas for 35 years.

Malaysia has a bio-diverse range of flora and fauna, and is also considered one of the 17 mega-diverse countries.

Society

Malaysia is a multi-ethnic, multi-cultural and multilingual society. The population as of February 2007 is 26.6 million consisting of 62% Malays, 24% Chinese, 8% Indians, with other minorities and indigenous peoples. Malay is the national language of the country. In the past, Malays wrote in Sanskrit or using Sanskrit-based alphabets. After the 15th century, Jawi (a script based on Arabic) became popular. Over time, Romanized script overtook Sanskrit and Jawi as the dominant script. This was largely due to the influence of the colonial education system, which taught children in Romanised writing rather than in Arabic script.

By constitutional definition, all Malays are Muslim. About 30% of the population are Malaysians of Chinese descent. Malaysians of Indian descent comprise about 8% of the population. About 90% of the Indian community is Tamils but various other groups are also present, including Malayalis, Punjabis and Gujaratis. There are also various non-Malay peoples who are designated as indigenous, mostly in East Malaysia. These make up about 7% of the population.

Non-Malay indigenous groups make up more than half of the state of Sarawak's population—constitute about 66% of Sabah's population—and also exist in much smaller numbers on the Peninsula, where they are collectively known as Orang Asli. The non-Malay indigenous population is divided into dozens of ethnic groups, but they share some general cultural similarities. Population distribution is uneven, with some 20 million residents concentrated on the Malay Peninsula, while East Malaysia is relatively less populated.

Due to the rise in labour intensive industries, Malaysia has 10 to 20% foreign workers with the uncertainty due in part to the large number of illegal workers, mostly Indonesian. There are a million legal foreign workers and perhaps another million unauthorised foreigners. The state of Sabah alone has nearly 25% of its 2.7 million population listed as illegal foreign workers.

Although the Malaysian constitution theoretically guarantees religious freedom, in practice the situation is not so simple. All ethnic Malays are Muslim as defined in the Malaysian constitution. Additionally, all non-Muslims who marry a Muslim must renounce their religion and convert to Islam. Meanwhile, Non-Muslims experience restrictions in activities such as construction of religious buildings and the celebration of certain religious events in some states. Malaysians tend to personally respect one another's religious beliefs, with inter-religious problems arising mainly from the political sphere. However, there is a growing divide because many Chinese and Indians feel oppressed by recent religiously-related political sentiments that threaten freedom of religion.

Healthcare

Malaysian society places importance on the expansion and development of healthcare, putting 5% of the government social sector development budget into public healthcare—an increase of more than 47% over the previous figure. This has meant an overall increase of more than RM 2 billion. With a rising and aging population, the Government wishes to improve in many areas including the refurbishment of existing hospitals, building and equipping new hospitals, expansion of the number of polyclinics, and improvements in training and expansion of telehealth. Over the last couple of years they have increased their efforts to overhaul the systems and attract more foreign investment.

The Malaysian healthcare system requires doctors to perform a compulsory three years service with public hospitals to ensure the manpower of these hospitals is maintained. Recently foreign doctors have also been encouraged to take up employment here. There is still, however, a compound shortage of medical workforce, especially that of highly trained specialists resulting in certain medical care and treatment only available in large cities. Recent efforts to bring many facilities to other towns have been hampered by lack of expertise to run the available equipment made ready by investments.

The majority of private hospitals are in urban areas and, unlike many of the public hospitals, are equipped with the latest diagnostic and imaging facilities. Private hospitals have not generally been seen as an ideal investment—it has often taken up to ten years before companies have seen any profits. However, the situation has now changed and companies are now looking into this area again, particularly in view of the increasing interest by foreigners in coming to Malaysia for medical care and the recent government focus to develop the health tourism industry.

Government and Politics

Malaysia is a federal constitutional elective monarchy. The federal head of state of Malaysia is the Yang di-Pertuan Agong, commonly referred to as the King of Malaysia. The Yang di-Pertuan Agong is elected to a five-year term among the nine hereditary Sultans of the Malay states; the other four states, which have titular Governors, do not participate in the selection.

The system of government in Malaysia is closely modelled on that of the Westminster parliamentary system, a legacy of British colonial rule. In practice however, more power is vested in the executive branch of government than in the legislative, and the judiciary has been weakened by sustained attacks by the government during the Mahathir era. Since independence in 1957, Malaysia has been governed by a multi-party coalition known as the Barisan Nasional (formerly known as the Alliance).

Legislative power is divided between federal and state legislatures. The bicameral parliament consists of the lower house, the House of Representatives or Dewan Rakyat (literally the "Chamber of the People") and the upper house, the Senate or Dewan Negara (literally the "Chamber of the Nation"). The 219-member House of Representatives are elected from single-member constituencies that are drawn based on population for a maximum term of 5 years. All 70 Senators sit for 3-year terms; 26 are elected by the 13 state assemblies, 2 representing the federal territory of Kuala Lumpur, 1 each from federal territories of Labuan and Putrajaya, and 40 are appointed by the king. Besides the Parliament at the federal level, each state has a unicameral state legislative chamber whose members are elected from single-member constituencies. Parliamentary elections are held at least once every five years, with the last general election being in March 2004. The cabinet is chosen from among members of both houses of Parliament and is responsible to that body.

State governments are led by chief ministers (Menteri Besar in Malay states or Ketua Menteri in states without hereditary rulers), who is a state assembly member from a majority party in the state assemblies.

Administrative divisions. Putrajaya is the administrative capital of Malaysia. The country has 13 states (Johor, Kedah, Kelantan, Melaka, Negeri Sembilan, Pahang, Perak, Perlis, Pulau Pinang, Sabah, Sarawak, Selangor, and Terengganu) and one federal territory with three components (city of Kuala Lumpur, Labuan, and Putrajaya)

Judiciary. The legal system is based on English common law. Judicial review of legislative acts in the Supreme Court is at the request of the supreme head of the federation. Malaysia has not accepted jurisdiction of the International Court of Justice. Islamic law is applied to Muslims in matters of family law. Judges to the Federal Court are appointed by the paramount ruler on the advice of the prime minister)

Economy

Southeast Asia has been a centre of trade for centuries. Various items such as porcelain and spices were actively traded even before Malacca and Singapore rose to prominence.

Later, as the British started to take over as administrators of Malaya, rubber and palm oil trees were introduced for commercial purposes. Over time, Malaysia became the world's largest major producer of tin, rubber, and palm oil. These three commodities, along with other raw materials, firmly set Malaysia's economic tempo well into the mid-20th century.

Instead of relying on the local Malays as a source of labour, the British brought in Chinese and Indians to work in on the mines, plantations and fill up the void in professional expertise. Although many of them returned to their respective home countries after their agreed tenure ended, some remained in Malaysia and settled permanently.

As Malaya moved towards independence, the government began implementing economic five-year plans, beginning with the First Malayan Five Year Plan in 1955. Upon the establishment of Malaysia, the plans were re-titled and renumbered, beginning with the First Malaysia Plan in 1965.

In the 1970s, Malaysia began to imitate the four Asian Tiger economies (Republic of Korea (South Korea), Republic of China (Taiwan), then British Crown Colony of Hong Kong and the Republic of Singapore) and committed itself to a transition from being reliant on mining and agriculture to an economy that depends more on manufacturing. With Japanese investment, heavy industries flourished and in a matter of years, Malaysian exports became the country's primary growth engine. Malaysia consistently achieved more than 7% GDP growth along with low inflation in the 1980s and the 1990s. Today, Malaysia is one of the world's largest computer hard disk manufacturing sites.

Malaysia is a relatively open state-oriented and newly industrialised market economy. The state plays a significant but declining role in guiding economic activity through macroeconomic plans. In 2007, the economy of Malaysia was the 3rd largest in Southeast Asia and 29th largest economy in the world by purchasing power parity with a growth rate of 5% to 7% since 2007.

Since the 1980s the industrial sector has led Malaysia's growth. The Malaysian economy recovered from the 1997 Asian Financial Crisis sooner than neighbouring countries, and has since recovered to the levels of the pre-crisis era. Inequalities exist between different ethnic groups, with a major issue being that the Chinese minority accounts for 70% of the country's market capitalisation, even though it only makes up about one third of it.

International trade, facilitated by the adjacent Strait of Malacca shipping route and manufacturing are both key sectors of the country's economy. Malaysia is an exporter of natural and agricultural resources, the most valuable exported resource being petroleum. At one time, it was the largest producer of tin, rubber and palm oil in the world. Manufacturing has a large influence in the country's economy, although Malaysia's economic structure has been moving away from it. In an effort to diversify the economy and make Malaysia's economy less dependent on exported goods, the government has pushed to increase tourism in Malaysia. As a result tourism has become Malaysia's third largest source of income from foreign exchange, although it is threatened by the negative effects of the growing industrial economy, with large amounts of air and water pollution along with deforestation affecting tourism. Malaysia has developed itself into a centre of Islamic banking. Knowledge-based services are also expanding. Malaysia's rapid economic growth and prosperity is reflected by the Petronas Towers, the headquarters of the national oil giant in Kuala Lumpur and, at one time, the tallest building in the world. While the pace of development today is not as rapid, it is seen to be more sustainable.

Infrastructure

The infrastructure of Malaysia is one of the most developed in Asia. Its telecommunications network is second only to Singapore's in Southeast Asia, with 4.7 million fixed-line subscribers and more than 30 million cellular subscribers. The country has seven international ports, the major one being the Port Klang. There are 200 industrial parks along with specialised parks such as Technology Park Malaysia and Kulim Hi-Tech Park. Fresh water is available to over 95 per cent of the population. During the colonial period, development was mainly concentrated in economically powerful cities and in areas forming security concerns. Although rural areas have been the focus of great development, they still lag behind areas such as the West Coast of Peninsular Malaysia. The telecommunication network, although strong in urban areas, is less available to the rural population.

Malaysia's road network covers 98,721 kilometres and includes 1,821 kilometres of expressways. The longest highway of the country, the North-South Expressway, extends over 800 kilometres between the Thai border and Singapore. The road systems in East Malaysia are less developed and of lower quality in comparison to that of Peninsular Malaysia. Malaysia has 118 airports, of which 38 are paved. The country's official airline is Malaysia Airlines, providing international and domestic air service alongside two other carriers. The railway system is state-run, and covers a total of 1,849 kilometres. Relatively inexpensive elevated Light Rail Transit systems are used in some cities, such as Kuala Lumpur. The Asean Rail Express is a railway service that connects Kuala Lumpur to Bangkok, and is intended to eventually stretch from Singapore to China.

Traditionally, energy production in Malaysia has been based on oil and natural gas. The country has 13 GW of electrical generation capacity. However, the country only has 33 years of natural gas reserves, and 19 years of oil reserves, while the demand for energy is increasing. In response, the government is expanding into renewable energy sources. Sixteen per cent of electricity generation is hydroelectric, the remaining 84 per cent being thermal. The oil and gas industry is dominated by state owned Petronas, and the energy sector as a whole is regulated by the Energy Commission of Malaysia, a statutory commission that governs the energy in the peninsula and Sabah.

National Security

Malaysia's strategic interests are viewed from three-tiers encompassing the areas of immediate vicinity, regional and global. The areas of its immediate vicinity comprise the land territories, territorial waters, airspace, the Exclusive Economic Zone (EEZ), the Straits of Malacca and its approaches, and the Straits of Singapore as well as the sea and air lines of communication connecting Peninsular Malaysia and Sabah and Sarawak.

The regional areas of interest to Malaysia cover Southeast Asia, including Andaman Islands as well as the South China Sea. Malaysia views any development affecting the region as invariably impinging her security and development. This is particularly significant as Malaysia shares either common land or sea boundaries or both with most of the ASEAN states. Any infringement to the region's security, whether in the form of intra-regional or extra-regional conflicts, will have consequential effects on Malaysia's security.

Malaysia's growing trade links, new markets for its products, increasing foreign investment and the acquisition of private enterprises with worldwide interests have broadened its interests beyond the immediate vicinity and the region. In view of this, it is in Malaysia's interest to ensure that global peace is maintained. Taking cognizance of its strategic and competing interests, Malaysia's defence revolves around the fundamental principles of Self-Reliance, Regional Cooperation and External Assistance.

Malaysia has asserted sovereignty over the Spratly Islands together with China, Philippines, Taiwan, Vietnam, and Brunei. Malaysia was not party to the March 2005 joint accord among the national oil companies of China, the Philippines, and Vietnam on conducting marine seismic activities in the Spratly Islands. Disputes continue over deliveries of fresh water to Singapore, bridge construction Singapore's land reclamation, maritime boundaries, and Pedra Branca Island/Pulau Batu Putih. Both parties agreed to arbitration on the island dispute within three years. The ICJ awarded Ligitan and Sipadan islands, also claimed by Indonesia and Philippines, to Malaysia but left the maritime boundary in the hydrocarbon-rich Celebes Sea in dispute, resulting in confrontations in March 2005 over concessions to the Ambalat oil block.

Separatist violence in Thailand's predominantly Muslim southern provinces prompted measures to close and monitor its border with Malaysia to stem terrorist activities. Philippines retains a claim to Malaysia's Sabah State in northern Borneo. In 2003, Brunei and Malaysia ceased gas and oil exploration in their disputed offshore and deepwater sea beds and negotiations have stalemated prompting consideration of international adjudication. Malaysia's land boundary with Brunei around Limbang is in dispute.

Piracy remains a problem in the Malacca Strait besides the issue of refugees from Indonesia and Burma. Malaysia is a regional transit point for some illicit drugs, though drug trafficking is prosecuted vigorously and carries severe penalties.

Even though it recognises the importance of regional cooperation and external assistance, Malaysia believes that self-reliance should continue to be the cornerstone of its defence. In this regard Malaysia will strive towards enhancing and developing its Armed Forces capabilities as well as promoting defence consciousness and patriotism among its citizens.

Armed Forces

In the early 1990s, Malaysia undertook a major programme to expand and modernize its armed forces. The role of the MAF is to defend the sovereignty and strategic interests of Malaysia from all forms of threat. It is responsible to assist the civilian authorities to overcome all international threats, preserve public order, assist in natural disasters and participate in national development programmes.

REPUBLIC OF MALDIVES

The Republic of Maldives is an island nation consisting of a group of atolls in the Indian Ocean. The Maldives is located south of India's Lakshadweep islands, and about seven hundred kilometres south-west of Sri Lanka. The Maldives' twenty-six atolls encompass a territory featuring 1,192 islets, roughly two hundred of which are inhabited by local communities. It is the smallest predominantly Muslim nation in the world.

The name "Maldives" derives from the Sanskrit *maladvipa*, meaning "garland of islands". Originally the inhabitants were Buddhist, but Islam was introduced in 1153. It later became a Portuguese (1558), Dutch (1654), and British (1887) colonial possession. In 1965, the Maldives obtained independence from Britain, and in 1968 the Sultanate was replaced by a Republic. However, in thirty-eight years, the Maldives have seen only three Presidents. Historically, Maldives had a strategic importance because of its location on the major maritime routes of the Indian Ocean. Sri Lanka and India have had cultural and economic ties with it for centuries.

The Maldives is the smallest Asian country in both population and land area. With an average ground level of 1.5 metres above sea level, it is the planet's lowest country. It is also the country with the lowest natural highest point in the world, at 2.4 metres. Forecasts of Maldives' inundation are a great concern for the Maldivian people.

History

Maldivian tradition suggests that the first settlers were Dravidian people, probably fishermen from the southwest coast of the Indian Subcontinent and the western shores of Sri Lanka. Buddhism came to the Maldives at the time of Emperor Ashoka's expansion and became the dominant religion until the 12th century AD. According to a legend, a prince named Koimala from India entered the Maldives from the North (Ihavandhu) and became the first king from the House of Theemuge. The ancient Maldivian Kings promoted Buddhism and the first Maldive writings and artistic achievements in the form of highly developed sculpture and architecture are from that period. The conversion to Islam began from the end of the 12th century AD. Over the centuries, the islands have been visited and their development influenced by sailors and traders from countries on the Arabian Sea and the Bay of Bengal.

From 1887 to 1965, Maldives was ruled by a succession of sultans. They were hereditary until 1932. Maldives remained a British crown protectorate until 1953 when the sultanate was suspended and the First Republic was declared under the short-lived presidency of Muhammad Amin Didi. Muslim conservatives in Male ousted his government, and during a riot over food shortages, Didi was beaten by a mob and died on a nearby island. In 1956 Britain obtained permission to reestablish its wartime airfield on Gan in the southernmost Addu Atoll on a 100-year lease and a payment of £2,000 a year, as well as some 44 hectares

Capital	-	Malé
Official language	-	Dhivehi
Government	-	Presidential republic
	-	President Abdulla Yameen
	-	Speaker of the Majlis Abdulla Shahid
	-	Chief Justice Ahmed Faiz
Formation	-	Independence from United Kingdom - 26 July 1965
Area	-	298 square kilometres
Population	-	328,536 (2012 estimate) Density 1,102/ square kilometre
GDP (PPP)	-	$2.841 billion (2011 estimate) Per capita $8,731
GDP (nominal)	-	$1.944 billion (2011 estimate) Per capita $5,973
Minister of Defence and National Security	-	Colonel (Retired) Mohamed Nazim
Chief of Defence Force	-	Major General Ahmed Shiyam

on Hitaddu for radio installations. In 1960 Maldives allowed Britain to continue at Gan and the Hitaddu for a thirty-year period, with the payment of £750,000 over the period of 1960 to 1965 for the purpose of Maldives' economic development.

In 1959 the inhabitants of the three southernmost atolls protested against the government. They formed the United Suvadive Republic and elected, Abdullah Afeef as president and Hithadhoo as capital of this republic. On 26 July 1965, Maldives gained independence from Britain, who retained the use of the Gan and Hitaddu facilities. After independence from Britain in 1965, the sultanate continued to operate for another three years under King Muhammad Fareed. On 11 November 1968, the monarchy was abolished and replaced by a republic, although this was a cosmetic change without any significant alteration in the structures of government. The official name of the country was changed from Maldive Islands to the Maldives in a progressive manner. Tourism began to be developed on the archipelago about five years later.

Elected to replace Nasir for a five-year presidential term in 1978 was Maumoon Abdul Gayoom, a former university lecturer and Maldivian ambassador to the United Nations. The peaceful election ushered in a period of political stability and economic development. The local populace benefited from increased tourism and the corresponding increase in foreign contacts involving various development projects. Gayoom's popularity remained strong, allowing him to win three more presidential terms, receiving more than 95 percent of the vote as the government did not allow any legal opposition.

During the 1970s, the economic situation in Maldives suffered a setback when the Sri Lankan market for Maldives' main export of dried fish collapsed. Adding to the problems was the British decision in 1975 to close its airfield on Gan in line with its policy of abandoning defence commitments east of the Suez Canal. A steep commercial decline followed. As a result, the popularity of Nasir's government suffered and the twenty-year period of authoritarian rule under Nasir abruptly ended in 1978 when he fled to Singapore. A subsequent investigation revealed that he had absconded with millions of dollars from the state treasury.

In November 1988, a group of Maldivians headed by Mr. Lutfee a small time businessman used Tamil mercenaries from Sri Lanka to stage a coup against President Gayyoom. After an appeal by the Maldivian government for help, the Indian military intervened against the mercenaries in order to reinstate Gayyoom in power. On the night of 3 November 1988, the Indian Air Force airlifted a parachute battalion group from Agra and flew them non-stop over 2,000 kilometres to the Maldives. The Indian paratroopers landed at Hulule and secured the airfield and restored the Government rule at Malé within hours. The brief, bloodless operation, labelled Operation Cactus, also involved the Indian Navy.

On 26 December 2004, the Maldives were devastated by a tsunami following the 2004 Indian Ocean earthquake. Only nine islands were reported to have escaped any flooding, while fifty-seven islands faced serious damage to critical infrastructure, fourteen islands had to be totally evacuated, and six islands were decimated. A further twenty-one resort islands were forced to shut down due to serious damage. The total damage was estimated at over 400 million dollars or some 62% of the GDP. A total of 108 people, including six foreigners, reportedly died in the tsunami. The destructive impact of the waves on the low-lying islands was mitigated by the fact there was no continental shelf or land mass upon which the waves could gain height. The tallest waves were reported 14 feet high.

On 16 January 2012, the Maldives military, on orders from President Nasheed, un-constitutionally arrested Judge Abdulla Mohamed, the chief justice of the Maldives Criminal Court, on charges he was blocking the prosecution of corruption and human rights cases against allies of former President Gayoom. On 7 February, Nasheed ordered the police and army to subdue the anti-government protesters and use force against the public. Police came out to protest against unlawful orders given to them. President Mohamed Nasheed resigned on 7 February 2012 by letter, and followed that with a televised public address informing Maldivians of his resignation and reasons thereof. However, within hours, Nasheed told foreign media that he was deposed by a military coup led by President Waheed. There have been disputes over exactly what happened that day. Nasheed's vice president, Mohammed Waheed Hassan, was sworn in as President in accordance with the Constitution at the Peoples majlis in front of the Chief Justice.

On 23 February 2012, the Commonwealth suspended the Maldives from its democracy and human rights watchdog while the ousting was being investigated, and backed Nasheed's call for elections before the end of 2012. On 8 October, Nasheed was arrested after failing to appear in court to face charges that he ordered the illegal arrest of a judge while in office. However, his supporters claim that this detention was politically motivated in order to prevent him from campaigning for the 2013 presidential elections. In the elections, finally held on 16 November 2013, the contest was between Maldivian Democratic Party candidate, Mohamed Nasheed and Progressive Party of Maldives candidate Abdulla Yameen. The latter emerged victorious.

Geography

The Maldives holds the record for being the flattest country in the world, with a maximum natural ground level of only 2.3 metres, though in areas where construction exists this has been increased to several metres. Over the last century, sea levels have risen about 20 centimetres. The ocean is likely to continue rising and this threatens the existence of Maldives. The Indian Ocean is particularly important for its diverse sea life and coral reefs, and the Maldives are among the richest locations in this regard.

Demographics

The Maldivian ethnic identity is a blend of the cultures reflecting the peoples who settled on the islands, reinforced by religion and language. Some social stratification exists on the islands. It is not rigid, since rank is based on varied factors, including occupation, wealth, Islamic virtue, and family ties. Traditionally, instead of a complex caste system, like the Vedic one, there was merely a distinction between noble (bçfulhu) and common people in the Maldives. Members of the social elite are concentrated in Malé.

Outside of the service industry, this is the only location where the foreign and domestic populations are likely to interact. The tourist resorts are not on islands where the natives live, and casual contacts between the two groups are discouraged.

A census has been recorded since 1905, which shows that the population of the country remained around 100,000 for the first seventy years of the last century. Following independence in 1965, the health status of the population improved so much that the population doubled by 1978, and the population growth rate peaked at 3.4% in 1985. By 2005, the population had reached 300,000, although the census in 2000 showed that the population growth rate had declined to 1.9%. Life expectancy at birth stood at 46 years in 1978, while it has now risen to 72 years. Infant mortality has declined from 127 per thousand in 1977 to 12 today, and adult literacy stands at 99%. Combined school enrolment stands in the high 90s.

The Maldives has one of the highest birth rates in the world. The result is that many islands have become overpopulated and are completely covered by homesteads. About 70,000 foreign nationals live in the country, mainly from the neighbouring South Asian countries of India, Sri Lanka, Bangladesh and Nepal.

Language and Culture

Maldivian culture is derived from a number of sources, the most important of which are its proximity to the shores of Sri Lanka and southern India. Thus the population is mainly a mix of Indo-Aryan, Dravidian and Semitic from the anthropological point of view. The official and common language is Dhivehi. The present-day written script is called Thaana and is written from right to left. English is used widely in commerce and increasingly as the medium of instruction in government schools. The language is from Indo-Iranian Sanskritic origin, which points at a later influence from the north of the subcontinent.

After the long Buddhist period of their history, Maldivians converted to Sunni Islam in the mid-12th century. Islam is the official religion of the entire population, as adherence to it is required for citizenship. In the island culture there are a few elements of African origin as well from slaves brought to the court by the royal family and nobles from their hajj journeys to Arabia in the past. There are islands like Feridhu and Maalhos in Northern Ari Atoll, and Goidhu in Southern Maalhosmadulhu Atoll where many of the inhabitants trace their ancestry to released African slaves.

Economy

In ancient times the Maldives were renowned for the cowries, coir rope, dried tuna fish (Maldive Fish), ambergris (Maavaharu) and coco de mer (Tavakkaashi). Local and foreign trading ships used to load these products in the Maldives and transport them to other harbours in the Indian Ocean.

Today tourism and fisheries form the two key components of the Maldivian economy. The country's shipping, banking and manufacturing sectors are growing at a considerable pace. Among the South Asian nations, the Maldives has the second highest per-capita GDP at 3,900 USD (2002 figure). Major trading partners include India, Sri Lanka, Thailand, Malaysia and Singapore. The development of tourism has fostered the overall growth of the country's economy. It has created direct and indirect employment and income generation opportunities in other related industries. Today, tourism is the country's biggest foreign exchange earner, contributing to 20% of the GDP. With eighty-seven tourist resorts in operation. The year 2006 recorded 467,154 tourist arrivals.

The mechanisation of the traditional fishing boat called "Dhoni" in 1974 was a major milestone in the development of the fisheries industry and the country's economy in general. A fish canning plant was installed in the island of Felivaru in 1977, as a joint venture with a Japanese firm. Moreover, the opening up of the Exclusive Economic Zone (EEZ) of the Maldives for fisheries has further enhanced the growth of the fisheries sector. Today, fisheries contribute over fifteen percent of the GDP and engage about thirty percent of the country's work force. It is also the second-largest foreign exchange earner after tourism.

Airports with two permanent-surface runways exist at Male and Gan. Air Maldives is national airline. Maldives has minimal domestic and international facilities with one television station; and one Indian Ocean International Telecommunications Satellite Corporation (Intelsat) earth station.

The major daily newspaper is Haveeru (North Side) in Male. Aafathis, is another daily in Dhivehi and English. Maldives also has a number of weekly and monthly publications as well as several news agencies and publishers. Hindi-language films, newspapers, and magazines from India are popular. The government radio station Voice of Maldives, established in 1962, broadcasts to the entire country in Dhivehi and English.

Administrative Divisions

The Maldives have been divided into 21 administrative divisions (20 administrative atolls and Malé city). In addition to a name, every administrative division is identified by the Maldivian code letters, such as "Haa Alif" for Thiladhunmati Uthuruburi (Thiladhunmathi North); and by a Latin code letter. The first corresponds to the geographical Maldivian name of the atoll. The second is a code adopted for convenience. It began in order to facilitate radio communication between the atolls and the central administration. As there are certain islands in different atolls that have the same name, for administrative purposes this code is quoted before the name of the island, for example: Baa Funadhoo, Kaafu Funadhoo, Gaafu-Alifu Funadhoo. Since most Atolls have very long geographical names it is also used whenever the name of the atoll has to be quoted short, for example in the atoll website names.

Each atoll is administered by an Atoll Chief (Atholhu Veriyaa) appointed by the President. The Ministry of Atoll Administration and its Northern and Southern Regional Offices, Atoll Offices and Island Offices are collectively responsible to the President for Atolls Administration. The administrative head of each island is the Island Chief (Katheeb), appointed by the President. The Island Chief's immediate superior is the Atoll Chief.

Politics

Politics in the Maldives takes place in the framework of a presidential republic, whereby the President is the head of government. The President heads the executive branch and appoints the cabinet. The President is nominated to a five-year term by a secret ballot of the Majlis (parliament), a nomination which is confirmed by national referendum.

The unicameral Majlis of the Maldives is composed of fifty members serving five-year terms. Two members from each atoll are elected directly by universal suffrage. Eight are appointed by the president, which is the main route through which women enter parliament. The country introduced political parties for the first time in its history in July 2005, six months after the last elections for the parliament.

Tourism

The Maldives archipelago possesses a truly unique geography. Nature has fragmented the archipelago into 1,190 tiny islands that occupy a mere one per cent of its 90,000 square kilometres of territory. Only 185 islands are home to its 300,000 population, while the other islands are used entirely for economic purposes of which tourism and agriculture are the most dominant. Tourism accounts for 28% of GDP and more than 60% of the Maldives' foreign exchange receipts. Over 90% of government tax revenue comes from import duties and tourism-related taxes. The development of tourism has fostered the overall growth of the country's economy. It has created direct and indirect employment and income generation opportunities in other related industries. The first tourist resorts were opened in 1972 with Bandos island resort and Kurumba Village.

The emergence of tourism in 1972 transformed the economy of the Maldives, moving rapidly from dependence on fisheries to tourism. In just three and a half decades, the industry has become the main source of income and livelihood of the people of the Maldives. Tourism is also the country's biggest foreign currency earner and the single largest contributor to the GDP. Today, there are 92 resorts in the Maldives hosting 600,000 tourists annually.

National Security

The Maldives National Defence Force is the combined security organisation responsible for defending the security and sovereignty of the Maldives, having the primary task of being responsible for attending to all internal and external security needs of the Maldives, including the protection of the Exclusive Economic Zone and the maintenance of peace and security. The National Security Service of about 2,000 members performs army, police, and maritime duties. The Republic of Maldives has no armed forces, faces no internal or external threat and is not involved in any international dispute. Threat perceptions include global factors like the threat to the environment, ozone depletion and global warming. Maldives has a Coast Guard Force with 400 Personnel.

Maldives' first-ever terror strike occurred on 29 September 2007, when an Islamist cell triggered an explosive device in Male's Sultan Park. Investigators discovered that the cell had connections with Lashkar-e-Taiba operatives at the Jamia Salafiyya in Faisalabad—a seminary that has produced key Lashkar commanders.

MYANMAR

Burma, officially the Union of Myanmar, is the largest country by geographical area in mainland Southeast Asia. Myanmar achieved independence from Britain on 4 January 1948, as the "Union of Burma." It became the "Socialist Republic of the Union of Burma" on 4 January 1974, before reverting to the "Union of Burma" on 23 September 1988. On 18 June 1989, the State Law and Order Restoration Council adopted the name "Union of Myanmar." This was recognised by the United Nations, but not by the US Government as this decision was not approved by any sitting legislature.

The flag of Myanmar is red with a blue rectangle in the upper hoist-side corner bearing, 14 white five-pointed stars encircling a cogwheel containing a stalk of rice; the 14 stars represent the seven administrative divisions and seven states. It is bordered by China on the north, Laos on the east, Thailand on the southeast, Bangladesh on the west, and India on the northwest, with the Bay of Bengal to the southwest. One-third of Myanmar's total perimeter, 1,930 kilometres, forms an uninterrupted coastline.

Myanmar's diverse population has played a major role in defining its politics, history and demographics in modern times. The country's culture, heavily influenced by neighbours, is based on Theravada Buddhism intertwined with local elements.

History

The Mon people are thought to be the earliest group to migrate into the lower Ayeyarwady valley and, by the mid-900s BC, were dominant in southern Burma. The Mons became one of the first in South East Asia to embrace Theravada Buddhism. The Tibeto-Burman speaking Pyu arrived later in the 1st century BC, and established several city states and established a small kingdom in Bagan in 849. Prosperous from trade, Bagan kings built many magnificent temples and pagodas throughout the country – many of which can still be seen today. Bagan's power slowly waned in 13th century and the Bagan empire was irreparably broken up into several small kingdoms:

- The Burman kingdom of Ava or Innwa (1364–1555), the successor state to three smaller kingdoms founded by Burmanized Shan kings, controlling Upper Burma.
- The Mon kingdom of Hanthawady Pegu or Bago (1287–1540), founded by a Mon-ized Shan King Wareru (1287–1306), controlling Lower Burma.
- The Rakhine kingdom of Mrauk U (1434–1784), in the west.
- Several Shan states in the Shan hills in the east and the Kachin hills in the north.

The Burmese under King Anaukpetlun (1605–1628) established a smaller kingdom based in Ava covering Upper Burma, Lower Burma and Shan states, but it experienced a slow and steady decline for the next 100 years.

King Bodawpaya (1782–1819) attempted to extend his kingdom towards India and captured then independent kingdom of Assam in 1819. The new conquests brought the Burmese adjacent to the

Capital	-	Naypyidaw
Largest city	-	Yangon (Rangoon)
Official language Recognised languages:	-	Burmese Jingpho, Kayah, Karen, Chin, Mon, Rakhine, Shan
Government	- - -	Unitary presidential constitutional republic President General Thein Sein Vice President Sai Mauk Kham Vice President Nyan Tun
Formation	-	Independence 4 January 1948 (from UK) New Constitution 30 March 2011
Area	-	676,578 square kilometres
Coastline	-	1,930 kilometres
Population	-	60,280,000 (2010 estimate) Density 73.9/square kilometre
GDP (PPP)	-	$89.461 billion (2012 estimate) Per capita $1,405
GDP (nominal)	-	$53.140 billion (2012 estimate) Per capita $854
Minister of Defence	-	Lt General Wai Lwin
C-in-C Armed Forces	-	Vice Senior General Min Aung Hlaing
C-in-C Army	-	General Soe Win
C-in-C Navy	-	Admiral Nyan Tun
C-in-C Air Force	-	General Myat Hein
C-in-C Air Defence	-	Brig Gen Myint Hiaing

British India. The British defeated the Burmese in the First Anglo-Burmese War (1824–1826). Burma had to cede Assam, Manipur, Rakhine (Arakan) and Tanintharyi (Tenessarim).

In 1852, the British attacked a much weakened Burma during a Burmese palace power struggle. After the Second Anglo-Burmese War, the British captured the remaining coastal provinces: Ayeyarwady, Yangon and Bago, naming the territories as Lower Burma.

The Third Anglo-Burmese War (1885) resulted in Upper Burma and Lower Burma being reunited, and Burma was administered as a single province within British India despite Burma's independent history and traditions. To stimulate trade and facilitate changes, the British brought in Indians and Chinese who quickly displaced the Burmese in urban areas. To this day Yangon and Mandalay have large ethnic Indian populations. Railroads and schools were built, as well as a large number of prisons including the infamous Insein Jail, then as now used for political prisoners. Burmese resentment was strong and was vented in violent riots that paralyzed Yangon on occasion all the way until the 1930s. Much of the discontent was caused by a perceived disrespect for Burman culture and traditions, for example, what the British termed the Shoe Question: the colonisers' refusal to remove their shoes upon entering Buddhist temples or other holy places.

On 1 April 1937, Burma became a separately administered territory, independent of the Indian administration. The vote for keeping Burma in India, or as a separate colony divided the populace, and laid the ground work for the insurgencies to come after independence. In the 1940s, the Thirty Comrades, commanded by Aung San, founded the

Burma Independence Army. The Thirty Comrades received training in Japan.

During World War II, Burma became a major frontline in the Southeast Asian Theatre. The British administration collapsed ahead of the advancing Japanese troops but, by July 1945, the British had retaken the country. Although many Burmese fought initially for the Japanese, some Burmese also served in the British Burma Army. The Burma Independence Army under the command of Aung San and the Arakan National Army fought with the Japanese from 1942–1944, but switched allegiance to the Allied side in 1945.

In 1947, Aung San became Deputy Chairman of the Executive Council of Burma, a transitional government. But in July 1947, political rivals assassinated Aung San and several cabinet members. On 4 January 1948, the nation became an independent republic, named the Union of Burma, with Sao Shwe Thaik as its first President and U Nu as its first Prime Minister. Unlike most other former British colonies and overseas territories, it did not become a member of the Commonwealth. A bicameral parliament was formed, consisting of a Chamber of Deputies and a Chamber of Nationalities.

Democratic rule ended in 1962 when General Ne Win led a military coup d'état. He ruled for nearly 26 years and pursued policies under the rubric of the Burmese Way to Socialism. In 1988, General Saw Maung staged a coup d'état and formed the State Law and Order Restoration Council (SLORC). In 1989, SLORC declared martial law after widespread protests. The military government finalised plans for People's Assembly elections on 31 May 1989.

In May 1990, the government held free elections for the first time in almost 30 years. The National League for Democracy (NLD), the party of Aung San Suu Kyi, won 392 out of a total 489 seats, but the election results were annulled by SLORC, which refused to step down. Led by Than Shwe since 1992, the military regime has made cease-fire agreements with most ethnic guerrilla groups. In 1997, the State Law and Order Restoration Council was renamed the State Peace and Development Council (SPDC).

On 23 June 1997, Myanmar was admitted into the Association of Southeast Asian Nations (ASEAN). On 27 March 2006, the military junta, which had moved the national capital from Yangon to a site near Pyinmana, officially named it Naypyidaw, meaning "city of the kings".

Mass public demonstrations started on 18 August 2007, when the government raised the price of gas and diesel oil by 500% in order to cover a budget deficit that resulted from a salary hike for civil servants. The junta's move of the Burmese capital to Pyinmana may also have contributed to the budget deficit.

On 19 September 2007, several hundred monks staged a protest march in the city of Sittwe. Larger protests in Rangoon and elsewhere ensued over the following days. Security became increasingly heavy handed, resulting in a number of deaths and injuries. By 28 September, internet access had been cut and journalists reputedly warned not to report on protests. Internet access was restored on 5 October.

The constitution of Burma, its third since independence, was drafted by its military rulers and published in September 2008. The country is governed as a presidential republic with a bicameral legislature, with a portion of legislatures appointed by the military and others elected in general elections. The current head of state, inaugurated as President on 30 March 2011, is Thein Sein.

The legislature, called the Pyidaungsu Hluttaw, is bicameral and made up of two houses: The 224-seat upper house Amyotha Hluttaw (House of Nationalities) and the 440-seat lower house Pyithu Hluttaw (House of Representatives). The upper house consists of 224 member of which 168 are directly elected and 56 are appointed by the Burmese Armed Forces while the lower house consists of 440 members of which 330 are directly elected and 110 are appointed by the armed forces. The major political parties are the National League for Democracy, National Democratic Force and the two backed by the military: the National Unity Party, and the Union Solidarity and Development Party.

Burma's army-drafted constitution was approved in a referendum in May 2008. The results, 92.4% of the 22 million voters with an official turnout of 99%, are considered suspect by many international observers and by the National league of democracy with reports of widespread fraud, ballot stuffing, and voter intimidation.

The elections of 2010 resulted in a victory for the military-backed Union Solidarity and Development Party and various foreign observers questioned the fairness of the elections. One criticism of the election was that only government sanctioned political parties were allowed to contest in it and the popular National League for Democracy was declared illegal and is still barred from political activities.

However, immediately following the elections, the government ended the house arrest of the democracy advocate and leader of the National League for Democracy, Aung San Suu Kyi, and her ability to move freely around the country is considered an important test of the military's movement toward more openness. After unexpected reforms in 2011, NLD senior leaders have decided to register as a political party and to field candidates in future by-elections.

In October, 2010, a new flag was adopted and the official name of the country changed to "Republic of the Union of Myanmar", replacing the old "Union of Myanmar" from 1989.

On 9 November 2010, Myanmar's ruling junta stated that the Union Solidarity and Development Party won 80% of the votes. This claim is widely disputed by pro-democracy opposition groups, asserting that the military regime engaged in rampant fraud to achieve its result. On 13 November 2010 the military authorities in Burma released the pro-democracy leader, Aung San Suu Kyi. The military junta was officially dissolved in 2011 and a nominally civilian government installed, though the military retains enormous influence.

Geography

Myanmar has an area of 678,500 square kilometres (land: 657,740 square kilometres and water: 20,760 square kilometres). Its land boundaries total 5,876 kilometres with Bangladesh (193 kilometres), China (2,185 kilometres), India (1,463 kilometres), Laos (235 kilometres) and Thailand (1,800 kilometres). It has a coastline of 1,930 kilometres. It has a strategic location near major Indian Ocean shipping lanes.

The climate of Myanmar is characterised as tropical monsoon with cloudy, rainy, hot, humid summers (southwest monsoon, June to September) and less cloudy, scant rainfall, mild temperatures, lower humidity during winter (northeast monsoon, December to April).

The terrain comprises central lowlands ringed by steep, rugged highlands. The highest point is Hkakabo Razi (5,881 metres). Myanmar's natural resources include petroleum, timber, tin, antimony, zinc, copper, tungsten, lead, coal, some marble, limestone, precious stones, natural gas and hydropower. 14.92% of the land is arable with only 1.31% under permanent crops. Irrigated land comprises 18,700 square kilometres. Myanmar is prone to natural hazards like destructive earthquakes and cyclones. Flooding and landslides are common during rainy season (June to September). The country also experiences periodic droughts. Current environmental issues include deforestation and industrial pollution of air, soil, and water. Inadequate sanitation and water treatment also contribute to disease

The Ayeyarwady delta, which is approximately 50,400 square kilometres in area, is largely used for rice cultivation.In the north, the Hengduan Shan mountains form the border with China. Three mountain ranges, namely the Rakhine Yoma, the Bago Yoma, and the Shan Plateau exist within Myanmar, all of which run north-to-south from the Himalayas. The mountain chains divide Myanmar's three river systems, which are the Ayeyarwady, Thanlwin, and the Sittang rivers. The Ayeyarwady River, Myanmar's longest river, nearly 2,170 kilometres long, flows into the Gulf of Martaban. Fertile plains exist in the valleys between the mountain chains. The majority of Myanmar's population lives in the Ayeyarwady valley, which is situated between the Rakhine Yoma and the Shan Plateau.

Myanmar's slow economic growth has contributed to the preservation of much of its environment and ecosystems. Forests, including dense tropical growth and valuable teak in lower Myanmar, cover over 49% of the country. Other trees indigenous to the region include rubber, acacia, bamboo, ironwood, mangrove, coconut and betel palm. In the highlands of the north, oak, pine and various rhododendrons cover much of the land. The lands along the coast support all varieties of tropical fruits. In the Dry Zone, vegetation is sparse and stunted.

People

The major Burmese ethnic groups are Burman 68%, Shan 9%, Karen 7%, Rakhine 4%, Chinese 3%, Indian

2%, Mon 2%, other 5%. The religions are Buddhist 89%, Christian 4% (Baptist 3%, Roman Catholic 1%), Muslim 4%, animist 1%, other 2%. Burmese is the major languages, though minority ethnic groups have their own languages. Myanmar has an estimated population of 47,382,633. The median age is 27 years with a population growth rate of 0.81%.

Myanmar has a population of about 55 million. Current population figures are rough estimates because the last partial census was taken in 1983. No trustworthy nationwide census has been taken in Myanmar since 1931. There are over 600,000 registered migrant workers from Myanmar in Thailand, and millions more work illegally. Burmese migrant workers account for 80% of Thailand's migrant workers. Myanmar has a population density of 75 persons per square kilometre, one of the lowest in Southeast Asia. Refugee camps exist along Indian-Burmese, Bangladeshi-Burmese and Burmese-Thai borders while several thousand are in Malaysia. Conservative estimates state that there are over 295,800 refugees from Myanmar, with the majority being Rohingya, Kayin, and Karenni.

Myanmar is ethnically diverse. The government recognizes 135 distinct ethnic groups. While it is extremely difficult to verify this statement, there are at least 108 different ethno-linguistic groups in Myanmar, consisting mainly of distinct Tibeto-Burman peoples, but with sizable populations of Daic, Hmong-Mien, and Austroasiatic (Mon-Khmer) peoples. The Bamar form an estimated 68% of the population.[10] 10% of the population are Shan. The Kayin make up 7% of the population. The Rakhine people constitute 4% of the population. Overseas Chinese form approximately 3% of the population. Mon, who form 2% of the population, are ethno-linguistically related to the Khmer. Overseas Indians comprise 2%. The remainder are Kachin, Chin, Anglo-Indians and other ethnic minorities. Included in this group are the Anglo-Burmese. Once forming a large and influential community, the Anglo-Burmese left the country in steady streams from 1958 onwards, principally to Australia and the U.K. Today, it is estimated that only 52,000 Anglo-Burmese remain in Myanmar.

Government and Politics

Executive branch. The country is governed as a presidential republic with a bicameral legislature, with a portion of legislators appointed by the military and others elected in general elections. The current head of state, inaugurated as President on 30 March 2011, is Thein Sein.

Legislative branch. Myanmar has a unicameral People's Assembly or Pyithu Hluttaw (485 seats; members elected by popular vote to serve four-year terms).

Judicial branch. Remnants of the British-era legal system are in place, but there is no guarantee of a fair public trial; the judiciary is not independent of the executive.

Major political parties in Myanmar are the National League for Democracy and the Shan Nationalities League for Democracy, although their activities are heavily regulated and suppressed by the military government. Many other parties, often representing ethnic minorities, exist.

Administrative Divisions

Myanmar is divided into seven states and seven divisions.

The Divisions are:

- Ayeyarwady Division
- Bago Division
- Magway Division
- Mandalay Division
- Sagaing Division
- Tanintharyi Division
- Yangon Division

The States are:

- Chin State
- Kachin State
- Kayin (Karen) State
- Kayah (Karenni) State
- Mon State
- Rakhine (Arakan) State
- Shan State

Economy

Under British administration, Myanmar was one of the wealthiest countries in Southeast Asia. It was once the world's largest exporter of rice. Myanmar also had a wealth of natural and labour resources. It produced 75% of the world's teak and had a highly literate population.

Myanmar is a resource-rich country, which suffers from pervasive government controls, inefficient economic policies and rural poverty. Steps in the early 1990s to liberalize the economy after decades of failure under the "Burmese Way to Socialism" stalled, and liberalisation measures were rescinded. Myanmar does not have monetary or fiscal stability. The economy suffers from serious macro-economic imbalances, inflation, multiple official exchange rates overvaluing the Burmese kyat, and a distorted interest rate regime.

After a parliamentary government was formed in 1948, Prime Minister U Nu disastrously attempted to make Burma a welfare state and adopted central planning. Rice exports fell by two thirds and mineral exports by over 96%. Plans were partly financed by printing money, which led to inflation. The 1962 coup d'état was followed by an economic scheme called the Burmese Way to Socialism, a plan to nationalise all industries, with the exception of agriculture. The catastrophic programme turned Burma into one of the world's most impoverished countries. Burma's admittance to Least Developed Country status by the UN in 1987 highlighted its economic bankruptcy.

After 1988, the regime retreated from totalitarian rule. It permitted modest expansion of the private sector, allowed some foreign investment, and received needed foreign exchange. All fundamental market institutions are suppressed. Private enterprises are often co-owned or indirectly owned by state.

Inflation is a serious problem for the economy. In recent years, both China and India have attempted to strengthen ties with the government for economic benefit. Many nations, including the United States and Canada, and the European Union, have imposed investment and trade sanctions on Burma. The United States has banned all imports from Burma. Foreign investment comes primarily from People's Republic of China, Singapore, South Korea, India, and Thailand.

The major agricultural product is rice which covers about 60% of the country's total cultivated land area.

Today, the country lacks adequate infrastructure. Goods travel primarily across the Thai border, where most illegal drugs are exported and along the Ayeyarwady River. Railways are old and rudimentary, with few repairs since their construction in the late 19th century. Highways are normally unpaved, except in the major cities. Energy shortages are common throughout the country including in Yangon. Burma is also the world's second largest producer of opium, accounting for 8% of entire world production and is a major source of illegal drugs, including amphetamines. Other industries include agricultural goods, textiles, wood products, construction materials, gems, metals, oil and natural gas. The Norwegian company Seadrill owned by John Fredriksen is involved in offshore oil drilling, expected to give oil and oil export revenues.

Rubies are the biggest earner; 90% of the world's rubies come from the country, whose red stones are prized for their purity and hue. Thailand buys the majority of the country's gems. Burma's "Valley of Rubies", the mountainous Mogok area, 200 kilometres north of Mandalay, is noted for its rare pigeon's blood rubies and blue sapphires.

Transportation

Myanmar has 85 airports, with 21 having paved runways. The country has 2,056 kilometres of gas pipelines and 558 kilometres of oil pipelines. The railways extend over 3,955 kilometres (most of it narrow gauge). The roadways extend 27,000 kilometres (paved–3,200 kilometres; unpaved–23,800 kilometres. Its waterways extend 12,800 kilometres.

The merchant marine of Myanmar has 34 ships (1000 GRT or over) 402,724 GRT/620,642 DWT, that include bulk carriers–8, cargo–18, passenger–2, passenger/cargo–3, roll on/roll off–2 and specialised tanker–1. (9 are foreign-owned: Germany 5, Japan 4). The major ports and terminals are Moulmein, Rangoon and Sittwe.

Armed Forces

Myanmar's armed forces are known as the Tatmadaw, which numbers 488,000. The Tatmadaw comprises the Army, the Navy, and the Air Force. The military is very influential in the country, with top cabinet and ministry posts held by military officers. Although official figures for Burmese military spending are not available, the Stockholm International Peace Research Institute, in its annual rankings, ranked Myanmar in the top 15 military spenders in the world. The country imports most of its weapons from Russia, Ukraine, China and India.

National Security

Over half of Myanmar's population consists of diverse ethnic groups with substantial numbers of kin beyond its borders. Despite continuing border committee talks, significant differences remain with Thailand over boundary alignment and the handling of ethnic rebels, refugees, and illegal cross-border activities. Civil wars have been a constant feature of Myanmar's socio-political landscape since independence in 1948. They are predominantly struggles for ethnic and sub-national autonomy and fighting has predominately taken place in areas around the ethnically Burman core region of the country where the majority of country's population resides. Ongoing conflicts include fighting between Kachin Independence Army and the government in Kachin State, the Rohingya armed groups in Arakan State as well as Shan, Lahu and Karen minority groups in the eastern half of the country. In 2005 Thailand sheltered about 121,000 Burmese refugees. Karens also protest Thai support for a Burmese hydroelectric dam on the Salween River near the border. Environmentalists in Myanmar and Thailand continue to voice concern over China's construction of hydroelectric dams upstream on the Nujiang/ Salween River in Yunnan Province.

Myanmar has about 550,000-1,000,000 refugees and internally displaced persons due to government offensives against ethnic insurgent groups near its borders. Most of them are ethnic Karen, Karenni, Shan, Tavoyan, and Mons.Myanmar is the world's second largest producer of illicit opium (estimated production 292 metric tons). The cultivation is estimated to be over 30,900 hectares. Lack of government will to take on major narco-trafficking groups and lack of serious commitment against money laundering continues to hinder the overall anti-drug effort. Myanmar is the major source of methamphetamine and heroin for regional consumption. The country is currently under Financial Action Task Force countermeasures due to continued failure to address its inadequate money-laundering controls.

Myanmar is building a research nuclear reactor near May Myo (Pyin Oo Lwin) with help from Russia. Myanmar is one of the signatories of the nuclear non-proliferation pact since 1992 and a member of the IAEA since 1957. The military junta had informed the IAEA in September 2000 of its intention to construct the reactor. The research reactor outbuilding frame was built by ELE steel industries limited of Yangon and water from Anisakhan/BE water fall will be used for the reactor cavity cooling system.

The 2012 Rakhine State riots are a series of ongoing conflicts between Rohingya Muslims and ethnic Rakhine in northern Rakhine State, Myanmar. The riots came after weeks of sectarian disputes and have been condemned by most people on both sides of the conflict. The immediate cause of the riots is unclear, with many commentators citing the killing of ten Burmese Muslims by ethnic Rakhine after the rape and murder of a Rakhine woman as the main cause. Whole villages were "decimated". Over 300 houses and a number of public buildings were razed. 650 Rohingyas were killed, 1,200 missing, and more than 80,000 displaced. According to the Myanmar authorities, the violence, between ethnic Rakhine Buddhists and Rohingya Muslims, left 78 people dead, 87 injured, and thousands of homes destroyed. It displaced more than 52,000 people. On 10 June 2012, a state of emergency was declared in Rakhine, allowing the military to participate in administration of the region. The Burmese army and police have been accused of targeting Rohingya Muslims through mass arrests and arbitrary violence. A number of monks' organisations that played a vital role in Burma's struggle for democracy have taken measures to block any humanitarian assistance to the Rohingya community.

In March 2012, a draft foreign investment law emerged, the first in more than 2 decades. Foreigners will no longer require a local partner to start a business in the country, and will be able to legally lease but not own property. The draft law also stipulates that Burmese citizens must constitute at least 25% of the firm's skilled workforce, and with subsequent training, up to 50-75%.

In 2012, the Asian Development Bank formally began re-engaging with the country, to finance infrastructure and development projects in the country. The United States, Japan and the European Union countries have also begun to reduce or eliminate economic sanctions to allow foreign direct investment which will provide the Burmese government with additional tax revenue.

NEPAL

Nepal is a landlocked nation in South Asia, bordering the People's Republic of China to the north and India to the south, east and west. Nepal previously had the distinction of being the world's only Hindu state, with over 80% of the people following this faith. However, on 18 May 2006 Nepal was declared a secular state.

The national flag consists of two vertically stacked crimson red triangles with blue borders. The upper portion has an eight-pointed disc rising out of a white crescent moon, and the bottom portion has a white sun. The moon and sun symbolize the eternal eyes of god, the red colour represents energy in action, and the blue border signifies Nepal's peaceful nature.

History

Founded in 1559, Gorkha was one among the hill states until the rule of Prithvi Narayan Shah (1743–75), when the Nepalese state was established. An astute military strategist, Shah obtained financial assistance and armaments from India and then created alliances with neighbouring states or purchased their neutrality. In fact, his forces even managed to repel British troops. On 29 September 1768, Gorkha troops entered Kathmandu during religious celebrations and took it without a fight. Intrigue and infighting among the royalty continued until 1846, when Jang Bahadur Kunwar, a military commander, established a dynasty of prime ministers that ruled until 1951. The Rana dynasty was a parallel monarchy in which the pre-eminent authority was the prime minister, a hereditary position. The monarchy was reduced to a ceremonial position that legitimized Rana rule and monarchs were either exiled or kept under house arrest. Rampant nepotism and inefficient administration handicapped political development. The Ranas provided some positive development, such as eliminating slavery, establishing schools and factories. On 8 January 1951, the last Rana oligarch, Mohan Shamsher, agreed to restore the king to power and hold elections. In February 1951, King Tribhuvan (r. 1911–55) returned to power.

From February 1951 numerous short-lived governments ruled either under an interim constitution or under King Tribhuvan and his successor, Mahendra (r. 1955–72). The kings regularly dismissed uncooperative or poorly functioning ministries and continually postponed elections. After popular protests, the king allowed the first national elections in February 1959. The Nepali Congress won. But the king dismissed this government in 1960, and instituted a *panchayat* (village council) government, a four-tiered system of representative government with traditional village-level councils at the local level and the National Panchayat at the national level. King Mahendra died in January 1972, and his successor, Birendra (r. 1972–2001), adopted a more liberal approach to government.

In May 1980, King Birendra held a national referendum on the *panchayat* system. He interpreted the narrow margin of support (54.7 percent voted in favour) as a need for political change. He allowed direct elections to the National Panchayat and Nepal once again underwent tumultuous change. Nepal's improving relations with China placed stress on its

Capital	-	Kathmandu
Official language	-	Nepali
Recognised languages:		Maithili, Nepal Bhasa, Bhojpuri, Tharu, Gurung, Tamang, Magar, Awadhi, Sherpa, Kiranti and other 100 different indigenous languages.
Government	-	Federal Republic
	-	President Ram Baran Yadav
	-	Prime Minister
	-	Chief Justice Khil Raj Regmi
Formation	-	Kingdom declared 21 December 1768
	-	State declared 15 January 2007
	-	Republic declared 28 May 2008
Area	-	147,181 square kilometres
Population	-	26,494,504 (2011 census) Density 180/square kilometre
GDP (PPP)	-	$39,899 billion (2012 estimate) Per capita $1,400
GDP (nominal)	-	$19,921 billion (2012 estimate) Per capita $743
Chief of Army Staff	-	General Gaurav Shumsher JB Rana

relations with India, and for this and other reasons India terminated trade and transit treaties in March 1989. After a long and rich history, during which the country splintered and coalesced under a variety of absolute rulers, Nepal became a constitutional monarchy in 1990. A new constitution was promulgated on 9 November 1990, with provisions for basic human rights, adult franchise, and a multiparty democracy with the king as a constitutional monarch. Elections were held in May 1991, and the Nepali Congress came to power.

In one of the most remarkable events in Nepal's history, Crown Prince Dipendra killed the king, queen, and other royal family members on 1 June 2001, reportedly over his choice of a bride. The crown passed to Gyanendra, Dipendra's uncle, who adopted a firm approach to political issues. When cease-fire talks with the Maoists ended in November 2001, King Gyanendra declared a state of emergency and sent the army into the conflict. This action intensified the conflict. The king dissolved parliament in May 2002 and later unconstitutionally released Deuba's government and assumed executive powers. In the face of unstable governments and a Maoist siege on the Kathmandu Valley in August 2004, popular support for the monarchy began to wane. A seven-party alliance government was installed, whose primary task is to change the constitution.

Following the 2006 democracy movement, the king agreed to relinquish the sovereign power back to the people and reinstated the dissolved House of Representatives on 24 April 2006. Using its newly acquired sovereign authority, on 18 May 2006, the newly resumed House of Representatives unanimously passed a motion to curtail the power of the king and declared Nepal a secular state.

The Maoist leader, Pushpa Kamal Dahal, known as "Prachanda", became the first prime minister of the Federal Democratic Republic of Nepal, having won an overwhelming vote in the Constituent Assembly elected in April. The first meeting of the Constituent Assembly on 28 May 2008 overwhelmingly voted for the abolition of the monarchy in the country and declared Nepal a Federal Democratic Republic. It thus abolished the 239-year-old monarchy. In June 2008 former King Gyanendra Shah departed from the palace, remaining in the country as an ordinary citizen.

The turning point in the change in Nepal was the April 2006 people's movement, when hundreds of thousands took to the streets for 19 successive days. The king was compelled to hand power back to the political parties, while a peace agreement emerged that ended the conflict, bringing the Maoists into an interim parliament and government and promising elections to a Constituent Assembly.

The people's movement also took the lid off social pressures often disregarded by Nepal's elites. Although established as a unitary Hindu kingdom, with politics directed from the Himalayan foothills, today around half the population live in the fertile southern plains and more than one-third are from over 50 indigenous, largely non-Hindu communities.

The Nepali Congress (NC) candidate Dr. Ram Baran Yadav was elected as the first President of republican Nepal, securing a comfortable majority in the presidential election held on 21 July 2008. The Communist Party of Nepal (Maoist) won the largest number of seats in the Constituent Assembly election held on 10 April 2008 and formed a coalition government which included most of the parties. Although acts of violence occurred during the pre-electoral period, election observers noted that the elections themselves were markedly peaceful.

The newly elected Assembly met in Kathmandu on 28 May 2008, and, after a polling of 564 Constituent Assembly members, 560 voted to form a new Government, with the monarchist Rastriya Prajatantra Party, which had four members in the assembly, registering a dissent note. At that point, it was declared that Nepal had become a secular and inclusive democratic republic. The King was thereafter given 15 days to vacate the Narayanhiti Royal Palace, in order to re-open it as a public museum.

However, political tensions and consequent power-sharing battles have continued in Nepal. In May 2009, the Maoist-led government was toppled and another coalition government with all major political parties barring the Maoists was formed. Madhav Kumar Nepal of the Communist Party of Nepal (Unified Marxist-Leninist) was made the Prime Minister of the coalition government.

On 27 May 2012, the country's Constituent Assembly failed to meet the deadline for writing a new constitution for the country. Prime Minister Baburam Bhattarai announced that new elections will be held on 22 November. One of the main obstacles has been disagreement over whether the states which will be created will be based on ethnicity.

Geography

Nepal is a landlocked country with India to the east, south, and west and China to the north. Its total land area is 147,181 square kilometres. Its boundary with China is 1,236 kilometres and with India is 1,690 kilometres. Nepal and China have no territorial disputes, but Nepal and India have several: possession of a 75-square-kilometre area called Kalapani, further complicated by its proximity to the Chinese border; the boundary of the Maha Kali River (Sarda River in India), with ramifications for development and distribution of hydropower and water resources; possession of 209 hectares of land after changes in the course of the Mechi River; and sovereignty over several areas comprising nearly 600 square kilometres along the border.

Mountains and rugged hills cover nearly 75 percent of Nepal. It has three main physiographic regions that run laterally across the country. In the south, the plains of the Terai Region cover about 23 percent of Nepal's total area and are the main agricultural and most densely populated region. The Hill Region covers about 42 percent of the total area and consists of hills, flat lands, and valleys. Farther north, the Himalayan Region covers nearly 35 percent of the total area with 200 peaks more than 6,000 metres in elevation and 13 peaks more than 8,000 metres high, including Sagarmatha (Mount Everest), the world's highest mountain (8,850 metres). Eight out of ten world's highest mountains are in Nepal. The major river systems are—from east to west—the Kosi (513 kilometres), Narayani (332 kilometres), and Karnali (507 kilometres) are major tributaries of the Ganges in India. Nepal lies within a subtropical monsoon climate zone. Climatic conditions and precipitation vary with elevation, ranging from tropical in the Terai plains to alpine and tundra in the northern mountain areas. Nepal's natural resource base is insufficient for its economic needs, and "scenic beauty" is seen as one of the most commercially important resources. Fuel resources are especially scarce. Permanent crop cultivation has reduced the proportion of land used for forest harvesting. Nepal has numerous environmental problems.

Society

No anthropological or linguistic survey of the population has ever been conducted. The names of ethnic groups are derived from the language they speak, and ethnic identity is based on various combinations of national origin, region, language, religion, and caste. The demographic composition is Hindus (59 percent), indigenous Janajatis (31 percent), Newars (5.5 percent), Muslims (4.3 percent), and others - Sikhs, Bengalis, Marwaris, and Jains (0.2 percent). Nepal has 92 languages spoken as mother tongues. Many languages are rarely spoken outside of specific areas, but knowledge of more than one language is common. Nepali is the national language and the most common mother tongue (spoken by 48.6 percent of the population), as well as the most common second language. Maithili is the second most common mother tongue (12.3 percent), and English is increasingly prominent as well as compulsory in public schools and universities.

Groups are the Brahman-Hill 12.5%, Magar 7%, Tharu 6.6%, Tamang 5.5%, Newar 5.4%, Kami 3.9%, Yadav 3.9%, other 32.7%, unspecified 2.8%. Nepali is the national language with 47.8% of the population speaking it as their first language. Other languages include Maithili 12.1%, Bhojpuri 7.4%, Tharu (Dagaura/Rana) 5.8%, Tamang 5.1%, Nepal Bhasa 3.6%, Magar 3.3%, Awadhi 2.4%, other 10%, White 2.6% unspecified 2.5%. Differences between Hindus and Buddhists have been in general very subtle and academic in nature due to the intermingling of Hindu and Buddhist beliefs. Both share common temples and worship common deities and many of Nepal's Hindus could also be regarded as Buddhists and vice versa. Gurkhas are from Nepal. Buddhism was relatively more common among the Newar. Among the other natives of Nepal, those most influenced by Hinduism were the Magar, Sunwar, Limbu and Rai. Hindu influence is less prominent among the Gurung, Bhutia, and Thakali groups, who employ Buddhist monks for their religious ceremonies.

Health indicators are poor by international standards, especially in rural areas. Disease prevalence is higher than in other South Asian countries. Nepal's Human Development Index (HDI) was 0.504 in 2002, ranking Nepal 140 out of 177 countries. Health-care facilities, hygiene, nutrition, and sanitation generally are poor and beyond the means of most, particularly in rural areas. Provision of health services is constrained by low government spending, rugged terrain, and lack of health education (which lowers the demand for health services).

Economy

Prior to 1990 economic relations were in the form of cross-border trade with India and China. Since 1990, the government has adopted market-oriented policies with greater liberalisation of the domestic economy and trade focusing on privatising state industries and creating joint-venture projects, particularly in financial institutions. The economy is characterised by dependence on agriculture, a poor export base, unbalanced regional development, dependence on foreign aid, excessive government control and regulation, and inefficient public enterprises and administration.

Hilly and mountainous terrain in the northern two-thirds of the country has made the building of roads and other infrastructure difficult and expensive. There were just over 8,500 km of paved roads, and one 59 km railway line in the south. Aviation is in a better state, with 48 airports, ten of them with paved runways. There is less than one telephone per 19 people; landline services are not adequate nationwide but concentrated in cities and district headquarters; mobile telephony is in a reasonable state in most parts of the country with increased accessibility and affordability.

Tourism is an important component of the economy, but the security situation has hurt the industry. Since the early 1990s, the government has abolished travel restrictions in some remote areas, constructed numerous tourist centres, and allowed access to 263 mountains. Most goods come either from or through India. Trade disputes with India have exacerbated a perpetual trade deficit and reduced Nepalese exports to India. Major imports include petroleum products, textiles, vehicles, fertilizer, crude palm oil, and machinery. More than 50 percent of imports come from India. Other important sources of imports are Singapore, China, Malaysia, and Indonesia.

Agriculture accounts for about 40% of Nepal's GDP, services comprise 41% and industry 22%. Agriculture employs 76% of the workforce, services 18% and manufacturing/craft-based industry 6%. Agricultural produce—mostly grown in the Terai region bordering India—includes tea, rice, corn, wheat, sugarcane, root crops, milk, and water buffalo meat.

Industry mainly involves the processing of agricultural produce, including jute, sugarcane, tobacco, and grain. Its workforce of about 10 million suffers from a severe shortage of skilled labour. The spectacular landscape and diverse, exotic cultures of Nepal represent considerable potential for tourism, but growth in this hospitality industry has been stifled by recent political events. The rate of unemployment and underemployment approaches half of the working-age population. Thus many Nepali citizens move to India in search of work; the Gulf countries and Malaysia being new sources of work. Nepal receives US$50 million a year through the Gurkha soldiers who serve in the Indian and British armies and are highly esteemed for their skill and bravery. The total remittance value is worth around US$1 billion, including money sent from the Persian Gulf and Malaysia, who combined employ around 700,000 Nepali citizens. A long-standing economic agreement underpins a close relationship with India. The country receives foreign aid from India, Japan, the United Kingdom, the United States, the European Union, China, Switzerland, and Scandinavian countries. Poverty is acute; per-capita income is less than US$470.

Infrastructure

Nepal's transportation system is poor. The mountainous terrain physically constrains development of the transportation network, and the government has lacked funds to maintain, improve and expand the transportation infrastructure, which has thus relied heavily on foreign funding. The transportation infrastructure is concentrated in the central and eastern parts of the Terai. Roads are Nepal's principal transportation mode. The total road length is 17,217 kilometres, including 4,781 kilometres paved, 4,703 kilometre gravel-covered, and 7,643 kilometres classified as fair weather roads.

Nepal's railroad system is small, outdated, and declining in use and quality. Two rail lines link to railheads in India. The passenger traffic is about 1.7 million per year and freight traffic, 21 tons. The railroad has lost money for years because of low fares, overstaffing, and political intervention. Civil aviation has been slow to develop. In 2005 Nepal had 44 airports of varying standards and only one international airport, Tribhuvan, near Kathmandu. The number of international tourists arriving by air was 288,356 in 2004.

Telecommunication penetration is now about 61.42% with mobile being 54.46%. Twelve months earlier the mobile penetration was 38.31%; this represents a growth rate of 42.15% for the mobile sector. However, the growth of fixed line telephony has been very low. Similarly, the numbers of subscribers to data/internet services represents 17.53% penetration rate. Most of the data service is accounted by GPRS users. Twelve months earlier the data/internet penetration was 10.05%, thus this represents a growth rate of 74.77%. In the broadcast media, the state operates 2 television stations as well as national and regional radio stations. There are roughly 30 independent TV channels registered, with only about half in regular operation. Nearly 400 FM radio stations are licensed with roughly 300 operational.

Government and Politics

Executive Branch: Executive power is held by the Council of Ministers, which is headed by the prime minister. The Council of Ministers is responsible for the general administration of the country. The Council of Ministers has a central secretariat consisting of 22 ministries and the secretariat of the National Planning Commission.

Legislative Branch: Nepal's legislature consists of a bicameral parliament. The lower house of parliament, the House of Representatives (Pratinidhi Sabha), has authority over the Council of Ministers and is regarded as the more powerful of the two houses. It has 205 members directly elected for five-year terms. The prime minister is the leader of the majority party and the country's chief executive. The upper house, the National Council (Rashtriya Sabha), has 60 members, appointed or indirectly elected to six-year terms.

Judicial Branch: The 1990 constitution established a three-tier court system consisting of 75 district courts, 16 appellate courts, and the Supreme Court. Village and municipal bodies may exercise quasi-judicial functions for minor offenses. The judiciary is widely regarded as becoming more autonomous, but it suffers from large case backlogs, insufficient finances and personnel, political intervention, poor demarcation of jurisdiction between courts, and biases based on caste and economic status.

Administrative Divisions: Nepal is divided into 14 zones and 75 districts, grouped into 5 development regions. Each district is headed by a fixed chief district officer responsible for maintaining law and order and coordinating the work of field agencies of the various government ministries. The 14 zones are:

Bagmati	Bheri	Dhawalagiri
Gandaki	Janakpur	Karnali
Koshi	Lumbini	Mahakali
Mechi	Narayani	Rapti
Sagarmatha	Seti	

Foreign Relations: Nepal's foreign policy has been directed toward preserving autonomy and addressing domestic economic and security issues. Nepal's most substantive international relations are with international economic institutions, such as the Asian Development Bank, the International Monetary Fund, the World Bank, and the South Asian Association for Regional Cooperation. The country also maintains strong political relations with India and China, usually attempting to balance one against the other. Relations with India are fraught with trade and border disputes and Indian suspicions that Nepalese and Pakistani rebels use Nepal as a haven to attack India. Relations with Bhutan have been strained since 1992 over the nationality and possible repatriation of refugees from Bhutan.

Armed Forces

Nepal's military consists of the Nepalese Army which includes the Nepalese Army Air Service, (the air force unit under it), and the Nepalese Police Force. Most of the equipment and arms are supplied by the India. Nepal has close ties with both of its neighbours, India and China. In accordance with a long standing treaty, Indian and Nepalese citizens may travel to each others' countries without a passport or visa. Nepalese citizens may work in India without legal restriction. Although Nepal and India typically have close ties, from time to time Nepal becomes caught up in the problematic Sino-Indian relationship. India considers Nepal as part of its realm of influence, and views Chinese aid with concern.

Nepal Army's participation in the UN peacekeeping operations spans a period of 50 years covering 31 UN Missions. The Nepal Army has contributed Force Commanders, military contingent, military observers and staff officers. Its most significant contribution has been of peace and stability in Africa. It has demonstrated its capacity of sustaining large troop commitments over prolonged periods. Presently, Nepal is ranked as the fourth largest troop contributing country to the UN.

PAKISTAN

The Republic of Pakistan borders Iran to the southwest, Afghanistan to the west and north, China to the northeast, and India to the east. The Arabian Sea marks Pakistan's southern boundary. Pakistan's exact size is debated because of its disputed border with India. According to the United Nations, the country has a total area of 796,095 square kilometres. This figure, however, does not include the Pakistan-administered portions of Jammu and Kashmir and the Northern Areas, with areas of 11,639 square kilometres and 72,520 square kilometres, respectively.

Pakistan proclaimed independence on 14 August 1947, from Britain. Pakistan's flag is green with a narrow vertical white band on its left side. A white crescent and star are in the centre of the green band. Green signifies the Muslim majority, white denotes minorities, the crescent represents progress, and the star symbolizes light and knowledge.

Pakistan shares borders with Afghanistan (2,430 kilometres), China (523 kilometres), India (2,912 kilometres), and Iran (909 kilometres). Afghanistan disputes the legitimacy of its border with Pakistan, and at times Afghanistan's governments have argued that all Pashtun (Pakhtun) territory in Afghanistan and Pakistan should be under Afghan control. Pakistan and India have disputed possession of Jammu and Kashmir since 1947, and the issue remains unresolved despite numerous cease-fire agreements. Jammu and Kashmir is split between the two countries by a border called the Line of Control. Pakistan's coastline totals 1,064 kilometres along the Arabian Sea.

Pakistan's history has been characterised by periods of military rule and political instability. It is still an undeveloped nation that faces problems with high levels of poverty and illiteracy. It is the sixth most populous country in the world and has the second largest Muslim population in the world after Indonesia. It also has the second largest Shia Muslim population in the world. It is the world's only Muslim-majority nuclear-powered country.

History

Muhammad Iqbal conceived the concept of a Muslim homeland called Pakistan ("Land of the Pure") in the 1920s, but the establishment of Pakistan was most advanced by Mohammad Ali Jinnah, a Bombay lawyer who proved to be a shrewd leader of the Muslim League political party. Jinnah claimed that India contained two nations, one Hindu and one Muslim, and that Muslims could not safely exist in a Hindu-dominated India. The degree to which Jinnah's objectives were motivated by religion is still debated, but his ideas resonated with Muslims who felt politically, economically, and socially discriminated against and with Muslims having theological interests in an Islamic state.

Pakistan was born as a bifurcated state in August 1947, divided by 1,600 kilometres of Indian soil and by economic and social divisions between a largely Bengali East Wing and a heavily Punjabi and Sindhi West Wing. The country also faced problems with absorbing millions of Muslim refugees from India, addressing substantial poverty, and establishing both a functioning government and a sense of national

Capital	-	Islamabad
Official languages	-	Urdu (National); English (Government)
Regional languages	-	Punjabi, Pashto, Sindhi, Seraiki, Brahui and Balochi
Government	-	Parliamentary Federal Republic
	-	President Mamnoon Hussain
	-	Prime Minister Nawaz Sharif
	-	Chief Justice Tassaduq Hussain Jillani
Formation	-	Independence from Britain - 14 August 1947
	-	Islamic Republic - 23 March 1956
Area	-	796,095 square kilometres (disputed)
Coastline	-	1,046 kilometres
Population	-	182,490,000 (2012 estimate) Density 227/square kilometre
GDP (PPP)	-	$514.559 billion (2012 estimate) Per capita $2,960
GDP (nominal)	-	$230.525 billion (2012 estimate) Per capita $1,410
Defence Minister	-	Khawaja Muhammad Asif
Chairman Joint Chiefs of Staff	-	General Rashad Mahmood
Chief of Army Staff	-	General Raheel Sharif
Chief of Navy Staff	-	Admiral Muhammad Asif Sandila
Chief of Air Staff	-	Air Chief Marshal Tahir Rafik Butt
Commander Strategic Forces	-	Lt Gen Syed Absar Hussain

unity over a geographically and ethnically divided state.

The founding fathers, Mohammad Ali Jinnah and Liaquat Ali Khan, passed away by 1951, and their deaths were precursors to the subsequent series of short-lived governments that changed just as often by military coup as by election. Pakistan was initially governed by a Constituent Assembly responsible for drafting a constitution and issuing legislation until the constitution went into force. However, the constitution's drafting was delayed by disagreements over how different regions would be represented and how the state would embody Islamic principles. Legislative paralysis prompted Governor General Ghulam Mohammad to dismiss the Constituent Assembly in 1954. This action is now seen as the beginning of "viceregal" politics in Pakistan, in which the military and civil bureaucracy, not elected officials, govern the country and maintain substantial influence over society and the provinces. A new Constituent Assembly wrote the first constitution in 1956 and reconstituted itself as the Legislative Assembly. However, regional rivalries between East and West Pakistan and ethnic and religious tensions threatened political stability, and on 7 October 1958, President Iskander Mirza disbanded the Legislative Assembly. Later that month, Mirza himself was overthrown by General Mohammad Ayub Khan.

Ayub Khan saw himself as a reformer who would bring much-needed stability to the country, and he started by establishing a system of local governments called Basic Democracies for communities to have meaningful input into politics. But Ayub quickly lost interest and turned toward the civil bureaucracy for policy advice and formation. A new constitution was promulgated in 1962, and it established a weak legislature (the National Assembly) and a president with substantial legislative, executive, and financial powers. Possibly the most notable event of Ayub's tenure was a 17-day war with India in 1965 over the Kashmir dispute. The 1965 war had the unintended consequences of interrupting impressive economic growth and deflating the military's confidence in its own abilities. Amid worsening societal and political problems, substantial popular opposition, and his own declining health, Ayub Khan resigned in 1969.

Subsequently, General Agha Mohammad Yahya Khan became president and chief martial law administrator, and he attempted to reinstitute parliamentary democracy. However, festering tensions over representation in the National Assembly led to civil war between East and West Pakistan in 1971. With Indian assistance, East Pakistan seceded and became the independent nation of Bangladesh. At the same time, India and West Pakistan fought a 14-day war which ended in a cease-fire agreement. Largely as a result of Pakistan's military losses, Yahya resigned in 1971, and Zulfiqar Ali Bhutto was appointed president, becoming the first civilian head of government in nearly two decades.

Bhutto lifted martial law, and a new constitution came into effect in August 1973. The constitution was heavily concerned with the role of Islam, the distribution of power between the federal and provincial governments, and the division of responsibilities between the president and prime minister, the latter assuming greater authority than before. Bhutto nationalised numerous industries, and the government's heavy involvement in the economy would have enduring economic repercussions. The country appeared to be democratising, but political opposition grew against Bhutto's repression of political opponents and alleged voting irregularities. In July 1977, Bhutto was overthrown, and General Mohammad Zia ul-Haq became chief martial law administrator. Bhutto eventually was sentenced to death on charges of conspiring to murder a political opponent and was executed in 1979.

Zia adapted the structure of Ayub Khan's Basic Democracies to a new system of local governments and also adopted various measures to create an Islamic state. When the Soviet Union invaded Afghanistan in 1979, Pakistan became the recipient of numerous Afghan refugees and large-scale foreign aid from the United States, China, Saudi Arabia, and others. The refugees and financial assistance continued until the war's end in 1989. Zia officially terminated martial law in 1985 by assuming the presidency and reinstating the 1973 constitution. However, he also added the Eighth Amendment, which empowered the president to appoint and dismiss the prime minister and provincial governors and to dissolve the national and provincial legislatures. When Zia died in an airplane crash in August 1988, Benazir Bhutto - head of the Pakistan People's Party (PPP) and daughter of Zulfiqar Ali Bhutto - became prime minister. Pakistan thus became the first Muslim country with a female head of government.

Bhutto's government was plagued by ethnic conflict, severe economic problems, and a lack of legislative support. In October 1990, Mian Nawaz Sharif, leader of the Islamic Democratic Alliance (IDA), became prime minister and faced the same problems that troubled Bhutto. In 1993 Bhutto's PPP won the National Assembly, and she once again became prime minister. However, in 1996 President Farooq Leghari dismissed Bhutto on charges of corruption, and in 1997 Nawaz Sharif replaced her. In 1998 India conducted nuclear tests, and two weeks later Pakistan reacted by detonating five nuclear devices. Many countries responded with condemnation and sanctions, but Pakistan felt that it finally possessed sufficient deterrent force against its perennial rival, India. Deterrence failed to hold, however, and in October 1999 India and Pakistan engaged in a limited conflict (the Kargil War), which Pakistan was widely seen as precipitating because of its suspected support of militants who entered Indian-held Kashmir from Pakistani-held Kashmir. The conflict proved to be embarrassing for the government, and, with the economy suffering tremendously, General Pervez Musharraf overthrew Nawaz Sharif on 12 October 1999.

Musharraf became both president and chief of army staff, and he further consolidated his power through various legal measures. After the 11 September 2001 terrorist attacks in the United States, Musharraf's government benefited from an infusion of economic and military aid, because Pakistan is seen as an important ally in the war on terrorism. However, Pakistan was widely suspected of complicity in a terrorist attack on India's parliament in December 2001. In an April 2002 national referendum, Musharraf's tenure as president was extended to 2007. In late 2004, Musharraf reneged on a previous commitment to relinquish his position as chief of army staff, much to the chagrin of many secular and religious political parties, who demanded that elections be held in early 2005.

In the 2007 general elections, the Pakistan Peoples Party (PPP) won 123 seats in the 342-seat National Assembly and Sharif's party came second with 91, while Pervez Musharraf's party came a poor third with 54 seats. Sharif's Pakistan Muslim League (Nawaz) won 8 provincial assembly seats, while the PPP won 7 provincial seats.

On 28 November 2007, nearly nine months before his resignation as president, Musharraf stepped down as army chief due to growing domestic and international pressure. Musharraf's appointee as army chief was General Ashfaq Kayani, a former chief of the powerful Inter-services Intelligence (ISI) and subsequently vice chief of the army. Soon after taking over, Kayani began slowly to reduce the army's role in civilian affairs, which had increased enormously under Musharraf. Within ten months of taking over as army chief, Kayani had selected six of the nine powerful corps commanders of Pakistan.

On 18 February 2008, Pakistan held general elections after Benazir Bhutto's assassination postponed the original date of 8 January 2008. The Pakistan Peoples Party won the majority of the votes and formed an alliance with the Pakistan Muslim League (N). On 7 August 2008, the PPP and the Pakistan Muslim League (N) agreed to force Musharraf to step down and begin his impeachment. Asif Ali Zardari and Nawaz Sharif, announced sending a formal request or joint charge sheet that he steps down, and impeach him through parliamentary process upon refusal. On 18 August 2008, in a speech defending his record, Musharraf announced his resignation.

By 9 September 2008 a new democratically elected political establishment came to power in Pakistan, ending nine years of military rule originating in the coup led by Army Chief General Pervez Musharraf, on 12 October 1999. Following a six-week emergency declared by Musharraf on 3 November 2007 (the President's grip on power had been weakened by public unrest led by lawyers), elections to the National Assembly and the four provincial assemblies took place on 18 February 2009. These elections had been delayed by six weeks due to the assassination, on 27 December 2007, of Benazir Bhutto, a former prime minister and the leader of the largest opposition party, the Pakistan People's Party (PPP). The new coalition government, formed largely by the PPP and the Pakistan Muslim League (Nawaz) led by former Prime Minister Nawaz Sharif, elected Yousaf Raza Gilani, a senior PPP politician, as prime minister on 24 March 2009. On 9 September Asif Ali Zaradari was sworn in as the president, completing the country's turbulent transition to democracy.

Pakistan's top priority, insofar as security is concerned, is to fight terrorism and Islamist militancy in the Federally Administered Tribal Areas (FATA) of Pakistan bordering Afghanistan. It is focusing on a three pronged policy towards the tribal areas comprising political dialogue, development and the

use of force, military operations which has had mixed results. The United States has expressed reservations about negotiating with Pakistan Taliban (Tehrik-e-Taliban Pakistan – TTP) militants, fearing it would reinforce the status of the tribal areas as a sanctuary for al-Qaeda and the Afghan Taliban in planning cross-border attacks into Afghanistan.

Notwithstanding US pressure on Pakistan to use its army and frontier corps more actively and effectively in the tribal areas and Swat in the Khyber-Pakhtunkhwa Province, Pakistani security forces in general remain unable or unwilling to effectively counter the resurgent Afghan and TTP militants, though there are over 112,000 troops deployed in the area. This has led to allegations of official Pakistani complicity – particularly by serving or retired members of the ISI – in providing assistance to the Afghan Taliban, which Pakistan has denied. Speculation has also arisen that the ISI provided Afghan Taliban militants details of the US military campaign, which in some cases enabled the fighters to escape US missile strikes in the tribal areas, and that the ISI was involved in the deadly suicide car bomb attack carried out by Jalaluddin Haqqani's Afghan Taliban, on the Indian Embassy in Kabul on 7 July 2008; this was denied by the Pakistan government.

Pakistan's military operations targeting the Taliban and al-Qaeda in the Bajaur Agency of the tribal areas have been relatively more effective. Since the start of the offensive in August 2008, the military's objective has expanded from defending its administrative headquarters at Khar to securing Bajaur Agency against the TTP. As a result of these operations an estimated 220,000 people were displaced from the area. At the same time, government backed tribal lashkars (militias) have begun mounting offensives against the Taliban, though their success appears limited so far. By the end of 2009, more than 3 million Pakistani civilians have been displaced by the ongoing conflict in North-West Pakistan between the government and Taliban militants.

Pakistan's major challenge is to build a consensus against terrorism and Islamist extremism among the political establishment. To effectively pursue the campaign on terror, the Pakistani military will need to balance growing US pressure for military strikes in the tribal areas with the Pakistani army's decreasing tolerance for such attacks. It also needs to ensure that the ensuing domestic political turbulence, heightened by the growing economic crisis, does not place the government at risk from the army. Since 2004, Pakistani armed forces are engaged in fighting against Pakistani Taliban groups.

The Pakistani general election of 2013 saw the Pakistan Muslim League (N) achieve a majority, following which Nawaz Sharif became elected as the Prime Minister of Pakistan, returning to the post for the third time after fourteen years, in a democratic transition.

Geography

Topography. Pakistan has a diverse array of landscapes spread among nine major ecological zones. Its territory encompasses portions of the Himalayas, Hindu Kush and Karakoram mountain ranges, making it home to some of the world's highest mountains, including K2, which at 8,611 metres above sea level is the world's second highest peak. Inter-mountain valleys make up much of the North-West Frontier Province, and rugged plateaus cover much of Balochistan Province in the west. In the east, expansive, irrigated plains along the Indus River cover much of Punjab and Sindh provinces, which have deserts as well (Cholistan in Punjab, Thar in Sindh).

Principal Rivers. The main rivers are the Indus (2,749 kilometres within Pakistan) and its tributaries. the Chenab (730 kilometres), Ravi (680 kilometres), Jhelum (611 kilometres), and Sutlej (531 kilometres). The navigable portions of these rivers are generally small and unconnected as a result of seasonal variations in water flows and the presence of substantial irrigation structures.

Natural Resources. Economically important natural resources include arable land, chromite, coal, copper, fireclay, gypsum, iron, limestone, oil, natural gas, rock salt, and silica sand.

Land Use. More than 40% of the working population is employed in agriculture, yet the per capita amount of agricultural land is declining, and there are significant natural limitations to increasing the quantity of arable land. The country's total land area is 79.6 million hectares, but only 59.3 million hectares have been surveyed. Out of the surveyed land area, 24.6 million hectares are classified as not available for cultivation, 3.6 million hectares are forest area, and 9.2 million hectares are unused but believed to be cultivable. Approximately 22 million hectares are used for cultivation, of which nearly 16 million hectares are actually sown, with the remainder left fallow. About 13.5 million hectares of the sown area are irrigated, and 6.5 million hectares are sown more than once per year. Most cultivable and irrigated land is located in the eastern provinces of Punjab and Sindh around the Indus River and its tributaries. Pakistan has an extensive but inefficient canal system for irrigation, and much of the crop area is rain fed, but precipitation tends to be unevenly distributed throughout the year.

Environmental Factors. Numerous environmental problems threaten the economy and the population's health, and there is little indication of their abatement. The availability of natural resources is limited by the dry climate and mountainous terrain, substantial population growth is increasing pressure on the resource base, and resource management has suffered from the emphasis on rapid economic growth and often-unregulated forms of economic productivity. As a result, human transformation of the environment is manifest in several problems. Population growth and poor water infrastructure have reduced per capita water availability from 53,000 cubic metres to 1,200 cubic metres, and heavy reliance on firewood has contributed to the world's second highest rate of deforestation. Poor agricultural practices have led to soil erosion, groundwater degradation, and other problems that have hindered crop output and contributed to health problems for rural communities. Solid waste burning, low-quality fuels, and the growing use of fuel-inefficient motor vehicles have contributed to air pollution that in some cities—such as Islamabad, Lahore, and Rawalpindi—has exceeded levels deemed safe by the World Health Organisation. The government has expressed concern about environmental threats to economic growth and social development and, since the early 1990s, has addressed environmental concerns with new legislation and institutions such as the Pakistan Environment Protection Council. Only 0.04% of the government's development budget goes to environmental protection.

The 2010 Pakistan floods began in July 2010 following heavy monsoon rains in the Khyber Pakhtunkhwa,

Sindh, Punjab and Balochistan regions of Pakistan and affected the Indus River basin. At one point, approximately one-fifth of Pakistan's total land area was underwater. According to Pakistani government data the floods directly affected about 20 million people, mostly by destruction of property, livelihood and infrastructure, with a death toll of close to 2,000. The number of individuals affected by the flooding exceeds the combined total of individuals affected by the 2004 Indian Ocean tsunami, the 2005 Kashmir earthquake and the 2010 Haiti earthquake.

Society

Population. Pakistan has a large, mostly rural population with a high rate of growth. The population growth rate expects it to double approximately every 26 years. The population is clustered in the eastern provinces of Punjab and Sindh, which contain 78.6% of the total population.

Ethnic Groups. Ethnic groups in Pakistan generally are categorised according to various combinations of religion, language, and sometimes tribe. Punjabis are the largest linguistic group (44.2% of the population) and often are divided into three occupational castes. Rajputs, Jats and Arains. Pakhtuns (15.4%) are the dominant ethnic group in the North-West Frontier Province, but Pakhtuns belong to different tribes or kinship groups and have no central governing authority. Sindhis (14.1%) are dominant in Sindh and are divided into occupational and caste groupings. Balochis (3.6%) are dominant in Balochistan and are divided into various eastern and western tribes. Other ethno-linguistic groups include the Seraikis, who live mostly in Punjab; Urdu-speaking Muhajirs, refugees from India and their descendants who migrated to Pakistan during the 1947 partition and are concentrated in Sindh; and Brahuis, a Dravidian language group in Sindh and Balochistan.

Languages. Urdu is the national language and the language of most print media. English has official status and often is regarded as the language of the elite and upwardly mobile. Urdu and English often are used in government and business. Punjabi is the most common language, spoken by 44.2% of the population, followed by Pakhtu (15.2%), Sindhi (14.1%), Siraiki (10.5%), Urdu (7.8%), and Balochi (3.8%). Smaller linguistic groups include the Hindko in the North-West Frontier Province, the Farsi-speaking Hazaras of Balochistan, and the Brahuis in Sindh and Balochistan. Language often articulates ethnic identity, and provincial boundaries are linguistically based. Urdu has been promoted as a means of unifying ethnic groups, but it is the mother tongue of only the Muhajirs. Furthermore, many groups perceive the establishment of Urdu as the national language as threatening to their employment potential, political participation, and ethnic identity.

Religion. The overwhelming majority of the population (96.3%) is Muslim, of whom approximately 95% are Sunni and 5% Shia. Sunnis and Shias are subdivided into numerous sects. Approximately 1.6% of the population is Hindu, 1.6% is Christian, and 0.3% belongs to other religions, such as Bahaism and Sikhism. Some 0.2% of the population is Ahmadiyya (also known as Qadiani), a small but influential sect that maintains some Islamic beliefs but is considered heretical by orthodox Muslims and is not recognised as Muslim by Pakistani law. The country was founded to promote religious freedom, and the constitution guarantees freedom of religion. However, Islam is the state religion, and the constitution states that religious practice is "subject to law, public order, and morality." The government also has Islamic institutions such as the Federal Shariat Court and the Council of Islamic Ideology, which advise politicians on the congruence of legislation with Islamic injunctions. It is debatable whether the government has established such institutions for religious or political reasons, but the government has promoted Islam as a means of unifying numerous ethnic groups. Nevertheless, political, economic, and religious differences have been manifested in occasionally violent conflicts between religious communities, particularly between Sunni and Shia militias.

Education and Literacy. Pakistan has low indicators of educational attainment, and education has been under-funded for decades. In 2001 the government announced plans to institute universal primary education by 2010 and 78% literacy by 2011. Free primary education is a constitutional right and is

compulsory in every province except Balochistan. In addition to public and private schools, an indeterminate number of mosque-administered *madrassas* provide free room, board, and theological education, which makes them an attractive option for poor families. Some madrassas are suspected of having links to religious militants, prompting the government to announce its intention of establishing greater regulation over these institutions.

Economy

Despite being a very poor country in 1947, Pakistan's economic growth rate was better than the global average during the subsequent four decades, but imprudent policies led to a slowdown in the late 1990s. Throughout the 1990s, Pakistan's economy suffered for a number of reasons, but from 2002 to 2004 the economy has recovered as a result of changes in government policies and the resumption of international lending. Economic statistics do not reflect the reality of the economy, because official economic data omit the informal economy, which is estimated to equal about 30% of the formal economy. Since independence, economic growth rates have been impressive but also have fluctuated widely. These fluctuations have occurred largely because successive governments have emphasised different sectors through changes in subsidies, regulations, and state ownership of industry. The government has shifted from state ownership of many industries and heavy regulation of the private economy to privatisation of some state industries, deregulation, facilitation of capital flows, and reforms of the financial system and monetary policy. Still, lax fiscal and monetary policies, infrastructural deficiencies, a poorly developed human resource base, and persistent market distortions that benefit a small elite of landowners, industrialists, and others undercut economic potential.

The structure of the Pakistani economy has changed from a mainly agricultural base to a strong service base. Agriculture now only accounts for roughly 20% of the GDP, while the service sector accounts for 53% of the GDP. Significant foreign investments have been made in several areas including telecommunications, real estate and energy. Other important industries include apparel and textiles (accounting for nearly 60% of exports), food processing, chemicals manufacture, and the iron and steel industries. The economic crisis of 2008 led Pakistan to seek more than $100 billion in aid in order to avoid possible bankruptcy. This was never given to Pakistan and therefore it had to depend on a more aggressive fiscal policy, backed by the IMF.

Mining and Minerals. Mining and minerals historically have been a weak economic sector. Since 2000 mining and quarrying have accounted annually for around 1.4% of GDP and employed an estimated 0.1% of the working population. Chromite is the only metallic ore that has been exploited on a commercial scale, but the country has substantial deposits of copper and iron ores as well. Pakistan also has significant deposits of non-metallic ores such as anhydrite, dolomite, gypsum, limestone, marble, and rock salt.

Industry and Manufacturing. Since the mid-1960s, the industrial sector has produced 19 to 25% of GDP, accounting for 24.5% of GDP in 2004. Manufacturing and construction dominate the industrial sector, accounting for around 19% of GDP. Various liberalisation reforms have been pursued since the early 1980s but have been hindered by substantial corruption, frequent raw material shortages, the government's tendency to provide generous concessions to particular sectors and a burdensome tax structure that has helped promote the development of the informal economy.

Energy. Economic growth, population growth, and rising urbanisation have increased energy demand, much of which is met by imported energy sources because of the country's limited domestic energy resources. Coal has provided around 5% of total domestic energy supply for decades, but most is of poor quality and generally is used in brick kilns. With regard to non-traditional sources, oil and natural gas have provided around 37 to 43% of total energy supplies each since the late 1970s, and the country is attempting to expand hydropower production. For decades, Pakistan has depended heavily on oil imports. Domestic oil provided 6.7% of total energy supplies, and domestic recoverable petroleum reserves have fallen to less than 50% of their estimated original amount. However, natural gas production has nearly doubled to 2.7 million cubic feet per day, providing 43.8% of the total energy supply. The government has considered pipelines that could import around 1.5 billion cubic feet of gas per day, but these plans are still under review. Hydropower has declined from 17.7% of total energy supply to 11.3%.

Services. The services sector accounts for about 50% of Pakistan's annual GDP. From 2000 to 2004, transportation, wholesale and retail trade, finance, public administration, defence, and services collectively provided about 52% of GDP. Services alone were about 9 to 10% of GDP. The services sector has suffered from many of the same problems as the industrial sector, such as political corruption and crippling tax rates, and sectoral growth has been limited by a dearth of educational resources and skilled labour.

Balance of Payments. Pakistan has had balance of payments difficulties for decades, largely as a result of current account deficits due to trade deficits.

External Debt. Estimates of the size of Pakistan's external debt vary by source. However, observers generally believe that the combination of poor tax administration, high government expenditures, and heavy dependence on external funds has resulted in massive fiscal deficits that, at times, have nearly crippled the economy and rendered Pakistan one of the world's most indebted countries.

Foreign Aid. The economy is heavily dependent on bilateral and multilateral aid, which substantially influences economic growth. After 11 September 2001, the United States and other countries dropped economic sanctions against Pakistan because of its potential role in the war on terrorism. Prior to 2000, Pakistan had never completed an International Monetary Fund (IMF) lending programme because of government unwillingness to comply with loan package conditions and political issues such as nuclear weapons tests or difficulties in Kashmir.

The growth of non-agricultural sectors has changed the structure of the economy, and agriculture now only accounts for roughly 20% of the GDP. The service sector accounts for 53% of the country's GDP, with wholesale and retail trade forming 30% of this sector. Large amounts of foreign investments have been made into several industries. The top industries in Pakistan are telecom, software, automotives, textiles, cement, fertilizer, steel, ship building, and more recently, aerospace.

Pakistan has accomplished many engineering feats such as construction of the world's largest earth filled dam Tarbela, the world's twelfth largest dam Mangla, as well as, with collaboration with China, the world's highest international road: the Karakoram Highway. There are also additional dams planned such as Kalabagh Dam, Diamer-Bhasha Dam, Munda, Akhori and Skardu Katzara.

Infrastructure

Roads. Roads, road traffic, and motor vehicles all have increased substantially since the early 1990s. According to government statistics, from 1994 to 2003 total road length increased from 196,877 to 251,845 kilometres, and highways increased, from 104,001 to 151,028 kilometres. The total number of

registered motor vehicles also increased from 3.5 million to 5.2 million, including 2.5 million motorcycles, 1.3 million automobiles, and 178,000 trucks. In the early 1990s, the government announced plans to shift passenger and freight traffic from roads to rail, but the declining quality and quantity of rail service continues to prompt increases in private and commercial use of roads.

Railroads. The railroad system is publicly owned, but government funding has been insufficient to maintain the system. Government figures indicate that operating revenues exceeded operating expenses from 1994 to 2003, but the deterioration in the quantity and quality of service suggests that major problems persist. From 1994 to 2003, the quantity of track kilometres fell from 8,775 to 7,791 kilometres, and route kilometres dropped from 12,625 to 11,515 kilometres. Of the track kilometres, 7,346 kilometres were 1.676-millimeter gauge, and 445 kilometres were 1.000-millimeter gauge. Passenger journeys peaked at 85 million in 1989 and declined until 1999, after which they increased to 72.4 million in 2003. Freight tonnage fell from 8 million tons in 1994 to 6.2 million tons in 2003. In the same period, the number of locomotives decreased from 676 to 577, and the quantity of coaches fell from 2,831 to 1,843. A proposed rail line connecting Pakistan with Iran has been stalled because of a lack of funding.

Ports. According to government statistics, the tonnage handled by ports increased from 30 million tons in 1994 to 41.2 million tons in 2003. In the same period, the number of twenty-foot-equivalent-units (TEUs) increased from 409,670 to 615,826. In 2004 Pakistan had two ports, Karachi and Port Qasim, both of which were upgraded in the 1990s. Karachi handles approximately 60% of import and export cargo and is linked by a daily container train to an inland terminal at Lahore. Port Qasim handles about 40% of import and export cargo. The first phase of a multipurpose port located at Gwadar on the

Balochistan coast is operational, with a second phase under construction. A deepwater port at Keti Bandar, 100 kilometres southeast of Karachi, is planned as part of a private power project.

Civil Aviation and Airports. Since the 1980s, the air network has expanded. Pakistan has 50 airports with permanently surfaced runways. Karachi, Lahore, Peshawar, Quetta, and Rawalpindi handle both international passenger and cargo flights, and Multan and Turbat handle international cargo. The major international airline is government-owned Pakistan International Airlines, and four other private airlines offer international passenger and cargo services.

Pipelines. The government currently is considering several proposed gas pipelines linking Pakistan with Afghanistan, India, Iran, Turkmenistan, and others. These proposals are still under consideration, partly because the proposed routes would go through areas of periodic civil unrest. Pakistan has a gas pipeline network with coverage of 56,400 kilometres in 1050 towns. It has nearly 1600 CNG stations and the gas throughput in Pakistan is 38 MMSCMD per day. The number of gas customers in Pakistan is estimated at 19 lakh, and Pakistan runs vehicles on CNG whose number is estimated at 15.60 lakh.

Telecommunications. From 1991 to 2002, the estimated number of radios increased only slightly from 10 to 10.2 million, and the estimated number of televisions was unchanged at 2.1 million. The government runs both Azad Kashmir Radio, with three stations, and Pakistan Broadcasting Corporation, with 35 stations. Three private radio stations also are in operation. Government-run Pakistan Television Corporation maintains four domestic television channels, and there are three private television broadcasters. Foreign channels are available by satellite and cable. Domestic phone service is poor. In the early 2000s, Pakistan had approximately 3.7 million telephones, 8 million cellular telephones, 600,000 personal computers, and 500,000 Internet users.

Government and Politics

Overview. The government is based on the much-amended constitution of 1973, which was suspended twice (in 1977 and 1999) and reinstated twice (in 1985 and 2002). According to the constitution, Pakistan is a federal parliamentary system with a president as head of state and a prime minister as head of government. The legislature, or parliament, is the Majlisi- Shoora (Council of Advisers), consisting of the Lower House, which is often called the National Assembly, and the Upper House, or Senate. National Assembly members are directly elected for five-year terms. Senate members are elected by provincial assemblies, with equal representation from each of the four provinces as well as representatives from the Federally Administered Tribal Areas and Islamabad Capital Territory. Both the Senate and National Assembly may initiate and pass legislation, but only the National Assembly can approve federal budgets and finance bills. However, parliament often has had little real political power. For example, in 2003 the only bill passed by the National Assembly was the national budget. Executive power lies with the prime minister and president. The prime minister is an elected member of the National Assembly and is the leader of the National Assembly's dominant party or coalition. However, the prime minister also is appointed formally by the president. The prime minister is assisted by a cabinet of ministers who are appointed by the president on the prime minister's advice. An electoral college composed of members of the national and provincial legislatures elects the president for a five-year term, and no individual may hold the office for more than two consecutive terms. By law the president must be a Muslim. The president acts on the advice of the prime minister but has the power to prevent passage of non-finance bills and may dissolve the National Assembly if he concludes that the government cannot operate according to the constitution. The Senate, however, cannot be suspended.

Politics in Pakistan often have not operated according to the constitution. The military and Civil Service of Pakistan frequently have been the pre-eminent actors in the country's power structure. Moreover, there has been some concern that Pakistan could become a "failed state" because of the apparent inability of any single entity to control the country, the weakened productivity of a population beset by years of economic difficulties, and continuing problems of communal conflict and terrorism. Ethnic and provincial tensions often are manifested in rivalries between political parties, and several governments have been ended by assassination or military coup rather than by formal, electoral change.

Religion has played an important role in politics, and religious differences have been very salient in Pakistani government and civil society. The government has consistently been faced with tensions of whether and how to synthesize Islamic principles into an essentially secular and Western form of government.

Administrative Divisions. Pakistan has four provinces—Balochistan, North-West Frontier Province, Punjab, and Sindh—and numerous federally administered areas. Provincial boundaries correspond with areas of numerically dominant linguistic groups, and provinces are divided into a total of 26 divisions that are further subdivided into 101 districts. Federally administered areas include the capital (Islamabad) and 13 Federally Administered Tribal Areas (FATAs).

Judicial and Legal System. The legal system is derived from English common law and is based on the much-amended 1973 constitution and Islamic law (sharia). The Supreme Court, provincial high courts, and other courts have jurisdiction over criminal and civil issues. The president appoints the Supreme Court's chief justice and formally approves other Supreme Court justices as well as provincial high court judges on the advice of the chief justice. The Supreme Court has original, appellate, and advisory jurisdiction, and high courts have original and appellate jurisdiction. The Federal Shariat Court determines whether laws are consistent with Islamic injunctions. Special courts and tribunals hear particular types of cases, such as drugs, commerce, and terrorism. Pakistan's penal code has limited jurisdiction in tribal areas, where law is largely derived from tribal customs.

Mass Media. Print media are published in 11 languages, but most are published in Urdu and Sindhi, and English language publications are numerous. The press generally publishes free from censorship and has played an active role in national elections, but journalists often exercise self-censorship as a result of arrests and intimidation by government and societal actors. Most print media are privately owned, but the government controls the National Press Trust, a major newspaper publisher, and the Associated Press of Pakistan, one of the two major news agencies.

Foreign Relations. Pakistan's primary foreign policy objectives are protection from external threats and the preservation of territorial integrity. Foreign alliances often have been based on mutual—and sometimes ephemeral—strategic interests. Contentious relations with India dominate foreign relations and are largely due to perennial tensions over Kashmir, which was the basis of wars in 1948, 1965, 1971, and 1999. Various talks have eased tensions but not mutual suspicions. China has perhaps been Pakistan's most consistent ally because of shared antipathies of other countries, such as India and Russia, but in the 1990s China assumed a more distant relationship as a result of India's growing military prowess, Russia's military decline, and other factors. China is alleged to have supplied Pakistan with nuclear weapons material, ostensibly to counter India's nuclear weapons. Relations with Afghanistan have been harmonious and tense, often simultaneously. The two countries have a disputed border, but Pakistan supported insurgents in Afghanistan against Soviet occupation in the 1980s and was a key ally of the Taliban in the 1990s. Since their 1971 war, Pakistan and Bangladesh typically have had close ties based largely on shared opposition to India. Relations with Islamic Middle Eastern countries generally have been close, but ties with largely Shia Iran have been strained. For countries outside South Asia and the Middle East, relations generally are based on Pakistan's perceived strategic value in the international system. After 11September 2001, the United States and other countries saw Pakistan as an important ally in fighting international terrorists operating in Afghanistan, and international aid increased substantially. Pakistan's relations with the United States have had important ramifications for the government's domestic support, particularly among some religious parties who perceive the government as acting against Islamic injunctions.

Armed Forces

The Pakistan Armed Forces consists of approximately 619,000 active personnel in the army (550,000), air force (45,000), and navy (24,000), as well as 513,000 reserves. Under the 1973 constitution, the federal government controls the armed forces, and the president is the commander in chief. The Ministry of Defence has a permanent staff of civil servants headed by the defence secretary general, and the minister of defence is a civilian member of the prime minister's cabinet. The Joint Chiefs of Staff Committee deals with problems concerning military aspects of state security and is charged with integrating and coordinating the army, navy, and air force. The committee's secretariat acts as the principal link between the service headquarters and the Ministry of Defence.

The Directorate for Inter-Services Intelligence (ISI) is of particular importance at the joint services level because it manages covert operations outside of Pakistan and because it has been involved in domestic politics, usually to keep track of the incumbent regime's opponents. The chief of the army staff (COAS) is the key power holder in the armed forces and is also one of the triumvirate that runs the country, along with the prime minister and president. The COAS usually operates from army headquarters in Rawalpindi. The military is forbidden constitutionally from acting independently of the elected political leadership in domestic matters. However, from 1947 to 2004 military generals have acted as head of state for nearly 30 years, and in times of civilian government the armed forces have routinely intervened on domestic and foreign policy issues. The military justifies its consistent involvement in politics as protection from malign foreign interests and corrupt and incompetent politicians. Although public opinion surveys are rare, it appears that the public dislikes military rule, yet consistently has a more favourable view of the military than of elected officials.

Because the military conducts its affairs with carefully defended secrecy, the degree to which army officers and personnel are religiously motivated is debated. However, Western analysts tend to conclude that whereas the military increasingly sees itself as serving Islam, the institution's decision making is still largely secular. Military intervention in politics is designed to limit civilian involvement in sensitive matters, such as Kashmir, nuclear disarmament, internal military personnel decisions, and defence spending. The military also is extensively involved in the economy, and military enterprises produce approximately 3% of the gross national product. Military enterprises include the Army Welfare Trust (AWT), whose assets include the Askari Bank, one of the country's largest financial institutions, and the Fauji Foundation, which is the country's biggest conglomerate. These and other military financial institutions often are exempt from taxes and regulations covering the manufacturing sector and asset disclosure.

With regard to military strategy, the military's budget and personnel have reduced strategy to largely defensive objectives, such as limited offensive tactics in bordering areas (particularly Kashmir), use of irregular forces, and deterring and countering possible attacks from foreign powers (particularly India). The military's history of far lower military expenditures and capabilities than India has prompted the military to attempt to impose high costs on India to force its withdrawal from Kashmir. Furthermore, the military hopes that its nuclear capabilities can reduce the disadvantages of its conventional forces. However, the theoretical deterrence between nuclear powers has not limited military engagement between India and Pakistan—as exemplified by the 1999 Kargil War—and analysts believe that Pakistan's military strategy historically has suffered from overly optimistic assessments of potential success and underestimations of diplomatic and military losses, as well as a lack of contingency planning.

Foreign Military Relations. Pakistan has sought to become an important actor in international politics, but its foreign military alliances often are intended to address matters with bordering countries. Other countries have established alliances with Pakistan to address their own strategic interests in South and Central Asia, and these alliances have tended to be ephemeral. Pakistan's military relationship with China started in the 1970s as a way of countering India, but China has softened its relations since India's military strength has increased. Still, Pakistan and China maintain a military relationship, including periodic joint military exercises. United States aid in the 1980s was significantly reduced after the Soviet Union pulled out of Afghanistan in 1989 but resumed after the 11 September 2001, terrorist attacks. Moreover, in March 2004 the United States granted Pakistan status as a major non-North Atlantic Treaty Organisation ally, which provides access to U.S. military equipment and cooperation. In fact, the United States is one of the largest suppliers of military equipment to Pakistan along with China and Russia. Pakistan's military relations with India have been contentious, and the two countries fought a limited conflict in Kashmir in 1999. However, under the 1999 Lahore Agreement the two countries provide each other with advance notification of missile tests, and in 2003 and 2004 they engaged in several high-level discussions that have eased tensions.

Nuclear Power

The first nuclear test performed by Pakistan, on 28 May 1998, was known as Project-706.

Nuclear power in Pakistan is provided by three licensed-commercial nuclear power plants. It is the first Muslim country in the world to construct and operate civil nuclear power plants. The Pakistan Atomic Energy Commission (PAEC), the scientific and nuclear governmental agency, is solely responsible for operating these power plants. The electricity generated by commercial nuclear power plants is 3.6% of electricity generated in Pakistan, compared to 62% from fossil fuel, 33% from hydroelectric power and 0.3% from coal. Pakistan is not a party to the Nuclear Non-Proliferation Treaty but is a member in good standing of the International Atomic Energy Agency.

The People's Republic of China has been a strong vocal and avid supporter of Pakistan's nuclear power generation programme from early on. In 2005, both Pakistan government and the Chinese government adopted an Energy Security Plan, calling for a huge increase in generating capacity to more than 160,000 MWe by 2030. Pakistan Government plans for lifting nuclear capacity to 8800 MWe, 900 MWe of it by 2015 and a further 1500 MWe by 2020. In June 2008, the Pakistani Government announced plans to build commercial nuclear power plants III and IV commercial nuclear power plants at Chashma, Punjab Province, each with 320–340 MWe and costing PKR 129 billion, 80 billion of this from international sources, principally China. A further agreement for China's help with the project was signed in October 2008, and given prominence as a counter to the US–India agreement shortly preceding it. Cost quoted then was US$ 1.7 billion, with a foreign loan component of $1.07 billion.

External Threat. The military and public generally view India as the nation's primary security threat, and opposition to India is often a greater source of social cohesion than either Islam or Urdu. India's far greater military capabilities have been a source of both fear and frustration, and many suspect that this imbalance has prompted Pakistan to engage Indian forces indirectly through supporting insurgents morally, financially, or otherwise. India is not the country's only security concern, as Pakhtun and Balochi irredentist movements in Pakistan's western provinces have contributed to sometimes-tense relations with neighbouring Afghanistan.

Police. Provincial governments are charged with police administration in their respective jurisdictions, and provincial police forces operate independently. The federal government is largely uninvolved in provincial police administration but controls police in federally administered and tribal areas. The federal minister of interior supervises police nationwide, and the Police Service of Pakistan (PSP) selects, trains, and assigns senior officers to provincial or central government agencies. Although service in the PSP is competitive and well paid, lower ranking police personnel often have accused of routine extortion, violating civil liberties, and acting to preserve the tenure of government officials rather than the rule of law. The quantity of overall crime and various types of crime (such as murder and banditry) have increased steadily over the years, and the extensive availability and use of automatic weapons in Pakistani society is often referred to as the "Kalashnikov Culture." The population generally does not perceive the police to be effective against crime or publicly accountable.

Internal Security and Terrorism. Pakistan has numerous categories of terrorism and internal threats, with most insurgent groups identifying themselves as religious or ethnic separatists. Some political parties represent distinct religious and ethnic communities, and rivalries among these parties have been violent. Violence between religiously identified groups is rarely based solely on differing religious doctrines but rather the different social, political, and economic statuses that correlate with religion. There are also concerns that Pakistan's nuclear arsenal could be seized by insurgents in an event such as a coup or assassination of the nation's president. However, the government claims that it has enacted security measures to prevent such a threat and that the numerical and political superiority of religious moderates over religious extremists is a substantial obstacle to the latter's access to Pakistan's nuclear weapons.

Human Rights. The government's human rights record is generally regarded as poor by domestic and international observers, although there have been some improvements since 2000. Security forces use excessive and sometimes lethal force and are complicit in extrajudicial killings of civilians and suspected militants. The police and military have been accused of engaging in physical abuse, rape, and arbitrary arrest and detention, particularly in areas of acute conflict. Although the government has enacted measures to counter these problems, abuses continue. Furthermore, courts suffer from lack of funds, outside intervention, and deep case backlogs that lead to long trial delays and lengthy pre-trial detentions. Many observers contend that Pakistan's legal code is largely concerned with crime, national security, and domestic tranquillity and less with the protection of individual rights. Provincial and local governments have arrested journalists and closed newspapers that report on matters perceived as socially offensive or critical of the government. Journalists also have been victims of violence and intimidation by various groups and individuals. In spite of these difficulties, the press publishes freely, although journalists often exercise self-restraint in their writing.

SINGAPORE

The Republic of Singapore is a city-state located on the south-central coast of the island of Singapore. 137 kilometres north of the equator, it consists of 63 islands. The country is highly urbanised with very little primary rainforest remaining, although more land is being created for development through land reclamation. It is separated from Malaysia by the Straits of Johor to its north and from Indonesia's Riau Islands by the Singapore Strait to its south. Singapore is the world's fourth leading financial centre and a cosmopolitan world city, playing a key role in international trade and finance. The port of Singapore is one of the five busiest ports in the world.

The Singaporean flag has two equal horizontal bands of red (top) and white; a vertical white crescent (closed portion toward the hoist side), partially enclosing five white-point stars arranged in a circle, positioned near the hoist side of the red band. The red band symbolizes universal brotherhood and the equality of men; the white band, purity and virtue. The crescent moon represents a young nation on the rise, while the five stars stand for the ideals of democracy, peace, progress, justice, and equality.

Singapore has a long history of immigration. It has a diverse population made up of Chinese, Malays, Indians, Asians of various descents, and Caucasians. 42% of the population in Singapore are foreigners who work and study there. Foreign workers make up 50% of the service sector. The country is the second most densely populated in the world after Monaco and is the most globalised country in the world.

History

The island of Singapore was known to mariners for centuries as an entrepôt and supply point for Malay, Thai, Javanese, Chinese, Indian and Arab traders. In 1819 Sir Thomas Stamford Raffles arrived as the lieutenant governor of the British enclave of Bencoolen (Bengkulu on the west coast of Sumatra) and an agent of the British East India Company. He obtained permission from the local Malay official to establish a trading post. He called it Singapore, after its ancient name, and opened the port to free trade and free immigration on the south coast of the island at the mouth of the Singapore River. At the time, Singapore had about 1,000 inhabitants. By 1827 Chinese had become the most numerous of Singapore's various ethnic groups.

In the 20th century, Singapore became a major point of disembarkation for hundreds of thousands of labourers brought in from China, India, the Dutch East Indies, and the Malay Archipelago, bound for tin mines and rubber plantations to the north. Singapore prospered as financial institutions, transportation, communications and government infrastructure expanded rapidly to support the booming trade and industry of the British Empire.

Japan attacked Malaya in December 1941, and by February 1942 the Japanese had taken control of both Malaya and Singapore. They renamed Singapore *Sh Çnan* ("Light of the South") and set about dismantling the British establishment. During the 1942–45 occupation period, a favourable view of the

Capital	-	City of Singapore
Official languages	-	English; Chinese; Malay; Tamil
Government	-	Parliamentary republic
	-	President Tony Tan Keng Yam
	-	Prime Minister Lee Hsien Loong
	-	Chief Justice Sundaresh Menon
Formation	-	Founding 6 February 1819
	-	Self-government 3 June 1959
	-	Independence from Britain 31 August 1963
	-	Merger with Malaysia 16 September 1963
	-	Separation from Malaysia 9 August 1965
Area	-	Total 716 square kilometres
Coastline	-	151 kilometres
Population	-	5,399,200 (2013 estimate) Density 7,540/square kilometre
GDP (PPP)	-	Total $327.557 billion (2012 estimate) Per capita $61,046
GDP (nominal)	-	Total $270.020 billion (2012 estimate) Per capita $50,323
Minister for Defence	-	Ng Eng Hen
Chief of Defence Forces	-	Lieutenant General Ng Chee Meng
Chief of Army	-	Major General Ravinder Singh
Chief of Navy	-	Rear Admiral Ng Chee Peng
Chief of Air Force	-	Major General Ng Chee Meng

colonial relationship had lapsed among the local population and upon the return of the British, resulted in demands for self-rule. In 1946 Singapore became a separate crown colony with a civil administration.

In 1957 Malaya was granted independence, and the next year the British Parliament elevated the status of Singapore from colony to state and provided for new local elections. The PAP swept the elections held in May 1959, and Lee Kuan Yew was installed as the first prime minister. In 1962 Singaporean voters approved the PAP's merger plan with Malaya, and on 16 September 1963, Singapore joined Malaya and the former British territories on the island of Borneo—Sabah and Sarawak—to form the independent Federation of Malaysia.

Between 1963 and 1965, Singapore was an integral part of the Federation of Malaysia. Lee declared Singapore's independence from Britain on 31 August 1963; dissolved the Legislative Assembly; and called for an election to obtain a new mandate for the PAP pro-merger government. In the end, the merger failed. As a state, Singapore did not achieve the economic progress it had hoped for, and political tensions escalated between Chinese-dominated Singapore and Malay-dominated Kuala Lumpur, the capital of Malaysia.

After separation from Malaysia on 9 August 1965, Singapore was forced to accept the challenge of forging a viable nation—the Republic of Singapore—on a small island with few resources beyond the determination and talent of its people. Under the leadership of Lee Kuan Yew and the PAP, the new nation met the challenge.

In 1967, Singapore joined Brunei, Indonesia, Malaysia, the Philippines, and Thailand in forming the Association of Southeast Asian Nations (ASEAN) for the purpose of promoting regional stability, economic development, and cultural exchange. In 1968 Britain announced its decision to withdraw from its military bases in Singapore within three years. By the 1970s, Singapore had achieved status as a world leader in shipping, air transport, and oil refining. Singapore was no longer dependent on peninsular Malaysia for its economic prosperity.

In the 1970s through the 1990s, Singapore experienced sustained economic growth. Along with Hong Kong, South Korea, and Taiwan, it was called one of the "Four Tigers" of Asian economic prosperity. Labour-intensive industries were relocated to other ASEAN nations and were replaced by high-technology industries and services. The PAP developed a stable and corruption-free government, marked by strong central development planning and social policies. Despite authoritarian governmental practices and one-party dominance, the PAP maintained its large popular mandate. A Singaporean identity, distinct from that of the Malay and Chinese, emerged as the nation increasingly integrated itself into the global economy. In 1990 Lee Kuan Yew stepped down as prime minister, and Goh Chok Tong, the first deputy prime minister and first minister of defence, took over as part of the succession to a new generation of leaders. After 14 years in office, in 2004 Goh stepped down in favour of Lee Hsien Loong, the minister of finance and son of Lee Kuan Yew. The elder Lee agreed to stay on as minister mentor and Goh as senior minister in order to oversee the transition of the new generation of leaders. Lee Hsien Loong was confirmed in office in a democratic election held on 6 May 2006.

Geography

Singapore is located in Southeast Asia between Malaysia and Indonesia at the narrowest point of the Strait of Malacca, one of the world's strategic sea routes connecting the Indian Ocean with the South China Sea. Lying off the southern tip of the Malay Peninsula, Singapore is connected to Malaysia by a causeway. The land area is 699 square kilometres; and water area is 10 square kilometres, for a total national area of 709 square kilometres. The area has increased through land reclamation and landfill projects along the coast. Since 1988 the total land area has increased by some 63 square kilometres.

Singapore is an island nation with no land boundaries. Malaysia lies to the north across the Johore Strait and Indonesia to the south across the Strait of Malacca. Singapore comprises one main island and 58 islets. The total coastline is 193 kilometres. Since 1988, the coastline has increased by 55 kilometres as a result of extensive land reclamation and landfill projects. The forest cover is only about 4,000 hectares, or 6.6% of the land area. The gently undulating central plateau contains a water catchment area and a nature preserve.

Only two degrees north of the equator, Singapore has a tropical climate. There are two monsoon seasons, the north-eastern (dry) monsoon from December to March and the south-western (wet) monsoon from June to September. Even between the monsoon seasons, afternoon and early evening thunderstorms frequently occur.

Singapore has no irrigated land, and none of the land is planted to permanent crops. More than 60% of the land is devoted to residential, industrial, commercial, institutional, and infrastructure spaces. The major environmental issues are industrial pollution, limited freshwater resources, waste disposal, and seasonal smoke and haze resulting from forest fires in Indonesia.

Society

Population. Ethnic Chinese make up 76.8% of the population. The remainder of Singapore's population is Malay (13.9%), Indian (mostly Tamil, 7.9%), or other (1.4%).

Languages. Singaporeans speak many different languages, and the majority speak at least two languages. Malay is the national language and one of the four official languages, along with Chinese, Tamil, and English. Chinese is the majority language, spoken by about 76% of the population. The government has promoted fluency in Mandarin Chinese. Other languages, in order of use, are Malay (about 15%), English (about 9%), and Tamil (about 4%).

Religion. Buddhists and Daoists make up 51.0% of the total, or 64.4% of the Chinese population and 13.9% of the "other" ethnic composition. Islam has the second largest following at 14.9%, or 99.6% of the Malay population. Christians represent 14.6% and Hindus 4.0%, or about 55.5% of the Indian population.

Education and Literacy. Literacy is estimated at 95% overall, and 57.8% of Singaporeans have secondary school diplomas or even higher qualifications. Singaporean students consistently rank in the top five in the world in the two major international assessments of mathematics and science knowledge. Singaporean students were ranked first in the 2011 Trends in International Mathematics and Science Study conducted by the International Association for the Evaluation of Educational Achievement and have been ranked top three every year since 1995. The country's two main public universities, the National University of Singapore and Nanyang Technological University, are among the top 100 in the world.

Health. The state of health in Singapore is good by international standards. Rising standards of living, high levels of education, good housing, safe water supply and sanitation, quality medical services, and the active promotion of preventive medicine all have helped to significantly boost the health of Singaporeans. Two health care delivery "cluster" systems are available to Singaporeans. The western cluster, the National Healthcare Group, provides comprehensive public health care through a network of four hospitals, one national centre, nine polyclinics, three specialty institutes, nine business divisions, and more than 11,000 staff members. The eastern cluster, Singapore Health Services, offers three hospitals, five national specialist centres, a network of primary health care clinics, and more than 12,000 staff members. Traditional Chinese medicine also is widely practiced.

Welfare. The Central Provident Fund is Singapore's compulsory national social security savings plan. It was established in 1955 to ensure the financial security of all workers either retired or no longer able to work. Citizens and permanent residents are eligible to participate. The government makes major expenditures for "social development."

Economy

In 2009, the Economist Intelligence Unit ranked Singapore the tenth most expensive city in the world in which to live—the third in Asia, after Tokyo and Osaka. Singapore is the 5th wealthiest country in the world in terms of GDP (PPP) per capita.

The economy depends heavily on exports refining imported goods, especially in manufacturing. Manufacturing constituted 26% of Singapore's GDP in 2005.The manufacturing industry is well-diversified into electronics, petroleum refining, chemicals, mechanical engineering and biomedical sciences manufacturing. Singapore is the busiest port in the world in terms of tonnage shipped. Singapore is the world's fourth largest foreign exchange trading centre after London, New York City and Tokyo. Singapore has been rated as the most business-friendly economy in the world, with thousands of foreign expatriates working in multi-national corporations. The city-state also employs tens of thousands of foreign blue-collared workers from around the world.

Singapore is a popular travel destination, making tourism one of its largest industries. About 9.7 million tourists visited Singapore in 2006. The Orchard Road district is the centre of shopping hub in Singapore. To attract more tourists, the government decided in 2005 to legalise gambling and to allow two Integrated Resorts to be developed at Marina South and Sentosa. Cuisine has been heavily promoted as an attraction for tourists.

Singapore is also growing its medical tourism sector. 230,000 foreigners sought medical care in the country in 2003 and Singapore Medical services are aiming to serve one million foreign patients annually by 2012. In doing so it is hoped to generate $3 billion in revenue and create at least 13,000 new jobs within the health industries.

Singapore is considered to be having the best quality of life in Asia and eleventh overall in the world. It possesses the world's ninth largest foreign reserves. The country also maintains armed forces that are technologically advanced and well-equipped. After a contraction of -6.8% in the 4th quarter of 2009, Singapore is now the fastest-growing economy in the world, with GDP growth of 17.9% in the first half of 2010.

Industry and Manufacturing. Industry accounted for 33.6% of the gross domestic product (GDP) in 2005. Singapore's primary industries in order of value are electronics, chemicals, oil drilling equipment, petroleum refining, rubber processing and rubber products, processed food and beverages, ship repair, and offshore platform construction. Manufacturing output grew by 12.8% in 2005 and employed 20.5% of the workforce.

Energy. Although Singapore is 100% dependent on imports of oil and natural gas, it ranks as one of the world's top three crude oil refining and trading hubs. Singapore's crude oil refining capacity is estimated at 1.3 million barrels per day. However, India, Malaysia, and Thailand are challenging Singapore's regional petroleum refining dominance. In keeping with government policy, natural gas usage is rising rapidly.

Banking and Finance. The Monetary Authority of Singapore is responsible for regulating the country's banking and investment sector. Singapore's stock exchange, the Singapore Exchange (SGX), has separate divisions for the trading of securities and derivatives.

Labour. Of 2.3 million Singaporeans employed 68.7% work in services, 20.5% are employed in manufacturing, 10.1% in construction, and 0.7% in other sectors. According to the Ministry of Manpower, the annual average unemployment rate was 3.1%.

Foreign Economic Relations. Located on the strategic Strait of Malacca, Singapore is a major trading hub and home to the world's busiest port. The nation's prosperity has been built on a free trade policy.

Imports. Singapore's imports totalled around US$210.7 billion in 2005. Machinery and equipment, mineral fuels, chemicals, and foodstuffs are Singapore's major import commodities. The major import partners in 2005 were Malaysia (13.7%), the European Union (11.6%), the United States (11.6%), China (10.3%), Japan (9.6%), Taiwan (5.9%), Indonesia (5.2%), Saudi Arabia (4.5%), South Korea (4.3%), and Thailand (3.8%).

Exports. Singapore's exports totalled US$241.9 billion in 2005. The major exports are machinery and equipment (especially electronic components and parts), consumer goods, chemicals, and mineral fuels and petroleum products (processed for re-export). The major export partners in 2005 were Malaysia (13.2%), the European Union (12.0%), the United States (10.2%), Hong Kong (9.4%), China (8.6%), Japan (5.5%), Thailand (4.1%), Taiwan (3.9%), and South Korea (3.5%). Singapore maintains a favourable balance of trade.

Foreign Investment. Most foreign direct investment is concentrated in manufacturing, financial services, and commerce and comes primarily from the United Kingdom (16.1%), the US (15.4%), and Japan (13.5%).

Infrastructure

Roads. Since Singapore is a small island with a high population density, the number of private cars on the road is restricted so as to curb pollution and congestion. Car buyers must pay for duties one-and-a-half times the vehicle's market value and bid for a Singaporean Certificate of Entitlement (COE), which allows the car to run on the road for a decade. Car prices are generally significantly higher in Singapore than in other English-speaking countries and thus only one in 10 residents owns a car. Singapore has a road system covering 3,356 kilometres, which includes 161 kilometres of expressways. The Singapore Area Licensing Scheme, became the world's first congestion pricing scheme, and included other complementary measures such as stringent car ownership quotas and improvements in mass transit. Upgraded and renamed Electronic Road Pricing, the system introduced electronic toll collection, electronic detection, and video surveillance technology.

Railroads. Singapore has only 23 kilometres of railroad track, all operated by Malaysian Railways and technically located on Malaysian territory per an agreement brokered in 1965. The line provides passenger service three times daily from Singapore's Keppel Station across a 1.2- kilometre causeway that spans the Johore Strait to the Malaysian mainland and Kuala Lumpur. Weekly luxury train service also is available from Keppel Station to Chang Mai and Bangkok, Thailand, with connections to Kuala Lumpur.

Rapid Transit. Singapore's principal public mass transit system is operated by Singapore Mass Rapid Transit (SMRT) Corporation, which also runs light rail, bus, and taxi services. The system has 16 underground stations, 34 elevated stations, and one station at grade and operates on two lines, the North-South and East- West lines. The Bukit Panjang Light Rail Transit system is a fully automated service that carried 37,800 passengers per day in FY 2005, using some 7.8 kilometres of elevated guideways and serving 14 stations. More than 1 billion passengers ride on SMRT and SBS Transit buses. SBS Transit, which started as a bus company (Singapore Bus Services) in 1973, began light rail and its mass rapid transit operations in 2003. By 2005 SBS was operating two mini-metro light-rail feeder lines and one full metro line—the North East Line—with 14 operational underground stations and 20 kilometres of track. SBS and SMRT metro lines intersect at key interchange points. Most Singaporean residents travel by foot, bicycles, bus, taxis and train. Two companies run the public bus and train transport system—SBS Transit and SMRT Corporation. There are almost a dozen taxi companies, who together put out 25,000 taxis on the road. Taxis are a popular form of public transport as the fares are relatively cheap compared to many other developed countries.

Ports. Singapore is a major international transport hub in Asia, positioned on many sea and air trade routes. The Port of Singapore, managed by port operators PSA International and Jurong Port, was the world's second-busiest port in 2005 in terms of shipping tonnage handled, at 1.15 billion gross tons, and in terms of containerised traffic, at 23.2 million twenty-foot equivalent units (TEUs). It is also the world's second-busiest, behind Shanghai, in terms of cargo tonnage with 423 million tons handled. In addition, the port is the world's busiest for transhipment traffic and the world's biggest ship refuelling centre.

Civil Aviation and Airports. Singapore is an aviation hub for Southeast Asia and a stopover on the Kangaroo route between Sydney and London. There are eight airports in the country, and Singapore Changi Airport hosts a network of 80 airlines connecting Singapore to 200 cities in 68 countries. It has been rated one of the best international airports by international travel magazines, including being rated as the world's best airport for the first time in 2006 by Skytrax.

Pipelines. Singapore has 139 kilometres of natural gas pipelines.

Telecommunications: Telecommunications policy, regulation, and promotion are the responsibility of a government agency, Infocomm Development Authority of Singapore. Postal and telecommunications services are provided by Singapore Telecommunications (SingTel), which is 68% owned by Temasek Holdings, a government holding company that is 32% privately owned. Seventeen FM stations and two shortwave stations broadcast to some 2.6 million radios. Seven television broadcast stations are in operation, and more than 1.3 million televisions were in use. Singapore had 1.85 million landline telephones and 4.2 million cellular phones (equivalent to some 978 subscribers per 1,000 population) in use in 2005. The highly touted telephone system uses submarine cables to Malaysia (both Peninsular Malaysia and Sabah), Indonesia, and the Philippines, as well as two earth satellite stations relaying to Intelsat satellites (one each) positioned over the Indian and Pacific oceans.

Government and Politics

Singapore is a parliamentary republic. The constitution for the State of Singapore promulgated on 3 June 1959, was amended in 1965 at independence. The presidency is largely ceremonial, and the prime minister is the most powerful political figure. The current prime minister, Lee Hsien Loong, however, has been in office since 2004, and serves under the advice of his father, long-time prime minister and now minister mentor, Lee Kuan Yew. The People's Action Party (PAP), founded in 1954, has governed without serious opposition since 1959.

Executive Branch. The largely ceremonial president and head of state is assisted by the Council of Presidential Advisers (CPA), a body established by constitutional amendment in 1991. The president is required to consult the CPA before he vetoes the government budget or appoints government nominees to key posts. In other matters, such as withholding assent to certain bills passed by parliament, appointments to statutory boards, and withholding concurrence in regard to detention of persons in times of national emergency, the president may use his discretion on consulting the CPA. The CPA has six members: two appointed by the president at his discretion, two nominated by the prime minister, one put forward by the chief justice of the Supreme Court, and another suggested by the chairman of the Public Service Commission. CPA members are appointed to initial six-year terms and can be reappointed for additional four-year terms.

The head of government is the prime minister. There is no set tenure for the office of prime minister. On the advice of the prime minister, the president appoints the other members of the cabinet. The cabinet, responsible collectively to the Parliament, oversees government policies and day-to-day administration of the affairs of state.

Legislative Branch. The unicameral 84-seat Singapore Parliament is modeled after the Westminster system of parliamentary democracy where members are voted in at regular general elections and the leader of the majority party is invited by the president to assume the post of prime minister. The prime minister then selects ministers from elected members of Parliament to form the cabinet, which in turn runs the executive branch of government. Parliament sits for five years from the date of its first session after a general election. Members are elected by universal suffrage. The constitution provides for group representation in Parliament of the Malay, Indian, and minority communities.

Judicial Branch. The judicial branch is headed by a Supreme Court, whose chief justice is appointed by the president on the advice of the prime minister. Other Supreme Court judges then are appointed by the president on the advice of the chief justice. The Supreme Court consists of the Court of Appeals and the High Court. Supreme Court judges or former Supreme Court judges can sit as judges on the Court of Appeals and the High Court, as designated by the president after consultation with the prime minister. Subordinate courts include criminal courts, criminal mentions courts (at which charges are first placed), and traffic, night, coroners', civil, and family courts, plus various other tribunals and services that support the subordinate court system. Although Singapore's laws are inherited from English and British Indian laws, and includes many elements of English common law, the government has also chosen not to follow some elements of liberal democratic values. There are no jury trials and there are laws restricting the freedom of speech that may breed ill will or cause disharmony within Singapore's multiracial, multi-religious society. Criminal activity is often punished with heavy penalties including heavy fines or caning and there are laws which allow capital punishment in Singapore for first-degree murder and drug trafficking. The Singapore government argues that Singapore has the sovereign right to determine its own judicial system and impose what it sees as an appropriate punishment, including capital punishment for the most serious crimes.

Administrative Divisions. Singapore is a unitary state with no administrative divisions. It has no provincial or local government although there are some advisory bodies.

Politics and Political Parties. The majority party, which has been in power since 1959, is the People's Action Party (PAP). Of the opposition parties, only the Workers' Party of Singapore (WP) and the Singapore Democratic Alliance (SDA), an umbrella group, hold seats in Parliament. The SDA consists of the Singapore National Malay Organisation (Pertuhan Kebangsaan Melayu Singapura—PKMS), National Solidarity Party (NSP), Singapore's People's Party (SPP), and Singapore Justice Party (SJP).

Mass Media. The media industry is regulated by the government's Media Development Authority. All newspapers in Singapore are required by law to be public companies and are regulated by the government. Major daily newspapers are published in various languages. English-language publications include the venerable *Straits Times*, founded in 1845; *Business Times*; and three tabloids, *The New Paper*, *Streats*, and *Today*. Chinese-language newspapers include *Lianhe Wanbao*, *Lianhe Zaobao*, *Shin Min Daily News*, and *Toh Lam Hhat*. Two other dailies are the Malay *Berita Harian* and Tamil *Tamil Murasu*. Weekly newspapers are offered in English and Malay, and most newspapers can be accessed on the Internet. There also is a lively magazine circulation with 17 domestic English, one Malay, and nine Chinese titles. Most broadcasting is produced by radio and television companies owned by the Media Corporation of Singapore and Radio Corporation of Singapore.

Foreign Relations. Singapore seeks to maintain a credible defensive military to support its foreign policy. It promotes good relations with its neighbours and any nation wishing to establish friendly relations. As a founding member of the Association of Southeast Asian Nations (ASEAN), Singapore is committed to maintaining a secure peaceful environment in and around Southeast Asia and in the Asia-Pacific region. After breaking off a long-term diplomatic relationship with the Republic of China on Taiwan in 1990, Singapore established relations with the People's Republic of China.

National Security

The Singapore Armed Forces (SAF) utilises technology as "force multipliers", especially in the area of C^4I integration, which will enable its various units to fight in an integrated manner. The Army, Air Force and Navy are linked via advanced data-links and networks to enable coordinated attacks and support for various units and forces. Technology is an important element in the SAF's transformation into a 3rd Generation Fighting Force.

The SAF acknowledges that technology is crucial for overcoming the limitations of Singapore's small population. Having consistently had one of the largest defence budgets in the Asia-Pacific region, Singapore has focused on maintaining its spending on sophisticated and superior weaponry. Research and experimentation to develop a technological edge began as early as 1971, even though the SAF then had only rudimentary capabilities. The effort started off with a three-man team. The SAF devotes considerable resources to defence research and development (R&D) and experimentation - 5% and 1% of the defence budget, respectively. Singapore's education system has also produced national servicemen who can be trained to operate SAF's sophisticated platforms and systems.

Because of the scarcity of open land on the main island, training involving activities such as live firing and amphibious landings is often carried out on smaller islands, barred to civilian access. This also avoids risk to the main island and the city. However, large-scale drills are considered too dangerous to be performed in the area, and since 1975 have been performed in Taiwan. Training is also held in about a dozen other countries.

Due to airspace and land constraints, the Republic of Singapore Air Force (RSAF) maintains a number of overseas bases in Australia, the United States, and France. The RSAF's 130 Squadron is based in RAAF Base Pearce, Western Australia, and its 126 Squadron is based in the Oakey Army Aviation Centre, Queensland. The RSAF has one squadron – the 150 Squadron – based in Cazaux Air Base in southern France. The RSAF also has a few overseas detachments in the United States, in San Diego, California, Marana, Arizona, Grand Prairie, Texas and Luke Air Force Base, among others

Foreign Military Relations. Singapore provides facilities for servicing foreign naval vessels, but its official policy disallows the establishment of a naval base on the island by another country. Singapore supports a strong US military presence in the Asia-Pacific region. Most of Singapore's major military imports have been purchased from the United States.

External Threat. Singapore faces a potential military threat from Malaysia if historical tensions were to re-emerge. In particular, Singapore fears that the Malaysian state of Johore could cut off its water supply, an act that would be regarded as a casus belli. Singapore also is concerned about the possibility of a terrorist strike.

Terrorism. Singapore perceives a threat from international terrorist organisations. It maintains a high level of readiness and cooperation in the area of counterterrorism. Particular emphasis has been placed on protective and preventive actions against attacks on critical infrastructure, cyber terrorism, and chemical and biological attacks. Maritime piracy, long a problem in the immediate area, is of special concern to Singapore.

Human Rights. The Ministry of Home Affairs' Internal Security Department enforces the Internal Security Act as a counter to potential espionage, international terrorism, threats to racial and religious harmony, and subversion. The government maintains effective control over all security activities, but there are some reports of human rights abuses of detainees by security forces. The government generally respects the human rights of its citizens, but, nevertheless, retains broad powers to limit citizen rights and to handicap the political opposition. Caning, in addition to imprisonment, has been a routine punishment for numerous offenses. Preventive detention has been used to deal with espionage, terrorism, organised crime, and narcotics. Citizens' privacy rights occasionally have been infringed, and the government has restricted freedom of speech and freedom of the press and limited other civil and political rights. Government pressure to conform has resulted in the practice of self-censorship by journalists. The government has instigated court proceedings and defamation suits against political opponents and critics. Such suits have consistently been decided in favour of the government, a phenomenon that inhibits political speech and action and leads observers to believe that the ruling party uses the judicial system for political purposes.

SRI LANKA

Sri Lanka is an island nation located about 31 kilometres off the southern coast of India. It declared its Independence from the United Kingdom on 4 February 1948 and became a Republic on 22 May 1972. Its largest city is Colombo.

Due to its location in the path of major sea routes, Sri Lanka is a strategic naval link between West Asia and South East Asia, and has been a centre of Buddhist religion and culture from ancient times. Today, the country is a multi-religious and multi-ethnic nation, with nearly a third of the population following faiths other than Buddhism, notably Hinduism, Christianity and Islam. The Sinhalese community forms the majority of the population, with Tamils, who are concentrated in the north and east of the island, forming the largest ethnic minority. Other communities include the Muslim Moors and Malays and the Burghers.

Famous for the production and export of tea, coffee, rubber and coconuts, Sri Lanka boasts a progressive and modern industrial economy and the highest per capita income in South Asia. The natural beauty of Sri Lanka's tropical forests, beaches and landscape, as well as its rich cultural heritage, make it a world famous tourist destination. Sri Lanka has one of the fastest economic growth rates of the world.

History

One of the first written references to the island is found in the Indian epic Ramayana, which described the emperor Ravana as monarch of the powerful kingdom of Lanka, which was created by the divine sculptor Vishwakarma for Kubera, the treasurer of the Gods. The main written accounts of the country's history are the Buddhist chronicles of Mahavansa and Dipavamsa. The earliest-known inhabitants of the island were probably the ancestors of the Wanniyala-Aetto people, also known as Veddahs and numbering roughly 3,000. Linguistic analysis has found a correlation of the Sinhalese language with the languages of the Sindh and Gujarat, although most historians believe that the Sinhala community emerged well after the assimilation of various ethnic groups. From the ancient period date some remarkable archaeological sites including the ruins of Sigiriya, the so-called "Fortress in the Sky".

Since ancient times Sri Lanka was ruled by monarchs, most notably of the Sinha royal dynasty that lasted over 2000 years. The island was also infrequently invaded by South Indian kingdoms and parts of the island were ruled intermittently by the Chola dynasty, the Pandya dynasty, the Chera dynasty and the Pallava dynasty. The island was also invaded by the kingdoms of Kalinga (modern Orissa) and those from the Malay Peninsula. Buddhism arrived from India in the 3rd century BCE, brought by Bhikkhu Mahinda, who is believed to have been the son of Mauryan emperor Ashoka. Mahinda's mission won over the Sinhalese monarch Devanampiyatissa of Mihintale, who embraced the faith and propagated it throughout the Sinhalese population.

Sri Lanka had always been an important port and trading post in the ancient world, and was increasingly frequented by merchant ships from the

Capital	-	Sri Jayawardenapura-Kotte
Largest city	-	Colombo
Official languages	-	Sinhala, Tamil
Ethnic groups	-	73.9% Sinhalese; 12.6% Tamil; 7.4% Moors; 5.2% Indian Tamil; 0.5% Others
Government	-	Democratic Socialist Republic
	-	President Mahinda Rajapaksa
	-	Prime Minister D.M. Jayaratne
	-	Chief Justice Mohan Peiris
Area	-	Total 65,610 square kilometres
Coastline	-	1,340 kilometres
Population	-	20,277,597 (2012 census) Density 323/square kilometre
GDP (PPP)	-	Total $127 billion (2012 estimate) Per capita $6,135
GDP (nominal)	-	Total $64,914 billion (2012 estimate) Per capita $3,139
Defence Minister	-	Gotabhaya Rajapakse
Chief of Army	-	Lt. Gen. Daya Ratnayake
Chief of Navy	-	Vice Admiral JSK Colombage
Chief of Air Force	-	Air Marshal Harsha Abeywickrama

Middle East, Persia, Burma, Thailand, Malaysia, Indonesia and other parts of Southeast Asia. The islands were known to the first European explorers of South Asia and settled by many groups of Arab and Malay merchants. A Portuguese colonial mission arrived on the island in 1505 headed by the Lourenço de Almeida the son of Francisco de Almeida. At that point the island consisted of three kingdoms, namely Kandy in the central hills, Kotte at the Western coast, and Yarlpanam (Anglicised Jaffna) in the north. The Dutch arrived in the 17th century. Although much of the island came under the domain of European powers, the interior, hilly region of the island remained independent, with its capital in Kandy. The British East India Company established control of the island in 1796, declaring it a crown colony in 1802, although the island would not be officially connected with British India. The fall of the kingdom of Kandy in 1815 unified the island under British rule.

European colonists established a series of tea, cinnamon, rubber, sugar, coffee and indigo plantations. The British also brought a large number of indentured workers from Tamil Nadu to work in the plantation economy. The city of Colombo was established as the administrative centre, and the British established modern schools, colleges, roads and churches that brought Western-style education and culture to the native people. Increasing grievances over the denial of civil rights, mistreatment and abuse of natives by colonial authorities gave rise to a struggle for independence in the 1930s. During World War II, the island served as an important Allied military base.

Following the war, popular pressure for independence intensified. On 4 February 1948 the country won its independence as the Commonwealth of Ceylon. Don Stephen Senanayake became the first Prime Minister of Sri Lanka. In 1972, the country became a republic within the Commonwealth, and the name was changed to Sri Lanka. On 21 July 1960 Sirimavo Bandaranaike took office as prime minister, and became the first female head of government in post-colonial Asia and the first female prime minister in the world.

From 1983 to 2009, there was an on-and-off civil war against the government by the Liberation Tigers of Tamil Eelam (LTTE), a separatist militant organisation who fought to create an independent state named Tamil Eelam in the North and East of the island. Both the Sri Lankan government and LTTE have been accused of various human rights violations.

The Sri Lankan government's military offensive against the LTTE intensified amidst cautious optimism that the group was on the verge of military defeat. On 16 January 2008 the government formally withdrew from the 2002 ceasefire on the basis that it was already dead in practice and that, rather than constraining the LTTE, it had given it time to rearm. This decision led to the withdrawal of the Norwegian-led Sri Lanka Monitoring Mission (SLMM).

Having successfully defeated the LTTE in the east by mid July 2007, the government's military strategy appeared to be to defeat them militarily by capturing their final stronghold in the north and then to negotiate a political settlement with the civilian Tamil community. In July 2008, Sri Lanka's army chief, Lt Gen. Sarath Fonseka, publicly announced that the LTTE had lost their conventional fighting capacity and would be defeat by mid-2009, indicating a delay in an earlier estimate of June 2008. Notwithstanding the offer of a unilateral ceasefire by the LTTE during the South Asian Association for Regional Cooperation (SAARC) Summit in Colombo (26 July-4 August 2008), the government refused to enter into any agreement with the militants.

The unrelenting government military offensive from August 2008 against the LTTE included the use of combat aircraft and helicopter gunships along with troops on the ground to regain territory. On 19 May 2009, the President of Sri Lanka officially claimed an end to the insurgency and the defeat of the LTTE, following the death of Velupillai Prabhakaran and much of the LTTE's other senior leadership. After the civil war ended the government of Sri Lanka called for re-development of the country. There are 300,000 Tamils that need to be resettled.

Sri Lanka has emerged from its 26-year war to become one of the fastest growing economies of the world.

Geography

The island of Sri Lanka lies in the Indian Ocean, to the southwest of the Bay of Bengal and to the southeast of the Arabian Sea. It is separated from the Indian subcontinent by the Gulf of Mannar and the Palk Strait. According to Hindu mythology, a land bridge to the Indian mainland, known as Rama's Bridge, was constructed during the time of Rama by the *vanara* architect Nala. Often referred to as Adam's Bridge, it now amounts to only a chain of limestone shoals remaining above sea level. According to geological surveys, this is a natural causeway which was formerly complete, but was breached by a violent storm in 1480. The teardrop-shaped island consists mostly of flat-to-rolling coastal plains, with mountains rising only in the south-central part. Amongst these are Sri Pada (Adams Peak) and the highest point Pidurutalagala, at 2,524 meters (8,281 ft). The Mahaweli Ganga (Mahaweli river) and other major rivers provide fresh water to the population.

Sri Lanka's climate can be described as tropical, and quite hot. Its position between 5 and 10 north latitude endows the country with a warm climate, moderated by ocean winds and considerable moisture. The mean temperature ranges from a low of 16°C in Nuwara Eliya in the Central Highlands to a high of 32°C in Trincomalee on the northeast coast, where temperatures may reach 38°C. The average yearly temperature for the country ranges from 28° to 30°C. The rainfall pattern is influenced by the monsoon winds of the Indian Ocean and Bay of Bengal. Some of the windward slopes receive up to 2,500 millimetres (98 in) of rain per month, but the leeward slopes in the east and northeast receive little rain. Periodic squalls occur and sometimes tropical cyclones bring overcast skies and rains to the southwest, northeast, and eastern parts of the island.

Government and Politics

The Constitution of Sri Lanka establishes a democratic, socialist republic in Sri Lanka, which is also a unitary state. The government is a mixture of the presidential system and the parliamentary system. The President of Sri Lanka is the head of state, the commander in chief of the armed forces, as well as head of government, and is popularly elected for a six-year term. In the exercise of duties, the President is responsible to the Parliament of Sri Lanka, which is a unicameral 225-member legislature. The President appoints and heads a cabinet of ministers composed of elected members of parliament. The President's deputy is the Prime Minister, who leads the ruling party in parliament and shares many executive responsibilities, mainly in domestic affairs.

Members of parliament are elected by universal (adult) suffrage based on a modified proportional representation system by district to a six-year term. The primary modification is that, the party that receives the largest number of valid votes in each constituency gains a unique "bonus seat." The president may summon, suspend, or end a legislative session and dissolve Parliament any time after it has served for one year. The parliament reserves the power to make all laws. On 1 July 1960 the people of Sri Lanka elected the first-ever female head of government in Prime Minister Sirimavo Bandaranaike. Her daughter Chandrika Kumaratunga served multiple terms as prime minister and as president from 1999 to 2005.

President Mahinda Rajapaksa, the fifth President, began his second term on 19 November 2010. In the election held two years before the end of his first six year term, he won with 57.8 per cent of the votes. His success in Presidential and Parliamentary Elections in January and April, 2010 came after a series of sweeping victories in elections to eight Provincial Councils by the United People's Freedom Alliance (UPFA) led by him. The UPFA now has an over two-thirds majority in parliament.

Administrative Divisions

Sri Lanka is divided into 9 provinces and 25 districts. Each province is administered by a directly-elected provincial council, as under:

Province	Capital	Districts
Central	Kandy	Kandy, Matale, Nuwara Eliya
North Central	Anuradhapura	Anuradhapura, Polonnaruwa
Northern	Jaffna	Jaffna, Kilinochchi, Mannar, Vavuniya, Mullativu
Eastern	Trincomalee	Ampara, Batticaloa, Trincomalee
North Western	Kurunegala	Kurunagala, Puttalam
Southern	Galle	Galle, Hambanthota, Mathara
Uva	Badulla	Badulla, Monaragala
Sabaragamuwa	Ratnapura	Kegalle, Rathnapura
Western	Colombo	Colombo, Gampaha, Kaluthara

The districts are further subdivided into Divisional Secretariats, and these in turn to Grama Sevaka divisions.

Economy

In the 19th and 20th centuries, Sri Lanka became a plantation economy, famous for its production and export of cinnamon, rubber and Ceylon tea, which remains a trademark national export. The development of modern ports under British rule raised the strategic importance of the island as a centre of trade. During World War II, the island hosted important military installations and Allied forces. However, the plantation economy aggravated poverty and economic inequality. From 1948 to 1977 socialism strongly influenced the government's economic policies. Colonial plantations were dismantled, industries were nationalised and a welfare state established. While the standard of living and literacy improved significantly, the nation's economy suffered from inefficiency, slow growth and lack of foreign investment.

From 1977 the UNP government began incorporating privatisation, deregulation and promotion of private enterprise. While the production and export of tea, rubber, coffee, sugar and other agricultural commodities remains important, the nation has moved steadily towards an industrialised economy with the development of food processing, textiles, telecommunications and finance. By 1996 plantation crops made up only 20% of export, and further declined to 16.8% in 2005 (compared with 93% in 1970), while textiles and garments have reached 63%. The GDP grew at an average annual rate of 5.5% during the early 1990s, until a drought and a deteriorating security situation lowered growth to 3.8% in 1996. The economy rebounded in 1997–2000, with average growth of 5.3%.

2001 saw the first recession in the country's history, as a result of power shortages, budgetary problems, the global slowdown, and continuing civil strife. Since the separatist war ended in May 2009 the Sri Lankan stock market has shown marked gains to be among the three best performing markets in the world. The Colombo Stock Exchange reported the highest growth in the world for 2003, and today Sri Lanka has the highest per capita income in South Asia.

In April 2004, there was a sharp reversal in economic policy after the government headed by Ranil Wickremesinghe of the United National Party was defeated by a coalition made up of Sri Lanka Freedom Party and the leftist-nationalist Janatha Vimukthi

Peramuna called the United People's Freedom Alliance. The new government stopped the privatisation of state enterprises and reforms of state utilities such as power and petroleum, and embarked on a subsidy programme called the Rata Perata economic programme. Its main theme to support the rural and suburban SMEs and protect the domestic economy from external influences, such as oil prices, the World Bank and the International Monetary Fund.

Sri Lanka still lags behind some of its neighbours including Maldives and Mauritius but is ahead of its giant neighbour India. Its economy grew by an average of 5% during the 1990s during the 'War for Peace' era. According to the Sri Lankan central bank statistics, the economy was estimated to have grown by 7% last year, while inflation reached 20%. Parts of Sri Lanka, particularly the South and East coast, were devastated by the 2004 Asian Tsunami. The economy was briefly buoyed by an influx of foreign aid and tourists, but this was disrupted with the re-emergence of the civil war resulting in increased lawlessness in the country and a sharp decline in tourism. But following the end of the three-decade long separatist war in May 2009 tourism has seen a steep rise. Also the end of war has ensured the rule of law in the whole of the island.

Demographics

Population density is the greatest in western Sri Lanka, especially in and around Colombo. There is a small population on the island of the Wanniyala-Aetto people, also known as Veddahs. These are believed to be the oldest and indigenous ethnic group to inhabit the island. The Sinhalese people form the largest ethnic group in the nation, composing approximately 81.9% of the total population. Tamils are concentrated in the North, East, Central and Western provinces of the country. Tamils who were brought as indentured labourers from India by British colonists to work on estate plantations, nearly 50% of whom were repatriated following independence in 1948, are called "Indian Origin" Tamils. They are distinguished from the native Tamil population that has resided in Sri Lanka since ancient times. Indian Tamils make up 5.1% of the Sri Lankan population and, Sri Lankan Tamils 4.3%. There is a significant population (8.0%) of Moors, who trace their lineage to Arab traders and immigrants from the Middle East. Their presence is concentrated in the cities and the central and eastern provinces. There are also small ethnic groups such as the Burghers (of mixed European descent) and Malays from Southeast Asia.

Languages and Religion

Sinhalese and Tamil are the two official languages of Sri Lanka. English is spoken by approximately 10% of the population, and is widely used for education, scientific and commercial purposes. Members of the Burgher community speak variant forms of Portuguese Creole and Dutch with varying proficiency, while members of the Malay community speak a form of creole Malay that is unique to the island.

Sri Lanka also enjoys significant religious diversity. Approximately 69% of Sri Lankans are adherents of Buddhism. Theravada Buddhism is the predominant school, with distinctive sects being widely followed. Buddhism in Sri Lanka has been deeply influenced by indigenous faiths and traditions, as well as the influences of prevailing Buddhist schools in South East Asia. The ancient and famous Sri Dalada Maligawa or "Temple of the Tooth" is the principal Buddhist Temple in Sri Lanka, and by tradition houses the Tooth of Buddha. Hinduism is practiced by 7.9% of the population, mainly from the Tamil community. Christianity is practiced by 7% of the population, especially by Burgher people though most Christians are Sinhalese or Tamils. While most Sri Lankan Christians are Catholics, there are also significant numbers who adhere to Dutch Reformed Church and the Anglican Communion. Islam in Sri Lanka is practiced by 8.5% of the population and its adherents are almost entirely Moors and Malays.

Transportation

Sri Lanka's road network consists of 35 A grade highways and one Controlled-access highway (E01). The railway network, operated by the state-run national railway operator, Sri Lanka Railways, spans 1,447 kilometres. Sri Lanka also has three deep-water ports, at Colombo, Galle, and Trincomalee, in addition to the newest port being built at Hambantota. The port at Trincomalee is the fifth largest natural harbour in the world. With a grant of 20 million dollars from the US and help from China, a space academy has been set up for the purpose of developing an indigenous space sector to launch satellites of other nations as well as of Sri Lanka. This dual use of launching technology will also serve to develop missile technology. On 26 September 2012 China launched Sri Lanka's first satellite, with plans for more launches in the coming years.Sri Lanka has 14 airfields.

Education

With a literacy rate of 92%, and 83% of the total population having had Secondary Education, Sri Lanka has one of the most literate populations amongst developing nations. An education system which dictates 9 years of Compulsory Schooling for every child is in place, with 99% of the children entering the first grade. In 1942 a special education committee proposed extensive reforms to establish an efficient and quality education system for the people. In recent decades, a large number of private and international schools have been established across the nation. The International Baccalaureate and General Certificate of Secondary Education are popular education programmes.

Most secondary schools in Sri Lanka provide education from grades 1 to 13 in the same institution. Students sit for the GCE Ordinary Level Examination (O/Levels) in grade 11 and the GCE Advanced Level Examination (A/levels) in grade 13. These schools are modelled on British colleges and universities. A majority of them are public, but a number of elite private schools do exist. While most reputed schools centred around large cities are usually single-sex institutions, rural schools tend to be coeducational.

Sri Lanka has a number of large public universities. They include the University of Colombo, the University of Kelaniya, the University of Sri Jayewardenepura, the University of Moratuwa, the University of Peradeniya, the University of Jaffna, the University of Ruhuna, the Eastern University of Sri Lanka, the Rajarata University of Sri Lanka, the Sabaragamuwa University of Sri Lanka, the Wayamba University of Sri Lanka and the Uva Wellassa University of Sri Lanka.

Armed Forces

The Sri Lanka Army has approximately 200,000 regular personnel, approximately between 20,000–40,000 reserve personnel and 18,000 National Guardsmen and comprises 13 operational divisions, one air-mobile brigade, one commando brigade, one special forces brigade, one independent armoured brigade, three mechanised infantry brigades and over 40 infantry brigades. From the 1980s to 2009 the army was engaged in the Sri Lankan civil war.

n November 2007, 114 members of the 950 member Sri Lankan Army peacekeeping mission in Haiti were accused of sexual misconduct and abuse. 108 members, including 3 officers of the 950-member-strong Sri Lanka peacekeeping contingent were implicated in alleged misconduct and sexual abuse.

The Sri Lanka Navy has four regional headquarters; Colombo (NAV WEST), Boossa (NAV SOUTH), Trincomalee (NAV EAST), and Karanger (NAV NORTH). The SLN recently set up OM NOR CEN, a headquarters to command naval units performing defence measures on land; especially in areas recaptured from rebels. The Sri Lanka Navy's primary mission is guarding the coastline, particularly in the island's north and east.

The Sri Lanka Air Force played a major role throughout the Sri Lankan Civil War. The SLAF operates more than 160 aircraft and has a projected trained strength of 27,400 airmen and 1,300 officers, who are from both regular and reserve service. The Sri Lanka Air Force has expanded to specialize mainly in providing air-support to ground forces, troop landing, and carrying out air strikes on rebel-held areas in the Northern and Eastern theatres, but is also capable of high- and low-level air defence.

Security Issues

The strategic importance of Sri Lanka emanates from its geo-strategic location in the Indian Ocean. Trincomalee, on the eastern coast of Sri Lanka, is one of the best natural harbours in the world. Adequate support facilities in terms of port and other infrastructure also exist in Sri Lanka to meet medium scale repairs and refits. Incumbent on the creation of facilities at Trincomalee, Sri Lanka has the potential to emerge as the maritime hub in the region for shipping traffic. Sri Lanka is in fact better placed to provide bunkering and other facilities to ships than Singapore, which has emerged as a maritime hub.

India has been extremely sensitive about the role of extra-regional players in Sri Lanka, which is separated from it by the narrow 24-kilometre wide Palk Strait. Given its geographical proximity, Sri Lanka is within the Indian security orbit. The common Tamil ethnicity in the two countries exerts a gravitational pull. Happenings in Sri Lanka, therefore, have direct bearing on India. The insurgency in Sri Lanka has its ramifications on the internal politics and security in the state of Tamil Nadu in India. India cannot afford to have any sort of military rivalry in its backyard. Though Indian has a policy of non-interference in Sri Lankan affairs, the geographical and cultural linkages make it an indispensable factor in the peace process. The bottom line for Indian security planners is that Indian can acquiesce to a divided Sri Lanka only at its own peril.

THAILAND

The Kingdom of Thailand is located in the centre of peninsular Southeast Asia. Burma is to the west, Laos to the north and east, Cambodia to the southeast, and Malaysia to the south. The south coast of Thailand faces the Gulf of Thailand, while the Isthmus of Kra is bordered on the west by the Andaman Sea (part of the Indian Ocean) and on the east by the Gulf of Thailand. Thailand has islands in the Andaman Sea and Gulf of Thailand. The largest, with provincial status, is Phuket, off the west coast; on the gulf side, the largest islands are Samui and Pangan.

The total land boundary is 4,863 kilometres in length, including borders with Burma (1,800 kilometres), Laos (1,754 kilometres), Cambodia (803 kilometres), and Malaysia (506 kilometres). A dispute between Thailand and Laos over Mekong River islands continues to delay completion of an agreement on the demarcation of their boundary. Thailand has significant differences with Burma over the alignment of their boundary. There are disputed sections of the Thai - Cambodia border where border markers are missing. Land mines, the remnants of former conflicts, are still to be found—sometimes with lethal consequences—along Thailand's borders with Cambodia and Laos. Although Thailand has no actual border dispute with Malaysia, terrorist and insurgent activities in the frontier area lead to frequent border closures and tight security. The coastline is 3,219 kilometres long (750 kilometres on the Andaman Sea and 2,469 kilometres on the Gulf of Thailand).

History

The traditional founding date of Thailand is 1238. Unlike other nations in Southeast Asia, Thailand was never colonised. Its flag consists of five horizontal bands of red (on top), white, blue (double width), white, and red. The red stripes represent unity of the nation, the white strips represent purity of religion, and the blue stripe in the centre represents the king.

In the 9th century B.C., Mon and Khmer people established kingdoms that included large areas of what is now Thailand. Much of what these people absorbed from contacts with South Asian peoples—religious, social, political, and cultural ideas and institutions—later influenced the development of Thailand's culture and national identity. In the 2nd century B.C., the Hindu-led state of Funan in present-day Cambodia and central Thailand had close commercial contact with India and was a base for Hindu merchant-missionaries. In the southern Isthmus of Kra, Malay city-states controlled routes used by traders and travelers journeying between India and Indochina (present-day Cambodia, Laos, and Vietnam).

In 1238 a Tai chieftain, Sri Intraditya, declared his independence from Khmer overlords and established a kingdom at Sukhothai in the Chao Phraya Valley in central Thailand. The people of the central plain took the name *Thai*, which means "free," to distinguish themselves from other Tai people still under foreign rule. The Kingdom of Sukhothai was

Capital	-	Bangkok
Official language	-	Thai
Government	-	Parliamentary democracy and Constitutional monarchy
	-	King Bhumibol Adulyadej Rama IX
	-	Prime Minister Yingluck Shinawatra
Constitutional monarchy	-	24 June 1932
Constitution	-	24 August 2007
Area	-	513,120 square kilometres
Coastline	-	3,219 kilometres
Population	-	66,720,153 (2011 estimate) Density 132.1/square kilometre
GDP (PPP)	-	$701.554 billion (2013 estimate) Per capita $10,849
GDP (nominal)	-	$424.985 billion (2013 estimate) Per capita $6,572
Defence Minister	-	Air Chief Marshal Sukampol Suwannathat
Chief of Armed Forces	-	General Prayuth Chan-ocha
Chief of Army	-	General Udomdej Sitabutr
Chief of Navy	-	Admiral Surasak Runroengrom
Chief of Air Force	-	Air Chief Marshal Prajin Jantong

completely absorbed by the rising new Thai Kingdom of Ayutthaya by 1438.

The city-state of Ayutthaya was founded in 1350 and established its capital in 1351 on the Chao Phraya River in central Thailand, calling it Ayutthaya, after Ayodhaya, the Indian city of the hero Rama in the Hindu epic *Ramayana*. In 1360 Ramathibodi (r. 1351–69) declared Theravada Buddhism as the official religion and compiled a legal code based on Hindu legal texts and Thai custom that remained in effect until the late nineteenth century. Ayutthaya became the region's most powerful kingdom, eventually capturing Angkor and forcing the Khmer to submit to Thai suzerainty. Rather than a unified kingdom, Ayutthaya was a patchwork of self-governing principalities and tributary provinces ruled by members of the royal family who owed allegiance to the king. The king, however, was an absolute monarch who took on god-like aspects. This belief in a divine kingship continued until the 18th century. The kingdom became increasingly sophisticated as new social, political, and economic developments took place.

Real reform occurred during the reign of Chulalongkorn (Rama V, r. 1868–1910). He introduced currency based taxes and a conscription-based regular army. In 1893 a centralised state administration replaced the semi-feudal provincial administration. The regime established European-style schools for children of the royal family and sent government officials, promising civil servants, and military officers to Europe for further education. The first railroad line was opened between Bangkok and Ayutthaya in 1897 and extended farther north in 1901 and 1909. To the south, rail connections were made in 1903, linking with British rail lines in Malaya. Although much diminished in territory by the 1910s, Siam preserved its independence, and the kingdom served as a buffer state between the British and French colonies.

Siam joined the Allies in declaring war against Germany during World War I (1914–18) and sent a small expeditionary force to the European western front. These actions won Siam favourable amendments to its treaties with France and Britain at the end of the war. Siam also gained, as spoils of war, impounded German ships for use in its merchant marine. Siam took part in the Versailles peace conference in 1919 and was a founding member of the League of Nations.

In May 1946, a new constitution was promulgated. It called for a bicameral legislature with a popularly elected lower house and an upper house elected by the lower house. The name Siam was officially restored. The civilian government's failure eventually led to the restoration of the military faction in a coup in November 1947. In 1955 SEATO's headquarters was established in Bangkok, and Thailand offered the United States the use of Thai military bases.

Anti-communism influenced Thailand's foreign affairs, and in 1961 Thailand, the Philippines, and newly independent Malaya (since 1963, Malaysia) formed the Association of Southeast Asia (ASA). In 1967 Thailand became a founding member of the Association of Southeast Asian Nations (ASEAN), a broader regional cooperative organisation that replaced the ASA.

The period from 1976 till 1992 saw military rule and limited Parliamentary government. Strict censorship continued, and the regime tightly controlled labour unions and purged suspected communists from the civil service and educational institutions. As a result, many students joined the communist insurgency.

In March 1992, with a new constitution in force new elections were held. Coups and elections continued periodically till 2006. The first-ever elections to the Senate were held in 2000, and, in January 2001 one party—the Phak Thai Rak Thai (Thai Loves Thai Party)—won an absolute majority in the House of Representatives. Because of widespread allegations of illegal election practices, new polling took place in February in some constituencies. The Thai Rak Thai, having merged with another party, since the January election, still won absolute majority of seats, but a coalition government—with the New Aspiration Party and Chat Thai—was established. Police Lieutenant Colonel Thaksin Chinnawat became prime minister. The Thai Rak Thai was further strengthened in 2002 when it absorbed many members of the New Aspiration Party.

In February 2005, the Thai Rak Thai won a 75% majority in the House of Representatives elections, and, for the first time, a single-party government was formed. The following year, however, there were mass protests calling for Thaksin's resignation over corruption issues. He called for early parliamentary elections in April 2006 that were boycotted by the major opposition parties and declared unconstitutional in May. Amidst growing protests, and without meeting much resistance, a military junta overthrew the interim government of Thaksin Shinawatra on 19 September 2006. The junta abrogated the constitution, dissolved Parliament and the Constitutional Court, detained and later removed several members of the government, declared martial law, and appointed one of the king's Privy Counsellors, General Surayud Chulanont, as the Prime Minister. The junta later wrote a highly abbreviated interim constitution and appointed a panel to draft a permanent constitution. The junta also appointed a 250-member legislature, called by some critics a "chamber of generals" while others claimed that it lacks representatives from the majority. In this interim constitution draft, the head of the junta was allowed to remove the prime minister at any time. The legislature was not allowed to hold a vote of confidence against the cabinet and the public was not allowed to file comments on bills. This interim constitution was later surpassed by the permanent constitution on 24 August 2007.

Martial law was partially revoked in January 2007. The ban on political activities was lifted in July 2007 following the 30 May dissolution of the Thai Rak Thai party. The new constitution was approved by a referendum on 19 August, which led to a return to democratic elections on 23 December 2007. The People's Power Party (Thailand), led by Samak Sundaravej formed a government with five smaller parties. Following several court rulings against him in a variety of scandals, and surviving a vote of no confidence, and protesters blockading government buildings and airports, in September 2008, Sundaravej was found guilty of conflict of interest by the Constitutional Court of Thailand (due to being a host in cooking TV programme), and ended his term in office. He was replaced by PPP member Somchai Wongsawat. On 2 December 2008, Thailand's Constitutional Court found the ruling Peoples Power Party guilty of electoral fraud, which led to the dissolution of the party according to the law. After defections from smaller parties the opposition Democrats Party was able to form a government, a first for the party since 2001. The leader of the Democrat party, and former leader of the opposition, Abhisit Vejjajiva was appointed and sworn-in as the 27th Prime Minister, together with the new cabinet on 17 December 2008.

In April 2010, a set of new violent protests by the Red Shirt opposition movement, possibly backed financially by fugitive former Prime Minister Thaksin

Shinawatra, resulted in 87 deaths (mostly civilian and some military) and 1,378 injured. When the army tried to disperse the protesters, it was met with automatic gunfire, grenades, and fire bombs from the opposition faction in the army, known as the "watermelon". This resulted in the army returning fire with rubber bullets and some live ammunition. During the time of the "red shirt" protests against the government, there were numerous grenade and bomb attacks against government offices and the homes of government officials.

On 3 July 2011, the oppositional Pheu Thai Party led by Yingluck Shinawatra (the youngest sister of Thaksin Shinawatra) won the general election by a landslide (265 seats in the House of Representatives).

Geography

Topography. In the north, the chief topographic features are high mountains along the borders with Burma and Laos and extending down the Isthmus of Kra to the southern border with Malaysia. The central plain, which extends to the Gulf of Thailand, is a lowland area drained by the Chao Phraya and its tributary rivers. The upland Khorat Plateau in the northeast drains into the River Mun. The narrow, tropical Isthmus of Kra runs from mainland Thailand to the border with peninsular Malaysia.

Principal Rivers. The principal river is the Chao Phraya, which, with its tributaries, drains about 33% of the national territory and flows south into a delta at Bangkok. The Mun and many other smaller upland rivers are tributaries of the Mekong, which forms the border between Thailand and Laos before flowing into Cambodia and Vietnam and into the South China Sea. Together, the Chao Phraya and Mekong systems sustain Thailand's agricultural economy and provide waterways for inland navigation.

Climate. A tropical country, Thailand has three distinct seasons. The first is a hot and dry season from February to May, with an average temperature of 34°C and 75% relative humidity. This season is followed by a rainy, cooler season brought by the southwest monsoon from June to September, with an average daily temperature of 29°C and 87% relative humidity. A cooler, dry season, caused by the northeast monsoon, lasts from November to January, with temperatures ranging from 32°C to less than 20°C and lower relative humidity. The Isthmus of Kra is always hot and humid and has the heaviest rainfall. The lightest rainfall is in the northeast.

Natural Resources. Thailand's major natural resources are fluorite, gypsum, lead, lignite, natural gas, rubber, tantalum, tin, and tungsten. Renewable resources include fish and timber.

Land Use. Roughly 20% of Thailand is covered by mountains and hills, the steepness of which generally precludes agriculture. Arable land accounts for nearly 27.5% of the total area. About 6.9% is planted to permanent crops with 49,860 square kilometres irrigated.

Environmental Factors. The depletion of the water table around Bangkok has led to land subsidence. Despite the annual southwest monsoon, Thailand is subject to drought. Other environmental issues include air pollution from vehicle emissions, water pollution from organic and factory wastes, deforestation, soil erosion, and wildlife population depletion from illegal hunting.

Society

Population. The largest population is in the northeast, with 20.7 million inhabitants and a population density of 122.9 persons per square kilometre. The central region, excluding Bangkok, has the next largest population, with 14 million inhabitants and a density of 137.8 persons per square kilometre. Bangkok itself has a population of 6.3 million inhabitants and a population density of 4,038 persons per square kilometre.

Ethnic Groups. People of Thai ethnicity make up 75% of the population. Another 14% are ethnic Chinese, and 4% are Malay, leaving 7% as uncategorised. Additionally, Thailand has refugees from Burma, many of them ethnic, non-Thai-speaking Karen who fled their country in the face of fighting between Karen rebels and Burmese troops.

Languages. Nearly 94% of the people speak Tai-Kadai (Daic) languages, with Thai (in various dialects) being predominant and the national and official language. Another 2% speak Austro-Asiatic languages, 2% speak Austronesian languages, 1% speak Tibeto-Burman languages, and 0.2% speak Hmong-Mien languages. Standard Thai is based on the dialect spoken in the Chao Phraya Valley. The Thai alphabet, with 44 consonants and 32 vowels, originated during the reign of King Ramkhamhaeng (Rama the Great, r. 1279–98) and is an adaptation of Mon and Khmer scripts derived from Indian Devanagari. Some 74 languages are spoken in Thailand, including numerous Thai dialects plus English, which is the secondary language among the well educated and is widely understood.

Religion. The predominant religion is Theravada Buddhism, representing about 94% of the practicing population and about 90% of all Thai people. Muslims represent 4.6%; Christians, 0.7%; Hindus, 0.1%; and Sikhs, Baha'i Faith, and others, 0.6%. Religious instruction is required at both the primary and secondary education levels.

Education and Literacy. The Ministry of Education supervises public and private education. The literacy rate in Thailand is 92.6%.

Health. Human immunodeficiency virus/acquired immune deficiency syndrome (HIV/AIDS) is a serious problem in Thailand. The Thai government has launched a well-funded, politically supported, and pragmatic response to the epidemic. Major infectious diseases in Thailand also include bacterial diarrhea, hepatitis, dengue fever, malaria, Japanese encephalitis, rabies, and leptospirosis.

Welfare. Thailand has social welfare and social insurance systems. Social welfare involves welfare services aimed at the poor, persons with disabilities, children, the elderly, women, minority hill tribes, and other disadvantaged individuals. The social insurance system provides sickness, maternity, disability, death, dependent child, old age, and unemployment benefits. There also is a social security system for private-sector employees and medical security and pension systems for public-service employees, employees of national enterprises, and military personnel.

Economy

Thailand is an emerging economy and considered as a newly industrialised country. After enjoying the world's highest growth rate from 1985 to 1996 – averaging 12.4% annually – increased pressure on Thailand's currency, the baht, in 1997, the year in which the economy contracted by 1.9% led to a crisis that uncovered financial sector weaknesses and forced the Chavalit Yongchaiyudh administration to float the currency, however, Prime Minister Chavalit Yongchaiyudh was forced to resign after his cabinet came under fire for its slow response to the crisis. The baht was pegged at 25 to the US dollar from 1978 to 1997; however, the baht reached its lowest point of 56 to the US dollar in January 1998 and the economy contracted by 10.8% that year. This collapse prompted the Asian financial crisis.

Thailand's economy started to recover in 1999, expanding 4.2% and 4.4% in 2000, thanks largely to strong exports. Growth (2.2%) was dampened by the softening of the global economy in 2001, but picked up in the subsequent years owing to strong growth in Asia, a relatively weak baht encouraging exports and increasing domestic spending as a result of several mega projects and incentives of Prime Minister Thaksin Shinawatra, known as Thaksinomics. Growth in 2002, 2003 and 2004 was 5–7% annually. Growth in 2005, 2006 and 2007 hovered around 4–5%. Due both to the weakening of the US dollar and an increasingly strong Thai currency, by March 2008, the dollar was hovering around the 33 baht mark.

Thailand exports an increasing value of over $105 billion worth of goods and services annually. Major exports include Thai rice, textiles and footwear, fishery products, rubber, jewellery, cars, computers and electrical appliances. Thailand is the world's no.1 exporter of rice, exporting more than 6.5 million tons of milled rice annually. Rice is the most important crop in the country. Thailand has the highest percentage of arable land, 27.25%, of any nation in the Greater Mekong Subregion. About 55% of the arable land area is used for rice production.

Substantial industries include electric appliances, components, computer parts and cars, while tourism in Thailand makes up about 6% of the economy. Prostitution in Thailand and sex tourism also form a de facto part of the economy. Cultural milieu combined with poverty and the lure of money have caused prostitution and sex tourism in particular to flourish in Thailand. One estimate published in 2003 placed the trade at US$4.3 billion per year or about 3% of the Thai economy. According to research by Chulalongkorn University on the Thai illegal economy, prostitution in Thailand in the period between 1993 and 1995 made up around 2.7% of the GDP. It is believed that at least 10% of tourist dollars are spent on the sex trade.

Thailand functions as an anchor economy for the neighbouring developing economies of Laos, Burma, and Cambodia. Thailand's recovery from the 1997–1998 Asian financial crisis depended mainly on exports, among various other factors. Thailand ranks high among the world's automotive export industries along with manufacturing of electronic goods.

Forty-nine percent of Thailand's labour force is employed in agriculture, however this is less than the 70% employed in 1980. Agriculture has been experiencing a transition from labour intensive and transitional methods into a more industrialised and competitive sector.[64] Between 1962 and 1983, the agricultural sector grew by 4.1% on average a year and continued to grow at 2.2% between 1983 and 2007. However, the relative contribution of agriculture to GDP has declined while exports of goods and services have increased. As of December 2011, the unemployment rate in Thailand stands at 0.4%.

Agriculture, Forestry, and Fishing. In 2006 agriculture, forestry, and fishing contributed less than 10% of gross domestic product (GDP) but employed about 39% of the workforce. Thailand is the world's leading exporter of rice and a major exporter of shrimp. Other agricultural products include coconuts, corn, rubber, soybeans, sugarcane, and tapioca. In 1985 Thailand officially designated 25% of the nation's land area for protected forests and 15% for timber production. Protected forests have been set aside for conservation and recreation, while production forests are available for the forestry industry.

Mining and Minerals. Thailand's major minerals include fluorite, gypsum, lead, lignite, natural gas, rubber, tantalum, tin, and tungsten. The main mineral export is gypsum.

Industry and Manufacturing. Thailand is becoming a centre of automobile manufacturing for the Association of Southeast Asian Nations (ASEAN) market. The expansion of the automotive industry has been a boon for domestic steel production. Thailand's electronics industry faces competition from Malaysia and Singapore, while its textile industry faces competition from China and Vietnam.

Tourism. Tourism makes a larger contribution to Thailand's economy (typically about 6% of GDP) than that of any other Asian nation. One of the negative side effects of Thailand's tourism industry is a burgeoning sex tourism industry and a related threat from human immunodeficiency virus/ acquired immune deficiency syndrome (HIV/AIDS).

Infrastructure

Roads. Thailand has 57,403 kilometres of roads, 56,542 kilometres of which were paved and 861 kilometres, unpaved. Streets in Bangkok are frequently gridlocked, with an overabundance of motor vehicles flowing into the central city via expressways.

Railroads. Railroads are operated under the State Railway of Thailand. In 2005 the system totaled an estimated 4,071 kilometres of narrow-gauge (1.000-metre gauge) track. Freight traffic is considered an important part of Thailand's domestic container transport to and from seaport and inland terminals.

Ports. Thailand's ports in order of size are Bangkok, Laem Chabang, Pattani, Phuket, Sattahip, Si Racha, and Songkhla. The Thai merchant fleet comprises 400 ships of 1,000 gross registered tons or more, including 145 cargo carriers, 91 petroleum tankers, 60 bulk carriers, 32 refrigerated cargo ships, 29 liquefied gas ships, 21 container ships, 14 chemical tankers, 6 passenger/cargo ships, 1 passenger ship, and 1 specialised tanker.

Inland and Coastal Waterways. Thailand has some 4,000 kilometres of navigable inland waterways, 92% of which, or 3,701 kilometres, are navigable by boats with drafts up to 0.9 metres. Thailand's long coastlines lend themselves to inter-coastal trade.

Civil Aviation and Airports. Thailand has an estimated 108 airports and three heliports. Bangkok International Airport at Don Muang, 24 kilometres north of the capital, is an important regional hub for pass-through flights and as a destination. About 80 airlines provide service to the Bangkok International Airport and carry a reported 25 million passengers and 700,000 tons of cargo a year. Since 1977, Thai Airways has been fully owned by the Thai government.

Pipelines. Thailand has 3,760 kilometres of gas pipelines and 379 kilometres of refined products pipelines.

Telecommunications. In 2002 the Thai government formed a new Ministry of Information and Communications to oversee all aspects of telecommunications. The ministry also is responsible for implementing the country's information technology policy, called IT 2010, which is designed to strengthen Thailand's telecommunications infrastructure as a means of promoting overall economic development. Thailand's telecommunications network suffers from delays and other shortfalls in the provision of telephone services as a result of inadequate investment. The quality and availability of telephone service are much better in Bangkok and other cities than in rural areas. Mobile telephones are much more prevalent than landline phones. State entities, including the police and military, and government allies own almost all television and radio stations and play an important role in determining programming content. The government's Public Relations Department requires that all Thai radio stations carry 30 minutes of official news prepared by Radio Thailand, the government's national radio network, twice daily. Radio Thailand has seven networks that specialize in such areas as news and information, public affairs, social issues, education, and foreign-language broadcasts. Thailand has five television channels, two of which are run by the central government, two by the army, and one by a private enterprise. Altogether, Thailand has 204 AM radio stations, 334 FM radio stations, 6 shortwave stations, and 111 television broadcast stations. Additionally, there are between 2,000 and 3,000 community radio stations, many of which operate outside the law by using frequencies restricted to government entities.

Government and Politics

Thailand is a constitutional monarchy with a democratically elected bicameral legislature.

Executive Branch. The constitutional monarch and head of state, since 9 June 1946, is King Bhumibol Adulyadej (Rama IX of the Chakri Dynasty). The Privy Council, which is still provided for in the interim constitution, is an 18-member constitutional body that advises the king on matters of legislation, government affairs, clemency, awards, and other matters requiring the king's signature. Under the interim constitution, executive governmental power is exercised through a cabinet headed by a prime minister appointed by the king (with the concurrence of the Council for National Security (CNS) chairman) and the 19 members of the Council of Ministers who head major ministries.

Legislative Branch. Legislative power is exercised through a bicameral National Assembly composed of the House of Representatives (Saphaputhan Ratsadon) and Senate (Wuthisapha). All legislative matters of national policy received the approval of the National Assembly and the signature of the king before becoming law. Members of both houses served four-year terms. The number of representatives is determined by the size of the population.

Judicial Branch. Thailand has a three-level court system collectively known as the Courts of Justice. At the top is the Supreme Court of Justice. Below it are the Court of Appeal and, at the third level, the Courts of First Instance, over which the Supreme Administrative Court, which was established in 1999, presides. The Courts of First Instance include the Central Administrative Court and 16 regional administrative courts. A new Constitutional Tribunal, composed of justices from the Supreme Court of Justice and the Supreme Administrative Court, was established on 1 October 2006, to replace the functions of the Constitutional Court. Judges of the Supreme Court of Justice and the Supreme Administrative Court are subject to Senate approval. Other judges are members of the career civil service and are not subject to parliamentary review. Administrative appellate and supreme administrative courts operate at higher levels. A separate Military Court deals with military personnel and persons arrested during periods of martial law. Islamic sharia courts hear civil cases involving members of the Muslim minority.

Administrative Divisions. Thailand has 76 provinces (*changwat*), including Bangkok Municipality. The provinces are divided into 795 districts (*amphoe*), 81 subdistricts (*king amphoe*), 7,255 rural administrative subdistricts (*tambon*), and 69,866 villages (*muban*).

Electoral System. There are no elections for the heads of state and government. The monarchy is hereditary and based on the Palace Law of Succession enacted in 1924, which allows the king to appoint his heir. If he has failed to do so, the Privy Council nominates an heir for National Assembly consideration. Officially, the king appoints the prime minister, who is normally the leader of the party that had an outright majority or organised a majority coalition in the House of Representatives. The Senate is also elected by popular vote for nonparty candidates.

Politics and Political Parties. Active political parties include the Phak Prachathipat Party (Democratic Party); Phak Mahachon Party (Great People's Party);

Phak Chat Thai Party (Thai Nation Party); and Thai Rak Thai Party (Thai Loves Thai Party).

Foreign Relations. Thailand's foreign policy includes support for the Association of Southeast Asian Nations (ASEAN) in the interest of regional stability and emphasis on a close and longstanding security relationship with the United States. It has signed but not ratified the United Nations Law of the Sea Treaty.

National Security

Armed Forces Overview. Under normal operating circumstances, the minister of defence and the supreme commander of the armed forces are at the top of the chain of command and maintain control; however, real power is held by the three service chiefs.

Foreign Military Relations. A long-standing ally of the United States, Thailand signed numerous bilateral defence and mutual security agreements between 1950 and 2003. Most Thai military equipment is from the United States, the United Kingdom, and China.

External Threat. Thailand faces a number of external threats from cross-border activities.

Those on the border with Burma involve the handling of ethnic rebels, refugees, and illegal crossings, often related to drugs and arms trafficking. There have been periodic armed border clashes between Thai and Burmese border guards. Some 98,000 Karen refugees live in camps on the Thai side of the Burma–Thailand border, and rebel members of this group have skirmished with Thai troops. Similarly, separatist insurgents in predominantly Muslim southern Thailand allegedly have operated from neighbouring Malaysia, leading to cooperation between the two governments and Malaysian arrests of separatist ringleaders. Thailand has periodically closed border areas where communist Cambodian insurgents at odds with the Phnom Penh government control neighbouring territory. The Cambodian government has accused Thailand of complicity with the insurgents.

Terrorism. Thailand has been confronted with terrorist violence, primarily in the predominantly Muslim southern provinces of Narathiwat, Pattani, and Yala, which border Malaysia. This separatist violence has led to border closures and security tightening with neighbouring Malaysia to inhibit terrorist activities. During 2006 violence in the southern provinces, and particularly violence aimed at public school teachers, sporadically forced the temporary closure of public schools and disrupted the educational process in those areas. Fears of terrorism against Thailand's own tourist resorts are another cause of concern.

Human Rights. Trafficking in women and children and forced prostitution and labour are serious problems in Thailand. It is conservatively estimated that between 200,000 and 300,000 men, women, and children—but particularly women and young girls—are engaged in prostitution as part of Thailand's illegal sex tourism industry. Of these, between 30,000 and 40,000 prostitutes are under the age of 18 years; this figure does not include foreign migrants, many of whom come from Burma, Cambodia, China, and Laos. Thai and migrant women also are trafficked to Japan, Malaysia, Singapore, Bahrain, Australia, South Africa, Europe, and the United States for prostitution and sweatshop labour. Men, women, and children from China and Southeast Asian neighbours also are trafficked for sweatshop, fishery, construction, farm, and industrial labour.

MILITARY BALANCE

AFGHANISTAN

Active	190,700 Paramilitary 149,650
Afghan National Army *184,700*	Five Regional Commands
Forces by Role	
Army	201 Corps (1 commando battalion; 2 infantry brigades; 1 mechanised brigade) 203 Corps (1 commando battalion; 4 infantry brigades) 205 Corps (1 commando battalion; 4 infantry brigades) 207 Corps (1 commando battalion; 3 infantry brigades) 209 Corps (1 commando battalion; 3 infantry brigades) 215 Corps (1 commando battalion, 3 infantry brigades) 111 Division (2 infantry brigades) 7 rapid reaction battalions
Special Forces	1 Special Forces group; 2 commando brigades
Combat Support	1 signals battalion
Equipment by Type	
Reconnaissance	**406 Recce** M117 ASV**; APC** 173 M113A2
Artillery	**Towed** 109: 122mm 85 D-30; 155mm 24 M114A1 **Missiles** SSM SS-1 Scud
Afghan Air Force	***6,000***
Equipment by Type	
Aircraft	**Transport**: 35: Medium 15 G-222 (C-27A) **Light** 20: 6 *Cessna* 182; 14 *Cessna* 208B **Training** 2 L-39 *Albatross*
Helicopters	**Anti-tank**: 11 Mi-35; **Support:** 46; 6 MD-530F; 40 Mi-17
Afghan National Police	149,650 (under control of Ministry of Interior) Includes Afghan Uniformed Police, Afghan National Civil Order Police, Afghan Border Police , Afghan Anti-Crime Police

International Security Assistance Force (ISAF) led by NATO is deployed in all regions since October 2006, with contributing NATO nations filling identified posts.

BANGLADESH

Army: 126,150

Forces by Role	
Armour	1 brigade (2 armoured regiments); 6 independent regiments
Infantry	7 division headquarters; 18 infantry brigades; 1 composite brigade
Special Forces	1 commando battalion
Artillery	20 regiments
Engineers	1 brigade
Signals	1 brigade
Aviation	2 squadrons
Air Defence	1 brigade

Equipment by Type	
Tanks	232: **Main Battle tanks** 174 Type-59; 58 Type-69 **Light tanks** 8 Type-62
Armoured Personnel Carriers	306: **APC (T)** 134 MT-LB; **APC (W)** 172; 155 BTR-80; 17 *Cobra*
Artillery	815: **Towed** 343: 170 105 mm; 114 pack howitzer 111 122 mm; 62 130 mm; **Mortars** 472: 81 mm; 82 mm; 120 mm
Anti-Tank	**Recoilless** 238 106 mm M-40A1
Aircraft	**Transport** 6; 5 Cessna 152; 1 Piper *Cheyenne*
Air Defence	**Surface-to-Air Missiles: SP** FM-90**; Man-portable** QW-2 **Guns Towed** 164 37 mm; 34 Type-59 (S-60); 132 Type 65/74

Navy: 16,900

Forces by Role

Headquarters located at Dhaka

Equipment by Type	
Frigates	**5** **FFGHM** 1: 1 *Bangabandhu* (ROK Modified *Ulsan*) with 2 twin launchers with Otomat Mk 2 AShM, 2 triple 324mm TT, 1 76mm gun (capacity: 1 AW109E helicopter) **FFG** 1: 1 *Osman* (PRC *Jianghu I*) with 2 quad launchers with HY-2 (CSS-N-2) *Silkworm* AShM, 2 RBU 1200, 2 twin 100mm gun **FF** 3: 2 *Abu Bakr* (UK *Leopard*) with 2 twin 115mm gun 1 *Umar Farooq* (UK *Salisbury* – training role) with 3 *Squid*, 1 twin 115mm gun
Patrol & Coast Combatants	42 **PSOH** 2 *Bijoy* (UK *Castle*) **PCFG** 4 *Durdarsha* (PRC *Huangfeng*) with 4 single launchers with HY-2 (CSS-N-2) *Silkworm* AShM **PCO** 6: 1 *Madhumati* (*Sea Dragon*); 5 *Kapatakhaya* (UK *Island*) **PCC** 3: 2 *Meghna* (fishery protection); 1 *Nirbhoy* (PRC *Hainan*) with 4 RBU 1200 **PBFG** 5 *Durbar* (PRC *Hegu*) with 2 single launchers with SY-1 AShM **PBFT** 4 *Huchuan* (PRC) with 2 single 533mm TT each with YU 1 Type 53 HWT **PBF** 4 *Titas* (ROK *Sea Dolphin*)

	PB 14: 2 *Akshay;* 1 *Barkat* (PRC *Shanghai III*); 1 *Bishkali;* 2 *Karnaphuli;* 1 *Salam* (PRC *Huangfen*); 7 *Shaheed Daulat* (PRC *Shanghai II*)
Mine Countermeasures	5; **MSO** 4*Shapla* (UK *River*); 1 *Sagar*
Amphibious Craft	11
	Landing Ships 1 **LSL**
	Landing Craft 10 : 2 **LCU**; 3 **LCVP**; 5 **LCM** (*Yuchin*
Logistics and Support	11; **AOR** 2 (coastal); **AR** 1; **AG** 1; **ATF** 1; **AGHS** 2 *Agradoot;* 1 *Anushandhan;* **YTM** 3
Training	1 *Shaheed Ruhul Amin*
Aviation	Light Helicopters 2AE109E *Power*
Facilities	Bases - Chittagong, Dhaka, Kaptai, Khulna and Mangla

Air Force: 14,000

Three major bases: **Bashar** (consists of Dhaka–Tejgaon and Dhaka-Kurmitola); **Matiur Rahman** (Jessore) and **Zahurul Haque** (Chittagong). **Kurmitola** is the main fast Jet fighter / FGA base. Tejgaon houses two helicopter squadrons. **Jessore** houses the transport squadrons, the Air Force Academy and the Flying Training Wing. **Bogra** has the flying instructors' school; **Chittagong** has a combat training / light attack squadron plus a helicopter squadron.

Forces by Role	
Fighter	1 squadron with MiG-29 *B* / MiG-29UB *Fulcrum*
FGA	1 squadron with F-7 MB, F-7B G *Airguard*
	1 squadron with FT-7 BG, FT-7B *Airguard*
Ground Attack	1 squadron with A-5C (Q-5III) *Fantan*; FT-6 (MiG-19 UTI) *Farmer*
Transport	1 squadron with An-32 *Club*
	1 squadron with C-130B *Hercules*
Training	1 squadron with L-39ZA *Albatros*
	1 squadron with PT-6
Transport Helicopters	2 squadrons with Mi-17 / MI-171/MI-171Mi-IV Hip
	1 squadron with Bell 212
	1 Squadron with Bell 206L *Long Ranger*
Equipment by Type	
Aircraft	70 combat capable
	Fighter 45:10 F-7MB *Airguard;* 11 F-7BG *Airguard* (recce capable) 6 MiG-29 *Fulcrum* ; 2 MiG-29 UB *Fulcrum;* 5 FT-7BG/FT-7B *Airguard*
	Anti-tank 18 A-5C
	Transport 7:3 *An-32 Club;* 4 C-130B *Hercules*
	Training 17: 7 L-39ZA *Albatross;* 10 PT-6 (CJ-6)
Helicopters	**Support** 14: MI-17 (Mi-8MT) *Hip H*
	Utility 9; Bell 206L *Long Ranger;* 11 Bell 212
Tactical Missiles	**AAM**: AA-2 *Atoll;* R-73 (AA-1 *Archer*); R-27R (AA-10 *Alamo*)

Paramilitary 63,900

Ansars	20,000
Armed Police	5,000 rapid action force
Bangladesh Rifles	38,000; Border Guard; 41 paramilitary battalions
Coast Guard	900
Patrol &Coastal Combatants	9; **PB** 4: *1 Ruposhi Bangla;* 1 *Shaheed Daulat;* 2 *Shetgang* **PBR** 5 *Pabna*

UN Deployments

Ivory Coast	13 observers, 1 infantry battalion, 1 engineer company, 1 signals company, 1 MP platoon, 1 field hospital
DRC	34 observers, 2 mechanised battalions, 1 aviation company, 1 engineer company
Lebanon	1 FFG, 1 PCO
Liberia	11 observers, 1 infantry battalion, 2 engineer companies, 1 logistics company, 1 MP platoon, 1 field hospital
South Sudan	1 engineer company, 1 field hospital
Sudan	12 observers, 1 infantry company, 1 logistics company
Timor Leste	3 observers
Western Sahara	7 observers, 1 field hospital

BHUTAN

Royal Bhutan Army 10,000

Forces by Role

Royal Bhutan Army	No.1 Wing - Tendu No.2 Wing - Damthang No.3 Wing - Goinichawa No.4 Wing - Yonphula No. 5 Wing - Samchi No. 6 Wing - Wangdi No. 7 Wing - Paro No. 8 Wing - Samchi No. 9 Wing - Geylephug No. 10 Wing - Deothang No. 11 Wing - Rimte No. 12 Wing - Wangdi No. 13 Wing - Deothang No. 14 Wing - Nanglam No. 15 Wing - Thimpu (RBG) No. 16 Wing - Gelegphug Training Wing - Tenchholing
Independent Companies	9 (Ha, Damthang, Gumchawa, Punakha, Kalikhola, Thimphu (2), Khakthang and Deothang)
Special Forces	6 companies
Wangchuk Lo Dzong Military Training School	Ha
Royal Bodyguards	Three companies - Royal Palace (Thimpu)
Forest Guards	
Army Aviation	1 Dornier DO-28; 7 Mil Mi-28 helicopters
Royal Bhutan Police	
Police Training Centres	3 (Jigmiling, Geylephug and Zilnon Namgyeling)
Airport Security Unit	Paro

CHINA

Armed Forces **2,285,000**	**Army 1,600,000; Navy 255,000; Air Force 330,000 Strategic Missile Forces 100,000, Paramilitary 660,000**

<u>**Organisations by Service**</u>

Strategic Missile Forces	Second Artillery Force (100,000+)
Offensive	28 launch brigades within 6 missile bases; organization varies by missile type; one testing and one training base 1 ICBM brigade with DF-4 3 ICBM brigades with DF-5A 1 ICBM brigade with DF-31 2 ICBM brigades with DF-31A 1 IRBM brigade with DF-3A 1 MRBM brigade with DF-21 7 MRBM brigades with DF-21A 2 MRBM brigades with DF-21C 1 MRBM brigade with DF-21D 4 SRBM brigades with DF-11A 4 SRBM brigades with DF-15 2 SSM brigade with DH-10 2 SSM training brigades
Missiles	**Strategic** 470 **ICBM** 66: 12 DF-31 (CSS-9) (1 brigade); 24 DF-31A (CSS-9 Modified) (2 brigades); 10 DF-4 (CSS-3) (2 brigades); 20 DF-5A (CSS-4 Modified) (3 brigades) **IRBM** 2 DF-3A (CSS-2 Mod) **MRBM** 122: 80 DF-21 (CSS-5) (5 brigades); 36 DF-21 (CSS-5 Modified) (2 brigades); 2 DF-3A (CSS-Modified) (1 brigade); 6 DF-21D (CSS-5 Mod 4 - ASBM) **SRBM** 216: 108 DF-11/M-11 **(**CSS-7 Modified**)** (4 brigades); 96 DF-15/M-9 (CSS-6) 225 (6 brigades) **LACM** 54: 54 CJ-10 (DH-10) (2 brigades)
Navy	**Submarines Strategic; SSBN 4** 1 *Xia* (with 12 JL-1 (CSS-N-3) strategic SLBM); 3 *Jin* (capacity 12 JL-2 (CSS-NX-4) strategic SLBM
Defensive Radar	**Strategic**: phased array radar; detection and tracking radars (covering Central Asia and Shanxi (northern border)) located in Xinjiang
Space	**Satellites** 52 **Communications** 4: 3 *Fenghuo* (*Zhongxing* – dual use telecom satellites for civil/military communications); 1 *Chinasat* 1A (*Zhongxing* 1A – reported dual use satellite for civil/military communications) **Navigation/Positioning/Timing** 17: 2 *Beidou*-1; 5*Beidou*-2(M); 3 *Beidou*-2(G); 4 *Beidou*-2 (IGSO) **ISR** 20: 1 *Haiyang* 2A; 17 *Yaogan Weixing* (remote sensing); 2 *Zhangguo Ziyuan* (ZY-2 - remote sensing)

ELINT/SIGINT 11: 8 *Shijian* 6 (4 pairs - reported ELINT/SIGINT role)

***People's Liberation Army* 800,000**

Group Army	**18** (strength from 30-65,000)
Military Regions	**7** **North East–Shenyang Military Region** 250,000

North–Beijing Military Region 300,000
West–Lanzhou Military Region 220,000
South-West–Chengdu–Military Region 180,000
South–Guangzhou Military Region 180,000:
Centre–Jinan Military Region 190,000
East–Nanjing Military Region 250,000

Forces by Role

Armoured	5 armoured divisions, 11 armoured brigades, 1 OPFOR armoured brigade
Mechanised Infantry	7 mechanized infantry divisions, 2 (high altitude) mechanized infantry divisions, 1 mechanized guards division, 1 light guards division, 9 mechanized infantry brigades, 1 (high altitude) mechanized infantry brigade 2 independent regiments
Motorized Infantry	10 motorized infantry divisions, 3 (high altitude) motorized infantry divisions, 1 (jungle) motorized infantry division, 19 motorized infantry brigades, 2 (high altitude) motorized infantry brigades
Mountain Infantry	2 (independent) brigades
Airborne	1 (manned by AF) corps (3 airborne divisions, 35,000 airborne)
Amphibious	2 amphibious assault divisions, 1 amphibious mechanized brigade
Artillery	2 artillery divisions, 17 artillery brigades
SSM	1 independent brigade; 9 (coastal defence) regiments
Air Defence	21 air defence brigades; 1 independent regiment
Engineers	1 independent brigade, 13 engineer regiments
Signals	50 regiments
EW	5 EW regiments
Aviation	6 aviation brigades; 4 aviation regiments, 2 training aviation regiments

Equipment by Type

Tanks	**MBT** 7,430+: 4,300 Type-59/Type-59D/Type-59-II; 300 Type-79; 500 Type-88A/B; 1,000 Type-96/Type-96A; 300 Type-96G; 500 Type-98A/Type-99; 30Type-99A2 **Light** 800: 200 Type-05 AAAV ZTD-05; 400 Type-62; 200 Type-63A **AIFV** 2,150: 500 Type-04 (ZBD-04); 250 Type-05 AAAV(ZBD-05); 700 Type-86/Type-86A (WZ-501); 750 Type-92;150 Type-92A **APC** 2,900 **APC (T)** 2,000: 1,650 Type-63/Type-63C; 350 Type-89 **APC (W)** 900: 100 Type-09 (ZBL-09); 500 Type-92B; 100 WZ-523
Artillery	12,367+ **SP** 1,821: **122mm** 1,371: 1,296 Type-70-I/Type-89/Type-07 PLZ-07; 75 Type-09 (PLC-09) **152mm** 324 Type-83; **155mm** 126Type-05 (PLZ-05) **Towed** 6,140: **122mm** 3,800 Type-54-1 (M-30) M-1938/Type-83/Type-60 (D-74)/Type-96 (D-30); **130mm** 234 Type-59 (M-46)/Type-59-I; **152mm** 2,106 Type-54 (D-1)/Type-66 (D-20) **Mortars** 50+: **120mm** 50 Type 05 (PLL-05) **MRL** 1,770+ **SP** 1,716+: **107mm** some **122mm** 1,620 Type 81/Type-89; **300mm** 96 Type-03 PHL-03 **Towed 107mm** 54 Type-63
Mortars	2,586 **Towed 81mm** Type-W87; **82mm** Type-53 (M-37)/ Type-67/Type-82; **100mm** Type-71 (reported); **120mm** Type-55 (incl SP); **160mm** Type-56 (M-160)
Anti-Tank	**Missiles SP** 276 HJ-9 *Red Arrow* 9 **Man-portable** HJ-73A/HJ-73B/HJ-73C/HJ-8A/C/E

	RCL 3,966: **75mm** Type-56; **82mm** Type-65 (B-10)/Type-78; **105mm** Type-75; **120mm** Type-98
	RL 62mm Type-70-1
	Guns 1,888: **100mm** 1,658: 1,308 Type-73 (T-12)/Type-86; 350 Type-02 PTL02 **120mm** 72 Type-89 SP
Aircraft	**Transport** 8 **Medium** 3 Y-8 **Light** 5 Y-7
Helicopters	**Anti-Tank** 42 Z-10, Z-19
	MRH 401: 22 Mi-17 *Hip H*; 33 Mi-17-V5 *Hip H*; 24 Mi-17-V7 *Hip H*; 8 SA316 *Alouette III*; 8 SA342L *Gazelle*; 80 Z-9/9B; 200 Z-9 WA; 26 Z-9W
	Transport 234 Heavy 21: 4 Mi-26 *Halo*; 7 SA321 *Super Frelon*; 10 Z-8 Medium 145: 50 Mi-8T *Hip*; 69 Mi-171; 8 Mi-172; 18 S-70C2 (S-70C) *Black Hawk* Light 68: 53 AS350 *Ecureuil*; 15 EC120
UAV	**ISR • Heavy** BZK-005; WZ-5 **Medium** ASN-105; ASN-206 **Light** ASN-104; W-50
Air Defence	SAM 302+:
	SP 290: 200 HQ-7A; 60 9K331 Tor-M1 (SA-15 *Gauntlet*); 30 HQ-6D *Red Leader*
	Man-portable HN-5A/HN-5B *Hong Nu*; FN-6/QW-1/ QW-2
	Guns 7,700+
	SP 25mm Type-95/Type-04; **35mm** Type-07 37mm Type-88; **57mm** Type-80
	Towed 23mm Type-80 (ZU-23-2); **25mm** Type-85; **35mm** Type-90 (GDF-002); **37mm** Type-55 (M-1939)/Type-65/Type-74; **57mm** Type-59 (S-60); **85mm** Type-56 (M-1939) KS-12; **100mm** Type-59 (KS-19)
Radar	**Land** *Cheetah*; RASIT; Type-378
	Missiles AShM HY-1 (CSS-N-2) *Silkworm*; HY-2 (CSS-C-3) *Seersucker*; HY-4 (CSS-C-7) *Sadsack*
	ASM KD-10
ARV	Type-73; Type-84; Type-85; Type-97; Type-654
	VLB KMM; MTU; TMM; Type-84A
	MW Type-74; Type-79; Type-81-II; Type-84
Reserves	
Armour	2 regiments
Infantry	18 divisions, 4 brigades, 3 independent regiments
Artillery	3 divisions, 7 brigades
Engineers	15 regiments, 1 pontoon bridge brigade, 3 pontoon bridge regiments
Anti-tank	1 brigade
Air Defence	17 divisions, 8 regiments
Logistic	8 brigades
Signals	10 regiments
Chemical	7 regiments
Combat Support	9 logistic brigades, 1 logistics regiment

Navy 215,000; 40,000 conscript (total 255,000)

North Sea Fleet	HQ Qingdao; 9 coastal defence districts **Support bases:** Qingdao (HQ), Lushun
East Sea Fleet	HQ Dongqian Lake (Ninsbo); 7 coastal defence districts; **Support Bases:** Fujian, Zhousnan, Dongqian Lake (Ninsbo)
South Sea Fleet	HQ Guangzhou; **Support Bases:** Yulin, Guangzhou, Zuanjiang

Equipment by Type

Submarines	65:
	Strategic SSBN 4: 1 *Xia* (capacity 12 JL-1 (CSS-N-3) strategic SLBM);

3 *Jin* (capacity 12 JL-2 (CSS-NX-4) strategic SLBM
Tactical 61
SSN 5:
3 *Han* (Type 091) with YJ-82 AShM, 6 single 533mm TT
2 *Shang* (Type 093) with 6 single 533mm TT (3rd vessel in build)
SSK 55:
12 *Kilo* (2 Project 877, 2 Project 636, 8 Project 636N) with 3M54 *Klub* (SS-N-27B *Sizzler*) ASCM; 6 single 533mm TT with up to 18 Test-71/96 HWT
20 *Ming* (4 Type 035, 12 Type 035G, 4 Type 035B) with 8 single 533mm TT
16 *Song* (Type 039/039G) with YJ-82 (CSS-N-8)
Saccade ASCM, 6 single 533mm TT
4 *Yuan* (Type 039A) with 6 533mm TT
3 *Yuan* II (Type 039B) with 6 533mm TT
SSB 1 Qing (SLBM trials)

Principal Surface Combatants 77

Aircraft Carrier 1 *Liaoning* (capacity 18-24 J-15 aircraft, 4 JL-9 aircraft, 17 Ka-28/Ka-31/Z-8S/Z-8JH/Z-8 AEW heptr)

Destroyers **14**
DDGHM 12:
4 *Hangzhou* (RUS *Sovremenny*) with 2 quad launcher with 3M80/3M82 *Moskit* (SS-N-22 *Sunburn*) AShM, 2 3K90 *Uragan* (SA-N-7 Grizzly) SAM, 2 twin 533mm ASTT, 2 RBU 1000 *Smerch* 3, 2 twin 130mm gun,(capacity either 1 Z-9C (AS-565SA *Panther*) helicopter or 1 Ka-28 *Helix* A heptr)
2 *Luyang* (Type 052B) with 4 quad launcher YJ-83 AShM, 2 single launcher with 3K90 *Uragan* (SA-N-7 *Grizzly*) SAM, 2 triple 324mm TT with Yu-7 LWT, 1 100mm gun, (capacity 1 Ka-28 *Helix* A hel)
2 *Luyang II* (Type 052C) with 2 quad launcher with YJ- 62 AShM, 8 sextuple VLS with HHQ-9 SAM, 2 triple 324mm TT with Yu-7 LWT, 1 100mm gun, (capacity 2 Ka-28 Helix A helicopter)
1 *Luhai* (Type 051B) with 4 quad launcher with YJ-83 AShM, 1 octuple launcher with HQ-7 SAM, 2 triple 324mm ASTT with Yu-7 LWT, 1 twin 100mm gun, (capacity 2 Z-9C (AS-565SA Panther)/Ka-28 Helix A helicopter)
2 *Luhu* (Type 052) 4 quad launcher with YJ-83 AShM, 1 octuple launcher with HQ-7 SAM, 2 triple 324mm ASTT with Yu-7 LWT, 2 FQF 2500, 1 twin 100mm gun, (capacity 2 Z-9C heptr)
DDGM 2:
2 *Luzhou* (Type 051C) with 2 quad launcher with YJ-83 (C-803) AShM; 6 sextuple VLS with SA-N-20 *Grumble* SAM, 1 100mm gun, 1 helicopter landing platform

Frigates **62**
FFGHM 29:
2 *Jiangkai* (Type 054) with 2 quad launcher with YJ-83 AShM, 1 octuple launcher with HQ-7 SAM, 2 triple 324mm TT with Yu-7 LWT, 2 RBU 1200, 1 100mm gun, (capacity 1 Ka-28 *Helix* A/Z-9C (AS-565SA *Panther)* helicopter)
13 *Jiangkai II* (Type 054A) with 2 quad launcher with YJ-83 AShM, 1 32-cell VLS with HQ-16 SAM (reported), 2 triple 324mm TT with Yu-7 LWT, 2 RBU 1200, 1 76mm gun, (capacity 1 Ka-28 *Helix* A/Z-9C (AS-565SA *Panther*) helicopter)
4 *Jiangwei I* (Type 053H2G) with 2 triple launcher withYJ-83 AShM, 1 sextuple launcher with HQ-61 (CSA-N-2)SAM, 2 RBU 1200, 1 twin 100mm gun, (capacity: 2 Z-9C (AS-565SA *Panther*) helicopter)
10 *Jiangwei II* (Type 053H3) with 2 quad launcher with YJ-83 AShM, 1 octuple launcher with HQ-7 SAM, 2 RBU 1200, 2 100mm gun, (capacity: 2 Z-9C (AS-565SA *Panther*) helicopter)

FFGH 1:
1 *Jianghu IV* (Type 053H1Q - trg role) with 1 triple launcher with SY-1 (CSS-N-1) *Scrubbrush* AShM, 4 RB 1200, 1 100mm gun, (capacity: 1 Z-9C (AS-565SA *Panther*) helicopter)
FFGM 4:
2 *Luda* III (Type 051DT) with 2 quad launcher with YJ-82/83 AShM, 1 octuple launcher with HQ-7 *Crotale* SAM, 2 FQF 2500, 2 twin 100mm guns
2 *Luda* III (Type 051G) with 2 quad launcher with YJ-82/83 AShM, 1 octuple launcher with HQ-7 *Crotale* SAM, 2 FQF 2500, 2 triple 324mm ASTT, 2 twin 100mm guns
FFG 28:
8 *Jianghu I* (Type 053H) with 2 triple launcher with SY-1 (CSS-N-1) *Scrubbrush* AShM, 4 RBU 1200, 2 100mm gun
5 *Jianghu II* (Type 053H1) with 1 triple launcher with SY-1 (CSS-N-1) *Scrubbrush* AShM, 2 RBU 1200, 1 twin 100mm gun, (capacity 1 Z-9C (AS-565SA) Panther hel)
3 *Jianghu III* (Type 053H2) with 8 YJ-1 (CSS-N-4) *Sardine* AShM, 4 RBU 1200, 2 twin 100mm gun
6 *Jianghu V* (Type 053H1G) with 1 triple launcher with SY-1 (CSS-N-1) *Scrubbrush* AShM, 2 RBU 1200, 1 twin 100mm gun
6 *Luda II* (Type 051) with 2 triple launcher with HY-2 (CSS-N-2) *Silkworm* AShM, 2 triple 324mm ASTT, 1 twin 130mm gun, (mine-laying capability)

Patrol and Coastal Combatants 211
PCFG 76
65+ *Houbei* (Type 022) with 2 quad launcher with YJ-83 (C-803) AShM
11 *Huangfen* (Type 021) with 2 twin launcher with HY-2 (CSS-N-3 *Seersucker*) AShM
PCG 26
6 *Houjian* (Type 037/II) with 2 triple launcher with YJ-1 (CSS-N-4 *Sardine*) AShM
20 *Houxin* (Type 037/IG) with 2 twin launcher with YJ-1 (CSS-N-4 *Sardine*) AShM
PCC 75
3 *Haijui* (Type 037/I) with 4 RBU 1200 (20 eff.)
50 *Hainan* (Type 037) with å4 RBU 1200 (20 eff.)
22 *Haiqing* (Type 037/IS) with 2 Type-87 (12 eff.)
PB 34 *Haizui/Shanghai III* (Type 062/I)

Mine Warfare 47
Mine Countermeasures 46
MCO 7: 6 *Wochi*; 1 *Wozang*
MSO 16 T-43
MSC 16 *Wosao*
MSD 7: 4 *Futi*-class (Type 312); 42 in reserve; 3 (other)
Minelayers 1 *Wolei*

Amphibious
Principal Amphibious Vessels **LPD** 2 *Yuzhao* (Type 071) (capacity 2 LCAC or 4 UCAC plus supporting vehicles; 500–800 troops; 2 helicopters - 2 further vessels launched)
Landing Ships 85
LSM 59:
10 *Yubei* (capacity 10 tanks or 150 troops)
1 *Yudeng* (Type 073) (capacity 6 tk; 180 troops)
10 *Yuhai* (capacity 2 tk; 250 troops)
30 *Yuliang* (Type 079) (capacity 5 tk; 250 troops)
10 *Yunshu* (Type 073A) (capacity 6 tk)
LST 26:
7 *Yukan* (capacity 10 tk; 200 troops)

	9 *Yuting* (capacity 10 tk; 250 troops; 2 hel)
	10 *Yuting II* (capacity 4 LCVP; 10 tk; 250 troops)
	Landing Craft 151
	LCU 120 *Yunnan*
	LCM 20 *Yuchin*
	LCAC 1
	UCAC 10
Logistics and Support	205:
	AORH 5: 2 *Fuqing*; 2 *Fuchi*; 1 *Nanyun;*
	AOT 50; 7 *Danlin*; 20 *Fulin*; 2 *Shengli*; 2 *Jinyou*; 18 *Fuzhou*
	AOL 5 *Guangzhou;*
	AS 8: 1 *Dazhi*; 5 *Dalang*; 2 *Dazhou*
	ASR 1 *Dajiang* with 2 SA-321 *Super Frelon;*
	ARS 2: 1 *Dadong*; 1 *Dadao;*
	AG 6: 4 *Qiongsha* (capacity 400 troops); 2 *Qiongsha* (hospital conversion);
	AK 23: 2 Yantai; 2 Dayun; 6 Danlin; 7 Dandao; 6 Hongqi
	AWT 18: 10 *Leizhou*; 8 *Fuzhou;*
	AGOR 5: 1 *Dahua*; 2 *Kan*; 1 *Bin Hai*; 1 *Shuguang;*
	AG1 1 *Dadie;*
	AGM 5 (space and missile tracking);
	AGS 6: 5 *Henlai*; 2 *Ganzhu;*
	AGB 4: 1 *Yanbing*; 3 *Yanha;*
	ABU 7 *Yannan*
	ATF 51: 4 *Tuzhong*; 10 Huiju; 1 *Daozha*; 17 *Gromovoy*; 19 *Roslavl;*
	AH 1 *Daishan*
	AX 2: 1 *Shichang*; 1 *Daxin*
	YDG 5 *Yen Pai*

Naval Aviation 26,000

<u>Forces by Role</u>	
Bomber	1 regiment with H-6DU/G; Y-8X
	1 regiment with H-6G
Fighter	1 regiment with J-7E
	1 regiment with J-81/J-8F
	1 regiment with J-7II
FGA	1 regiments with J10-AS
	1 regiment with J-11B/BS
	1 regiments with Su-30Mk2
Attack	2 regiments with JH-7
	3 regiments with JH-7A
ELINT/ Reconnaissance	1 regiment with Y-8J/Y-8JB
Maritime Patrol	1 regiment with SH-5
Transport	2 regiments with Y-8/Y-7
Training	1 regiment with HY-7/K-8
	1 regiment with HY-7/HJ-5
	1 regiment with CJ-6
	1 regiment with JJ-6/JJ-7
Helicopters	1 regiment with Mi-8; Ka-28; Ka-31
	1 regiment with AS365; Ka-28; Z-8; Z-8A/JH/S

<u>Equipment by Type</u>	
Aircraft	341 combat capable
	Bombers 30 H-6G
	Fighter 72: 24 J-7E *Fishbed*; 24 J-8F *Finback*; 24 J-8H *Finback*
	FGA 200: 120 JH-7/JH-7A; 24 J-10A/S; 4+ J-11B/BS; 24 Su-30MK2

	Flanker
	ASW 4 SH-5
	ELINT 7: 4 Y-8JB *High New* 2; 3 Y-8X
	AEW&C 6: 4 Y-8J; 2 Y-8W *High New* 5
	ISR 7 HZ-5
	Tanker 3 H-6DU
	Transport 66: **Medium** 4 Y-8 **Light** 62: 50 Y-5; 4 Y-7; 6 Y-7H; 2 Yak-42
	Training 106+: 38 CJ-6; 5 HJ-5*; 21 HY-7; 14 JJ-6*; 4 JJ-7; 12 JL-8; 12+ JL-9
Helicopters	**ASW** 44: 19 Ka-28 *Helix* A; 25 Z-9C
	AEW 10: 9 Ka-31; 1 Z-8 AEW
	SAR 6: 4 Z-8JH; 2 Z-8S
	Transport 43 **Heavy** 35: 15 SA321 *Super Frelon*; 20 Z-8/Z-8A;3 Z-8JH
	Medium 8 Mi-8 *Hip*
UAV	**ISR Heavy** BZK-005, **Medium** BZK-007
Missiles	**AAM** • IR PL-5; PL-9; R-73 (AA-11 *Archer*) **SARH** PL-11 IR/SARH R-27 (AA-10 *Alamo*) **ARH** R-77 (AA-12 *Adder*) **ASM** Kh-31A (AS-17B *Krypton*); YJ-61 (CAS-1 *Kraken*); YJ-8K (CSS-N-4 *Sardine*); YJ-83K (CSSC-8 *Saccade*)
Bombs	Conventional: Type-200-4/Type-200A
	Laser-Guided: LS-500J
	TV-Guided: KAB-500KR; KAB-1500KR

Marines ***10,000***

<u>**Forces by Role**</u>	
Army	3 (amphibious role) divisions
Marine Infantry	2 brigades (*each:* 1 special ops battalion, 1 AD battalion, 1 mechanized infantry battalion, 2 reconnaissance battalions, 2 artillery battalions, 2 tank battalions)

<u>**Equipment by Type**</u>	
Tanks	**Light tanks** 124 Type-05 AAAV (ZTD-05)
APC	**APC (T)** 248 Type-05 AAAV (ZBD-05)
Artillery	40
	Towed: 122mm Type-83; **MRL 107mm** Type-63
Anti-tank	**Missiles** HJ-73, HJ-8
Air Defence	**SAM MANPAD** HN-5 *Hong Nu/Red Cherry*

Air Force ***330,000***

The PLA Air Force (PLAAF) branches - Aviation, SAM, AAA and Airborne.

Military region air force (MRAF)	7
	13 division level command posts
Air Divisions	29 (including up to 4 regiments, each with 10-15 aircraft, 1 maintenance unit, transport and training aircraft)
Headquarters Air Force	1 air division (34th,VIP Transport) with II-76 MD, Tu-154M, B-747, CRJ200, Y8, Y7, An-30; 100th, 101st, 102nd Regiments; Air Force Flight Test Regiment
North Beijing MRAF	1 air division (7th fighter)
Northeast-Shenyang MRAF	1 air division (1st fighter)
West-Lanzhou MRAF	1 air division (6th fighter)
Centre – Ninan MRAF	1 air division (5th attack)
East-Nanjing MRAF	1 air division (3rd fighter)

South-Guangzou MRAF	1 air division (2nd fighter)
Southwest-Chengdu MRAF	1 air division (4th airlift)

Forces by Role

Bomber	1 regiment with H-6/K (with YJ-63 cruise missile)
	5 regiments with H-6A/M
Fighter	6 regiment with J-7 Fishbed
	6 regiments with J-7E *Fishbed*
	3 regiments with J-7G *Fishbed*
	1 regiment with J-8B *Finback*
	2 regiments with J-8F *Finback*
	3 regiments with J-8H *Finback*
	1 regiment with Su-27SK/UBK *Flanker*
	6 regiments with J-11/*Su-27UBK*
	4 regiment with *J-11B/BS*
Fighter/Ground Attack	3 regiments with *Su-30MKK Flanker*
	7 regiments with *J-10A/S*
	2 regiments with J-7E *Fishbed*
	2 regiments with J-8H *Finback*
Ground Attack	4 regiments with *JH-7A*
	4 regiments with *Q-5C/D/E Fantan*
Electronic Warfare	1 regiment with Y-8CB/G/XZ
	1 regiment with Y-8CB/G
ISR	1 regiment with JZ-8F *Finback*
	1 regiment with Y-8H1
Airborne EW & Control	1 regiment with KJ-200/KJ-2000/Y-8T
Combat Search & Rescue	1 regiment with Mi-171; Z-8
Tanker	1 regiment with H-6U
Transport	1 (VIP) regiment with B-737; CRJ-200/700
	1 (VIP) regiment with B-737; Tu-154M; Tu-154M/D
	1 regiment with Il-76MD *Candid B*
	3 regiments with Y-7
	1 regiment with Y-8
Training	2 regiments with H-6H
	5 regiments with CJ-6/-6A/-6B; H-5; HJ-5; Y-7; JL-8
Transport Helicopters	1 regiment with AS332 *Super Puma* (VIP)
Air Defence	3 SAM divisions
	2 mixed SAM/ADA divisions
	9 SAM brigades
	2 mixed SAM/ADA brigades
	2 ADA brigades
	9 independent SAM regiments
	1 independent ADA regiments
	4 independent SAM battalions

Equipment By Type

Aircraft	1,903 combat capable
	Bombers up to 82 H-6A/E/H/K/M
	Fighter 842: 216 J-7 *Fishbed;* 192 J-7E *Fishbed*; 120 J-7G Fishbed; 24 J-8B *Finback;* 48 J-8F *Finback;* 96 J-8H *Finback;* 95 J-11; 43 Su-27SK *Flanker;* 32 Su-27UBK *Flanker*
	FGA 543: 240 J-10A/S; 110 J-11B/BS Flanker; 120 JH-7/JH-7A; 73 Su-30MKK *Flanker*
	Anti-tank 120 Q-5C/D/E *Fantan*
	EW 13: 4 Y-8CB *High New* 1; 7 Y-8G *High New* 3; 2 Y-8XZ *High New* 7
	ELINT 4 Tu-154M/D *Careless*

	ISR 51: 24 JZ-6; 24 JZ-8 *Finback*; 3Y-8H1 **AEW&C** 8+: 4+ KJ-200; 4 KJ-2000 C2 5: 2 B-737; 3 Y-8T *High New* 4 **Tanker** 10 H-6U **Transport** 326 **Heavy** 10 Il-76MD *Candid* B Medium 40+ Y-8; **Light** 239: 170 Y-5; 41 Y-7/Y-7H; 20 Y-11; 8 Y-12 **PAX** 31: 9 B-737 (VIP); 5 CRJ-200; 5 CRJ-700; 12 Tu-154M *Careless* **Training** 950: 400 CJ-6/-6A/-6B; 50 JJ-7; 40 JL-8
Helicopters	**MRH** 22: 20 Z-9; 2 Mi-17-V5 *Hip H* **Transport** 28: **Heavy** 18+ Z-8 (SA321) **Medium** 6 AS-332 *Super Puma* (VIP); 4 *Bell* 214; 4 Mi-8 *Hip;*
UAV ISR	**Heavy** CH-1 *Chang Hong; Chang Kong* 1; *Firebee* **Light** *Harpy*
SAM	600 **SP** 300+: 24 HD-6D; 60+ HQ-7; 32 HQ-9; 24 HQ-12 (KS-1A); HQ-16; 32 S-300PMU (SA-10B *Grumble*); 64 S-300PMU1 (SA-20 *Gargoyle*); 64 S-300PMU2 (SA-20 *Gargoyle*) **Towed** 300+ HQ-2 (SA-2) *Guideline* Towed/HQ-2A/HQ-2B (A) **Guns** 16,000 100mm/85mm **Missiles AAM • IR** PL-2B‡; PL-5B/C; PL-8; R-73 (AA-11 *Archer*); **SARH** PL-11 **IR/SARH** R-27 (AA-10 *Alamo*); **ARH** PL-12; R-77 (AA-12 *Adder*) **ASM** KD-88; Kh-29 (AS-14 *Kedge*); Kh-31A/P (AS-17 Krypton); Kh-59 (AS-18 Kazoo); YJ-91 (Domestically produced Kh-31P variant) **LACM** YJ(KD)-63; CJ-10 (in development)

15th Airborne Corps	
Special Forces	1 SF unit
Reconnaissance	1 reconnaissance regiment
Air Manoeuvre	2 AB divisions (2 AB regiment; 1 artillery regiment) 1 AB division (1 AB regiment; 1 artillery regiment)
Combat Support	1 signals group
Combat Service Support	1 logistics group
Equipment	**AIFV** 130 Type-03 (ZBD-03) **Artillery** 108 **Towed** 122mm 54 Type-96 (D-30) **MRL Towed** 107mm 54 Type-63 **Mortars** 82mm **Anti-tank SP** HJ-9 *Red Arrow* 9
Cyber	*The PLA has devoted much attention to information warfare over the past decade, both in terms of battlefield EW and wider, cyber warfare capabilities. The main doctrine is the 'Integrated Network Electronic Warfare' document, which guides PLA computer network operations and calls for the combination of network warfare and EW tools at the start of a conflict in order to paralyse (or at least degrade) an opponent's C4ISR capabilities. China's cyber assets fall under the command of two main departments of the General Staff Department (GSD). Computer network attacks and EW would in theory come under the 4th Department (Electronic Countermeasures), and computer network defence and intelligence gathering comes under the 3rd Department (Signals Intelligence). The 3rd Department is supported by a variety of 'militia units' comprising both military cyber warfare personnel and civilian hackers. The PLA also has a 'Cyber Blue Team' designed to improve the PLA's 'ability to safeguard internet security.'*

Paramilitary 660,000 active

People's Armed Police ***660,000***

Internal Security ***400,000***	14 (mobile) divisions 22 (mobile) independent regiments Some fire fighting and garrison units
Border Defence ***260,000***	30 divisions HQ 110 (border) regiments 20 (marine)

Equipment by Type

Patrol and Coastal Combatants 154

PCO 16; **PB/PBF** 138

China Marine Surveillance Patrols China's EEZ

Equipment by Type

Patrol and Coastal Combatants 68

PSO 6; **PCO** 14; **PB/PBF** 48

Maritime Safety Administration (MSA)

Various tasks including aid to navigation

Equipment By Type

Patrol and Coastal Combatants 207

PB 207

Fisheries Law Enforcement Command (FLEC)

Enforces Chinese fishery regulations

Equipment by Type

Patrol and Coastal Combatants 133+

PSO 4; **PCO** 11; **PB/PBF** 118+

Ministry of Public Security

Police	*45 divisions (14 each with 4 regiments, remainder no standard organisation; 1–2 divisions per province)*
Commissars 69,000+	

UN Peacekeeping	**Observers:** Ivory Coast, Cyprus, Democratic Republic of Congo, Gulf of Aden, Lebanon, Liberia, Middle East, South Sudan, Sudan, Western Sahara, Timor-Leste
	Missions: Democratic Republic of Congo (1 engineer company; 1 field hospital); **Lebanon** (1 engineer company; 1 field hospital); **Liberia** (1 engineer company; 1 transport company; 1 field hospital); **Sudan** (2 engineer companies; 1 transport company; 1 field hospital)
	Deployment: **Gulf of Aden** – 2 FFGHM and 1 AORH

INDIA

Armed Forces **1,325,000**

Organisations by Service

Strategic Forces Command	In charge of all nuclear assets
Forces by Role	1 Missile Group with *Agni I* 1 Missile Group with *Agni II* 1 Missile Group with *Agni IIII* 2 Missile Groups with SS-150/SS-250/SS-350 *Prithvi*;
Equipment by Type **Strategic Missiles**	 **54** **ICBM** *Agni V* **IRBM** 12: 80-100 *Agni I*; 12: 20-25 *Agni-II*; *Agni III* **SRBM** 30: SS-150 *Prithvi I*/SS-250 *Prithvi* II; SS-350 *Dhanush* (naval); PJ-10 *Brahmos*. **LACM** *Nirbhay*
Space	**Satellites . ISR** 1 *Cartosat 2A*; 2 RISAT

Army 1,130,000

Forces By Role **Regional Commands**	 Northern (Udhampur) Western (Chandimandir) Central (Lucknow) Southern (Pune) Eastern (Kolkata) South Western (Jaipur)
Training Command	ARTRAC (Shimla)
Corps HQ	13; (3 strike corps, 10 holding corps)
Armoured	Three divisions (*each:* 3 armoured brigades; one SP artillery brigade with 1 medium regiment, 2 SP artillery regiments) 8 independent armoured brigades 60 armoured regiments (10 regiments each with 45 T-90S; 35 regiments each with 45 T-72M1; 8 regiments each with 45 T-55; 7 regiments each with 45 *Arjun)*
Mechanised infantry	25 battalions
Infantry	4 RAPID (Reorganised Army Plains Infantry Divisions) (*each:* one armoured brigade, one mechanised infantry brigades, two infantry brigades) 20 infantry divisions (*each:* one artillery brigade, 3-5 infantry brigades); 8 independent brigades; 14 mountain divisions (*each:* 1+ artillery brigade and 3-4 infantry brigades); 2 independent mountain brigades; 319 battalions
Special Forces / Airborne	1 independent para brigade; 8 Special Forces battalions; 5 airborne battalions
Artillery	3 divisions (*each:* 2 artillery brigade with 3 medium artillery and 1 composite SATA/MRL regiments); 15 independent artillery brigades **Medium artillery** 80 regiments

Self-Propelled medium artillery 3 regiments
Field artillery 82 regiments
Self-Propelled field artillery 3 regiments
Mountain artillery 51 regiments
Mortar 10 regiments
MRL 5 regiments
SSM 2 regiments; 1 *Agni* regiment; 1 *BrahMos* regiment

Engineers 4 brigades; 56 regiments
Helicopters 14 squadrons
Anti-tank helicopters 5 squadrons
Air Defence Artillery 8 brigades
5 regiments with 320 ZU-23-2 (some Self-Propelled)
30 regiments with 1,920 L40/70 (*each:* 4 Air Defence batteries);
12 SAM regiments; 2 groups (*each:* 2-5 SAM batteries)

Territorial Army 6 Ecological battalions
37 Departmental units (from government ministries)
25 Infantry battalions
20 Air Defence regiments with 1,280 L40/60

<u>Equipment by Type</u>

Tanks 3,274
124 *Arjun;* 715 T-55 (being retired); 1,950 T-72M1; 485 T-90S; (1,100 various models in store)

Reconnaissance 110 BRDM-2 each with AT-4 *Spigot*/AT-5 *Spandrel*; *Ferret* (used for internal security duties along with some indigenously built armoured cars)

AIFV 1,455
350 BMP-1; 980 *Sarath* (BMP-2); 125 BMP-2K
APC 649 APC (W) 157+ OT-62/OT-64; PPV 179: 165 *Casspir*; 14 *Yukthirath* MPV

Artillery 9,682
SP 20: **130mm** 20 M-46 *Catapult*; **152mm** 2S19 *Farm*
Towed 2,970+: **105mm** 1,350+: 600+ IFG Mk1/Mk2/Mk3 (being replaced); up to 700 LFG; 50 M-56 **122mm** 520 D-30; **130mm** 600 M-46; (500 in store) **155mm** 500: 300 FH-77B; 200 M-46 (upgrade)
MRL 192: **122mm** 150 BM-21/LRAR 214mm 14 *Pinaka*; **300mm** 28 9A52 *Smerch*
Mortars 6,520
SP 120mm E1
Towed 6,520: **81mm** 5,000+ E1 120mm 1,500 AM-50/E1 160mm 20 M-58 *Tampella*

Anti-tank **Missiles** SP 9K111 (AT-4 *Spigot*); 9K113 (AT-5 *Spandrel*)
Man-portable 9K11 (AT-3 *Sagger*) (being phased out); 9K111 (AT-4 *Spigot*); 9K113 (AT-5 *Spandrel*); *Milan 2*; RCL 84mm *Carl Gustav*; **106mm** 3,000+ M40A1 (10 per inf bn)

Helicopters **MRH** 232: 40 *Dhruv*; 12 *Lancer*; 120 SA315B *Lama* (*Cheetah*); 60 SA316B *Alouette III (Chetak)*

Air Defence **SAM** 3,300
SP 680: 180 2K12 *Kub* (SA-6 *Gainful*); 50+ 9K33 *Osa* (SA-8B *Gecko*); 200 9K31 *Strela-1* (SA-9 *Gaskin*); 250; 9K35 *Strela-10* (SA-13 *Gopher*)
Man-portable 2,620: 620 9K32 *Strela-2* (SA-7 *Grail* – being phased out)‡; 2,000 9K31 *Igla-1* (SA-16 *Gimlet*)
Guns 2,395
SP 155: **23mm** 75 ZSU-23-4; ZU-23-2 (truck-mounted); **30mm** 20-80 2S6 *Tunguska*
Towed 2,240: **20mm** *Oerlikon* (reported); 23mm 320 ZU-23-2; **40mm** 1,920 L40/70

UAV	**ISR Medium** 26: 14 *Nishant*; 12 *Searcher* Mk I/Mk II
Radar	**Land** 38: 14 AN/TPQ-37 *Firefinder*; BSR Mk.2; 24 *Cymbeline*; EL/M-2140; M113 A1GE *Green Archer* (mor); **MUFAR**; *Stentor*
Amphibious	2 LCVP
Missiles	**IRBM** 24: 12 *Agni* I (80-100 msl);12 *Agni-II* (20-25 msl); Agni-III **SRBM** 30: 30 SS-150 *Prithvi I*/SS-250 *Prithvi II* **LACM** 8–10 PJ-10 *BrahMos*
AEV	BMP-2; FV180
ARV	T-54/T-55; VT-72B; WZT-2; WZT-3
VLB	AM-50; BLG-60; BLG T-72; Kartik; MTU-20; MT-55;*Sarvatra*
MW	910 MCV-2

***Navy* 58,350 (including 7,000 Naval Aviation and 1,200 Marine Commandos)**

<u>Forces by Role</u>	
Commands	Fleet HQ New Delhi Western (Mumbai) Eastern (Vishakhapatnam) Southern (Kochi) Andaman & Nicobar (Port Blair)
<u>Equipment by Type</u>	
Submarines	**Tactical** 14 **SSN** 1 *Chakra* (RUS *Nerpa*) with 4 single 533mm TT with 3M54 *Klub* (SS-N-27 *Sizzler*) SLCM, 4 single 650mm TT with T-65 HWT; (RUS lease agreement) **SSK** 13 4 *Shishumar* (GER T-209/1500) with 8 single 533mm TT 4 *Sindhughosh* (FSU *Kilo*) with 6 single 533mm TT 4 *Sindhughosh* (FSU *Kilo*) with 6 single 533mm TT with 3M54 *Klub* (SS-N-27 *Sizzler*) SLCM
Principal Surface Combatants 22	
Aircraft Carriers	**CV** 1; 1 *Viraat* (UK *Hermes*) (capacity 30 *Sea Harrier* FRS Mk1 FGA aircraft each with *Sea Eagle* tactical ASM;7 Ka-27 ASW helicopter/*Sea King* MK42B ASW helicopter) **CV** 2; 1 *Vikramaditya* (Russia *Gorshkov* (capacity 24 MiG 29KFGA aircraft each with *Sea Eagle* tactical ASM;7 Ka-28 ASW / Ka-31 AEW / HAL Dhruv helicopters)
Destroyers	11 **DDGHM** 6 3 *Delhi* with 4 quad launcher with 3M-24 *Uran* (SS-N-25 *Switchblade*) AShM, 2 single launcher with 3K90 *Uragan* (SA-N-7 *Gadfly*) SAM, 5 single 533mm ASTT, 1 100mm gun, (capacity either 2 *Dhruv* helicopter /Sea King Mk42A ASW helicopter) 3 *Shivalik* with 1 octuple VLS with 3M54 *Klub* (SSN-27 *Sizzler*) ASCM, 1 octuple VLS with *Barak* SAM, 6 single launcher with 3K90 *Uragan* (SA-N-7 *Gadfly*) SAM, 1 76mm gun, (capacity 1 *Sea King* Mk42B ASW helicopter) **DDGM** 5 2 *Rajput* (FSU *Kashin*) with 2 twin launcher with R-15M *Termit* M (SS-N-2C Styx) AShM, 2 twin launcher with M-1 *Volna* (SA-N-1 *Goa*) SAM, 5 single 533mm ASTT, 2 RBU 6000 *Smerch* 2, 1 76mm gun, (capacity 1 Ka-25 *Hormone*/Ka-28 *Helix* A helicopter) 1 *Rajput* (FSU *Kashin*) with 2 twin launcher with PJ-10 *BrahMos* ASCM, 2 single launcher with R-15M *Termit* M (SS-N-2C *Styx*)

AShM, 2 twin launcher with M-1 *Volna* (SA-N-1 *Goa*) SAM, 5 single 533mm ASTT, 2 RBU 6000 *Smerch* 2, 1 76mm gun, (capacity 1 Ka-25 *Hormone*/Ka-28 *Helix* A helicopter)
2 *Rajput* (FSU *Kashin*) with 1 octuple VLS with PJ-10 *BrahMos* ASCM, 2 twin launcher with R-15M *Termit* M (SS-N-2C *Styx*) AShM, 2 octuple VLS with *Barak* SAM. 1 twin launcher with M-1 *Volna* (SA-N-1 Goa) SAM, 5 single 533mm ASTT, 2 RBU 6000 Smerch 2, 1 76mm gun, (capacity 1 Ka-25 *Hormone*/Ka-28 *Helix* A helicopter)
Frigates 12
FFGHM 11
3 *Brahmaputra* with 4 quad launcher with SS-N-25 *Switchblade* AShM, 1 octuple VLS with *Barak* SAM, 2 triple 324mm ASTT, 1 76mm gun, (capacity 2 SA316B *Alouette III (Chetak)/Sea King* Mk42 ASW helicopter)
3 *Godavari* with 4 single launcher with R-15 *Termit* M (SS-N-2D *Styx*) AShM, 1 octuple VLS with *Barak* SAM, 2 triple 324mm ASTT, 1 76mm gun, (capacity 2 SA316B *Alouette III (Chetak)/Sea King* MK42 ASW helicopter)
3 *Talwar* I with 1 octuple VLS with 3M54 *Klub* (SS-N-27 *Sizzler*) AShM, 6 single launcher with 3K90 *Uragan* (SA-N-7 *Gadfly*) SAM, 2 twin 533mm ASTT, 2 RBU 6000 *Smerch* 2, 2 CADS-N-1 *Kashtan* CIWS, 1 100mm gun, (capacity 1 *Dhruv*/Ka-31 *Helix B* AEW helicopter /Ka-28 *Helix A* ASW helicopter)
FFH 1
1 *Nilgiri* with 2 triple 324mm ASTT, 2 twin 114mm gun (capacity 1 SA316B *Alouette III (Chetak)* helicopter /*Sea King* Mk42 ASW helicopter)

Patrol & Coastal Combatants 59
Corvettes 24
FSGM 20
4 *Khukri* with 2 twin launcher with R-15M *Termit* M (SSN- 2C Styx) AShM, 2 twin launcher with 9K32M *Strela*-2M (SA-N-5 *Grail*) SAM, 1 76mm gun, 1 helicopter landing platform (For *Dhruv*/SA316 *Alouette III (Chetak)*
4 *Kora* with 4 quad launcher with 3M24 Uran (SS-N-25 *Switchblade*) AShM, 1 quad launcher with 9K32M *Strela*-2M (SA-N-5 *Grail)* SAM, 1 76mm gun, 1 hel landing platform (For *Dhruv*/SA316 *Alouette III (Chetak)*)
10 *Veer* (FSU *Tarantul*) with 4 single launcher with R-15 *Termit* M (SS-N-2D *Styx*) AShM, 2 quad launcher (manual aiming) with 9K32M *Strela*-2M (SA-N-5 *Grail*), 1 76mm gun
2 *Prabal* (mod *Veer*) each with 4 quad launcher (16 eff.) each with 3M24 *Uran* (SS-N-25 Switchblade) AShM, 1 quad launcher (manual aiming) with 9K32M Strela-2M (SA-N-5 *Grail*) SAM, 1 76mm gun
FSM 4
4 *Abhay* (FSU *Pauk II*) with 1 quad launcher (manual aiming) with 9K32M Strela-2M (SA-N-5 *Grail*) SAM, 2 twin 533mm ASTT, 2 RBU 1200, 1 76mm gun
PSOH 6 *Sukanaya* (capacity 2 HAL *Chetak*)
PCC 16: 6 *Trinkat* SDB MK 5; 5 SDB Mk 3; 10 *Car Nicobar*
PBF 8 *Super Dvora*
PB 5: 3 *Plascoa* 1300 (SPB); 2 SDB Mk 3

Mine Warfare 8
MSO 8 *Pondicherry* (FSU *Natya*)

Amphibious 17
LPD 1; *Jalashwa* (US *Austin* Class) (capacity up to 6 support helicopters); either 9 LCM or 4 LCM and 2 LCAC; 5 LCVP; 930 troops)

	LS 10
	LSM 5 *Kumbhir* (FSU *Polnocny* C) (capacity 5 MBT or 5 APC; 160 troops)
	LST 5: 2 *Magar* (capacity 15 MBT or 8 APC or 10 trucks; 500 troops; 3 *Magar* Mod (capacity 11 MBT or 8 APC or 10 trucks; 500 troops)
	Landing Craft: LCU 8 *Vasco da Gama* MK2 / 3 LC (capacity 2 APC; 120 troops)
Logistics and Support	50
	AORH 4: 1 *Aditya* (mod *Deepak*); 2 Deepak; 1 *Jyoti;*
	AOL 6
	ASR 1
	AWT 2
	AGOR 1 *Sagardhwani*
	AGHS 8 *Sandhayak;*
	AGS 1 *Makar*
	ATF 1
	AP 3 *Nicobar*
	AX 4 1 *Krishna* (UK *Leander*) 1 *Tir;* 2 AXS;
	YPT 1
	YDT 3
	YTL/YTM 15

Naval aviation 7,000

<u>**Forces by Role**</u>	
FGA	1 squadron with *Sea Harrier* FRS MK51
	1 squadron with MiG-29K *Fulcrum*
ASW	5 squadrons with Ka-31 *Helix B*; Ka-25 *Hormone;* Ka-28 (Ka-27PL) *Helix A*; *Sea King* MK42A/*Sea King* MK42B; HAL *Chetak* (SA-316B) *Alouette III*
Maritime Reconnaissance	2 squadrons with Il-38 *May*; Tu-142M *Bear F*; Do-228-201; B-2 *Defender*
Search and Rescue	1 squadron with *Sea King* MK42C; HAL *Chetak* (SA-316B) *Alouette III* (several in SAR role)
Transport	1 squadron with HAL-784M
Communications	1 squadron with Do-228
	1 squadron with HS-748M (HAL-784M)
Training	2 squadrons with HJT-16 MKI *Kiran*; HJT-16 MKII *Kiran II*; HPT-32 *Deepak*
Transport Helicopter	1 squadron with UH-3H *Sea King*
UAV	1 squadron with *Searcher* Mk II, 4 *Heron*
<u>**Equipment by Type**</u>	
Aircraft	34 combat capable
	Fighter 15 Mig-29K *Fulcrum*
	FGA 10 *Sea Harrier* FRS MK51
	ASW 9 5 Il-38 *May*; 4 Tu-142M *Bear*
	MP 14 Do-228-201
	Transport 37: 17 BN-2 *Islander*, 10 Do-228, 10 HS-748 HAL-784M
	Training 12: 6 HJT-16 MKI, 6 HJT-16 MKII *Kiran II6*
Helicopters	**AEW** 9: 9 KA-31 *Helix B*
	SAR 6: 6 *Sea King* MK42C
	MRH 53: 4 Dhruv; 26 SA316B *Alouette III (Chetak)*; 23SA319 *Alouette III*
	Utility 49; *Dhruv* ALH, 6 HAL *Chetak* (SA-316B), 25 *Alouette III*; (some in SAR role)
UAV	12: 8 *Searcher* Mk II, 4 *Heron*

Missiles	**ASM**: *Sea Eagle*; KH-35/*Sea Skua* **AAM**: R-550 *Magic 2*/R-550 *Magic* tactical AAM
Marines	1,200; Amphibious 1 brigade; Commando 1 (marine) force *Sagar Prahari Bal* (SPB) newly raised

Air Force *127,200*

Air Commands	Western (New Delhi) Central (Allahabad) Southern (Trivandrum) Eastern (Shillong) South Western (Gandhinagar) Training (Bangaluru) Maintenance (Nagpur)
Forces by Role	
Fighter	3 squadrons with MiG-29B *Fulcrum*, MiG-29UB *Fulcrum*
FGA	4 squadrons with *Jaguar* IB/IS 8 squadrons with MiG-21bis/*Bison* 3 squadrons with MiG-21M/MF *Fishbed* 6 squadrons with MiG-27ML *Flogger* 9 squadrons with Su-30 MK1 *Flanker* 3 squadrons with M-2000H (M-2000E) *Mirage*
Maritime attack	1 squadron with *Jaguar* S (I) with *Sea Eagle* ASM
AEW/AWACS	1 squadron with IL-76 TD *Phalcon*
Reconnaissance	1 squadron with Gulfstream IV
Transport	1 squadron with C-130J *Super Hercules* 5 squadrons with An-32 *Cline* 1 squadron with B-737; B-737BBJ; EMB-145BJ 4 squadrons with Do-228; HS-748 2 squadrons with Il-76 *Candid*
Tankers	1 squadron with Il-78 *Midas*
Attack helicopters	2 squadrons with Mi-25 *Hind D*/Mi-35 *Hind*
Helicopters	4 squadrons with ALH *Dhruv* 8 squadrons with Mi-8 *Hip* 6 squadrons with MI-17 *Hip H*/ Mi-17 IV 1 squadron with 10 Mi-26 *Halo* 1 squadron with Mi-26 (Halo) 3 squadrons with HAL *Cheetah* (SA-315B) Lama 5 squadrons with HAL *Chetak* (SA-315B)
Training	1 squadron with *Tejas* some squadrons with HJT-16 MKI *Kiran*; HPT-32 *Deepak*; MiG-21; Mig-21bis; Mig-21M/MF; Mig-21FL; Mig—27Ml; Mig-23BN; Jaguar IS/2-IM; *Hawk* Mk132 AJT 56
UAV	5 squadrons with *Searcher* MK II
SAM	25 squadrons with S-123M *Pechora* (SA-3B) *Goa* 6 squadrons with OSA-AK (SA-8B *Gecko*) 2 squadrons with *Akash* 10 flt with SA-18 *Gimlet*
Equipment by Type	
Aircraft	870 combat aircraft **Fighter** 63: 57 MiG-29 *Fulcrum*; 7 MiG-29UB *Fulcrum*; FGA 698: 14 *Jaguar* IB; 82 *Jaguar* IS; 10 *Jaguar* IM; 31 *MiG-21bis*; 119 MiG-21 *Bi-son*; 54 MiG-21M *Fishbed*; 16 MiG-21MF *Fishbed*; 40 MiG-21U/UM *Mon-gol*; 127 MiG-27ML *Flogger* J2; 40 *Mirage* 2000E (2000H) **AEW&C:** 3 IL-76 TD *Phalcon* **Reconnaissance:** 3 *Gulfstream* IV SRA-4

Tanker: 6 IL-78 *Midas*
Transport 238: 24 Il-76 Candid; 105 An-32 Cline; 6 B-707; 4 B-737; 20 BAe-748; 51 Do-228; 4 EBM-135BJ
PAX 33: 6 B-707; 4 B-737; 3 B-737bBJ; 20 HS-748
Training 241: 36 Hawk Mk 132AJT; 120 HJT-16 MKI; 56 HJT-16 MKII Kiran II

Helicopters
Anti-Tank: 20 Mi-25 *Hind D*/Mi-35 *Hind*
Support 210; 0 *Dhruv*; 4 Mi-26 Halo (Hy Tpt); 102 Mi-8, 72 Mi-17 (Mi-8 MT) Hip H; 60 HAL *Cheetah* (SA-315B) *Lama* SA-315; 48 HAL *Chetak* (SA-316B) *Alouette* III

UAV
some *Searcher* MK II

Air Defence
SAM S-125 *Pechora* (SA-3B) *Goa*
SP 9K33 Osa-AK (SA-8B) *Gecko*
Man-portable 9K310 *Igla-1* (SA-16 *Gimlet*)

Missiles
ASM AM-39 *Exocet*; AS-11; AS-11B (ATGW); AS-12 *Kegler*; AS-17 *Krypton*; As-30; AS-7 *Kerry*; *Sea Eagle*
ARM AS-11; AS-11B (ATGW); AS-12 *Kegler*; AS-17 *Krypton*
AAM AA-10 *Alamo*; AA-11 *Archer*; AA-12 *Adder*; AA-7 *Apex*; AA-8 *Aphid*; R-550 *Magic*; Super 530D

Coast Guard 9,550
(under Director General – Ministry of Defence)

Regional Commands
Mumbai, Chennai, Port Blair (11 districts)

Forces by Role
Air
9 squadrons

Equipment by Type
Patrol & Coastal Combatants
76
PSOH 12: 2 *Sankalp*; 4 *Samar*; 3 *Samudra*, 3 *Vishwas*
PCO 7 *Vikram*
PCC 23: 8 *Priyadarshini*; 3 *Rajshree* (additional vessels in build);; 1 *Rani Abbakka* (additional vessels in build); 7 *Sarojini-Naidu*
PCF 2 *Cochin*
PBF 13 *Interceptor*
PB 19: 3 *Jija Bai* (mod) 1; 6 *Tara Bai*; 10 (various)
Amphibious UCAC 6 *Griffon* 8000

Aircraft
Transport 24: 24 Do-228

Helicopters
Utility SA-316 17: 17 HAL *Chetak* (SA-316B) *Alouette*

Cyber
National agencies include the Computer and Emergency Response Team (CERT-In), which has authorised designated individuals to carry out penetration tests against infrastructure. The Defence Information Assurance and Research Agency (DIARA) is mandated to deal with cyber-security related issues of the armed services and defence ministry. All services have their own cyber security policies, and headquarters maintain information security policies. In 2005, the Indian Army raised the Army Cyber Security Establishment and in April 2010 set up the Cyber Security Laboratory at the Military College of Telecommunications Engineering in Mhow (under the Corps of Signals). There is no Indian national cyber security strategy.

Rashtriya Rifles 65,000
(Ministry of Defence)
60 battalions (in 20 Sector HQ)

Paramilitary ***1,300,600***

Assam Rifles	64,000; Ministry of Home Affairs 7 HQ; 42 battalions
Border Security Force 230,000; (Ministry of Home Affairs)	170 battalions Small arms, light artillery, some anti-tank weapons **Artillery: Mortars** 942 81 mm **Aircraft**: some transport (air support)
Central Industrial Security Force (Ministry of Home Affairs)	94,350 (lightly armed security guards only) Guards public-sector locations
Central Reserve Police Force (Ministry of Home Affairs)	230,000 Internal security duties, only lightly armed, deployable throughout the country 2 Mahila (women) battalions 125 battalions 13 rapid action force battalions

Defence Security Corps **31,000** provides security at Defence Ministry sites

Indo-Tibetan Border Police (Ministry of Home Affairs)	36,300 Tibetan border security SF/guerrilla warfare and high altitude warfare specialists 30 battalions
National Security Guards **7,350**	Anti-terrorism contingency deployment force, comprising elements of the armed forces, CRPF and Border Security Force
Special Protection Group **3,000**	Protection of ministers and senior officials
Railway Protection Force **70,000**	
Shastra Seema Bal **31,554**	Guards Indo-Nepal/Bhutan borders
Special Frontier Force **10,000**	Mainly ethnic Tibetans
State Armed Police **450,000**	For duty primarily in home state only Some battalions with infantry weapons and equipment 24 (India Reserve Police; Commando-trained) battalions

Reserve organisations

Civil Defence 500,000	Fully trained in 225 towns in 32 states Some units for NBC defence
Home Guards	487,821 reservists (actual) (515,000 authorised) In all states except Arunachal Pradesh and Kerala; men on lists, no training. Not usually armed in peacetime -weapons held in state armouries. Used for civil defence, rescue and fire-fighting teams in wartime.

Paramilitary special battalions 6 battalions to protect tea plantations in Assam

Foreign Missions

Afghanistan
(2 companies ITBP for protection for road construction project)
Arabian Gulf and Indian Ocean
(2 FFG on maritime security operations)
Tajikistan
(Forward Operating Base) Farkhar

UN Missions

Observers
(Ivory Coast, Democratic Republic of Congo, Sudan, Timor-Leste, Lebanon, Syria/Israel, Tajikistan)

Peace Keeping
Democratic Republic of Congo (3 mechanised infantry battalions; 1 infantry battalion; 1 helicopter unit; 1 field hospital) Lebanon (1 infantry battalion; 1 field hospital)
South Sudan (1 infantry battalion; 1 engineer company; 1 aviation unit; 1 transport company; 1 field hospital)

INDONESIA

Armed Forces 302,000 Army 300,400; Navy 65,000; Air Force 30,100
Paramilitary 281,000; Reserves 400,000

Organisations by Service

Army 300,400

Military Area Commands 13 (*KODAM*)

Forces by Role

Mechanised	3 armoured cavalry battalions
	6 cavalry battalions
Light	1 infantry brigade (1 cavalry & 3 infantry battalions)
	2 infantry brigades (1 commando & 2 infantry battalions)
	5 infantry brigades (3 infantry battalions)
Infantry	45 battalions
	8 commando battalions
Field Artillery	12 battalions
Engineers	7 battalions
Aviation	1 composite aviation squadron
Helicopters	1 squadron
Air Defence	6 battalions
	3 SAM units
Combat Service Support	4 construction battalions

Special Forces Command (*KOPASSUS*) 5, 000
3 groups (*total:* 2 commando/parachute units, 1 counter-terrorist unit (Unit 81), 1 training unit, 1 intelligence unit

Strategic Reserve Command	(*KOSTRAD*) 40,000
Armoured	2 armoured cavalry battalions
Infantry	2 division HQ
	3 brigades (3 commando & 5 infantry battalions);
Airborne	3 brigades (3 AB battalions)
Field Artillery	2 regiments (6 battalions)
Air Defence	2 battalions
Engineers	2 battalions

Equipment by Type

Light tanks	**350**: 275 AMX-13 (being upgraded); 15 PT-76; 60 Scorpion 90
Reconnaissance	**142:** 55 Ferret (13 upgraded); 69 Saladin (16 upgraded); 18 VBL
Armoured Fighting Vehicles	22 BMP-2
	APC 541: **APC (T)** 90: 75-AMX-VCI; 15 FV433 *Stormer*
	APC (W) 459: 14 APR-1; 150 *Anoa*; 22 *Black Fox*; 40 BTR-40; 34 BTR-50PK; 22 *Commando Ranger*; 45 FV603 *Saracen*; 60 LAV-150 *Commando;* 32 VAB-VTT
Artillery	1079
	Towed 115: **105mm** 110; KH-178 60 M-101; 50 M-56; **155mm** 5 FH-88
	Mortars 955: **81mm** 800; **120mm** 135: 75 Brandt; 80 UBM 52
	MLR 70mm 9 NDL-40
Anti-Tank	**Missiles** SS-11; 100 *Milan*; 9M14M (AT-3 *Sagger*)

	Recoilless 135: **106mm** M-40 45: 45 M-40A1; **90mm** 90: M-67
Rocket launcher	**89mm** 700: 700 LRAC
Aircraft	**Transport** 9: 1 BN-2A *Islander*; 6 NC-212 (CASA 212) *Aviocar*; 2 Rockwell *Turbo Commander* 680
Helicopters	**Anti-tank**: 6 Mi-35 Hind
	Support 16 Mi-17 *Hip*
	Utility 30: 12 Bell 412 *Twin Huey*; 18 Mi-17V5 *Hip*
	Training 12 Hughes 300C
Air Defence	**Missiles**
	SP 2 Kobra (125 GROM-2); TD-2000B *Giant Bow* II
	Towed 93; 51 *Rapier*; 42 RBS-70413
	Man-portable QW-3
	Guns .Towed 411: **20mm** 121 Rh 202; **23mm** *Giant Bow*; **40mm** 90 L/70; **57mm** 200 S-60
ARV	9: 2 AMX-13; 6 AMX-VCI; 3 BREM-2; *Stormer*; T-54/T-55
VLB	12: 10 AMX-13; *Leguan*; 2 *Stormer*

Navy 65, 000

Eastern Fleet	HQ located at Surabaya; 13 bases
Western Fleet	HQ located at Teluk Ratai (Jakarta); 10 bases
Commands	Riau (West); Papua (East); Makassar (Central)
Forward Operating Bases	1 Kupang (West Timor); 1 Tahuna (North Sulawesi)

Equipment by Type

Submarines	**Tactical** SSK 2: 2 *Cakra* each with 8 single 533mm TT with 14 SUT HWT
Principal Surface Combatants	11
Frigates	**FFGHM** 7
	6 *Ahmad Yani* each with 2 Mk-141 Harpoon quad (8 eff.) each with RGM-84A *Harpoon* tactical SSM, 2 SIMBAD twin manual each with *Mistral* SAM, 2 triple 324mm ASTT (6 eff.) each with Mk 46 LWT, 1 76mm gun, (capacity either 1 HAS-21 *Wasp* ASW helicopter or 1 NBo-105 (Bo-105) utility helicopter)
	1 *Hajar Dewantara* (training) with 2 twin (4 eff.) each with MM-38 *Exocet* tactical SSM, 2 single 533mm ASTT each with SUT HWT, (capacity 1 NBo-105 (Bo-105) utility helicopter)
	FFGM 4
	4 *Sigma* each with 2 *Tetral* quad (8 eff.) *Mistral* SAM, each with 4 MM-40 *Exocet* Block II tactical SSM, 2 triple 324mm ASTT (6 eff.) 176mm gun, 1 helicopter landing platform
Patrol & Coastal Combatants	72
Corvettes	19
	FSGH 1
	1 *Nala* with 2 twin launcher with MM-38 Exocet AShM, 1 twin 375mm A/S mor, 1 120mm gun (capacity 1 lt helicopter)
	FSG 2
	2 *Fatahillah* each with 2 twin launcher with MM-38 *Exocet* tactical SSM, 2 B515 ILAS-3/Triple 324mm ASTT (2-6 eff.) with 12 A 244 / Mk 46, 1 2 tube *Bofors* 375mm (2 eff.) 1 120 mm gun
	FSM 16
	16 *Kapitan Patimurat* each with 4x1 400mm ASTT, Twin each with SA-N-5 *Grail* SAM 2 RBU 6000 *Smerch* 2(24 eff.), 1 57mm gun
	PCFG 4 *Mandau* each with 4 MM-38 Exocet tactical SSM
	PCT 4 Singa each with 2 Single 533mm TT
	PCC 4 *Kakap*; 4 *Todak*
	PBG 4

	2 *Clurit* with 2 twin launcher with C-705 AShM
	2 *Waspada* with 2 twin launcher with MM-38 *Exocet* AShM
	PB 33 *1 Cucut*; 13 *Kobra*; 1 *Krait*; 8 *Sibarau*; 10 *Viper*
Mine Warfare	11
	MCO 2 *Pulau Rengat*
	MSC 9*Palau Rote*
Amphibious	**LPD** 5**:** 1 *Dr Soeharso* (Ex-*Tanjung Dalpele*; capacity 2 LCU/LCVP; 13 tanks; 500 troops); 4 *Makassar* (capacity 2 LCU / LCVP; 13 tank; 500 troops; 2 AS332L *Super Puma*
	LST 26: 1 *Teluk Amboina* (capacity 16 tanks; 200 troops); 12 *Teluk Gilimanuk*; 7 *Teluk Langsa* (capacity 16 tanks; 200 troops); 6 *Teluk Semangka* (capacity 17 tanks); 200 troops)
	Craft: 54 LCU
Logistics and Support	32
	AGF 1 *Multatuli*
	AORLH 1 Arun (UK Rover)
	AOT 3: 2 *Khobi*; 1 *Sorong*
	AKSL 4
	AGOR 7: 5 *Baruna Jaya*; 1 *Jalanidhi*; 1 *Burujulsad*
	AGHS 1
	ATF 2
	AXS 2 (Training)
	AP 8: 1 *Tanjung Kampani* (troop transport); 1 *Tanjung Nusanive* (troop transport); 5 *Karang Pilang* (troop transport)
	YTM 3

Marines ***20,000***

Forces by Role	
Special Forces	1 battalion
Amphibious	2 marine groups (1 cavalry regiment, 3 marine battalions, 1 artillery regiment, 1 combat support regiment, 1 CSS regiment)
	1 marine brigade (3 battalions)

Equipment by Type	
Tanks	**Light tanks 55**: 55 PT-76
Reconnaissance	21 BRDM
AIFV	83**:** 24 AMX-10P; 10 AMX-10 PAC 90; 37 BM-3F; 12 BTR-80A
APC (W)	100 BTR-50P
Artillery	59
	Towed 50 **105mm** 22 LG1 MK II **122mm** 28 M-38
MRL	**122mm** 9 RM-70
Mortars	**81mm**
Air Defence	**Guns 150: 40mm** L/60/L/70, **57mm** S-60

Naval Aviation *1,000*

Equipment by Type	
Aircraft	**MP** 23: 3 CN-235 MPA; 14 N-22B *Searchmaster* B; 6 N-22SL *Searchmaster* L
	Transport 28; 21 C 212-200 *Aviocar*, 2 DHC-5 *Buffalo*, 3 TB-9 *Tampico*, 2 TB-10 *Tobago*
Helicopters	**ASW 9**: HAS-1 *Wasp*
	Support 6 AS-332, 6 NAS-322L *Super Puma*
	Utility 28; 9 EC-120B *Colibri*; NB-Bell 412, 2 *Twin Huey*, 17 NBO-105

Air Force 30,100

Operational Commands	2: East and West; plus Training Command
<u>Forces By Role</u>	
Fighter	1 squadron with F-5E *Tiger* II; F-5F *Tiger* II 1 squadron with F-16A/B *Fighting Falcon*
FGA	1 squadron with Su-30 MKI *Flanker* (multi-role); Su-27SK *Flanker* 3 squadrons with *Hawk* MK109; *Hawk* MK209
Ground Attack	1 squadron with EMB-314 (A-29) *Super Tucano*
Maritime Reconnaissance	1 squadron with B-737-200
Transport	1 VIP squadron with B-707; *Cessna* 401; *Cessna* 402; F-28-1000; F-28-3000; L-100-30; SC.7 3M *Skyvan* (survey); 4 *Cessna* 207 *Stationair* 1 squadron with C-130H/H-30 *Hercules* L-100-30 1 squadron with C-212 (NC 212) *Aviocar* 1 squadron with F-27-400M *Troopship*; CN-235-M
Tanker	1 squadron with KC-130B *Hercules*
Training	3 squadrons with AS-202 *Bravo*; SF-260M/SF-260W *Warrior*; T-34C *Turbo Mentor*
Helicopter	2 squadrons with S-58T; NAS-322L (AS-332L) *Super Puma* (VIP/CSAR); NAS-330 (SA-330) *Puma* (1 NAS-330SM VIP); EC-120B *Colibri*
<u>Equipment By Type</u>	
Aircraft	69 combat capable
Fighter	22: 12 F-5; 8 F-5E *Tiger* II; 4 F-5F *Tiger* II; 7 F-16A *Fighting Falcon*; 3 F-16B *Fighting Falcon*
Fighter Ground Attack	10: 2 Su-27SK *Flanker*; 3 Su-27SKM *Flanker*; 2 Su-27MK *Flanker*
Maritime Patrol	5: 3 B-737-200; 2 CN-235M-220 MPA
Tanker	1 KC-130B *Hercules*
Transport	40: **Medium** 15: 4 C-130B *Hercules*; 3 C-130H *Hercules*; 6 C-130H-30 *Hercules*; 2 L-100-30; **Light** 19: 2 CN-295; 2 C-212 *Aviocar*; 5 CN-235-110; 6 F-27-400M Troopship; **PAX** 5: 1 B-737-200; 1 B-737-800BBJ; 1 F-28-1000; 2 F-28-3000;
Utility	6: 2 *Cessna* 172; 4 *Cessna* 207 *Stationair*
Training	118: 39 AS-202 *Bravo*; *Hawk* MK53 7 KT-1 7: 7 KT-1B SF-260 19: 19 SF-260M/SF-260W *Warrior* T-34 20: 20 T-34C *Turbo Mentor* T-41
Helicopters	**SAR** 10: 10 S-58T **Support** 16; AS-332 5: 5 NAS-322L (AS-332L) *Super Puma* (VIP/CSAR) NAS-330 (SA-330) *Puma* 11 (1 NAS-330SM VIP) **Utility** EC-120 12: 12 EC-120B *Colibri*
Missiles	**Tactical ASM**; AGM-65 *Maverick* **AAM** AIM-9: AIM-9P *Sidewinder*; **SARH** R-27 (AA-10 *Alamo*); **ARM** Kh-31P (AS-17A *Krypton*)
Special Forces (Paskhasau)	3 Wings (6 Special Operations squadrons) 4 independent companies

Paramilitary 280,000 active

Naval Auxiliary Service

Patrol & Coastal Combatants	71: **PCC** 65 *Kal Kangen*; **PCI** 6 *Carpentaria*

Customs

Patrol & Coastal Combatants	65: **PBF** 15; **PB** 50

Marine Police

Patrol and Coastal Combatants	37: **PSO** 2 *Bisma*; **PCC** 14 *Bango*; **PBF** 3 *Gagak*

Police 280,000 (including 14,000 Police mobile brigade (BRIMOB) organised in 56 companies, including Counter terrorism unit (Gegana)

Equipment By Type

APC (W)	34 *Tactica*
Aircraft	Transport 5: 2 *Beech* 18; 2 NC-212 (CASA-212) *Aviocar*; 1 Rockwell *Turbo Commander* 680
Helicopters Utility	22: 3 Bell 206 JetRanger; 19 NBO-105 (BO-105)

KPLP (Coast and Seaward Defence Command)
Responsible to Military Sea Communications Agency

Equipment By Type

Patrol & Coastal Combatants	**11**; **PCO** 2 *Arda Dedali* **PB** 9: 4 *Golok* (SAR); *5 Kujang*
Logistics and Support	**ABU** 1 *Jadayat*
Reserve Organizations	**Kamra People's Security** 40,000 (report for 3 weeks; basic training each year; part time police auxiliary)
UN Missions	**Observers:** Georgia, Lebanon, Liberia, Nepal, Sudan, Democratic Republic of Congo, Haiti **Units:** Democratic Republic of Congo (1 engineer coy), Lebanon (1 infantry battalion, 1 MP company, 1 field hospital)

IRAN

***Armed Forces* 523,000 (Army 350,000 Islamic Revolutionary Guard Corps 125,000 Navy 18,000 Air 30,000) Paramilitary 40,000**

Armed Forces General Staff coordinates two parallel organisations: the regular armed forces and the Revolutionary Guard Corps

Reserves 350,000 **(Army 350,000, ex-service volunteers)**

Army 130,000	220,000 conscript (total 350,000)

Forces by Role

5 corps-level regional HQ	1 commando division 4 armoured divisions 2 mechanised divisions 4 infantry divisions
Special Forces	1 commando division (3 commando brigades) 6 commando brigades 1 Special Forces brigade
Armoured	7 armoured brigades
Mechanised	16 mechanised brigades
Light	13 infantry brigades
Air Manoeuvre	1 AB brigade
Aviation	Some aviation groups
Artillery	5 artillery groups

Equipment by Type
Totals include those held by IRGC Ground Forces.
Some equipment serviceability in doubt

Tanks	**MBT** 1,663+; 150 *Zulfiqar;* 480 *T-72Z;* 150 M60A1; 75+ T-62; *100 Chieftain* Mk3/Mk5; 540 *T-54/T-55/Type-59/Safir-74; 168* M47/M48 **Light Tanks** 80+: 80 *Scorpion; Towsall* RECCE 35 EE-9 *Cascavel* **AIFV** 610: 210 BMP-l; 400 BMP-2 with 9Klll *Fagot* (AT-II *Spigot)* **APC** 640+: **APC (T)** 340+: 140 *Boragh* with 9Kll1 *Fagot* (AT-4 *Spigot);* 200 M 113; BMT-2 *Cobra* **APC (W)** 300+: 300 BTR-50/BTR-60; *Rakhsh*
Artillery	8,798+ **SP** 292+: 122mm 60+: 60 2S1 *Carnation; Raad-l (Thunder* 1) 155mm 150+: 150 M109; *Raad-2 (Thunder* 2) 170mm 30 M-1978; 175mm 22 M107; 203mm 30 M110 **Towed** 2,030+; 105mm 150: 130 M101A1; 20 M-56; 122mm 640: 540 D-30; 100 Type-54 (M-30) M-1938, 130mm 985 M-46; 152mm 30 D-20; 155mm 205: 120 GHN-45; 70 M114; 15 Type-88 WAC-21; 203mm

	20 M115, MRL 1,476+: 107mm 1,300: 700 Type-63; 600 HASEB *Fadjr* 1; 122mm 157: 7 BM-11; 100 BM-21; 50 *Arash/Hadid/Noor;* 240mm 19: 10 *Fadjr* 3; 9 M-1985; 330mm *Fadjr 5* **Mortars** 5,000: 60mm; 81mm; 82mm; 107mm M-30; 120mm M-65
Anti-tank	**Missiles • Man-portable** 9K11 *Malyutka* (AT-3 *Sagger/I-Raad),* 9K111 *Fagot* (AT-4 *Spigot);* 9K113 *Konkurs* (AT-5 *Spandral/ Towsan-1); Saeqhe* 1; *Saeqhe* 2; *Toophan;.Toophan* 2 **RCL** 200+: 75mm M-20; 82mm B-10; 106mm 200 M-411, 107mm B-11
Aircraft	**Transport** 17 Light 16: 10 Cessna 185; 2 F-77 *Friendship;* 4 *Turbo Commander* 690 PAX 1 *Falcon 20*
Helicopters	**Anti-tank** 50 AH-IJ *Cobra* **Transport** 173: Heavy 20 CH-47C *Chinook;* Medium 25 Mi-171, Light 128: 68 Bell 205A (AB-205A); 10 Bell 206 *Jet Ranger* (AB-206); 50 Bell 214
UAV	**ISR** Medium *Mohajer* 3/4; Light *Mohajer* 2; *Ababil*
Air Defence	**SAM SP** 10+: HQ-7; 10 *Pantsyr* S-1E (SA-22) *Greyhound)* **Man-portable** 9K36 *Strela-3* (SA-14 *Gremlin);* 9K32 *Strela-2* (SA-7 Grail) *Misaq* 1 (QW-1 *Vanguard); Misaq* 2 (QW *11); Igla-S* (SA-24 *Grinch*); HN-54 **Guns** 1,122; **SP** 180: 23mm 100 ZSU-23-4; 57mm 80 ZSU-57-2 **Towed** 942 14.5mm ZPU-2; ZPU-4; 23mm 300 ZU- 23-2; 35mm 92 *Skyguard;* 37mm M-1939; 40mm 50 L/70; 57mm 200 S-60; 85mm 300M1939 **Missiles • Tactical** SSM 30 CSS-8 (175 msl); *Shahin-1/Shahin-2; Nazeat; Oghab*
ARV	20+: BREM-1; 20 *Chieftain* ARV; M578; *T-54/55* ARV
VLB	15: 15 *Chieftain* AVLB
MW	*Taftan 1*

***Iranian Revolutionary Guard Corps* 125,000+**

Iranian Revolutionary Guard Corps Ground Forces 100,000+

Controls *Basij* paramilitary forces. Lightly manned in peacetime. Primary role: internal security; secondary role: external defence, in conjunction with regular armed forces.

<u>**Forces By Role**</u>

Command	31 provincial corps HQ (2 in Tehran)
Manoeuvre	31 independent brigades (each brigade allocated 10 Basij militia battalions for operations

Iranian Revolutionary Guard Corps Naval Forces 20,000+ (including 5,000 Marines)

<u>**Forces by Role**</u>

Combat Support	Some artillery batteries Some AShM batteries with HY-2 (CSS-C-3 *Seersucker*)

Equipment by Type

In addition to the vessels listed the IRGC operates a substantial number of patrol boats with a full-load displacement below 10 tonnes, including 40 *Boghammar*-class vessels and small *Bavar*-class wing-in-ground effect air vehicles

Patrol and Coastal Combatants 113

PBFG 46: 5 *China Cat* with 2 twin lnchr with C-701/*Kosar* AShM
10 *Thondor* (PRC *Houdong*) with 2 twin lnchr with C-802 (CSS-N-8 *Saccade*) AShM
25 *Peykaap II* (IPS-16 mod) with 2 single lnchr with C-701 (*Kosar*) AShM
6 *Zolfaghar* (*Peykaap* III/IPS-16 mod) with 2 single lnchr with C-701 (*Kosar*)/C-704 (*Nasr*) AShM
PBF 35: 15 *Peykaap I* (IPS -16); 10 *Tir* (IPS 18); £10 *Pashe* (MIG-G-1900)
PB 20 *Ghaem*
PTG 12

Amphibious — **Landing Ships** 4
2 *Hejaz* (mine-laying capacity)
2 MIG-S-5000

Logistics and Support — **AP** 3 *Naser*

Missiles — **Tactical** AShM C-701 (*Kosar*); C-704 (*Nasr*); C-802; HY-2 (CSS-C-3 *Seersucker*)

Iranian Revolutionary Guard Corps Marines 5,000+

Forces by Role

Manoeuvre — **Amphibious** 1 marine brigade

Iranian Revolutionary Guard Corps Air Force

Controls Iran's strategic missile force

Forces by Role

Missile — 1 brigade with *Shahab*-l/2
1 battalion with Shahab-3; *Ghadr-l; Sajjil*-2

Equipment by Type

Missile — **Tactical MRBM** 12+: 12+ *Shahab-3/Ghadr-l*; *Sajjil-2*
SRBM 18+: some *Fateh* 110; 12-18 *Shahab-l*/2 (200-300)
SSM Some *Zelzal*

Navy 18,000 — HQ at Bandar-e Abbas

Equipment by Type

In addition to the vessels listed the Iranian Navy operates a substantial number of patrol boats with a full-load displacement below 10 tonnes.

Submarines 29

Tactical 21:
SSK 3 Kilo (RUS Type 877EKM) with 6 single 533mm IT
SSC 1 *Fateh*
SSW 17: 16 *Qadir* with 2 single 533mm IT: 1 *Nahang*
SDV 8: 5 *Al Sabehat* (SF insertion and mine-laying capacity); 3 other

Patrol and Coastal Combatants	69 (+ 50 small craft under 10 tonnes) **Corvettes** 6: **FSGM** 3 *Jamaran* (UK Vosper Mk 5) with 2 twin lnchr with CSS-N-4 *Sardine* AShM, 2 lnchr with SM-l SAM, 2 triple 324mm ASIT, 1 76mm gun, 1 hel landing platform **FSG** 4 3 *Alvand* (UK Vosper Mk 5) with 2 twin lnchr with CSS-N-4 *Sardine* AShM, 2 triple 324mm ASIT, 1 114mm gun 1 *Bayandor* (US PF-103) with 2 twin lnchr with C-802 AShM, 2 triple 324rnm ASIT, 2 76mm gun **FS** 1 Bayandor (US PF-I03) with 2 76mm gun **PCFG** 14 *Kaman* (FRA *Combattante* II) with 1-2 twin lnchr with C-802 AShM **PBFG** 8: 4 Mk13 with 2 single lnchr with C-704 (*Nasr*) AShM, 2 single 324 mm TT 4 *China Cat* with 2 single lnchr with C-701 (*Kosar*) AShM **PBF** 16: 15 *Kashdom* II; 1 MI55 **PB** 22: 3 *Kayvan*; 6 MkII; 10 MkIII; 3 *Parvin* **PTF** 3 *Kajami* (semi-submersible)
Mine Warfare	**Mine Countermeasures** 5: **MSC** 3: 2 Type-292; 1 *Shahrokh* (in Caspian Sea as trg ship) **MSI** 2 *Riazi* (US *Cape*)
Amphibious	**Landing Ships** 13: **LSM** 3 *Farsi* (ROK) (capacity 9 tanks; 140 troops) **LST** 4 *Hengam* (capacity 9 tanks; 225 troops) **LSL** 6 *Fouque*
Landing Craft	10: **LCAC** 7: 6 *Wellington*; 1 *Iran* **LCT** 2 **LCU** 1 *Liyan* 110
Logistics and Support	47 **AB** 12 *Hendijan* (also used for coastal patrol) **AE** 2 *Delvar* **AFD** 2 *Dolphin* **AG** 1 *Hamzah* AK 3 *Delvar* **AORH** 3: 2 *Bandar Abbas*; 1 *Kharg* **AWT** 5: 4 *Kangan*; 1 *Delvar* **AX** 2 *Kialas* **YTB** 17
Missiles • Anti-ship	C-701 (*Kosar*); C-704 (Nasr); C-802/A (*Noor*/ *Ghader*); *Ra'ad* (coastal defence)

Marines 2,600

Forces by Role

Manoeuvre Amphibious	2 marine brigades

Naval Aviation **2,600**

Equipment by Type

Aircraft	3 combat capable **ASW** 3 P-3F *Orion* **Transport** 16 Light 13: 5 00-228; 4 F-27 *Friendship;* 4 *Turbo Commander* 680 PAX 3 *Falcon* 20 (ELINT)
Helicopters	**ASW** 10 SH-3D *Sea King* MCM 3 RH-53D *Sea Stallion* **Transport • Light** 17: 5 Bell 205A (AB-205A); 2 Bell 206 *JetRanger* (AB-206); 10 Bell 212 (AB-212)

Air Force 30,000 (including 12,000 Air Defence)

Forces by Role

Serviceability probably about 60% for US aircraft types and about 80% for PRC/Russian aircraft. Includes IRGC Air Force equipment.

Fighter	1 squadron with F-7M *Airguard;* JJ-7 *Mongol* A 2 squadrons with F-14 *Tomcat* 2 squadrons with MiG-29AIUB *Fulcrum*
Fighter Ground Attack	1 squadron with *Mirage* F-1E; F-5E/F *Tiger* II 1 squadron with Su-24MK *Fencer* 0 5 squadrons with F-4D/E *Phantom* II 3 squadrons with F-5E/F *Tiger* II
Maritime Patrol	1 squadron with P-3MP *Orion*
ISR	1 (det) squadron with RF-4E *Phantom* II
Search & Rescue	Some flights with Bell-214C (AB-214C)
Tanker/Transport	1 squadron with B-707; B-747; B-747F
Transport	1 squadron with B-707; Falcon 50; L-1329 *Jetstar;* Bell 412 2 squadrons with C-130E/H *Hercules* 1 squadron with F-27 *Friendship; Falcon 20* 1 squadron with IL-76 *Candid;* An-140 (Iran-140 *Faraz)*
Training	1 squadron with Beech *F33NC Bonanza* 1 squadron with F-5B *Freedom Fighter* 1 squadron with PC-6 1 squadron with PC-7 *Turbo Trainer* Some units with EMB-312 *Tucano;* MPI-17 *Mushshak;* TB21 *Trinidad;* TB-200 *Tobago*
Transport Helicopter	1 squadron with CH-47 Chinook Some units with *Bell* 206A *JetRanger* (AB-206A); *Shabaviz* 2-75; *Shabaviz* 2061
Air Defence	16 battalions with MIM-23B I-HAWK/*Shahin* 5 squadrons with FM-80 (*Crotale*); *Rapier; Tigercat;* S-75M *Volkhov* (SA-2 Guideline); S-200 *Angara* (SA-5 *Gammoll*), FIM-92A *Stinger;* 9K32 *Strela-2* (SA-7 Grail); 9K331 *Tor*-M1 (9A-15 *Gauntlet*)

Equipment by Type

Aircraft	334 combat capable
Fighter	184+: 20 F-5B *Freedom Fighter;* 55+ F-5E *Tiger* 11/F-5F *Tiger* II; 24 F-7M *Airguard;* 43 F-14 *Tomcat;* 36 MiG 29A/U/UB *Fulcrum;* 6 *Azarakhsh*
Fighter Ground Attack	111: 65 F-4D/E *Phantom* II; 10 *Mirage* F-1E; 30 Su 24MK *Fencer* D; 6 *Saegheh*
Anti-tank	13: 7 Su-25K *Frogfoot;* 3 Su-25T *Frogfoot;* 3 Su-25UBK *Frogfoot*

ASW	5 P-3MP *Orion*
ISR	6+ RF-4E Phantom II
Tanker Transport	3: 1 B-707; 2 B-747
Transport	117: **Heavy** 12 Il-76 *Candid*; **Medium** 19 C-130E/11 *Hercules*; **Light** 75: 11 An-74TK-20; 5 An-140 (Iran-140 *Faraz*) (45 projected); 10 F-27 *Friendship*; 1 L-1329 *Jetstar*; 10 PC-6B *Turbo Porter*; 8 TB-21 *Trinidad*; 4 TB-200 *Tobago*; 3 *Turbo Commander* 680; 14 Y-7; 9 Y-12; **PAX** 11: 2 B-707; I B-747; 4 B-747F; 1 *Falcon* 20; 3 *Falcon* 50
Training	151: 25 *Beech* F33A/C *Bonanza*; 15'EMB-312 *Tucano*; 15 JJ-7; 25 MFI-17 *Mushshak*; 12 *Parastu*; 15 PC-6; 35 PC-7 *Turbo Trainer*; 't T-33
Helicopters	**MRH** 32: 30 Bell 214C (AB-214C); 2 Bell 412 **Transport** 4+: Heavy 2+ CH-47 *Chinook*; Light 2+: 2 *Bell* 206A *Jet Ranger* (AB-206A); some *Shabaviz* 2-75 (indigenous versions in production); some *Shabaviz* 2061
Air Defence	**SAM** 529+: 250 FM-80 (*Crotale*); 30 Rapier; 15 *Tigercat*: 150+ MIM-23B I-*HAWK*/*Shahin*; 45 S-75 Dvina (SA-2 *Guideline*); 10 S-200 *Angara* (SA-5 *Gammon*); 29 9K33 I *Tor*-M1 (SA-15*Gauntlet*) **Man-portable** FIM-92A Stinger; 9K32 *Strela*-2 (SA-7 *Grail*); **Guns •Towed** 23mm 2U-23; 37mm *Oerlikon* **Missiles ASM** AGM-65A *Maverick*; Kh-25 (AS-10 *Karen*); Kh-29 (AS-14 *Kedge*); C-801K AShM **ARM** Kh-58 (AS-11 *Kilter*) **AAM • IR** PL-2A; PL-7; R-60 (AA-8 *Aphid*); R-73 (AA-11 *Archer*): AIM-9 *Sidewinder*; IRISARH R-27 (AA-1I! *Alamo*) SARH AIM-54 *Phoenix*; AIM-7 *Sparrow*

Air Defence Command

Established to co-ordinate army, air force and IRGC air-defence assets. Precise composition unclear.

Paramilitary 40,000-60,000

Law-Enforcement Forces 40,000-60,000 (border and security troops);
450,000 on mobilisation (including conscripts)
Part of armed forces in wartime

Patrol and Coastal Combatants	**PB** 90
Aircraft	**Transport**: 2 *Iran*-140; some *Cessna* 185/*Cessna* 310
Helicopters	**Utility** 24 AB-205 (*Bell* 205)/AB-206 (*Bell* 206) *Jet Ranger*

Basij Resistance Force up to 1,000,000 on mobilisation

Paramilitary militia, with claimed membership of 12.6 million; perhaps 1 million combat capable; in the process of closer integration with IRGC Ground Forces,

Forces by Role

2,500 militia battalions (claimed, limited permanent membership)

Cyber

Iran is believed to have a developed capacity for cyber operations, The precise relationship of groups such as the 'Iranian Cyber Army' to regime

and military organisations is unclear, but the former has launched hacking attacks against a number of foreign organisations. In 2012, Tehran established a Joint Chiefs of Staff Cyber Command with emphasis on thwarting attacks against Iranian nuclear facilities. In June 2012, the head of the Civil Defence Organisation announced that plans to develop a cyber-defence strategy were under way.

Deployment

Gulf of Aden and Somali Basin Navy: 1 FSG; 1 AORH
Sudan UN • UNAMID 2 observers

MALAYSIA

Armed Forces ***109,000***	(Army 80,000; Navy 14,000; Air Force 15,000) Paramilitary 24,600 Reserves 51,600 (Army 50,000, 1,000 Air Force 600) Paramilitary 244,700
Army 80,000	2 Military Regions 4 Area Commands (divisions)
Forces by Role	
Armour	5 regiments
Mechanised infantry	5 regiments
Infantry	9 brigades; 36 battalions
Special Forces	1 brigade (3 Special Forces battalions)
Airborne	1 brigade (Rapid Deployment Force) (1 light tank squadron, 1 light artillery regiment, 3 airborne battalions, 1 engineer squadron)
Artillery	2 medium regiments 7 field artillery regiments 1 MRL regiment 1 locating regiment
Air Defence	3 regiments
Engineers	5 regiments
Helicopters	1 squadron
Reserves	
Territorial Army	Police 5 (highway safety) battalions Infantry 16 regiments
Equipment by Type	
Tanks	48 *Twardy* PT-91M **Light Tanks** 21 *Scorpion* 90
Reconnaissance	296: **AML** 130 AML-60/90; 92 *Ferret* (60 mod) 74 SIBMAS **AIFV** 44: 31 ACV 300 *Adnan (Bushmaster);* 13 ACV300 *Andan*
APC	787 **APC (T)** 265: 149 ACV300 *Adnan* (including variants); 13 FV4333 *Stormer*; 63 K-200A; 40 K-200A1 **APC (W)** 522: 32 *Anoa*; 300 *Condor* (including variants); 150 LAV-150 *Commando*; 30 M3 *Panhard*; 10 VBL
Artillery	424 **Towed** 134 **105mm** 130: 130 Model 56 pack howitzer **155mm** 34: 12 FH-70; 22 G-5 **MRL** 36: 36 *ASTROS II* (equipped with **127mm** SS-30) **Mortar** 254: 254 **81mm** SP 14: 4 K281A1; 10 ACV300-S; **120mm SP** 8 ACV-S **81mm**: 232
Anti-tank	**SP** 8 ACV300 *Baktar Shikan*; K263 **Man-portable** 60+: 18 AT-7 9K115 *Saxhorn*; 24 *Eryx*; 18 *Baktar Shikan* (HJ-8); METIS-M; C90-CRRB **RCL** 260: **106mm** 24: 24 M-40; **84mm** 236: 236 *Carl Gustav* **RL 73mm** 584: 584 RPG-7 *Knout*
Amphibious Craft	**LCA** 165: 165 *Damen* assault craft 540 (capacity 10 troops)
Helicopters	**Utility** 20: 9 SA-316B *Alouette III;* 11 A109

Air Defence	**SAM** 15 *Jernas (Rapier 2000)* **Man-portable** 48+: *Anza*; SA-18 *Grouse (Igla)*; *Starburst*; **Guns.Towed** 60: **35mm**: 24 GDF-005 towed **40mm**: 36 L40/70
AEV	9: 3 MID-M; 6 WZT-4
ARV	41: *Condor*; 15 ACV300; 4 K-288A1; 22 SIBMASS
VLB	5: *Leguan*; 5 PMCz-90

Navy 14,000

Forces by Role	Naval HQ located at Lumut Regional Command 1 Kuantan – East Coast Regional Command 2 Kota Kinabalu – Borneo Regional Command 3 Langkawi - West Coast
Equipment by Type	
Submarines	**Tactical SSK** 2 *Tunku Abdul Rahman* (*Scorpene*) each with 6 single 533mm torpedo tubes
Principal Surface Combatants	10
Frigates	10 **FFGHM** 2 2 *Lekiu* (capacity 1 *Super Lynx* utility helicopter) each with 2 B515 *ILAS-3* triple 324mm each with 1 *Sting Ray* LWT, 2 quad (8 eff.) each with 1 MM-40 *Exocet* tactical SSM, 1 *Sea Wolf* VLS with 16 *Sea Wolf* SAM **FFG** 2 2 *Kasturi* each with 2 twin (4 eff.) each with MM-38 Exocet tactical SSM, 1 Mle 54 *Creusot-Loire* 375mm Bofors (6 eff.), 1 100 mm gun, 1 helicopter landing platform **FF** 6 6 *Kedah* (MEKO) each fitted for MM-40 *Exocet* tactical SSM; each fitted for RAM CIWS and 1 76mm gun (Further 4 of class in build)
Patrol & Coastal Combatants	37
Corvettes	**FSGM** 4 4 *Laksamana* each with 2 B515 *ILAS-3* triple 324mm each with A244 LWT, 1 quad (4 effective) with 12 *Aspide* SAM, 3 twin (6 effective) each with 1 Mk 2 *Otomat* SSM, 1 76mm gun **PCFG** 4 4 *Perdana* (*Combattante* II) each with 2 single with 1 MM-38 *Exocet* tactical SSM, 1 57mm gun **PBG** 4 4 *Handalan* (Spica-M) each with 2 twin (4 eff.) each with MM-38 *Exocet* tactical SSM, 157mm gun **PBF** 17 *Tempur* **PB** 8: 6 *Jerong* (Lurssen 45); 2 *Sri Perlis*
Mine Warfare	**MCO** 4: 4 *Mahamiru*
Amphibious	**LS LST** 1: 1 *Sri Inderapura* (capacity 10 tanks; 400 troops) **AGHS (Survey) /AGOS** 2 **Amphibious Craft** 115: 115 LCM/LCU
Logistics and Support	13: **AOR** 2; **AG** 1; **ARS** 2; **AGS** 2; **ATG** 2
Training	**AX** 1; **AXS** 1; **AP** 2
Naval Aviation	160
Helicopters	**ASW** 6 Super *Lynx* **Utility** AS-555 *Fennec*
Special Forces	
Naval commandos	1 unit

***Air Force** 15,000*

Air Operational HQ	2 Air Divisions Training and Logistics Command Integrated Area Defence Systems HQ
Forces by Role	
Fighter	2 squadrons with MiG-29N (MiG-29) *Fulcrum*
FGA	1 squadron with F/A-18D *Hornet* 1 squadron with Su-30MKM *Flanker* 2 squadrons with *Hawk* MK108; *Hawk* MK208
FGA / Reconnaissance	1 squadron with F-5E *Tiger II*/F-5F *Tiger II*; RF-5E *Tigereye*
Maritime	1 squadron with Beech 200T *Maritime Patrol*
Special Forces	1 (Air Force Commando) unit (air field defence)
Transport	2 squadrons with KC-130H *Hercules* (tanker); C-130H *Hercules*; C-130H-30 *Hercules*; Cessna 402B (2 modified for aerial survey) 1 (VIP) squadron with B-737-700 BBJ; BD700 *Global Express*; F-28 *Fellowship*; *Falcon* 900; 2 S-61N; S-70A *Black Hawk*; A-109 1 squadron with 6 CN-235
Training	1 training school with MB-339A; MD3-160; PC-7 MK II *Turbo Trainer*; SA-316 *Alouette III*
Helicopters	4 (Transport/SAR) squadrons with S-61A-4 *Nuri*; S-61N; S-70A *Black Hawk*
SAM	1 squadron with *Starburst*
Equipment by Type	
Aircraft	67 combat capable
Fighter	21: 8 F-5F *Tiger II; 11* MiG-29N *Fulcrum*
FGA	26: 8 F/A-18D *Hornet; 8 Hawk* MK108; 12 Su-30 MKM
Reconnaissance	2: 2 RF-5E *Tigereye*
Maritime	4: 4 Beech 200T *Maritime Patrol*
Tanker	2 KC-130H *Hercules*
Transport	32; 1 *Airbus* A319CT; 1 B-737-700 BBJ BD700 *Global Express* 1 C-130 12: 4 C-130H *Hercules*; 8 C-130H-30 *Hercules* CN-235 6 *Cessna* 402 9: 9 *Cessna* 402B (2 modified for aerial survey) F-28 *Fellowship; 1 Falcon* 900
Training	101: 15 *Hawk* MK208; 8 MB-339AB; 8 MB-339C; 20 MD3-160 2 MiG-29U *Fulcrum;* 30 PC-7/18; 30 PC-7 MK II *Turbo Trainer*
Helicopters	**ASW** 20 S-61A-4 *Nuri* **Support** 8: 4 S-61N; 4 S-70A *Black Hawk* **Utility** 9: 1 A-109; 8 SA-316 *Alouette III*
UAV	**Tactical** 3 *Eagle;* 150; *Aludra*
Air Defence	**SAM Man-portable**: *Starburst* **Missile Tactical: ASM**: AGM-65 *Maverick;* AGM-84D *Harpoon* **AAM**: AA-10 *Alamo*; AA-11 *Archer*; AIM-7 *Sparrow*; AIM-9 *Sidewinder*

***Paramilitary** 24,600*

***Police-General Operations Force** 18,000*

Forces	
Police	5 brigade HQ; 2 (Aboriginal) battalions; 19 battalions; 4 independent companies
Special Operations	1 battalion

Equipment by Type

Reconnaissance	100 S52 *Shorland* **APC (W)** 170: 140 AT105 *Saxon*; 30 SB-301

Malaysian Maritime Enforcement Agency (MMEA) 4,500

1 MMEA HQ Putrajaya with designated control for the Malaysian Maritime Zone, which is divided into 5 Maritime Regions (Northern Peninsula; Southern Peninsular; Eastern Peninsular; Sarawak; Sabah) and sub-divided into a further 19 Maritime Districts

Equipment by Type

Patrol & Coastal Combatants	84 **PSO** 2 *Langkawi* with 1 heptr landing platform **PBF** 12: 10 MRTP 16; 2 *Penggalang* **PB** 70: 15 *Gagah*; 4 *Malawali*; 2 *Nusa*; 1 *Peninjau*; 5 *Ramunia*; 2 *Rhu*; 4 *Semilang*; 15 *Sipadan* (*ex-Kris/Sabah*); 8 *Icarus* 1650; 10 *Pengawal*; 4 *Penyelamat*
Logistics and Support	**AX** 1 *Marlin*
Aircraft	**MP 2** *Bombardier* 415MP
Helicopters	**MRH** 3 *Dauphin* AS-365

Marine Police 2,100

Equipment by Type

Patrol & Coastal Combatants	132 **PBF** 12 6 *Sangitan; 6 Stan Patrol* **PB/PBR**120
Logistics and Support	8: 2 AT; 6 Transport
Facilities	Bases at Kuala Kemaman, Penang, Tampoi and Sandakan

Police Air Unit

AircraftTransport	7: 7 PC-6 *Turbo-Porter* **Utility** 10: 4 Cessna 206; 6 Cessna 208 *Caravan I*
Helicopters	**Support AS-355** 2: 2 AS-355F *Ecureuil II* **Utility BELL 206** 1: 1 Bell 206L *Long Ranger*

Area Security Units (R) 3,500

Auxiliary General Operations Force

Paramilitary	89 units
Border Scouts (R)	1,200 in Sabah and Sarawak

People's Volunteer Corps 240,000 reservists (some 17,500 armed)

Customs Service

Patrol & Coastal Combatants	23 **PBF** 10 **PB** 13
UN Missions	**Observers:** Democratic Republic of Congo, Lebanon, Liberia, Nepal, South Sudan, Sudan, Timor-Leste, Western Sahara **Units:** Lebanon (1 mechanised infantry battalion)

MYANMAR

Armed Forces ***406,000*** *(Tatmadaw)*

Army ***375,000***

<u>**Organization**</u>	
Regional Commands	12
<u>**Forces by Role**</u>	
Light Infantry	10 division headquarters; 100 infantry battalions
Armour	10 battalions
Airborne	1 brigade
Infantry	337 battalions (regional commands)
Artillery	22 artillery regiments; 37 independent companies
Engineers	6 combat engineer battalions; 54 field engineer battalions
Air Defence	7 battalions
Intelligence	40 companies
Signals	45 battalions
<u>**Equipment by Type**</u>	
Tanks	160: 10 T-55; 50 T-72; 100 Type-63/Type-69
Light Tanks	105 Type-63
Reconnaissance	115: 45 *Ferret*; 40 Humber *Pig*; 30 *Mazda*
Armoured Personnel Carriers	361 **APC (T)** 331 Type-85; 55 Type-90 **APC (W)** 20 *Hino* **PPV** 10 MPV
Artillery	404 **SP 155mm** 30 B-52 NORA **Towed** 264: **105mm** 132: 36 M-56; 96 M101; **122mm** 100 D-30; **130mm** 16 M-46; **140mm**; **155mm** 16 *Soltam* MRL 30: **107mm** 30 Type-63; **122mm** BM-21; **240mm** M-1991 **MRL** 80: **107mm** 30 Type-63; **122mm** BM-21 **Mortars** 80: **82mm** Type-53 (M-37); **120mm** 80+: 80 Soltam; Type-53 (M-1943)
Anti-Tank	**Recoilless** 1,000; **106mm** M-40A1; 84mm 1,000 Carl Gustav **73mm**; RPG-7 *Knout* **Guns** 60; **57mm** 6-Pdr; **76.2mm** 17 pdr
Air Defence	**Missiles** HN-5 *Hong Nu/Red Cherry*; SA-16 *Gimlet* **Guns** 46: **SP 57mm** 12 Type-80; **Towed** 34: **37mm** 25 Type-74; **40mm** 10 M-1

Navy ***16,000***	Headquarters located at Yangon
<u>**Equipment by Type**</u>	
Principal Surface Combatants	3
Frigates	**FFG** 3: 1 *Aung Zeya* with 2 twin launcher with C-802 AShM, 1 76mm gun 2 *Mahar Bandola* (PRC Type-0531H1) with 2 triple launchers with HY-2 (C-201) *Seersucker* AShM, 2 RBU 1200, 2 tin 100mm gun
Patrol & Coastal Combatants	99
Corvettes	**FS** 3 *Anawrahta* each with 1 76mm gun

	PCG 6 *Houxin* each with 2 twin (4 eff.) each with 4 C-801 (CSS-N-4) *Sardine* tactical SSM
	PBG 4 *Myanmar* each with 2 twin (4 eff.) each with 4 C-801 (CSS-N-4) *Sardine* tactical SSM
	PCO 2 *Indaw*
	PCC 9 *Hainan*
	PB 18: 3 PB-90; 6 PGM 401; 6 PGM 412; 9 *Myanmar*; 3 *Swift*
	PBR 57: 4 *Sagu*; 9 Y-301, 1 Y-301; 43 (various)
Amphibious Craft	18: 8 **LCU**; 10 **LCM**
Logistics and Support	18 **AOT** 1; **AK** 1; **AKSL** 5: **AGS** 2; **ABU** 1; **TPT** 9
Facilities	Bases located at Bassein, Mergui, Moulmein, Seikyi, Rangoon (Monkey Point), Sittwe
Naval Infantry	1 battalion

Air Force 15,000

Forces by Role	
Fighter	3 squadrons with MiG-29B *Fulcrum*; F-7 (Mig-21F *Fishbed* C; FT-7 (JJ-7) Mongol A: MiG-29 *UB Fulcrum*
Ground Attack	2 squadrons with A-5M (Q-5II) *Fantan*
Transport	1 squadron with An-12 *Cub*; F-27 *Friendship*; FH-227; PC-6A *Turbo Porter* / PC-6B *Turbo Porter*
Training/Liaison	2 squadrons with G-4 *Super Galeb*; PC-7 *Turbo Trainer*; PC-9 1 squadron with Ce-550 *Citation II*; Cessna 180 *Skywagon*; K-8 *Karakoram*
Helicopters	4 squadrons with PZL W-3 *Sokol* Mi-17 (Mi-8MT) *Hip H*; PZL Mi-2 *Hoplite*; Bell 205; Bell 206 *Jet Ranger*; SA-316 *Alouette III*
Equipment by Type	136
Fighter	69: *8 MiG-29B Fulcrum; 50 F-7 Airguard*
FGA	22 A-5M (Q-5II) Fantan
Transport	15: 2 An-12 *Cub*; 1 Ce-550 *Citation II*; 3 F-27 *Friendship*; 4 FH-227; 5 PC-6A *Turbo Porter* / PC-6B *Turbo Porter*
Utility	4 Cessna 180 *Skywagon*
Training	57: 10 FT-7 (JJ-7) Mongol A: 12 G-4 Super Galeb; 12 K-8; 2 MiG-29UB *Fulcrum*; 12 PC-7 *Tourbo Trainer*; 9 PC-9
Helicopters	**Support** 39: 10 PZL W-3 *Sokol*; 11 Mi-17 (Mi-8 MT) *Hip H**; 18 PZL Mi-2 *Hoplite* **Utility** 27: 12 Bell 205; 6 Bell *Jet Ranger*; 9 SA-316 *Alouette III*

Paramilitary 107,250

People's Police Force 72,000

People's Militia 35,000

People's Pearl and Fishery Ministry	250
Patrol & Coastal Combatants	**PBR** 6: *Carpentaria*

NEPAL

Army 95,750

Forces by Role

Army	6 Division HQ; 1 (valley) command
Infantry	16 brigades (63 infantry battalions) 32 independent companies
Special Forces	1 brigade (1 AB battalion, 1 mechanised battalion, 1 ranger battalion, 1 independent Special Forces battalion)
Artillery	1 brigade (4 artillery regiments)
Air Defence	2 AD regiments; 4 independent AD companies
Engineers	5 engineer battalions
Royal Guards	1 MP battalion

Equipment By Type

Reconnaissance	40: 40 *Ferret*
Armoured Personnel Carriers	**APC (W)** 40: 40 *Casspir*
Artillery	109 **Towed** 39 75 mm 6 pack; 94 mm; 5 3.7 inch (mountain training), 105 mm 28; 8 L-118 Light Gun; 14 pack how **Mortars** 70+: 81 mm, 120 mm
Air Defence	**Guns** 32; 14.5 mm Towed, ZPU 30: Type-56 (ZPU-4) 37 mm (PRC) 40 mm 2 L/60

Air Wing 320

Aircraft	**Transport** 5: 1 BAe-748; 2 M-28 *SkyTruck*; 2BN2T *Islander*
Helicopters	**MRH** 9: 1 *Dhruv*; 2 *Lancer*; 3 Mi-17-1V *Hip H*; 1 SA315B *Lama* (*Cheetah*); 2 SA316B *Alouette III* **Transport** 3 Medium 1 SA330J Super *Puma Light* 2 AS350B2/B3 *Ecureuil*

Paramilitary 62,000

Armed Police Force 15,000
Ministry of Home Affairs

Police Force 47,000

UN Missions	**Observers:** Chad, Ivory Coast, Democratic Republic of Congo, Haiti, Liberia, Lebanon, Middle East, Sierra Leone, South Sudan, Sudan, Timor-Leste, Western Sahara **Units: Congo** (1 mechanised infantry battalion, 1 engineer company); **Haiti** (1 infantry battalion); **Lebanon** (1 infantry battalion); **Liberia** 1 MP platoon; **South Sudan** (1 infantry battalion)

PAKISTAN

Army 550,000

Strategic Assets	**National Command Authority** for control of nuclear weapons. It has two committees – Employment Control; and Development Control. The Strategic Plans Division (SPD) acts as the secretariat and formulates nuclear policy, strategy and doctrine, and strategic plans for deployment and employment.
Army Strategic Forces Command	12,000-15,000
Strategic Missiles	60 **MRBM** 30 *Ghauri-I Hatf-V*; *Ghauri-II Hatf-VA*; *Shaheen-II Hatf-VI* 2; *Babur* **SRBM** 30 *Ghaznavi*; 50 *Hatf-III*; *Shaheen-I Hatf-IV*; *Hatf-VII*; **LACM** some *Babur Hatf-VIII*
Forces by Role	
Army	9 corps headquarters (Mangla, Multan, Lahore, Karachi, Rawalpindi, Peshawar, Quetta, Gujranwala, Bahawalpur) Northern Areas Command (Gilgit)
Armoured	2 divisions; 7 (independent) brigades
Mechanised	2 mechanised infantry divisions; 1 (independent) mechanised brigade
Infantry	18 divisions; 1 (area) command; 5 (independent) brigades
Special Forces	2 group (4 Special Forces battalions)
Artillery	9 (corps) brigades; 5 independent brigades
Engineers	7 brigades
Aviation	1 (VIP) squadron; 5 (composite) squadrons
Helicopters	10 squadrons
Air Defence	1 command; 3 Air Defence groups (8 Air Defence battalions)
Equipment by Type	
Tanks	2,411: 265 MBT 2000 *Al-Khalid*; 320 T-80UD; 51 T-54/T-55; 1,100 Type-59; 400 Type-69; 275+ Type-85; (270 M48A5 in store)
Armoured Personnel Carriers	1,390 **APC (T)** 1,260: 1,160 M113; 100 Type 63 **APC (W)** 120 BTR-70/BTR-80
Artillery	4,607 **SP** 375: **155mm** 315: 200 M109/M109A2; 115 M109A5 **203mm** 60 M110/M110A2 **Towed** 1,659: **105mm** 329: 216 M101; 113 M-56; **122mm** 570: 80 D-30 (PRC); 490 Type-54 M-1938; **130mm** 410Type-59-I; **155mm** 322: 144 M114; 148 M198; 30 *Panter* **203mm** 28 M115 **MRL** 88: **107mm** Type 81; **122mm** 52+: 52 Azar (Type-83); some KRL-122 **300mm** 36 A100 **Mortars** 2,350: **81mm**; **120mm** AM-50; M-61
Anti Tank	**SP** M901 TOW **Man-portable** 11,100: 10,500 HJ-8/TOW; 600 9K119 *Refleks* (AT-11 *Sniper*) **RCL** 75mm Type-52; **106mm** M40A1 **RL 89mm** M20 **Guns 85mm** 200 Type-56 (D-44)

Aircraft	**ISR** 30 Cessna O-1E *Bird Dog* **Transport** Light 14: 1 Beech 200 *King Air*; 1 Beech 350 *King Air*; 3 Cessna 208B; 1 Cessna 421; 1 Cessna 550 *Citation*; 1 Cessna 560 *Citation*; 2 *Turbo Commander* 690; 4 Y-12(II) **Training** 90 Saab 91 *Safir* (50 obs; 40 liaison)
Helicopters	**Anti-tank** 42: 25 AH-1F *Cobra* with TOW; 16 AH-1S *Cobra*; 1 Mi-24 *Hind* **MRH** 114: 10 AS550 *Fennec*; 6 AW139; 26 *Bell* 412EP *Twin Huey*; 40+ Mi-17 *Hip H*; 12 *SA315B Lama*; 20 SA319 *Alouette III* **Transport** 59 Medium 36: 31 SA330 *Puma* ; 4 Mi-171; 1 Mi-172 Light 23: 5 Bell 205 (*UH-1H Iroquois*); 5 Bell 205A-1 (AB-205A-1); 13 Bell 206B *Jet Ranger II* **Training** 22: 12 Bell 47G; 10 Hughes 300C
UAV	**ISR** Light *Bravo; Jasoos; Vector*
Air Defence	**SAM** **SP** some M113 with RBS-70 **Man-portable** 2,990+: 2,500 Mk1/Mk2; 60 FIM-92A Stinger; HN-5A; 230 Mistral; 200 RBS-70 **Guns Towed** 1,934: 14.5mm 981; **35mm** 248 GDF-002/GDF-005 (with 134 *Skyguard* radar units); **37mm** 310 Type-55 (M 1939)/ Type-65; **40mm** 50 L/60; **57mm** 144 Type-59 (S-60); **85mm** 200 Type-72 (M-1939) KS-12
Radar	**Land** AN/TPQ-36 *Firefinder* (arty, mor); RASIT (veh, arty); SLC-2
Missiles	**Strategic** **MRBM** 30 *Ghauri/Ghauri II (Hatf-5);* some *Shaheen-2 (Haft-6* - in test) **SRBM** 30 *Ghaznavi (Hatf-3* - PRC M-11); up to 10 *Shaheen-1 (Hatf-4);* **LACM** some *Babur (Hatf-7* - in development) **Tactical • SRBM** 105+: *105 Hatf-1*; some *Abdali (Hatf-2);*
ARV	117: 65 Type 653; *Al Hadeed*; 52 M88A1; T-54/T-55
VLB	M47M; M48/60
MW	*Aardvark* Mk II

Navy 22,000 (including 1,400 Marines and 2,000 Maritime Security Agency)

Equipment by Type	
Submarines	8 **SSK** 5: 2 *Hashmat* (French *Agosta* 70) each with 4 x1 533 mm ASTT each with 20+ F17P HWT/UGM- 84 *Harpoon* tactical USGW; 3 *Khalid* (French *Agosta* 90B) each with 1x533 mm ASTT each with SM-39 *Exocet* tactical USGW **SSI** 3: 3 MG110 SSI each with 2 single 533mm TT
Principal Surface Combatants	
Frigates	10 **FFGHM** 3 3 *Sword (PRC Type 054)* with 2 quad launcher with YJ-83 AShM, 1 octuple launcher with HQ-7 SAM, 2 triple 324mm ASTT with Mk 46 LWT, 1 76mm gun, (capacity 1 Z-9C *Haitun* helicopter) **FFGH** 4 4 *Tariq* (UK *Amazon*) (capacity 1 *Lynx* Utility Helicopter) each with 2 single each with TP 45 LWT,2 Mk-141 *Harpoon* twin each with 1 RGM-84D *Harpoon* tactical SSM, 1 114 mm gun **FFHM** 2 2 *Tariq* (capacity 1 *Lynx* Utility Helicopter) (D184, D186) each with 2 triple 324 mm ASTT (6 effective) each with Mk 46 LWT, 1 sextuple (6 effective) with LY-60 (*Aspide*) SAM, 1 114 mm gun;

FFH 1
1 *Alamgir* (US *Oliver Hazard Perry*) with 2 triple 24mm ASTT with Mk46 LWT, 1 76mm gun

Patrol & Coastal Combatants 12
PBFG 2 *Zarrar* each with 4 single each with RGM-84 *Harpoon* AShM
PBG 4: 2 *Jalalat* II with 2 twin launcher with C-802 (CSS-N-8 *Saccade*) AShM
2 *Jurrat* with 2 twin launcher with C-802 (CSS-N-8 *Saccade*) AShM
PBF 4: 2 *Kaan* 15
PB 2: 1 *Larkana*; 1 *Rajshahi*

Mine Warfare 3: 3 *Munsif* (French *Eridan*)

Amphibious **Landing Craft** • UCAC 4 *Griffon* 2000

Logistics and Support 11
AORH 2
1 *Fuqing* with 1 SA-319 Alouette III utility helicopter
1 *Moawin* with 1 Sea King MK45 ASW helicopter
AOT 3: 1 *Attock*; 2 *Gwadar*
AGS 1 *Behr Paima*
YTM 4

Facilities

Bases Karachi; Ormara; Gwadar

Marines 1,400

Commando 1 group

Naval aviation Aircraft 7 combat capable
ASW 9: 3 *Atlantic*, 4 P-3C *Orion*
MP 6: F-27 MK 200MPA
Transport 1 Hawker 850XP

Helicopters **ASW** 12: 5 *Sea King Mk45* ASW; 7 Z-9C *Haitun*
Utility 4; 4 SA-319B *Alouette III*

Missiles Anti-ship AM-39 *Exocet*

Air Force 70,000

Regional Commands
Northern (Peshawar)
Central (Sargodha)
Southern (Faisalabad)

Forces By Role

Fighter
1 squadron with *Mirage* IIIEP/OD (*Mirage* IIID)
1 squadron with F-16A *Fighting Falcon*/F-16B
3 squadrons with F-7PG/ FT-7PG *Airguard*
2 squadrons with F-7PG/F-7P *Skybolt*

Fighter Ground Attack
2 squadrons with JF-17 *Thunder* (FC-1)
1 squadron with F-16C/D Block 52 *Fighting Falcon*
3 squadrons with *Mirage* 5 (5PA)

ASW 1 squadron with Mirage 5PA2/5PA3 with AM-39 *Exocet* AShM

AEW&C 1 squadron with Saab 2000/Saab 2000 *Erieye*

ELINT / ECM 1 squadron with *Falcon* 20F

SAR
6 squadrons with SA-316 *Alouette III*
1 squadron with Mi-171 (SAR/Liaison)

Tanker 1 squadron with Il-78 *Midas*

Transport
1 squadron with C-130/C-130B *Hercules*
1 VIP squadron with B-707; Cessna 560XL *Citation Excel*; CN-235M-220; F-27-200 Friendship; Falcon 20E; Gulfstream IVSP
1 (communications) squadron with EMB-500 *Phenom* 100; Y-12 (II)

Training	2 OCU squadrons with F-7P/FT-7P *Skybolt* 1 OCU squadron with *Mirage III/Mirage 5* 1 OCU squadron with F-16A/B *Fighting Falcon* 1 squadron with FT-5 1 squadron with K-8 *Karakoram* 2 squadrons with MFI-17 2 squadrons with T-37C *Tweet*
Surface to Air Missiles	1 battery with CSA-1 (SA-2) *Guideline*; 9K310 *Igla-1* (SA-16 *Gimlet*) 6 batteries each with 24 *Crotale*

Equipment by Type

Aircraft	423 combat capable
Fighter	200: 29 FC-1/JF-17 *Thunder*; 50 *Mirage* III EP; 54 F-7PG (F-7 MG) *Airguard*; 75 F-7P *Skybolt*; 46 F-16A/F-16B *Fighting Falcon*; 12 F-16 C/D; (18 F-16CD; 12F-16 C6F-16D .
Fighter Ground Attack	174: 12 F-16C Block 52 *Fighting Falcon*; 6 F-16D Block 52 *Fighting Falcon*; 29+ JF-17 *Thunder* (FC-1 - 150+ on order); 7 *Mirage IIID (Mirage IIIOD)*; 63 *Mirage IIIE* (IIIEP); 40 *Mirage 5* (5PA)/5PA2; 3 *Mirage 5D* (5DPA)/5DPA2; 10 *Mirage 5PA3* (ASuW)
ISR	10 *Mirage* IIIRP (Mirage IIIR)
ELINT / ECM	2 Da-20 *Falcon;* 4 ZDK-03 AWACS
AEW&C	3: 2 Saab 2000 *Erieye* (2 more on order); 1 ZDK-03
Tanker	4 Il-78 Midas
Transport	34 **Medium** 16: 5 C-130B *Hercules*; 10 C-130/E *Hercules;* 1 L-100-20 **Light** 13: 1 Cessna 560XL *Citation Excel;* 4 CN-235M-220; 4 EMB-500 *Phenom* 100; 1 F-27- 200 *Friendship*; 2 Y-12 (II) **PAX** 5: 1 B-707; 1 *Falcon 20E*; 2 *Gulfstream* IVSP; 1 Saab 2000
Training	139: 39 K-8 Karakorum; 80 MFI-17B Mushshak; 20 T-37C Tweet
Helicopters	19; 4 Mi-171, 15 SA-316 *Alouette III*
Missiles	150 **Towed:** 144 *Crotale*; 6 CSA-1 (SA-2) *Guideline* **Man-portable**: SA-16 *Gimlet*
Radar - Land	51: 6 **AR-1** (AD radar low level); *Condor* (AD radar high level); FPS-89/100 (AD radar high level); **MPDR** 45: 45 MPDR 45/MPDR 60/MPDR 90 (AD radar low level); **TPS-43G** (AD radar high level)Type 514 (AD radar high level)
Anti-Ship Missiles	AGM-65 *Maverick*; AM-39 *Exocet*
Air-to-Air Missiles	AIM-9L *Sidewinder*/AIM-9P *Sidewinder*; R-Darter Super 530
Unmanned Aerial Vehicle	**MQ-1** Predator; *Baaz*; *Ababeel*

Facilities	4 Radar air control sectors 7 Radar control and reporting station

Paramilitary 304,000 active

Coast Guard

Patrol & Coastal Combatants	5; **PB** 1; **PBF** 4
Miscellaneous Boats/Craft	23

Frontier Corps 65,000 (under Ministry of Interior)	Balochistan and Khyber Pakhtunkhwa

Forces By Role

Armoured reconnaissance	1 independent squadrons

Paramilitary	11 regiments (*total:* 40 paramilitary battalions)
<u>**Equipment By Type**</u>	
APC	**APC (W)** 45: 45 UR-416
<u>**Maritime Security Agency**</u> 2,000	
Principal Surface Combatants	
Destroyers	**DD** 1: 1 *Nazim* (US *Gearing*) with 2 triple 324mm TT, 1 twin 127mm gun
Patrol & Coast Combatants	10 **PCO** 4 *Barkat* **PB** 6: 2 *Subquat* (PRC Shanghai); 1 *Sadaqat* (ex-PRC Huangfen) ; 3 (various)
National Guard 185,000	
Janbaz Force	
Mujahid Force	
National Cadet Corps	
Women Guards	
Northern Light Infantry 12,000	
Paramilitary	3 battalions
Pakistan Rangers	40,000 (Ministry of Interior)
UN Missions	**Observers:** Ivory Coast, Democratic Republic Of Congo, Liberia, Sudan, Timor Leste, Western Sahara **Units**: **Ivory Coast** (1 infantry battalion; 1 engineer company; 1 transport company); **Democratic Republic of Congo** (3 mechanised infantry battalions; 1 infantry battalion); **Liberia** (3 infantry battalions; 3 engineer companies; 1 field hospital); **Sudan** 1 engineer company

SINGAPORE

Armed Forces 72,500	(**Army** 50,000; **Navy** 9,000; **Air Force** 13,500) **Paramilitary** 75,100 **Reserves** 312,500 (Army 300,000 5,000 Air 7,500) Paramilitary 44,000

Army ***15,000****; 35,000 conscripts (total 50,000)*

<u>Forces by Role</u>

1 Rapid Deployment division (1 infantry brigade, 1 amphibious brigade (3 amphibious battalions),
1 air mobile brigade)
1 division (mixed active/reserve formations)
3 Combined Arms division (each: 2 infantry brigades (each: 3 infantry battalions), 1 armoured brigade, 1 reconnaissance battalion, 2 artillery battalions, 1 AD battalion, 1 engineer battalion)

Reconnaissance	4 battalions
Infantry	8 battalions
Commando	1 battalion
Artillery	4 battalions
Engineer	4 battalions
Intelligence	1 battalion
Reserves	9 infantry brigades included in mixed active/inactive reserve formations listed above; 1 operational reserve division with an additional infantry brigade; People's Defence Force Commands with 12 infantry battalions

Mechanised	6 battalions
Reconnaissance / light armoured	6 battalions
Infantry	56 battalions
Commando	1 battalion
Artillery	12 battalions
Engineer	8 battalions

<u>Equipment by Type</u>

Tanks	96: **MBT** 100 *Tempest (Centurion)*; 96 *Leopard*; 80-100 **Light tanks** 350 AMX-13 SM1
Reconnaissance	22 AMX-10 PAC 90
AIFV	**372:** 22 AMX-10 P 90; 100 AV-81 *Terrex*; 250 IFV-25; M-113A1/ M-113A2 (some with 40mm AGL, some with 25mm gun)
APC	1,695: **APC (T)** 1,400+: 250 IFV-40/50; 700+ M113A1/M113A2; 400+ ATTC Bronco **APC (W)** 280: 250 LAV-150 Commando/V-200 Commando; 30 V-100 Commando PPV 15 *Maxx Pro Dash*
Artillery	798 **SP 155mm** 54 SSPH-1 *Primus* **Towed** 88: **105mm** (37 LG1 in store); **155mm** 88: 18 FH-2000; 18 Pegasus; 52 FH-88 **MRL 227mm** 18 HIMARS **Mortars** 638+

	SP 90+ **81mm**; **120mm** 90: 40 on *Bronco*; 50 on M113
	Towed 548 **81mm** 500 **120mm** 36 M-65 **160mm** 12 M-58 *Tampella*
Anti-tank	**Missile Man-portable** 60: 30 *Milan*; 30 *Spike* MR
	RCL 290: **84mm** 200 Carl Gustav; **106mm** 90 M40A1
	RL 67mm *Armbrust*
Air Defence	**SAM** 75+
	SP *Mistral*; RBS-70; 9K38 *Igla* (SA-18 *Grouse*) (on V-200/M-113)
	Man-portable *Mistral*; RBS-70; 9K38 *Igla* (SA-18 *Grouse*)
	Guns 34
	SP 20mm GAI-C01
	Towed 34 **20mm** GAI-C01; **35mm** 34 GDF (with 25 *Super-Fledermaus* fire control radar)
UAV	**ISR** Light Skylark
RADAR	**Land** AN/TPQ-36 *Firefinder*; AN/TPQ-37 *Firefinder* (arty, mor); 3 *ARTHUR* (arty)
AEV	80: 18 CET; 54 FV180; 8 M728
ARV	*Bionix; Bueffel*; LAV-150; LAV-300
VLB	*Bionix*; LAB 30; *Leguan*; M2; M3; 12 M60
MW	910-MCV-2; *Trailblazer*

<u>Facilities</u>

Training camps	3 (including infantry, artillery and armoured) located in Taiwan (Republic of China), 1 (artillery, combat engineers) located in Thailand; 1 located in Brunei

***Navy 3,000**; 1,000 conscript; 5,000 active reservists (total 9,000)*

<u>Equipment by Type</u>

Submarines	**Tactical SSK** 5:
	3 *Challenger* each with 4 single 533mm TT
	1 *Challenger* (trg role) with 4 single 533mm TT
	1 Archer (SWE *Västergötland* class) (AIP fitted) with 6 single 533mm TT for *WASS Black Shark* LWT
Principal Surface Combatants	6
Frigates	**FFGHM** 6 *Formidable* each with 8 RGM-84 *Harpoon* SSM, 2 octuple (32 eff.) VLS with *Aster* 15 SAM, 1 76mm gun, (capacity for 1 S-70B *Sea Hawk*)
Patrol & Coastal Combatants	35
	Corvettes FSGM 6: 6 *Victory* each with 2 triple ASTT (6 effective), 2 octuple (16 effective) each with 1 *Barak* SAM, 2+ Mk 140 *Harpoon* quad (8 effective) each with 1 RGM-84C *Harpoon* tactical SSM, 1 76mm gun
	PCO 11: 6 *Fearless* each with 2 *Sadral* sextuple each with *Mistral* SAM 5 *Fearless* each with 2 *Sadral* sextuple each with *Mistral* SAM, 1 76mm gun
	PBF 6
	PBI 12
Mine Warfare	**MHC** 4: 4 *Bedok*
Amphibious	**LPD**: 4 *Endurance* (capacity 350 troops; 18 MBTs; 4 LCVP; 2 helicopters) (with helicopter deck) each with 2 Twin (4 effective) each with *Mistral* SAM, 1 76mm gun
	Landing Craft 34 LCU; LCU 100 LCVP
Logistics and Support	2
	AR 1 *Swift Review*
	Training 1

Facilities	**Bases** located at Changi and Tuas (Jurong)

Air Force *13,500; 3,000 conscript; 7,500 reservists (total 21,000)*

Forces by Role	
Fighter Ground Attack	2 squadrons with F-5S *Tiger II*; 9 F-5T *Tiger II* (secondary GA role) 3 squadrons with F-16C *Fighting Falcon*/F-16D *Fighting Falcon* 1 squadron with F-155 G *Eagle*
Reconnaissance	1 squadron with 8 RF-5S *Tiger*
Reconnaissance /transport	1 squadron with 4 KC-130B *Hercules* (tanker/transport); 1 KC-130H *Hercules*; 5 C-130H *Hercules* (2 Elint); 1 squadron with 9 F-50 *Maritime Enforcer* (4 transport, 5 MR)
Airborne Early Warning	1 squadron with 4 E-2C *Hawkeye*
Tanker	1 squadron with 4 KC-135R *Stratotanker*
Training	1 squadron with F-16C/D at Luke AFB, AZ; AH-64D *Apache* located at Marana, (AZ), US-47D *Chinook* located at Grand Prairie, (TX)US; F-15 at Mountain Home (ID), US on F-15E, and then F-15SG 1 squadron with A-4 SU Super *Skyhawk*; TA-4SU *Super Skyhawk*; 1 squadron with PC-21
Helicopters	1 squadron with AB-205A (Bell 205A); UH-1H *Iroquois*; 1 squadron with CH-47SD *Super D Chinook*; 2 squadrons with AS-332M *Super Puma* (including SAR); AS-532UL *Cougar*; 2 squadrons with AH-64D *Apache*; AS-550A2 *Fennec*/AS-550C2 *Fennec*
Unarmed Aerial Vehicles	2 squadrons with *Searcher MkII* 1 squadron with *Hermes 450* (Staffed by personnel from all three services)

Equipment by Type	
Aircraft	140 combat capable
Fighter	29: F-5 37: 28 F-5S *Tiger II*; 9 F-5T *Tiger II* (GA role)
Fighter Ground Attack	84: 24 F-15SG Eagle; 20 F-16C Fighting Falcon; 40 F-16D Fighting Falcon
Anti-tank	14: 4 A-4SU *Super Skyhawk*; 4 A-4SU; 10 TA-4SU *Super Skyhawk*; 4 A-4SU
Reconnaissance	8 RF-5S *Tiger*
Maritime Reconnaissance	9 F-50 *Maritime Enforcer* (4 transport, 5 MR)
Airborne Early Warning	4 G550-AEW
Tanker	5; 1 KC-130B *Hercules* (tanker/transport); 4 KC-135R *Stratotanker*
Transport	9; 5 C-130H *Hercules* (2 Elint); 4 F-50
Training	19 PC-21
Helicopters	**Anti-tank** 19 AH-64D *Apache* **ASW** 6 S-70B *Sea Hawk* **Support**: 40: 18 AS-332M *Super Puma* (including 5 SAR); 10 CH-47SD *Super D Chinook;* **Utility** 54: 12 AS-532UL *Cougar;* 6 AB-205A (Bell 205A); 24 UH-1H *Iroquois*
UAV	some *Hermes* 450; 40 *Searcher* MK II
Missiles	**Tactical: ASM**; AGM-45 *Shrike*; *Hellfire*; AGM-65B/G *Maverick*; AGM-84 *Harpoon*; AM-39 *Exocet* **AAM:** AIM-120C *AMRAAM* in store (US); AIM-7P *Sparrow*; AIM-9N *Sidewinder*AIM-9P *Sidewinder*

Air Defence Group

<u>Forces by Role</u>	
Air Defence	1 ADA squadron with *Oerlikon* 1 AD squadron with MIM-23 HAWK 1 AD squadron with *Rapier-Blindfire*
<u>Equipment by Type</u>	
Missiles	**Tactical ASM**: AGM-45 *Shrike* AGM-65; AGM-65B *Maverick*; AGM-65G *Maverick;* AGM-84 *Harpoon;* AAM AIM-120; AIM-120C *AMRAAM* in store (US) **AIM:** AIM-7P *Sparrow;* AIM-9N *Sidewinder*/AIM-9P *Sidewinder*
Air Force Systems Bde	
<u>Forces by Role</u>	
Air Defence	1 AD squadron with radar (mobile) 1 AD squadron with LORADS
Divisional Air Def Arty Bde	attached to army divs
<u>Forces by Role</u>	
Air Defence	1 AD battalion with *Mistral* 1 AD battalion with 9K38 *Igla* (SA-18 *Grouse*) 3 AD battalion with RBS-70
<u>Equipment by Type</u>	**SAM** 36 **Towed** *Mistral;* RBS-70 **Man-portable** 9K38 *Igla (SA-18 Grouse)*

Paramilitary *75,100 active*

Civil Defence Force *1,600 regulars, 3,200 conscripts, 23,000 reservists; 54,000+ volunteers; 1 construction brigade (2,500 conscripts)*

Singapore Police Force *8,500; 3,500 conscript; 21,000 reservists (total 33,000)*

Singapore Gurkha contingent *1,500*	(6 companies)
Cyber	*The Singapore Ministry of Defence has long identified the potential damage that could be caused by cyber attacks, with this concern perhaps more acute following its adoption of the Integrated Knowledge-based Command and Control (IKC2) doctrine, designed to aid the transition of Singapore's Armed Forces to a 'third generation' force. Meanwhile, Singapore established the Singapore Infocomm Technology Security Authority (SITSA) on 1 October 2009, as a division within the Internal Security Department of the Ministry of Home Affairs (MHA). Its main responsibilities will be dealing with cyber terrorism and cyber espionage, as well as operational IT security development.*
<u>Deployment Overseas</u>	
Australia	**Air Force:** 230 personnel **Aircraft: Training** 27: 27 S-211 **Helicopters**: 12 AS-332 *Super Puma* Spt/AS-532 *Cougar* Utility **Facilities:** School - 1 with 12 AS-332 *Super Puma* Spt/AS-532 *Cougar* utility (flying training) located at Oakey, 1 with 27 S-211 training aircraft (flying training) located at Pearce
Brunei	**Air Force:** 500 personnel; 1 helicopter detachment with 5 UH-1H *Iroquois* **Facilities:** School - 1 (training)
France	**Air Force:** 200 personnel; some training squadron with 6 A-4SU *Super Skyhawk;* 10 TA-4SU *Super Skyhawk*

Taiwan (Republic of China)	**Army:** Training camp - 3 (including infantry, artillery and armoured)
Thailand	**Army:** Training camp - 1 (Artillery, combat engineers)
United States	**Air Force: Aircraft • FGA** 24: 12 F-16C *Fighting Falcon*/F-16D *Fighting Falcon* on lease located at Cannon AFB, (NM), US; 12 on lease located at Luke AFB, (AZ), US **Helicopters: Anti-tank AH-64**: some AH-64D *Apache* located at Marana, (AZ); **Support: CH-47** 6+: 6+ CH-47D *Chinook* located at Grand Prairie, (TX) **Navy • Support facility located at Singapore USPACOM:** 1 logistic support squadron located at Singapore

SRI LANKA

Army ***200,000***

Forces by Role	
Divisional HQ	12
Armoured	1 brigade
Armoured Reconnaissance	3 regiments
Air Mobile	1 brigade
Infantry	34 brigades
Special Forces	1 independent brigade
Commando	1 brigade
Field Artillery	9 regiments
Engineers	4 regiments
Signals	5 regiments
Equipment By Type	
Tanks	**MBT** 62: 62 T-55AM2/T-55A
Reconnaissance	15: 15 *Saladin*
AIFV	62: 13 BMP-1; 49 BMP-2 **APC (T)** 30:Type-63/85/89 **APC (W)** 31 *Buffel*; 105 *Unicorn*; 25 BTR-80/ BTR-80A; 20 Type-92
Artillery	908 **Towed** 96: **122 mm**; **130mm** 30 Type-59-I; **152mm** 46 Type-66 (D-20) **MRL** 28; **122mm** RM-70 *Dana*; 6 KRL-122 **Mortars** 784: 520 **81mm**; 209 **82mm**; 55 **120mm** M-43
Anti-tank	**RCL** 40; 10 **105mm** M-65; 30 **106mm** M-40; **Guns** 8 **85mm** Type-56 (D-44)
UAV	1: 1 *Seeker*
Radar	**Land** 2: 2 AN/TPQ-36 *Firefinder* (artillery)
ARV	16 VT-55
VLB	2 MT-55

Navy ***15,000***

Forces by Role	
Headquarters	Colombo
Equipment by Type	
Patrol & Coastal Combatants	138 **PSOH** 1 *Sayura* (IND *Vigraha*) **PCG** 2 *Nandimithra* (ISR *Sa'ar* 4) with 3 single launcher with 1 GII Gabriel II AShM, 1 76mm gun **PCO** 2: 1 *Reliance*; 2 *Sagara* (IND *Vikram*) **PCC** 1 *Jayesagara* **PBF** 87: 26 *Colombo*; 3 *Dvora*; 3 *Killer* (ROK); 6 *Shaldag*; 14 *Super Dvora* (Mk1/II/III); 3 *Simonneau*; 5 *Trinity Marine*; 27 *Wave Rider* **PB** 18: 4 *Cheverton*; 2 *Prathapa* (PRC mod *Haizhui*); 3 *Ranajaya* (PRC *Haizhui*); 1 *Ranarisi* (PRC mod *Shanghai* II); 5 *Weeraya* (PRC *Shanghai* II); 3 (various) **PBR** 27
Amphibious	**Landing Ships • LSM** 1 *Yuhai* (capacity 2 tanks; 250 troops)

	Landing Craft 8
	LCU 2 *Yunnan*
	LCM 2
	LCP 3 *Hansaya*
	UCAC 1 M 10 (capacity 56 troops)
Logistics and Support	2: 1 **AP;** 1 **AX**
Facilities	
Bases	Northern Command located at Kankesanthurai Southern Command located at Galle North Central Command located at Medawachiya HQ and Western Command located at Colombo Main base and Eastern Command located at Trincomalee

Air Force 28,000

Forces by Role	
Fighter	1 squadron with F-7BS/GS, FT-7
Fighter Ground Attack	1 squadron with MiG-27M *Flogger J2*; MiG-23UB *Flogger* 1 squadron with *Kfir* C-2; 2 *Kfir* C-7/*Kfir* TC-2 1squadron with K-8 *Karakorum*
Transport	1 squadron with An-32B *Cline*; BAe-748; 1 squadron with Beech 200 *Super King Air*; Y-12 (II)
Anti-tank Helicopters	1 squadron with Mi-24V *Hind E*;
Training	1 squadron with PT-6 (CJ-6); *Cessna* 150L
Utility Helicopters	1 squadron with MI-17 (Mi-8) *Hip H*; 1 squadron with Bell 206 *Jet Ranger* 1 (VIP) squadron with Mi-35P *Hind*; Bell 212
ISR UAV	1 squadron with *Blue Horizon*-2 1 squadron with *Searcher II*
Equipment by Type	
Aircraft	30 combat capable
Fighter	8: 3 F-7BS; 4 F-7GS; 1 FT-7
Ground Attack	15: 4 *Kfir* C-2; 2 *Kfir* C-7; 2 *Kfir* TC-2; 6 MiG-27M *Flogger J2*; 1 MiG-23UB *Flogger* C
Transport	23; 5 An-32B *Cline*; BAe-748 2 Beech 200 *Super King Air* 1; 2 C-130K *Hercules;* 6 Cessna 421C *Golden Eagle*;Y-12
Training	14: 7 K-8 *Karakorum*; 7 PT-6
Helicopters	**Anti-tank** 11; MI-24 1: 1 Mi-24V *Hind E*; MI-35 12 Support MI-8 7: 3 MI-17 (Mi-8MT) *Hip H* **Utility** 12: 2 Bell 206 *JetRanger*; 2 Bell 212; 6 Bell 412 *Twin Huey* (VIP)
UAV	**Medium** some Blue Horizon-2; Searcher II
Air Defence	**Guns • Towed** 27: **40mm** 24 L/40; **94mm** 3 (3.7in)

Paramilitary 62,200

Home Guard 13,000
National Guard 15,000
Police Force 30,200; 1,000 (women); 30,400 reservists (total 61,600)

Ministry of Defence Special Task Force 3,000 (anti-guerrilla unit)

UN Missions	**Observers**: Democratic Republic of Congo, South Sudan, Sudan, Western Sahara **Units**: Haiti (infantry battalion); Lebanon (infantry company)

THAILAND

Armed Forces 360,850	**(Army 245,000; Navy 69,850; Air Force 46,000)** **Paramilitary 113,700** **Reserves 200,000; Paramilitary 45,000**
Organisations by Service	
Army	*130,000; 115,000 conscript (total 245,000)* 4 Regional Army HQ 3 Corps HQ
Forces by Role	
Armour	3 divisions
Armoured Infantry	1 division
Rapid Reaction	1 force (1 battalion per region)
Mechanised Infantry	5 divisions
Special Forces	1 division and 1 regiment
Infantry	3 divisions
Artillery	1 division
Air Defence Artillery	1 division (6 battalions)
Engineers	1 division
Helicopters	some flights
Economic development	4 divisions
Reserves	
Infantry	4 division HQ
Equipment by Type	
Tanks	283 **MBT** 53 M-60A3; 105 M-60 A1; 50 Type-69 (training in store); 105 M-48A5 **Light Tanks** 194: 24 M-41; 104 *Scorpion* (50 in store); 66 *Stingray*
Reconnaissance	32: M1114 *HMMWV;* S52 32: 32 S52 Mk 3
Armoured Personnel Carriers	1,140 **APC (T)** 880; M-113 340: 340 M-113A1/M-113A3 Type-85 **APC (W)** 160: 18 *Condor;* LAV 142: 142 LAV-150 *Commando*
Artillery	2,555 **Towed** 577; 340 **105mm**; 24 LG1 MK II; 200 M-101 Mod 12 M-102; 32 M-618A2; **130mm** 54 Type-59-I ; **155mm** 183; 42 GHN-45 A1; 48 M-114; 61 M-198; 32 M-71 32 **SP 155mm** M-109 20: 20 M-109A2 **MRL 130mm**: some Type-85 **Mortars** 1,900 **SP** 33; **81mm** 21 M125A3; **107mm** M106A3; **120mm** 12 M1064A3 **Towed** 1,867: **81mm**; **107mm** M106A1; **120mm** 12 M1064
Anti-tank	**Missiles** 318 **SP** 18 M-901A5 **Man-portable** 300 M47 *Dragon* **Recoilless** 180; **106mm** 150: 150 M-40; **75mm** 30: 30 M-20; **Rocket Launchers** M-72 *LAW*
Aircraft	**Reconnaissance: Observation** 40: 40 Cessna O-1A *Bird Dog* **Transport** 19; 2 Beech 1900C, Beech 200 *Super King Air* 2; CASA 212 *Aviocar* 2 *Jetstream* 41; 2 Short 330UTT 2

	Utility: U-17 10: 10 U-17B TRG 33 MX-7 18: 18 MX-7-235 *Star Rocket* T-41 15: 15 T-41B *Mescalero*
Helicopters	**Anti-tank** 7 AH-1F *Cobra*
	MRH 3 Mi-17V-5 *Hip H*
	Transport 201: **Heavy** 5 CH-47D *Chinook* **Medium** 6 UH-60L *Black Hawk* **Light** 190: 92 Bell 205 (UH-1H *Iroquois*); 28 Bell 206 *Jet Ranger*; 37 Bell 212 (AB-212); 3 *Enstrom* 480B
	Training: 42 Hughes 300C
Unarmed Aerial Vehicles	**Reconnaissance: Tactical**: *Searcher*
Air Defence	**SAM Static**: *Aspide*
	Man-portable: some FIM-43 *Redeye* HN-5: some HN-5A
	Guns 202 20mm 48
	SP 24: 24 M-163 *Vulcan*
	Towed 148: 24 M-167 *Vulcan* 37mm 52: 52 Type-74 40mm 78: 30 M-1 /M-42 SP; 48 L/70 57mm 24: 6 Type-59 (S-60)
Radar	**Land**: 36; AN/TPQ *Firefinder* (Artillery, mortar); RASIT (vehicle, artillery)
ARV	43: 22 M88A1; 6 M88A2; 10 M113; 5 Type-653; WZT-4
VLB	Type-84
MW	*Bozena; Giant Viper*

Navy *44,000 (including Naval Aviation, Marines, Coastal Defence); 25,850 conscript (total 69,850)*

Equipment by Type

Principal Surface Combatants	11
Aircraft Carrier	**CVH** 1: 1 *Chakri Naruebet* (capacity 9 AV-8A *Harrier* FGA aircraft; 6 S-70B *Seahawk* ASW helicopters)
Frigates	10
	FFGHM 2
	2 *Naresuan* (capacity either 1 S-70B-2 *Seahawk* ASW helicopters or 1 *Super Lynx* utility helicopters) each with 2 Mk 141 *Harpoon* quad (8 eff.) each with 1 RGM-84A *Harpoon* tactical SSM, 2 triple 324mm TT (6 eff.), 1 8 cell Mk 41 VLS with 1 RIM-7M *Sea Sparrow* SAM, 1 127mm gun
	FFGM 4
	2 *Chao Phraya* each with 4 twin (8 eff.) each with 1 CSS-N-4 *Sardine* tactical SSM, 2 (4 eff.) non-operational each with 1 HQ-61 (CSA-N-2) SAM non-operational, 2 RBU 1200 (10 eff.), 2 twin 100mm gun (4 eff.), 2 twin 37mm gun (4 eff.), 1 helicopters landing platform
	2 *Kraburi* (capacity 1 AB-212 (Bell 212) utility helicopters) each with 2 twin (4 eff.) each with 1 HQ-61 (CSA-N-2) SAM, 4 (8 eff.) each with 1 CSS-N-4 *Sardine* tactical SSM, 2 RBU 1200 (10 eff.), 1 twin 100mm gun (2 eff.), 2 twin 37mm gun (4 eff.)
	FFGH 2
	2 *Phuttha Yotfa Chulalok* (capacity 1 AB-212 (Bell 212) utility helicopters) (leased from US) each with 2 Twin ASTT (4 eff.) with 22 Mk 46 LWT, 1 Mk16 Mk 112 octuple with 1 RGM-84C *Harpoon* tactical SSM, tactical ASROC, 1 127mm gun
	FF 2
	1 *Makut Rajakumarn* with 2 triple ASTT (6 eff.), 2 114mm gun
	1 *Pin Klao* with 6 x1 324mm ASTT, 3 76mm gun 2 *Tapi* each with 6 x1 324mm ASTT each with Mk 46 LWT, 1 76mm gun
Patrol & Coastal Combatants	84
Corvettes	7
	FSG 2
	2 *Rattanakosin* each with 2 triple ASTT (6 eff.), 1 *Albatros* octuple with 1 Aspide SAM, 2 Mk 140 *Harpoon* quad (8 eff.) each with 1

PENTAGON'S SOUTH ASIA DEFENCE AND STRATEGIC YEAR BOOK

RGM-84A *Harpoon* tactical SSM, 1 76mm gun
FS 5
3 *Khamronsin* each with 2 triple ASTT (6 eff.), 1 76mm gun;
2 *Tapi* each with 6 single 324mm ASTT each with Mk 46 LWT, 176mm gun; 2 *Pattani* each with 176mm gun
PCFG 6
3 *Prabparapak* each with 2 single each with 1 GI *Gabriel* 1 tactical SSM, 1 triple (3 eff.) with GI *Gabriel* 1 tactical SSM, 140mm gun, 157mm gun
3 *Ratchari* each with 2 twin (4 eff.) each with MM-38 *Exocet* tactical SSM, 176mm gun
PCO 5: 3 *Hua Hin* each with 220mm gun, 176mm gun; 2 *Pattani* with 1 76mm gun
PCC 9: 3 *Chon Buri* each with 276mm gun each with 140mm gun, 176mm gun; 6 *Sattahip* each with 140mm gun, 176mm gun
PBF 4
PB 53: 7 T-11; 9 *Swift*; 3 T-81; 9 T-91; 3 T-210; 13 T-213; 1 T-227; 3 T-991; 3 T-994

Mine Warfare 17
MCC 2: 2 *Bang Rachan*
MCM Support 1 *Thalang*
MCO 2 *Lat Ya*
MSR 12

Amphibious
LPD 1 *Anthong* with 1 76mm gun (capacity 2 heptrs; 19 MBT; 500 troops)
LS 2 *Sichang* with 1 heptr landing platform (capacity 14 MBT; 300 troops)
Landing Craft 56
LCU 13: 3 *Man Nok*; 6 *Mataphun* (capacity either 3-4 MBT or 250 troops); 4 *Thong Kaeo*
LCVP 12
LCM 24
LCA 4
UCAC 3 *Griffon* 100TD

Logistics and Support 14
AORH 1 *Similan* (1 helicopter),
AOR 1 *Chula*
AOL 5: 4 *Prong*; 1 *Samui*
AWT 1
ABU 1
TRG 1
YPT 2
YTM 2

Facilities
Bases at Bangkok, Sattahip, Songkhla, Phang Nga, Nakhon and Phanom

Naval Aviation *1,200*

Fighter Ground Attack 7: 5 AV-8A *Harrier*; 2 TAV-8A *Harrier*

Reconnaissance
Observation 9: 9 *Sentry* 02-337
MP 10: 5 DO-228-212; 2 F-27 MK 200MPA*; 2 P-3T (P-3A) *Orion*
Transport F-27 2: 2 F-27-400M *Troopship*
Utility 8: 2 CL-215-III; 4 GAF N-24A *Search Master;* 1 UP-3T (UP-3A) *Orion*

Training 16: 14 **TA-7**; 4 TA-7C *Corsair II* TAV-8 2: 2 TAV-8A *Harrier*

Helicopters	**ASW** 8: 6 S-70B *Seahawk;* 2 S-76B Super Lynx 2 **Utility** 15: AB-212 (Bell 212) 5 Bell 214 5: 5 AB-214ST S-76 5: 5
Missiles	**Tactical ASM**: AGM-84 *Harpoon*
Marines 23,000	1 division HQ
Forces by Role	
Reconnaissance	1 battalion
Amphibious assault	1 battalion
Infantry	2 regiments
Combat Support	1 regiment (1 Air Defence Artillery battalion, 3 Field artillery battalions)
Equipment by Type	
APC	**APC (W) LAV** 24: 24 LAV-150 *Commando* **AAV** 33: 33 LVTP-7
Artillery	**Towed** 48: 36 **105mm**; 12 GC-45 **155mm**
Anti-tank	**Missiles** 22: M47 *Dragon* **TOW** 24; 24 HMMWV
Air Defence	**Guns** 14: **12.7mm**
Air Force 46,000	4 air divisions, 1 Flying Training school
Forces by Role	
Fighter	2 squadron with 35 F-5E *Tiger II*/F-5F *Tiger II*, 2 F-5B 3 squadrons with F-16A *Fighting Falcon* 1 squadron with L-39ZA/MP *Albatros*
FGA	1 squadron with *Gripen* C/D
Ground Attack	1 squadron with *Alpha Jet* 1 squadron with AU-23A *Peacemaker* 1 squadron with L-39ZA/MP *Albatros*
Reconnaissance/ELINT	1 squadron with 3 IAI-201 *Arava*, 2 Learjet 35A
AEW&C	1 squadron with Saab 340 *Erieye*
Transport	1 squadron with 9 Basler *Turbo-67;* 15 GAF N-22B *Nomad;* 1 squadron with 4 BAe-748; 3 G-222; 1 squadron with 7 C-130H *Hercules;* 5 C-130H-30 *Hercules*
VIP	1 (Royal Flight) squadron with A-310-324; Airbus A319CJ; 1 B-737-200; BAe-748; 737-400; Beech 200 *Super King Air;* SA-226AT *Merlin IV/IVA;* AS-532A2 *Cougar MKII;* AS-332L *Super Puma;* Bell 412 *Twin Huey*
Utility	1 squadron with L-392A
Liaison	1 squadron with Beech 65 *Queen Air;* Beech E90 *King Air;* Rockwell *Commander* 500; Cessna 150; T-41D *Mescalero*
Survey	1 squadron with 3 SA-226AT *Merlin IV/IVA;* GAF N-22B *Nomad*
Training	CT-4B/E *Airtrainer;* PC-9; Bell 206B *JetRanger II*
Helicopters	2 squadron UH-1H *Iroquois* 1 squadron Bell 412 *Twin Huey*
Equipment by Type	
Aircraft	163 combat capable
Fighter/Ground Attack	88: **F-5** 49: 31 F-5E *Tiger II*/F-5F *Tiger II*, 2 F-5B **F-16** 50: 41 F-16A *Fighting Falcon;* 9 F-16B *Fighting Falcon*
Transport	59: A-310 1: 1 A-310-324 A-319CJ 1B-737 3: 1 B-737-200; 2 B737-400 BAe-748 6 *Basler* Turbo-67 9 Beech 200 *Super King Air* 2 Beech 65 *Queen Air* 2 Beech 90 1: 1 Beech E90 *King Air* C-130 12: 7 C-130H *Hercules;* 5 C-130H-30 *Hercules* G-222 3 IAI-201 *Arava* 3 LEARJET 35 2: 2 *Learjet* 35A Rockwell *Commander* 500 3 SA-226 6: 6 SA-226AT *Merlin IV/IVA*

Utility	37: 22 AU-23A *Peacemaker*; 15 GAF N-22B *Nomad*
Training	119: 10 Alpha Jet; 29 CT-4B/E *Airtrainer*; 3 Cessna 150 L-39 46: 46 L-39ZA/MP *Albatros* PC-9 23 T-41 12: 12 T-41D *Mescalero*
Helicopters	**Support** 19: 3 AS-332L *Super Puma*; 3 AS-532A2 *Cougar MKII*; 13 Bell 212 **Utility** 28 Bell 206 6: 6 Bell 206B *JetRanger II* Bell 412 *Twin Huey* 2 UH-1 20: 20 UH-1H *Iroquois*
Missiles	**Tactical AAM**: AIM-120 *AMRAAM* **AIM-9**: AIM-9B *Sidewinder*/AIM-9J *Sidewinder Python III; ASM: AGM-65 Maverick*

Paramilitary *113,700 active*

Border Patrol Police *41,000*

Marine Police *2,200*

Patrol and Coastal Combatants 92

	PCO 1 *Srinakrin* **PCC** 2 *Hameln* **PB** 43: 2 *Chasanyabadee*; 1 *Yokohama*, 1 *Sriyanont*; 1 *Burespadoogkit*; 3 *Cutlass*; 35 (various) **PBR** 46

National Security Volunteer Corps *45,000*

Police Aviation *500*

Aircraft	6 combat capable **ATK** 6 AU-23A *Peacemaker* **Transport** 16 Light 15: 2 CN-235; 8 PC-6 Turbo-Porter; 3 SC-7 3M Skyvan; 2 Short 330UTT **PAX** 1 F-50
Helicopters	**MRH** 6 Bell 412 Twin Huey **Transport** Light 67: 27 Bell 205A; 14 Bell 206 *Jet Ranger*; 20 Bell 212 (AB-212)

Provincial Police *50,000 (including 500 Special Action Force)*

Thahan Phran (Hunter Soldiers) *20,000*

Paramilitary	13 regiments

Volunteer Irregular Force

UN Missions	**Observers**: Sudan, UNMOGIP **Deployment: Arabian Sea & Gulf of Aden –** CTF-151: 1 PCO; 1 AORH

MILITARY SPENDING IN SOUTH ASIA

Military Expenditure in Pakistan

In local currency (Rs in billions)																				
Year	1988	1989	1990	1991	1992	1993	1994	1995	1996	1997	1998	1999	2000	2001	2002	2003	2004	2005	2006	2007
Value	47	51	59	70	82	90	98	112	124	132	140	147	154	170	188	207	232	263	287	[307]
At 2005 constant (USD in millions)																				
Year	1988	1989	1990	1991	1992	1993	1994	1995	1996	1997	1998	1999	2000	2001	2002	2003	2004	2005	2006	2007
Value	2,896	2,894	3,054	3,270	3,472	3,467	3,379	3,434	3,430	3,285	3,281	3,311	3,320	3,553	3,819	4,077	4,248	4,412	[4,517]	4,465
As percentage of GDP																				
Year	1988	1989	1990	1991	1992	1993	1994	1995	1996	1997	1998	1999	2000	2001	2002	2003	2004	2005	2006	2007
Value	6.2	6	5.8	5.8	6.1	5.7	5.3	5.3	5.1	4.9	4.8	3.9	3.7	3.9	3.9	3.7	3.5	3.4	3.2	

Military Expenditure in Sri Lanka

In local currency (Rs in billions)																				
Year	1988	1989	1990	1991	1992	1993	1994	1995	1996	1997	1998	1999	2000	2001	2002	2003	2004	2005	2006	2007
Value	4.7	4.1	7	10	13	15	19	35	38	37	42	40	57	54	49	47	56	61	81	105
At 2005 constant (USD in millions)																				
Year	1988	1989	1990	1991	1992	1993	1994	1995	1996	1997	1998	1999	2000	2001	2002	2003	2004	2005	2006	2007
Value	257	198	270	368	412	442	513	863	807	716	751	676	904	755	625	562	626	612	713	804
As percentage of GDP																				
Year	1988	1989	1990	1991	1992	1993	1994	1995	1996	1997	1998	1999	2000	2001	2002	2003	2004	2005	2006	2007
Value	2.1	1.6	2.1	2.8	3	3.1	3.4	5.3	5	4.2	4.1	3.6	4.5	3.9	3.1	2.7	2.8	2.6	2.9	

Notes:

1. The figures for Sri Lanka for 2000 do not fully reflect a special allocation of Rs 28 billion made for war-related expenditure.
2. The figures for these countries are for current spending only (they exclude capital spending).
3. The figures for these countries do not include military pensions.

Military Expenditure in India

In local currency (Rs in billions)																				
Year	1988	1989	1990	1991	1992	1993	1994	1995	1996	1997	1998	1999	2000	2001	2002	2003	2004	2005	2006	2007
Value	152	172	184	196	210	252	279	316	351	416	492	598	642	689	717	761	812	982	1,102	1,193
At 2005 constant (USD in millions)																				
Year	1988	1989	1990	1991	1992	1993	1994	1995	1996	1997	1998	1999	2000	2001	2002	2003	2004	2005	2006	2007
Value	11,440	12,219	12,036	11,238	10,740	12,131	12,185	12,550	12,778	14,144	14,757	17,150	17,697	18,313	18,256	18,664	19,204	22,273	23,615	24,249
As percentage of GDP																				
Year	1988	1989	1990	1991	1992	1993	1994	1995	1996	1997	1998	1999	2000	2001	2002	2003	2004	2005	2006	2007
Value	2.1	1.6	2.1	2.8	3	3.1	3.4	5.3	5	4.2	4.1	3.6	4.5	3.9	3.1	2.7	2.8	2.6	2.9	

Note: The figures for India include expenditure on the paramilitary forces of the Border Security Force, the Central Reserve Police Force, the Assam Rifles and the Indo-Tibetan Border Police but do not include spending on military nuclear establishments.

Military Expenditure in Bangladesh

In local currency (Taka in millions)																				
Year	1988	1989	1990	1991	1992	1993	1994	1995	1996	1997	1998	1999	2000	2001	2002	2003	2004	2005	2006	2007
Value	9,104	10,663	11,143	12,071	14,396	16,105	19,021	21,582	23,076	25,863	28,436	31,277	33,377	34,020	34,105	36,150	39,630	43,005	46,950	..
At 2005 constant (USD in millions)																				
Year	1988	1989	1990	1991	1992	1993	1994	1995	1996	1997	1998	1999	2000	2001	2002	2003	2004	2005	2006	2007
Value	347	379	377	384	442	480	538	554	578	615	624	647	675	675	655	657	659	669	684	
As percentage of GDP																				
Year	1988	1989	1990	1991	1992	1993	1994	1995	1996	1997	1998	1999	2000	2001	2002	2003	2004	2005	2006	2007
Value	1	1.1	1	1	1.1	1.2	1.2	1.3	1.3	1.3	1.3	1.3	1.2	1.1	1.1.	1.1	1.1	1	1	

Military Expenditure in Nepal

In local currency (Rs in millions)

Year	1988	1989	1990	1991	1992	1993	1994	1995	1996	1997	1998	1999	2000	2001	2002	2003	2004	2005	2006	2007
Value	834	988	1,114	1,320	1,607	1,801	1,939	2,064	2,242	2,417	2,789	3,239	3,648	4,837	6,621	7,951	9,756	11,153	[11,004]	[10,604]

At 2005 constant (USD in millions)

Year	1988	1989	1990	1991	1992	1993	1994	1995	1996	1997	1998	1999	2000	2001	2002	2003	2004	2005	2006	2007
Value	39.9	43.5	45.3	46.4	48.3	50.3	50	49.4	49.2	52.1	52.9	57.1	62.8	81.1	108	122	146	156	[143]	[132]

As percentage of GDP

Year	1988	1989	1990	1991	1992	1993	1994	1995	1996	1997	1998	1999	2000	2001	2002	2003	2004	2005	2006	2007
Value	0.9	1	0.9	0.9	0.9	0.9	0.9	0.9	0.8	0.8	0.8	0.8	0.9	0.9	1.1	1.5	1.6	1.8	1.9	[1.7]

Military Expenditure in Afghanistan

In local currency (Afghani in millions)

Year	1988	1989	1990	1991	1992	1993	1994	1995	1996	1997	1998	1999	2000	2001	2002	2003	2004	2005	2006	2007
Value	..	..	..	..	..	..	..	..	..	..	..	..	..	..	..	..	5,440	5,521	6,223	10,255

At 2005 constant (USD in millions)

Year	1988	1989	1990	1991	1992	1993	1994	1995	1996	1997	1998	1999	2000	2001	2002	2003	2004	2005	2006	2007
Value	..	..	..	..	..	..	..	..	..	..	..	..	..	..	..	..	123	111	119	181

As percentage of GDP

Year	1988	1989	1990	1991	1992	1993	1994	1995	1996	1997	1998	1999	2000	2001	2002	2003	2004	2005	2006	2007
Value	..	..	..	..	..	..	..	..	..	..	..	..	..	..	..	..	″	1.9	1.5	1.5

1. The figures for Afghanistan are for core budget expenditure on the Afghan National Army. If spending from the external budget, paid for directly by military aid, were included, then the total military spending would be more than six times higher.

Notes:

1. In the financial year 1998-99, Nepal's additional expenditure on paramilitary forces was Rs 3315 million.
2. Figures for these countries do not include spending on paramilitary forces.

SOUTHERN ASIA DEFENCE EXPENDITURE DATA

Country	Population (millions)	Armed Forces Total	GDP (US$ billion)			Per capita (US$)			Growth (%)			Defence Budget (US$)		
			2010	2011	2012	2010	2011	2012	2010	2011	2012	2010	2011	2012
Afghanistan	30.4	340,350	17.7	18.3	19.8	596	602	653	8.23	5.77	5.22	2.96bn	2.49bn	2.09bn
Bangladesh	161.1	220,950	..	113.8	118.7	..	707	737	6.38	6.51	6.05	1.34bn	1.25bn	1.49bn
Bhutan	742,737	10,000	1.26	1.41	1.48	1,880	1,978	2,121	7.12	11.76	7.5	..	..	..
China	1,314.1	2,255,000	6.8tr	7.3tr	8.25tr	4,414	5,435	6,142	10.33	9.24	7.83	88.8bn	90.2bn	102bn
India	1,110.3	1,325,000	1.64tr	1.83tr	1.95tr	1,394	1,519	1,618	10.09	6.84	4.86	29.7bn	36.1bn	38.5bn
Iran	78.868	523,000	..	482.43	483.78	..	6,117	6,134	..	2.04	-0.94	..	26.94bn	23.9bn
Maldives	328,536	...	1.36	1.94	2.06	3,932	5,973	6,336	..	..	..	..	41m	45mn
Myanmar	47.4	581,000	46.1	51.44	54.05	854	942	990	5.45	5.53	6.20	1.76bn	2.04bn	2.27bn
Nepal	25.2	69,000	17.96	18.98	19.42	609	635	650	4.55	3.88	4.63	241m	269m	238bn
Pakistan	152.8	619,000	202	210.22	230.5	1,079	1,105	1,211	3.76	3.04	3.68	5.16bn*	5.21bn*	5.78bn*
Sri Lanka	16.7	151,000	49.4	58.8	59.77	2,345	2,761	2,782	8.01	8.26	6.75	1.86bn	1.97bn	1.46bn

CONVENTIONAL MILITARY STRENGTH

Country	Regular	Paramilitary	Tanks (1)	APCs (2)	Combat Ac (3)	Attack Heptrs	Principal Surface Combatants (4)	Patrol and Coastal Combatants	Subs (5)	Amph (6)
China	2,285,000	660,000	7,400	4,350	1,693	38	78	211	71	239
Indonesia	302,000	400,000	350	519	67	-	11	67	2	31
Malaysia	109,000	51,600	48	784	74	-	10	37	2	1
Myanmar	406,000	107,250	160	361	136	-	1	99	0	18
Singapore	72,500	312,500	96	1,695	148	19	6	35	5	4
Thailand	305,860	200,000	283	1,140	163	3	11	83	0	8
Afghanistan	170,700	136,100	no data	173	no data	13	0	0	0	0
Bangladesh	157,050	63,900	232	248	74	14	5	42	0	11
Bhutan	10,000	0	0	0	0	0	0	0	0	0
India	1,325,000	1,155,000	3,215	1,455	798	22	21	61	15	18
Nepal	95,750	62,000	0	53	0	-	0	0	0	0
Pakistan	642,000	304,000	2,411	1,320	453	42	10	12	8	0
Sri Lanka	160,900	5,500	62	221	31	11	0	139	0	1
Iran	520,000	350,000	1,620	1,400	320	570	256		14	
Russia	1,027,000	20,000,000	23,000+	27,190+	2,080	1,589+	62	74	67	45+
USA	1,498,157	1,082,718	8,023+	28,454	4,269	5,289	106	16	71	32
Australia	54,747	19,915	149	1,728	109	113	12	14	6	3

Notes: All figures are estimates and include some equipment held in store. Figures are not shown for coast guard and paramilitary forces.

1. Main battle tanks.
2. Includes light tanks, light armoured vehicles, armoured personnel carriers, infantry mobility vehicles and infantry fighting vehicles.
3. Includes fighters, bombers and armed maritime patrol aircraft.
4. Includes corvettes, frigates, destroyers, cruisers and aircraft carriers.
5. Includes nuclear and conventional submarines.
6. Amphibious ship categories, including: tank landing ship, medium landing ship, heavy landing ship, amphibious landing platform, landing ship logistic and helicopter, landing ship dock, assault landing ship and landing ship helicopter and dock.

ECONOMIC INDICATORS

	Afghanistan	Bangladesh	Bhutan	China	India	Iran
Surface area (sq km)	647,500	147,570	38,394	9,596,960	3,287,260	1,745,150
Coastline (km)	..	580	..	14,500	7,516	2,440
Forest area (sq km)	13,500	14,394	32,598	2,096,239	685,790	110,750
Forest area (% of land area)	2.06	11.05	84.9	22.47	23.06	6.8
Agricultural land (% of land area)	58.12	70.12	13.54	55.65	60.47	30.06
Agricultural land (sq km)	379,100	91,280	5,200	5,191,482	1,797,990	489,570
Population growth (annual %)	2.72	1.2	1.68	0.47	1.36	1.11
Population density (sq km)	54.15	1,069	49	144	363	45.9
Rural population (% of total)	76.45	71.6	64.43	49.49	68.7	30.91
Urban population growth rate (%)	4	2.9	3.88	3.03	2.54	1.31
Life expectancy (years)	49	63	67	73	65	73
Birth rate (per 1,000 people)	43.08	19.96	20.06	11.93	21.82	16.78
Net migration	-381,030	-2,908,015	16,829	-1,884,102	-2,999,998	-185,650
Population <14 years	46.08	30.67	28.84	19.07	30.21	22.72
Population 15-64 years	51.66	64.70	66.33	72.55	64.79	72.01
Population >65 years	2.25	4.62	4.82	8.36	4.99	5.25
Age ratio (% of working age population)	93.54	..	50.76	37.82	54.33	38.85
Energy imports, net (% of energy use)	..	19	..	8.61	25.12	-67.55
Energy use (kg of oil equivalent per capita)	..	145	..	1,806.92	565.63	2,816.76
Export of goods/services % of GDP)	18.10	15	26	31.37	23.88	33.05
Imports of goods & Services (% of GDP)	63.36	21	55	27.30	30.33	24.65
Trade (% of GDP)	81.46	54.51	92.41	58.67	54.21	57.71
Telephone users (%)	0.04	..	..	21.15	2.62	37.12
Mobile phone subscribers (%)	54.26	84.3	4.8	73.18	71.9	74.92
Internet users (%)	5	5	21	38	11	21
GDP (PPP) ($ million)	33,277	272,273	4,026	11,347,450	4,530,860	
GDP (per capita at PPP)($)	1.280	1,906	5,787	8,422	3,783	
GDP growth (annual %)	5.73	6.7	5.57	9.3	7	4.62
External trade balance (% of GDP)	-45.25	-8.70	-24.67	4.06	-6.44	8.39
FDI (net inflow % of GDP)	0.434	0.712	0.946	3.0	1.718	1.63
Gross domestic savings (% of GDP)	-19.837	16.44	25.23	52.51	34.61	41.09
Gross national expenditure (% of GDP)	145.25	108.70	124.67	95.93	106.44	91.60
Govt. consumption expenditure (% of GDP)	11.5	5.8	20.0	13.1	11.7	..
Electric power consumption (kWh per capita)	..	104	..	2,943.79	616.20	2,652.31
Motor vehicles (per 1,000 people)	28	21.92	34	57.71	14	..
Roads (km)	37,475	21,269	6,920	4,008,229	3,929,439	198866
Paved roads (%)	27.5	9.5	40	40	47	80
Railway lines (km)	..	2,835	..	66,239	63,974	6,073

Economic Indicators (contd).

	Maldives	Myanmar	Nepal	Pakistan	Sri Lanka
Surface area (sq km)	298	676,578	147,180	796,100	65,610
Coastline (km)	2,002	1,930	..	1,046	1,340
Forest area (sq km)	10	314,634	36,360	16,440	18,454
Forest area (% of land area)	3	48.16	25.36	2.13	29.42
Agricultural land (% of land area)	23	19.22	29.71	34.44	41.78
Agricultural land (sq km)	79	125.580	42,590	265,500	26,200
Population growth (annual %)	1.6	0.84	2	1.79	1.04
Population density (sq km)	1,066	80.13	186	229.27	332.78
Rural population (% of total)	58.88	66.77	83.00	63.78	84.87
Urban population growth rate (%)	4.08	2.58	3.76	2.72	1.60
Life expectancy (years)	76	65	69	65	74
Birth rate (per 1,000 people)	16.63	17.03	23.65	26.92	17.76
Net migration	-53	-500,000	-100,000	-1,999,998	-249,998
Population <14 years	25.78	25.27	35.50	34.83	24.89
Population 15-64 years	68.96	69.55	60.26	60.83	66.69
Population >65 years	5.24	5.16	4.22	4.33	8.41
Age ratio (% of working age population)	45.00	43.76	65.92	64.39	49.93
Energy imports, net (% of energy use)	..	0.84	71.74	23.98	43.87
Energy use (kg of oil equivalent per capita)	..	-60.95	12.07	487.31	477.89
Export of goods/services % of GDP)	95	269.53	17	16	23.06
Imports of goods & Services (% of GDP)	83	0.12	31	15	37.61
Trade (% of GDP)	223.98	0.30	41.70	19.229	60.66
Telephone users (%)	7.52	.10	2.77	3.23	17.14
Mobile phone subscribers (%)	165.72	2.57	43.80	61.61	87.07
Internet users (%)	59	0.12	9	9	15
GDP (PPP) ($ million)	2,859	..	38,302	487,607	117,282
GDP (per capita at PPP)($)	8,793	..	1,439	2,753	5,620
GDP growth (annual %)	7.46	13.64	3.88	2.95	8.25
External trade balance (% of GDP)	3.02	0.059	-23.01	-5.07	-14.55
FDI (net inflow % of GDP)	13.73	..	0.49	0.62	1.61
Gross domestic savings (% of GDP)	1.71	12.108	8.617	8.00	15.834
Gross national expenditure (% of GDP)	138.69	99.940	123.90	105.07	114.55
Govt. consumption expenditure (% of GDP)	..	..	9.6	7.9	14.8
Electric power consumption (kWh per capita)	..	121.12	92.69	456.63	449.18
Motor vehicles (per 1,000 people)	27.7	5.41	..	17.54	19.86
Roads (km)	100	34,337	17,433	262,256	114,093
Paved roads (%)	88	12	56	72	..
Railway lines (km)	..	3,336	..	7,791	1,491

TERRORISM

TERRORISM IN SOUTH ASIA

Introduction

In recent years, global terrorist activities have been converging on South Asia, which has become the hardest-hit region-the "source" and "hotbed" of the international terrorist attacks. Governments of South Asian countries have adopted various measures to intensify their crackdown on terrorist activities and tried to maintain the social stability within their nations. Since 2009, India, Sri Lanka and Bangladesh have achieved some progress in their counter-terrorist efforts, and terrorist activities have lost some momentum in these countries. However, the Afghan government continues to struggle in controlling the political situation in the country, Pakistan is beset by internal and external difficulties, and the US-led Af-Pak strategy has not yielded significant results. So far, the Taliban in both Pakistan and Afghanistan have continued to carry out their militant activities. The fight between terrorism and counter-terrorism is still very fierce.

Main Features of Current Terrorist Activities

In recent years, the frequency of violent terrorist attacks has remained high in the South Asian region due to unstable domestic situations, weak government control and the impact of underlying ethnic and religious tensions. The Pakistan-Afghanistan border areas have become the main bases for terrorist organizations such as al Qaeda, the Taliban and the Lashkar-e-Taiba. Terrorist activities in South Asia have the following characteristics:

- South Asia has become the most important centre of terrorist activities in the world. The terrorist activities in this region have remained large in number and scale, with the tendency of localization and close collaboration through regional networks. According to the statistics of the South Asia Terrorism Portal, the world had seen another 145 terrorist incidents, causing 803 deaths and 1,563 injuries. 81 of these terrorist incidents had taken place in South Asia, making up 58 per cent of the world's total. At the same time, terrorist activities have become more localized. The Taliban activities have spread to a large part of Afghan territory. The Pakistan Taliban continues to launch terrorist attacks one after another in the heartland of the country. The terrorist organization, Lashkar-e-Taiba, in the Kashmir region, has greatly enhanced its capabilities to launch terrorist activities. The trend of Talibanization in both Afghanistan and Pakistan, the regionalization of the Taliban and the localization of the Indian terrorist groups are becoming more prominent.
- Terrorists have strengthened their collaboration through regional networks. Terrorist organizations in South Asia have collaborated more closely with each other and formed regional networks across Afghanistan, Pakistan, India, Bangladesh and other countries. They have also joined hands with other international terrorist forces like al Qaeda, receiving funds from the Middle East, recruiting personnel from Central Asia, and thus forming bases of international terrorist activities. The Lashkar-e- Taiba has set up affiliates in India, Afghanistan and Bangladesh, and has evolved from a jihad organization in India-controlled Kashmir, into a regional terrorist organization with the range of activities expanding to the surrounding areas.
- Terrorist activities in South Asia have demonstrated the vicious spill-over effects in Afghanistan and Pakistan. The activities of the al Qaeda have become more covert and it pays more attention to exporting its action mode and terrorist ideology. The core circle of al Qaeda has speeded up working hand in glove with the local extremist forces in Afghanistan and Pakistan. The Haqqani network in Afghanistan, the Lashkar-e- Taiba in Kashmir and the Pakistani Taliban are becoming increasingly interwoven and symbiotic by providing support to each other. Some terrorist forces have aligned or affiliated themselves with al Qaeda as its branches, creating terrorist networks spanning over 70 countries around the world. For example, the Iraqi al Qaeda was founded in September 2004 and the al Qaeda in the Islamic Maghreb in Northern Africa was established in September 2006. Moreover, al Qaeda is also making better use of the Internet to spread and export terrorism and extremist ideology.
- Due to geographical, ethnic and economic reasons, many young people are being

recruited by terrorist organizations to receive terrorist training in the border areas between Afghanistan and Pakistan. On completion of their training and indoctrination, they form the backbone of forces used to carry out terrorist activities. Should terrorist forces support each other and coordinate their activities, a new round of integration and regrouping may take place, which will subject the regional security situation to serious challenges.

- *Fidayeen*-type attacks have become the main pattern of terrorist activities and terrorist methods are getting more sophisticated. Since the 26/11 terrorist attacks in Mumbai in 2008, attacks similar to a *fidayeen* pattern and characterized by careful planning and multi-pronged and well coordinated small-group attacks causing widespread devastation and destruction have become the first choice of terrorists. In 2009, most terrorist attacks with big casualties in South Asia were *fidayeen*-type ones. Out of the 19 massive terrorist attacks, 13 were *fidayeen*-type attacks, making up 70 per cent of the total, which include the 11/2 armed attack on Kabul, 3/ 3 attack against the Sri Lankan cricket team in Lahore, 30/3 attack on the Lahore police school, 27/5 attack on the Lahore police department, and the 10/10 attack on the Pakistani Army headquarters. In these terrorist attacks, terrorists demonstrated skill and tactics such as good coordination, successful breaking-through of defences, and multi-pronged assaults. For instance, in both cases of terrorist attacks on the Lahore police school on 30 March and on Pakistani Army headquarters on 10 October, terrorists launched a surprise assault at the entrances, created chaos and simultaneously divided themselves into several small groups to occupy strongholds and hijack hostages to confront the security forces. When surrounded and cornered they resorted to suicide by detonating explosives strapped to them. What merits more attention is that while the *fidayeen*-type attacks are increasingly directed against the important government and military facilities, more and more attacks are also being conducted against the living quarters of military personnel around military targets. In the deadly 10/10 terrorist attacks on the Pakistani Army headquarters and the 15/10 attacks on the police, terrorists disguised themselves as policemen and suddenly assaulted the heavily-guarded military places by employing various means. Terrorist activities in South Asia have proved that it will be very difficult to prevent *fidayeen*-type terrorist attacks.

Trend of Terrorist Activities

The counterterrorism situation in South Asia has undergone some important changes in its dynamics. Since the beginning of last year, Pakistan has expanded the range of its counter-terrorism targets, not only hitting the Pakistan Taliban but also striking the ringleaders of the Afghan Taliban and al Qaeda within Pakistan. Simultaneously, Pakistan has stepped up mopping up operations against militants of the Pakistan Taliban within the country. After cleaning up the Taliban militants in the tribal areas of Southern Waziristan at the end of 2009, it has ended its operations in the tribal areas of Bajaur in March and killed Maulana Faqir Mohammed, the ringleader of the region. Additionally, India has thwarted several plots of terrorist attacks, Bangladesh is engaging in cleaning up the religious extremist forces in the country and Sri Lanka has taken tight precautions against terrorist attacks by the remnants of the Tamil Tigers. These new developments are conducive to weakening the capabilities of terrorist groups to carry out terrorist activities.

However, on the whole, terrorist activities in South Asia cannot be held in check in a short time. On the one hand, although terrorist organizations in the region have suffered some losses, they will not stop their terrorist activities easily. As a matter of fact, they will try to seek every opportunity to take revenge by launching more terrorist attacks. Terrorist attacks happened one after another in Jaipur of India on 13 February 2010, in Kabul on 26 February 2010 and Kandahar of Afghanistan and in Lahore of Pakistan on the same day of 13 March 2010. These attacks demonstrated that terrorist organizations in South Asia will continue or even intensify their attacks.

Supporting this trend is the fact that regional counter-terrorism efforts are handicapped in various ways. First, the effectiveness of Pakistani counter-terrorism operations remains to be seen. Since April 2009, the Pakistani military has been carrying out cleanup operations against terrorists in the Swat area, containing the momentum of the Pakistan Taliban expanding to the interior of the country. So far, the Pakistani military has ousted militants of Pakistan Taliban in South Waziristan and killed some important figures. But judging from actual results of counter-terrorism operations of the Pakistani military, it killed or captured only a very limited number of terrorists. The majority of their effective strength in Pakistan has actually been preserved and transferred to other places. The supremacy of the Pakistani military does not automatically mean it can take the initiative in the fight against terrorists in the battlefield. The effectiveness of its combat against terrorists seems doubtful because it is also restrained by factors other than the military, namely those of political, economic and social nature. The democratically-elected Pakistan coalition government has been weak and troubled by internal strife, which hinders counter-terrorism efforts in the country.

The goal of realizing internal stability in Afghanistan is still not in sight. The efficiency of the American military operations in Afghanistan is limited by the difficult terrain there. It is no easy job to eliminate al Qaeda in such a short period of time and given that the Taliban mingle easily with the Afghan populace. Furthermore, the number and quality of the Afghan security forces cannot be greatly improved in such little time to shoulder heavy responsibilities effectively. It is not easy to achieve the goal of letting the Afghans run Afghanistan effectively in a short time. The country is desperately poor and divided into many tribes. No previous Afghan central government has exercised effective control over the entire country.

In a nutshell, the security situation in Afghanistan cannot be improved in the short run, and the hotbed that breeds terrorism in South Asia will, unfortunately, continue to exist for a long time.

Against the backdrop of the complicated relations between countries in the region, some terrorist activities have been aimed at sowing the seeds of discord and sabotaging relations, especially between India and Pakistan. These two countries are the largest and second largest states respectively in the South Asian subcontinent, with a total population of over 1.25 billion. The two countries have been at loggerheads with each other since their independence and have already fought three wars against each other. Terrorist groups in the region do not want to see a peaceful and stable South Asia and try to seek gains from the tensions between these two countries. Their activities have in fact, contributed to worsening relations between India and Pakistan. The process of reconciliation between the two sides has stalled bringing the two nations, which is the exact result terrorist organizations in the region want to see.

The spillover of terrorist activities in South Asia is evident in the surrounding regions and many other parts of the world as well. China, as a neighbouring country of South Asia, has suffered a lot from terrorists related to organizations like al Qaeda, Afghanistan Taliban and Pakistan Taliban. The terrorist organization East Turkistan Islamic Movement (ETIM) is supported and funded by al Qaeda and Taliban in one way or another. Some of its members were trained in Afghanistan and on the Pakistani side of the Pakistan and Afghanistan border area by al Qaeda and Taliban. This terrorist organization has sent terrorists into China and masterminded terrorist attacks mainly in Xinjiang Uygur Autonomous Region time and again.

SOUTH ASIA FATALITIES—2005-2013

Year	Civilians	Security Forces	Terrorists	Total
2005	2,063	920	3,311	6,294
2006	2,803	1,725	4,504	9,032
2007	31,28	1,504	6,145	10,777
2008	3,653	2,342	14,632	20,627
2009	14,197	2,738	12,703	29,638
2010	2,571	844	6,016	9,431
2011	3,173	962	3,284	7,419
2012	3,270	871	2,902	7,043
2013	3,313	833	2,094	6,240
Total	**38,171**	**12,739**	**55,591**	**106,501**

2013

	Civilians	Security Forces	Terrorists	Total
BANGLADESH				
Islamist	163	14	97	274
Left Wing	2	0	17	19
Bangladesh (Total)	165	14	114	293
BHUTAN				
	0	0	0	0
INDIA				
Jammu and Kashmir	19	59	94	172
Left Wing	152	101	145	398
North East	72	19	121	212
Rest of India	25	0	1	26
India (Total)	266	179	361	808
NEPAL				
	0	0	0	0
PAKISTAN				
	2,880	640	1,619	5,139
SRI LANKA				
	0	0	0	0
Grand Total*	**3,313**	**833**	**2,094**	**6,240**

INDIA
TERRORIST INCIDENTS – 2013

8 Jan 2013 Almost a dozen of Pakistani troopers breached the Line of Control (LoC) at Mankot sector in Mendhar tehsil of Poonch District, ambushed an Indian Army patrol, killed two Indian troopers (beheading one of them, while mutilating other), injured another two of them, and took the head of one while fleeing back to Pakistan occupied Kashmir (PoK). The killed troopers were identified as Lance Naik Hem Raj and Lance Naik Sudhakar Singh.

Reports suggest that Lashkar-e-Toiba (LeT) founder and Jama'at-ud-Da'awa (JuD) chief Hafiz Muhammad Saeed provoked the Pakistani soldiers to fire on Indian troops as part of his plans to begin jihad (holy war) in Kashmir. Reports say Saeed was inciting LeT's BATs (Border Action Teams), consisting of jihadis and trained militants to step up activity along the LoC. Also, Hafiz Saeed and Hizb-ul-Mujahideen (HM) 'supreme commander' Syed Salahuddin have reportedly told a delegation of separatists leaders from Jammu and Kashmir that armed militancy would revive in the Valley in 2014.

At least nine Central Reserve Police Force (CRPF) personnel, one Jharkhand Jaguar trooper, four civilians and two Communist Party of India-(Maoist) cadres were killed as Maoists attack SFs at Karmatiya forests of Latehar District. Around 300 CRPF and Jharkhand Jaguar personnel treaded deep into the Karmatiya jungles as part of a combing operation when Maoists started indiscriminate firing from tree tops and hills. Over 600 Maoists, led by senior leaders, were present in the Latehar jungles. CPI-Maoist central committee member Arvind was the leader behind the attacks, said Police sources. Many of the Maoists were dressed like SF personnel.

9 Feb 2013 Parliament House attack (13 December 2001) case convict Mohamad Afzal Guru was hanged to death at Tihar Central Jail in New Delhi at 8 am.

21 Feb 2013 16 people were killed and 117 were injured in the twin blasts in Dilsukhnagar area of Hyderabad City (Hyderabad Urban District). The blasts took place at a local bus stop and a Canteen, which were about 150 metres from each other, at 6.58pm and 7.01pm respectively. Preliminary investigations reveal that the IEDs (improvised explosive device) were placed on bicycles causing explosions at both the places.

22 Feb 2013 The CPI-Maoist cadres triggered a landmine blast killing eight persons - six Police personnel, one Special Police Officer (SPO) and one civilian - at Majhauliya village in Gaya District of Bihar. The Security Forces were on patrolling duty during the ongoing process of selection of gram sevikas when the blast took place near the Koili culvert between Roshanganj and Imamganj areas at around 1pm.

13 Mar 2013 Two *fidayeen* (suicide attackers) stormed a Central Reserve Police Force camp in Bemina area of Srinagar city killing five troopers and injuring 10 others, including seven troopers and three civilians. The two terrorists, who carried out the attack, were also killed. Though Hizb-ul-Mujahideen (HM) claimed responsibility for the attack, investigations indicate that the militants were of Pakistani origin and belonged to the Lashkar-e-Toiba (LeT).

4 Apr 2013 Seven CPI-Maoist cadres were killed in an encounter with the Police near Bhatpar village in Bhamragad division of Gadchiroli District.

Five personnel of the Jharkhand Armed Police were killed when cadres of the CPI-Maoist opened fire at a village market in Chainpur in Gumla District. Two villagers were also reported to have been shot dead but the Government officials did not confirm this.

12 Apr 2013 Four CPI-Maoist cadres, a Policeman and two villagers were killed in an encounter between the Maoists and Commandos of an anti-Naxal unit, C-60, in a forest of Dhanora in Gadchiroli District. Several LWEs were injured in the firing but bodies of three women and one male rebel were recovered.

16 Apr 2013 10 CPI-Maoist cadres were killed in an encounter with Security Forces (SFs) in the forest area of Puarti village in Sukma District. SFs recovered dead bodies of nine out of 10 cadres killed. Seven of the 10 killed were identified as members of the North

Telangana Special Zonal Committee (NTSZC).

17 Apr 2013 17 people, including 11 Policemen, were injured in a bomb blast barely 50 metres from the Bhartiya Janata Party (BJP) party office in Bangalore (Karnataka). Union Ministry of Home Affairs (MHA) called the blast "a terrorist attack".

18 Apr 2013 A Pune court awarded death penalty to Indian Mujahideen (IM) operative Mirza Himayat Inayat Baig in the German Bakery blast case of 13 February 2010, which killed 17 and wounded 64. Inayat Baig, the lone arrested accused in the German Bakery blast was convicted by a sessions court in Pune on 15 April for criminal conspiracy, murder and other charges.

26 Apr 2013 Militants in the evening laid an ambush and killed four Policemen personnel near Haigam locality along the Sopore-Kupwara road in Baramulla District. Inspector General of Police A G Mir said that four Policemen were on their way to Haigam to probe a complaint of robbery when they were ambushed by militants in a lane of the village. Baleeg-ud-Din, 'spokesperson' of Hizb-ul-Mujahideen (HM), through a phone call to a local new agency claimed responsibility of the attack. The militants took away three AK-47 rifles from the slain troopers.

29 Apr 2013 Seven CPI-Maoist cadres were killed in a gun battle with Security Forces (SFs) in Latehar District. SFs recovered three dead bodies, while the Maoists reportedly managed to flee with four dead bodies.

17 May 2013 At least seven villagers, one trooper of the Commando Battalion for Resolute Action (CoBRA) and a CPI-Maoist cadre were killed in cross-firing between Security Forces and Maoists in the forest near Edesmeta village of Bijapur District. Police said that some of the killed villagers were suspected to be members of the Jan Militia group of CPI-Maoist.

20 May 2013 Five coal labourers were reportedly shot dead by armed militants, suspected to be from United Achik Liberation Army (UALA), in Nangalbibra region of South Garo Hills District in retaliation for the quarry owner's failure to pay up extortion money on time. The armed group is said to have served demand notes on coal mine owners throughout Nangalbibra region in the month of April and amounts ranging from INR 500000 to INR 10 million had been demanded by the outfit.

24 May 2013 Four Security Force personnel and a militant were killed in an encounter at Buchoo village located in Tral area of Pulwama District.

25 May 2013 Top Congress leaders, including State Congress Chief Nand Kumar Patel, senior Congress leader Mahendra Karma (founder of Salwa Judum, an anti-Maoist vigilante group) and former Congress Member of Legislative Assembly, Uday Mudliyar, were among 28 persons killed when heavily-armed Communist Party of India-Maoist (CPI-Maoist) cadres ambushed a convoy of the leaders inside a dense forest in Sukma District. Former Union Minister V C Shukla was among 30 others injured in the incident.

13 Jun 2013 In an armed attack on a passenger train, a group of around 200 CPI-Maoist cadres targeted the Dhanbad-Patna Intercity Express at the Bhalui halt near Jamui District, killing three persons, including two Security Force personnel and a civilian, and injuring six passengers. At least 500 passengers were said to be in the train. The Maoists decamped with three rifles, including one AK 47 and two INSAS rifles.

24 Jun 2013 Eight Army personnel were killed and 11 others sustained injuries when two heavily armed Hizb-ul-Mujahideen (HM) militants ambushed an Army convoy in Hyderpora area of Srinagar. While fleeing from the ambush site the militants also opened fire and hurled a grenade on Police and CRPF check point near Barzulla Bridge in the city, injuring a Police Officer and a CRPF trooper.

27 Jun 2013 Eight Communist Party of India-Maoist (CPI-Maoist) cadres were shot dead by Security Forces (SFs) in an encounter in the forests of Latehar District. The State Director General of Police Rajeev Kumar said five Maoists were killed in the gun battle when they opened fire on one group of security personnel while other three died in a gunfight against another group of security men in Kumandih forest of the same District.

7 Jul 2013 At least two monks, a Burmese and a Tibetan, were injured in a coordinated terror attack, in and around the Mahabodhi Temple (the Temple of the Great Awakening, where Buddha is believed to have attained enlightenment) Complex at Bodh Gaya in the Gaya District of Bihar. Ten low-intensity serial blasts occurred between 5:30 and 5:58 am at and around the World Heritage site. A total of 13 bombs were placed there. Two live bombs were detected and defused at the Complex, while a third bomb was recovered near the Royal Residence hotel at Baiju

Bigaha village, about four kilometres from the Mahabodhi Temple. Examination of three unexploded bombs revealed that small LPG cylinders had been used as containers to pack explosives suspected to be a mix of ammonium nitrate, potassium and sulphur, and, according to the National Security Guard's explosive experts.

Six CPI-Maoist cadres were killed in an encounter with Police near Etapalli tehsil in Gadchiroli District.

17 Jul 2013 At least three Special Auxiliary Police (SAP) troopers and two guards of a private road construction company were killed and seven others injured when an armed group of over 125 CPI-Maoist cadres attacked a base camp of the company at Goh in Aurangabad District.

6 Aug 2013 Personnel of Pakistan Army's Border Action Team (BAT) along with a group of 20 heavily armed terrorists entered 450-metres deep into the Indian Territory along the Line of Control (LoC) in the Poonch sector of Jammu and Kashmir (J&K). The intruders ambushed an Indian Army patrol consisting of six soldiers, killing five of them and injuring another.

13 Aug 2013 Three Chhattisgarh Armed Force (CAF) troopers, including a head constable, and a CPI-Maoist cadre were killed in an hour long encounter between the Maoists and Security Force personnel at Kaushalnagar in the Bastar District.

16 Aug 2013 LeT operative Abdul Karim Tunda arrested from the Indo-Nepal border. Tunda is accused of masterminding over 40 bomb blasts in New Delhi, Panipat, Sonepat, Ludhiana, Kanpur and Varanasi between December 1996 and January 1998. In the Indian dossier handed over to Pakistan after the 26 November 2008, Mumbai attacks, Tunda was ranked 15. The dossier also claims he is connected to Jaish-e-Mohammed (JeM) and Jamat-ud-Dawa (JuD) apart from the LeT.

28 Aug 2013 Yasin Bhatkal alias Mohammad Ahmed Siddibappa Zarrar alias Imran alias Asif alias Shahrukh, Indian Mujahideen's (IM) 'operational chief' on Indian soil, was arrested by Indian agencies from Nahar chowk at Raxaul in the East Champaran District of Bihar along the India-Nepal border. He was arrested along with another IM cadre, identified as Asadullah Akhtar alias Haddi.

13 Sep 2013 At least nine migrant labourers were killed and 11 others were injured in an explosion inside a working shed located on the slab cover put up over Naga Nullah (drain) at Nagamapal in Imphal West District. All the labourers were engaged by Simplex Project Limited, Kolkata, which has been entrusted with the task of laying the slabs over Naga Nullah as well as to build the embankment'.

14 Sep 2013 At least 14 Communist Party of India-Maoist (CPI-Maoist) cadres were killed in an encounter with Police at Silakota village in the Podia Block of Malkangiri District. The gun battle, which lasted for several minutes, took place in a forest close to the border with Chhattisgarh.

25 Sep 2013 The Army foiled an infiltration bid by militants at the Line of Control (LOC) in the Keran Sector of Kupwara District, killing 12 militants in the operation.

26 Sep 2013 At least 13 persons were killed in two separate suicide attacks carried out by a *fidayeen* squad of militants in Kathua and Samba Districts. The militants first killed four policemen and a civilian in an attack at the Hiranagar Police Station in Kathua District; then they hijacked a truck, killing its helper, and reached the Army Camp at Mesar in Samba District. There they killed four Army personnel, including the Second-in-Command of the 16th Cavalry, Lieutenant Colonel Bikramjeet Singh. The three militants were killed later.

30 Sep 2013 At least seven militants were killed in the ongoing Operation Shala Bhata in the Keran Sector of Kupwara District during the week. Five soldiers were also injured. The operation was launched on September 24 following reports that well-entrenched group of 35-40 militants and Pakistani 'special troops' have infiltrated in the region.

17 Oct 2013 Communist Party of India-Maoist (CPI-Maoist) cadres detonated a cane bomb - a trademark Improvised Explosive Device (IED) used by them - to blow up a vehicle, killing all its seven occupants near Pathara village in Aurangabad District.

27 Oct 2013 Seven persons, including one militant were killed, and 100 others were injured in eight serial bomb blasts near Gandhi Maidan, the venue of Bharatiya Janata Party (BJP) Prime Ministerial candidate Narendra Modi's rally in Patna, minutes before he reached there to address a huge gathering. Eight explosive devices with timers went off between 9.30am and 12.25pm as part of a serial bomb attacks suspected to be the handiwork of Indian Mujahideen (IM).

3 Nov 2013 Seven people were killed and 10 others were seriously injured when suspected Garo National Liberation Army (GNLA) militants fired on a group of people at Gendapara village in Goalpara District in Assam.

3 Dec 2013 Eight policemen on patrolling duty were killed in an attack carried out by the Communist party of India-Maoist (CPI-Maoist) near Nabinagar in Aurangabad District. They were travelling in a jeep that was blown up by a landmine on its way from Nabinagar to Tandwa.

26 Dec 2013 Five persons were killed and several others were injured when a bomb kept on a bicycle went off on a road connecting Jalpaiguri town (Jalpaiguri District) with National Highway (NH)-31. Police said they suspected the Kamtapur Liberation Organisation (KLO), which observes its Martyrs' Day on December 28.

27 Dec 2013 Karbi Peoples' Liberation Tiger (KPLT) militants killed four people, including three Naga women, attacking a Naga village, in the Chokihola area of Karbi Anglong District. The militants set ablaze some houses and opened indiscriminate firing. A Naga militant outfit, Rangma Naga Hills Protection Force (RNHPF), had retaliated and launched a counter-attack on the KPLT militants, killing two of the KPLT militants.

PAKISTAN
TERRORIST INCIDENTS – 2013

1 Jan 2013 At least four persons were killed and more than 50 others injured when an Improvised Explosive Device (IED) planted in a parked motorcycle exploded near Ayesha Manzil within the precincts of Gulberg Police Station in Karachi

Pakistani has suffered 896 deadly incidents of suicide bombings which have killed 5,243 innocent people and injured 11,221 others between January 1, 2002 and December 31, 2012. Statistically speaking, the staggering death toll (of 5,243) means that the human bombs were able to kill 476 people every year on average and 40 people each month since 2002.

6 Jan 2013 89 militants and 13 civilians among 102 persons killed during the week in FATA.

32 civilians and three SFs among 35 persons killed during the week in Sindh.

10 Jan 2013 At least 117 persons were killed and over 216 injured in three separate bomb blasts in Quetta, the provincial capital of Balochistan.

32 civilians and 11 militants among 44 persons killed during the week in KP.

At least 30 members of the Tablighi Jamaat were killed and more than 70 were injured in a suicide blast inside the Tablighi Markaz located on the Takhta Band Road in Mingora city, the headquarters of Swat District of Khyber-Pakhtunkhwa.

17 SFs and 14 militants among 34 persons killed during the week in FATA.

33 civilians and one militant among 34 persons killed during the week in Sindh.

At least 16 persons, including two activists of the Pakistan People's Party (PPP), a supporter of the Muttahida Qaumi Movement (MQM) and eight labourers, were shot dead in separate incidents in Karachi.

13 Jan 2013 A roadside bomb killed 14 soldiers in Dosali village, 50 kilometres south of Miranshah in North Waziristan Agency of Federally Administered Tribal Areas (FATA).

14 Jan 2013 Three khasadar (tribal police) personnel, captured by militants during a clash in Kohikhel area of Shalobar, were beheaded.

21 Jan 2013 23 civilians and 10 SFs among 37 persons killed during the week in FATA.

13 bullet-riddled bodies of local people belonging to three families were also found in Alamgudar and Dogra areas of Bara populated by Sepah Afridi tribe.

23 civilians and three SFs among 28 persons killed during the week in Sindh.

22 Jan 2013 At least 11 persons, including a Policeman and a medical superintendent of the Sindh Government Hospital, were killed in separate incidents of violence in Karachi.

25 Jan 2013 At least four people, including a Deputy Superintendent of Police (DSP) and two Policemen, were killed in an Improvised Explosive Device (IED) blast in Bakhtiar Goth, New Muzaffarabad Colony in Karachi.

28 Jan 2013 75 militants and four civilians among 82 persons killed during the week in FATA.

24 civilians and eight SFs among 35 persons killed during the week in Sindh.

1 Feb 2013 Twenty-eight Shia persons were killed and 46 others injured when a suicide bomber struck outside a mosque just after the Friday prayers in Pat Bazaar in Hangu Town (Hangu District).

2 Feb 2013 Thirty six persons were killed when Tehreek-e-Taliban Pakistan (TTP) suicide bombers attacked an Army camp in Sarai Naurang area of Lakki Marwat District in Khyber Pakhtunkhwa.

4 Feb 2013 71 militants and 32 civilians among 103 persons killed during the week in FATA.

40 civilians and 14 SFs among 67 persons killed during the week in Khyber Pakhtunkhwa.

47 civilians and eight militants among 56 persons killed during the week in Sindh.

13 civilians and seven militants among 24 persons killed during the week in Balochistan.

11 Feb 2013 38 militants and 21 civilians among 59 persons killed during the week in FATA.

26 civilians and five militants among 33 persons killed during the week in Sindh.

16 Feb 2013 A remote-controlled bomb targeting Shias Hazaras killed 84 persons, including women and children, and injured more than 169 others in Hazara town of Quetta, the provincial capital of Balochistan.

18 Feb 2013 50 militants and 10 civilians among 60 persons killed during the week in FATA.

40 civilians and two SFs among 42 persons killed during the week in Sindh.

12 civilians and nine militants among 27 persons killed during the week in Khyber Pakhtunkhwa.

23 Feb 2013 At least six labourers working on the Makran Coastal Highway, which links the area to Karachi, were lined up and shot dead by unidentified assailants in the Shadi Kaur area of Gwadar District in Balochistan.

25 Feb 2013 32 civilians and seven militants among 41 persons killed during the week in Sindh.

32 militants and three civilians among 37 persons killed during the week in FATA.

17 civilians and eight militants among 25 persons killed during the week in Balochistan.

3 Mar 2013 At least 45 persons were killed and another 70 were injured in a huge explosion that ripped through a Shia-majority neighbourhood in Karachi (Karachi District), the provincial capital of Sindh.

4 Mar 2013 78 civilians and five militants among 86 persons killed during the week in Sindh.

32 militants and three civilians among 36 persons killed during the week in FATA.

11 Mar 2013 55 militants and five civilians among 60 persons killed during the week in FATA.

18 Mar 2013 36 militants and three Security Forces among 39 persons killed during the week in FATA.

A Policeman and three civilians were killed and 49 persons, including a woman additional district and session's judge, were injured in a suicide attack in a judicial complex in Peshawar.

19 Mar 2013 At least 46 militants, including an Uzbek 'commander', were killed in twin suicide attacks on the Tehreek-e-Taliban Pakistan (TTP) in the headquarters of the Ansarul Islam (AI) in Bagh area of Tirah Valley in Khyber Agency.

21 Mar 2013 At least 17 persons were killed and 34 others injured in a car bomb explosion in the Jalozai camp for Internally Displaced Persons (IDPs) in Nowshera District of Khyber Pakhtunkhwa.

23 Mar 2013 A suicide bomber rammed a water tanker bomb at a military check post, killing 17 Security Forces and one civilian while injuring 20 others near Miranshah, the main town in North Waziristan Agency, in Federally Administered Tribal Areas (FATA).

24 Mar 2013 60 militants and 17 Security Force Personnel among 78 persons killed during the week in FATA.

23 civilians and two SFs among 26 persons killed during the week in KP.

1 Apr 2013 16 militants and four SF Personnel among 21 persons killed during the week in FATA.

8 Apr 2013 46 militants and five civilians among 55 persons killed during the week in FATA.

11 Apr 2013 19 persons, including nine soldiers, seven militants and two volunteers of Tawheedul Islam (TI), a pro-Government armed group, were killed during heavy fighting between troops and militants at a flashpoint near the Afghan border in Tirah Valley.

15 Apr 2013 137 militants and 32 Security Force Personnel among 171 persons killed during the week in FATA.

At least nine militants and a soldier were killed in a clash between the SFs and militants in Dabori area of Orakzai Agency.

16 Apr 2013 At least 11 militants and a soldier were killed in clashes at Kago Kamar locality of Dabori area in Orakzai Agency. Also, at least nine soldiers were killed and eight others injured in a suicide attack on a military vehicle and nearby roadside checkpoint in the Saidgai area of NWA.

16 persons were killed and more than 35 injured when a suicide bomber targeted the senior Awami National Party (ANP) leader Ghulam Ahmad Bilour and his nephew Haroon Bilour in Mundabheri area of Yakatut in Peshawar (Peshawar District), the provincial capital of Khyber Pakhtunkhwa. While Ghulam Ahmad Bilour, contesting from the NA-1, Peshawar, received minor injuries, Haroon Bilour, contesting from the PK-3, escaped unhurt.

19 Apr 2013 At least five militants were killed in retaliatory action by Security Forces when militants try to ambush security personnel in the Dabori area of Orakzai Agency. In addition, at least four persons were killed and eight others injured in a rocket attack on an election rally in Wana town of South Waziristan Agency (SWA).

20 Apr 2013 A female suicide bomber blew herself up outside a hospital in Khar, the main town of Bajaur Agency, and killed at least four persons and injured four others.

21 Apr 2013 41 militants and 15 SFs among 70 persons killed during the week in FATA.

A roadside bomb targeting a military convoy killed four Army soldiers and injured four more in Mir Ali town of North Waziristan Agency (NWA) in Federally Administered Tribal Areas (FATA).

26 Apr 2013 Former President General (retired) Pervez Musharraf is formally arrested over the murder case of former Prime Minister Benazir Bhutto. Musharraf will remain in his villa on the edge of Islamabadwhere he is already under a two-week house arrest over his decision to sack judges when he imposed emergency rule in November 2007.

27 Apr 2013 At least six people, including an Assistant Sub-Inspector (ASI), were killed while a religious cleric was injured in separate acts of violence across the Karachi (Karachi

District), the provincial capital of Sindh.

28 Apr 2013 36 civilians and 7 SFs among 44 persons killed during the week in Sindh.

29 Apr 2013 The dead bodies of three missing Security Force (SF) personnel were found in Adamkot area of North Waziristan Agency.

3 May 2013 Federal Investigation Agency (FIA) prosecutor Chaudhry Zulfizar Ali handling the 26/11 Mumbai (India) attacks case and former Prime Minister Benazir Bhutto's assassination case was shot dead by unidentified assailants in the busy commercial area of Karachi Company in Islamabad, the federal capital nation. Ali was heading for an anti-terrorism court in Rawalpindi for a hearing of the Bhutto assassination case when he was attacked.

5 May 2013 36 militants and eight SFs among 46 persons killed during the week in FATA.

32 civilians and three SFs among 36 persons killed during the week in Sindh.

6 May 2013 Twenty-three persons were killed and more than 70 others injured in a blast at the election rally of Jamiat Ulema-e-Islam-Fazl (JUI-F) candidates at a *Madrassa* in Sewak village in Kurram Agency.

7 May 2013 At least 12 persons were killed and 35 others were injured in a remote-controlled blast when a candidate of the Fazlur Rehman led Jamiat Ulema-e-Islam (JUI-F) was conducting his election campaign in Doaba Town of Hangu District. Five persons, including Pakistan People's Party (PPP) leader Muhammad Zahir Shah Khan, were killed in a remote-controlled bomb blast near the Babagam village in Maidan area of Lower Dir District.

Three activists of Muttahida Qaumi Movement (MQM), identified as Qasim Saeed, Anis Ilyas and Bilal Ahmed, were shot dead and one other, identified as Muhammad Hussain was injured by unidentified assailants in Jumma Goth area within the premises of Ibrahim Hydri Police Station of Karachi.

8 May 2013 Two Policemen, a woman and a suicide bomber were killed and another militant arrested with a suicide vest during an encounter in Rasheed Garhi area of Peshawar. Also, a Policeman and two women were killed and 27 others injured as a suicide bomber rammed his explosives-laden car into Domail Police Station in Bannu city of same District.

10 May 2013 Nine militants and three soldiers were killed in a gunfight in Parachamkani area of Kurram Agency on May 10. In addition, four persons were killed and 21 others injured in a bomb blast occurred at the Khwaja Jan Chowk in Miranshah bazaar of NWA near the election offices of candidates for the NA-40 seat.

11 May 2013 At least 14 persons were killed and 61 others injured in three separate bomb blasts in Karachi.

At least 15 persons were killed and 20 others were injured when unidentified assailants attacked the convoy of the candidate of PB-28 Syed Khadim Hussain's nephew in Naseerabad District.

12 May 2013 At least 16 persons were killed in a blast that ripped through a passenger bus in Miranshah town of North Waziristan Agency (NWA) of Federally Administered Tribal Areas (FATA).

Balochistan Inspector General of Police Mushtaq Sukhera narrowly escaped a suicide attack in the high security zone on Zarghoon Road in Quetta, the provincial capital of Balochistan, that killed at least six persons and injured 46 others.

13 May 2013 5 civilians and 18 militants among 67 persons killed during the week in FATA.

28 civilians and eight SFs among 38 persons killed during the week in Khyber Pakhtunkhwa.

29 civilians and four militants among 36 persons killed during the week in Sindh.

20 civilians and five SFs among 26 persons killed during the week in Balochistan.

16 May 2013 Three soldiers and two civilians were killed while six others sustained injuries in a bomb attack followed by firing on a Security Forces' convoy on the Kohat Road near Sra Khawra area of Matani in Peshawar, the provincial capital of Khyber Pakhtunkhwa.

17 May 2013 27 civilians and six SFs among 33 persons killed during the week in KP:

21 persons were killed and around 120 others sustained injuries in separate bomb blasts during the Friday prayer at two mosques in Baz Darra village in Palai Union Council of Malakand District in Khyber Pakhtunkhwa.

19 civilians and two SFs among 23 persons killed during the week in Sindh.

23 May 2013 13 persons, including 12 Balochistan Constabulary personnel, were killed and 17 others sustained injuries in an explosion caused by a bomb rigged to a rickshaw near Link Badini Road in the proximity of Bhossa Mandi on Eastern Bypass in Quetta, the capital of Balochistan.

At least six persons, including five women, were killed and two others sustained injuries in a firing incident on Noorpur Road in Bakra Mandi area of Sibi District.

24 May 2013 At least six Policemen were killed and a

District Police Officer (DPO) and his guard were injured when militants attacked their vehicles with rockets on the Indus Highway in Mattani area of Darra Adamkhel District of Khyber Pakhtunkhwa

At least three persons were killed in a suicide attack, targeting Hazi Hayatullah, leader of Afghan religious outfits Jamatul Dawa Alquran and Sunnah, on Pajagi Road in Saeedabad area of Peshawar (Peshawar District), the provincial capital of KP..

27 May — 29 civilians, three militants and one SF among 33 persons killed during the week in Sindh.

13 SFs, five civilians and four militants among 22 persons killed during the week in KP

The Tehreek-e-Taliban Pakistan (TTP) issued a fresh threat to assassinate former President General (retired) Pervez Musharraf, currently detained in his palatial farmhouse in Islamabad, over a string of high-profile cases. In a video posted on the jihadi website Umar Media, TTP spokesman Ehsanullah Ihsan said, "Soon we will punish this Satan (Musharraf) to death for his wicked deeds. From Balochistan to Waziristan, Musharraf engulfed this country in blood and fire. He is the killer of hundreds of innocent students of Lal Masjid." This is the second video issued by the TTP with a threat against Musharraf. Before Musharraf returned to Pakistan from self-exile in March, the TTP had issued a video that said the militants had formed a special squad of suicide bombers and snipers to kill him.

29 May 2013 — The Army and Paramilitary Forces killed 15 militants and destroyed five hideouts located in Parachamkani area of Kurram Agency FATA. In addition, at least six militants, including the 'deputy chief' of the Tehreek-e-Taliban Pakistan (TTP) Wali-ur-Rehman, were killed in a United State (US) drone strike in Chashma village near Miranshah town of North Waziristan Agency.

31 May 2013 — At least 34 militants and three Security Forces (SFs) were killed in gunfight in an area between the Kurram and Khyber Agencies.

3 Jun 2013 — 110 militants and fife SFs among 115 persons killed during the week in FATA.

10 Jun 2013 — 42 militants and six Security Force personnel among 48 persons killed during the week in FATA.

27 civilians and four SF among 31 persons killed during the week in Sindh.

12 Jun 2013 — At least seven persons, including two activists of the MQM and a Police Constable, were killed in separate incidents in Karachi.

13 Jun 2013 — 30 civilians among 40 persons killed during the week in Sindh

At least 12 persons, including two Policemen and an MQM activist were killed in separate incidents in Karachi.

15 Jun 2013 — Five people were killed in separate acts of violence in Karachi.

At least 24 people, including 14 female students, four nurses and three FC personnel, Quetta Deputy Commissioner Abdul Mansor Khan, were killed and 27 others injured when unidentified terrorists carried out blasts in Quetta, the provincial capital of Balochistan. The militants first blew up a bus of Sardar Bahadur Khan (SBK) Women University when it was inside the parking lot of the university. Thereafter, they triggered blast inside the Bolan Medical College (BMC) hospital in Quetta where the victims had been taken for treatment and further action. At around 7pm, the third blast was heard from the BMC Complex.

18 Jun 2013 — At least 35 persons, including a newly-elected Member of Provincial Assembly (MPA) Imran Mohmand, were killed and over 57 others injured when a suicide bomber blew himself up at a funeral prayer in Shah Zaman Qala village of Shergarh town in Mardan District.

19 Jun 2013 — At least six Security Force personnel were killed and three others injured when a convoy of the forces came under attack in Sra Khawra area of Matani town in outskirts of Peshawar. The sources said four of the militants were also shot dead when the SF personnel retaliated.

18 Jun 2013 — At least six persons, including MQM and Pakistan People's Party (PPP) workers, were killed in separate incidents in Karachi.

21 Jun 2013 — At least nine persons were killed in separate incidents in Karachi.

22 Jun 2013 — At least 12 persons, including three Policemen and two activists of the Muttahida Qaumi Movement (MQM), were killed in separate incidents in Karachi.

23 Jun 2013 — A total of 11 persons, including 10 foreign tourists-cum-mountaineer, were killed when militants wearing paramilitary uniforms attacked a base camp of Nanga Parbat mountain range in Bonar area of Diamer District in Gilgit Baltistan region of Pakistan occupied Kashmir (PoK). One Pakistani woman guide was also killed in the incident. Tehreek-e-Taliban Pakistan (TTP) 'spokesperson' Ehsanullah Ehsan while claiming the responsibility said that killing was revenge against the United States' (US) drone attacks and killing of TTP 'deputy chief' Waliur Rehman Mehsud. He also

revealed that a new faction of the outfit, named Junud-e-Hafsa, carried out the attack.

24 Jun 2013 50 civilians and 16 militants among 73 persons killed during the week in Khyber Pakhtunkhwa.

36 civilians and three SFs among 40 persons killed during the week in Sindh

25 Jun 2013 The Federal Investigation Agency (FIA) submitted a *challan* against former President General (retired) Pervez Musharraf in the Anti-Terrorism Court (ATC-I), declaring him prime accused in former Premier Benazir Bhutto murder case. The FIA presented the charge sheet against Musharraf and listed him as the main accused in the light of a statement recorded by US journalist Mark Siegel. (Bhutto was killed on 27 December 2007. Pervez Musharraf is also facing charges in connection with the murder of Nawab Akbab Bugti in 2006 and 2007 judges case, and is currently under 'house arrest' at his farmhouse turned jail at Chak Shahzad on the outskirts of Islamabad.)

26 Jun 2013 A bomb attack targeting a Sindh High Court judge killed at least 10 persons, including two Rangers, six Policemen and the driver of the judge's car, and injured 15 others, including the judge, near Burns Road in Karachi.

28 Jun 2013 At least three persons, including a woman, were killed and 18 others injured when dozens of Lyari gangsters carried out an armed attack in streets of Kharadar area in Karachi.

29 Jun 2013 At least five persons were killed in separate incidents in Karachi.

1 Jul 2013 28 people were killed and over 60 others sustained wounds when a suicide bomber blew himself up near an Imam Bargah (Shia place of worship) in Aliabad area of Hazara Town in Quetta, Balochistan. The suicide bomber detonated the explosive strapped to his body when he was stopped from entering the premises of the Imam Bargah Abu Talib.

22 civilians and 10 SFs among 33 persons killed during the week in Sindh.

In 2013, till June, around 273 people were abducted from various parts of the metropolis and their bodies were later found dumped in gunny bags. The recovered bodies carried marks of severe torture before they were being shot, tortured to such extent that many of them are still lying unidentified in morgues. As many as 92 bodies were recovered from Lyari and its adjoining areas including Baghdadi, Chakiwara, Eidgah, Pak Colony, Kharadar, Old Golimar, Garden and Kalri. The remaining bodies were recovered from other areas including Malir, Gulshan-e-Iqbal, Nazimabad, Rizvia, Landhi, Khokhrapar, Shah Faisal Colony and Orangi.

8 Jul 2013 26 civilians and five militants among 32 persons killed during the week in Sindh: At least five persons were killed in separate incidents of target killing in Karachi.

18 militants and five civilians among 28 persons killed during the week in FATA.

19 Jul 2013 At least seven people, including two Policemen and two Awami National Party (ANP) workers, were shot dead in separate incidents of targeted killing across Karachi.

22 Jul 2013 5 militants and 10 SFs among 51 persons killed during the week in FATA.

20 civilians and five militants among 28 persons killed during the week in Sindh.

23 Jul 2013 Four persons were killed in separate incidents of violence in different areas of Karachi.

24 Jul 2013 Suicide bombers and armed militants mounted an attack on the local office of Inter-Services Intelligence Agency (ISI) in high security zone of Sukkur Barrage Colony in the Sukkur town of Sukkur District, sparking a shootout that killed eight persons, including four terrorists, three ISI officials and a civilian, and injured 50 others.

Five persons were killed in separate incidents of violence in different areas of Karachi.

26 Jul 2013 At least 48 persons were killed and 100 others were injured in a coordinated twin suicide attacks at Parachinar in the Kurram Agency.

27 Jul 2013 At least seven Pakistan Coast Guards personnel were killed and an equal number of them sustained injuries in an attack carried out by unidentified armed militants at a check post located in the Sundsar area of Gwadar District.

29 Jul 2013 53 civilians and 29 militants among 82 persons killed during the week in FATA.

17 civilians and eight SFs among 26 persons killed during the week in Balochistan.

19 civilians and four militants among 26 persons killed during the week in Sindh.

24 persons, including 12 Policeman, five militants, four prisoners, and three civilians, were killed in the attack and the counter attack by the Security Forces when TTP militants stormed the Central Prison at Dera Ismail Khan in the Khyber Pakhtunkhwa (KP) Province.

5 Aug 2013 17 militants and 16 SFs among 36 persons killed during the week in Khyber Pakhtunkhwa.

16 civilians and 8 SFs among 26 persons killed during the week in Sindh.

6 Aug 2013 At least 14 persons, including three SF personnel, were killed on August 6 in an attack by Baloch Liberation Army (BLA) militants on five passenger buses in the Machh area of Bolan District.

8 Aug 2013 Thirty eight persons, including 21 Police officials, were killed and 40 others were injured in a suicide blast at a funeral in the Police Lines area of Quetta.

9 Aug 2013 At least 10 persons were killed and 15 others injured when unidentified militants attacked the Jamia Masjid Farooqia in Quetta.

12 Aug 2013 41 civilians and 24 SFs among 76 persons killed during the week in Balochistan.

20 Aug 2013 Rawalpindi Special Anti-Terrorism Court (ATC) Judge Chaudhry Habibur Rahman while hearing the December 2007 murder case of former Prime Minister Benazir Bhutto indicted the former President General (retired) Pervez Musharraf. "He was charged with murder, criminal conspiracy for murder and facilitation for murder," said public prosecutor Chaudhry Azhar. However, Pervez Musharraf denied the charges.

26 Aug 2013 51 civilians and three militants among 56 persons killed during the week in Sindh.

1 Sep 2013 44 civilians and two SFs among 47 persons killed during the week in Sindh.

8 Sep 2013 30 civilians and eight militants among 44 persons killed during the week in Sindh.

15 Sep 2013 Major General, Sanaullah Khan, and, lieutenant colonel, Tauseef, were killed along with a soldier, Irfan Sattar, in an improvised explosive device (IED) explosion in the Upper Dir District of Khyber Pakhtunkhwa near Pak-Afghan Border. Major General Sanaullah was the general officer commanding Swat Division. Tehreek-e-Taliban Pakistan (TTP) 'spokesman' Shahidullah Shahid claimed responsibility for the attack.

19 Sep 2013 Three persons were killed and 20 others injured in a hand grenade attack near a mosque in the Sarband area of Peshawar.

21 Sep 2013 12 militants were killed and two soldiers were injured in a shootout near the Pak-Afghan border in Lower Dir District.

22 Sep 2013 81 persons were killed and 145 others injured when two suicide attackers blew themselves up at the end of Sunday service at All Saints Church near Qissa Khawani bazaar in Peshawar (Peshawar District), the provincial capital of Khyber Pakhtunkhwa.

25 Sep 2013 Security Forces killed five militants in a retaliatory fire after the militants attacked their camp with rockets in the Janni Khel area of Bannu District.

27 Sep 2013 19 persons were killed and 42 others injured when a bomb exploded on a bus carrying Government employees at Gulbela area on Charsadda Road of Peshawar.

29 Sep 2013 A car bomb blast killed at least 42 persons and injured 100 others in the Kissa Khawani Bazaar area of Peshawar (Peshawar District), the provincial capital of Khyber Pakhtunkhwa.

The alleged Somali mastermind of the attack on a Kenyan mall connected with jihadists while studying in Pakistan and later fought in Afghanistan and Kashmir, The Washington Post report said. Mukhtar Abu Zubeyr, known as Godane, earned a scholarship in the 1990s to study in Pakistan, where he "connected with jihadist circles". Godane then travelled to "Afghanistan to train and fight, as well as to Kashmir", the report added.

2 Oct 2013 At least 17 militants were killed and several others were injured when a suicide bomber ran a vehicle full of explosives into the 'headquarters' of Mullah Nabi Hanfi group of the Tehreek-e-Taliban Pakistan (TTP) in the Spin Tall area of Hangu District in Khyber Pakhtunkhwa (KP). Mullah Nabi Hanfi was a 'commander' of the Hangu chapter of the TTP before switching sides and joining the Government's counter-insurgency efforts.

16 Oct 2013 10 people, including Khyber Pakhtunkhwa Law Minister Israrullah Gandapur, were killed and over 30 others were injured when a suicide bomber struck a festive gathering at the residence of Gandapur in the Kolachi area of Dera Ismail Khan District. Israrullah Gandapur was elected as an independent candidate during the 2013 General Elections and later joined the Pakistan Tehreek-e-Insaf (PTI).

21 Oct 2013 Seven persons, including two women - one civilian and one Police constable - were killed and another 16 were injured when militants triggered an Improvised Explosive Device (IED) explosion targeting the Jaffar Express train in the Notal area of Naseerabad District in Balochistan Province.

29 Oct 2013 Unidentified armed militants killed nine persons, including three women and two children, in an attack at the residence of a local tribal leader in the Loti Zain area of Dera Bugti District. An unnamed levies official said that the house belonged to a pro-government tribesman

1 Nov 2013 Hakimullah Mehsud, the 'chief' of the Tehreek-e-Taliban Pakistan (TTP), was killed in a US drone strike in the Dandy Darpakhel area, five kilometers north of Miranshah, the main town of North Waziristan Agency

(NWA), in Federally Administered Tribal Areas (FATA). Intelligence officials said Hakimullah was leaving from a meeting at a mosque when the drone targeted their vehicle. Five militants, including Abdullah Bahar Mehsud and Tariq Mehsud, both key militant 'commanders' and close aides of the TTP chief, were also killed in the attack.

11 Nov 2013 The 'chief fundraiser' of the Haqqani Network, Nasiruddin Haqqani, was shot dead by unidentified militants in Islamabad, the Afghan Taliban said.

29 civilians and 27 militants among 57 persons killed during the week in Sindh.

15 Nov 2013 10 persons were killed and over 78 injured in sectarian clashes that erupted during a Muharram (the mourning period observed by the Shias, commemorating the tragedy of Karbala) procession in Rawalpindi. The incident occurred when the mob turned against the Police personnel deputed in the area for security.

23 Nov 2013 Thousands of people led by Pakistan Tehreek-e-Insaf (PTI) protesting US drone strikes blocked a road in Peshawar (Khyber Pakhtunkhwa) used to truck NATO troop supplies and equipment in and out of Afghanistan. PTI chief Imran Khan while condemning the drone attacks said that his party would block NATO supplies in Pakistan forever.

8 Dec 2013 22 civilians and 16 militants killed during the week in Sindh.

19 Dec 2013 Troops mounted helicopter and mortar attacks on militants in North Waziristan Agency of Federally Administered Tribal Areas (FATA), where officials said that at least 33 militants and three civilians have been killed.

At least five soldiers were killed and 34 others were wounded when a suicide bomber rammed his explosive-laden car into a military checkpoint in the Mir Ali tehsil of Miranshah in North Waziristan Agency.

TERRORISM DATA – INDIA

State-wise Fatalities in Left-wing Extremism: 2013

States	Civilians	SFs	LWE	Total
Andhra Pradesh	6	1	1	8
Assam	0	0	0	0
Bihar	7	10	0	17
Chhattisgarh	43	26	23	92
Jharkhand	29	24	42	95
Karnataka	0	0	0	0
Madhya Pradesh	0	0	0	0
Maharashtra	8	3	26	37
Odisha	8	1	1	10
Uttar Pradesh	0	0	0	0
West Bengal	0	0	0	0
Total	**101**	**65**	**93**	**259**

Parameters of LWE/CPI-Maoist Violence in Bihar: 2011-2012

Parameters	2011	2012
No. of incidents	316	166
Police Informers' Killed (Out of total civilians killed)	12	13
No. of encounters with police	17	12
No. of attacks on police (including landmines)	13	7
No. of Naxalites arrested	428	422
No. of Naxalites surrendered	26	42
Total no. of arms snatched	4	2
Total no. of arms recovered	171	151
Arms training camps held	12	5
No of Jan Adalats held	17	10

Source: MHA.

State-wise Left Wing Extremist Violence 2009-2012

State	2009		2010		2011		2012	
	Incidents	Deaths	Incidents	Deaths	Incidents	Deaths	Incidents	Deaths
Andhra Pradesh	66	18	100	24	54	09	67	13
Bihar	232	72	307	97	316	63	166	44
Chhattisgarh	529	290	625	343	465	204	370	109
Jharkhand	742	208	501	157	517	182	480	163
Madhya Pradesh	1	8	7	1	8	0	11	0
Maharashtra	154	93	94	45	109	54	134	41
Odisha	266	67	218	79	192	53	171	45
Uttar Pradesh	8	2	6	1	1	2	2	0
West Bengal	255	158	350	258	92	45	6	0
Others	5	0	5	0	6	1	8	0
TOTAL	**2,258**	**908**	**2,213**	**1,005**	**1,760**	**611**	**1,415**	**415**

Source: MHA Annual Report, 2012-13.

Other Parameters of LWE/CPI-Maoist Violence in Chhattisgarh: 2011-2012

Parameters	2011	2012
No. of incidents	465	369
Police Informers' Killed (Out of total civilians killed)	91	35
No. of encounters with police	99	88
No. of attacks on police (including landmines)	75	76
No. of Naxalites arrested	509	397
No. of Naxalites surrendered	20	26
Total no. of arms snatched	29	17
Total no. of arms recovered	108	91
Arms training camps held	24	24
No of Jan Adalats held	13	16

Source: MHA.

Fatalities in LWE/ CPI-Maoist Violence in Bihar: 2005-2013

Years	Civilians	SF Personnel	LWE/CPI Maoists	Total
2005	25	29	52	106
2006	16	5	19	40
2007	23	21	5	49
2008	35	21	15	71
2009	37	25	16	78
2010	54	24	20	98
2011	39	3	19	61
2012	16	10	15	41
2013	2	7	0	9
Total	**247**	**145**	**161**	**553**

Left Wing Extremists Killed, Arrested Surrendered 2007-2012

Years	Naxalites Killed	Naxalites Arrested	Naxalites Surrendered	Total
2007	141	1,456	390	1,987
2008	199	1,743	400	2,342
2009	220	1,981	150	2,351
2010	172	2,916	266	3,354
2011	99	2,030	394	2,523
2012	74	1,882	440	2,396
Total	**905**	**12,008**	**2,040**	**14,953**

Source: MHA.

Jammu and Kashmir: Fatalities in Terrorist Violence 1988-2013

	Civilians	Security Force Personnel	Terrorists	Total
1988	29	1	1	31
1989	79	13	0	92
1990	862	132	183	1177
1991	594	185	614	1393
1992	859	177	873	1909
1993	1023	216	1328	2567
1994	1012	236	1651	2899
1995	1161	297	1338	2796
1996	1333	376	1194	2903
1997	840	355	1177	2372
1998	877	339	1045	2261
1999	799	555	1184	2538
2000	842	638	1808	3288
2001	1067	590	2850	4507
2002	839	469	1714	3022
2003	658	338	1546	2542
2004	534	325	951	1810
2005	521	218	1000	1739
2006	349	168	599	1116
2007	164	121	492	777
2008	69	90	382	541
2009	55	78	242	375
2010	36	69	270	375
2011	34	30	119	183
2012	16	17	84	117
2013	19	59	94	172
Total*	**14671**	**6092**	**22739**	**43502**

Parameters of LWE/CPI-Maoist Violence in Jharkhand: 2011-2012

Parameters	2011	2012
No. of incidents	517	479
Police Informers' Killed (Out of total civilians killed)	35	32
No. of encounters with police	42	43
No. of attacks on police (including landmines)	23	21
No. of Naxalites arrested	380	377
No. of Naxalites surrendered	17	6
Total no. of arms snatched	17	30
Total no. of arms recovered	165	162
Arms training camps held	24	12
No of Jan Adalats held	54	23

Source: MHA.

While most parameters appeared to be comparable over the two years, there was a considerable decrease in arms training camps held by the Maoists, and the organization of 'Jan Adalats' ('People's Courts', kangaroo courts organized by the Maoists), suggesting that the Maoist networks were under some pressure, resulting in a decline in political mobilization and recruitment.

Incidents of Attacks on Economic Targets by LWE Extremists in Jharkhand: 2008-2012

	2008	2009	2010	2011	2012
Railways	7	17	13	10	2
Telephone Exchange	10	14	6	8	3
Mining	4	2	6	2	0
Pole transmission	0	0	1	0	0
Panchayat Bhawan	0	7	4	0	1
School Building	4	37	7	6	0

Source: MHA.

Fatalities in Left-Wing Extremist Violence in Maharashtra: 2005-2013

Years	Incidents	Civilians	SF Personnel	LWE	Total
2005	94	29	24	3	56
2006	98	39	3	19	61
2007	94	22	3	5	30
2008	68	17	5	9	31
2009	154	41	52	4	97
2010	94	35	10	3	48
2011	109	44	10	3	57
2012	134	27	14	4	45
2013	-	8	3	26	37

Fatalities Left-Wing Extremism (LWE) Violence in Manipur: 2001-2013

Years	Civilians	Security Force Personnel	Terrorists	Total
2001	70	25	161	256
2002	36	53	101	190
2003	27	23	148	198
2004	40	41	127	208
2005	138	50	143	331
2006	107	37	141	285
2007	150	40	218	408
2008	131	13	341	485
2009	77	18	321	416
2010	26	8	104	138
2011	25	10	30	65
2012	25	12	73	110
2013	2	0	1	3
Total	**854**	**330**	**1,909**	**3,093**

Fatalities involving Manipur PLA—2003-2013*

Years	Civilians	Security Force Personnel	Terrorists	Total
2003	0	2	14	16
2004	0	6	15	21
2005	1	13	10	24
2006	7	12	34	53
2007	4	1	12	17
2008	1	1	4	6
2009	0	4	15	19
2010	0	1	3	4
2011	0	0	5	5
2012	0	1	2	3
2013	0	3	0	3
Total	**13**	**44**	**114**	**171**

Fatalities in Terrorist Violence in India's Northeast: 2005-2013

Years	Civilians	SFs	Terrorists	Total
2006	232	92	313	637
2007	457	68	511	1036
2008	404	40	607	1051
2009	270	40	542	852
2010	77	22	223	322
2011	79	35	132	246
2012	90	18	209	317
2013	9	3	26	38
Total	**1,618**	**318**	**2,563**	**4,499**

Fatalities in Left-Wing Extremism (LWE) Violence in Odisha: 2005-2013

Year	Civilians	SFs	Maoists	Total
2005	13	1	3	17
2006	3	4	16	23
2007	13	2	8	23
2008	24	76	32	132
2009	36	32	13	81
2010	62	21	25	108
2011	36	16	23	75
2012	27	19	14	60
2013	13	5	23	41
Total	**227**	**176**	**157**	**560**

Assam: Insurgency related killings 1992-2013

Years	Civilians	Security Force Personnel	Terrorists	Total
1992	80	34	19	133
1993	74	24	33	131
1994	173	35	63	271
1995	170	73	27	270
1996	302	87	62	451
1997	285	85	167	537
1998	531	72	180	783
1999	214	77	212	503
2000	366	65	327	758
2001	264	59	283	606
2002	138	32	275	445
2003	212	12	281	505
2004	194	24	136	354
2005	149	10	83	242
2006	96	35	43	174
2007	269	19	149	437
2008	224	16	133	373
2009	175	21	196	392
2010	48	12	98	158
2011	34	15	45	94
2012	32	4	55	91
2013	25	4	52	81
Total	**4,055**	**815**	**2,919**	**7,789**

Manipur: Insurgency Related Killings 1992-2013

Years	Civilians	Security Force Personnel	Terrorists	Total
1992	84	30	51	165
1993	266	91	66	423
1994	189	98	63	350
1995	183	64	74	321
1996	117	65	93	275
1997	233	111	151	495
1998	87	62	95	244
1999	89	64	78	231
2000	93	51	102	246
2001	70	25	161	256
2002	36	53	101	190
2003	27	23	148	198
2004	40	41	127	208
2005	138	50	143	331
2006	107	37	141	285
2007	150	40	218	408
2008	131	13	341	485
2009	77	18	321	416
2010	26	8	104	138
2011	25	10	30	65
2012	25	12	73	110
2013	21	5	26	52
Total	**2,214**	**971**	**2,707**	**5,892**

Meghalaya: Insurgency Related Killings 1992-2013

Years	Civilians	Security Force Personnel	Terrorists	Total
1992	0	0	0	0
1993	0	0	0	0
1994	4	0	0	4
1995	7	0	0	7
1996	3	4	0	7
1997	3	0	1	4
1998	5	14	1	20
1999	5	17	0	22
2000	12	7	17	36
2001	24	8	8	40
2002	29	18	17	64
2003	26	5	27	58
2004	7	5	23	35
2005	2	1	26	29
2006	7	0	17	24
2007	4	1	13	18
2008	0	1	12	13
2009	1	0	4	5
2010	3	0	17	20
2011	11	10	8	29
2012	27	2	19	48
2013	19	9	22	50
Total	**199**	**102**	**232**	**533**

Mizoram: Insurgency Related Killings: 1992-2013

Years	Civilians	Security Force Personnel	Terrorists	Total
1992	0	0	0	0
1993	0	0	0	0
1994	0	0	0	0
1995	0	0	0	0
1996	0	0	0	0
1997	0	4	0	4
1998	0	0	0	0
1999	0	0	0	0
2000	2	5	0	7
2001	4	7	1	12
2002	0	0	0	0
2003	0	1	0	1
2004	0	1	0	1
2005	2	0	0	2
2006	1	0	1	2
2007	2	0	6	8
2008	0	4	1	5
2009	1	0	0	1
2010	0	0	0	0
2011	1	0	0	1
2012	0	0	0	0
2013	0	0	0	0
Total	**13**	**22**	**9**	**44**

Tripura: Insurgency related killings 1992-2013

Years	Civilians	Security Force Personnel	Terrorists	Total
1992	59	18	21	98
1993	148	28	7	183
1994	206	22	10	238
1995	178	34	45	257
1996	140	31	18	189
1997	205	50	19	274
1998	214	25	26	265
1999	240	41	22	303
2000	453	16	45	514
2001	239	31	42	312
2002	94	43	38	175
2003	195	39	61	295
2004	66	38	63	167
2005	34	8	31	73
2006	11	19	30	60
2007	10	5	21	36
2008	7	4	17	28
2009	9	1	1	11
2010	0	2	1	3
2011	1	0	0	1
2012	0	0	2	2
2013	0	0	0	0
Total	**2,509**	**455**	**520**	**3,484**

Nagaland: Insurgency related killings: 1992-2013

Years	Civilians	Security Force Personnel	Terrorists	Total
1992	34	33	29	96
1993	62	43	68	173
1994	110	26	56	192
1995	80	25	108	213
1996	144	48	112	304
1997	104	38	218	360
1998	26	14	72	112
1999	26	4	118	148
2000	13	4	84	101
2001	25	2	76	103
2002	5	2	29	36
2003	3	3	31	37
2004	35	1	22	58
2005	9	0	31	40
2006	10	1	81	92
2007	20	0	88	108
2008	42	2	101	145
2009	7	0	11	18
2010	0	0	3	3
2011	7	0	8	15
2012	6	0	55	61
2013	7	0	17	24
Total	**775**	**246**	**1,418**	**2,439**

Punjab: Insurgency related killings 1992-2013

Years	Civilians	Security Force Personnel	Terrorists	Total
1981	13	2	14	29
1982	13	2	7	22
1983	75	20	13	108
1984	359	20	77	456
1985	63	8	2	73
1986	520	38	78	636
1987	910	95	328	1333
1988	1949	110	373	2432
1989	1168	201	703	2072
1990	2467	476	1320	4263
1991	2591	497	2177	5265
1992	1518	252	2113	3883
1993	48	25	798	871
1994	2	0	76	78
1995	0	0	11	11
1996	0	0	3	3
1997	56	2	1	59
1998	0	0	0	0
1999	0	0	0	0
2000	18	0	0	18
2001	1	0	0	1
2002	5	0	0	5
2003	0	0	0	0
2004	0	0	0	0
2005	0	0	0	0
2006	0	0	0	0
2007	7	0	0	7
2008	0	0	0	0
2009	0	0	0	0
2010	0	2	2	4
2011	0	0	0	0
2012	0	0	2	2
2013	0	0	0	0
Total	**11,783**	**1,750**	**8,098**	**21,631**

TERRORISM DATA – PAKISTAN

Fatalities in Terrorist Violence in Pakistan 2003-2013

Years	Civilians	Security Force Personnel	Terrorists/ Insurgents	Total
2003	140	24	25	189
2004	435	184	244	863
2005	430	81	137	648
2006	608	325	538	1,471
2007	1,522	597	1,479	3,598
2008	2,155	654	3,906	6,715
2009	2,324	991	8,389	11,704
2010	1,796	469	5,170	7,435
2011	2,738	765	2,800	6,303
2012	3,007	732	2,472	6,211
2013	2,880	640	1,619	5,139
Total	**18,035**	**5,462**	**26,779**	**50,276**

2013

Months	Civilians	Security Force Personnel	Terrorists/ Insurgents	Total
January	414	70	265	749
February	360	44	201	605
March	249	43	193	485
April	230	88	234	552
May	283	81	185	549
June	326	62	104	492
July	240	68	149	457
August	224	62	62	348
September	292	46	71	409
October	127	37	70	234
November	130	38	85	253
December	5	1	0	6
Total	**2,880**	**640**	**1,619**	**51,39**

Shia Killings in Pakistan: 2002-2013

Years	Incidents	Killed
2002	4	6
2003	4	24
2004	8	129
2005	10	86
2006	9	60
2007	28	258+
2008	23	150
2009	17	183
2010	34	245
2011	24	136
2012	115	399
2013	39	410
Total	**315**	**2,086**

Pakistan Region-wise

Region	Civilians	SFs	Terrorists	Total
Balochistan	700	133	97	930
FATA	305	188	1,152	1,645
KP	594	160	161	915
PoK	-	-	-	-
Gilgit-Baltistan	12	6	0	18
Punjab	61	4	8	73
Sindh	1,208	149	201	1,528
Total	**2,880**	**640**	**1,619**	**5,139**

Fatalities in FATA: 2009-2013

Years	Civilians	SFs	Militants	Total
2009	636	350	4,252	5,238
2010	540	262	4,519	5,321
2011	488	233	2,313	3,034
2012	549	306	2,046	2,901
2013	305	188	1152	1,645
Total	**2,225**	**1,151**	**13,202**	**16,578**

Fatalities in Balochistan: 2004-2013

Years	Civilians	SFs	Terrorists	Total
2004	67	21	2	90
2005	71	14	28	113
2006	226	82	142	450
2007	124	27	94	245
2008	130	111	107	348
2009	152	88	37	277
2010	274	59	14	347
2011	542	122	47	711
2012	690	178	86	954
2013	700	133	97	930
Total	**2,406**	**715**	**558**	**3,679**

Fatalities in Sindh: 2010-2013

Years	Civilians	Security Force Personnel	Militants	Total
2010	777	61	158	996
2011	1,082	61	68	1,211
2012	1,318	118	117	1,553
2013	109	14	6	129
Total*	**3,286**	**254**	**349**	**3,889**

Fatalities in Khyber Agency: 2008-2013

Years	Civilians	SFs	Militants	Total
2008	34	5	122	161
2009	120	48	623	791
2010	180	56	331	567
2011	204	49	203	456
2012	257	46	464	767
2013	43	12	312	367
Total*	**838**	**216**	**2055**	**3109**

Fatalities in Quetta: 2004-2013

Years	Incidents	Killed
2004	13	64
2005	47	14
2006	52	41
2007	104	95
2008	81	62
2009	94	82
2010	83	153
2011	114	240
2012	148	205
2013	117	369
Total	**853**	**1325**

Drone attacks in Pakistan: 2005-2013

Year	Incidents	Killed	Injured
2005	1	1	0
2006	0	0	0
2007	1	20	15
2008	19	156	17
2009	46	536	75
2010	90	831	85+
2011	59	548	52
2012	46	344	37
2013	22	148	29
Total	**277**	**2,548**	**301+**

Fatalities in Peshawar and KP: 2007-2013

Years	Civilians	SFs	Terrorists	Total Fatalities in Peshawar	Total Fatalities in KP	Percentage of Fatalities in Peshawar
2007	48	11	8	67	986	6.79%
2008	95	29	38	162	2201	7.36%
2009	317	61	42	420	5497	7.64%
2010	70	16	43	129	1202	10.73%
2011	169	16	45	230	1206	19.07%
2012	161	49	35	245	656	37.34%
2013	282	61	17	360	850	42.35%

Fatalities in Karachi: 2010-2013

Years	Civilians	Security Force Personnel	Terrorists	Total
2010	777	61	158	996
2011	1,079	61	68	1,208
2012	1,295	118	117	1,530
2013	1,094	121	124	1,339
Total	4,245	361	467	5,073

CHINA BORDER/ TERRITORIAL ISSUES

CHINA AND ITS BORDER/TERRITORIAL ISSUES

Country	Length (in kms)	Details	Status	Comments
Afghanistan	76	Abuts the 'Wakhan Corridor" in Afghanistan with the Tashkurgan Tajik Autonomous County (Kashgar District) of the province of Xinjian in China	Sino-Afghan border delimited as part of a secret treaty in November 1963, whose terms have never been published.	China is developing infrastructure on its side of the border, including a 75-km road built less than 10-km from the border funded by its Ministry of Defence.
Bhutan	470	Despite cultural and religious ties to Tibet, Bhutan has maintained a close relationship with India, on whom it is dependent for external matters and defence.	The border is unresolved, particularly the western and eastern tri-junctions where Bhutan, China and India meet. China also claims the Doklam plateau in Western Bhutan and has made numerous intrusions.	Negotiations have been conducted between Bhutan and China over three decades to demarcate the border but are yet to be successfully concluded.
Brunei	Maritime Boundary	Differences over sovereignty claims which remain unclear, which could be as much as 43,272 sq. kms	Geographically, over 1600 kms separate Hainan province of China and Brunei. Politically and economically, their relations are less extensive than other ASEAN nations.	Due to absence of tensions the contested sovereignty claims have received scant attention
India	3,439	The border, referred to as the Line of Actual Control is one of the longest in the world, under dispute. The area of the land under dispute tops 135,000 sq kms over which the two sides have even gone to war.	Disagreement over the status of Tibet is at the heart of the dispute ever since it was annexed by China in the 1950s and ceased to be a political buffer between the two countries. India can expect no respite from Chinese pressure as the solution to the dispute appears intractable.	China's salami tactics – upping the ante in small, measured increments – makes the situation tense from time to time. While China is unwilling to accept the status quo, trade between to the two is increasing. The issue now goes beyond territory to environmental concerns and control of natural resources.
Indonesia	Maritime Boundary	Geographically, 1,482 kms separate Hainan province of China and Indonesia's Natuna islands. Overlaps exist between maritime claims of the two states over an area of about 98,000 sq kms.	Indonesia has rejected all Chinese overtures to engage in bilateral delimitation talks over the "invisible boundary". However, there have been a number of incidents over illegal Chinese fishing activities in the South China Sea.	The area of the South China Sea has rich recoverable reserves of natural gas, which are at the heart of the dispute. (Estimated to be 46 trillion cu ft). At its core is the Spratly Islands.

(Contd.)

Country	Length (in kms)	Details	Status	Comments
Japan	Claims over EEZ and disputes over the Senkaku/ Diaoyu and Okinotori islands	The principal territorial and maritime disputes between China and Japan are: 1) The group of islands in the East China Sea known to the Chinese as Diaoyu and to the Japanese as Senkaku. 2) Delimitation of the maritime boundary in the East China Sea and exploitation of the oil and gas resources, notably the fields called Chuiuiao in Chinese and Shirakaba in Japanese. 3) Okinotori, a tiny formation that Japan claims is an island capable of generating claims to EEZ and continental shelf rights. China, while not contesting Japan's ownership of Okinotori, refuses to recognize it as an island for extended maritime claims.	Both states are parties to the 1982 United Nations Convention on the Law of the Sea (UNCLOS). It states that a nation can claim an exclusive economic zone (EEZ) to a distance of 200 nm from coastal baselines, and also a continental shelf to the limits of its natural prolongation of its land territory to the outer edge of its continental margin up to 350 nm or 100 nm seaward of the 2,500 metre depth contour. However, since the East China Sea is only 360 nm across at its widest point, this precludes any easy solution to the dispute.	Control over the Senkaku islands might convey EEZ rights to 68,686 sq kms and to Okinotori some 400,000 sq kms. Repeated efforts at compromise have failed. A joint "consensus" reached in 2008 has stalled, and both sides have rejected the suggestion that their territorial and maritime disputes be submitted to international arbitration. The Japanese government maintains that the territorial issue has been settled, while China, seemingly a power on the rise relative to Japan, has little incentive to compromise. Acting as a mitigating factor on these disputes is the fact that China is Japan's largest trading partner.
Kazakhstan	1,700	The border had 944 sq kms in dispute. In agreements between 1994 and 1998, the border was changed by only 187 sq kms, with China securing 43 % of the land under dispute while Kazakhstan got title over 57 %.	This resolution appears to show Beijing's willingness to compromise. However, relative to the total size of their territories China is arguably the winner.	In 2009 Beijing requested Kazakhstan to lease almost one million hectares of land to Chinese farmers to grow soya beans and rapeseed, which has created new concerns throughout Central Asia over a policy of gradual Chinese encroachment.
Korea	1,415	China's 1,400 km land border with North Korea was established by means of an as-yet secret Sino-DPRK treaty in 1963.	While the border is formally undisputed, a number of issues regarding control of the waterways, ports, islands, and mountain territories in the border region have emerged since the 1950s and continue to be unresolved to this day.	China fears being flooded by North Korean refugees in the event of the collapse of the DRPK government. Should the two Koreas ever merge, the validity of the current Sino-Korean border might be challenged by a newly reunified Korea. There are outstanding maritime disputes between China and South Korea, though the two states have sought to manage their competing claims and friction over access to marine resources by their fishing fleets through the establishment of a joint fishing zone in the Yellow Sea.

(Contd.)

Country	Length (in kms)	Details	Status	Comments
Kyrgyzstan	858	In 1999 China and Kyrgyzstan settled their dispute along border, with Bishkek ceding almost 1,240 sq kms of land to Beijing.	In 2001, rumours surfaced claiming that Kyrgyzstan President Askar Akayev had reaped personal financial gains from the deal provoking uproar in Kyrgyzstan and energized the opposition movement, forcing Akayev to flee the country in 2005.	Kyrgyzstan's economic relations with Beijing have grown, and the creation of the Shanghai Cooperation Organization appears to be pulling the country away from its traditional ties to Moscow. Russia has tried to limit China's influence through regional organizations such as the Collective Security Treaty Organization. In 2011, Russia tried to lure Kyrgyzstan back into its orbit by agreeing to expand the Moscow-led Customs Union to include Kyrgyzstan, which could weaken Bishkek's commercial relations with Beijing.
Laos	423	The Sino-French Border Agreement of 1895 between China and French possessions in SE Asia delimited and demarcation the Sino-Lao boundary which is largely based on water-courses and watersheds, where possible. A Treaty and Supplementary Protocol, in 1991, established a Border Commission which completed its work in 1992.	The border is undisputed. Laos is strategically well-placed to constitute one or more east-west land bridges linking northern Myanmar and Thailand to ports on the South China Sea, as well as allowing the development of north-south trade routes from Yunnan Province. The extent to which Laos can retain full sovereign control over its territory along the Sino-Laos border remains to be seen.	There has been a growth of Chinese-owned and operated factories, plus a large Chinese casino located in the Laotian border town of Boten. According to some reports, Chinese owners have refused to allow Laotian officials to inspect these businesses, much less to regulate their activities. This is worrying for the Laotian government.
Malaysia	Maritime Boundary	The dispute over maritime boundaries has arisen due to China's apparent claim to all of the South China Sea, as shown on Chinese maps that depict the nine-dashed line, an area of approximately 2,225,420 sq kms.	The maritime boundary has yet to be delimited and the territorial dispute in the South China Sea has yet to be resolved. In particular, the sovereignty over the Spratly Islands, which include numerous small islands scattered over 240,000 sq kms of water.	China is reluctant to move quickly to settle the dispute over the Spratly islands. The Malaysian government is reluctant to joint development of them. Instead, it is actively exploiting marine resources in the disputed area, maintaining a military presence and commercial development. Malaysia's 2009 decision for a joint submission with Vietnam to the UN Commission on Limits of the Continental Shelf interferes with China's claims.

(*Contd.*)

Country	Length (in kms)	Details	Status	Comments
Mongolia	4,645	Clarified on 25 December 1962, when they signed an agreement officially delimiting the Sino-Mongolian border.	China's enormous economic growth has given Beijing considerable economic leverage over Mongolia, making any Chinese attempt to take additional border territory or annex Mongolia outright highly unlikely.	If Mongolia hopes to avert Chinese domination and guarantee its border and territorial integrity, it needs to adopt duties on foreign goods and regulate foreign, specifically Chinese, capital, to avoid becoming merely an economic satellite of China.
Myanmar	2,200	In 1988, a second treaty settled the remaining disputes along the border.	A Sino-Burmese boundary treaty delimiting the bulk of their mutual border was signed on 1 October 1960, and ratified a year later, where China secured approximately 114 sq km of disputed territory. While most of the Sino-Myanmar border remains unchanged, the "provisional western extremity" still awaits the settlement of the Sino-Indian boundary.	Domestic rebellion in the Han Chinese-dominated Kokang region of Myanmar has led to border tensions, as approximately 50,000 ethnic Han Chinese have fled to China during the past ten years. During 2010, China was even forced to deploy additional troops to this tense border region to halt the further flow of refugees.
Nepal	1,415	Myanmar's boundary with China is still not fully settled, since defining the tri-junction with India is contingent on the resolution of the Sino-Indian dispute.	The as-yet unfinished boundary line between China and Nepal relates to seven Nepalese counties bordering on Tibet.	The two tri-junctions - where the Nepalese, Chinese, and Indian territories meet - have yet to be negotiated on both the western and eastern ends of Nepal as a consequence of the Sino-Indian dispute. There are also a number of bilateral disputes between the PRC and Nepal, including over the exact ownership of Mount Everest.
Pakistan	523	Boundary delimitation and demarcation between Nepal and China began during October 1961. Pakistan is one of China's only firm allies along its southern border. Sino-Pakistani relations are dominated by the notion of "special relationship" or "entente cordiale."	Since settling their shared border through secret negotiations in 1963, they have avoided any boundary disputes. The relationship has proven remarkably durable during the past fifty years, including Beijing's decision to provide Pakistan with nuclear technology, and Pakistan's assistance to Beijing in furthering the PRC's presence in the Indian Ocean via the deep-water port at Gwadar.	The challenge of transnational terrorism and Islamic fundamentalism has posed a threat to Sino-Pakistani border diplomacy since the mid-1990s, but Beijing's pipeline plans and anticipated linkage with the Karakoram Highway denote even greater cooperation, making the Sino-Pakistani border stable.

(Contd.)

Country	Length (in kms)	Details	Status	Comments
Philippines	Maritime Boundary	Un-delimited maritime boundaries and overlapping maritime claims are an enduring source of tension between the Philippines and China, despite rapidly expanding economic ties and talk of a "golden age of partnership" in bilateral relations. The dispute over the South China Sea tends to dominate their interactions.	China asserts territorial sovereignty over numerous islands in the South China Sea, especially the Spratly islands, on historic grounds. The Philippines claims sovereignty over several of the same islands, which it refers to as the Kalayaan Island Group (KIG). They also contest sovereignty over Scarborough Shoal, in the South China Sea.	Philippine relations with China, while increasingly strong, especially in economic terms, can in political and diplomatic terms be characterized largely as cautious at best, and even hostile at times.
Russia	4,300	The Sino-Russian border demarcation in 2008 represented a massive economic opportunity to many, but also a potential future threat. Despite being formally settled, Russia's border with China is potentially dangerous. It is a dividing line between two equally imperial but very different cultures.	Moscow's relationship with Beijing remains both a foundation stone of Russia's geopolitical architecture and also a vital economic partnership. It is tempered, however, by a deep unease about the sustainability of the border in the face of a rising China, which has in effect made Russia the front line of Europe versus Asia.	Beijing may reopen historical iniquities and the legitimacy of 19th century treaties, in which huge territories were seized by Russia. To many Russians living in the Russian Far East China represents a source of labour, investment, goods, and opportunities to develop eastern Siberia's 65 % of Russia's prospective petroleum reserves, 85 % of its natural gas reserves, almost all its diamonds, 70 % of its gold, and large reserves of coal, timber, and other natural resources.
Taiwan	Territorial and Maritime claims	Separated by the 161 km wide Taiwan Strait, China and Taiwan's border dispute is complex. For much of its post-1949 history the Republic of China (ROC) on Taiwan claimed all of-mainland China plus Mongolia as its sovereign territory.	Taipei's hopes of retaking the mainland have diminished, but it has territorial claims and actual control over a number of small islands off the coast of China, including Jinmen (formerly Quemoy) and Mazu, as well as the Pratas islands. It also retains control over the largest island in the Spratlys, Itu Aba (Taiping Island). The PRC claims not only all of the offshore islands controlled by Taiwan, but all the islands of the ROC proper, such as the Penghu (formerly the Pescadores), Green (Lu Dao), and Orchid (Lan Yu) islands.	The two governments agree with each other, however, on many South China Sea territorial and maritime claims against other Asian nations. Indeed Beijing and Taipei have cooperated in the past against other claimants in the South China Sea. Further, it was, in fact, the ROC that first published a map in 1947 including the infamous eleven-dashed line claiming the majority of the South China Sea, a claim that the PRC later adopted in its nine-dashed line map.

(*Contd.*)

Country	Length (in kms)	Details	Status	Comments
Tajikistan	400	Tajikistan, in January 2011, ratified an agreement with China concerning the border, bringing an end to more than a decade of negotiation and well over a century of dispute. The normalization of the Tajik-China border in 1999 specified that Tajikistan cede to China 200 sq km, and in 2002 a second agreement increased this to 1,122 sq kms, mainly in the Pamir mountains.	Tajikistan's chief negotiator, Foreign Minister Hamrokhon Zarifi, heralded it as a great success, explaining that it was far less territory (only about 5 %) than the 28,000 sq kms that had previously been in dispute. The Tajikistan government's political opponents saw it differently, since this equalled 0.78 % of Tajikistan's entire territory of 143,100 sq kms.	If current economic trends continue, however, the resolution of the Tajik-China border issues will prove to be of comparatively small significance in comparison with the ever-growing importance of Chinese political and economic influence in Tajikistan.
Vietnam	1,350	Vietnam's border relations with China include both land and sea boundaries. Beijing and Hanoi started full normalization of bilateral relations in 1991.	The major land dispute along the two countries' mutual border is over 227 sq km. In 1999, the two countries agreed to split these areas, with Vietnam receiving just under 113 sq kms and China just over 114 sq kms. The sea disputes encompass both maritime areas in the Gulf of Tonkin and competing sovereignty claims over the Paracel and Spratly archipelagos in the South China Sea.	While an agreement dividing the Gulf of Tonkin was reached in 2000, and a joint-fishing zone was established, disputes on other maritime issues remain unresolved. Further, China's claim within the so-called nine-dashed lines in the South China Sea overlap with Vietnam's claims to EEZ and continental shelf areas immediately to the east of Vietnam's coastline. Bilateral tensions have periodically increased due to actions in and relating to the South China Sea.

MISSILES SURVEY

MISSILES SURVEY

Recent developments in ballistic and cruise missile technology in South Asia show an increasingly alarming rate of proliferation. These developments are the result of matured national programmes whose continuation and developments have been supported by political leaderships as well as popular support. States involved in missile proliferation have also either already acquired a nuclear military capability or are suspected to be in the final stages of acquiring such. Consequently, the security impact is serious and this environment of proliferation can threaten the progress of welfare and sustainable economic prosperity in the countries involved. Ballistic and cruise missile systems are viewed not only as cost-effective weapons but also as symbols of national power. In addition, they present an asymmetric threat. Many ballistic and cruise missiles are armed with weapons of mass destruction.

China has the most active and diverse ballistic missile development programme in the world. It is developing and testing offensive missiles, forming additional missile units, qualitatively upgrading certain missile systems, and developing methods to counter ballistic missile defences. China's ballistic missile force is expanding in both size and types of missiles. New theatre missiles continue to be deployed, while the ICBM force is adding the CSS-10 Mod 1 (DF-31) and CSS-10 Mod 2 (DF-31A) ICBMs. The new DF-21D is the world's first anti-ship ballistic missile or ASBM. Future ICBMs probably will include some with multiple independently-targetable re-entry vehicles, and the number of ICBM nuclear warheads capable of reaching the United States could expand to well over 100 within the next 15 years.

India and Pakistan continue to develop new short and long-range ballistic missiles. Pakistan has tested its solid-propellant Shaheen 2 MRBM six times since 2004 and India has tested its new solid-propellant Agni III IRBM three times since 2006. India has stated that the solid-propellant Agni II MRBM is ready for deployment.

Land-attack cruise missiles (LACMs) are highly effective weapon systems that can present a major threat to military operations. At least nine countries are involved in LACM production and many missiles will be available for export.

Ballistic missiles are generally categorized into four classes: Short-range (SRBM), which have a range of up to 1, 000 kilometres; Medium-range (MRBM), with range of approximately 1, 000-3,000 kilometres; Intermediate-range (IRBM), which have operational ranges of approximately 3,000-5,500 kilometres, and; Intercontinental-range (ICBM), which can travel upwards of 5,500 kilometres.

Ballistic missiles offer deep targeting and highly effective penetration capabilities that can destroy military, political, and economic assets. They are also regarded as the best solution to carry weapons of mass destruction (WMD). Logistically, the ease of operations allowed by ballistic missiles compared to aircraft makes them indisputably useful weapons systems to have in the military arsenal. By acquiring such capabilities, the entire opponent country is made into a battle field, where economic, political, military and civilian targets can be simultaneously targeted much more easily at any time, regardless of how these targets are defended.

Ballistic missiles are the ideal weapon to deliver nuclear warheads because these do not depend on highly accurate targeting for effectiveness. That said, nuclear powers in the region have achieved sophisticated terminal guidance systems which deliver greater targeting accuracy.

China's long-term, comprehensive transformation of its military forces is improving its capacity for force projection and Chinese ballistic missiles play a key role in China's military efforts. China currently deploys the nuclear-armed CSS-2, CSS-5 Mod 1, and CSS-5 Mod 2 for regional nuclear deterrence. China is also acquiring new conventionally-armed MRBMs to conduct precision strikes at longer ranges. These systems are likely intended to hold at risk, or strike, logistics nodes and regional military bases including airfields and ports. Notably, China is developing an anti-ship ballistic missile (ASBM) based on a variant of the CSS-5.

India continues to develop and improve its ballistic missiles. The solid-propellant Agni II MRBM is ready for deployment. The new solid-propellant Agni III IRBM has been flight-tested three times since 2006. Indian missile developers have also stated that they have the capability to produce an ICBM, with a range of about 5,500 kilometres.

Pakistan continues to improve the readiness and capabilities of its Army Strategic Force Command and individual Strategic Missile Groups through training exercises that include live missile firings. Pakistan has tested its solid-propellant Shaheen 2 MRBM six times since 2004, and this missile system is probably deployed.

China—Ballistic Missiles

Category	Designation	Range (kms)	Payload	Assessed Nos.
SRBMs	DF-15/M-9/CSST-600 DF-11/M-11/CSS-X-7	600 300	950 kgs; 350kT 800 kgs; 350kT	350-400 700-750
MRBMs	DF-3/CSS-2 DF-21/21A/CSS-5(Mod 1 & 2)	3,000 2,100	2,150 kgs; 3.3MT 600 kgs; 350kT	15-20 60-80
IRBMs	DF-4/CSS-3	5,400	2,200 kgs; 3.3MT	15-20
ICBMs	DF-5/5A DF-31/31A	13,000 7,200/11,200	3,200 kgs; 4-5MT (?); 200Kt MIRV	20 <20
SLBM	JL1/ JL2	1,000+ 7,200	600 kgs; 350kT 700 kgs; 300kT	12 60(?)

China—Cruise Missiles

Category	Designation	Range (kms)	Payload	Assessed Nos.
LACM	ALCM+GLCM			
	Kh-55/AS-15(Kent)	3000		(?)
	HN-1/HN-2	600/1500	350 kgs; 90kT	300(?)
	DH-10	1500		150-300
	YJ-63			400-500
	Tianjin-1	600-1000		
ASCMs	YJ-62			120
	Styx/CSS-N-2			100
	Sunburn/SS-N-22			100+
	Sizzler SS-N-27			50(?)

Missile Programme Drivers—China

- The Taiwan Issue
- China-US Relations.
- Relations with Russia.
- Japan and South Korea.
- India.

China Missiles—Main Features

- 1300+ missiles, majority short range, conventionally armed.
- 40 ICBMs, ranges 7200-13000 kilometres.
- 90-120 M/ IRBMs, all land-based.
- Only SLBM (JL-1) not successful.
- New SLBM tested, awaiting Jin Class SSBN.
- Missiles are "not targeted at specific countries in peacetime."
- Prior to mutual "No-targeting" agreement, half of ICBM inventory was targeting US.
- Chinese missiles based on original buy-outs from the USSR/Russia.
- Modern Russian-supplied ASCMs.
- About 120 missiles of the total inventory are nuclear capable.

India—Missiles

Name	Missile/Propulsion	Warhead	Payload (kgs)	Range (kilometres)
Prithvi-I/SS-150	Ballistic/Liquid fuel	Conventional/ Nuclear	1,000	150
Prithvi-II/SS-250	Ballistic/Liquid fuel	Conventional/Nuclear	500	250
Dhanush/Prithvi-III/SS-350	Ballistic/Liquid fuel	Conventional/Nuclear	NK	350
Agni-(TD)	Ballistic/2Stage Hybrid	Nuclear	1,000	1,200 - 1,500
Agni-I	Ballistic/Solid-fuel	Nuclear	1,000	700 - 800
Agni-II	Ballistic/Solid-fuel	Nuclear	1,000	2,000 - 2,500
Agni-III	Ballistic/Solid-fuel	Nuclear	NK	3,500 - 4,000
Agni-V	Ballistic/Solid-fuel	Nuclear	NK	5,000
Brahmos/PJ10	Ballistic/2Stage Hybrid Engine	Conventional	200 - 300 280 - 300	Sh/Sm/Gr/Air
Nirbhay	Cruise	Conventional	NK	1,000
K-15 Sagarika	2stage SLBM	Conventional/Nuclear	600	700
Shourya	Ballistic/Solid/Canisterised	Conventional/Nuclear	>500	600

Missile Programme Drivers—India

- Long land border with both China and Pakistan.
- History of territorial wars with both.
- Both nuclear weapon states.
- Strong China-Pakistan relations.
- Transfer of missile and nuclear technology.
- India's NFU policy.
- Triad doctrine.

Pakistan—Missiles

Type	Designation	Propulsion	Range (kms)	Payload (kgs)
SRBM	Hatf–1/1A/	Solid-Fuel	60-80/100	500
	Hatf-2/Shadoz	Solid-Fuel	300	500
	Hatf-3/DF-11/M11 Ghaznavi	Solid-Fuel	280	800
	Hatf-4DF-15 Shaheen	Solid-Fuel	600-800	500
	Hatf-6/M18/ Shaheen-II	Solid-Fuel	2,000	500
	Hatf V/Ghauri/Nodong	Liquid-Fuel	1,200-1,300	1,000
	Ghauri-II	Liquid-Fuel	1,700	
	Ghauri-III	Liquid-Fuel	2,500-3,500	
LACM	Hatf-VII/DH-10/Babur		700	
ALCM	Hatf-VIII/Ra'ad		350	

Pakistan Missiles—Main Features

- Chinese and North Korean assistance.
- Efforts under way for cruise missile-delivery systems.
- Chinese selectively abide by the MTCR; e.g. air-launched missiles are excluded.
- Currently Pak still dependent on China and DPRK for propellant, critical components and technological aspects.
- The Ghaznavi (/M11) and Shaheen-I are operational.
- Shaheen II development is complete and induction and service trials completed.
- Ghauri II is likely to be completed soon.
- Pakistan also keeps missiles and warheads de-mated as well as separated.
- Warheads are believed to stored in disassembled state.

Missile Programme Drivers—Pakistan

- Indo-centric threat perception.
- Perception of Indian superiority in conventional forces.
- Nuclear deterrent meant to deter conventional attack.
- Long land border, Navy irrelevant.
- Major Indian value targets within range of fighter-bombers.

NUCLEAR SURVEY

NUCLEAR SURVEY

Table 1: Military and Nuclear Weapons Expenditures (US $ bn, 2010 exchange rates)

	Total Military Spending (2010)	Nuclear Weapons (2011, estimated)	
		Core Cost	Full Cost
USA	687	34.0	61.3
Russia	53-86	9.8	14.8
China	129	6.4	7.6
France	61	4.7	6.0
UK	57	4.5	5.5
India	35	3.8	4.9
Israel	13	1.5	1.9
Pakistan	7.9	1.8	2.2
North Korea	8.8	0.5	0.7
Total	**1052-1085**	**67.0**	**104.9**

Note: Core costs refer to researching, developing, testing, operating, maintaining and upgrading the nuclear arsenal (weapons and delivery vehicles) and the nuclear command-control-communications and early warning infrastructure.
Full costs add unpaid/deferred health and environmental costs, missile defences assigned to defend against nuclear weapons, and nuclear threat reduction and incident management. Air defences, anti-submarine warfare and nuclear weapons-related intelligence and surveillance expenses are not included.

Source: Bruce Blair and Matthew A. Brown, "World Spending on Nuclear Weapons Surpasses $1 Trillion Per Decade" (Washington DC: Global Zero, June 2011). Available at: http://www.globalzero.org/en/page/cost-of-nukes

Table 2: The World's Nuclear Arsenals (2012)

	Strategic		Other		To be Dismantled	Total by Country	Yield Range (kt)	Total Yield (Mt)
	Deployed	Reserve	Deployed	Reserve				
USA	1722	2450	200	300	3100	7772	Sub-kt-455	535
Russia	1799	700	0	860-1040	5500	8859-9039	Sub-kt-1000	773
China	200	40	-	-	-	240	184-240	294
France	300		-	-	-	300	100-300	55
UK	160	65	-	-	-	225	100	21
Israel	80	-	-	-	-	80		1.6-12
India	80-100	-	-	-	-	80-100	15-200	1
Pakistan	90-110	-	-	-	-	90-110	Sub-kt-50	1.7
DPRK	-	-	-	-	-	-	Sub-kt-8	0.05
Totals	**4431**-4471	3255	200	1160-1340	8600	17646-17866		1682-1693

All figures are based on S.N. Kile, et al., "World Nuclear Forces," *SIPRI Yearbook 2012: Armaments, Disarmament and International Security* (Oxford: Oxford University Press, 2012), pp. 307–44 unless otherwise noted below. All figures are estimates.

CHINA

China's nuclear capabilities are primarily controlled by the Second Artillery Corps (SAC) of the People's Liberation Army (PLA), which also controls China's land-based conventional missile force. It is directly commanded by China's highest-level military organization, the Central Military Commission (CMC). China is thought to have roughly 240 nuclear warheads and 180 nuclear-capable missiles and aircraft of various types.[1] SAC is organized into six ballistic missile bases and several subordinate brigades deployed throughout China.

China's 2008 defence white paper indicated that SAC "is mainly responsible for deterring other countries

[1] Hans M. Kristensen and Robert S. Norris, "Chinese Nuclear Forces, 2011:' Bulletin of the Atomic Scientists 67 (November/December 2011): 81-87, http://bos.sagepub.com/content/67 16/81.

from using nuclear weapons against China, and for conducting nuclear counterattacks and precision strikes with conventional missiles."[2] Furthermore, according to the white paper:

The Second Artillery Force sticks to China's policy of no first use of nuclear weapons, implements a self-defensive nuclear strategy, strictly follows the orders of the CMC, and takes it as its fundamental mission the protection of China from any nuclear attack. In peacetime the nuclear missile weapons of the Second Artillery Force are not aimed at any country. But if China comes under a nuclear threat, the nuclear missile force of the Second Artillery Force will go into a state of alert, and get ready for a nuclear counterattack to deter the enemy from using nuclear weapons against China. If China comes under a nuclear attack, the nuclear missile force of the Second Artillery Force will use nuclear missiles to launch a resolute counterattack against the enemy either independently or together with the nuclear forces of other services.[3]

China's Second Artillery would use their weapons as part of Beijing's "active defense" military doctrine. This is a concept under which limited offensive measures may be employed as necessary to safeguard core strategic interests, even though those strategic goals are viewed as inherently defensive—such as protecting China's maritime periphery.

China is also developing the DF-21D is the world's first anti-ship ballistic missile or ASBM. The PLA Navy (PLAN) is strengthening its "nuclear counter-attack" capabilities.[4] The eventual deployment of China's sea-based forces appears to be intended to serve as a complement to the Second Artillery's land-based nuclear missiles and to further strengthen the survivability of China's strategic deterrent.

China is modernizing its nuclear missile force in order to enhance the survivability and credibility of its deterrent. China has progressed to one of the world's most impressive nuclear and conventional ballistic missile programmes (see Table A.I). China now has "the most active and diverse ballistic missile development program in the world."[5] In addition, China is developing and testing offensive missiles, forming additional missile units, qualitatively upgrading certain missile systems, and developing methods to counter ballistic missile defences.

The key drivers of changes in the nuclear missile force structure is China's concern about the credibility of its traditional nuclear deterrent posture in the face of improvements in adversary intelligence, surveillance, and reconnaissance (ISR) capabilities; conventional precision strike capabilities; and missile defence capabilities. Beijing is therefore modernizing its nuclear missile forces to enhance their survivability, increase their striking power, and counter perceived advances in U.S. missile defence capabilities.[6]

A Second Artillery publication—*Intimidation Warfare*—states that deterrence must be carefully calibrated to maximize the chances of achieving the desired results. If the level of threat is too low, it will fail to influence the enemy; if it is too high, there is an equally serious risk of deterrence failure because the enemy may lash out in desperation. Similarly, in another passage it is stated that deterrence operations could accidentally trigger escalation if they are poorly timed: "Whether the timing for conducting the military deterrence of the missile forces is correctly chosen will directly affect the progress of deterrence and its outcome, If the appropriate timing is chosen, then deterrence will deter the enemy, contain the eruption of war, and obtain the objective of peace with the small price of deterrence. If inappropriate timing is chosen, then deterrence may cause the situation to deteriorate, even leading to the eruption and escalation of war."[7]

China deploys the DF-3 (CSS-2) intermediate-range ballistic missile (IRBM) and the DF-21 and DF-21A (CSS-5 Mod 1 and CSS-5 Mod 2) medium-range ballistic missiles (MRBMs) for regional nuclear deterrence missions. China has 14-18 DF-3 (CSS-2), which was first deployed in 1971 and is a single-stage, liquid propellant IRBM with a maximum range

---

[2] Information Office of the State Council of the People's Republic of China, "Chinas National Defense in 2008:' Beijing, January 2009, 29, http://www.fas.org/programslssp/nukes/2008DefenseWhitePaper- Jan2009.pdf.

[3] Ibid. The white paper also states, "The conventional missile force of the Second Artillery Force is charged mainly of the task of conducting medium- and long-range precision strikes against key strategic and operational targets of the enemy."

[4] Ibid., 24.

[5] National Air and Space Intelligence Center, "Ballistic and Cruise Missile Threat;" NA-SIC-I031-0985-09, Wright-Patterson Air Force Base, OH, April 2009, 3.

[6] See Yao, "Chinese Nuclear Policy and the Future of Minimum Deterrence"; Chu Shulong and Rong Yu, "China: Dynamic Minimum Deterrence;' in *The Long Shadow: Nuclear Weapons and Security in 21st Century Asia*, ed. Muthiah Alagappa (Stanford, CA: Stanford University Press, 2008), 161-87.

[7] See PLASAF, *Dierpaobing zhanyixue* [The science of Second Artillery campaigns]; Zhao, *Shezhan-dao-dan weishe zongheng tan*) [Intimidation warfare: Comprehensive survey of missile intimidation].

Table 3: China's Nuclear Missile Force Structure

Type	NATO Designation	Year Deployed	Range (km)	Warhead × Yield (Kt)	No. of Warheads
Land-based missiles					
DF-3A	CSS-2	1971	3100	1 x 3300	16
DF-4	CSS-3	1980	5400(+)	1 x 3300	12
DF-5A	CSS-4 Mod 2	1981	13000(+)	1 x 4000-5000	20
DF-21A	CSS-5 Mod ½	1991	2150	1 x 200-300	60
DF-31	CSS-10 Mod 1	2006	7200	1 x 200-300 (?)	10-20
DF-31A	CSS-10 Mod 2	2007	11200	1 x 200-300 (?)	10-20
Submarine-launched ballistic missiles					
JL-1	CSS-NX-3	1986	1000(+)	1 x 200-300	12
JL-2	CSS-NX-14	–	ca. 7400	1 x 200-300 (?)	36
Aircraft					
Hong-6	B-6	1965	3100	1 x bomb	20
Others	–	–	–	1 x bomb	20
Total					**ca. 240**

Source: Stockholm International Peace Research Institute, *SIPRI Yearbook 2011: Armaments, Disarmament and International Security* (New York: Oxford University Press, 2011), 342.

Note: IRBM = intermediate-range ballistic missile; MRBM = medium-range ballistic missile; ICBM = intercontinental ballistic missile; MIRV = multiple independently targetable re-entry vehicle; SLBM = submarine launched ballistic missile.

of about 3,000 kilometres. The DF-3 (CSS-2) is "transportable" but has "limited mobility." It could be nearing retirement from service.

China has transitioned to a more survivable, road-mobile theatre nuclear force featuring the DF-21 (CSS-5 Mod 1) and DF-21A (CSS-5 Mod 2) MRBMs. The PLA has about 60-80 nuclear-armed DF-21 (CSS-5 Mod 1) and DF-21A (CSS-5 Mod 2) MRBMs and 70-90 associated launchers. Both are two-stage, solid propellant, road-mobile missiles with maximum ranges of more than 1,750 kilometres.

The silo-based DF-5 (NATO designation CSS-4) ICBM, a two-stage, liquid propellant missile, has been the mainstay of China's intercontinental nuclear deterrence force since its initial deployment in 1981. China currently deploys about 20 silo-based DF-5 ICBMs, which have a range of at least 13,000 kilometres.

China has also fielded two road-mobile ICBMs, the DF-31 and DF-31A. The DF-31 (CSS-10 Mod 1) is a three-stage, solid propellant, road-mobile ICBM with a maximum range of more than 7,200 kilometres. The DF-31 will replace China's aging limited-range DF-4 missiles. Deployed on a mobile erector launcher (MEL), the DF-31 is likely intended to mainly cover targets in Russia and Asia. China conducted the first developmental flight test of the DF-31 in August 1999.

The DF-31A (CSS-10 Mod 2) is a three-stage, solid propellant, road-mobile ICBM with a maximum range of more that) 11,200 kilometres. China began deploying it in 2007.

China has about 16-24 of its older and shorter-range, liquid-fuelled DF-4 (CSS-3) ICBMs. The DF-4 is a two-stage, liquid propellant missile with a range of about 5,400 kilometres. The DF-4 can be deployed as a silo-based system, but it is also transportable. China has about 10-15 Iaunchers.

China is developing additional ICBMs - a new road mobile ICBM, possibly capable of carrying a multiple independently targeted re-entry vehicles (MIRV).

China has conducted 45 nuclear tests. Estimates of the current number of Chinese nuclear warheads vary, but China is believed to have manufactured a total of between 200 and 300 warheads, roughly 50 of which have been used for nuclear tests. Currently, approximately 155 of those are believed to be prepared for deployment.

A number of Chinese missile bases are reportedly within range of northern India: DF-3As and DF-21s are stationed in Kunming, Yunnan province and Delingha, Qingha province; and DF-4s at Delingha, Huaihua area in Hunan province and Luoyang area of Henan province. Nuclear-capable DF-21Cs are also reportedly deployed near Delingha. The only plausible targets for DF-21 missiles at Delingha are cities in India. India is also the only nuclear power in range of the Kunming base. Claims by some India analysts that China has nuclear weapons in Tibet are denied by China and unconfirmed by independent sources.

China is improving its nuclear forces to bypass US missile defences, and is reportedly exploring the technology for a rudimentary missile defence system. It tested an anti-satellite missile in 2007 and missile interception technology in 2010, which some Chinese analysts suggest is being developed with Indian missiles in mind. However, China is modernising and expanding its nuclear capabilities more slowly than its conventional military.

INDIA

The organizations concerned with research and development for India's nuclear weapons are controlled by the Department of Atomic Energy (DAE), which was set up in 1954. It functions under the direct control of the Prime Minister and includes facilities to be part of

India's nuclear weapons programme, including nuclear reactors, reprocessing facilities, and enrichment facilities.

India became a declared nuclear weapon state in May 1998, although it had maintained a capability to assemble nuclear explosive devices and had developed a delivery capability, both in terms of aircraft as well as missiles, several years previously. In May 1998, this capability was finally translated into an explicit and declared nuclear weapon status through a series of nuclear tests.

India has a credible theory of how its nuclear weapons may be used which is spelt out in its nuclear doctrine formulated, on 4 January 2003, at a meeting of the Cabinet Committee on Security (CCS). Since then, it has put in place a triad of land-based, air-delivered and submarine-based nuclear forces and delivery assets to conform to its declared doctrine of no-first-use and retaliation only.

India has a command and control infrastructure that can survive a first strike and a fully secure communication system that is reliable and hardened against radiation or electronic interference. A number of redundancies have been created to strengthen survivability. India today has a long-range ballistic missile capability and a submarine-based missile capability. These capabilities will be further improved as time goes on and more resources become available. In all these respects, significant progress has been achieved.

As regards the current status of India's nuclear deterrent and its command and control system, at least two legs of the triad referred to in the nuclear doctrine are already in place. These include a modest arsenal, nuclear-capable aircraft and missiles both in fixed underground silos as well as those which are mounted on mobile rail and road-based platforms. These land-based missiles include both *Agni*-II (1,500 km) as well as *Agni*-III (2,500 km) missiles. The range and accuracy of further versions for example, *Agni* V (5,000 km) which was tested successfully only recently, will improve with the acquisition of further technological capability and experience. The third leg of the triad, which is submarine-based, is a work in progress. India needs at least three *Arihant* class nuclear submarines so that at least one will always be at sea. Submarine-based missiles systems have been developed and tested in the form of the *Sagarika* but these are still relatively short in range. It is expected that a modest sea-based deterrence will be in place by 2015 or 2016.There is also a major R&D programme which has been in place since 2005, for the development of a new, longer range and more accurate generation of submarine-based missiles which are likely to ready for deployment around 2020.

The National Command Authority is in charge of India's nuclear deterrent. At its apex is the Political Council which is headed by the Prime Minister and includes all the ministerial members of the Cabinet Committee on Security such as the Ministers of Defence, Home and External Affairs. Below the Political Council is the Executive Council which is headed by the National Security Advisor and includes the Chiefs of the three armed forces, the C-in-C of India's Strategic Forces Command, among others. There is an alternate National Command Authority which would take up the functions of nuclear command in case of any contingency when the established hierarchy is rendered dysfunctional. The NCA has access to radiation hardened and fully secured communications systems where, too, redundancies have been put in place as back-up facilities.

In order to support the NCA, a Strategy Programme Staff has been created in the National Security Council Secretariat to carry out general staff work for the National Command Authority. This unit is charged with looking at the reliability and quality of our weapons and delivery systems, collate intelligence on other nuclear weapon states particularly those in the category of potential adversaries and work on a perspective plan for India's nuclear deterrent in accordance with a ten year cycle. The Strategy Programme Staff has representatives from the three services, from the Science and Technology establishment and other experts from related domains, including External Affairs. A Strategic Armament Safety Authority has been set up to review and to update storage and transfer procedures for nuclear armaments, including the submarine-based component. It will be responsible for all matters relating to the safety and security of nuclear and delivery assets at all locations. This will function under the direct authority of the NCA.

The National Command Authority works on a two-person rule for access to armaments and delivery systems. Regular drills are conducted to examine possible escalatory scenarios, surprise attack scenarios and the efficiency of response systems under the no-first-use limitation. Specialized units have also been trained and deployed for operation in a nuclearized environment.

Table 4: India's Nuclear Forces (2012)

Type	Range (km)	Payload (kg)	Status
Ballistic Missiles (Land-based)			
Prithvi I/II	150/ 250	800/ 500	Weapons system entered service in 1994. Prithvi I has nuclear capability and Prithvi II is also believed to do so. Approx. fewer than 50 launchers deployed.
Agni I	700	1000	Entered service in 2004
Agni II	2000	1000	Entered service in 2004
Operational status uncertain			
Agni III	3000	1500	Operational since 2011
Agni IV	>3000	1000	Under development
Agni V	>5000	1000	Under development
Ballistic Missiles (Sea-based)			
Dhanush	350	500	Under development
K-15	700	500-600	Under development
K-4	3500	1000	Under development
Aircraft			
Mirage 2000H Vajra	1850	6300	Aircraft is capable of delivering nuclear gravity bombs

Source: SIPRI.

PAKISTAN

Since its nuclear tests in May 1998, Pakistan has been rapidly developing and expanding its nuclear arsenal. It is producing highly enriched uranium (HEU) and plutonium—the key ingredients for nuclear weapons—and is increasing its capacity to produce plutonium by building new reactors. It is also testing and deploying a diverse array of nuclear-capable ballistic and cruise missiles, with ranges from 60 to 2000 kilometres.

Pakistan is believed to have received in the early 1980s a first generation Chinese weapon design that used HEU.[8] Pakistan is moving from an arsenal of weapons based wholly on HEU to greater reliance on lighter and more compact plutonium-based weapons. The shift is being made possible by a rapid expansion in plutonium production capacity, with two production reactors under construction to add to the two reactors that are currently operating. Pakistan is also moving from aircraft-delivered nuclear bombs to nuclear-armed ballistic and cruise missiles; and from liquid-fuelled to solid-fuelled medium range missiles. Pakistan has received direct assistance from China for both its nuclear weapons and missile programmes, and from North Korea for its missile programme.

Estimates of Pakistan's nuclear weapons stockpile have grown as it continues to produce fissile material for nuclear weapons and to expand its fissile material production capacity, especially for plutonium. As of 2011, the US government estimates Pakistan's stockpile to range from 90 to over 110 weapons.[9]

Table 5: Growth of Pakistan's Nuclear Arsenal, 1998–2011

Year	1998	1999	2000	2001	2002	2003	2004
Estimated weapons	2	8	14	20	26	32	38

(Contd.)

Year	2005	2006	2007	2008	2009	2010	2011
Estimated weapons	44	50	60	70	80	90	100

Source: Adapted and updated from Robert S. Norris and Hans Kristensen, *"Global Nuclear Weapons Inventories, 1945–2010,"* Bulletin of the Atomic Scientists, July/August 2010, Vol. 66, No. 4, pp. 77–83.

Pakistan is in the process of developing a range of delivery systems for its nuclear weapons. It has a number of short-range, medium, and longer range road-mobile ballistic surface-to-surface missiles (SSMs) in various stages of development. It also is moving from liquid-fuelled missiles to solid-fuelled missiles. Pakistan has received assistance from North Korea and China with its missile programme.

Pakistan Army's Strategic Force Command has tested both short- and long-range missiles. The *Abdali* missile, with a range less than 200 km, is a simple solid-fueled missile that Pakistan began testing in 2002. In January 2003, the liquid-fueled *Ghauri* missile (*Hatf V*) was inducted into the army. It is derived from the Democratic People's Republic of Korea (DPRK)'s *No-Dong* missile. Work on the *Ghauri* missile started in the early 1990s and the first test was carried out in 1998.

The 750 km-range solid-fuelled *Shaheen-I* was handed over to the military in March 2003. It is derived from the Chinese M-11 missile and China may have

[8] Hans M. Kristensen and Robert S. Norris, "Pakistan's Nuclear Forces, 2011," *Bulletin of the Atomic Scientists*, July 2011, pp. 91–99.

[9] David E. Sanger and Eric Schmitt, "Pakistani Nuclear Arms Pose Challenge to U.S. Policy," *New York Times*, 31 January 2011.

provided missile components, 34 intact M-11 missiles, and "blueprints and equipment...to build a plant for making missiles," as well as technical assistance with further development of this missile.[10]

Pakistan has also developed a second generation of ballistic missile systems. *Shaheen*-II is a 2000 km-range solid-fuel missile, first tested in 2004. In 2011, Pakistan carried out the first test of a possible battlefield nuclear missile, the 60 km-range *Nasr* missile, described in an official statement as able to carry "nuclear warheads of appropriate yield" and as "consolidating Pakistan's deterrence capability at all levels of the threat spectrum."[11] Pakistan is also developing a nuclear-capable ground-launched cruise missile (*Babur*) and an air-launched cruise missile (*Ra'ad*) with ranges of about 600 km and 350 km respectively.

There is little public information about the storage and deployment of Pakistan's nuclear weapons. It is believed that "missiles are not mated with warheads and the fissile cores are not inserted into the warheads themselves."[12] Reports suggest that while warheads are kept in component form, possibly by "isolating the fissile 'core' or trigger from the weapon and storing it elsewhere...all the components are stored at military bases."[13]

Pakistan and India each year exchange lists of nuclear facilities as part of their 1988 Agreement on the Prohibition of Attack against Nuclear Installations and Facilities.[14] These lists are not made public, however. They may include both military and civilian nuclear facilities.

Table 6: Pakistan's Nuclear Weapon Delivery Systems, 2012

Type	Range (km)	Payload (kg)	Status
Ballistic Missiles (Land-based)			
Abdali (Hatf-2)	180	200-400	Under development
Ghaznavi (Hatf-3)	290	500	Entered service in 2004.
Fewer than 50 launchers deployed			
Shaheen I (Hatf-4)	600-800	750-1000	Entered service in 2004
Fewer than 50 launchers deployed			
Shaheen II (Hatf-6)	2500	(approx. 1000)	Under development
Ghauri I (Hatf-5)	1200	700-100	Entered service in 2003
Fewer than 50 launchers deployed			
Nasr (Hatf-9)	60	–	Under development
Cruise Missiles			
Babur (Hatf-7)	600	400-500	Under development
Ra'ad (Hatf-8)	350	–	Under development. Air-launched
Aircraft			
F-16A/B	1600	4500	Currently being upgraded
Mirage III/V	2100	4000	

Source: Hans Kristensen and Robert S. Norris, *"Pakistan Nuclear Forces 2011,"* Bulletin of the Atomic Scientists, Volume 67, No. 4, pp. 91-99.

Pakistan has developed an extensive nuclear infrastructure that allows it to produce both HEU and plutonium for weapons.

Table 7: Pakistan's Nuclear Weapon Storage and Deployment Sites

Facility name/location	Province	Weapons	Function
Fatejhang National Defence Complex	Punjab	SSM	Missile development and potential warhead storage capability
Masroor Weapons Depot	Sindh	Various	Storage of bombs for Mirage Vs at Masroor Air Base, and warheads for SSMs
Sargodha Weapons Depot	Punjab	Various	Storage site for bombs for F-16s at Sargodha Air Base, and warheads for SSMs
Shanka Dara Missile Complex	Punjab	SSM	Missile development and potential warhead storage capability
Near Quetta Air Base	Balochistan	Bombs	Storage site with underground facilities in high-security weapons storage area
Wah Ordnance Facility	Punjab	Various	Warhead production, disassembly and dismantlement facility

Source: Robert S. Norris and Hans Kristensen, *"Worldwide Deployments of Nuclear Weapons, 2009,"* Bulletin of the Atomic Scientists, *November/ December 2009.*

[10] Shirley A. Kan, "China and Proliferation of Weapons of Mass Destruction and Missiles: Policy Issues," Congressional Research Service, Report RL31555, 13 December 2007.

[11] Press Release No. PR94/2011-ISPR, Pakistan Inter Services Public Relations Directorate, Rawalpindi, 19 April 2011.

[12] *Nuclear Black Markets: Pakistan, A.Q. Khan and the Rise of Proliferation Networks*, International Institute of Strategic Studies, London, 2007, p. 33.

[13] Joby Warrick, "Lack of Knowledge about Arsenal may Limit U.S. Options," *Washington Post*, 11 November 2007.

[14] Under this agreement, India and Pakistan are to "refrain from undertaking, encouraging or participating in, directly or indirectly, any action aimed at causing the destruction of, or damage to, any nuclear installation or facility in the other country." The term "nuclear installation or facility" includes "nuclear power and research reactors, fuel fabrication, uranium enrichment, isotopes separation and reprocessing facilities as well as any other installations with fresh or irradiated nuclear fuel and materials in any form and establishments storing significant quantities of radio-active materials." Each year on 1 January the two countries exchange a list giving the latitude and longitude of its nuclear installations and facilities and changes.

Table 8: Pakistan's Fissile Material Related Facilities

Location	Facility Type	Material
Dera Ghazi Khan	Uranium mine, ore concentration plant, conversion plant	Uranium
Kahuta	Enrichment (Khan Research Laboratories)	HEU
Gadwal (Wah)	Enrichment (secondary plant)	HEU
Chaklala	Enrichment (pilot plant)	HEU
Sihala	Enrichment (pilot plant)	HEU
Golra	Enrichment (pilot plant)	HEU
Khushab–I	Heavy-water reactor 40–50MWt	Plutonium
Khushab–II	Heavy-water reactor 40–50MWt	Plutonium
Khushab–III	Heavy-water reactor 40–50 MWt (under construction)	Plutonium
Khushab–IV	Heavy-water reactor 40–50 MWt (under construction)	Plutonium
Chashma (Khushab)	Reprocessing facility (under construction)	Plutonium
Rawalpindi	Reprocessing facility–I (New Laboratories)	Plutonium
Rawalpindi	Reprocessing facility–II (New Laboratories))	Plutonium
Khushab–I and II	Tritium production	Tritium
Chashma (Kundian)	Reactor fuel-fabrication plant	
Multan	Heavy-water production facility	
Khushab	Heavy-water production facility	

Source: Adapted and updated from Nuclear Black Markets: Pakistan, A.Q. Khan and the Rise of Proliferation Networks, *International Institute of Strategic Studies*, London, 2007.

The Strategic Plans Division (SPD) has responsibility for strategic weapons development and nuclear weapons planning and operations, as well as security of the nuclear complex. It also has an arms control group. The nuclear weapons development and production infrastructure managed by SPD has three broad divisions: the A.Q. Khan Research Laboratory (Kahuta) produces enriched uranium; the Pakistan Atomic Energy Commission is responsible for uranium mining, fuel fabrication, reactor construction and operation, and spent fuel reprocessing to produce plutonium; and the National Development Complex is responsible for weapons and delivery system research and production.[15]

Pakistan's nuclear weapons are assigned to its Arm Strategic Force Command, which has responsibility for ballistic and cruise missiles, and the Air Force Strategic Command, which deals with nuclear armed aircraft. Pakistan has a Naval Strategic Force Command, charged with exercising "technical, training, and administrative control over the strategic delivery systems," but it is not known if this command has yet been issued any nuclear weapons.[16] Pakistan may seek to put nuclear-armed cruise missiles on some of its submarines, or modify existing naval missiles to be nuclear capable.[17]

Pakistan releases no information on its nuclear weapon budget. Historically, the government has not even provided a breakdown of its overall military spending plans to parliament as part of the annual national budget. The annual military budget was debated in parliament in 2008 for the first time since 1965.[18]

The secrecy about the history and scale of the nuclear weapon and missile programmes, the extent of external technical and material support, and the effect of indirect support through military and economic aid means the full cost of Pakistan nuclear weapons programme cannot be estimated with any reliability. There was a significant increase in nuclear weapon spending after 2000 (when SPD was established).

A more recent estimate suggests Pakistan's nuclear spending could be about $800 million per year as of 2011, and possibly as much as $2 billion per year if health and environmental costs are included—and projected to rise significantly because of Pakistan's expanding nuclear programme.[19]

Assuming that Pakistan spends on the order of 0.5% of GDP on its nuclear weapons, suggests that in 2009 nuclear weapon programme spending amounted to about $2.2 billion a year (the GDP was about $441 billion in purchasing power parity, and $162 billion in nominal terms).[20] For 2011, the nominal GDP was $211 billion, about $484 billion in purchasing power parity terms. This would suggest that in 2011 Pakistan spent about $2.4 billion on its nuclear weapons programme.

[15] Key facilities in Pakistan's nuclear weapons program infrastructure are described in *Nuclear Black Markets: Pakistan, A.Q. Khan and the Rise of Proliferation Networks, op.cit.*

[16] Ibid.

[17] Eric Schmitt and David E. Sanger, "U.S. Says Pakistan Made Changes to Missiles Sold for Defense," *New York Times*, 30 August 2009.

[18] Haroon Rashid, "Pakistan Reveals Defence Spending," *BBC*, 11 June 2008.

[19] Bruce G. Blair & Matthew A. Brown, "World Spending on Nuclear Weapons Surpasses $1 Trillion Per Decade," *Global Zero Nuclear Weapons Cost Study*, June 2011, http://www.globalzero.org/files/scott/Global%20Zero%20Cost%20Study,%20June%202011.pdf.

[20] For Pakistan's GDP in purchasing power terms in recent years, see for example "Pakistan: Country Report," Economist Intelligence Unit, December 2011. Similar figures are given by the CIA World Factbook, https://www.cia.gov/library/publications/theworld-factbook/geos/pk.html.

For Pakistan to spend about $2.5 billion per year on its nuclear weapons is feasible. The annual official military spending for 2011–2012 was budgeted at Rs. 444.2 billion, a 30% increase from the previous year.[21] Reports suggest this military budget does not include military pensions and various other direct and indirect costs associated with the armed forces and that including these costs would increase Pakistan's total military budget for 2011 to around Rs. 675 billion (about $21 billion, using current purchasing power parity exchange rates).[22]

This would suggest that, in purchasing power terms, as of 2011, Pakistan spent the equivalent of about 10% of its conventional military budget on nuclear weapons. Pakistan is not reliant only on its own resources to support its military spending, including on nuclear weapons, or to meet its development needs. Since 2001, Pakistan has received an estimated $22 billion in military and economic assistance from the United States, of which over $14 billion was military assistance and over $7 billion was economic aid of various kinds.[23]

Reflecting its concerns after September 2001 about the vulnerability of Pakistan's nuclear weapon and fissile materials to seizure by Islamist militants, the United States has provided Pakistan on the order of $100 million worth of assistance to secure its nuclear weapons, facilities, and materials.[24] This has included "training of Pakistani personnel in the United States and the construction of a nuclear security training centre...[and] a raft of equipment from helicopters to night-vision goggles to... fencing and surveillance systems, and equipment for tracking nuclear material if it left secure areas."[25]

Despite extensive foreign military assistance, Pakistan's effort to sustain its conventional and nuclear military programmes has come at increasingly great cost to the effort to meet basic human needs and improve living standards. Pakistan's economic and social development expenditure in 2010–2011 was Rs. 617 billion, i.e. about 10% less than the spending on conventional military forces.[26] The 2011 budget increased military spending by over Rs. 50 billion, but cut social and economic development spending by Rs. 100 billion.

---

[21] Kamran Yousaf, "Budget 2011–2012: Defence spending up by 12%," *Express Tribune*, 4 June 2011.

[22] Ansar Abbasi, "Real Figure of Defence Budget," *The News*, 12 June 2010.

[23] K. Alan Kronstadt, "Pakistan-U.S. Relations: A Summary," Congressional Research Service, Report R41832, 21 October 2011.

[24] David E. Sanger and William J. Broad, "U.S. Secretly Aids Pakistan in Guarding Nuclear Arms," *New York Times*, 18 November 2007.

[25] Ibid.

[26] "Highlights," *Pakistan Economic Survey 2010-2011*, Finance Division, Government of Pakistan, Islamabad, http://www.finance.gov.pk/survey/chapter_11/Highlights.pdf.

SPACE SURVEY

CHINESE SPACE PROGRAMME

Introduction

China's first satellite was launched in 1970 (*Dong Fang Hong*). Most of the launches are of Chinese communications, weather, remote sensing, navigation, or scientific satellites. Some of those satellites may be for military applications, or are dual use. Some were commercial launches for foreign countries or companies, primarily placing communications satellites into orbit. China launched its first astronaut, or "taikonaut," when a *Shenzhou* 5 achieved Earth orbit with Chinese astronaut Yang Liwei. Lt. Col. Yang landed on 16 October 2003, after a 21 hour 23 minute flight. China's first lunar probe was successful in 2007 and it's first Space Laboratory, *Tiangong*-1, was successfully launched in 2011.

China has three space launch sites: Jiuquan (also called Shuang Cheng-tzu) in the Gobi desert; Xichang, in southeastern China (near Chengdu); and Taiyuan, south of Beijing. Jiuquan was China's first launch site, and is used for launches of a variety of spacecraft, including those related to the human spaceflight programme. Xichang, inaugurated in 1984, is used for launches into geostationary orbit (above the equator), primarily communications satellites. Taiyuan, opened in 1988, is used for launches into polar orbits (that circle the Earth's poles), primarily weather and other Earth observation satellites. China has several different launch vehicles; most are called *Chang Zheng* (CZ, meaning Long March). Versions of the CZ 2 are used at Jiuquan; the CZ 2F is used for launches associated with its human spaceflight program. Versions of the CZ 3 and some CZ 2 variants are used at Xichang. CZ 4 is used at Taiyuan.

The People's Republic of China successfully completed its second human spaceflight mission on 17 October 2005. China is only the third country, after Russia and the United States, able to launch people into space. Its first human spaceflight was in 2003 when a single astronaut, or "taikonaut," made a flight lasting slightly less than a day. The 2005 flight lasted five days, and involved two taikonauts.

The Space Programme

China considers Space as a significant symbol of the nation's strength. In 2006, China celebrated the 50th Anniversary of its Aerospace Industry and published goals to combine and streamline military and civilian research organisations to promote its scientific development. China's stated purposes for its goals are to:

1. Unveil the development of China's space programme to the world; and
2. Enhance international Space cooperation in order to develop its economy and realize modernisation.

The government stated that the exploration and utilisation of Outer Space should be for peaceful purposes. Expenditures on Space programmes have increased from US$1.5 billion in 2007 to US$2.24 billion in 2010. Indications are that China is now accelerating investment in a satellite-based navigation system, human spaceflight, and Space-based Solar Power.

China has a comprehensive system for Space development seen by the launch of a spacecraft with three astronauts, one woman and two men, who returned safely after spending 13 days on a mission that made it the third nation to dock a manned spacecraft to another craft in orbit. The *Shenzhou* 9 space capsule landing, broadcast on CCTV television on 29 June 2012, included displays of manual and automatic docking, represented an important leap forward for China's space programme's aim to construct a space station in orbit by the year 2020.

China plans to launch a piloted space capsule to rendezvous and dock with an experimental space laboratory as a trial run for an eventual docking with a future Chinese space station. Some analysts believe the Chinese human spaceflight programme is driven by military objectives.

The upcoming docking mission is an intermediate step in a 30-year Chinese plan to construct a national space station. The plan emerged from a contentious internal debate that began in March 1986 and engaged hundreds of Chinese experts in many fields, as well as the leadership of numerous Chinese institutions. The goal of constructing a space station, as opposed to going to the moon was set very early in Chinese deliberations. The "guiding thought" behind China's space station plan was summed up in a set of four-character Chinese phrases that can be translated as: "Can't Not Do It, Can't Do It Big, Start with a Capsule, Smooth and Steady Development."

China's future space station will be small compared to the International Space Station. No final design has been approved and many technical decisions are yet to be made but China's space station is now estimated by some programme planners to be in the range of 60 to 80 metric tons: five to six times less massive than the International Space Station. An experimental space station module, still in the design phase, is planned to be launched and tested in 2016. The final station currently being discussed is a modular design constructed by linking together several of these modules, which will each be approximately 20 tons. Chinese studies of foreign experience constructing and maintaining space stations suggest China needs to keep its station small enough to be efficiently supplied and supported by China's available means of transport. The most intense debates about the long-term future of Chinese space technology centred on this question of transportation.

Figure 1: Artist's Rendering of Potential Chinese Space Station Design

Construction is Anticipated to Begin Around 2020

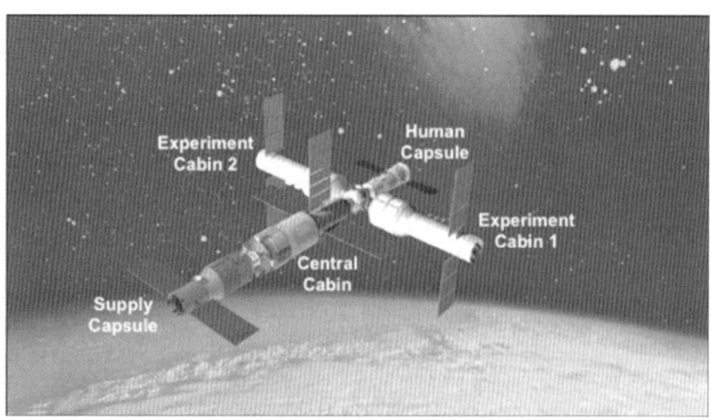

Programme planners successfully completed a remote controlled docking of the unpiloted *Shenzhou* 8 space capsule and the *Tiangong* 1 experimental space laboratory in November 2011. The *Shenzhou* 9 mission, in June 2012, was designed to test the ability to conduct a piloted docking between a *Shenzhou* capsule occupied by three Chinese astronauts and the same *Tiangong* 1 experimental space laboratory.

China also appears ready to adopt a less cloistered approach to at least one of its space facilities. The new launch site on Hainan Island is being promoted as a tourist attraction, and will be surrounded by museums, theme parks, golf courses and luxury housing.

China decided to build a space station because it did not want to fall behind other nations in the development of space technology. The Chinese space station programme has already accomplished many of its goals. It has helped China develop a robust national space infrastructure, motivated a new generation of Chinese scientists and engineers to participate in the development of that infrastructure, and demonstrated China's national commitment to being a significant player in space.

It will be another decade before China completes its space station. Difficult and dangerous work remains to be done. The leadership of China's space programme does not appear to be in a hurry and is not rushing to beat the United States to the moon or anywhere else. It is following the long-term plan it began two decades ago to build a space station.

China's Human Spaceflight Programme

The *Shenzhou* spacecraft design is patterned after Russia's Soyuz spacecraft, although the Chinese insist that the spacecraft are made entirely in China. *Shenzhou* consists of three modules: the descent module, a service module, and an orbital module. At the end of the primary mission, the descent module and service module detach from the orbital module. The service module positions the descent module correctly for re-entry and fires its engines to initiate descent. It detaches from the descent module and disintegrates in the atmosphere as the descent module returns to Earth. The orbital module typically remains in orbit for several months. It has its own propulsion system, allowing it to make manoeuvres. On some of the test flights, experiments were carried on the orbital module in addition to those in the descent module. Four orbital test flights of the *Shenzhou* spacecraft were conducted without crews between 1999 and 2003, in preparation for the flight of *Shenzhou* 5.

China launched its second human spaceflight mission on 12 October 2005. Carrying two taikonauts, Fei Junlong and Nie Haisheng, the *Shenzhou* 6 descent module successfully returned to Earth on 17 October after about five days (115 hours and 32 minutes). In addition to learning more about human spaceflight in general, the crew carried out scientific experiments. The *Shenzhou* 6 orbital module remains in orbit.

Chinese officials have been quoted discussing a three-step human spaceflight plan: send humans into Earth orbit, dock spacecraft together to form a small laboratory, and ultimately build a large space station.

Military Space Activities

Chinese officials routinely call for using space for peaceful purposes, and argue against the militarisation of space in settings such as the U.N. Conference on Disarmament. However, China's remote sensing, communications, and navigation satellites satisfy both military and civilian objectives. The Chinese space programme is conducted by the China Aerospace Science and Technology Corporation (abbreviated CASC by the Chinese), a state-owned enterprise that develops and manufactures strategic and tactical missiles in addition to spacecraft, launch vehicles, and other aerospace products.

Figure 2: Chinese Launch Space Facilities.

At a latitude of approximately 19° the new launch facility near the city of Wenchang on Hainan Island is better suited for lifting heavy payloads into space than the existing launch sites at Jiuquan, Xichang and Taiyuan.

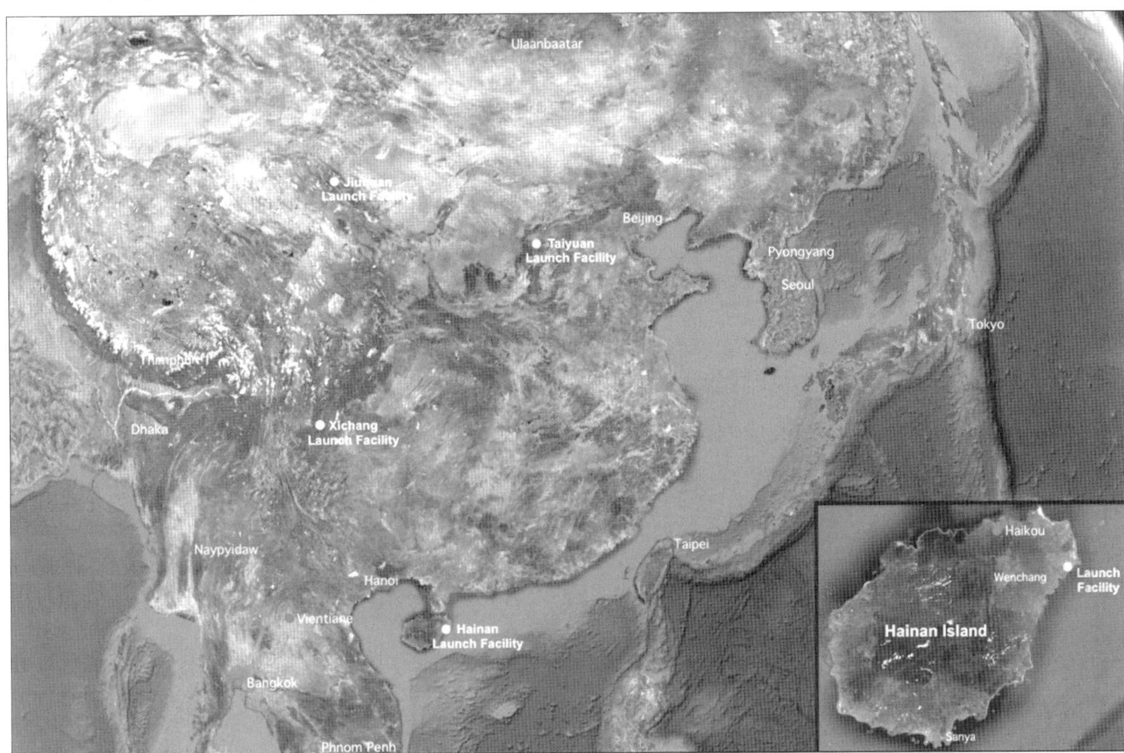

It is assessed that China will eventually deploy advanced imagery, reconnaissance, and Earth resource systems with military applications. China is working on, and plans to field, anti-satellite systems, including conducting research to develop ground-based laser anti-satellite weapons.

Lunar Programme

In December 2011, China published a blueprint outlining its ambitions in outer space. The launch, on 2 December, of Chang'e-3 shows that it remains on track. Named for the legendary Chinese goddess who is said to live on the moon, China's moon mission involves both a lander vehicle and a small, wheeled rover. China will be the third nation to land a wheeled vehicle on the moon, after the Soviet Union and the United States.

The moon rover is named Yutu ("Jade Rabbit") for the legendary rabbit that is a lunar companion for the goddess Chang'e. Yutu carries solar panels for electrical power. A mast on top carries the communications antenna as well as 3D stereo cameras. A robot arm on the front of the rover has spectrometers on it for taking measurements of lunar soil. The rover has six wheels in a rocker-bogie configuration similar to that used by NASA rovers such as the Mars rover Curiosity.

International Cooperation

China is very interested in international cooperation in space and has cooperative arrangements with several countries, including Russia, Brazil, and Europe.

INDIAN SPACE PROGRAMME

Introduction

The Indian Space Research Organisation (ISRO)

India uses its satellites communication network – one of the largest in the world – for applications such as land management, water resources management, natural disaster forecasting, radio networking, weather forecasting, meteorological imaging and computer communication. Business, administrative services, and schemes such as the National Informatics Centre (NICNET) are direct beneficiaries of applied satellite technology.

The INSAT-2 satellites provide telephone links to remote areas; data transmission for organisations, mobile satellite service communications for private operators, railways, and road transport; and broadcast satellite services. India's EDUSAT (Educational Satellite) was launched in 2004 for adult literacy and distance learning applications in rural areas.

The IRS satellites have applications with the Indian Natural Resource Management programme, with regional Remote Sensing Service Centres in five Indian cities, and with Remote Sensing Application Centres in 20 Indian states that use IRS images for economic development applications.

India's satellites and satellite launch vehicles have had military spin-offs. While India's Prithvi missile is not derived from the Indian space programme, the intermediate range Agni missile is drawn the SLV-3. The IRS and INSAT satellites were primarily intended and used for civilian-economic applications, but they also offered military spin-offs.

ISRO has applied its technology to "telemedicine", directly connecting patients in rural areas to medical professionals in urban locations via satellites. It has also helped implement India's Biodiversity Information System, completed in October 2002. The IRS-P5 (CARTOSAT-1) was equipped with high-resolution panchromatic equipment to enable it for cartographic purposes. It was followed by the IRS-P6 developed also for agricultural applications.

Research Facilities

Facility	Location (s)	Description
Physical Research Laboratory	Ahmedabad	Solar planetary physics, infrared astronomy, geo-cosmo physics, plasma physics, astrophysics, archaeology, and hydrology are some branches of study at this institute. An observatory at Udaipur also falls under the control of this institution.
Semi-Conductor Laboratory	Chandigarh	Research & Development in the field of semiconductor technology, micro-electromechanical systems and process technologies relating to semiconductor processing.
National Atmospheric Research Laboratory	Chittoor	Fundamental and applied research in Atmospheric and Space Sciences.
Space Applications Centre	Ahmedabad	Aspects of practical use of space technology, including geodesy, satellite-based telecommunications, surveying, remote sensing, meteorology, environment monitoring etc. It also operates the Delhi Earth Station.
North-Eastern Space Applications Centre		Shillong Developmental support to North East in specific application projects using remote sensing, GIS, satellite communication and space science research.

Test Facilities

Facility	Location (s)	Description
Liquid Propulsion Systems Centre	Bangalore, Thiruvananthapuram, Mahendragiri (near Tirunelveli)	Testing and implementation of liquid propulsion control packages and helps develop engines for launch vehicles and satellites. Testing is largely conducted at Mahendragiri. It also constructs precision transducers.

Construction and Launch Facilities

Facility	Location	Description
ISRO Satellite Centre	Bangalore	Venue for implementing indigenous spacecraft in India. The satellites Aryabhata, Bhaskara, APPLE, and IRS-1A were constructed at this site. The IRS and INSAT satellite series are under development here.
Laboratory for Electro-Optics Systems	Bangalore	Development of attitude sensors for all satellites. High precision optics for cameras and payloads in all ISRO satellites are developed here.
Satish Dhawan Space Centre	Sriharikota	Launching site for India's satellites. Also the main launch base for sounding rockets and home to India's largest Solid Propellant Space Booster Plant (SPROB) and Static Test and Evaluation Complex (STEX).
Vikram Sarabhai Space Centre	Thiruvananthapuram	The largest ISRO base. It is also the main technical centre and venue of development of the SLV-3, ASLV, and PSLV series. It supports the Thumba Equatorial Rocket Launching Station and the Rohini Sounding Rocket programme. It is also developing the GSLV series.
Thumba Equatorial Rocket Launching Station	Thiruvananthapuram	For launch sounding rockets.

Tracking and Control Facilities

Facility	Location (s)	Description
Indian Deep Space Network (IDSN)	Bangalore	Receives, processes, archives and distributes spacecraft health data and payload data in real time. Can track and monitor satellites to very large distances, even beyond the Moon.
National Remote Sensing Centre	Hyderabad	Applies remote sensing to manage natural resources and study aerial surveying.
Indian Space Research Organisation Telemetry, Tracking and Command Network	Bangalore (headquarters) and a number of ground stations throughout India and World.	Software development, ground operations, Tracking Telemetry and Command (TTC), and support. It has Tracking stations throughout the country and in Port Louis (Mauritius), Bearslake (Russia), Biak (Indonesia) and Brunei.
Master Control Facility	Bhopal; Hassan	Geostationary satellite orbit raising, payload-testing, and in-orbit operations. It has earth stations and Satellite Control Centre (SCC) for controlling satellites. A second MCF-like facility named 'MCF-B' is being constructed at Bhopal.

Lunar Exploration

Chandrayaan-1 was India's first mission to the moon. The unmanned lunar exploration mission included a lunar orbiter and an impactor called the Moon Impact Probe. India launched the spacecraft using a modified version of the PSLV i.e. C11 on 22 October 2008 from Satish Dhawan Space Centre, Sriharikota. The vehicle was successfully inserted into lunar orbit on 8 November 2008. It carries high-resolution remote sensing equipment for visible, near infrared, and soft and hard X-ray frequencies. Over its two-year operational period, it surveyed the lunar surface to produce a complete map of its chemical characteristics and 3-dimensional topography. The polar regions were of special interest, as they might contain ice. The lunar mission carried five ISRO payloads and six payloads from other international space agencies including NASA, ESA, and the Bulgarian Aerospace Agency, which were carried free of cost. The Chandrayaan-1 became the first lunar mission to discover existence of water on the moon.

Mangalyaan Mission

Mars Orbiter Mission (MOM), informally called Mangalyaan ("Mars-craft"), is a Mars orbiter that was successfully launched into Earth orbit on 5 November 2013 by ISRO. The mission is a "technology demonstrator" project aiming to develop the technologies required for design, planning, management and operations of an interplanetary mission.

The spacecraft, with a 1,350 kg lift-off mass, has a

single solar array with three panels of 1400 x 1800 mm capable of generating 750 watts of power in the Martian orbit. It will also be equipped with a 36 AH Lithium-ion battery for power storage. For attitude and orbit control, the spacecraft will be equipped with four reaction wheels, eight thrusters of 22 Newton each and a 440 Newton liquid rocket engine.

- India is the sixth country to launch a mission to Mars after the US, Russia, Europe, Japan and China;
- If the mission is successful, India will be the first Asian country to do so;
- The spacecraft is expected to take nearly 300 days to reach the Martian orbit;
- The spacecraft will be placed in an orbit of 500 × 80,000 km around Mars;
- Scientists have drawn up plans to insert the satellite into an orbit around Mars on 22 September 2014.

ISRO Space Missions, 2012-17

ISRO has planned 58 space missions during 2012-17, at a cost of Rs 39,750 crore, encompassing 33 satellite missions and 25 launch vehicle missions. While several new missions will be launched on the communication front, an interesting one will be GSAT 7 that is a communication satellite for 'special users'.

India's advanced communication satellite GSAT-10 to augment telecommunication, direct-to-home broadcasting and radio navigation services was launched on board Ariane-5 rocket from Europe's spaceport in French Guiana in South America.

GSAT-10 also has a navigation payload—GAGAN (GPS aided Geo Augmented Navigation)—that would provide improved accuracy of GPS signals (of better than seven metres) to be used by Airports Authority of India for civil aviation requirements. This is the second satellite in INSAT/GSAT constellation with GAGAN payload after GSAT-8, launched in May 2011.

TALKING TO THE TALIBAN

TALKING TO THE TALIBAN

Introduction

Incidents of violence and terrorism have been on the rise in Pakistan. It has adopted various policy options, including military, political and socio-economic, to counter the rising terrorism and militancy. One such policy instrument has been the signing of peace agreements with the militant outfits in Khyber Pakhtunkhwa (KPK) and the Federally Administered Tribal Areas (FATA). Peace deals have been an important tool in Pakistan's conflict management strategy because of their history as a non-military option and their resonance with the tribal culture.

The FATA has become the epicentre of international terrorism in recent years. Located along the 2,400 kilometre-long rugged border separating Afghanistan and Pakistan, FATA has provided Al-Qaeda, the most hunted terrorist group in the world, with a robust and resilient sanctuary. Thus the situation in Pakistan's tribal areas is not only complicated because of the porous border, and complex administrative structure but also explosive due to its trans-national and international linkages. The ground zero of terrorism is now in FATA as it is the de facto headquarters of the global jihad movement. It is the single most important base of Al-Qaeda's operations, where its leaders, trainers and planners are located. Also, the leadership of Afghan Taliban, Pakistani Taliban, the East Turkistan Islamic Movement (ETIM), Islamic Movement of Uzbekistan (IMU), Islamic Jihad Group (ITU), the Libyan Islamic Fighters Group (UFG) and a dozen other groups are located in FATA. Both their operational and ideological leaders are protected by the Pakistani Taliban.

The developments in FATA are playing an important role enabling in shaping the global and regional threat environment. Hundreds of secular tribal leaders have been killed and Taliban-like religious leaders have come to power. Today, there are new groups and new players. TTP has emerged as the most dominant player and its constituents present an unprecedented challenge even to a well-structured and well-led Pakistani military and the US intelligence community.

A Complex Administrative Structure

The tribal areas and Khyber Pakhtunkhwa have complex and diverse administrative structures with seven tribal agencies of FATA and six Frontier Regions (FRs); six Provincially Administered Tribal Areas (PATA) districts and three PATA enclaves, 18 settled districts and one hybrid area (Malakand Agency). FATA consist of seven agencies: Bajaur, Mohmand, Khyber, Orakzai, Kurram, North Waziristan and South Waziristan. These agencies are administered by the federal government through the Khyber Pakhtunkhwa Governor and Political Agents. There are six transitional areas wedged between the tribal agencies and the settled districts of Khyber Pakhtunkhwa which are called Frontier Regions (FRs). These are FR Peshawar, FR Kohat, FR Bannu, FR Tank, FR Dera Ismail Khan and FR Lakki. The FRs are administered by the provincial government through the district coordination officer (DCO) of the respective settled district, who exercises powers comparable to those of a political agent in FATA.

The six PATA districts, i.e., Chitral, Upper Dir, Lower Dir, Shangla, Buner and Swat, were carved out of the erstwhile princely states in 1969. Administered provincially, an act of the federal parliament or the provincial assembly cannot be extended to them unless so directed by the Khyber Pakhtunkhwa Governor. The three PATA enclaves are the former princely state of Amb, Kala Dhaka (in Mansehra district) and the tribal area of Kohistan district.

The 17 settled districts of Khyber Pakhtunkhwa are managed by the provincial government without any specific role for the Governor. The Malakand protected area is unique in the sense that it is called an agency but has no political agent. The administration is run by a *Nazim* (administrator) and a DCO. However, no district police officer or police stations are present there. Under articles 246 and 247 of the Constitution, the parliament cannot legislate for FATA and PATA unless the President so directs. Legislators from FATA can legislate for the whole country but not for their own region.

Patterns of Militancy

The militancy bordering the Pak-Afghan border has spread into various directions. It is raging in the seven tribal agencies, six Frontier Regions, six PATA districts, 18 settled districts of Khyber Pakhtunkhwa and other parts of Pakistan in varying shades and intensity. The Taliban from Afghanistan have found a sanctuary in the tribal areas where they come to rest and recover, replenish their revenues, recruit new cadres, hibernate in the winter and infiltrate into Afghanistan in the summer.

The insurgency in Afghanistan operates on three fronts. The northern front, where mainly Hizb-e-Islami militants are active, spans Nurestan, Konar, Laghman and Nangarhar provinces of Afghanistan as well as parts of Pakistan across the border. The central front, comprising foreign fighters (Arabs and Central Asians), covers the Afghan provinces of Khost, Paktia and Paktika as well as Bajaur area of Pakistan. The southern front, which mainly comprises of Afghan Taliban, is based in Helmand, Kandahar, Zabol and Uruzgan provinces of Afghanistan as well as parts of Balochistan.

Militants from Pakistan's border areas have been linked to a range of international terrorist attacks and plots, such as the July 2005 bombings in London, the foiled 2006 plot against transatlantic commercial flights, the foiled plots in Germany and Denmark in 2007, and the 2008 arrest of terrorism suspects in Spain.

Estimates of the number of foreign fighters present in the tribal areas are varied. They include Saudis, Uzbeks and Chechens, Yemenis, Egyptians, Algerians, Tunisians, Iraqis, Libyans and Jordanians. Recent estimates suggest that the number of foreign militants in FATA is between 3,500 and 5,000. These militants constantly keep changing their locations to avoid US drone strikes and military operations by the Pakistan Army. Chinese Uyghur militants of the East Turkistan Movement, Uzbek rebels from Islamic Movement of Uzbekistan, and Chechens are among those operating in the tribal belt.

The Situation in the Federally Administered Tribal Areas

In 1893, with a view to divide and weaken the 11 main Pashtun tribes and turn Afghanistan into a buffer zone between the British and Russian empires, the British diplomat Sir Henry Mortimer Durand established the Durand Line which serves as the border between Pakistan and Afghanistan. In 1901, the British Raj imposed on the tribal areas a series of laws, known as the Frontier Crimes Regulations (FCR), which were ostensibly based on tribal customs (*riwaj*) and the Pashtun code of ethics known as *Pashtunwali*. According to the FCR, the people were free to govern their internal affairs according to tribal codes, while the colonial administration held authority in what were known as 'protected' and 'administered' areas only.

In the last 60 years, the state has failed to invest either in human development or physical infrastructure of FATA to bring it at par with other parts of Pakistan. The development indicators show a bleak 17% literacy rate, one doctor for every 8,000 people and only 100 high schools compared to 500 *madrassas*.

According to the 1973 Constitution of Pakistan, FATA remains under the direct executive authority of the President. Laws framed by the National Assembly do not apply there unless specifically ordered by the President. Some of the draconian clauses in the FCR violate human rights and democratic principles. These include:

a) Section 21: Collective responsibility of the tribe empowers the administration to punish the whole tribe for individual misconduct.
b) Section 22: Territorial responsibility empowers the administration to impose fine on an entire village for an individual's offence.
c) Section 40: A preventive provision pertaining to good conduct under which individuals can be detained for years without recourse to appeal.

The governance of each tribal agency rests with a Political Agent (PA), who is the administrative head of an agency, arbitrator of inter-tribal disputes, armed with judicial powers and supervisor of development, etc. The government functions through tribal intermediaries: *maliks* (representatives of the tribes) and *lungi* holders (representatives of the clans).

The traditional *jirga* system is becoming an ineffective instrument for local conflict resolution because the poor and more vulnerable segments of society cannot afford to convene a *jirga* due to its expensive formalities such as the cost of hospitality of the *jirga* members. In most cases *jirga* decisions favour the richer or the more influential party.

Some recent changes in the traditional power structures of FATA have become a serious source of instability. Firstly, the influx of Arab *'mujahideen'* in the 1980s and of Taliban and Al Qaeda militants since 2001 brought political Islam, money, and illegal economic activity to the region and buttressed the emergent Islamist leadership. Secondly, migration of the population to the settled areas of Pakistan and the booming oil economies in the Gulf has injected substantial remittances to families which in the past had relatively low social status in the tribal society. These families now seek power and influence in consonance with their new financial status. Migrants have also become acutely conscious of inequities in the tribal areas and have garnered greater appreciation for the rights that Pakistani citizens enjoy everywhere except FATA. Thirdly, the role of the *mullah* and political Islam has expanded into FATA and adjoining areas. The prominence of the *mullah* and the collapse of the *malik* system is one of the most important changes in FATA in the recent years.

Finally, US-led military operations in Afghanistan and Iraq and action by the Pakistan Army in the tribal areas have contributed to the growth of Islamism and even Islamist militancy in the region. It is difficult for many tribal residents to understand how the *mullahs* and militants, who were once considered heroes and given support in the bid to drive Soviet troops out of Afghanistan, are now branded as villains.

Military Operations and Peace Agreements

To purge its tribal areas of foreigner and local militants, the Pakistani military launched *Operation Meezan* in 2002 and entered FATA for the first time since the country's independence in 1947. Some 80,000 military and paramilitary troops were deployed in FATA.

In March 2004, under intense US pressure, Pakistan Army launched an operation in Kaloosha village near Wana, the administrative headquarters of South Waziristan, with the belief that a surgical operation would eradicate the militants. However, the militants ambushed the troops, inflicted heavy losses on them and took officials hostage. Due to increasing casualties on both sides as well as high public resentment resulting from indiscriminate shelling, the government soon opted for a peace deal with the militants.

Shakai Agreement

The signing of peace agreements with pro-Taliban militants started with the Shakai agreement, which the government signed with Nek Muhammad and other militant commanders at Shakai, South Waziristan on 27 March 2004. Nek, a charismatic Yargulkhel Wazir, was a battle-hardened commander of the Taliban who provided sanctuary to the chief of Uzbek militants Tahir Yaldochev in the military operation in Kaloosha.

The main clauses of the agreement were that the government would:

- Release all individuals taken prisoner during the military operation.
- Pay compensation for casualties as well as for collateral damage caused during the operation.
- Not take action against Nek Muhammad and other wanted individuals.
- Allow foreign *'Mujahideen'* to live peacefully in Waziristan.
- Local *'Mujahideen'* would not resort to any action against the land and government of Pakistan.

In response, the *'Mujahideen-e-Waziristan'* (fighters from Waziristan) would not take part in any action in Afghanistan.

In the peace agreement, the militants were given a status equal to the government. The peace accord failed because of disagreements over registration of foreigners with the authorities. The government claimed that the militants were required to register 'foreign fighters' in the area. However, the militants claimed that there was no such clause in the agreement.

On 11 June 2004, the military operation was re-launched. Nek Muhammad was killed by a missile launched from a US drone on 19 June 2004. The agreement remained in place for less than 50 days. The agreement led to the tribal dissidents morphing into a powerful militant group which became a permanent feature of the tribal landscape and further reinforced polarisation. Pakistan's strong support for the stance of the US in the war on terror and reliance on the use of military means further militarised the situation.

Sararogha Peace Deal

The militancy, which was hitherto restricted to areas inhabited by the Ahmadzai Wazir tribes of South Waziristan, spread to the Mehsud-dominated areas of South Waziristan by the spring of 2004. The two Mehsud commanders spearheading the militancy in their respective areas were Abdullah and Baitullah. The government opted for another peace deal in a bid to bring calm to the Mehsud territories. The deal was inked between pro-Taliban militant Baitullah Mehsud and the government of Pakistan through the mediation of a local *jirga* at Sararogha, South Waziristan, on 22 February 2005.

The agreement was signed by Baitullah Mehsud and members of the local *jirga*. The six clauses of the written agreement were:

- Baitullah and his group would neither harbour nor support any foreign fighter in their area.
- Baitullah and his supporters would not attack any government functionary nor damage official property. They would also not create any hindrance in development activities.
- The government would not take action against Baitullah and his supporters for their past actions. However, they would be dealt

with according to the law if they were found to be involved in any terrorist or criminal activities in the future.

- Any culprit found in the Mehsud area would be handed over to the government.
- All the issues not covered by the agreement would be resolved with mutual consultation between the political administration and the Mehsud tribe.
- In case of violation of any clause of the agreement, the political administration was empowered to take legal action.

The agreement did not cover cross-border infiltration or attacks in Afghanistan. There was no clause concerning the surrender of foreign fighters nor was there any provision that militants would surrender their weapons. The agreement became controversial after reports emerged that money had been paid to the militants during the negotiations. Also, Abdullah Mehsud, the second most important militant commander in the region, opted out of the agreement.

Miranshah Peace Accord

The militancy that began in the Ahmadzai Wazir territories of South Waziristan in 2003 spread to the Uthmanzai Wazir areas of North Waziristan in 2005. The government writ receded in North Waziristan as the militants attacked security forces personnel and convoys. The political administration was effectively restricted to government buildings. When the cost of military options exceeded the benefits, the government opted for a 16-point peace deal with the militants of North Waziristan on 5 September 2006.

The undertakings by the Uthmanzai Wazirs, including local Taliban, religious leaders, elders and tribesmen, included:

- There would be no attacks on law enforcement personnel and government property. There would be no targeted killings.
- No parallel administration would be established in the area and the government's writ would prevail. In case of any problem, the political administration in consultation with the Uthmanzai tribes would resolve the issue according to the traditions and the FCR.
- There would be no cross-border militant activities in Afghanistan. However, there would be no restriction on crossing the border for trade/business and for meeting relatives according to the local *riwaj*.
- There would be no terrorist activity in the districts adjacent to North Waziristan.
- All foreigners residing in North Waziristan would either leave Pakistan or remain peaceful according to the prevailing law and the current agreement. All the clauses of the agreement would also apply to the foreigners in the tribal agency.
- All captured government property during the operation including vehicles, weapons or any other equipment would be returned.

The government's undertakings included:

- All individuals apprehended during the operation would be released and would not be arrested again on the previous charges.
- The government would release all political benefits.
- The government would remove all newly-established checkpoints on the roads and would post Levies and Khasadar personnel on the old checkpoints as was done in the past.
- The government would return all vehicles, weapons and other equipment captured during the operation.
- The government would stop all land/air operations and all issues would be resolved according to the local traditions.
- The government would pay compensation for collateral damage to the affected persons.
- There would be no restrictions on carrying weapons according to the tribal tradition. However, restrictions would continue to be imposed on heavy weapons.
- Implementation of the agreement would begin with the withdrawal of the army from the check posts to the barracks.

In the agreement, a 10-member committee was to be established comprising clerics/elders and representatives of the political administration. It was to be responsible for establishing a link between the government and the Uthmanzai tribes and review and ensure the implementation of the agreement. Any individuals or group not abiding by the agreement or disrupting peace in Waziristan was to be proceeded against. The agreement was signed by Hafiz Gul Bahadar, Maulana Sadiq Noor and Maulana Abdul Khaliq.

During the signing ceremony of the agreement in the soccer stadium of Miranshah, security cover was provided by the militants while their flag was fluttering over the scoreboard of the stadium. An unspecified amount of money was transferred from Pakistani government to the militants. A vague term "foreigners", a euphemism for Al Qaeda and other foreign militants, was used. Some 100 mid-level Taliban and Al Qaeda commanders and foot soldiers were released from custody.

The peace deal broke down on 20 May 2007.

Khyber Agency Pact

While the insurgency incubated and matured in Waziristan, militancy in Khyber Agency had been raging on Deobandi-Barelvi fault-lines for several years. This militancy remained restricted to Bara subdivision and Tirah Valley of Khyber Agency. The main militant outfits in the area were *Lashkar-e-Islam*, led by Mangal Bagh; *Ansarul Islam*, led by Qazi Mehboob; and *Amr Bil Maroof Wa Nahi Anil Munkir* (promotion of virtue and prevention of vice), headed by Haji Namdar. These groups were mainly 'moral brigades' and not part of the Tehreek-e-Taliban Pakistan, the umbrella organisation of Taliban militants in the country.

The Khyber Agency, which borders Afghanistan on one side and the Khyber Pakhtunkhwa (KP) province on the other, is important not only because the main supply route of the NATO and US forces in Afghanistan passes through it, but also because of its proximity to Peshawar, the KP capital. To counter the impending danger of the militants consolidating their position in Peshawar and to keep the NATO supply line via Khyber Pass open, the government launched Operation Siraat-e- Mustaqeem (right path) in 2008. However, the immediate trigger for this operation was the abduction of 16 Christians, including two priests, on 21 June 2008 by Lashkar-e-Islam. After several days of military action, the operation came to an end and a peace deal was signed by the government, represented by the political agent, and an 18-member *jirga* of Afridi tribes.

According to the agreement:

- Law enforcement agencies and government property would not be targeted. There would be no targeted killings.
- Armed patrol would be the prerogative of the government.
- No parallel administration would be set up. Any problems would be resolved through the FCR according to the local tradition.
- There would be no incursions into Peshawar district and other settled areas.
- Any foreigner in Bara sub-division would leave Pakistan.
- Government officials and law enforcement personnel would not be threatened. The tribes and *Khasadars* would be responsible for the protection of the roads in accordance with *riwaj*.
- *Khasadars* and government officials would be allowed to work and would not be threatened or forced to quit their jobs.
- Development work would not be impeded.
- Guarantees for peaceful behaviour would be given by the concerned tribe.
- No training camp would be operated against Pakistan. Action against any militant camp including would be taken by the concerned tribe and the government in accordance with traditions.
- Display of unlicensed weapons in government offices and Bara bazaar would be banned except for those authorised by the Peace Committee of Afridi tribes.
- No propaganda against Pakistan and its institutions in the form of pamphlets or CDs would be allowed.
- Heavy weapons would not be allowed in the tribal territories.

On the day of peace deal, five Frontier Corps personnel were killed and three wounded in Khyber Agency. Mangal Bagh insisted on continuing his struggle against criminal elements in Bara. The timing of the operation was significant in that regard, launched as it was before the Prime Minister's visit to the US. (Lashkar-e-Islam leader Mangal Bagh alleged that the aim of the operation was to please the US). The operation targeted "empty buildings [used by] banned organisations," and "not a single leader or fighter [of these organisations] was captured."

Swat Agreements

The Provincially Administered Tribal Areas (PATA) of KP comprise mainly of six districts: Swat, Shangla, Upper Dir, Lower Dir, Chitral and Buner which previously constituted the princely states of Swat, Dir and Chitral. In 1969 PATA regulations were imposed which were quashed by the Supreme Court in 1994. This abolished the customary tribal courts based on local traditions and replaced them with the civil law of Pakistan. This sparked an uprising spearheaded by Sufi Muhammad, leader of *Tehrik-e-Nifaz-e-Shariat-e-Muhammadi* (movement for the implementation of *Shariah* law). The TNSM said it wanted imposition of *Shariah* which the then government promised. There was a similar uprising in the region in 1999. In 2002, Sufi was arrested while entering Pakistan after fighting alongside the Taliban against the US forces in Afghanistan. In Sufi's absence his more radical son-in-law Fazlullah, nicknamed 'Mullah Radio' because of his speeches on illegal FM radio channels, became active. The violence by Fazlullah's militant group in Swat precipitated a military operation there in 2007.

The first peace deal in Swat was struck on 20 April 2008 between the Awami National Party-led provincial government and followers of the TNSM led by Sufi Muhammad. The government accepted the right of every Muslim to 'peacefully' work for the enforcement of *Shariah*. The TNSM dissociated itself from the elements attacking the security forces and a *fatwa* was issued against attacks on security personnel which were considered against Islamic teachings. The TNSM renewed its pledge to support the state institutions and enable the state to restore its writ in the region. The agreement paved the way for the release of Sufi Muhammad, who had been in jail since February 2002.

The second Swat peace agreement was signed on 21 May 2008 between Swat militants operating under the command of Fazlullah and the Awami National Party-led government after achieving consensus on several issues. It was a 16-point handwritten accord in Urdu. During the negotiations, the Swat chapter of the Taliban was represented by their spokesperson Muslim Khan, Ali Bakht, Maulana Muhammad Amin, Mehmood Khan and Nisar Khan, while the government team consisted of senior ministers Bashir Bilour and Rahimdad Khan, NWFP Environment Minister Wajid Ali Khan, Awami National Party (ANP) provincial President Afrasiab Khattak and MPA Shamshir Ali.

The clauses of the agreement stated:

- The militants agreed to accept and honour the writ of the federal and provincial governments.
- *Shariah* would be implemented in Malakand Division in letter and spirit.
- The militants would not criticize or abuse the religion of other citizens.
- Cases of imprisoned militants would be reviewed and a decision about their release made.
- Personnel of law enforcement agencies, government officials, buildings and installations, police stations, police officials, Police Lines, army, Frontier Corps, Frontier Constabulary, bridges, roads and electricity installations would not be attacked. There would be a ban on private militias. The Taliban would denounce and disown suicide attacks, remote-controlled bomb blasts and bomb blasts in all private or government buildings and shops.
- The army would be gradually sent back to the barracks in accordance with the prevailing situation.
- All foreign militants would be handed over to the government. The militants would not attack barber shops or markets visited by women.
- The government would look into the damage caused during the security forces' operations and compensate all the deserving victims.
- The Taliban would not oppose campaigns to vaccinate children against polio and other diseases, and would not obstruct women's education.
- There would be a complete ban on display of weapons and only licensed weapons allowed.
- Incidents of abduction and vehicle theft and snatching would be condemned and eliminated and all those places where militants and suicide bombers were trained or explosives were made would be dismantled.
- In line with the rules of the authorised license, there would be permission to talk on FM radio channels.
- The local Taliban would cooperate with the government in investigation of incidents of murder, robbery and other crimes.
- The government would take action in the area against oppressors, those taking bribe, adulterers, thieves, dacoits and kidnappers in order to rid the society of such elements.
- An Islamic university would be set up, which would be run by a joint government-Taliban committee.
- An 11-member joint committee was named to ensure the implementation of the agreement. The members of the committee included Wajid Ali Khan, MPA Dr Shamshir Ali, the Malakand Range deputy inspector general of police, the Swat district police officer and the Swat district coordination officer from the government side and Maulana Muhammad Amin, Ali Bakht, Muslim Khan, Mehmood Khan and Nisar Khan from the Taliban.

The agreement failed to mention anything about Taliban commander Fazlullah or whether he had been granted amnesty. Hard-core Jihadi elements such as Jaish-e-Muhammad and non-local militants, mostly from Punjab, started violating the agreement almost instantly. Immediately after the agreement, a militant commander, Said Jamal, announced establishment of a *Shariah* court in Swat for settling local disputes. Only hours before the signing of the Swat peace deal, two girls' schools were torched and a policeman shot dead. The militants continued running training camps in the hills. They carved out 'no-go' areas and nominated their 'governors' there.

As many as 400 Swat policemen resigned after the peace deal, most likely because they feared reprisal attacks by militants. The Swat militants had reportedly said that they would not abide by the peace agreement if a similar deal was not reached with the Tehrik-e-Taliban in Waziristan, a stipulation which was not included in the Swat peace deal.

Diverging Views

According to the militants, every time a peace agreement is at hand, US drones strike the tribal areas. Also, Pakistan Army is fighting Washington's war against its own people, and is killing innocent tribesmen. Therefore, the 'Mujahideen' would continue 'jihad' against US-led forces in Afghanistan and if Pakistan tries to stop them, they would fight against Pakistani forces as well.

The three core Pakistani defence concerns are to contain Indian hegemony; not to permit development of pressures which would threaten retention of nuclear weapons by Pakistan; and retention of leverage over political developments in Afghanistan and to have a pro- Pakistan government in that country.

Most analysts described the peace deals as tactical moves by the militants to gain advantage from the government without changing their violent ways. Ceasefires were used to erect a parallel system of government complete with *Shariah* courts, taxation, and recruitment of militants' own 'police' force. Thus, peace deals weaken Pakistani state institutions and prolong the insurgency rather than curtailing it and there has been no reduction in violence.

If peace is to be measured in terms of the number of attacks on the military and paramilitary forces, then the tribal areas remained mostly peaceful in the immediate aftermath of signing of peace agreements. However, target killings of tribal elders, sporadic attacks on government installations, torching and bombing of girls' schools, beheadings of alleged criminals, closing down of barbershops, bombing of CD shops and intermittent displays of force by the militants continued.

The decisions on the peace agreements in the tribal areas were made entirely by the military. The basic flaw with the agreements, both in Ahmadzai Wazir and Mehsud areas, was that they were between the military and the militants and focused mainly on areas of concern for the military, i.e., attacks on security forces personnel. In return, the militants were offered a free hand in the area. Such agreements also gave an equal status to the militants as a party vis-à-vis the state. The government further undermined its position by signing the pact in the quarters of the militants which according to the tribal traditions of *Nanawatay* meant that the government was responsible for the entire crisis.

No verification mechanisms were put in place to ensure that the militants follow through on their commitments, such as not indulging in cross-border infiltration. Weak enforcement mechanisms were in place in case the militants reneged on any promise. This was mainly because the militants were armed to the teeth and the tribes that were expected to enforce the agreements lacked the capacity and the weapons to match the militants' force. It was obvious from the outset that the local trial elders could pose little challenge to the militants who were fighting troops from armies of nearly 50 countries in Afghanistan.

Lessons

Operation *Rah-e-Nijat* (path of salvation) started by the Pakistan security forces and backed by the political leadership in October 2009 is still not culminated or achieved its goals in South Waziristan. Nearly one million Mehsud and Burki tribesmen have borne the brunt of the ongoing operation.

Operation *Rah-e-Nijat* is not the first operation of its kind launched in Waziristan; the region has been observing many operations since 2002-3 like Operation Mizan, Zalzala, etc, and the most disturbing one in terms of displacement of people and destruction is Operation Rah-e-Nijat, which is spread in a vast area for a long span of time. An estimated 60,000 houses, markets and education institutions have been affected due to the ongoing military operation.

Military operations are being considered the sole tool to root out militancy from the constitutionally deprived tribal areas, but this panacea is no more a practical phenomenon due to their subsequent miserable effects.

From mid-2011 to March 2012, the United States tried encouraging Taliban members to work with the Afghan government. Those talks also failed. Negotiating with stubborn insurgents who set moral guidelines on end goals render it challenging for both sides to negotiate and fight simultaneously; and apply force to back diplomacy and vice versa. Fragmentation among opponents is frustrating when commitments are not met. It is also puzzling why a few ideologues prefer endless pursuit of power, at any cost, over peace and stability.

There are some lessons in having a dialogue with militants. Clear conditions and moral guidelines must be set at the beginning and stuck to. These need not be preconditions. The talks should be designed to create a series of confidence-building measures, consistent with the future of the people.

It is hard to fight and negotiate at the same time. When the Taliban cut off discussions, they are normally having a hard time motivating their fighters while talks were taking place. Talking and fighting simultaneously are challenges for the government. Force must be backed by diplomacy, and diplomacy must be backed by force.

Article 1 of the Pakistan Constitution recognises FATA as being a part of the country but Article 247 (b) takes it out of the purview of parliament and makes the president its sole custodian. Constitutionally the president is empowered to administer it the way he likes, continue administering it as presently done through the draconian FCR (Frontier Crimes Regulations), make it a separate province or merge it with the Khyber Pakhtunkhwa province. Other laws of the land do not apply there nor does the Supreme Court have any jurisdiction there. All matters are settled through the provisions of the FCR which are completely different to the laws on the statute books applicable to the rest of the country. Another important thing to bear in mind is the fact that FATA is administered and not governed. In FATA there is no such thing as government – of the type in the rest of the country. This needs to be rectified.

Recent Developments

Mullah Fazlullah, the recently appointed chief of the Tehrik-e-Taliban Pakistan (TTP), is not new to the scene. But his background differs from that of his predecessors, who were Mehsuds from the Federally Administered Tribal Areas (Fata). Fazlullah comes from the Tehrik-e-Nifaz-e-Shariat-e-Mohammadi (TNSM — Movement for the Enforcement of Islamic Law), which has its roots in the Malakand Agency. The movement's initial programme is evident from its name, but its methods have changed over time.

The TNSM was founded in 1989 by Maulana Sufi Muhammad, a native of Dir, a former princely state of the Malakand Agency. Once a member of the Jamaat-e-Islami, Sufi Muhammad soon eschewed electoral politics (though he had participated in it to become a local elected official). He grew in influence after the Supreme Court decision of 1994, which deprived the local executive authorities of their judicial powers and merged the Provincially Administered Tribal Areas (PATA) into the legal mainstream. The discontented Khans and Maliks of the PATA then rallied around him. In November 1994, the TNSM staged an armed operation and forced the government to promulgate the *Sharia* Regulation, making the *Sharia* the primary source of law. Aftab Sherpao, then chief minister of the North West Frontier Province, was compelled to make substantial concessions.

In September-October 2001, the TNSM marshalled about 10,000 militants to aid the Taliban in fighting the post-9/11 Western (and Northern Alliance) military attacks. Its poorly armed foot soldiers crossed the Durand Line and came under a hail of bombs. When Sufi Mohammad returned to Pakistan, he was arrested and imprisoned. The TNSM was banned.

The movement continued to function under the leadership of his son-in-law, Mullah Fazlullah, who began to broadcast his sermons on the radio from Swat, his stronghold. These sermons gained an enormous following and Fazlullah soon became known as "Mullah Radio". The TNSM then pursued its career with the blessings of all political parties. As the 2002 elections approached, they attempted to share the TNSM's popularity, particularly in the Swat Valley. But the TNSM only backed Islamic parties affiliated with the Muttahida Majlis-e-Amal — which returned the favour. The rescue operations undertaken by the movement in the wake of the 2005 earthquake further polished its image.

The turning point came in 2007. After the storming of the Red Mosque, the TNSM struck up an alliance with the TTP of Baittullah Mehsud. In late October, about 4,500 TNSM combatants took control of some 60 villages in the Swat Valley, which they subjected to cultural policing operations and Shariah courts. The formidable army response forced the TNSM to enter into negotiations.

The TNSM went back on the offensive in 2008. Its troops took control of the valley in a wave of unspeakable violence and *Sharia* courts started operating in the region. Girls were prevented from attending school (their schools were the first to be demolished), women were no longer to appear in public, men had to grow beards. As a result, about a third of the valley's 1.7 million inhabitants fled towards the south. By late 2008, the Swat Valley, a place known for its picturesque tourist attractions, was virtually under the complete control of TTP representatives.

The ISI then decided to release Sufi Mohammad to hammer out a ceasefire agreement with him. In February 2009, the provincial government (dominated by the ANP Pashtun nationalists since 2008) and the militants agreed to a truce, according to which the *Sharia* became law in Malakand Division in exchange for an end to the violence. But in April, the TNSM violated the agreement it had only just signed, on the pretence that the government had not allowed it to appoint the judges of *Sharia* courts. The ISI again turned to Sufi Mohammad, but he had become hostage to the TTP, which was not in favour of any agreement.

The movement then extended its control over the Swat Valley, into the districts of Lower Dir, Shangla and Buner, about 65 miles from Islamabad. Apart from its usual methods, of which women and girls were the principal victims, they stepped up punitive executions, hanging their opponents from trees and at traffic circles as an example. This campaign caused nearly millions to flee and prompted the army— now with public approval—to launch an assault. According to some sources, the operation left 128 dead among security forces, but about 1,500 militants were killed. Along with a massive deployment of army troops, helicopters and fighter planes were used to crush resistance. The scale of the damage prevented many refugees from returning to their devastated towns and villages. For the first time, Pakistan was experiencing a civil war some 65 miles from its capital, but it still did not manage to break the back of the TNSM. Fazlullah found sanctuary in Afghanistan.

From the Afghan provinces of Nuristan and Kunar, Fazlullah launched raids across the Durand line. In September 2013, the TTP claimed responsibility for the killing of Major General Sanaullah, GOC Malakand division, and Lieutenant Colonel Tauseef Ahmed in Upper Dir district, near the Afghan border. This assassination was attributed to Fazlullah because these regions were part of his battlefield— and because he was notoriously opposed to the peace talks Nawaz Sharif had initiated (by targeting a Pakistani general, he consolidated Kayani's reluctance to talk). Indeed, the negotiation process will probably be suspended on the Pakistani side, or will follow the stop-and-go pattern of the Swat discussions in 2008-09.

The appointment of Fazlullah may also be revealing of the lack of interest for meaningful negotiations on the Afghan side. While there were apparently several candidates for replacing Hakimullah Mehsud, Fazlullah has been selected not only by a representative *shura* but also by Mullah Omar. In October 2012, US soldiers had arrested Latif Mehsud —Hakimullah's right-hand man—in Afghanistan, which suggests relations between the Afghan Taliban and the TTP had already become more intense. Eventually, with the prospect of NATO forces leaving the battleground in 2014, both may fully converge and target not only the Afghan National Army but also Pakistan—from Afghanistan.

The politicians of Pakistan have denounced the assassination of Hakimullah Mehsud as an attack on the peace talks between Islamabad and the TTP. The Pakistan army (which probably approved of the drone strike beforehand) is not actively supporting. The killing of the elder son of the founder of the Haqqani network near Islamabad has also killed the prospect of peace talks.

Conclusion

The fact that 'peace' agreements were followed by military operations against the militants in the same area is a testimony to their failure. There are also inherent problems in dealing with the militants. Firstly, the Pakistani Taliban was founded as a militant armed organisation and lacks a political wing. Secondly, they were compartmentalised. Hence, agreements in one or more agencies could not be taken as a comprehensive peace deal. Thirdly, the ideologically motivated non-state actors did not believe in borders and boundaries; fighting for causes and not countries. As things stand, Pakistan has ceded some 30,000 square kilometres of its 796,095 square kilometres to various terrorist-insurgent conglomerates. When the Pakistan army decided to use force, they suffered major losses while attacking militant sanctuaries in the Federally Administered Tribal Areas of Pakistan and Afghan border regions. While both these major options, talks and conflict, fail to provide results, achieving peace seems a distant proposition.

In most of the agreements, the government negotiated from a position of weakness, demanding too little and offering too much. A predetermined sense of siege drove the government negotiators to agree to the militants' terms in a rush. This not only left the militants walking away with more than they had hoped for, but also led to eventual military operations after the collapse of the agreements that compounded the miseries for the local population. Any agreement should be signed from a position of strength by the government. The militants would fear a breakdown of talks as much as the government does.

The local tribes/population that bore the brunt of collapse of the so-called peace agreements were not involved in the agreements. The only objective that the state wanted to achieve was to secure an end to attacks on the security forces. It seemed to have been taken for granted that if there were no more attacks on the security forces everything else would automatically fall into place. On the contrary, the militants grew in strength and did not brook dissent from the local population, and undermined public welfare through schools, hospitals and development projects.

The civilian administration and citizens of the tribal areas would have to be involved in the key decisions regarding the peace agreements so that they consider the concerns of the local population. The objective must be the welfare of the population and a state of affairs for the local people where access to rights such as health, education and a dignified existence.

There should be an independent structure and mechanism to disarm and demobilize the militants and reintegrate them into society. The programme should involve surrender of all weapons other than rifles and pistols that the tribal people traditionally carry.

Any peace deal would be short-lived if the context in which violence is perpetrated remains unchanged. So far, peace deals have been signed by both parties to gain time, only to resume fighting a few months later. The government requires strong action to purge the areas of criminal elements who have found safe havens in the tribal belt in order to wean off support for the militants, and to prevent them from setting up their own 'justice systems'. Peace can be tenuous at best in any area where human rights are not respected and the people feel that they do not have a stake in the system. FATA has long remained a hub of criminal activity and weapons and narcotics trafficking. The state institutions should be strengthened to deal with these problems instead of leaving the people to fend for themselves.

FATA should be integrated into mainland Pakistan through a constitutional package involving extension of the Political Parties Act to the region. In no way should the rights of a citizen residing in FATA be less than those enjoyed by Pakistani citizens elsewhere in the country. The state should not have a separate system for FATA. Policing and action against criminals and militants should be the domain of the state and the tribesmen should not be asked to police or hunt for criminals. Writ of the higher judiciary should also be extended to FATA.

To contain the militancy, Pakistan has taken measures which have not worked because of the archaic administrative set up in the tribal belt, the emphasis on military means and absence of political support for policies, actions under external compulsions rather than on account of domestic needs, trans-national character of the insurgency and negotiating from a position of weakness.

Pakistan needs a comprehensive counter-insurgency policy based on three pillars: military, political and economic. Priority should be given to integrate the tribal areas into Pakistan through political and administrative reforms. Such policies should prioritize national interest with strong political and public backing. Institutions need to be strengthened to enable the people to not only live in peace but also to access justice.

INDIA-CHINA BORDER AGREEMENTS

Agreement on the Maintenance of Peace and Tranquillity Along the Line of Actual Control in the India-China Border Areas

7 September 1993

The Government of the Republic of India and the Government of the People's Republic of China (hereinafter referred to as the two sides), have entered into the present Agreement in accordance with the Five Principles of mutual respect for sovereignty and territorial integrity, mutual non-aggression, non-interference in each other's internal affairs, equality and mutual benefit and peaceful coexistence and with a view to maintaining peace and tranquillity in areas along the line of actual control in the India-China border areas.

1. The two sides are of the view that the India-China boundary question shall be resolved through peaceful and friendly consultations. Neither side shall use or threaten to use force against the other by any means. Pending an ultimate solution to the boundary question between the two countries, the two sides shall strictly respect and observe the line of actual control between the two sides. No activities of either side shall overstep the line of actual control. In case personnel of one side cross the line of actual control, upon being cautioned by the other side, they shall immediately pull back to their own side of the line of actual control. When necessary, the two sides shall jointly check and determine the segments of the line of actual control where they have different views as to its alignment.

2. Each side will keep its military forces in the areas along the line of actual control to a minimum level compatible with the friendly and good neighbourly relations between the two countries. The two sides agree to reduce their military forces along the line of actual control in conformity with the requirements of the principle of mutual and equal security to ceilings to be mutually agreed. The extent, depth, timing, and nature of reduction of military forces along the line of actual control shall be determined through mutual consultations between the two countries. The reduction of military forces shall be carried out by stages in mutually agreed geographical locations sector-wise within the areas along the line of actual control.

3. Both sides shall work out through consultations effective confidence building measures in the areas along the line of actual control. Neither side will undertake specified levels of military exercises in mutually identified zones. Each side shall give the other prior notification of military exercises of specified levels near the line of actual control permitted under this Agreement.

4. In case of contingencies or other problems arising in the areas along the line of actual control, the two sides shall deal with them through meetings and friendly consultations between border personnel of the two countries. The form of such meetings and channels of communications between the border personnel shall be mutually agreed upon by the two sides.

5. The two sides agree to take adequate measures to ensure that air intrusions across the line of actual control do not take place and shall undertake mutual consultations should intrusions occur. Both sides shall also consult on possible restrictions on air exercises in areas to be mutually agreed near the line of actual control.

6. The two sides agree that references to the line of actual control in this Agreement do not prejudice their respective positions on the boundary question.

7. The two sides shall agree through consultations on the form, method, scale and content of effective verification measures and supervision required for the reduction of military forces and the maintenance of peace and tranquillity in the areas along the line of actual control under this Agreement.

8. Each side of the India-China Joint Working Group on the boundary question shall appoint diplomatic and military experts to formulate, through mutual consultations, implementation measures for the present Agreement.

The experts shall advise the Joint Working Group on the resolution of differences between the two sides on the alignment of the line of actual control and address issues relating to redeployment with a view to reduction of military forces in the areas along the line of actual control. The experts shall also assist the Joint Working Group in supervision of the implementation of the Agreement, and settlement of differences that may arise in that process, based on the principle of good faith and mutual confidence.

9. The present Agreement shall come into effect as of the date of signature and is subject to amendment and addition by agreement of the two sides.

Signed in duplicate at Beijing on the Seventh day of September 1993 in the Hindi, Chinese and English languages, all three texts having equal validity.

[Signed:]

R. L. Bhatia Minister of State for External Affairs Republic of India

Tang Jiaxuan Vice-Foreign Minister People's Republic of China

Agreement Between the Government of the Republic of India and the Government of the People's Republic of China on Confidence-Building Measures in the Military Field Along the Line of Actual Control in the India-China Border Areas

29 November 1996

The Government of the Republic of India and the Government of the People's Republic of China (hereinafter referred to as the two sides),

Believing that it serves the fundamental interests of the peoples of India and China to foster a long-term good-neighbourly relationship in accordance with the 'five principles of mutual respect for sovereignty and territorial integrity, mutual non-aggression, non-interference in each other's internal affairs, equality and mutual benefit and peaceful co-existence,

Convinced that the maintenance of peace and tranquillity along the line of actual control in the India-China border areas accords with the fundamental interests of the two peoples and will also contribute to the ultimate resolution of the boundary question,

Reaffirming that neither side shall use or threaten to use force against the other by any means or seek unilateral military superiority,

Pursuant to the Agreement between the Government of the Republic of India and the Government of the People's Republic of China on the Maintenance of Peace and Tranquillity along the Line of Actual Control in the India-China Border Areas, signed on 7 September, 1993,

Recognizing the need for effective confidence building measures in the military field along the line of actual control in the border areas between the two sides,

Noting the utility of confidence building measures already in place along the line of actual control in the India-China border areas,

Committed to enhancing mutual confidence and transparency in the military field, Have agreed as follows:

ARTICLE I

Neither side shall use its military capability against the other side. No armed forces deployed by either side in the border areas along the line of actual control as part of their respective military strength shall be used to attack the other side, or engage in military activities that threaten the other side or undermine peace, tranquillity and stability in the India-China border areas.

ARTICLE II

The two sides reiterate their determination to seek a fair, reasonable and mutually acceptable settlement of the boundary question. Pending an ultimate solution to the boundary question, the two sides reaffirm their commitment to strictly respect and observe the line-of actual control in the India-China border areas. No activities of either side shall overstep the line of actual control.

ARTICLE III

The two sides agree to take the following measures to reduce or limit their respective military forces within mutually agreed geographical zones along the line of actual control in the India-China border areas:

(1) The two sides reaffirm that they shall reduce or limit their respective military forces within mutually agreed geographical zones along the line of actual control in the India-China border areas to minimum levels compatible with the friendly and good neighbourly relations between the two countries and consistent with the principle of mutual and equal security.

(2) The two sides shall reduce or limit the number of field army, border defence forces, paramilitary forces and any other mutually agreed category of armed force deployed in mutually agreed geographical zones along the line of actual control to ceilings to be mutually agreed upon. The major categories of armaments to be reduced or limited are as follows: combat tanks, infantry combat vehicles, guns (including howitzers) with 75 mm or bigger calibre, mortars with 120 mm or bigger calibre, surface-to-surface missiles, surface-to-air missiles and any other weapon system mutually agreed upon.

(3) The two sides shall exchange data on the military forces and armaments to be reduced or limited and decide on ceilings on military forces and armaments to be kept by each side within mutually agreed geographical zones along the line of actual control in the India-China border areas. The ceilings shall be determined in conformity with the requirement of the principle of mutual and equal security, with due consideration being given to parameters such as the nature of terrain, road communication and other infrastructure and time taken to induct/de-induct troops and armaments.

ARTICLE IV

In order to maintain peace and tranquillity along the line of actual control in the India-China border areas and to prevent any tension in the border areas due to misreading by either side of the other side's intentions:

(1) Both sides shall avoid holding large scale military exercises involving more than one Division (approximately 1 5,000 troops) in close proximity of the line of actual control in the India-China border areas. However, if such exercises are to be conducted, the strategic direction of the main force involved shall not be towards the other side.

(2) If either side conducts a major military exercise involving more than one Brigade Group (approximately 5,000 troops) in close proximity of the line of actual control in the India-China border areas, it shall give the other side prior notification with regard to type, level, planned duration and area of exercise as well as the number and type of units or formations participating in the exercise.

(3) The date of completion of the exercise and deinduction of troops from the area of exercise shall be intimated to the other side within five days of completion or de-induction.

(4) Each side shall be entitled to obtain timely clarification from the side undertaking the exercise in respect of data specified in Paragraph 2 of the present Article.

ARTICLE V

With a view to preventing air intrusions across the line of actual control in the India-China border areas and facilitating overflights and landings by military aircraft:

(1) Both sides shall take adequate measures to ensure that air intrusions across the line of actual control do not take place. However, if an intrusion does take place, it should cease as soon as detected and the incident shall be promptly investigated by the side operating the aircraft. The results of the investigation shall be immediately communicated, through diplomatic channels or at border personnel meetings, to the other side.

(2) Subject to Paragraphs 3 and 5 of this Article, combat aircraft (to include fighter, bomber, reconnaissance, military trainer, armed helicopter and other armed aircraft) shall not fly within ten kilometres of the line of actual control.

(3) If either side is required to undertake flights of combat aircraft within ten kilometres from the line of actual control, it shall give the following information in advance to the other side, through diplomatic channels:
   (a) Type and number of combat aircraft;
   (b) Height of the proposed flight (in meters);
   (c) Proposed duration of flights (normally not to exceed ten days);
   (d) Proposed timing of flights; and
   (e) Area of operations, defined in latitude and longitude.

(4) Unarmed transport aircraft, survey aircraft and helicopters shall be permitted to fly up to the line of actual control.

(5) No military aircraft of either side shall fly across the line of actual control, except by prior permission. Military aircraft of either side may fly across the line of actual control or overfly the other side's airspace or land on the other side only after obtaining the latter's prior permission after providing the latter with detailed information on the flight in accordance with the international practice in this regard. Notwithstanding the above stipulation, each side has the sovereign right to specify additional conditions, including at short notice, for flights or landings of military aircraft of the other side on its side of the line of actual control or through its airspace.

(6) In order to ensure flight safety in emergency situations, the authorities designated by the two sides may contact each other by the quickest means of communications available.

ARTICLE VI

With a view to preventing dangerous military activities along the line of actual control in the India-China border areas, the two sides agree as follows:

(1) Neither side shall open fire, cause bio-degradation, use hazardous chemicals, conduct blast operations or hunt with guns or explosives within two kilometres from the line of actual control. This prohibition shall not apply to routine firing activities in small arms firing ranges.

(2) If there is a need to conduct blast operations within two kilometres of the line of actual control as part of developmental activities, the other side shall be informed through diplomatic channels or by convening a border personnel meeting, preferably five days in advance.

(3) While conducting exercises with live ammunition in areas close to the line of actual control, precaution shall be taken to ensure

that a bullet or a missile does not accidentally fall on the other side across the line of actual control and causes harm to the personnel or property of the other side.

(4) If the border personnel of the two sides come in a face-to-face situation due to differences on the alignment of the line of actual control o any other reason, they shall exercise self-restraint and take all necessary steps to avoid an escalation of the situation. Both sides shall also enter into immediate consultations through diplomatic and/or other available channels to review the situation and prevent any escalation of tension.

ARTICLE VII

In order to strengthen exchanges and cooperation between the military personnel and establishments in the border areas along the line of actual control, the two sides agree:

(1) To maintain and expand the regime of scheduled and flag meetings between their border representatives at designated places along the line of actual control;
(2) To maintain and expand telecommunication links between the border meeting points at designated places along the line of actual control;
(3) To establish step-by-step medium and high-level contacts between the border authorities of the two sides.

ARTICLE VIII

(1) Should the personnel of one side cross the line of actual control and enter the other side because of unavoidable circumstances like natural disasters, the other side shall extend all possible assistance to them and inform their side, as soon as possible regarding the forced or inadvertent entry across the line of actual control. The modalities of return of the concerned personnel to their own side shall be settled through mutual consultations.
(2) The two sides shall provide each other, at the earliest possible, with information pertaining to natural disasters and epidemic diseases in contiguous border areas which might affect the other side. The exchange of information shall take place either through diplomatic channels or at border personnel meetings.

ARTICLE IX

In case a doubtful situation develops in the border region, or in case one of the sides has some questions or doubts regarding the manner in which the other side is observing this Agreement, either side has the right to seek a clarification from the other side. The clarifications sought and replies to them shall be conveyed through diplomatic channels.

ARTICLE X

(1) Recognizing that the full implementation of some of the provisions of the present Agreement will depend on the two sides arriving at a common understanding of the alignment of the line of actual control in the India-China border areas, the two sides agree to speed up the process clarification and confirmation of the line of actual control. As an initial step in this process, they are clarifying the alignment of the line of actual control in those segments where they have different perceptions. They also agree to exchange maps indicating their respective perceptions of the entire alignment of the line of actual control as soon as possible.
(2) Pending the completion of the process of clarification and confirmation of the line of actual control, the two sides shall work out modalities for implementing confidence building measures envisaged under this Agreement on an interim basis, without prejudice to their respective positions on the alignment of the line of actual control as well as on the boundary question.

ARTICLE XI

Detailed implementation measures required under Article I to Article X of this Agreement shall be decided through mutual consultations in the India-China Joint Working Group on the Boundary Question. The India-China Diplomatic and Military Expert Group shall assist the India-China Joint

ARTICLE XII

This Agreement is subject to ratification and shall enter into force on the date of exchange of instruments of ratification. It shall remain in effect until either side decides to terminate it after giving six months' notice in writing.

It shall become invalid six months after the notification.

This Agreement is subject to amendment and addition by mutual agreement in writing between the two sides.

Signed in duplicate in New Delhi on 29 November, 1996 in the Hindi, Chinese and English languages, all three texts being equally authentic.

In case of divergence, the English text shall prevail.

Agreement Between the Government of the Republic of India and the Government of the People's Republic of China on the Political Parameters and Guiding Principles for the Settlement of the India-China Boundary Question

11 April 2005

The Government of the Republic of India and the Government of the People's Republic of China (hereinafter referred to as the two sides),

Believing that it serves the fundamental interests of the peoples of India and China to foster a long-term constructive and cooperative partnership on the basis of the Five Principles of Peaceful Co-existence, mutual respect and sensitivity for each other's concerns and aspirations, and equality,

Desirous of qualitatively upgrading the bilateral relationship at all levels and in all areas while addressing differences through peaceful means in a fair, reasonable and mutually acceptable manner,

Reiterating their commitment to abide by and implement the Agreement on the Maintenance of Peace and Tranquillity along the Line of Actual Control in the India-China Border Areas, signed on 7 September 1993, and the Agreement on Confidence Building Measures in the Military Field along the Line of Actual Control in the India-China Border Areas, signed on 29 November 1996,

Reaffirming the Declaration on Principles for Relations and Comprehensive Cooperation between India and China, signed on 23 June 2003,

Recalling that the two sides have appointed Special Representatives to explore the framework of settlement of the India-China boundary question and the two Special Representatives have been engaged in consultations in a friendly, cooperative and constructive atmosphere,

Noting that the two sides are seeking a political settlement of the boundary question in the context of their overall and long-term interests,

Convinced that an early settlement of the boundary question will advance the basic interests of the two countries and should therefore be pursued as a strategic objective,

Have agreed on the following political parameters and guiding principles for a boundary settlement:

ARTICLE I

The differences on the boundary question should not be allowed to affect the overall development of bilateral relations. The two sides will resolve the boundary question through peaceful and friendly consultations. Neither side shall use or threaten to use force against the other by any means. The final solution of the boundary question will significantly promote good neighbourly and friendly relations between India and China.

ARTICLE II

The two sides should, in accordance with the Five Principles of Peaceful

Coexistence, seek a fair, reasonable and mutually acceptable solution to the boundary question through consultations on an equal footing, proceeding from the political perspective of overall bilateral relations.

ARTICLE III

Both sides should, in the spirit of mutual respect and mutual understanding, make meaningful and mutually acceptable adjustments to their respective positions on the boundary question, so as to arrive at a package settlement to the boundary question. The boundary settlement must be final, covering all sectors of the India-China boundary.

ARTICLE IV

The two sides will give due consideration to each other's strategic and reasonable interests, and the principle of mutual and equal security.

ARTICLE V

The two sides will take into account, inter alia, historical evidence, national sentiments, practical difficulties and reasonable concerns and sensitivities of both sides, and the actual state of border areas.

ARTICLE VI

The boundary should be along well-defined and easily identifiable natural geographical features to be mutually agreed upon between the two sides.

ARTICLE VII

In reaching a boundary settlement, the two sides shall safeguard due interests of their settled populations in the border areas.

ARTICLE VIII

Within the agreed framework of the final boundary settlement, the delineation of the boundary will be carried out utilising means such as modern cartographic and surveying practices and joint surveys.

ARTICLE IX

Pending an ultimate settlement of the boundary question, the two sides should strictly respect and observe the line of actual control and work together to maintain peace and tranquillity in the border areas. The India- China Joint Working Group and the India-China Diplomatic and Military Expert Group shall continue their work under the Agreements of 7 September 1993 and 29 November 1996, including the clarification of the line of actual control and the implementation of confidence building measures.

ARTICLE X

The Special Representatives on the boundary question shall continue their consultations in an earnest manner with the objective of arriving at an agreed framework for a boundary settlement, which will provide the basis for the delineation and demarcation of the India-China boundary to be subsequently undertaken by civil and military officials and surveyors of the two sides.

ARTICLE XI

This Agreement shall come into force as of the date of signature and is subject to amendment and addition by mutual agreement in writing between the two sides.

Signed in duplicate in New Delhi on 11 April, 2005, in the Hindi, Chinese and English languages, all three texts being equally authentic.

In case of divergence, the English text shall prevail.

For the Government of the Republic of India

For the Government of the People's Republic of China

New Delhi, 11 April 2005

Agreement Between the Government of the Republic of India and the Government of the People's Republic of China on the Establishment of a Working Mechanism for Consultation and Coordination on India-China Border Affairs

17 January 2012

The Government of the Republic of India and the Government of the People's Republic of China (hereinafter referred to as the "two sides");

Firmly believing that respecting and abiding by the Line of Actual Control pending a resolution of the Boundary Question between the two countries as well as maintaining and strengthening peace and tranquility in the India-China border areas is very significant for enhancing mutual trust and security between the two countries, for resolving the Boundary Question at an early date and for building the India-China Strategic and Cooperative Partnership for Peace and Prosperity;

Desiring to materialize the spirit of the Agreement between the Government of the Republic of India and the Government of the People's Republic of China on the Maintenance of Peace and Tranquility Along the Line of Actual Control in the India-China Border Areas signed on 7th September 1993, the Agreement between the Government of the Republic of India and the Government of the People's Republic of China on Confidence Building Measures in the Military Field Along the Line of Actual Control in the India-China Border Areas signed on 29th November 1996 and the Protocol between the Government of the Republic of India and the Government of the People's Republic of China on Modalities for the Implementation of Confidence Building Measures in the Military Field Along the Line of Actual Control in the India-China Border Areas signed on 11th April 2005;

Aiming for timely communication of information on the border situation, for appropriately handling border incidents, for earnestly undertaking other cooperation activities in the India-China border areas, have agreed as follows:

ARTICLE I

The two sides agree to establish a Working Mechanism for Consultation and Coordination on India-China Border Affairs (hereinafter referred to as "the Working Mechanism") to deal with important border affairs related to maintaining peace and tranquillity in the India-China border areas.

ARTICLE II

The Working Mechanism will be headed by a Joint Secretary level official from the Ministry of External Affairs of the Republic of India and a Director General level official from the Ministry of Foreign Affairs of the People's Republic of China and will be composed of diplomatic and military officials of the two sides.

ARTICLE III

The Working Mechanism will study ways and means to conduct and strengthen exchanges and cooperation between military personnel and establishments of the two sides in the border areas.

ARTICLE IV

The Working Mechanism will explore the possibility of cooperation in the border areas that are agreed upon by the two sides.

ARTICLE V

The Working Mechanism will undertake other tasks that are mutually agreed upon by the two sides but will not discuss resolution of the Boundary Question or affect the Special Representatives Mechanism.

ARTICLE VI

The Working Mechanism will address issues and situations that may arise in the border areas that affect the maintenance of peace and tranquility and will work actively towards maintaining the friendly atmosphere between the two countries.

ARTICLE VII

The Working Mechanism will hold consultations once or twice every year alternately in India and China. Emergency consultations, if required, may be convened after mutual agreement.

ARTICLE VIII

This Agreement shall come into force on the date of its signature. It may be revised, amended, or terminated with the consent of the two sides. Any revision or amendment, mutually agreed by the two sides, shall form an integral part of this Agreement.

Signed in duplicate in Hindi, Chinese and English languages at New Delhi, on 17 January 2012, all three versions being equally authentic. In case of divergence the English text shall prevail.

Agreement Between the Government of the Republic of India and the Government of the People's Republic of China on Border Defence Cooperation

The Government of the Republic of India and the Government of the People's Republic of China (hereinafter referred to as the 'two sides'),

Firmly believing that the India-China Strategic and Cooperative Partnership for Peace and Prosperity serves the fundamental interests of the people of the two countries,

Reiterating that neither side shall use its military capability against the other side and that their respective military strengths shall not be used to attack the other side,

Reaffirming that neither side shall use or threaten to use force against the other side by any means nor seek unilateral superiority,

Having accepted the principle of mutual and equal security,

Acknowledging the need to continue to maintain peace, stability and tranquility along the line of actual control in the India-China border areas and to continue implementing confidence building measures in the military field along the line of actual control,

Recognizing the importance of materializing the spirit of the *Agreement between the Government of the Republic of India and Government of the People's Republic of China on the Maintenance of Peace and Tranquillity Along the Line of Actual Control in the India-China Border Areas* signed on 7th September 1993, the *Agreement between the Government of the Republic of India and the Government of the People's Republic of China on Confidence Building Measures in the Military Field Along the Line of Actual Control in the India-China Border Areas* signed on 29th November 1996, the *Protocol between the Government of the Republic of India and the Government of the People's Republic of China on Modalities for the Implementation of Confidence Building Measures in the Military Field Along the Line of Actual Control in India-China Border Areas* signed on 11th April 2005 and the *Agreement between the Government of the Republic of India and the Government of the People's Republic of China on the Establishment of a Working Mechanism for Consultation and Coordination on India-China Border Affairs* signed on 17th January 2012,

Have agreed as follows:

ARTICLE I

The two sides shall carry out border defence cooperation on the basis of their respective laws and relevant bilateral agreements.

ARTICLE II

The two sides shall implement border defence cooperation in the following ways:

1. Exchange information-including information about military exercises, aircrafts, demolition operations and unmarked mines-and take consequent measures conducive to the maintenance of peace, stability and tranquillity along the line of actual control in the India-China border areas,
2. Jointly combat smuggling of arms, wildlife, wildlife articles and other contrabands,
3. Assist the other side in locating personnel, livestock, means of transport and aerial vehicles that may have crossed or are possibly in the process of crossing the line of actual control in the India-China border areas,
4. Work with the other side in combating natural disasters or infectious diseases that may affect or spread to the other side,
5. Any other way mutually agreed upon by the two sides.

ARTICLE III

Border deference cooperation visualized in this agreement shall be implemented through the following mechanisms:

1. Flag meetings or border personnel meetings at designated places along the line of actual control in the India-China border areas.
2. Periodic meetings between officers of the relevant Military Regions of China and Army Commands of India and between departments responsible for military operations.
3. Periodic meetings of the representatives of the Ministry of Defence of the Government of India and the Ministry of National Defence of the People's Republic of China.
4. Meetings of the Working Mechanism for Consultation and Coordination on India-China Border Affairs.
5. Meetings of the India-China Annual Defence Dialogue.

ARTICLE IV

In implementing border defence cooperation and to facilitate contacts and meetings between relevant organizations, the two sides may establish Border Personnel Meeting sites in all sectors, as well as telephone contacts and telecommunication links at mutually agreed locations along the line of actual control. The two sides may also consider establishing a Hotline between the military headquarters of the two countries. Specific arrangements shall be decided upon through mutual consultations between the two sides.

ARTICLE V

In order to enhance understanding and cooperation between the border defence forces of the two sides, each side may invite the other side for joint celebrations on major national or military days or festivals and organize cultural activities, non-contact sports events and small scale tactical exercises along the line of actual control in the India-China border areas. In addition, the two sides may also conduct joint military training exercises, at Army level, in each other's country on a regular basis. The theme of such joint exercises will be decided through mutual consultations.

ARTICLE VI

The two sides agree that they shall not follow or tail patrols of the other side in areas where there is no common understanding of the line of actual control in the India-China border areas.

ARTICLE VII

In case a doubtful situation arises with reference to any activity by either side in border areas where there is no common understanding of the line of actual control, either side has the right to seek a clarification from the other side. In such cases, the clarification shall be sought and replies to them shall be conveyed through any of the mechanisms established under *Article III* of this Agreement.

ARTICLE VIII

The two sides agree that if the border defence forces of the two sides come to a face-to-face situation in areas where there is no common understanding of the line of actual control, both sides shall exercise maximum self-restraint, refrain from any provocative actions, not use force or threaten to use force against the other side, treat each other with courtesy and prevent exchange of fire or armed conflict.

ARTICLE IX

The two sides shall implement this Agreement without prejudice to their respective positions on the alignment of the line of actual control as well as on the boundary question.

ARTICLE X

This Agreement shall come into force on the date of its signature. It may be revised, amended or terminated with the consent of the two sides. Any revision or amendment, mutually agreed by the two sides, shall form an integral part of this Agreement.

Signed in duplicate in Hindi, Chinese and English languages at Beijing on the 23rd day of October month of 2013, all three versions being equally authentic. In case of divergence, the English text shall prevail.

For the Government of the Republic of India

For the Government of the People's Republic of China

JOINT STATEMENT OF THE REPUBLIC OF INDIA AND THE PEOPLE'S REPUBLIC OF CHINA

12 April 2005

H.E. Mr. Wen Jiabao, Premier of the State Council of the People's Republic of China, is currently paying a state visit to the Republic of India from 9 to 12 April 2005 at the invitation of H.E. Dr. Manmohan Singh, Prime Minister of the Republic of India.

During the visit, Premier Wen Jiabao held talks with Prime Minister Dr. Manmohan Singh, called on President Dr. A.P.J. Abdul Kalam and Vice President Shri Bhairon Singh Shekhawat, and met with Chairperson, United Progressive Alliance Smt. Sonia Gandhi. External Affairs Minister Shri K. Natwar Singh and Leader of Opposition, Lok Sabha Shri L.K. Advani will call on him. Premier Wen paid a visit to Bangalore and will deliver a speech at the Indian Institute of Technology in New Delhi.

Leaders of the two countries had an in-depth exchange of views in a sincere, friendly and constructive atmosphere and reached broad consensus on bilateral relations and international and regional issues of common concern.

The two sides reviewed the friendly contacts and progress in their bilateral relations in recent years and agreed that India-China relations have entered a new stage of comprehensive development. Both sides noted with satisfaction that with the frequent exchange of visits between leaders of the two countries, the process of building trust and understanding has gained momentum. Rapid growth of trade and economic cooperation has been coupled with the expansion of exchanges and cooperation in other fields. The two sides have made incremental progress in addressing outstanding issues. The two sides have also maintained good communication and collaboration in international and regional affairs. Both sides agreed that India and China have made satisfying progress in developing their long-term constructive and cooperative partnership.

The two sides recalled the Declaration on Principles for Relations and Comprehensive Cooperation between the two Prime Ministers on 23 June 2003 and reiterated that the Declaration provided a shared vision of bilateral relations and an agreed framework for cooperation.

In the light of the development of their bilateral relations, in order to promote good neighbourliness, friendship and mutually beneficial cooperation and taking into account the profound changes in the regional and international situation, the two sides agreed that India-China relations have now acquired a global and strategic character. The leaders of the two countries have, therefore, agreed to establish an India-China Strategic and Cooperative Partnership for Peace and Prosperity.

Such a partnership is based on the principles of Panchsheel, mutual respect and sensitivity for each other's concerns and aspirations, and equality; provides a sound framework for an all-round and comprehensive development of bilateral relations based on mutual and equal security, development and prosperity of the two peoples; and contributes to jointly addressing global challenges and threats. It reflects the readiness of the two sides to resolve outstanding differences in a proactive manner without letting them come in the way of the continued development of bilateral relations.

The two sides agreed that high-level exchanges between the governments, parliaments and political parties of the two countries play an important role in expanding overall bilateral cooperation. They conveyed their determination to maintain and strengthen the momentum of such exchanges in future and agreed to hold regular meetings between the leaders of the two countries. In this context, the two sides also reiterated their intention to promote regular ministerial-level exchanges and make full use of the India-China strategic dialogue and other bilateral dialogue mechanisms.

The year of 2005 marks the 55th anniversary of the establishment of diplomatic relations between India and China. To mark the occasion, the two countries will organize a series of commemorative activities. It was noted that "Cultural Festival of China" was currently underway in India and that a corresponding "Cultural Festival of India" would be organised in China later in the year. The two sides would also organize other cultural activities to further promote mutual awareness and deepen the friendship between the two peoples. The two sides declared 2006 as the "year of India-China friendship".

Both sides expressed satisfaction with strengthened exchanges in the area of culture, and affirmed that mutual understanding and cultural exchanges would facilitate development of cooperation in other areas as well. In order to reinforce traditional cultural links, an agreement was concluded for the construction of an Indian-style Buddhist temple at Luoyang in Henan Province of China.

The two sides stressed that an all-round expansion of India-China economic cooperation, including trade and investment, constitutes an important dimension of a stronger India-China relationship. The two countries agreed to make joint efforts to increase the bilateral trade volume to US$ 20 billion or higher by 2008. The two sides welcomed the report of the Joint Study Group (JSG) that was set up to examine the potential complementarities between the two countries in expanded trade and economic cooperation. The JSG in its Report has identified a series of measures related to trade in goods, trade in services, investments and other areas of economic cooperation, and recommended their expeditious implementation to remove impediments and facilitate enhanced economic engagement between India and China. The two Prime Ministers tasked the Ministerial-level India-China Joint Economic Group (JEG) to consider these recommendations and coordinate their implementation. For this purpose, the two sides will make their best endeavour to hold the next meeting of the JEG within the next six months. The JSG has also recommended an India-China Regional Trading Arrangement, comprising of trade in goods and services, investments, identified understandings for trade and investment promotion and facilitation, and measures for promotion of economic cooperation in identified sectors. The Prime Ministers agreed to appoint a Joint Task Force to study in detail the feasibility of, and the benefits that may derive from, the India-China Regional Trading Arrangement and give recommendations regarding its content.

Both sides noted that the Agreement on the Establishment of a Financial Dialogue Mechanism would further facilitate the dynamic and diversifying economic cooperation between the two sides. They will continue consultations on concluding the Bilateral Investment Promotion and Protection Agreement.

The two sides noted with satisfaction that the two countries have signed the SPS Protocols for the export of grapes and bitter gourd from India to China. The two sides also agreed to constitute a Joint Working Group to implement expeditiously the MOU on Application of SPS between the Chinese General Administration of Quality Supervision, Inspection and Quarantine and the Indian Ministry of Agriculture.

China positively evaluates market access for Indian rice to the Chinese market and will launch as early as possible the risk analysis procedure of the Indian rice in accordance with relevant Chinese laws and regulations.

The two sides agreed to further promote the cooperation in the spheres of education, science and technology, healthcare, information, tourism, youth exchange, agriculture, dairy development, sports and other fields on the basis of mutual benefit and reciprocity. The two sides decided to establish an India-China Steering Committee on Scientific and Technological Cooperation chaired by their Ministers for Science and Technology, and start consultations on an agreement on mutual recognition of academic certificates and degrees between India and China. The two sides announced the launching of regular youth exchange activities. China will invite 100 Indian youth to China within the year of 2005 and hold an exhibition this year on advanced and applicable technologies in India.

The two sides recognised the importance of strengthening mutual connectivity and agreed to jointly work towards further enhancement of direct air and shipping links, tourism and people-to-people contacts. It was noted with satisfaction that an MOU on major liberalisation of civil aviation links between India and China was concluded during the visit.

The two sides will continue to cooperate in exchanging flood-season hydrological data of the trans-border rivers as agreed between them.

In response to concerns expressed by the Indian side, the Chinese side agreed to take measures for controlled release of accumulated water of the landslide dam on the river Parechu, as soon as conditions permit. It was noted with satisfaction that an agreement concerning the provision of hydrological data on Sutlej/Langqen Zangbo was concluded during the visit and that the two sides had also agreed to continue bilateral discussions to finalize at an early date similar arrangements for the Parlung Zangbo and Lohit/Zayu Qu Rivers.

The two sides agreed to cooperate in the field of energy security and conservation, including, among others, encouraging relevant departments and units of the two countries to engage in the survey and exploration of petroleum and natural gas resources in third countries.

The two sides noted the useful exchanges and interaction in the military field and decided to further promote such exchanges and interaction. They agreed that broadening and deepening of defense exchanges between the two countries was of vital importance in enhancing mutual trust and understanding between the two armed forces, and to ensuring a peaceful environment in which they could pursue their respective national development objectives. The two sides decided to further strengthen effective contacts and exchanges in this field.

During the visit, the two sides exchanged views on the India-China boundary question and reiterated their readiness to seek a fair, reasonable and mutually acceptable solution, through equal and friendly consultations and proceeding from the overall interests of bilateral relations. They expressed satisfaction over the progress made in the discussions between the Special Representatives of the two countries and welcomed the conclusion of the Agreement on the Political Parameters and Guiding Principles for the Settlement of the Boundary Question. Both sides are convinced that an early settlement of the boundary question will advance the basic interests of the two countries and should therefore be pursued as a strategic objective. They expressed their commitment to the mechanism of Special Representatives for seeking a political settlement of the boundary question in the context of their long-term interests and the overall bilateral relationship.

Pending a final resolution, the two sides will continue to make joint efforts to maintain peace and tranquility in the border areas in accordance with the Agreements of 1993 and 1996. Both sides agreed that while continuing the discussions between the Special Representatives, it is also important that the Joint Working Group (JWG) continues its work to seek an early clarification and confirmation of the Line of Actual Control (LAC). Progress made so far on the clarification of the LAC in the India-China border areas was noted. It was agreed to complete the process of exchanging maps indicating their respective perceptions of the entire alignment of the LAC on the basis of already agreed parameters, with the objective of arriving at a common understanding of the alignment, as soon as possible.

The two sides expressed satisfaction at the progress achieved in the implementation of the Agreements of 1993 and 1996 and agreed to fully implement them expeditiously. Towards that end, they concluded a Protocol on Modalities for the Implementation of Confidence Building Measures in the Military Field along the Line of Actual Control in the India-China Border Areas.

The Indian side reiterated that it recognised the Tibet Autonomous Region as part of the territory of the People's Republic of China and that it did not allow Tibetans to engage in anti-China political activities in India.

The Indian side recalled that India was among the first countries to recognize that there is one China and its one China policy remains unaltered. The Indian side stated it would continue to abide by its one China policy.

The Chinese side expressed its appreciation for the Indian positions.

Both sides reviewed with satisfaction the implementation of the memorandum on the border trade through the Nathula Pass between the Tibet Autonomous Region of the People's Republic of China and the Sikkim State of the Republic of India.

The two sides noted with satisfaction that through friendly consultations an agreement in principle had been reached between the two countries to solve the long-pending issue of property originally belonging to Indian Consulate General in Shanghai with the Chinese side agreeing to provide a plot of land in lieu of the premises of the original Consulate General of India.

As two large developing countries, both India and China were aware of each other's important role in the process of promoting the establishment of a new international political and economic order. Both sides share common interests in the maintenance of peace, stability and prosperity in Asia and the world at large, and share the desire to develop closer and more extensive understanding and cooperation in regional and international affairs.

The two sides are supportive of democratisation of international relations and multilateralism, stand for the establishment of a new international political and economic order that is fair, rational, equal and mutually beneficial, and promote North-South Dialogue and South-South Cooperation. The two sides believe that the international community should eliminate poverty, narrow the gap between North and South, and achieve common prosperity through dialogue and cooperation.

The two sides reiterated the importance of the United Nations in global peace, stability and common development and expressed their determination to continue their efforts, together with the international community, in strengthening the UN system to develop a sound multilateral basis to address global issues. Both India and China agree that reform of the United Nations should be comprehensive and multi-faceted and should put emphasis on an increase in the representation of developing countries. The Indian side reiterated its aspirations for permanent membership of the UN Security Council. The Chinese side also reiterated that India is an important developing country and is having an increasingly important influence in the international arena. China attaches great importance to the status of India in international affairs. It understands and supports India's aspirations to play an active role in the UN and international affairs. The two sides reaffirmed their readiness to conduct close consultations and cooperation in the process of UN reforms.

The two sides, aware of the threats posed by terrorism to the peace and security of the two countries and the whole world, resolutely condemn terrorism in any form. The struggle between the international community and global terrorism is a comprehensive and sustained one, with the ultimate objective of eradication of terrorism in all regions. This requires strengthening the global legal framework against terrorism. Both sides noted the positive outcome of the meetings held so far of their bilateral dialogue mechanism on counter-terrorism and agreed to further strengthen and consolidate their discussions and cooperation. It was agreed to hold the next meeting of the dialogue mechanism on counter-terrorism later this year.

Both sides agreed to conduct regular exchange of views on major international and regional issues, strengthen cooperation in the WTO and other international multilateral organisations, and to continue the consultations on other issues of common concern. They agreed to work together to preserve stability and growth in the global economy and reduce disparities between developed and developing countries. They supported an open, fair, equitable and transparent rule-based multilateral trade system and resolved to safeguard the legitimate rights and interests of the developing countries.

Aware of their linked destinies as neighbours and the two largest countries of Asia, both sides agreed that they would, together, contribute to the establishment of an atmosphere of mutual understanding, trust and cooperation in Asia and the world at large, and facilitate efforts to strengthen multilateral coordination mechanisms on security and cooperation.

During the visit, the two sides signed and/or released the following documents:

i. Agreement on Political Parameters and Guiding Principles for the Settlement of the India-China Boundary Question
ii. Report of India-China Joint Study Group on Comprehensive Trade and Economic Cooperation
iii. Protocol on Modalities for the Implementation of CBMs in the Military Field Along the Line of Actual Control in the India-China Border Areas
iv. Agreement on Mutual Administrative Assistance and Cooperation in Customs Matters
v. MOU on the Launch of the India-China Financial Dialogue
vi. MOU on Civil Aviation
vii. Protocol of Phytosanitary Requirement for Exporting Grapes from India to China
viii. Protocol of Phytosanitary Requirement for Exporting Bitter Gourds from India to China
ix. MOU on Provision of Hydrological Information of the Sutlej /Langqen Zangbo River in Flood Season by China to India.
x. Protocol on India-China Film Cooperation Commission
xi. MOU on Cooperation between the Indian Council of World Affairs and the Chinese People's Institute of Foreign Affairs
xii. Memorandum on the Construction of an Indian-style Buddhist Temple on the Western side of the White Horse Temple in Luoyang, China

The two sides believed that Premier Wen Jiabao's highly successful State visit to the Republic of India marked a new level of India-China relationship and opened a new chapter in the friendly relations and cooperation between the two countries.

Premier Wen Jiabao, on behalf of the Chinese Government and people, expressed his appreciation to the Government and the people of India for their warm hospitality, and invited Prime Minister Manmohan Singh to visit China at a mutually convenient time. Prime Minister Manmohan Singh appreciated the invitation and accepted it with pleasure. The Indian side also reiterated the invitation to President Hu Jintao to visit India. The exact time of the visit will be decided through diplomatic channels. "

INDIA-CHINA DEFENCE COOPERATION AND MILITARY ENGAGEMENT

Defence cooperation and military engagement between India and China are aspects of the complex mix of conflict and cooperation approach to bilateral relations between the two Asian giants. It is based on the presumption that there is a security dilemma between the two countries. However, it recognises the framework and postulates of what is called cooperative security. It argues that India-China defence cooperation and military engagement are not only possible but also desirable. For these two biggest developing nations of the world, peace and friendship between them are not only in their mutual interests, but also important for bringing peace, stability and prosperity to South Asia.

Military engagements between countries across the world are increasingly becoming an important aspect of the bilateral relations between them. It is not only symbolic of maturing of their relationship but also builds trust and confidence between the defence forces which may prove useful during any joint military operation such as fighting terrorism or natural disasters like flood and earthquake. Military engagement is possible when there is higher degree of friendship and cooperation at the political level between the two governments and their defence forces. If approaches to study of international politics and more particularly to study of bilateral relationship between two countries can be broadly categorised as realists and liberal institutionalist, then advocates of Confidence Building Measures (CBMS) like defence cooperation and military engagement can be put in the category of the latter nomenclature. Liberal institutionalists as distinguished from the realists point out that international cooperation is not only possible but also highly desirable because it reduces transaction costs and makes interstate relations more predictable.[1]

Both India and China have military engagements with a number of countries, besides between two of them. The rationale and raison d'etre for defence cooperation and military engagement between the two countries can hardly be overemphasised given the fact that the two countries fought a war in 1962 and they share a common border of 3488 kilometres which remains undefined and disputed even after having thirteen rounds of fresh parleys. There exists, what is called, a persistent security dilemma between the two countries. Although, there had been no major conflict between the countries after 1962, there have been reports of border incursions from time to time, and tension have also built up across the border. In the post-1962 period, and after the restoration of the diplomatic relations between the two countries in 1976, the relationship between the two reached its nadir when the Sumdorong Chu incident took place in 1986.

This incident brought the two countries almost to the brink of war, which in turn impelled the two sides to explore ways and means for defence cooperation and military engagement.

It is in this backdrop that it is significant to revisit the achievements between India and China in the field of defence cooperation and military engagement particularly at a time when these achievements built over the years as consequences of greater political engagement at various levels between the two countries and their leaders. It is regrettable, however, that the defence cooperation and military engagement between the two countries face challenges in the wake of the reports relating to the denial of visa to a senior Indian army officer on the grounds that he controls allegedly a disputed region of India. As a response, media reported Government's decision to keep the military exchanges between the two countries on hold till the visa issue is amicably settled through diplomatic channels. India's Defence Minister, A. K. Anthony, however, in a statesmanlike manner allayed the anxiety regarding the uncertainties about the military exchanges between the two countries.

Agreement on Maintenance of Peace and Tranquillity, 1993

The consolidation of diplomatic relations between the two countries with the path breaking visit of the then Prime Minister Rajiv Gandhi to China in December 1988, established the Joint Working Group (JWG), the groundwork for defence cooperation and military engagement.

A milestone in the military relationship between the two countries was the visit of Sharad Pawar, the then

[1] Keohan, Robert O., ed., *Neorealism and Its Critics*, New York: Colombia University Press, 1986.

Defence Minister to China in July 1992. It was the first ever visit by a Defence Minister of India to China. During the visit it was agreed to develop academic, military, scientific and technological exchanges between the two countries. It is also believed that during Mr. Pawar's visit, the Chinese military leadership emphasised the importance of forced reduction in the border region due to prohibitive cost. The visit fructified in the signing of the Agreement on the Maintenance of Peace and Tranquillity along the Line of Actual Control (LAC) in the India-China Border area on 7th September 1993 during the visit of the then Prime Minister P.V. Narashima Rao. The Agreement[2] was indeed a breakthrough. In view of its importance, it is worthwhile to elucidate the salient features of the Agreement in greater detail.

In the first place, the Agreement affirmed the view that the India-China boundary question shall be resolved through peaceful and friendly consultations and that neither side shall use or threaten to use force against the other by any means. Yet another important high light of the Agreement was that it stipulated 'pending an ultimate solution of the boundary question between the two countries, the two sides shall strictly observe the LAC between the two sides and that no activities of either side shall overstep the line of actual control. In case of personnel of one side cross the line of LAC, upon being confirmed by the other side, they shall immediately pull back to their own side of the LAC. It further provided that when necessary, the two sides shall jointly check and determine the segments of the LAC when they have different views as to its alignment

Secondly, the agreement stipulated that each side will keep its military forces in the area along the LAC to a minimum level compatible with the friendly and good neighbourly relations between the two countries. It further iterated that the two sides agreed to reduce their military forces along LAC in conformity with the requirement of the principle of mutual and equal security to ceilings to be mutually agreed, and that the reduction of military forces shall be carried out by stages in mutually agreed geographical locations sector-wise within the areas along the LAC.

Thirdly, as regards military exercise, the Agreement mentioned that each side shall give the other prior notification of the military exercises of specified levels near the LAC permitted under the Agreement. Fourthly, in case of contingency or other problems arising in the areas of LAC, the two sides shall deal with them through meetings and friendly consultations between border personnel of the two countries. Fifthly, the two sides also agreed in the accord to take adequate measures to ensure that air intrusions across the line of actual control do not take place and that the two sides shall undertake mutual consultation in case intrusions occur.

As a follow up of this agreement, a senior level Chinese military delegation aimed at fostering CBMs between the defence forces of the two countries made a six day goodwill visit to India in December 1993.

CBM's in LAC, 1996

Three years later, the Agreement on Maintenance of Peace and Tranquillity along the LAC in India-China Border Area was followed by the Agreement Between the Government of Republic of India and the Government of the People's Republic of China on Confidence Building Measures in the military field along the LAC in the India-China Border Areas on 29th November 1996 during the visit of Chinese President Ziyang Zemin to India. This Agreement while reiterating and reaffirming the intent and spirit of the 1993, state agreement, inter-alias, as Confidence Building Measures, envisaged the following:[3]

1. The major categories of armament to be reduced or limited include combat tanks, infantry combat vehicles, guns (including howitzers) with 75 mm or bigger calibre, mortars with 120mm or bigger calibre, surface-to-surface missiles, surface-to-air missiles and any other weapon system.
2. The two sides shall exchange data on the military forces and armaments to be reduced or limited and decide on ceilings on military forces and armaments to be kept by each side within agreed geographically zones along the line of actual control in the India-China border.

In order to maintain peace and tranquillity along the line of actual control in the India-China border areas and to prevent any tension in the border areas due to misreading by either side of the other side's intentions, Article IV of the Agreement provided the following:

1. Both sides shall avoid holding large-scale military exercises involving more than one

[2] 2Chellaney, Brahma, *Asian Juggernaut*, Harper, 2010, pp. 296-300.

[3] Ibid., pp. 301-308.

Division (approximately 15,000 troops) in close proximity of the line of actual control in the India-China border areas. However, if such exercises are to be conducted, the strategic direction of the main force involved shall not be towards the other side.

2. If either side conducts a major military exercise involving more than one Brigade Group (approximately 5000 troops) in close proximity of the line of actual control in the India-China border areas, it shall give the other side prior notification with regard to type, level, planned duration and area of exercise as well as the number and type of units or formations participating in the exercise.
3. The date of completion of the exercise and de-induction of troops from the area of exercise shall be intimated to the other side within five days of completion or de -induction.
4. Each side shall be entitled to obtain timely clarification from the side undertaking the exercise in respect of date specified in Paragraph 2 of the present Article.

With a view to preventing air intrusions across the LAC in the India-China border areas and facilitating over flights and landings by military aircraft, Article V provides that—

(1) Both sides shall take adequate measures to ensure that air intrusions across the line of actual control do not take place. However, if an intrusion does take place, it should cease as soon as detected and the incident shall be promptly investigated by the side operating the aircraft. The results of the investigation shall be immediately communicated, through diplomatic channels or at border personnel meetings, to the other side.

(2) Subject to paragraphs 3 and 5 of this Article, combat aircraft (to include fighter, bomber, reconnaissance, military trainer, armed helicopter and other armed aircraft) shall not fly within ten kilometres of the line of actual control.

(3) If either side is required to undertake flights of combat aircraft within ten kilometres from the line of actual control, it shall give the following information in advance to the other side, through diplomatic channels:
   a) Type and number of combat aircraft;
   b) Height of the proposed flight (in metres);
   c) Proposed duration of flights (normally not to exceed ten days);
   d) Proposed timing of flights; and
   e) Area of operations, defined in latitude and longitude.

(4) Unarmed transport aircraft, survey aircraft and helicopters shall be permitted to fly up to the line of actual control.

(5) No military aircraft of either side shall fly across the line of actual control, except by prior permission. Military aircraft of either side may fly across the line of actual control or overfly the other side's airspace or land on the other side only after obtaining the latter's prior permission after providing the latter with detailed information on the flight in accordance with the international practice in this regard.
Notwithstanding the above stipulation, each side has the sovereign right to specify additional conditions, including at short notice, for flights or landings of military aircraft of the other side on its side of the line of actual control or through its airspace.

(6) In order to ensure flight safety in emergency situations, the authorities designated by the two sides may contact each other by the quickest means of communications available.

Similarly, with a view to preventing dangerous military activities along the line of actual control in the India-China border areas, Article VI stipulates that:

(1) Neither side shall open fire, cause biodegradation, use hazardous chemicals, conduct blast operations or hunt with guns or explosive within two kilometres from the line of actual control. This prohibition shall not apply to routine firing activities in small arms firing ranges.

(2) If there is a need to conduct blast operations within two kilometres of the line of actual control as part of developmental activities, the other side shall be informed through diplomatic channels or by convening a border personnel meeting, preferably five days in advance.

(3) While conducting exercises with live ammunition in areas close to the line of actual control, precaution shall be taken to ensure that a bullet or a missile does not accidentally fall on the other side across the line of actual control and cause harm to the personnel or property of the other side.

(4) If the border personnel of the two sides come in a face-to-face situation due to differences

on the alignment of the line of actual control of any other reason, they shall exercise self-restraint and take all necessary steps to avoid an escalation of the situation. Both sides shall also enter into immediate consultations through diplomatic and/or other available channels to review the situation and prevent any escalation of tension.

Article VII of the agreement envisages the following:

a) To maintain and expand the regime of scheduled and flag meetings between their border representatives at designated places along the line of actual control;
b) To maintain and expand telecommunication links between the border meeting points at designated places along the line of actual control; and
c) To establish step-by-step medium and high-level contacts between the border authorities of the two sides.

Article VIII of the Agreement provides the following guidelines:

1. Should the personnel of one side cross the line of actual control and enter the other side because of unavoidable circumstances like natural disasters, the other side shall extend all possible assistance to them and inform their side, as soon as possible regarding the forced or inadvertent entry across the line of actual control. The modalities of return of the concerned personnel to their own side shall be settled through mutual consultations.
2. The two sides shall provide each other, at the earliest possible, with information pertaining to natural disasters and epidemic diseases in contiguous border areas which might affect the other side. The exchange of information shall take place either through diplomatic channels or at border personnel meetings.

Article X mentions following provisions:

1. Recognising that the full implementation of some of the provisions of the present Agreement will depend on the two sides arriving at a common understanding of the alignment of the line of actual control in the India-China border areas, the two sides agree to speed up the process clarification and confirmation of the line of actual control. As an initial step in this process, they are clarifying the alignment of the line of actual control in those segments where they have different perceptions. They also agree to exchange maps indicating their respective perceptions of the entire alignment of the line of actual control as soon as possible.
2. Pending the completion of the process of clarification and confirmation of the line of actual control, the two sides shall work out modalities for implementing confidence-building measures envisaged under his Agreement on an interim basis, without prejudice to their respective positions on the alignment of the line of actual control as well as on the boundary question.

Thus, it can be seen from various provisions of different agreements and accords signed between India and China that every conceivable aspect of military contingency has been thoughtfully anticipated and ways and means to deftly handle them without precipitating the matter have been envisaged. It was against this backdrop of signing of various agreements providing for CBMS that a slew of visits at various levels between the two countries were given further impetus. The most significant of the visit was that of the then Defence Minister, George Fernandes to China in April 2003. The visit of Mr. Fernandes took place after the gap of more than one decade and also helped ease the post Pokhran tension.

Defence cooperation and military engagement between the two countries further received a boost during the visit of the then Prime Minister Atal Behari Vajpayee to China in June 2003. It may be recalled that during the erstwhile short-lived Janata regime, Vajpayee had visited China in 1979. He, however, had to cut short his visit to China when war broke out between China and Vietnam as a mark of solidarity with the latter. The joint declaration between the two countries signed on 23 June 2003, *inter alia*, mentioned that "...they agreed on the need to broaden and deepen defence exchanges between the two countries, which will help enhance and deepen mutual understanding and trust between the two armed forces. They confirmed that the exchange of visits by their Defence Ministers and of military officials at various levels should be strengthened".[4]

Protocols on CBM's along the LAC, 2005

The upward swing of defence cooperation and military engagement between the two countries was given a further impetus during the visit of Chinese

[4] Ibid., p. 317.

Premier Wen Jiabao in April 2005 in the protocol between the Government of the Republic of India and the Government of the People's Republic of China on modalities for the implementations of Confidence Building Measures in the military field along the LAC in the India-China border areas signed on 11 April 2005. This Protocol sought to further elucidate certain provisions of the 1996 confidence building accord while reiterating verbatim of some of the bilateral commitments in the accord. Some of the amplified provisions which merits attentions are as under:

Article III of the Protocol envisages the following provisions:[5]

a) In the event of an alleged air intrusion of its controlled air space by the military aircraft of the other side, either side may seek a Flag Meeting within 48 hours of the alleged air intrusion in order to seek a clarification. The investigation shall be completed by the other side and its results communicated through a Flag Meeting within a period of four weeks.
b) If a military aircraft of either side is required to fly across the Line of Actual Control or to overfly the airspace of the other side, prior permission shall be sought from the other side according to procedures and formats to be mutually agreed upon.
c) If a military or civilian aircraft of either side is required to fly across the Line of Actual Control or to land on the other side of the Line of the LAC in an emergency situation, the two sides will ensure flight safety in such a situation by adhering to procedures to be mutually agreed upon.

Article V provides the following:

a) Both sides shall hold two additional border meetings each year at *Spanggur Gap* in the Western Sector, *Nathula Pass* in the Sikkim Sector and *Bum La* in the Easter Sector respectively in celebration of the National Day or Army Day of either side. Specific arrangements shall be decided through consultation between the border forces of the two sides.
b) Both sides are in principle to expand the mechanism of border meeting points to include *Kibithu-Damai* in the Eastern Sector and *Lipulekh Pass/Qiang La* in the Middle Sector. The precise locations of these border meetings points will be decided through mutual consultations.
c) Both sides shall conduct exchanges between the relevant Military Regions of China and Army Commands of India. Specific arrangements shall be decided upon through mutual consultations between the relevant agencies under the Ministries of Defence of the two sides.
d) Both sides shall strengthen exchanges between institutions of training of the two armed forces, and conduct exchanges between institutions of sports and culture of the two armed forces. Specific arrangements shall be decided upon through mutual consultations between the relevant agencies under the Ministries of Defence of the two sides.

Memorandum of Understanding, 2006

It was against this background of what may be called the heightened engagement between the two countries that the then Defence Minister Pranab Mukherjee visited China on a five-day visit in May/June 2006 and held wide ranging talks with Chinese leaders including Chinese Premier Wen Jiabao and his Chinese counterpart General Cao Gangchaum.

The high point of the visit was the signing of the Memorandum of Understanding (MOU) which is first ever of its kind between the two countries. The MOU envisages for the establishment of a mechanism to ensure frequent and regular exchanges between leaders and officials of the Defence Ministries and the armed forces of the two countries in addition to developing an annual calendar for holding regular joint military exercises and training programmes. In the past few years, the two countries had conducted joint naval manoeuvres, but the interaction between the ground forces has been limited to border meetings and mountaineering expeditions and there had been no interaction between the air forces of the countries. Prior to this the MOU signed between the two countries, thus, aimed at addressing these imperatives. The Defence Minister also visited the sensitive Lanzhou Military Area Command which controls the largest physical area of China's seven military regions. The region holding the nuclear research and missile testing facilities in the Chinese west comes under the Command of this area. Mr. Mukherjee's visit to the head quarters of the Lanzhou Military Command was a significant step in the process of building bilateral trust and confidence on part of China.[6]

[5] Ibid., pp. 322-327.

[6] Author's script broadcast in the External Service Division of All India Radio on 12th June 2006.

These gains were further consolidated during the visit of Chinese President Hu Jintao to India in November 2006. In the Joint Declaration signed between the two countries on 21st November, it was mentioned that 'the exchange of visits in the field of defence has resulted in the building of mutual trust and enhancement of mutual understanding between the defence establishments of the two countries. Both sides shall fully implement the provisions of the Memorandum of Understanding for exchanges and cooperation in the field of defence signed on 29 May 2006, which provides a sound foundation and institutional framework for further development of defence cooperation.'[7]

Certain concrete steps were taken as a follow-up of the CBM's. For example, Armed Forces of India and China held a warm meeting at a new border point in Arunachal Pradesh, on 18th November 2006, on the eve of President Hu Jintao's visit to India. The two sides met at Kibithu in Anjwa district of Arunachal Pradesh, and discussed modalities for the conduct of troops along the border. An official press release claimed, "The meeting and exchanges were characterised by great warmth and bonhomie. It marks another milestone in the growing relationship and military exchanges between the armed forces of the two countries." Border meetings between personnel of the armed forces of the two countries have traditionally been held at Chusul in Ladakh, Nathu La in Sikkim, and Bum La in Kamang district of Arunachal Pradesh.[8]

Hand-in-Hand 2008: The India-China Joint Military Exercise

Encouraged by the success of the first ever joint military exercise between China and India is Kunming in Yunnan in 2007, a week long China-India joint antiterrorists training kicked off on 6 December 2008 in Belgaun in Karnataka with performance of the Chinese Tai Chai and Indian martial arts. *Qin Xiangyon*, in charge of the Chinese soldiers participating in the sessions, said during the opening ceremonies that the joint training was aimed at promoting the two army's mutual understanding and trust. He also said that it was a way for the armies to develop their friendship, and expand the fields for exchanges and cooperation. After the ceremony, Chinese and Indian soldiers displayed their weapons. Moreover, Chinese soldiers performed tai chi and anti-terror shooting skills, while their Indian counterparts put on display the country traditional martial arts. Commenting on the importance of the joint military exercise Quyang Wei, a professor at the University of National Defence said in an exclusive interview to Xinhua that 'China and India are the world's biggest developing countries. Peace and Friendship between them is not only in the interests of both the countries, but also important for bringing peace, stability and prosperity to South Asia.

Highlighting the need for the joint training, the Chinese Defence Ministry spokesman Huang Xueping said that such training 'was intended to enhance mutual understanding and trust and advance development of relations between Chinese and Indian armies.' Emphasising the importance of such exercises Lt. General Ma Xiaotions, Head of the Chinese Military Observer delegation and also the Deputy Chief of the PLA said that 'it showcased the resolution of the two sides to safeguard regional peace and stability and create a harmonious environment for development together.'[9] Coming from the mouth of a very senior PLA functionary, the statement should be taken very seriously. An editorial in *China Daily* hailed the joint training programme and said,' China and India are looking after their fences, turning the Himalayas, the highest mountains on the earth, into a friendly border,'[10]

The joint military exercise was carried out according to the Memorandum of Understanding for Exchange and cooperation in the field of Defence signed in 2006 and listed in the annual exchange plan for 2008.

Defence cooperation between India and China maintained a healthy momentum during the year 2009. The Chief of Naval Staff attended the International Fleet Review 2009 at Qingdao from 21-24 April 2009. Indian participation included guided missile destroyers INS Mumbai and INS Ranveer, the guided missile corvette INS Khanjar and the tanker INS Jyoti. Chinese "Shenzhen" Missile Destroyer made port call at the Kochi port from 8-11 August, 2009. The Deputy Chief of General Staff of China's visit was reciprocated by Indian Army Chief Gen. BC Joshi's visit to China in July 1994. Since then, regular exchanges have been taking place at various levels. Liberation Army of China visited India in December 2009. The Defence Secretary led a high

[7] Suo motto statement by Shri Pranab Mukherjee, Minister of External Affairs on 'Chinese President's visit to India in Lok Sabha on 28th November 2006.

[8] *The Hindu*, 21st November, 2006.

[9] News from China, Vol. xx, No. 12, December 2008.

[10] Available at http://expressindia.com, accessed on 21st September 2010.

level Indian delegation for the third Annual Defence Dialogue held in Beijing on 6 January 2010.[11]

Although these military engagement and CBM's have somewhat helped in diffusing tension across the border, incidents regarding border incursions are reported from time to time. Every month, the Indo-Tibetian Border Police (ITBP) reports around a dozen unannounced Chinese military patrols in the disputed border area, and this number have not decreased over the last decade. Most of these incidents are inoffensive. Often border-guards do not even make direct contacts, but leave behind subtle traces of their presence, like piles of stones, cigarette packets, or cans. From time to time, Chinese military officials reportedly enter the Indian side of LAC in civilian clothes and vehicles. Almost on a weekly basis, small Chinese boats tour around Lake Pangong Tso in Ladakh.[12]

In more recent times, India is worried about a significant increase in the number of stand-offs between Indian and Chinese border patrols and more aggressive posturing by Chinese soldiers along the border. The latest standoff between the two sides along the LAC was sometime in early September 2010, when Chinese soldiers brought a bulldozer into a disputed area in the Ladakh region to construct a road. Even after the Indian side objected to it and asked the Chinese to take it back, the People's Liberation Army (PLA) unduly delayed the withdrawal of the machine and took it away only about four days later. The delay of the Chinese was unusual, but it fell into the trend they have noticed this summer of greater assertiveness by People's Liberation Army soldiers, reported a leading newspaper quoting senior officials. The 2010 summer has already recorded an almost 100 per cent increase in the number of stand-offs between the patrols of the two sides. These peaceful standoffs were reported from Depsang, Demchok and Pangong Tso areas of Ladakh region in recent times.[13] Tension on account of border-intrusions arises because of non-demarcation of LAC, which needs to be addressed by both sides. It is essential, therefore, that the border talks between the two countries should take place.

Although the denial of visa by China to the senior Indian Army Officer has cast a shadow over the military engagement and defence dialogue between the two countries, there is a perception among a section of strategic community and in the media that both sides should work amicably out an exit route of the diplomatic impasse sooner than later for the larger interest and in particular to the tricky border issue in which the PLA seems to have an upper hand in China.[14] At the writing of this article, it seems there are veiled signs of conciliation between the two countries. While newspaper reports suggest that Beijing might take a second look at the visa issue, the government of India has given the go ahead for an official visit by the Indian Coast Guard chief Vice-Admiral Anil Chopra to Shanghai in October. He will be the first high-ranking military official to visit China since Lt General Jaswal was denied permission to lead a military delegation to Beijing in July this year.[15] It is also pertinent to mention that although not reported in the media, a group of senior journalists from China visited India in September this year. The journalists also had free and frank discussions with the scholars at the Institute for Defence Studies and Analyses (IDSA), New Delhi. Military engagement which China had suspended with the United States earlier on the ground of supply of arms to Taiwan is going to be resumed, according to news reports. All these point out that military exchange between the two countries may be revived at some stage sooner than later.

Conclusion

In conclusion, it can be said that defence cooperation and military engagement between India and China is an aspect of the complex mix of conflict and cooperation approach to bilateral relations between the two Asian giants. It is based on the presumption that there is a security dilemma between the two countries. It recognizes the framework and postulates of what is called cooperative security. China's acquiescence for military engagement and defence cooperation with India is another aspect of China's overall strategy of so-called peaceful and harmonious rise, which it initiated and pursues, arguably to project China as a soft-power, but really to consolidate its economic muscles and to use it as a leverage to enhance its influence, particularly at a time when there is greater degree of mutual economic inter-dependence between China and India.

---

[11] Ministry of External Affairs, Government of India, *Annual Report, 2009-2010.*

[12] Jonathan Holslag, *The Persistent Military Security between China and India, Journal of Strategic Studies: Vol. 32, No. 6, December 2009, p.817.*

[13] *The Times of India*, 27th September 2010.

[14] *The Hindu*, "India to Engage China's Military as Influence Expands", 20th September 2010.

[15] *Indian Express*, 29th September 201010. The US Army Regulation No.8-29 of 25 Feb 05.

DRDO

Leading the Way in Taking India's Defence Strength to New Heights

India today has a proud position among the elite nations in the world, being: One of the FOUR countries to have multi-level Strategic Deterrence Capabilities; Among FIVE countries to have its own Ballistic Missile Defence (BMD) program; Among SIX countries to have developed a nuclear- powered Submarine; Among SEVEN countries to have developed its own Main Battle Tank (MBT) and indigenous 'Fourth plus' generation Combat Aircraft; and among select few countries to have its own Electronic Warfare & multi-range Radar program.

These and many more world class weapon systems, platforms, military equipment and related materials are based on cutting edge technologies developed by DRDO, the Defence Research Development Organization (http://drdo.gov.in). DRDO is the R&D wing of the Ministry of Defence, Govt of India, with over 55 years of innovation and R&D and a vision to empower India with cutting-edge defence technologies. It's mission is to achieve self-reliance in critical defence technologies and systems, while equipping the armed forces with state-of-the-art weapon systems and equipment. DRDO has led the design, development and production of state-of-the-art weapon systems, military equipment and soldier support systems, in accordance with requirements laid down by the three Services. DRDO is headed by Scientific Advisor to Raksha Mantri (SA to RM), who is also the Secretary, Department of Defence R&D and Director General DRDO. Dr. DS Kothari, the eminent scientist and educationist was the first to head the Organization which is currently headed by Shri Avinash Chander. The SA to RM is supported by Director Generals (Technology Clusters) and CCR&Ds (Chief Controllers Research & Development). Each DG (Technology Clusters) heads a specific technology cluster of laboratories, whereas CCR&Ds look after specific corporate functions.

DRDO has led these products to production by the Indian public and private sector industries, including SMEs (small and medium enterprises), all through, taking them along in the journey of building self-reliance. In its journey from a state of near zero knowledge or technology base and a non-existent industrial base in post-independence era, when even nuts, bolts and sewing needles had to be imported, DRDO has been moving in close association with the armed forces, academic institutions, research organizations and industries, to achieve its prime objective of building indigenous capabilities and self-reliance in cutting edge defence technologies. These products and technologies have been instrumental in overall industrial growth in the crucial segment of defence industries; taking the share of indigenous content of items approved for acquisition by our armed forces to over 55%. The production value of systems based on DRDO technologies that have been inducted / approved for induction into Services (excluding strategic systems) stands at over ₹1,60,000 crore. Besides, exhaustive infrastructure for design, development, testing and comprehensive evaluation of weapon systems, and related materials has been created as national assets.

The impact of these technologies on employment generation and on national economy can be envisioned from the fact that in most cases, these indigenous products cost much lower than imported counterparts and have been developed at a fraction of the cost of development in most other countries.Thus, for example, just about ₹7500 crores have been spent so far on the development of 'Tejas', the Air Force version of Indian Light Combat Aircraft. The unit cost of 'Tejas', a 'Fourth plus' generation combat aircraft for which production has

Tejas Combat Aircraft

commenced, is expected to be far less than any comparable fighter aircraft in the world. It is noteworthy that, at about ₹10,000 crore, the annual budget of defence R&D is less than 5.5% of India's total defence budget. This is far less than that of United States (about 12%), China (about 20%), and most other countries. DRDO's accomplishments are result of hard work and dedicated efforts of a relatively small work force comprising just about 7500 DRDS scientists and about 19,000 technical and support personnel, working in its 60 R&D laboratories, establishments and work centers. Indeed, this committed work force being its most valuable asset, DRDO lays great emphasis on their selection process, post induction training and career long professional development, providing an excellent meritorious career.

Many of the DRDO developed technologies have found civil applications too and are benefiting the society, with multiplying effect on employment generation and economic growth. Packaged ready to eat nutritious food, Explosive Detection Kit, and bio-digester are such examples where advanced technologies developed for Indian soldiers has found way for commercial exploitation.

DRDO has entered into a new phase of delivery of state of the art systems and critical technologies to the nation and has made significant achievements in recent years. DRDO's prowess in strategic systems touched new heights with the launch of India's long range strategic missile Agni 5. Agni 3 joined Agni 1, Agni 2 & 'Prithvi 2' in the arsenal to strengthen India's strategic might, while Agni 4 and Agni 5 are being readied for induction. Over 70 launches of major missile systems have demonstrated DRDO's strength and operational readiness. The long range cruise missile, Nirbhay had its maiden flight proving the required critical technologies. In establishing a credible two layer Ballistic Missile Defence system, a series of successful interceptions, mostly with direct hit, have demonstrated its reliability. Production clearance of Bo5 underwater system, incorporating many novel technologies, proving the reliability of the system, was another breakthrough. INS Arihant, India's first indigenous nuclear powered submarine, with its nuclear reactor having achieved criticality, is gearing up for seaward trials. In the arena of tactical systems, induction of Akash, the medium range air defence system with multi-target, multi directional capability is another shining achievement.

BrahMos, the best supersonic cruise missile in operation, is designed to be launched from land, air, sea and sub-sea platforms, with high speed and precision of attack. Its Block II version with target discrimination capability, and Block III version with steep diving capability even at supersonic speeds have been developed making BrahMos a deadly weapon. Prahar, a novel, highly-manoeuvrable precision strike, Surface-to-Surface tactical missile capable of being fired in salvo mode is all set to extend the reach of our artillery fire to over 150 kilometres, filling the gap between Pinaka rockets and Prithvi Missile. India's first Light Weight Multi-role Supersonic Combat Aircraft Tejas, a 4th Plus Generation contemporary fighter aircraft having recorded over 2,500 flawless take offs and landings, was demonstrated during "Iron Fist", a fire power demonstration exercise of the Indian Air Force. Having undergone extensive weapon trials, extreme weather trials, high altitude & sea level trials and achieving Initial operational clearance, 'Tejas' is now ready for induction. The LCA Navy, capable of operating from aircraft carrier ship, had its maiden flight in April 2012. Integration of mission systems with the much needed AEW&CS platform fitted with indigenous Active Electronically Scanned Array radar antenna is another significant achievement of DRDO. The systems are undergoing comprehensive flight tests. Avionics upgrades of MiG 27, Jaguar and Sukhoi-30 aircrafts were indigenously accomplished, significantly enhancing their combat capabilities. India's first indigenously designed & developed aircraft engine Kaveri is undergoing Certification Tests after a series of successful flight trials. Successful development of an indigenous Wankel rotary engine for UAVs and its flight demonstration on

Agni-3 Launch

"UAV Nishant" is another achievement. Two regiments have been equipped with the Main Battle Tank Arjun. The Arjun Mark-II, with about 80 improved features and developed in a record time of two and half years, has entered advanced phase of User Trials. Thermo-baric ammunition capable of delivering simultaneous fragmentation, thermal and blast effect has been developed for MBT Arjun to further boost its firepower. A number of Battlefield support systems including Armoured Amphibious Dozer, Armoured Engineering Reconnaissance Vehicle and Tracked Armoured Ambulance are now in production. A new Modular Bridging System capable of yielding single span of up to 46 metres and capable of bearing load up to 70 tons is undergoing user trials.

Among naval sensors, very high degree of self-reliance has been achieved with design development, and induction of sonars meeting needs of Indian Navy. USHUS, an Advanced Active-cum-Passive integrated sonar system, NAGAN, an active-cum-passive towed-array sonar & HUMSA-NG, a new generation hull-mounted sonar for ships; are integrated with their respective platforms. Among the weapon systems, VARUNASTRA, a heavy weight torpedo, underwent extensive sea trials on its way to induction. Radars and electronic warfare systems are another area of DRDO's technological strength, exemplified by the development, production and acceptance of WLR, an advanced electronically scanned pulse Doppler weapon locating radar; 3D TCR, a 3-dimensional tactical control radar; Bharani, a Low Level Lightweight Radar and ASLESHA, a 3D Low Level Lightweight Radar. Completion and acceptance of Varuna, a modern ESM system for Navy with capability to intercept and process all modern radars including LPI radars was another step in achieving self-reliance in the field of Electronic Warfare.

A series of secure communication systems based on Software Defined Radio, ranging from hand-held sets, to aircraft and ship-based systems have been developed. The compact system is capable of operating on multiple frequency bands, avoiding need for multiple systems. The light-weight integrated Multi-function Sight, for surveillance and speedy engagement of targets was accepted for induction. An electro-optical fire control system EON-51 for the Navy is another achievement. An advanced Holographic Sight facilitating accurate aiming with both eyes open, has been developed for the INSAS rifle. Design and fabrication of System on Chip (SoC) for mission computers and its integration with On-Board Computers for major missile systems and aeronautical platforms, was another significant milestone.

DRDO has played a pioneering role in the development of special materials for defence requirements. Recent achievements include production of light armour for the Mi-17 helicopter and more than 30,000 tons of DMR steel for Indian Navy. The setting up of a Titanium sponge production facility at KMML is a boost for aeronautical, missile and space programmes. Alive to the needs of emerging war scenarios DRDO has taken up development of Unmanned War Machines as a major thrust area and has made significant achievements, including the delivery of state-of-the-art Remotely Operated Vehicle Daksh, an invaluable asset for bomb disposal, series of successful flights of long endurance UAV Rustom -1 in its final configuration and demonstration of an advanced Autonomous Underwater Vehicle. A series of mini and micro UAVs have also been developed. Bulk production orders have been received for Submarine Escape Suite for the Navy, Combat Free Fall System for Paratroopers and Lightweight Helicopter Oxygen System for the Air Force. An On-board Oxygen Generation System (OBOGS) has also been developed. Series production of Computerised Pilot Selection System (CPSS) for comprehensive evaluation of candidates has been handed over to users.

Development of Solar Powered Modular Green Shelters was another significant achievement in supporting our soldiers. The NBC Reconnaissance Vehicle designed for 'surveillance and on-site collection & analysis of samples from contaminated environment', was handed over to the users. Sonar technologies for detection of ships and underwater threats were innovatively employed to develop Sanjeevini, a life-detector to locate victims trapped under debris or a bore-well and 'Tarangini', a portable device to measure depth and bottom hardness in water bodies.

All these endeavours had a single-minded focus: to transform India into a world-class centre for design development and production of defence systems and technologies, ensuring freedom from denial regimes and external controls.

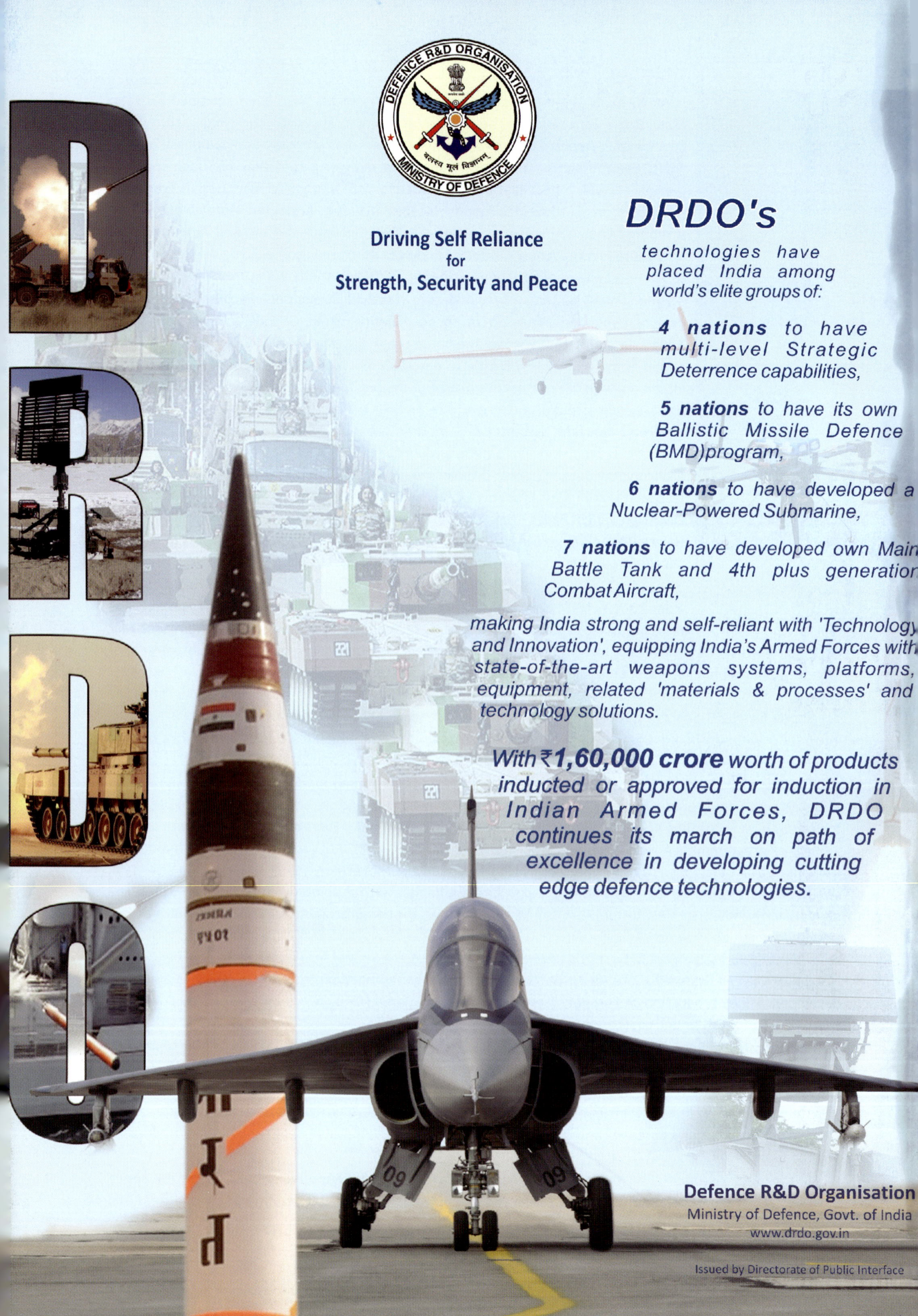
DEFENCE R&D ORGANISATION
MINISTRY OF DEFENCE
Driving Self Reliance
for
Strength, Security and Peace
DRDO's
technologies have placed India among world's elite groups of:
4 nations to have multi-level Strategic Deterrence capabilities,
5 nations to have its own Ballistic Missile Defence (BMD)program,
6 nations to have developed a Nuclear-Powered Submarine,
7 nations to have developed own Main Battle Tank and 4th plus generation Combat Aircraft,
making India strong and self-reliant with 'Technology and Innovation', equipping India's Armed Forces with state-of-the-art weapons systems, platforms, equipment, related 'materials & processes' and technology solutions.
With ₹1,60,000 crore worth of products inducted or approved for induction in Indian Armed Forces, DRDO continues its march on path of excellence in developing cutting edge defence technologies.
Defence R&D Organisation
Ministry of Defence, Govt. of India
www.drdo.gov.in
Issued by Directorate of Public Interface

NEW RELEASE

Book released by Vice President of India Shri M. Hamid Ansari

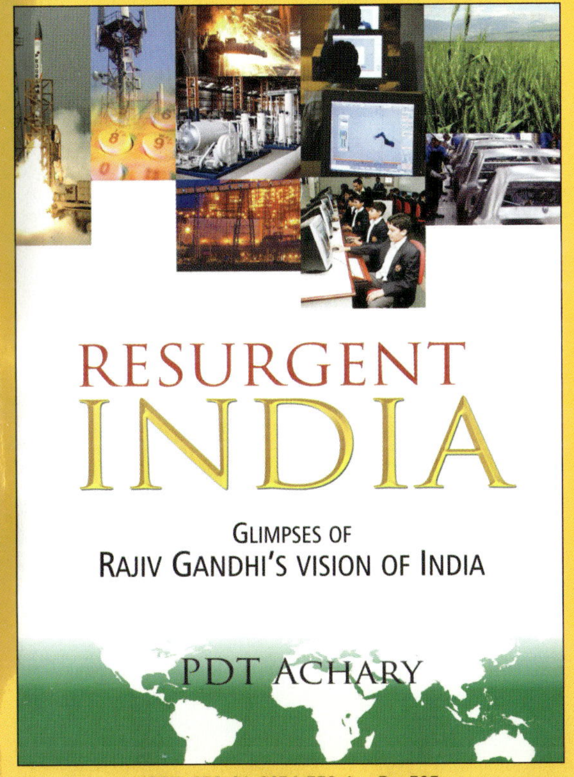

ISBN: 978-81-8274-753-1 • Rs. 595

ISBN: 978-81-8274-736-4 • Rs. 695

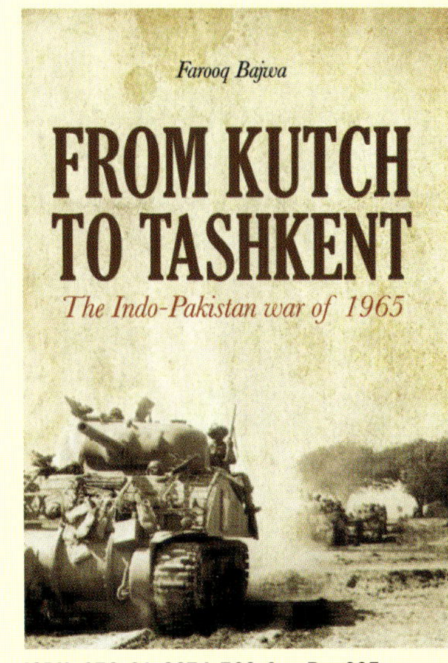

ISBN: 978-81-8274-760-9 • Rs. 695

ISBN: 978-81-8274-723-4 • Rs. 895

ISBN: 978-81-8274-740-1 • Rs. 995

ISBN: 978-81-8274-743-2 • Rs. 395

ISBN: 978-81-8274-739-5 • Rs. 1995

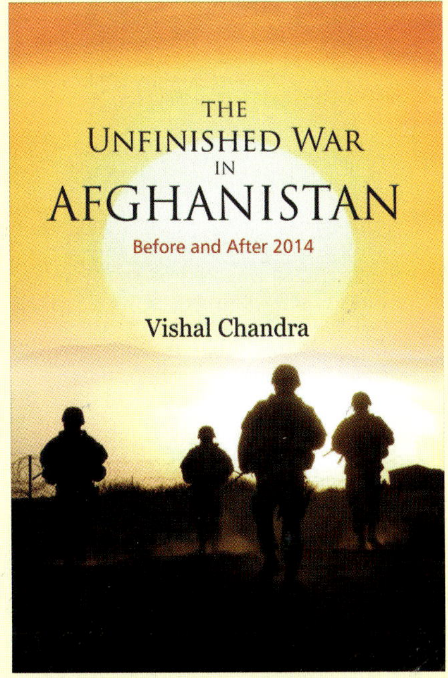

ISBN: 978-81-8274-762-3 • Rs. 995

HISTORY DIVISION, MINISTRY OF DEFENCE,
GOVERNMENT OF INDIA

OFFICIAL HISTORY OF THE INDIAN ARMED FORCES IN THE SECOND WORLD WAR 1939-45

SERIES OF 8 BOOKS

A Series of 24 volumes describing the role of the Indian Armed forces had been published by the History Division, Ministry of Defence some sixty years back. Eight of these volumes, which describe major operations conducted by the Indian troops, have been out of stock for some time. Pentagon Press, who have published many titles of military interest, have now come out with a reprint of these volumes as there is a great demand for them among readers. The volumes have been nicely printed and aesthetically bound. It is hoped that the series would go far in familiarising the new generation of Indians with matters military.

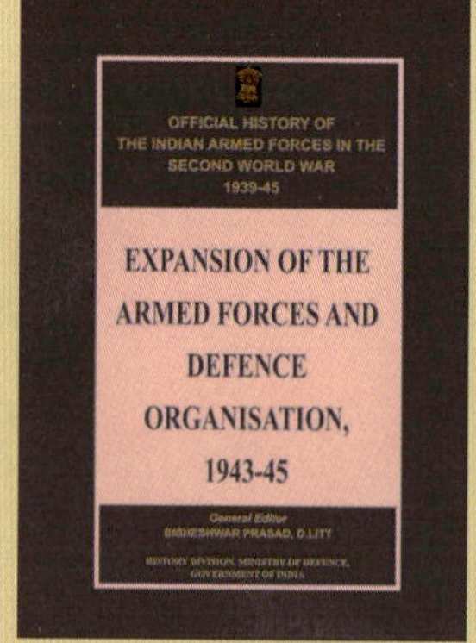

EXPANSION OF THE ARMED FORCES AND DEFENCE ORGANISATION1943-45

978-81-8274-661-9 • Rs. 990

THE ARAKAN OPERATION

978-81-8274-662-6 • Rs. 990

CAMPAIGN IN WESTERN ASIA

978-81-8274-663-3 • Rs. 990

CAMPAIGNS IN SOUTH EAST ASIA 1941-42

978-81-8274-664-0 • Rs. 990

THE NORTH AFRICAN CAMPAIGN

978-81-8274-665-7 • Rs. 990

EAST AFRICAN CAMPAIGN 1940-41

978-81-8274-666-4 • Rs. 790

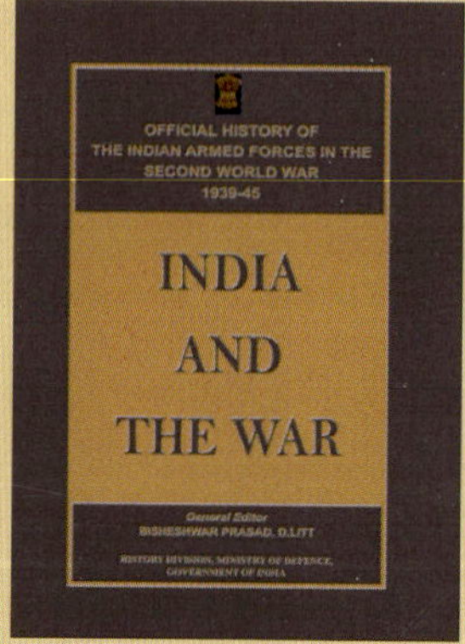

INDIA AND THE WAR

978-81-8274-667-1 • Rs. 790

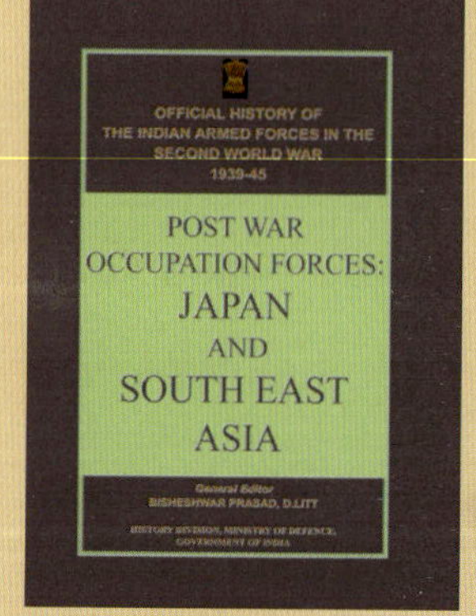

POST WAR OCCUPATION FORCE: JAPAN AND SOUTH EAST ASIA

978-81-8274-668-8 • Rs. 990

PENTAGON PRESS

206, Peacock Lane, Shahpur Jat, New Delhi-110 049 (India)
Phones: +91-11-64706243, 26491568 • Telefax: +91-11-26490600
email: rajan@pentagonpress.in • www.pentagonpress.in